The Origins and Growth of Criminology

The International Library of Criminology, Criminal Justice and Penology
Series Editors: Gerald Mars and David Nelken

Titles in the Series:

The Origins and Growth of Criminology
Piers Beirne

The Psychology and Psychiatry of Crime
David Canter

Crime and the Media
Richard V. Ericson

Psychological Explanations of Crime
David P. Farrington

Terrorism
Connor Gearty

Criminal Careers, Vols I & II
David F. Greenberg

Social Control: Aspects of Non-State Justice
Stuart Henry

Professional Criminals
Dick Hobbs

Computer Crime
Richard Hollinger

Street Crime
Mike Maguire

Occupational Crime
Gerald Mars

Gender, Crime and Feminism
Ngaire Naffine

White-Collar Crime
David Nelken

Organized Crime
Nikos Passas

Criminal Statistics: Their Use and Abuse
Kenneth Pease

Police, Vols I & II
Robert Reiner

Victimology
Paul Rock

Prosecution
Andrew Sanders

Drugs, Vols I & II
Nigel South

Sex Crimes
Donald West

The Origins and Growth of Criminology

Essays on Intellectual History, 1760-1945

Edited by

Piers Beirne

Professor of Sociology & Legal Studies
University of Southern Maine

Dartmouth

Aldershot · Brookfield USA · Hong Kong · Singapore · Sydney

Published by
Dartmouth Publishing Company Limited
Gower House
Croft Road
Aldershot
Hants GU11 3HR
England

Dartmouth Publishing Company
Old Post Road
Brookfield
Vermont 05036
USA

British Library Cataloguing in Publication Data
Origins and Growth of Criminology: Essays
on Intellectual History, 1760–1945. –
(International Library of Criminology &
Criminal Justice)
 I. Beirne, Piers II. Series
 364.09

Library of Congress Cataloging-in-Publication Data
The Origins and growth of criminology : essays on intellectual
 history, 1760–1945 / edited by Piers Beirne.
       p. cm. — (The International library of criminology and
 criminal justice)
     Includes bibliographical references and index.
     ISBN 1-85521-418-0
     1.Criminology—History. I. Beirne, Piers. II. Series.
 HV6021.075 1994
 364′.09—dc20   93-37293
                                                                          CIP

ISBN 1 85521 418 0

Printed in Great Britain by Galliard (Printers) Ltd, Great Yarmouth

Contents

Acknowledgements

The editors and publishers wish to thank the following for permission to use copyright material.

Greenwood Publishing Group Inc. for the essay: Gil Geis and Colin Goff (1986), 'Edwin H. Sutherland's White-Collar Crime in America: An Essay in Historical Criminology', *Criminal Justice History*, **7**, pp. 1–31. Reprinted with permission.

Dorie Klein (1982), 'The Etiology of Female Crime: A Review of the Literature' in Barbara R. Price and Natalie Sokoloff (eds), *The Criminal Justice System and Women*, New York: Clark Boardman, pp. 35–60.

Kluwer Academic Publishers for the essay: James Messerschmidt (1987), 'Feminism, Criminology and the Rise of the Female Sex "Delinquent" 1880–1930', *Contemporary Crises*, **11**, pp. 243–63.

Oxford University Press for the essays: Philip Jenkins (1984), 'Varieties of Enlightenment Criminology', *The British Journal of Criminology*, **24**, pp. 112–29; David Garland (1988), 'British Criminology Before 1935', *The British Journal of Criminology*, **28**, pp. 1–17; Jon Snodgrass (1976), 'Clifford R. Shaw and Henry D. McKay: Chicago Criminologists', *The British Journal of Criminology*, **16**, pp. 1–19.

Pergamon Press Limited for the essay: David B. Young (1983), 'Cesare Beccaria: Utilitarian or Retributivist?', *Journal of Criminal Justice*, **11**, pp. 317–26.

M. E. Sharpe Inc. for the essay: Piers Beirne and Alan Hunt (1990), 'Lenin, Crime and Penal Politics, 1917–1924', in Piers Beirne, *Revolution in Law: Contributions to the Development of Soviet Legal Theory, 1917–1938'*, pp. 99–135.

The University of Chicago Press for the essays: Piers Beirne (1987), 'Adolphe Quetelet and the Origins of Positivist Criminology', *American Journal of Sociology*, **92**, pp. 1140–69; John H. Laub and Robert J. Sampson (1991), 'The Sutherland-Glueck Debate: On the Sociology of Criminological Knowledge', *American Journal of Sociology*, **96**, pp. 1402–40.

Every effort has been made to trace all the copyright holders, but if any have been inadvertently overlooked the publishers will be pleased to make the necessary arrangements at the first opportunity.

Series Preface

The International Library of Criminology, Criminal Justice and Penology, represents an important publishing initiative designed to bring together the most significant journal essays in contemporary criminology, criminal justice and penology. The series makes available to researchers, teachers and students an extensive range of essays which are indispensable for obtaining an overview of the latest theories and findings in this fast changing subject.

This series consists of volumes dealing with criminological schools and theories as well as with approaches to particular areas of crime, criminal justice and penology. Each volume is edited by a recognised authority who has selected twenty or so of the best journal articles in the field of their special competence and provided an informative introduction giving a summary of the field and the relevance of the articles chosen. The original pagination is retained for ease of reference.

The difficulties of keeping on top of the steadily growing literature in criminology are complicated by the many disciplines from which its theories and findings are drawn (sociology, law, sociology of law, psychology, psychiatry, philosophy and economics are the most obvious). The development of new specialisms with their own journals (policing, victimology, mediation) as well as the debates between rival schools of thought (feminist criminology, left realism, critical criminology, abolitionism etc.) that contribute overviews offering syntheses of the state of the art. These problems are addressed by the INTERNATIONAL LIBRARY in making available for research and teaching the key essays from specialist journals.

GERALD MARS
Visiting Professor of Risk Management, Cranfield University

DAVID NELKEN
Visiting Professor of Law (Criminology), University College London

Introduction

The collection of essays in this volume is designed to make more readily accessible otherwise quite disparate material on the intellectual history of criminology, a topic in which there has been renewed interest in recent years. Its scope is the lengthy period that begins with the polemical writings of the 18th-century French and Italian *philosophes* and which ends with the consolidation of an erstwhile-scientific criminology in the United States. To situate this somewhat differently, the 14 essays here deal with a period that stretches from roughly 1760 to 1945.

In compiling the contents of this collection, I have been especially mindful of three considerations. First, I was asked, as editor, to gather material on the intellectual history of criminology that had been published in the last ten or so years and which had originally appeared in journal articles rather than in monographs. By and large, the material here reflects that missive. Second, I have tried to favour material that is sensitive to the issue of 'presentism', namely, the tendency to reconstitute past intellectual concerns according to those of the present. That tendency is clearly an affront to an adequate historiography, for to understand the past through the lenses of the present is necessarily to misunderstand it. At the same time, I have avoided material that embodies a voyeuristic fascination with museum pieces in intellectual history – presentism's unnamed antithesis ('pastism'?).

Third, and finally, I have tried to include material that opposes two sorts of conventional claims about the understanding of concept formation in criminology, one 'externalist', the other 'internalist'. Against externalist approaches, on the one hand, it must be objected that the origins and growth of the conceptual content and explanatory structure of criminology cannot adequately be understood either as mere representations of the power relations peculiar to modernity or as unmediated expressions of the epistemological divisions wrought by state practices in the asylum, the clinic and the prison. In other words, the whys, the hows, and the whens of the invention of concepts and ideas can never properly be understood if one views them as simply being parasitic on external events. The difficulty with internalist approaches, on the other hand, is that the key concepts and discursive techniques of criminology were not invented, and did not develop, as logical or even inevitable products of scientific research programmes. Most of the essays in this volume do not assume, therefore, that any of the explanatory claims of criminology has any objective truth.

In what follows I have grouped the essays under three broad headings: (I) The Enlightenment: Cesare Beccaria's *Of Crimes and Punishments*, (II) The Rise of Positivist Criminology and (III) The Growth of Criminology in the U.S., 1880–1945. However, these headings reflect more the need to impose some order on the work that happens recently to have been done on the intellectual history of criminology than they do the chief phases in the development of modern criminology. Indeed, elsewhere I have tried to challenge conventional views about the broad periods of classical criminology and positivist criminology, especially the alleged epistemological rupture between them and the correct periodization of the emergence of positivism.

I. The Enlightenment: Cesare Beccaria's *Of Crimes and Punishments*

The four essays in Part I are each concerned to reconsider the merits of the key text in the development of classical criminology, Cesare Beccaria's (1738–1794) short and anonymously-published treatise, *Of Crimes and Punishments* (*Dei delitti e delle pene*) of 1764.

In Chapter 1, Graeme Newman and Pietro Marongiu argue that a key trend in the history of penological reform, from Maconochie to Osborne, is one of fleeting success swiftly followed by institutional failure and eventually the demise of the reformers themselves. To this trend Beccaria has been a lonely exception, his myth of greatness and good practical effect providing hope and purpose for penologists in the same way that the members of any culture create larger myths in order to infuse their lives with meaning. The authors claim that the 'myth of Beccaria' is actually enabled by several longstanding myths that have been attached to the contents of *Of Crimes and Punishments* (hereinafter *OC&P*). First, the main arguments of *OC&P* are ambiguous and contradictory. Thus, they point out that, whereas Beccaria has been revered as a retributivist, in fact his retributivism was cast within a utilitarian model ('this served to sanitize the less appealing deterrent assumptions of the utilitarian position he advocated'). Whereas Beccaria is regarded as a humanitarian reformer, in fact he advocated corporal punishment and seems to have supported the use of judicial torture, in appropriate cases, provided that it was regulated by law. And whereas Beccaria is revered for his utter rejection of capital punishment, his grounds for so doing are entirely contradicted by his support for penal servitude for life.

The liberal 'spirit' bequeathed by Beccaria, the authors continue, is actually an illusion. Whereas Beccaria is credited with having introduced a penal philosophy that abolished 18th-century physical brutality and with having replaced it with humane imprisonment, in fact he was responsible for introducing a nightmarish and ever-expanding system in which more and more of the population are even now incarcerated. Indeed, the reason that the 'enlightened' European monarchy and nobility championed *OC&P* is that they quickly realized how efficiently its principles, if implemented, would preserve the social order and their political rule.

In Chapter 2, David Young focuses on one of the key points later developed by Newman and Marongiu – and with which they largely disagree. Young takes issue with the long-standing view that *OC&P* was chiefly a utilitarian work whose principles were largely directed to deterrence and to the happiness of the entire community. While those principles are present, Young agrees, the essential framework of *OC&P* was retributivist in its basic ideas. Young explicates this argument by examining five aspects of *OC&P*: (1) its establishment of the sovereign's right to punish; (2) its methods for determining relative offence severity and for explaining variations in responses to a crime; (3) its views on the aims of punishment; (4) its treatment of the rights of criminals, especially in relation to capital punishment, and (5) its concern with establishing a just society, in which rights and obligations would be equally distributed among all the citizenry, as the proper context for an equitable system of criminal justice.

Chapter 3 is Piers Beirne's 'Inventing Criminology: The "Science of Man" in Cesare Beccaria's *Dei Delitti e Delle Pene* (1764)'. The thesis of this essay unfolds in four stages. Firstly, it is claimed that in the last 200 years the predominant images of *OC&P* have been constructed more in terms of its practico-juridical effects than in terms of its actual discursive features. Instead, second, the persistent misrepresentation of Beccaria's arguments in *OC&P*

is actively encouraged by the ambiguity of many of the author's own positions and by the obscure and disingenuous style of much of his prose – common enough textual practices in the dangerous publishing conditions that existed during much of the Enlightenment. Only with considerable difficulty, therefore, can the nature and intended objects of Beccaria's discourse be discerned. Third, Beccaria's chief aim in *OC&P* is shown to have been the application to crime and penal strategies of the 'science of man', a deterministic discourse implicitly at odds with conventional assumptions about the exclusively humanist and volitional bases of 'classical criminology'. In making this claim, finally, the author fundamentally challenges the existing interpretations of the context and object of Beccaria's book.

In 'Varieties of Enlightenment Criminology' (Chapter 4), Philip Jenkins argues that Beccaria's ideas were reactionary in comparison with those contained in the revolutionary and materialist writings of the anarchist William Godwin (1756–1836) and the atheist Marquis de Sade (1740–1814). Where Beccaria sought to cultivate a model bourgeois society founded on the promotion of private property and industry, Godwin identified private property as the greatest criminogenic institution and therefore demanded its abolition. A just society, Godwin reasoned, required the abolition of government, the decentralization of authority and merely the 'restraint' of criminals. De Sade, himself no stranger to the inside of gaols, even condemned the very centrepiece of Beccaria's reforms in *OC&P*, namely, imprisonment. To imprison poor thieves, de Sade reasoned, was to punish the weak simply for trying to recapture what had once belonged to them. In setting *OC&P* against the writings of some of Beccaria's contemporaries, therefore, Jenkins concludes that the former is a monument to conservative penal policies, the first great attempt to repress crime without altering the social conditions that produce it.

II The Rise of Positivist Criminology

The five essays in Part II deal with the rise of positivist discourses about crime – discourses that situate crime in relation to the body, the social and the mind. They begin with Piers Beirne's essay 'Adolphe Quetelet and the Origins of Positivist Criminology', which shows how the latter arose with the labours of the Franco-Belgian moral statisticians. In the 1820s their work included some of the focal concerns in penality and the statistical movement, two domains that coincided in a common issue, namely, the regulation of the dangerous classes. The apparent failure of French penal strategies to regulate the conduct of the dangerous classes, when conjoined with an expansion in the scope of the statistical movement to include empirical social research, provided the structure and much of the substantive content of the criminology of the moral statisticians, especially so for Adolphe Quetelet's social mechanics of crime. Its structure was formed by the relentless application of the methods of the natural sciences to the moral phenomena lodged in the official records of crime. Its content comprised an empirical examination of the effects of different social environments on those individuals – drawn largely from the dangerous classes – who passed through the successive tiers of the administration of justice. Its outcome was a positivist discourse about '*Homo criminalis*' which included such concepts as 'criminal character' and 'criminal propensities' and which looked to the causal influence on crime of such factors as age, gender, class and race. Eventually, it nurtured a rigid binary opposition between normality and deviation.

In Chapter 6, Pasquale Pasquino begins with a few peremptory words uttered in 1885 by the Italian positivist Enrico Ferri that registered a new object of penal science, namely, *Homo criminalis*. This object Pasquino contrasts with *Homo penalis*, the administrative object of classical criminology. Whereas the *Homo penalis* of classical and administrative penology was a free-will subject undistinguishable from all other citizens, the *Homo criminalis* of criminology was and is an object that differs radically and in more or less complex ways from the 'normal' population of law-abiding citizenry. Whereas nothing needed to be known or explored about *Homo penalis*, the distinct, disordered and dangerous *Homo criminalis* needed to be investigated with all the tools of positivist science. It is around this figure of *Homo criminalis*, Pasquino reasons, that criminology derived its vocation and its punitive rationality.

In 'British Criminology before 1935' (Chapter 7), David Garland describes the growth of a modern scientific criminology in Britain. By 'scientific' Garland refers to the actors' definitions of the term rather than his own; in fact, he suggests that the positivist criminology that developed in Britain differed in crucial ways from Lombrosianism or Comteanism. British criminology developed in a psychiatric and medico-legal framework, a therapeutically-oriented discipline that was deeply committed in seemingly practical ways to existing institutions of criminal justice and which, compared with its continental counterparts, appeared profoundly conservative. From the outset, the British tradition of scientific criminology had the support of the prison establishment and the medical profession. Garland relates how this tradition grew out of a psychiatric classification of offenders; then, after about 1895, how it confronted the more complex world of penal-welfare institutions, and finally how, after the 1914–1918 War, it emphasized the importance of individual character and specialized treatment. Garland discusses the importance of Cyril Burt's *The Young Delinquent* of 1925, a lengthy tome that for a large popular audience combined statistical methods with 'commonsense' psychiatry and was the exemplar of the hodge-podge development of early British criminology.

In 'From Marx to Bonger: Socialist Writings on Women, Gender, and Crime' (Chapter 8), James Messerschmidt shows how, when they referred to crime, early socialist writers such as Marx and Engels tended to concentrate on the economic and class relations of production and to ignore reproductive relations such as procreation, socialization and everyday subsistence. Messerschmidt points out that while, in the early 19th century, many utopian socialist feminists had stressed the mutual dependence of class and gender oppression, Marx and Engels blindly argued that gender oppression was caused by class oppression. Textual evidence is offered, from Marx's and Engels's writings and from those of other early socialists such as Achille Loria and Willem Bonger, to show how their class-based and 'gender-less' theories dominated their views of women and crime. Marx and Engels, for example, held the view that women who commit crime (such as prostitution) are but particular cases who respond, like other workers, to the demoralized conditions of life brought on by capitalist class relations. Such a view necessarily fails to explain, Messerschmidt concludes, the important differences that exist in the types of crime respectively committed by men and women.

In Chapter 9, Piers Beirne and Alan Hunt investigate an important saga in the legal and political history of Soviet Marxism, namely, Lenin's influential pronouncements on crime and penality made during the critical period of early Bolshevik power between October 1917 and his death in mid-1924. Three key elements in this discourse are identified: (1) a largely positivist view of criminality in socialist and communist societies, including 'red-collar crime';

(2) support for various neoclassical strategies in Bolshevik penality, such as the decriminalization of certain common crimes, the use of fines and suspended sentences, and of socially useful labour paid at trade union rates; and, (3) a simultaneously coherent and contradictory fusion, within the penal complex, of strategies of law and terror in, respectively, the 'normal' and the 'exceptional' state. The authors suggest that, like his view on the constitution of Soviet society, Lenin's attitude towards penality stemmed from the complex interplay of authoritarian and libertarian tendencies in his political theory. These tendencies, both progressive and reactionary, are identified and discussed as they unfolded in the early years of Bolshevik power.

III The Growth of Criminology in the U.S., 1880–1945

The six essays in Part III address an immense subject that, especially from the Civil War to the rise of the school of social ecology in 1920's Chicago, still sorely lacks historical comment. In Chapter 10, Nicole Hahn Rafter identifies the origins of criminology in the U.S. in the doctrines of the movement in criminal anthropology which flourished in the 1890s. Three groups in particular are highlighted: (1) the European 'originators' who generated the theory, including the Hungarian Moriz Benedikt and the inventor of the concept of the born criminal, Cesare Lombroso; (2) the 'channelers' who provided access to the originators' work, including the New York physician E.P. Fowler, the American Institute of Criminal Law and Criminology, who arranged for Henry P. Horton to translate Lombroso's *Crime: Its Causes and Remedies* in 1918, and the English eugenist Havelock Ellis, whose *The Criminal* of 1890 did more than any other book to promulgate criminal anthropology; and, (3) 'U.S. criminal anthropologists' whose texts included MacDonald's (1893) *Criminology*, Henderson's (1893) *Introduction to the Study of the Dependent, Defective and Delinquent Classes*, and Parsons's (1909) *Responsibility for Crime*.

Hahn Rafter outlines much of the core content of U.S. criminal anthropology: its obsession with scientific status, its concept of the born criminal, its development of a hierarchy of criminal types, and its partial support of the eugenics programme. She concludes her essay with the provocative suggestion that many of criminology's subsequent identity crises, up to and including the present – e.g., its lack of focus and its failure to demarcate theoretical and institutional boundaries – stem from the fact that its origins lay in the incoherent dogma of criminal anthropology.

In 'Feminism, Criminology and the Rise of the Female Sex "Delinquent", 1880–1930' (Chapter 11), James Messerschmidt demonstrates how ideological currents within criminology sometimes contribute to social movements whose aim is to control the behaviour of a particular social group. In this case he outlines how, in the 1860s and 1870s, feminists organized a campaign against the masculine-defined state regulation of prostitution. In the process of their campaign these feminists converged with, and were then coopted by, the conservative social purity movement which viewed prostitution as 'white-slave traffic'. According to Messerschmidt, feminists who concentrated on the alleged passivity and innocence of young women, and how they were coerced into prostitution by evil men, did so at the expense of understanding the limited choices available to working-class girls in a patriarchal capitalist society.

Messerschmidt describes how, during the Progressive era, major U.S. cities established vice commissions whose targets were prostitution and the sexual immorality of young women, including flappers. Despite the relatively enlightened criticism of University of Chicago criminologist Frances Kellor, many criminologists actively participated in vice commission objectives in the sense of constructing and developing the category of 'female sex delinquency'. Criminologists' explanations of this new deviant category varied, in more or less complex ways, and depended on whether, for example, they subscribed to the biologism of Lombrosianism or to the environmentalism of incipient sociological accounts. In any event, criminologists participated in the construction of a new deviant category and in the incarceration of its incumbents.

Some of these themes are developed in Dorie Klein's essay, 'The Etiology of Female Crime: A Review of the Literature' (Chapter 12). Klein bemoans the fact that the history of American criminology from approximately 1900 to 1960 is not one in which women have figured very prominently; she thus sets out to explore that small group of writings that does focus on women. The specific authors discussed by Klein include Lombroso, W.I. Thomas, Freud, Kingsley Davis and Otto Pollak. Klein argues that, despite obvious analytical differences among these authors, their writings on women represent a tradition that shared certain assumptions in terms of theoretical groundwork. One assumption is that criminality is the result of individual physiological or psychological characteristics. This assumption, in turn, is built on two others: first, that individual characteristics are unaffected by economic, social and political forces and, second, that all women have in common a certain nature. Since they locate the aetiology of female crime at the level of the individual, so too the authors in this tradition assume that the remedies for criminality lie in individual adjustment rather than social change. Klein shows how these several assumptions usually embodied a moral position that masqueraded as science.

The next two essays deal with important aspects of the work of the person who is often referred to as the 'Dean' of American criminology, Edwin Sutherland. In Chapter 13, Gilbert Geis and Colin Goff report the intellectual and institutional developments that led to the publication of Sutherland's epochal *White-Collar Crime* of 1949. They describe how, when and why Sutherland's singlehanded determination to expose and understand corporate violations led to his coining of the term 'white-collar criminal' (in 1936), his empirical research on corporate violations between 1928 and 1934, and his famous Presidential Address of 1939 to the American Sociological Society, which showed him increasingly preoccupied with theoretical questions concerning the nature of crime. Thereafter, Geis and Goff describe Sutherland's continuing research on white-collar crime with the help of graduate students at Indiana University, his debate with Paul Tappan as to whether white-collar crime really is crime, and the saga of *White-Collar Crime*'s publication and chequered reception.

In Chapter 14, John Laub and Robert Sampson examine Sutherland's debate with Sheldon and Eleanor Glueck concerning the causes of crime and the proper methodological and theoretical tools for criminology. Through a detailed analysis of textual materials, both published and unpublished, the authors provide the several contexts necessary for understanding Sutherland's longstanding and bitter debate with the Gluecks; these include their isolation at Harvard Law School as well as Sutherland's intense dislike of individualistic and psychiatric explanations of crime and his sociological imperialism. Despite Sutherland's resounding victory against the Gluecks, and despite contemporary silence about the latter's research on delinquency in the history of American criminology, Laub and Sampson argue convincingly that the tradition established by the Gluecks lies at the heart of much work in criminology today.

Finally, in 'Clifford R. Shaw and Henry D. McKay: Chicago Criminologists', Jon Snodgrass outlines the contributions to criminology of these two famous Chicago sociologists. Snodgrass divides their work in Chicago into three parts: (1) the collection of autobiographies of juvenile delinquents, (2) the ecological distribution of delinquents, and (3) the delinquency prevention programme known as the Chicago Area Project. Providing in rich detail some biographical commentary on both Shaw and MacKay and their respective work styles, Snodgrass examines the main aspects of their 1942 book, *Juvenile Delinquency and Urban Areas*, offers some criticism of it, and concludes with a discussion of the development of the Chicago Area Project.

Part I
The Enlightenment: Cesare Beccaria's
Of Crimes and Punishments

[1]

PENOLOGICAL REFORM AND THE MYTH OF BECCARIA*

GRAEME NEWMAN
State University of New York at Albany

PIETRO MARONGIU
University of Cagliari, Sardinia, Italy

Beccaria is widely acknowledged as one of penology's great reformers. This paper analyzes aspects of Beccaria's life and works and concludes that the adoration afforded Beccaria by penologists far outweighs the actual contributions he made to penology. Many of the reforms that occurred during the eighteenth century can as easily be ascribed to social and political conditions as to Beccaria's work. When compared with the works of other great reformers of the eighteenth century, such as Voltaire or Bentham, Beccaria's works are less profound. The myth of Beccaria nonetheless presides over the modern paradigm of liberal penology.

One can scarcely find a textbook on criminology without a passage of adoration for the "father of modern criminology," Cesare Beccaria. A few examples of this blind worship will suffice. Sheldon Glueck (1965:4) unabashedly classified Beccaria's "genius" with that of Galileo, Newton, and Darwin. Lawrence Friedman (1973), influential historian of American law, refers to Beccaria as a "great reformer." John Conrad (1985:77–78) calls Beccaria a "savant" and "an admirable and modest 18th century Italian." In 1985 the United Nations devoted a sizable part of its Seventh Congress on the Prevention of Crime and Treatment of Offenders to the worship of Beccaria. A recent convention in Milan to commemorate the 250th anniversary of Beccaria's birth was an exercise in ritual adoration. Those speakers from countries that had abolished the death penalty felt obliged to state that abolition had been achieved because of Beccaria's influence (Harding, 1988). Others referred to him as "a prophet" (Mueller, 1988). Only one paper attempted a critical assessment of Beccaria's role as "innovator" (Modona, 1988).

Conrad (1985:77) also announced that he knew "of no detractors of Beccaria." Indeed, at the time he wrote his comments that was almost true. We have been able to find few sources in English critical of Beccaria and his works (see Jenkins, 1984; Sellin, 1976:66). The most widely cited exposition of Beccaria's works devotes a mere 2 pages out of 103 to a critical analysis

---

* We wish to express our thanks to W. Byron Groves and Piers Beirne for their helpful criticisms of earlier drafts of this paper.

NEWMAN AND MARONGIU

(Phillipson, 1970:102–103). And if one looks to criticisms made against Beccaria by the great philosophers, such as Kant and Hegel, one finds very little recognition of it in modern textbooks on penology (see Young, 1983, for a review; also Kant, 1983:168–170; Maestro, 1973:128).

We think that the idea of Beccaria as a great reformer is a myth slavishly adhered to by modern penologists. In this paper, we will argue that his "inspiration" has been a kind of hero worship that has been used to justify certain reforms as admirable. Further, we will show that the treatise for which Beccaria is so famous not only is full of irresovable contradictions, but holds within it reactionary, antireformist doctrines. Finally, we will argue that the majority of reforms that occurred during and soon after Beccaria's treatise can as easily be ascribed to prevailing social and political conditions as to Beccaria or his tract.

We should make clear at the outset that we do not deny the influence and standing of Beccaria and his work in penology. We seek, rather, to analyze his life and work critically and to determine why, in the light of our analysis, he has achieved such stature in penological literature. We examine both his life (that is, his character) and his intellectual contribution (that is, *On Crimes and Punishments* [1764], his *Treatise*) because the two are inextricably linked in what has become an established tradition in penological thought. That is to say, he is regarded in all texts as a *reform-er*, and he is often referred to as "the father" of modern criminology. We examine Beccaria and his work, therefore, as sociocultural phenomena. His intellectual contributions should not be separated from his social and cultural period nor, by implication, from his character. Although we believe that this approach should apply to all previous thinkers in criminology, we argue that it applies even more to one who is thought of as a *reform-er* and whose human example is so often held up to us as the "light."

In order to simplify our presentation, we first consider Beccaria as a reformer, and then consider his intellectual contributions to reform. We quickly demonstrate, however, that the concept of reform is virtually impossible to pin down and that the content of "intellectual" contributions may be as much "emotional" (or perhaps more accurately "spiritual") as they are "rational."

THE GREAT REFORMER: DOES BECCARIA MEASURE UP?

The period during which Beccaria wrote was of great significance in Europe: the three decades prior to the French Revolution, the culmination of a century in which the ethos of the utilitarians overturned the Christian ethos. Instead of accepting suffering as the natural state of man, happiness was proclaimed in its stead. The great utilitarians of the century, such as

THE MYTH OF BECCARIA   327

Voltaire, Montesquieu, Helvetius, and Diderot, not only linked the logic of government to the happiness of individuals, but carried forth this principle to an overwhelming concern for the "common man." Crane Brinton (1959:293–328) has demonstrated that this concern for the common man formed the core of the humanitarian "movement" of the eighteenth century. The sick, the weak, the poor, the criminal, the mentally ill, all came to be seen in a different light. Their plight was now society's responsibility, as well as God's.

Many of the utilitarians were, and are, recognized social reformers, of whom the most famous is Voltaire. By *reformers* we mean that they were the most outspoken of the intellectuals in their criticism of the status quo and in their advocacy of change, and they were brave enough to accept the consequences of their activism—often banishment or prison. Some were more extreme than others. Some were revolutionaries in the sense that they advocated the complete overthrow of the established order and law, such as de Sade and Robespierre (who helped design and carry out a revolution). Many of the great thinkers were well educated because they were fortunate enough to be of noble birth. They were not "workers" rising up in revolution in the Marxist sense. For this reason they have sometimes been called "bourgeois intellectuals" by critical criminologists (see, for example, Taylor et al., 1973:1–9; Vold and Bernard, 1986:18–35).

Other writers have compared Beccaria with reformers of his time. Maestro (1942), for example, has compared him with Voltaire, and Jenkins (1984) has compared him with the Marquis de Sade.[1] In these great thinkers, we have two quite distinct positions on the continuum of "liberal to radical."[2]

The Marquis de Sade, who wrote a little later than Beccaria and who lived in prison, largely, through the French Revolution, provides a fascinating contrast to both Voltaire and Beccaria. Among other things, he argued for the virtual abolition of all laws.[3] For expounding these ideas de Sade paid dearly: some 17 years in prison, 10 of them in the Bastille, served at various times throughout his lifetime (Lely, 1970). De Sade showed great courage in setting forth his ideas, and he was clearly prepared to accept their consequences.[4] In contrast, Jenkins (1984) has argued that Beccaria's ideas were

---

1. Phillipson (1923:1–106) has compared him with Bentham and Romilly only obliquely. In a brief passage in which he summarizes criticisms of Beccaria's logic, Phillipson observes that Bentham was "an acuter logician" (p. 103).

2. We use the term "liberal" intentionally because it has been argued that twentieth-century liberalism had its beginning in the Enlightenment of the eighteenth century (see Crane Brinton, 1959).

3. This is a greatly simplified account of his many views. For the best explication of his arguments on law and criminal justice, violence and libertinage, see his provocative play, "Philosophy in the Bedroom," published in various collections of his works.

4. De Sade, a strong supporter of the revolution and secretary of Robespierre's Jacobin Club, broke with the latter when appointed chair of the *Section des Piques*, the body

328   NEWMAN AND MARONGIU

essentially supportive of the status quo. The fact that they were embraced so quickly by sovereigns supports this view.

Voltaire was less radical than de Sade, though very much devoted to reform. Reformers are not, perhaps by definition, radicals; rather, they have sufficient faith in the system to try to change it rather than subvert it. Although this is perhaps a fine distinction, it is reasonably applied to the French Encyclopaedists, who depended on the favors of the sovereign for their existence, or at least were beholden to the established social structure for their inherited wealth. Voltaire, a rich noble in his own right, suffered at the hands of the sovereign on many occasions. He was arrested, jailed, and forced into exile as a result of many of his writings and plays.

The breadth and depth of Voltaire's writings are tremendous. Because of his conflict with the authorities, however, Voltaire had little direct influence with the sovereign.[5] When he turned his attention to questions of criminal law reform, he developed a unique strategy. His technique was to take up the cause of particular legal cases and fight them publicly. The most famous case he argued was that of the execution of Jean Calas by breaking on the wheel. Calas had been convicted of murdering his father, who had in actual fact committed suicide. Voltaire claimed a clear perversion of justice in this case. His relentless campaign eventually succeeded, and the sovereign was forced to restore the family honor of Calas. To influence the virtually all-powerful sovereigns to intervene in this and other cases by using what amounted to "public pressure," as we would call it today, was no small feat in the eighteenth century. Voltaire was the quintessential reformer.

It is easy to demonstrate that Beccaria was no great reformer in the sense that we have outlined. Compared with Voltaire, Beccaria hardly measures up. He was not a modest savant, as Conrad (1985) suggests; rather, he was lazy, timid, and reclusive.[6] Indeed, the *Treatise* was first published anonymously because of Beccaria's fear of reprisals. It is well known that Beccaria

---

responsible for conducting trials of those to be executed. On August 2, 1793, he stormed out of the meeting, decrying the mass executions. For this he was returned to the Bastille, where he remained until Robespierre was executed on October 15, 1794. (See Gillette, 1966:38.)

5. For a character study of Voltaire, see Torrey (1962). There appears to be no single book that reviews all of Voltaire's works, possibly because they were so vast (one French collection runs to 52 volumes) and covered incredible breadth of moral philosophy, science, poetry, religion, metaphysics, literature, theater, history, and political philosophy.

6. The introduction by Paolucci to the currently available English translation of Beccaria clearly documents this. However, Conrad (1985) has argued that this is an unreliable or biased source. Although Paolucci may have had an axe to grind, there are plentiful sources to support the characterization of Beccaria as lazy, timid, and reclusive. Even Marcello Maestro (cited by Conrad as contradicting this view) acknowledges this: "a tendency to laziness and melancholy, which was indeed a characteristic of [Beccaria's] temperament" (Maestro, 1942:53). That Maestro should acknowledge this is quite impressive,

THE MYTH OF BECCARIA   329

had to be cajoled and pushed into writing anything at all, including the *Treatise* (Cantu, 1862:149). Only after the *Treatise* became popular and widely accepted by a number of sovereigns did Beccaria consent to publish the document in his name.

Beccaria was invited to visit with the Encyclopaedists in France, but the visit was a disaster. He remained in France for only six weeks, hardly communicating with any of the great reformers.[7] That he had little direct contact or correspondence with the French reformers is surely significant. Beccaria failed to campaign for the reforms he advocated. His was hardly the behavior of a reformer, it seems to us. From the many accounts of Beccaria's life we have reviewed, the person that emerges is one of fickle and spoilt character, certainly not one of magnanimity or modesty or commitment to principle.

The fact remains, though, that the ideas as expressed in the *Treatise* quickly penetrated the criminal laws, debates about penology, and criminology throughout Europe, including England, and the United States. Maestro (1942) shows clearly that this would not have happened without the strong advocacy of the *Treatise* by Voltaire, perhaps the most influential reformer of the period. Beccaria's views were almost a perfect fit with Voltaire's. The preamble to the *Treatise* established a view of the role of religion almost identical to Voltaire's: it should have a role, but not an all-pervasive one, and certainly not fanatical. He sought to separate crime from morality. Beccaria's ideas on the role of the sovereign were also similar to Voltaire's: He recommended a carefully reserved role for sovereigns. Beccaria attacked the judiciary, not the sovereignty. Voltaire found in Beccaria much that he could use in his campaigns. One could conclude that it was Voltaire who made Beccaria famous, just as it was the Verri brothers who made him a writer.

BECCARIA AND BENTHAM

Some have suggested that Bentham was a disciple of Beccaria. This claim is made on the basis of Bentham's sentimental reference to Beccaria: "Oh, master, first evangelist of reason. . . ." As H.L.A. Hart (1982) has shown, however, the relation between Bentham and Beccaria is very complex. Bentham read Beccaria's *Treatise* when he was about 19 and probably wrote his *Rationale of Punishment* when he was about 29. Hart argues, but admits it is

---

since this biography is somewhat biased toward the adoration of Beccaria. The extensive work of Cantu (1862:153) clearly documents the evidence of Beccaria as reclusive, shy, and cowardly: "[Beccaria] . . . was careless in his handwriting and spelling . . . too lazy to write . . ." (*negletto nella scrittura e nell'ortographia . . . pigro della scrivere . . .*). Romangoli (1985:xxiv–xxvi) describes Beccaria as "cowardly," "moody" (*pavido e ombroso*), "inept" (*pigrizia e inettitudine*) , and "lazy" (*debole e pigro*). (Our translation.)

7. Maestro (1973) does his best to demonstrate that it was homesickness for his wife that caused his return. This is doubtful when one considers that after his wife died, some eight years after his return from Paris, he remarried within two months of her death.

speculative, that therefore Beccaria must have had a profound effect on Bentham's young mind. He suggests even further that there are examples of Bentham's "unconscious borrowing" from Beccaria. However, the passage in which Bentham displays his adoration continues on to note that Helvetius had actually provided Beccaria with most of the grist for his ideas.[8]

Bentham was also highly critical of Beccaria on a number of points, some of them profoundly philosophical. Although he admired Beccaria's work because it was "based on reason," he also pointed out that "even in his work there is some reasoning drawn from false sources" (Bentham, 1975:40). Further, he was highly critical of Beccaria's failure to develop his general points in detail, to the point that Hart (1982:49) observed that Bentham thought Beccaria to be "rather a lazy man." Their differences were profound, as Hart shows—and probably were such because Beccaria was not prepared to go to the logical extreme in his utilitarianism as was Bentham. Although Hart notes that certain ideas buried in footnotes to Beccaria's *Treatise* may have sparked Bentham's entire theory of fictions, for example, we can never really know which came first. But it is apparent that Bentham's was an incredibly advanced view of the role of law and legislation, and his theory of legal and other types of fictions must surely be seen as paradigm breaking. They presaged many new developments in the philosophy of language, and even the very latest shift in legal theory to the semiology of law (see Milovanovic, 1988).

One must realize that Beccaria's *Treatise* was so general that it is possible to link it to just about any theory. Bentham was certainly indebted to Beccaria for inspiration, but his work is far more extensive and profound than Beccaria's.

THE TREATISE: FORM AND CONTENT

A critical appraisal of the substance of *On Crimes and Punishments* is difficult to make, because it is a document full of many obscurities and contradictions (which become worse when translated into English). The vagueness of many of the terms used and the level of generality of the document make it difficult to pin down the substance. Some say that it is this level of generality that constitutes its genius. Others say that its form is the result of the particular way in which it was written.

There are various speculations about how the *Treatise* was written. One is a suspicion that Beccaria did not write the document, but the accuracy of this accusation turns on what is meant by the word "write." As far as we can

---

8. ". . . you who have raised your Italy so far above England, and I would add above France, were it not that Helvetius, without writing on the subject of laws, had already assisted you and provided you with your fundamental ideas . . ." (quoted in Maestro, 1973:131).

ascertain, it would seem that Beccaria had great difficulty writing. When he did, he wrote pieces here and there, "on scraps of paper," as Pietro Verri noted. Our guess is that Beccaria had put down notes resulting from the many discussions he had with the Verris and their visitors about the criminal law, and that the Verris had then urged Beccaria to put these scraps together into a book. Beccaria apparently spent a long time trying to do that, without accomplishing very much. Eventually, Pietro Verri collected the various pieces and organized them into an essay. So, whether Beccaria "wrote" the *Treatise* is difficult to say. Most of the passages, it would be fair to say, Beccaria probably wrote. But the document as a whole was produced by Verri, perhaps as Beccaria's "editor" or "ghostwriter." This could explain why much of the *Treatise* is disjointed. One section often does not follow the other. In fact, far from being a simple and clear document, the *Treatise* is complicated, inconsistent, and disorganized. Those who claim the document is simple and clear have probably never read it, though they may have read summaries of it, such as that by Phillipson (1923), who totally reorganized the ideas to make a more coherent presentation. A long letter written by Pietro Verri on November 1, 1765, describes the process in detail. It is so revealing, we quote it here in full:

> And now I will satisfy you on the subject of the book *On Crimes and Punishments*. The book is by the Marquis Beccaria. I gave him the subject; the majority of the ideas are the result of conversation which took place everyday between Beccaria, Alessandro, Lambertenghi and myself. In our society we pass the evening in the same room, each of us working. Alessandro is working on the *Storia d'Italia*, I have my political and economic works, Beccaria was bored and bored with others. Desperately, he asked me for a subject and I suggested this to him, because I knew it was an excellent one for an eloquent and very imaginative man. But he knew nothing about our criminal systems. Alessandro, who was *Protector of Prisoners*, promised to help him. Beccaria began to write his ideas on sheets of paper, and we encouraged him so much that he set down a great many ideas; every afternoon we took a walk and we talked of the errors in criminal law, we had discussions, questions, and then, at night, he did his writing; but it is so tiring for him to write that after an hour he cannot go on. When he had all the material collected, I wrote it down and we gave order to it, so to form a book. The difficulty was to publish such delicate matters without having trouble. I sent it to Mr. Aubert in Leghorn, who had published my *Meditazioni sulla felicita*. I sent the manuscript in April last year [1764] and we received the first copy in July 1764 (Maestro, 1942:54).

The date of this letter is important. Most biographers claim that the Verri brothers, especially Pietro, spread vicious lies about Beccaria's difficulty in writing the *Treatise*, because of jealousy over the fame that the book brought him. However, the split between the two friends did not occur until after Beccaria's trip to Paris, which occurred in 1766.

As a result of Beccaria's immodest behavior at Paris, Pietro Verri became very much upset. It seems that Beccaria failed to acknowledge the considerable assistance given him by the Verris, particularly Pietro's help, which most biographers are now agreed was accurately portrayed in the letter quoted above.[9] That is, Verri provided Beccaria with the topic. Almost all of the ideas emerged from their group discussions, so it was as if Beccaria wrote notes each day as a student would in a classroom. Verri then arranged the notes into a whole. At least by today's academic standards, Beccaria should have unambiguously acknowledged this input. It is clear that he did not, which resulted in resentment on the part of Pietro Verri:

> I would never expect this kind of ingratitude from any man, let alone from Beccaria, who is famous solely because of me. A man originally worthless, without a name, who, through me, had his vices and defects covered over by my enthusiastic friendship. He doesn't deserve this glory, because it was I who provided him with it.[10]

Beccaria has also been charged with plagiarism, or as one recent writer called it, "cribbing" (Masur, 1989:52). This charge was widely communicated by Pietro Verri after the Paris trip, when he became most resentful. Beccaria had not only failed to acknowledge his input, but also took complete credit for the extensive *Apologia* written in rebuttal to Facchinei (1765), a Jesuit who attacked the *Treatise* as being antichurch. There is absolutely no doubt that Pietro Verri wrote the entire *Apologia*. The embittered Pietro Verri planned "to find out in Montesquieu etc . . . all the things he took from them, in order to denounce him as a plagiarist." But his brother Alessandro advised that this was too risky; rather, he should make a rational criticism of the book, without showing much anger (Valeri, 1969:143; our translation).

One cannot plagiarize ideas, though one can steal them. There were few new ideas in the book (and for those that were, it took the sharp intellect of Bentham to give them form). They were taken from the prevailing ideas of the great French reformist thinkers. One cannot fault Beccaria on this. Rather, by today's standards, he was writing a "textbook," drawing on contemporary social thought. His fault was that he did not document his

---

9. There are varying degrees of interpretation of this letter. Marcello Maestro sees nothing wrong with Beccaria's behavior. Others attend more closely to Beccaria's minimal input into the *Treatise*. As Valeri notes: "[Verri] suggested to his friend, always weak and indecisive, the idea for the work . . . pushed him to write it, overcoming his natural laziness . . . Verri recopied in his own hand, the most confused pages . . ." (Valeri, 1969:113, our translation). And further, "[Verri] was the loving obstetrician of a difficult birth . . ." (1969:113, our translation).

10. Letter by Pietro Verri to Alessandro Verri, December 16, 1766 (from Valeri, 1969:145, our translation).

THE MYTH OF BECCARIA   333

sources. The fact is that Beccaria's behavior—by standards then and now—is ethically tainted and ought to be explicitly recognized as such by modern writers in penology. Instead, twentieth-century writers seem to assume that Beccaria's accomplishments in other areas cancel out his lapse in moral integrity. Indeed, one recent history of criminology does not even recognize the controversy over the writing of the *Treatise* (Jones, 1986).

EVALUATING THE TREATISE

Rather than go through the document section by section, we will concentrate on those sections for which Beccaria has become so famous. We should also point out that we are not questioning here the importance of the *Treatise* in laying out such basic principles of judicial policy as clarity of the law; no punishment without trial; detention pending trial should be fixed by law; without certainty of guilt, no person should be condemned; verdicts and proofs of guilt should be public; and secret accusations should not be permitted. These principles are stated in sections I through XI of the *Treatise*.

It must be recognized, however, that although these principles are often ascribed to Beccaria they were part of the general reformist approach and juridical enlightenment expounded by various thinkers before Beccaria published his *Treatise*. For example, in his 1748 *Spirit of Laws* Montesquieu had already written in favor of clarity of the law, not to mention Voltaire's ardent opposition to secret accusations (e.g., the Calas case). Moreover, the practice of secret accusations had never held sway in England, because it was the only European country that never adopted the inquisitorial system (derived from the Roman Church).[11] In this particular respect, Beccaria could hardly "reform" English penal law, notwithstanding Bentham's proclamations of him as his "*lucerna*" (light).

UTILITARIAN OR RETRIBUTIVIST?

Few texts have attended to the relationship between Beccaria and utilitarian theory, even though the utilitarian origins of much of modern sociological theory in general, and crime and punishment theory in particular, have distinct and traceable roots in that intellectual tradition.[12] The work of Durkheim, for example, probably the single most influential work on much

---

11. Nor was torture, as such, though *peine forte et dure* a practice resembling torture was in vogue (Newman, 1985).

12. There are many strains of utilitarian theory. See, for example, Lyons (1965). Different variations have appeared at different times throughout history, though it is safe to say that utilitarian theories of the eighteenth century were essentially hedonistic, focusing on the teleological (as opposed to deontological) aspects of utilitarianism. Obedience to rules (often associated with "rule utilitarianism" by twentieth-century philosophers) can be seen as an important and unstated assumption in many of the eighteenth-century utilitarian theories. However, because of their adherence to the social contract, they tended to see

deviance and punishment theory in criminology, is heavily influenced by utilitarian theory.

The definitional problems in distinguishing between retributivism and utilitarianism make for much confusion in understanding Beccaria's position. Young (1983:10) argues that Beccaria is essentially a retributivist and only secondarily a utilitarian. He reaches this conclusion largely as a result of defining retribution very broadly, and by more or less taking anything that Kant and Hegel said about punishment as definitional of retribution. However, the supreme role of the sovereign or State that both Hegel and Kant allowed in the role of punishment is not an essential element of retribution (Newman, 1985:193). Seen within its socio-historical context, Beccaria's similar treatment of the State is essentially posturing in order to avoid being put in jail.

Young (1983) also claims that assessing seriousness of crimes only by their consequences, which Beccaria does, is commensurate with retributivism. As one of us has noted, one type of retributivism may be in line with this view, ("secular retribution") if it is used as a simple matching formula to connect crime with punishment (Newman, 1983). However, in general, the consequentialist structure of this model makes it a very doubtful element of retributive logic. Barbara Wooton (1963), perhaps the strongest twentieth-century advocate of utilitarian criminal justice, has used injury and damage as the main criteria for matching punishments to crimes. By far the dominant ethic of retribution historically has been to require individual guilt (i.e., evil intent) of the actor in order to (1) justify punishing the actor in the first place—the offender must be shown to have consciously intended the act and (2) match the punishment to the offender's guilt ("religious retribution," see Newman, 1983). The damage done by the act is important, but secondary. Whether one agrees with Young's interpretation turns on the emphasis one puts on the teleological structure of Beccaria's arguments. Beccaria's views are probably close to "rule utilitarianism," which is not pure utilitarianism, but is primarily utilitarian nonetheless (see note 12).

Beccaria's utilitarian assumptions are particularly interesting because they appear to contradict some of his other "administrative" postulates. We can see these in his famous concluding sentence that has captivated generations of readers:

> In order for punishment not to be, in every instance, an act of violence of one or of many against a private citizen, it must be essentially public, prompt, necessary, the least possible in the given circumstances, proportionate to the crimes, dictated by the laws (Beccaria, 1963:99).

---

rules as an evil imposition, necessary only to maintain order, but certainly not as matters of morality in themselves (as argued by deontologists such as Kant).

THE MYTH OF BECCARIA   335

Retributivists would certainly agree that a punishment should be proportionate to the crime. That is their credo—some would say their only credo. However, it is contradicted by the utilitarian view that the pain of the punishment must outweigh the pleasure of the offense. This is in fact what is hidden by Beccaria's use of the words "least possible" and "necessary." What is the necessary condition for punishment—the breaking of a law? Retributivists would say so. But utilitarians, who are forward looking, are interested in preventing future crimes. This is why they have long advocated increasing punishments for second and subsequent offenses and why they advocate punishment by example—general deterrence (the reason for Beccaria's insistence that the punishment be public).

These punishment policies directly contradict the idea of proportionate punishments. Rather, their thrust is toward applying punishment that is greater than the crime. In other words, disproportionate punishments. Indeed, Beccaria notes, "the evil which [punishment] inflicts has only to exceed the advantage derivable from the crime," and this is stated in the section entitled "Mildness of Punishments." There is nothing whatsoever in these utilitarian views that guarantees mildness of punishments. On the contrary, the utilitarian principles espoused guarantee an increasingly severe punishment. Beccaria seems to realize this when he advocates that the "scale of punishments should be relative to the state of the nation itself."[13] This proposal must be seen as a posturing toward those who ran the nations of his day, mainly the sovereigns of Europe. A moment's reflection also reveals it to be entirely lacking in moral value: It would seem to allow for approval of the killing of 20,000 people during the French Terror since that reflected the state of the nation.

In sum, Beccaria incorporated the retributive justification for punishment into a utilitarian model. This served to sanitize the less appealing deterrent assumptions of the utilitarian position he advocated. That is, by advocating "proportionate" punishment, he was able to make his position seem just. But it is clear that he did not have in mind the kind of "just deserts" advocated by modern retributivists.

THE CLASSICAL SCHOOL AND JUDICIAL DISCRETION

Beccaria has been described as the founder of the "classical school" of criminology. This school is usually characterized as one that is "administrative" (Vold and Bernard, 1986) in its approach, and this is contrasted in

---

13. This statement is followed by a virtually incomprehensible passage that seems to claim that as the "social state" develops, so sensibilities will become greater, thus the force of punishment will diminish. Paolucci, in a footnote to his translation, refers to the passage in Montesquieu that he thinks Beccaria may have been trying to interpret. This was that there appeared to be no difference in the spirit of inhabitants between countries with severe punishments and those with mild punishments (Beccaria, 1963:44).

336   NEWMAN AND MARONGIU

many textbooks with the "scientific" or "positive school," which developed under the leadership of Lombroso, and later Ferri, in Italy. Beccaria's "administrative" criminology is seen as rooted in his critique of judicial discretion.

Beccaria did severely criticize judicial discretion, but he rather simply advocated that judges' discretion be replaced by very specific laws. But who would make those laws, and how specific could they get? Once again, the *Treatise* plays right up to the sovereigns, who, along with handpicked groups of nobles, essentially made the laws of Europe. Beccaria was simply removing the discretion of judges to a next and higher level. There was every reason for the sovereigns and nobles to look kindly on a proposal that advocated giving them more power. It is also understandable why it was not popular with the church, for this represented one more step toward taking power away from the church (which heavily influenced court procedures) and putting it in the hands of the secular elite.

Paolucci (see Beccaria, 1963) argues that Beccaria knew very little of courts and judges and that his claim that many of the problems of the criminal process were caused by the abuse of judicial discretion was simply unfounded. When France developed legislation based on Beccaria's proposals, the laws proved unworkable and resulted in many injustices. The laws could not possibly take into account all the human and situational circumstances in which offenses occurred.

MILDNESS OF PUNISHMENTS?

It appears that Beccaria did not advocate mild punishments at all. There are two glaring examples of this in his argument against the death penalty, which we discuss below. For the moment, we ask whether it is consistent for an enlightened reformer of his time to advocate corporal punishment. Section XXVI of the *Treatise* clearly advocates just this:

> Some crimes are acts of aggression against the person, others against property. The penalties for the first should always be corporal punishments (Beccaria, 1963:68).

Beccaria fails to specify what corporal punishments he approves. Does one assume that he had no criticism of the current practices (e.g., whipping, breaking on the wheel, removing bodily parts with red-hot pincers)? Instead, in this section he moves on to advocate equal punishments for both the nobleman and the "least citizen." Once again, he manages to play both tunes at once. Corporal punishments for violent crimes, but let's have equality for all.[14]

---

14. His position on equality before the law is also difficult and inconsistent. This passage seems to anticipate the position he took as a member of the commission for the new Lombard Code, published in 1791. On that commission he contradicted the principle of

THE MYTH OF BECCARIA   337

TORTURE

Beccaria achieved much of his fame because of his opposition to torture:

> [torture] tends to confound all relations to require that man be at the same time accuser and accused, that pain be made the crucible of truth as if its criterion lay in the muscles and sinews of the miserable wretch (Maestro, 1973:31).

Some have criticized Beccaria's definition or use of the concept of torture, but we agree with his definition.[15] That is, torture is the use of physical and mental pain to extract information, usually confessions or identification of collaborators.[16] In this sense it confounds the punishment with the process of finding guilt. In contrast, corporal punishment, which is often confused with torture, is the application of physical pain after, and separate from, the finding of guilt and pronouncement of sentence.

Beccaria was actually ambiguous on the use of torture, however. Although he railed against the use of pain to obtain confessions and to accuse collaborators, we find in the section on "Suggestive Interrogations, Depositions" a statement that directly contradicts this view:

> a person, who, under examination, obstinately refuses to answer the questions asked of him deserves a punishment that should be fixed by law, and of the severest kind, so that men may not thus fail to provide the necessary example which they owe to the public (Beccaria, 1963:28).

According to his own definition of torture, this statement actually advocates it. The only palliative is that the "punishment be fixed by law." The punishments used in the tortures (that is, the physical punishments and the procedures for administering them) of the Holy Inquisition were carefully spelled out and very specific according to Canon Law. The mere fact that the punishments are legislated does not rule out the use of torture.

Torture also has an essentially "public" character, as noted by Peters (1985:3–7): "The lawyers and historians . . . all find a common element in torture: it is torment inflicted by a public authority for ostensibly public purposes. . . . Its history is part of legal procedure as well as later governmental

---

equal law for all by advocating different punishments for different kinds of people: "the distinction of classes in the case of minor crimes is necessary in order to bring about the desired equality" (Maestro, 1973:145).

15.   Footnote by Paolucci (Beccaria, 1963:31), who criticized Beccaria for equating torture with trials by ordeal. As he notes, this followed closely the work of the Verris on torture. However, since Beccaria concentrates on torture as a guilt-finding process, this equation holds. The only substantial criticism Paolucci uses to back his accusation is that "it was a desperate abuse of the rationalistic desire to secure the "consent of the governed." This hardly detracts from Beccaria's argument.

16.   For an extensive discussion of the distinction between corporal punishment and torture, see Newman (1983); see also Pietro Marongiu (1987).

338   NEWMAN AND MARONGIU

exercise of power" (see also Sheleff, 1987). Although Beccaria defines torture only as a means to extract information or confessions, in the same section he writes that the political aim of punishment is "to terrorize" (*Qual'e il fine politico delle pene? Il terrore altri uomini*). This seems to be the same utilitarian aim of torture throughout history.

Finally, Beccaria's proposal of perpetual slavery (as we discuss below) appears to be consistent with his utilitarian approach. This may be regarded as an especially cruel form of punishment because it allows for complete control over the entire life and body of condemned persons.[17]

THE DEATH PENALTY

More than his views on torture, Beccaria is revered for his "absolute" opposition to the death penalty. Indeed, his biographers say, this position was even more extreme than those of other reformers of the time, such as Voltaire and Montesquieu. Beccaria's famous argument against the death penalty was that the sentence of slavery was more severe and therefore a greater deterrent than death. We question him on several counts.

First, penal slavery was a devious way of inflicting death. Sellin (1976:66) has described Beccaria's argument against the death penalty as "specious." The conditions made it quite likely that the offender would die. This was especially so when time was served in ships' galleys. In fact, galley slavery was considered appropriate for a "capital offense." It is not clear, therefore, how "absolute" Beccaria's opposition to the death penalty was, since many would die as a result of the punishments he proposed.

Second, his argument that penal slavery was a greater deterrent than death is questionable (Sellin, 1976:66). Because of the extremely painful ways that death was inflicted during his time, it is difficult to see how the punishment of penal slavery would be any *more* deterrent. He is thus led to advocate horrible punishments in order to demonstrate the deterrent value of slavery. He notes: ". . . it is not the intensity of the pain that has the greatest effect on the mind, but its continuance . . ." (Van den Haag, 1975:224). Brutalization in the name of deterrence is clearly advocated by Beccaria when he approvingly notes that prisoners are placed "in chains and fetters, under the club, under yoke, in an iron cage; and despair seems rather the beginning than the end of their misery. . . ."[18] And he concludes that "this is the advantage of the punishment of slavery, it scares more the ones who see it than the ones who suffer it" (Beccaria, 1963:59).

---

17.   For a more extensive account of the problem of torture in Beccaria's time, see Verri (1988). This is the basic work used by Alesssandro Manzoni (Beccaria's grandson) in his well-known book, *Storia della colonna infame.*

18.   Our translation: *"fra i ceppi o le catene, sotto il bastone, sotto il giogo, in una gabbia di ferro; il disperato non finisce i suoi mali, ma li comincia"* (Beccaria, 1963:59).

THE MYTH OF BECCARIA   339

We can see that his arguments here deeply contradict his previous claims to advocate mild punishments. In fact, he had argued in other parts of the *Treatise* that harsh punishments worked against deterrence. His only response to this criticism could be that penal slavery was less harsh than death as then inflicted, yet his argument was the opposite.

Beccaria made two other arguments against the death penalty that are popular today. First, that the death penalty is irrevocable. However, the alternative he advocates, penal slavery for life, cannot be revoked either, unless there is a way to turn back the clock. Obviously, one could apply the same criticism to his advocacy of corporal punishments. Second, he claimed that execution was a form of "legalized murder." Once again, according to this argument, penal slavery must be regarded as "legalized kidnapping." He later added another argument when serving on the commission for the Lombard Code. This was that "absolute proofs sufficient for sentencing a man to death do not exist . . . not even the confession of the accused . . ." (Maestro, 1973:144–150). He was strongly criticized by other members of the commission for this extreme stand.

In sum, we can see that the main arguments of the *Treatise* that have been revered by criminologists and penologists are in actual fact hopelessly ambiguous and in many cases self-contradictory. If we are correct in our characterization of Beccaria and of the *Treatise* for which he is so famous, the challenging question is why he and/or the *Treatise* are so revered. On this question we can only speculate, but we do have a number of possible explanations.

BECCARIA AND HISTORY

There is little doubt that Beccaria's ideas were used and promulgated by many other reformers at the time. His phrase "greatest happiness for the greatest number" found its way into many essays. Jeremy Bentham probably made that statement famous. The *Treatise* was widely promulgated and used by the great reformers. In that sense it had an enormous effect. Jenkins (1984) explains its popularity in the eighteenth century simply by the fact that the reforms advocated by Beccaria were already in the process of emerging as part of the overall spirit of enlightenment of the century.

In addition, *punishment* of the body was in the process of being replaced with *control* of the body, as so well demonstrated by Foucault (1979). The reasons for this transformation are complex, but one identified by Foucault was the need in a rapidly growing industrial society for disciplined workers. Foucault manages to draw together the growth of the organized society—through education, the military, and later the factory—to produce a disciplined work force. The by-product of this drastic transformation of society was to focus punishment away from the body and onto controlling the lives of

340   NEWMAN AND MARONGIU

the accused. Penal slavery and prison were natural consequences of this ethos. Thus, it can be seen that there were massive historical changes under way that created a climate in which Beccaria's "reforms" could flourish. His opposition to the death penalty and advocacy of penal slavery and prison were exactly in step. His plea for "mildness of punishments" suited perfectly the transformation from bodily focused punishments to those that manipulated or controlled the person. The utilitarian ethos—control—was served admirably by Beccaria's strong advocacy of deterrence.

Those sovereigns who quickly embraced his *Treatise* had already shown their inclination toward reform. These included Empress Catherine II of Russia, Grand Duke Leopold of Tuscany, and Frederick II of Prussia. However, the major policy advocated by Beccaria—removal of discretion from judges—actually led to placing greater power in the hands of the State. His solution to the discretion problem was to enact very specific laws in their place. As has been noted by modern experts on sentencing, all this does is shift the discretion from one level to another, in this case the legislative body. One can see that this "reform" is hardly a reform. Instead, it leads to the concentration of power in the hands of the sovereign. Or, if the State is ruled more by the legislative body (such as in England and, after the Revolution, France), the laws become unwieldy and inflexible because they must account for an incredible amount of detail and must be acted on by political bodies (the legislatures), which are renowned for having difficulty in reaching decisions. In fact, the 1795 Code of Misdemeanors and Punishments enacted in France in the third Brumaire, year IV (October 25, 1795), fixed specific and unalterable punishments giving the judge not the slightest choice. This code proved unworkable because it was impossible for any code to foresee the wide range of circumstances that might occur in each case. This inflexibility was eventually removed with the revisions brought about by the Napoleonic Codes (Maestro, 1942:140–147). That the Napoleonic Codes represented a definite "break with the horrors of the past," as Maestro says, there can be no doubt. But it is another thing to claim that it was Beccaria and his *Treatise* that were responsible for this break. The French Revolution, after all, came about as a result of many complex historical conditions. It was this revolution that produced the situation in which Beccaria's policies could be applied. One could say that Beccaria wrote the right thing at the right time.

THE "SPIRIT" OF BECCARIA

Some commentators on Beccaria who are aware of the weaknesses in logic of the *Treatise* have argued that it is not the logic that is so important, but rather its "heart." By using this more general interpretation of Beccaria, they are able to point to its "liberating" influence on almost every criminal code in the world that they identify as "enlightened." There is no mistaking that

THE MYTH OF BECCARIA   341

those who would characterize themselves as "liberal" in their views of criminal justice seem to embrace Beccaria's general spirit of reform.

Liberals embrace Beccaria's general position that favors milder punishments along with the utilitarian assumption that the infliction of pain and suffering on criminals is evil in itself. This spirit has continued through to the present with the strong movement this century toward the rehabilitation of offenders and the treatment model in penology. The treatment model, though under fierce attack, nevertheless still dominates the language of penology. Colleges still teach courses called "corrections," rarely courses on "punishment." What is it about this spirit of liberalism that makes it endure so?

Part of the answer lies within utilitarian philosophy itself. It rests on a profound contradiction. On the one hand, the utilitarians from Beccaria to Bentham advocate the least possible punishment. Yet at the same time they advocate an all-pervasive preventive and deterrent approach, such that it requires massive intervention by the State to enforce such a program. While they give lip service to the old utilitarian ethic of the social contract (one gives up only a small portion of one's self-interest to the State so that all may pursue their individual interests), they advocate policies that require the State to become larger and larger and to intervene more and more in the private lives of individuals. That the utilitarians of the eighteenth century should have promoted a policy that directly enhanced the power of the State is puzzling, given that the evidence for abuse of power by the State was all round them, and certainly one of the factors that led to the French Revolution and the social unrest that occurred in England.

It is within this framework that one should consider the transformation of penology that occurred in relation to Beccaria and the other utilitarians. The belief is that milder punishments resulted from their reforms. By what measure does one conclude that punishments are milder today than in Beccaria's time? It would seem that the product of the eighteenth-century reforms was prison, a solution to crime that has spread like an infectious disease. Is this punishment milder than the several corporal punishments applied in the eighteenth century? Is the proportion of punishments to crimes demonstrably more just? If one takes the massive prison terms that are dealt out for nonviolent crimes in most states of the United States and other countries, one must remain skeptical. It is true that the aggravated forms of the death penalty no longer exist in this century (that is various slow and bloody ways of inflicting death, such as drawing and quartering)—though there is aggravation of a different, and mental, kind given the delays in carrying out a death sentence that are typical of this punishment today. As Foucault (1979) argued, the focus shifted at the end of the eighteenth century from the body to the soul.

So the "spirit" of Beccaria is very much a ghost. One is unable to make

342   NEWMAN AND MARONGIU

clear statements as to what this spirit represents as far as reforms are concerned. One learns that "reforms" are exactly that: They herald changes
that leave basic structures untouched. The contribution that this spirit has
made, however, has resulted in a complex ideology that shields the true
nature of what it is that society does to criminals. The utilitarian ethos makes
it possible to claim that society is liberal and enlightened in its dealing with
criminals since it approves of milder punishments, when at the same time it
promotes penal policies and practices that directly oppose this ethic: the massive use of prisons, the aggravated penalty of death row.

The prejudice that "we are better today" in treating criminals than in Beccaria's time seems to stem from the idea that punishments today are much
more in proportion to the crimes than they were in the eighteenth century
and before. This idea is clearly open to question. Who is to say that the
aggravated death penalty of the eighteenth century, such as breaking on the
wheel, was out of proportion for the crime of murder in the first degree? The
only argument one hears to support such a thesis is "we don't do that today,
therefore it is wrong." Not only were punishments "violent" in the eighteenth century, but many other aspects of daily life were "violent." Surgery,
for example, required the drastic spilling of blood and infliction of pain. The
pain and suffering of various diseases was far more widespread than today.
Thus, it may have been entirely natural—indeed in proportion—for society of
that time to accept aggravated forms of the death penalty for certain crimes.

In conclusion, while Beccaria and others argued for the proportionality of
punishments to crimes, the range or scale on which to base this proportionality was never discussed by Beccaria (although it was considered in detail by
Bentham). There can be little doubt that the Enlightenment of which Beccaria was a part brought about change in many aspects of social and political
life, including the forms of penal punishment. But it is quite another thing to
claim that the resulting punishments were *milder*. It is impossible to tell
whether prison as it is massively used today is a milder punishment than
various corporal punishments (and even the death penalty) that were used in
the eighteenth century. And it is even less possible to guess whether more or
fewer people are punished today than yesterday. Foucault (1979) hints that
many more people today are subject to the discipline of the State than was the
case in the eighteenth century and before. We can only speculate on this.
But certainly it is a self-indulgent assumption to believe that the changes
brought in by the Enlightenment are in any way morally better or more liberal than the period before it.

Is it unfair to judge Beccaria by today's standards? We have trodden a
particularly thorny path trying to evaluate Beccaria and his work relative
both to his own historical period and to the penological values that seem to be
held in the twentieth century. We admit that this is ambitious and does very

THE MYTH OF BECCARIA 343

much complicate matters, but we do so in order to avoid two intractable philosophical problems.

First, we must, of course, try to understand his ideas and character in their social and historical context. But to leave it at that would open us to a grave criticism of relativism. For it would not be possible to go beyond simply observing his contributions. It would make it, strictly speaking, illogical to apply his ideas and values to the twentieth century, since by the relativistic argument they apply only to that specific historical and social period. The common solution to this problem is to superimpose an additional theory that posits *direction* in history (as, for example, in Marx's historical materialism) so that one can evaluate a particular historical period in terms of where things are today. We have contrasted Beccaria's "reforms" with the values held today by those who advocate reform (probably most academic and practitioner penologists).

Second, relativism is the enemy of transtemporal value. In response to it, we have tried at least to leave open the possibility of a value position that transcends time—the "human spirit," which allows one to make judgments of any time period. If one is unable to do this, one is unable to pronounce the torture of the eighteenth century as "evil." And if one is unable to do that, one is equally unable to pronounce the scourge of prisons as "evil." In this sense, it would only be "fair" to judge Beccaria by this transcending standard if one is able to identify it. But the history of philosophy gives one no sure footing when it comes to identifying transcendent values.

Liberal values have been attached to Beccaria, not only by his contemporaries (who had more justification to do so) but also by penologists of this century. In this sense it is fair to evaluate Beccaria in the light of modern ideas of reform. In doing so, however, one unearths the inadequacies of a supposedly enlightened position because one finds, as we have demonstrated in this paper, that values and positions are ascribed to Beccaria and his work that he demonstrably did not have. We have tried to show in this paper how penology, a supposedly social *science*, has participated in the creation of its own myth.

BECCARIA THE HERO

Our final explanation of the myth of Beccaria as the great reformer is more speculative and requires that we stand back and appraise the nature of penology and criminology itself as a "movement" or a "discipline." In his analysis of paradigms and paradigm shifts in science, Kuhn (1970) showed how entrenched certain paradigms can become. These paradigms were often presided over by the works of "great men." It may be that the role of "great men" has been to shore up the dominant paradigm, giving to it a certain sacred status. In this way it becomes much more difficult to question the

344   NEWMAN AND MARONGIU

paradigm either from a value-oriented position or even scientifically, because to question the paradigm comes very close to "sacrilege" or "blasphemy." We suggest, therefore, that the Great Beccaria is needed by penology to preside over a rickety paradigm full of contradictions and unsure of its basic values.

Lest we end on such a negative note, let us make a final observation. If one examines the history of reformers in penology, one finds that their stories are almost to a person stories of fleeting success, followed by abysmal failure both personal and institutional (see Eriksen, 1975). From Maconachie to Osborne, the story of their reform campaigns has been one of only brief success in bringing about change, followed by an often ruthless societal destruction of the reformers themselves. In contrast, Beccaria appears to be one of the few "success stories" in the otherwise depressing history of penological reformers. It may well be that the myth of Beccaria functions to provide hope and purpose for penologists, in the same way that larger myths in a culture provide meaning for peoples' lives (Becker, 1973). Without these myths, culture could not survive, nor the people in it. These conclusions seem to point to the need to study penology as a culture as well as a science.

REFERENCES

Beccaria, Cesare
       1963   On Crimes and Punishments, trans. H. Paolucci. 1764. New York: Bobbs–Merrill.

Becker, Ernest
       1973   The Denial of Death. New York: Free Press.

Bentham, Jeremy
       1975   The Theory of Legislation. 1874. Dobbs Ferry, N.Y.: Oceana Publications.

Brinton, Crane
       1959   A History of Western Morals. New York: Harcourt Brace.

Cantu, Cesare
       1862   Beccaria e il Diritto Penale. Florence: G. Barbera.

Conrad, John
       1985   Research and development in corrections. Federal Probation (Sept.): 76–78.

Eriksen, Thorsten
       1975   The Reformers. New York: Elsevier.

Facchinei
       1765   Note e osservazioni sul libro dei delitti e delle pene, Venice.

Foucault, Michel
       1979   Discipline and Punish: The Birth of the Prison. New York: Vintage Books.

Friedman, Lawrence M.
       1973   A History of American Law. New York: Simon & Schuster.

Gillette, Paul J.
       1966   The Complete Marquis de Sade. Vol. 1. Los Angeles: Holloway House.

THE MYTH OF BECCARIA 345

Glueck, Sheldon
1965   Beccaria and criminal justice. Harvard Law School Bulletin Jan.

Harding, Richard
1988   The abolition of capital punishment in Australia. Paper presented at International Congress on Cesare Beccaria and Modern Criminal Policy, Milan.

Hart, H.L.A.
1982   Essays on Bentham. New York: Oxford University Press.

Jenkins, Philip
1984   Varieties of enlightenment criminology: Beccaria, Godwin, de Sade. British Journal of Criminology 24(2):112–130.

Jones, David
1986   History of Criminology. New York: Greenwood.

Kant, Immanuel
1983   La Metafisica dei Costumi, trans. Giovanni Vidari. Bari: Laterza.

Kuhn, Thomas
1970   The Structure of Scientific Revolutions. Chicago: University of Chicago Press.

Lely, Gilbert
1970   The Marquis de Sade, trans. Alex Brown. New York: Free Press.

Lyons, David
1965   Forms and Limits of Utilitarianism. London: Oxford University Press.

Maestro, Marcello
1942   Voltaire and Beccaria as Reformers in Criminal Law. New York: Columbia University Press.
1973   Cesare Beccaria and the Origins of Penal Reform. Philadelphia: Temple University Press.

Marongiu, Pietro
1987   Tortura e punizione: Osservazioni preliminari. In Atti del Primo Congresso Nazionale della Societa Italiana do Psychiatria Forense. Cagliari: Vallasimus.

Masur, Louis P.
1989   Rites of Execution. New York: Oxford University Press.

Milovanovic, Dragan
1988   A Primer in the Sociology of Law. New York: Harrow and Heston.

Modona, Guido Neppi
1988   L'utile sociale nella concezione penalistica di Cesare Beccaria. Paper presented at International Congress on Cesare Beccaria and Modern Criminal Policy, Milan.

Mueller, Gerhard
1988   Cesare Beccaria and the social significance of his concept of criminal policy. Paper presented at International Congress on Cesare Beccaria and Modern Criminal Policy, Milan.

Newman, Graeme
1983   Just and Painful. New York: Macmillan.
1985   The Punishment Response. 2nd ed. New York: Harrow and Heston.

346   NEWMAN AND MARONGIU

Peters, Edward
    1985   Torture. New York: Basil Blackwell.

Phillipson, Coleman
    1970   Three Criminal Law Reformers: Beccaria, Bentham and Romily. 1923.
               New Jersey: Patterson Smith.

Romangoli, Sergio (ed.)
    1985   Cesare Beccaria: Opere. Rome: Sansoni Superbiblioteca, Vol. 1.

Sellin, Thorsten
    1976   Slavery and the Penal System. New York: Elsevier.

Sheleff, Leon Shoskolsky
    1987   Ultimate Penalties. Columbus: Ohio State University Press.

Taylor, Ian, Paul Walton, and Jock Young
    1973   The New Criminology. New York: Harper & Row.

Torrey, Norman
    1962   The Spirit of Voltaire. New York: Oxford University Press.

United Nations
    1985   The Italian Contribution to the Development of Modern Criminal Policy:
               Reason and Humanity in Cesare Beccaria's Thought. Seventh Congress on
               the Prevention of Crime and Treatment of Offenders, Milan, August
               26–September 6, 1985.

Valeri, Nino
    1969   Pietro Verri. Florence: Felice le Monnier.

Van den Haag, Ernest
    1975   Punishing Criminals. New York: Basic Books.

Verri, Pietro
    1988   Osservazioni sulla Tortura. 1776. Milan: Rizzoli.

Vold, George B. and Thomas J. Bernard
    1986   Theoretical Criminology. 3rd ed. New York: Oxford University Press.

Wooton, Barbara
    1963   Crime and Criminal Law. London: Stevens and Sons.

Young, David B.
    1983   Cesare Beccaria: Utilitarian or retributivist? Journal of Criminal Justice
               11:317–326.

Graeme Newman is a professor at the School of Criminal Justice, State University of
New York at Albany. He is the author of *Just and Painful: A Case for the Corporal Punishment of Criminals* (1983), *Understanding Violence* (1979), *The Punishment Response*
(1978), and *Comparative Deviance: Law & Perception in Six Cultures* (1976).

Pietro Marongiu is Associate Professor of Criminology in the School of Medicine, University of Cagliari, Sardinia, Italy. He is the author of *Teoria e Storia del Banditismo
Sociale in Sardegna* (*Theory and History of Social Banditry in Sardinia*, 1981).

The authors have also coauthored *Vengeance: The Fight Against Injustice* (1987).

[2]

Journal of Criminal Justice, Vol. 11, pp. 317-326 (1983)
Pergamon Press. Printed in U.S.A.

CESARE BECCARIA: UTILITARIAN OR RETRIBUTIVIST?

DAVID B. YOUNG

Department of History
Central Missouri State University
Warrensburg, Missouri 64093

ABSTRACT

Ever since Cesare Beccaria's On Crimes and Punishments *first appeared in 1764, it has been common to regard its author as a theorist of criminal jurisprudence who stressed considerations of utility to the exclusion of considerations of justice. There is strong evidence for this view, and Beccaria was in many ways a forerunner of Bentham. There is, however, another side to Beccaria that has often been overlooked. In the way in which he established the right of the sovereign to punish and in his concern for the rights of the criminal (rights which no consideration of utility could override), Beccaria showed that he was much closer to the outlook commonly associated with Kant and Hegel than one would at first suspect. Though there were utilitarian aspects to his thought, Beccaria may be considered basically a retributivist who incorporated certain obvious, though by no means dominant, utilitarian themes into his work. In blending utilitarianism and retributivism, Beccaria was usually consistent, and he usually gave greater emphasis to the former.*

At least since the eighteenth century, most major works on criminal justice have been either retributivist or utilitarian in nature, and the division continues today between those who support a retributivist justice model and those who uphold a utilitarian deterrence model. Retributivism, often associated with social contract and natural rights doctrines, maintains that a criminal *deserves* to be punished because he has violated a legal system from which everyone benefits. Whether on contractarian or other grounds, retributivists usually hold that the legal system must in some sense be viewed as having been willed or accepted by the criminal himself. Since the criminal has taken advantage of the benefits of the system while failing to bear the corresponding burden of obedience and self-restraint, he merits some sort of deprivation (punishment) in return so that the balance of benefits and burdens will again be equal (Murphy,1979: 77–81). Immanuel Kant (1965: 99–104), whose *Metaphysical Elements of Justice* was severely critical of Beccaria, was a champion of this point of view in the eighteenth century. A generation later, Hegel (1969: 70–71,.246), though of course no believer in contractarianism or natural rights, was likewise a spokesman for retributivism. Indeed, Hegel contended that a criminal had a *right* to be punished: a right, that is, to be treated as a responsible moral agent who may be called to account for his actions rather than as an animal to be manipulated with threats of deprivation.[1] In our own day, Herbert Morris (1973: 54–62), Jeffrie Murphy (1979: 77–81), and John Rawls (1971: 241, 314–316, 575–576) have been among the leading advocates of the Kantian, and, to some extent, the Hegelian position.

Utilitarians, on the other hand, have generally argued that the future, not the past, should be the main concern of any criminal justice system. The justification for punishing those who break the law is to maximize the total happiness of the people in the community. From a utilitarian point of view, punishment is chiefly a deterrent, both for the criminal himself and for others. If punishing certain actions or certain classes of actions will not increase the sum total of happiness, punishment should not be used; if it will maximize the collective pleasure, then it should be employed (Benn, 1973: 30–31).[2] From such a perspective, considerations of rights, desert, and obligation are at most of secondary importance.[3] Helvétius (1759: passim., esp. 33–186), who, by Beccaria's own account, exercised a great influence on the Italian reformer, was an early exponent of utilitarianism, though Helvétius's great work, De l'esprit, did not deal with criminal justice as such. Of course, the outstanding champion of utilitarianism in the late eighteenth and early nineteenth centuries was Jeremy Bentham, who was lavish in his praise of Beccaria (Bentham, 1970: 298, note a; Halévy, 1955: 20–22). In more recent times, Lady Wootton (1963: 32–57), among others, has carried the banner of utilitarianism. Further, one may note that most of those who have advocated therapy as a comprehensive approach to criminal justice have usually stood on utilitarian grounds. Karl Menninger (1968: 91–92, 138–139, 204, 277, 312) and B.F. Skinner (1953: 182–193, 446–449; 1971, passim., esp. 228–235), to mention only two, have simply taken it for granted that the sole purpose of the system of criminal justice is to increase the happiness of the criminal himself and of the community

at large. To the extent that they consider the contentions that a criminal may be a responsible agent deserving of punishment, or that an offender may be a bearer of rights which no consideration of utility can override, they reject them as quaint and "unscientific" (Menninger, 1968: 17; Skinner, 1971: 230–232).[4]

The degree to which a satisfactory theory of criminal justice can or should incorporate both retributivist and utilitarian elements has been the subject of much discussion. Hegel (1969: 67–73) was concerned with this matter in the early nineteenth century. In more recent times, John Rawls (1955: 3–32) and Stanley I. Benn (1973: 29–31) have addressed themselves to the issue. Both retributivism and utilitarianism contain valuable insights, and even those in one camp or the other who totally reject the arguments of their opponents run some very grave risks. Even committed retributivists have sometimes used certain utilitarian arguments, and vice versa (Murphy, 1979: 82–83).

THE INTERPRETATION OF BECCARIA

Ever since Cesare Beccaria's *On Crimes and Punishments* first appeared in 1764, it has been common both to acknowledge its importance as a milestone in criminal law and to see its author as a utilitarian who advocated changes in established practice solely in order to maximize social happiness. Thus, in defending the book against one of its Italian critics in 1765, Beccaria's close friends, the brothers Pietro and Alessandro Verri (1965) argued that Beccaria had never questioned the *right* of the sovereign to use any form of coercive power, but merely the *utility* of certain forms of coercion. Thus Bentham (Ms. No. 32, Univ. Col., London, as cited in Halévy, 1955: 21) himself addressed an unusually impassioned apostrophe to Beccaria:

Oh my master, first evangelist of Reason, you who have raised your Italy so far above England, and I would add above France, were it not that Helvétius, without having written on the subject of laws, had already provided you with your fundamental ideas; . . . you who have made so many useful excursions into the path of utility, what is there left for us to do?—Never to turn aside from that path.

Most modern students have accepted a similar point of view (Valsecchi, 1934; 135; Zarone, 1971. *passim.;* Maestro, 1973: 158), and such a noted legal scholar as George Fletcher (1978: 100–102) has no qualms at all in lumping Beccaria and Bentham together in the same category. Even those writers such as Franco Venturi ("Introduction" to Beccaria, 1965b: xiv–xvi), the foremost modern student of the Italian Enlightenment, who have recognized the natural rights and contractarian elements in Beccaria have tended to suggest that Beccaria was not fully consistent and that he simply oscillated between contractarian and utilitarian ideas, perhaps giving greater prominence to the latter (S. Romagnoli, "Introduzione" to Beccaria, 1958: vol.1, lxx–lxxii; Barriè, 1959: 436–437).

Of course it would be foolish to deny that there is a large dose of utilitarianism in Beccaria. His propensity to calculate pleasure and pain in mathematical terms, for instance, reminds one of Bentham and probably endeared him to the Englishman more than anything else (Beccaria, 1965a: 15–22, 40–42, 47–49, 94–96). What will be argued here, however, is that Beccaria was fundamentally a retributivist, that he incorporated utilitarian ideas into his work, albeit in a secondary capacity, and that, within a basically retributivist framework, he was usually, though not always, consistent in his use of utilitarian principles. An examination of five aspects of Beccaria's work will help to establish these contentions: (1) the way in which he establishes the sovereign's right to punish; (2) the methods that he uses to determine the relative severity of different crimes and to explain how the response to the same offense may vary; (3) his views on the goal or purpose of punishment; (4) his treatment of the rights of the criminal, especially: (a) in his examination of capital punishment, but also (b) in his considera-tion of the matter in other contexts; and finally (5) his concern with the justice or injustice of the social setting in which a criminal justice system must function.

THE RIGHT TO PUNISH

Beccaria's position begins to appear when one examines the way in which he establishes the right to punish. The question of how one can justify the authority of one human being to coerce another (and punishment is the most extreme form of coercion) is central to political thought, and the answer that any writer furnishes is of cardinal importance. Beccaria (1965a: 11–13) founded all such authority on a hypothetical social and political contract among independent individuals, and that in itself should put the reader on guard against a purely utilitarian interpretation. The contract which Beccaria envisioned, however, was quite unlike the total surrender of primitive freedom which Rousseau (1964: 360–362; Salvatorelli, 1945: 53–54), and Kant (1965:80–81) had in mind. Individuals, argued Beccaria (1965a: 13), give up only the "least possible portion" of their liberty in order to enjoy the remainder more securely. In Beccaria's eyes, laws ought to be regarded as the terms of the social contract, the conditions on which people unite. Further, they should be seen as having been willed by all members of a community. Coercion is justifiable only against someone who violates these conditions from which everyone benefits (Beccaria, 1965a: 12–13). In other words, a criminal is someone who derives benefits from the law without paying the price of obedience; in the process, he has violated the conditions which he himself helped to establish, at least ostensibly. He deserves, therefore, to have some deprivation inflicted upon him to restore the equitable distribution of benefits and burdens. Beccaria's justification for criminal sanctions is clearly retributivist: the reason for using such coercion is that the guilty party has violated the rights of others in a manner that harms society as a whole (Beccaria, 1965a:

11–15, 20–22). Beccaria did not attempt a utilitarian justification of the general right to punish.

It is interesting to note that Beccaria's view in this respect is similar to that of Kant (1965: 99–100), and it is especially close to Hegel's. To be sure, Hegel would have nothing to do with a social contract, but he did argue that the only way to establish an overall justification of punishment as an institution is to view punishment as the just desert of someone who has violated right as such in flouting the rights of a given person or persons (Hegel, 1969: 67–69).

THE RELATIVE SIGNIFICANCE OF CRIMES

In measuring the relative importance of different offenses, Beccaria turned to other principles. Jeffrie Murphy (1979: 84–85) has observed that the greatest weakness of retributivism is its inability to establish a satisfactory hierarchy of severity among crimes. If a violation of right or a failure of reciprocity is what constitutes a crime, then, *on a purely formal level*, petty theft is just as wrong, just as unfair, as murder. Several decades after *On Crimes and Punishments* first appeared, Hegel (1969: 68–69, 246–247, 273–274) suggested that, while the only reason for punishing a criminal at all is that he has flouted right as such, the only standard for judging the gravity of any sort of offense is the harm done to the community. This was Beccaria's view precisely. Like Hegel, Beccaria (1965a: 22–23, 33–38) rejected other criteria, such as the intrinsic wickedness of the criminal, as standards by which to measure crimes. Only a utilitarian criterion, the standard of the damage affected or attempted against society, could be appropriate, he held. Both differed from Kant in this respect. Kant (1965: 100–101), notorious for his defense of the *lex talionis*, argued that a criminal should receive precisely what he has meted out and that the gravity of his crime should be judged by the evil inherent in his will. In a long passage implicitly critical of the Kantian view, Hegel

(1969: 68–72) seemed to side with Beccaria, denying that a criminal's inward viciousness should be taken into account when weighing the importance of his offense.

In this regard, one may observe that Beccaria and Hegel were at one in maintaining that the degree of punishment for specific crimes may vary precisely because the social harm resulting from a given offense varies with the condition of the community. In a barbarous and precariously organized society, a seemingly minor infraction may be severely chastised because even trivial crimes upset the social order. In modern and more firmly cemented communities, Beccaria (1965a: 4–6, 59–61, 98–100, 104) and Hegel (1969: 274) agreed, punishments can be and ought to be milder because the same misdeeds that might destroy a savage community have only a slight impact on a civilized one. In this matter, both differed from Kant. Presumably, Kant (1965: 100–101) believed that the *lex talionis* in the form in which he defended it was universally and eternally valid.

THE GOAL OF PUNISHMENT

If Beccaria were a utilitarian in measuring crimes, he was likewise a utilitarian in discussing the purpose of punishment. When he treated that topic, he tended to move away from the idea that the purpose of punishment is to restore a balance of benefits and burdens, the idea implicit in his justification of the sovereign's right to punish at all. Instead, he turned to a rather extreme utilitarianism which was not always consistent with some of his other principles and which sometimes led to unfortunate results.

Beccaria (1965a: 31) explicitly declared that the goal of punishment is to diminish crime by means of deterrence. Retributivists in general have usually been prepared to admit some utilitarian considerations among the purposes of punishment. In particular, both Kant (1965: 100) and Hegel (1969: 71, 246) contended that it is all well and good if punishment does indeed have the effect of reducing crime, *provided* that one remember that the criminal is a responsible moral agent who is being punished for his decision to violate the law; the chief reason behind his punishment must be justice, not utility. On no account, Kant especially held, should a convicted criminal be considered *merely* as a means to the goal of diminishing crime, however desirable that end might be (Murphy, 1979: 82–91).

In a passage of which Kant no doubt approved, Beccaria (1965a: 50) declared, "There is no liberty whenever the law in some cases permits a man to cease to be a *person* and to become a *thing*" (my translation; emphasis in original). In discussing the end of punishment, however, Beccaria did sometimes tend to think of criminals as objects which could be used to lessen crime through the example of their suffering. In his infatuation with utilitarian calculation, he overlooked the humanity of the criminal. In particular, when discussing the benefits of a life sentence at hard labor as a replacement for the death penalty, Beccaria (1965a: 38, 43–44, 46–47) spoke of a convicted felon as a beast of burden, the sight of whose torment would induce people to refrain from crime more effectively than the spectacle of an execution would. In speaking this way, Beccaria lost sight of the view of the criminal as a responsible moral agent punished for his transgressions, not merely an object lesson. Marx (1973: 92) once posed a rhetorical question that cut to the heart of utilitarian theories of punishment: "Now what right have you to punish me for the intimidation or amelioration of others?" Though even a retributivist theory should not ignore the practical results of punishment, Beccaria was sometimes so carried away with the thought of deterrence that he would have been at a loss to answer such a question.

THE QUESTION OF RIGHTS

Capital Punishment

Beccaria, of course, is well known for advocating more moderate punishments

than the brutal ones commonly employed in his day (Beccaria, 1965a: 19–22, 55–56, 59–61, 70–71). In particular, he became famous (or infamous) for calling for the abolition of the death penalty, a step for which both Kant (1965: 104–105) and Hegel (1969: 246) reproached him. Certainly Beccaria did employ utilitarian arguments against judicial cruelty. In discussing the death penalty, for instance, he contended that capital punishment was an ineffective deterrent (Beccaria, 1965a: 65–69). Again following Montesquieu (1949: 252–253), Beccaria (1965a: 60–65) held that a society accustomed to moderate punishments will be dissuaded from crime by such chastisements quite as much as barbarous people will be deterred by their habitually cruel punishments. Beccaria's conclusion was one which Bentham (1970: 158–159, 179) endorsed wholeheartedly: excessive punishments are wrong in that they inflict pain to no purpose; they are useless in that lesser penalties will achieve the same result with less suffering. More fundamental than such utilitarianism, however, was a retributivist aspect of Beccaria's advocacy of moderate punishments. In this regard, he thought of people not as units of pleasurable and painful sensations whose purpose is simply to maximize social happiness, but rather as responsible bearers of rights, as beings who, by virtue of being human, can make certain claims which no consideration of utility can override. Certain punishments, Beccaria (1965a: 43–44, 55–56, 60, 62–63, 82, 96–97) held, violate such rights, regardless of their utilitarian value.

On several occasions, Beccaria addressed himself to the question of natural (or human) rights, notably the right of self-defense. His case against judicial torture and against compelling prisoners to testify against themselves was largely based on the contention that such proceedings violate the natural right of every person to preserve his own being (Beccaria, 1965a: 38, 43–44, 46–47). Likewise, his most compelling argument against the death penalty rested on grounds of right, not utility. The state's right to punish, he maintained, is based upon the surrender of liberty made in the original social contract, and any punishment which exceeds this is a violation of the rights of the criminal. Who, asked Beccaria (1965a: 62), ever would have given another person the right to kill him?

Critics have often pounced on this contractarian rights argument. One of Beccaria's first Italian detractors, the monk Ferdinando Facchinei (1965: 170) declared in 1765 that one might just as well argue that no one would ever grant the sovereign the right to punish him in any manner. Kant (1965: 104–105) was particularly scornful of what he deemed Beccaria's sophistry, maintaining that a criminal is executed, not because he has willed to be put to death, but because he has willed an act which deserves capital punishment. Hegel (1969: 246) seconded Kant on this score.

Beccaria's argument, though, is not as weak as it may first appear. He held that death is a punishment fundamentally different from any other, if, indeed, it is a punishment at all, properly speaking. The Roman poet Lucretius, after all, did have a point: death is not a misfortune that befalls you or a deprivation that is inflicted upon you; it is the *end* of you. Beccaria (1965a: 62–63) held that capital punishment is an act of annihilation, not coercion; it is an act of war, not of legal justice. Though the state may well have the right to coerce, it is anything but clear that the sovereign has the right, except perhaps in cases of treason or open rebellion, to make war upon its own citizens.[5] Fundamentally, Beccaria was convinced that all persons have a right to life, a right which can be overridden only in extreme cases of self-defense (Beccaria, 1965a: 11–15, 62–70). Some modern authors, notably Thomas W. Satre (1975: 75–87), have sought to develop an argument along similar lines. Whatever the merits of the case, it is clear that, like the retributivist Kant, Beccaria was concerned with respecting the human rights of the criminal, even in inflicting punishment.

In *On Crimes and Punishments*, Beccaria (1965a: 32–36, 73–75, 91–93) spoke of the right of a condemned person to rectify any judicial error, a natural extension of the right of self-preservation. He returned to this theme some thirty years later, employing it as another argument against the death penalty. In a memorandum which he prepared in 1792 in his capacity as a civil servant for the Austrian rulers of his native Lombardy, Beccaria ("Vota . . . della giunta delegata per la riforma del sistema criminale nella Lombardia austriaca riguardante la pena di morte," in Beccaria, 1958, vol. 2: 739–740) pointed out that, unlike other punishments, the death penalty is inherently irrevocable. He suggested that since a convicted person should enjoy the right to clear himself, such a final penalty amounted to an abridgement of that right. Only in cases of absolute certainty, only if there were no possibility of any error at all, could a court put convicted criminals to death. Since humans are not infallible, however, Beccaria concluded that there can never be sufficient certainty to warrant killing a condemned person. The irrevocability of the death penalty is one of the strongest arguments against it, and modern writers opposed to capital punishment have frequently relied upon this point (Black, 1974: 8–12; Murphy, 1979: 238–244). Like many such modern polemicists, Beccaria was concerned with retributivist themes, with respecting the rights of the accused, even if it should happen that the death penalty served a utilitarian purpose.

Other Punishments

Beccaria said relatively little about specific punishments other than the death penalty in *On Crimes and Punishments*. He examined that subject, however, in a memorandum he prepared in 1791 concerning a new Austrian law code that was to be applied in Lombardy ("Brevi riflessione intorno al codice generale sopra i delitti e le pene, per cio che riguarda i delitti politici," in Beccaria, 1958, vol. 2: 709, 717). He was particularly troubled by "degrading punishments" (*pene infamante*), including flogging, the pillory, and public labor. He was absolutely convinced that they should not be used for petty offenses (*delitti politici*), and he strongly implied that they should not be used at all. Certainly he had to be concerned about what he thought the authorities in Vienna would accept as well as about what he believed to be the truth, and consequently he employed all sorts of arguments to buttress his case (Maestro, 1973: 146). At one point, he contended that the mild and gentle disposition of the Lombards made degrading punishments useless and even pernicious, and, seeming to forget his insistence on equality before the law, he asserted that persons of quality should be exempted from such punishments because of their special sensibilities (Beccaria, 1958: vol. 2, 709–713). At bottom, though, he clearly believed that penalties such as these should not be used precisely because they were degrading, the embodiment of disrespect for the humanity of the offender. Debasement and shame, he declared, should arise from the crime itself, not from the punishment (Beccaria, 1958: vol. 2, 710, 717). Kant, who was thoroughly committed to respecting the rights of the criminal, might well have entertained a higher opinion of Beccaria had he known of this memorandum.

THE SOCIAL CONTEXT OF PUNISHMENT

Perhaps the least attractive feature of many retributivist theories, including those of Kant (1965: 100–108) and Hegel (1969: 66–73) has been a certain smugness, a tendency to assume that established institutions do in fact embody ideal conditions (Morris, 1973: 55–57). Too often, retributivists have assumed that a just system of benefits and burdens is already in place, so that, when a criminal is punished, a fair balance is restored. In fact, of course, such has not been and is not necessarily the case, and modern retributivists like Jeffrie Murphy (1979: 93–115) and John Rawls (1971: 314–315, 575–577) have been at pains to argue that a system of retributive justice can work only when there is a just social context.

Though Beccaria was a retributivist in many respects, he did not overlook the actual conditions in which a criminal justice system must function. Marx (1973: 93) once commented that, though the systems of Kant and Hegel were the best philosophies of criminal law at a formal level, both German thinkers had largely ignored the actual inequities around them. If a criminal were to be punished for violating a system of rules that supposedly represented his own will in some fashion, Marx observed, there really would be no reason to assume that he had ever willed those rules in any manner whatever if he derived no benefit from them. As Herbert Morris (1973: 56) has put it, "To the extent that the rules are thought to be to the advantage of only some, or to the extent that there is a maldistribution of benefits and burdens, then the difference between coercion [in the sense of simply forcing one person to do the will of another] and law disappears." Beccaria was keenly aware of such maldistribution in his own day; he knew of the special privileges given to the nobility and the clergy and of the harshness of the law toward the propertyless and uneducated. Hence he made a strong case that persons who were held to be nothing in the eyes of existing laws and institutions had no reason and no obligation to respect them. Imagining the argument which someone in his own country and time might make for turning to crime, Beccaria (1965a: 66) put the following words in the offender's mouth:

> What are these laws which I must respect and which leave such a great distance between me and the rich man? He denies me a penny which I ask of him, and he excuses himself by exhorting me to work, something with which he himself is unfamiliar. Who made these laws? Rich and powerful men who have never deigned to visit the squalid hovels of the poor. . . . Let us break these bonds which are so deadly for the majority and useful only to a handful of indolent tyrants; let us attack injustice at its source. I shall revert to my natural state of independence, and for a time I shall live free and happy by the fruits of courage and industry. . . . King of a small band, ... I

shall see those tyrants grow pale and tremble in the presence of a man whom they, with insulting ostentation, set at a lower level than their horses and dogs. (My translation)

With passages such as this, Beccaria's book amounted to a call, not simply for legal reform in the narrow sense, not just for equality before the law, but for a society of equals in which rights and obligations would be equitably distributed and the law could indeed be regarded as the will of each and every citizen (Beccaria, 1965a: 9–15, 96–97). Only in such a society could a retributive system of criminal law that respected the rights of all have an opportunity to achieve real justice.

SUMMARY AND CONCLUSION

Contrary to common opinion, then, Beccaria was basically a retributivist, quite close at many points to Kant and Hegel. Like Kant and unlike utilitarians, he founded the right to punish on a hypothetical social contract and the criminal's violation of its conditions. Without inconsistency, Beccaria, like Hegel, introduced utilitarian considerations in establishing the measurement of specific offenses. In dealing with the purpose of punishment, Beccaria did tend to become engrossed in utilitarian calculation of deterrence, permitting the criminal to assume the role of a thing, an object lesson, rather than a person. Beside that, however, one must set his very nonutilitarian concern for the human rights of the offender, even (or especially) when inflicting punishment. Finally, unlike Kant and Hegel, but like some modern retributivists, Beccaria was deeply concerned with the social context of criminal justice and convinced that the law could achieve its objectives only in a society where benefits and burdens were fairly distributed and the law could indeed be regarded as the will of all.

To be sure, there is a strong dose of utilitarianism in Beccaria, and, from his own point of view, Bentham had ample reason to praise the Italian reformer. Proponents of a deterrence model of criminal justice can find much to admire in *On Crimes and Punishments*. Bentham's praise and Kant's criticisms, however, should not blind the modern reader to the deep, underlying foundation of retributivism on which Beccaria's work rests. Advocates of a justice model can find even more to admire in Beccaria.

ACKNOWLEDGMENTS

The author wishes to express his deep gratitude to Professor Jeffrie Murphy, formerly of the University of Arizona, for his instruction and guidance in the philosophy of crime and punishment. He also wishes to thank the National Endowment for the Humanities for sponsoring a postdoctoral seminar in Tucson during the summer of 1980 which enabled him to profit from Professor Murphy's scholarship a well as from the insights of the other seminar participants.

An earlier version of this article was presented at the annual meeting of the Academy of Criminal Justice Sciences in 1982, and the author wishes to thank the other participants in the panel on "Roots of a Discipline: Historical and Theoretical" for their comments and suggestions.

NOTES

[1] Perhaps the most moving case for a criminal's right to be punished has been made by the contemporary Swiss author Friedrich Duerrenmatt in his novel *Traps*. The main character finds himself on "trial" at a strange dinner party in a private home. "Convicted" of murdering his boss, he vehemently rejects his "defense attorney's" plea that he is not responsible for his actions and is incapable of guilt, and he insists as strongly as he can that he has a right to be punished. The novel may be read at many levels, but certainly the most important is a forceful and effective literary statement of Hegel's position.

[2] One should note that utilitarians, as a rule, do *not* appeal to social contract theories, for such theories usually involve at least a hypothetical surrender of individual rights to the community and/or the sovereign who represents the community. David Hume (1965: 255–273) utterly rejected social contract doctrines, and most later utilitarians have followed his lead. As for human rights, Jeremy Bentham (1971: 155) declared, "*Natural rights* is simple nonsense: natural and imprescriptable rights, rhetorical nonsense—nonsense upon stilts" (emphasis in original). For Bentham (1971: 153–156), the only rights a person had were thoe which the community allowed in order to maximize happiness. Again, later utilitarians have usually followed the lead of their master.

Utilitarian considerations, of course, have been at the heart of economic models of criminal justice (Landes, 1971; Posner, 1972: *passim.;* Monzingo, 1977).

Those who advocate a therapeutic model, of course, do differ significantly from traditional utilitarians. Authors such as Bentham, for instance, would agree with the retributivists that punishment should be proportional to the crime, though their reasons for holding this view would be quite different from those advanced by Kant or Murphy. In a therapy model, however, the whole notion of proportionality between offense and response ceases to make any sense at all. Therapy, rather, should be proportional to the "disease," not to the overt offense. Other differences could be cited as well. The point here is that champions of therapy as a comprehensive approach to crime are not prepared to allow anything but utilitarian considerations as a basis for a criminal justice system (Murphy, 1979: 147–158).

In accordance with his principles, Beccaria (1965a: 62–63) conceded that the sovereign does have the right to put a citizen to death if and when that citizen's very existence constitutes a clear danger to the entire community. Such an execution, however, would amount to an act of war, an ultimate act of self-defense, rather than an act of ordinary justice.

REFERENCES

Barriè, O. (1959). *La cultura politica nell'età delle riforme.* In *Storia di Milano,* vol. 12, *L'età delle riforme,* ed. G. Treccani degli Alfieri, pp. 419–456. Milan: Fondazione Treccani degli Alfieri per la Storia di Milano.

Beccaria, C. (1958). *Opere,* ed. S. Romagnoli, 2 vols. Florence: Sansoni.

——— (1965a). *Dei delitti e delle pene. Con una raccolta di lettere e documenti relativi alla nascita dell'opera e alla sua fortuna nel'Europa del Settecento,* ed. F. Venturi. Turin: Einaudi.

——— (1965b). *Des délits et des peines,* ed. F. Venturi; trans. M. Chevallier. Geneva: Librairie Droz.

Benn, S.I. (1973). Punishment. In *The encyclopedia of philosophy,* ed. P. Edwards, vol. 7, pp. 29–31. New York: Macmillan.

Bentham, J. (1970). *An introduction to the principles of morals and legislation,* ed. J.H. Burns and H.L.A. Hart. London: Athlone.

——— (1971). Anarchical fallacies. In *Natural law in political thought,* ed. P.E. Sigmund, pp. 153–156. Cambridge, MA: Winthrop.

Black, C.L. (1974). *Capital punishment: The inevitability of caprice and mistake.* New York: W.W. Norton.

Facchinei, F. (1965). *Note ed osservazioni sul libro intitolato Dei delitti e delle pene.* Excerpted in C. Beccaria, *Dei delitti e delle pene. Con una raccolta . . . ,* ed. F. Venturi, pp. 164–177. Turin: Einaudi.

Fletcher, G. (1978). *Rethinking criminal law.* Boston: Little, Brown.

Halévy, E. (1955). *The growth of philosophical radicalism,* trans. M. Morris. Boston: Beacon Press.

Hegel, G.W.F. (1969). *Hegel's philosophy of right,* ed. and trans. T.M. Knox. Oxford: Oxford University Press.

Helvétius, C.A. (1759). *De l'esprit.* Paris:Durand.

Hume, D. (1965). Of the original contract. In D. Hume, *Hume's ethical writings,* ed. A. MacIntyre, pp. 255–273. New York: Macmillan.

Kant, I. (1965). *The metaphysical elements of justice. Part I of the metaphysics of morals,* ed. and trans. J. Ladd. Indianapolis: Bobbs-Merrill.

Landes, M. (1971). An economic analysis of the courts. *J. of Law and Econ.* 14:61–107.

Maestro, M. (1973). *Cesare Beccaria and the origins of penal reform.* Philadelphia: Temple University Press.

Marx, K. (1973). Capital punishment. In *Punishment and rehabilitation,* ed. J.G. Murphy, pp. 91–94. Belmont, CA: Wadsworth.

Menninger, K. (1968). *The crime of punishment.* New York: Viking.

Montesquieu, C.L. de Secondat, Baron de (1949). *Lettres persanes.* In C.L. de Secondat, Baron de Montesquieu, *Oeuvres complètes,* ed. R. Caillois, vol. 1, pp. 129–373. Paris: Bibliothèque de la Pléiade.

Monzingo, J.E. (1977). Economic analysis of the criminal justice system. *Crime and Delinq.* 23:257–269.

Morris, H. (1973). Persons and punishment. In *Punishment and rehabilitation,* ed. J.G. Murphy, pp. 40–64. Belmont, CA: Wadsworth.

Murphy, J.G. (1979). *Retribution, justice, and therapy.* Dordrecht and Boston: D. Reidel.

Posner, R.A. (1972). *Economic analysis of law.* Boston: Little, Brown.

Rawls, J. (1955). Two concepts of rules. *The Philosophical Rev.* 64:3–32.

——— (1971). *A theory of justice.* Cambridge, MA: Harvard University Press.

Rousseau, J.-J. (1964). *Du contract social.* In J.-J. Rousseau, *Oeuvres complètes,* ed. B. Gagnebin and M. Raymond, vol. 3, pp. 347–470. Paris: Bibliothèque de la Pléiade.

Salvatorelli, L. (1945). *Il pensiero politico italiano dal 1700 a 1870.* Turin: Einaudi.

Satre, T.W. (1975). The irrationality of capital punishment. *The Southwestern J. of Phil.* 6:75–87.

Skinner, B.F. (1953). *Science and human behavior.* New York: Macmillan.

———— (1971). *Beyond freedom and dignity.* New York: Alfred A. Knopf.

Valsecchi, F. (1934). *L'assolutismo illuminato in Austria e in Lombardia*, vol. 2, *La Lombardia.* Bologna: Nicola Zanichelli.

Verri, P., and Verri, A. (1965). *Risposta ad uno scritto che s'intitolato Note ed osservazioni sul libro Dei delitti e delle pene.* Excerpted in C. Beccaria, *Dei delitti e delle pene. Con una raccolta . . .* , ed. F. Venturi, pp. 178–186. Turin: Einaudi.

Wootton, B. (1963). *Crime and criminal law.* London: Stevens and Sons.

Zarone, G. (1971). *Etica e politica nell'utilitarianismo di Cesare Beccaria.* Naples: Istituto per gli Studi Storici.

[3]

INVENTING CRIMINOLOGY: THE "SCIENCE OF MAN" IN CESARE BECCARIA'S *DEI DELITTI E DELLE PENE* (1764)*

PIERS BEIRNE
University of Southern Maine

This paper challenges existing images of the context and object of Cesare Beccaria's (1764) Dei delitti e delle pene. *It offers textual and other evidence that the chief object of Beccaria's famous treatise was the application to crime and penality not of humanism and legal rationality, as convention holds, but of the Scottish-inspired "science of man." This latter was a deterministic discourse whose key principles—utilitarianism, probabilism, associationism, and sensationalism—implicitly defy conventional assumptions about the volitional basis of classical criminology. The paper thus questions* Dei delitti's *proper place in the history of criminology and, in so doing, casts doubt on the very existence of a distinctive "classical criminology."*

When you have any thing to obtain of present dispatch, you entertain; and amuse the party, with whom you deal, with some other Discourse; that he be not too much awake, to make Objections.

Francis Bacon in Sermones Fideles (1632)

In recent work I have tried to uncover the process of concept formation in the early history of criminology (Beirne, 1987a, 1987b, 1988; Beirne and Hunt, 1990). About the origin and development of positivist criminology, in particular, I have opposed two sets of conventional claims. First, against externalist claims, I have argued that the origins of the conceptual content and explanatory structure of positivist criminology cannot adequately be understood either as mere representations of the power relations peculiar to modernity or as unmediated expressions of the epistemological divisions wrought by state practices in the asylum, the clinic, and the prison. Second, against internalist claims, I have argued that the key concepts and discursive techniques of positivist criminology did not develop as logical or even inevitable products of scientific development. Rather, the key concepts emerged from some of the focal concerns of the domains of penality and the statistical

---

* This paper was presented at the annual meetings of the American Society of Criminology, Baltimore, Maryland, November 1990. Research for it was enabled by the generosity of the National Endowment for the Humanities (Fellowship #FB-26796) and by the provision of a Visiting Scholarship at the Institute of Criminology at Cambridge University. For their cautions, I am most grateful to Susan Corrente, David Garland, Alasdair MacIntyre, Jim Messerschmidt, Ray Michalowski, and Graeme Newman.

movement, which, during the Restoration (1814–1830) in France, coincided in the issue of the regulation of the "dangerous classes." Positivist criminology, I have suggested, was originally a multifaceted, nineteenth-century discourse based on economism, biologism, and mental hereditarianism; its chief objects ("criminal man," "criminality," and "criminal character") were demarcated by epistemological boundaries dividing the "normal" from the "pathological."[1]

In developing this description I have assumed, as have most other scholars (e.g., Vold and Bernard, 1986:10–15), the truth of the hallowed distinction between positivist criminology and the dominant discourse about crime that preceded it, namely, classical criminology. By convention, classical criminology was a mid- to late-eighteenth-century discourse couched in the rhetoric of classical jurisprudence; its chief object, as found in the works of Beccaria, Bentham, Romilly, and others, is held to have been the construction of a rational and efficient penal calculus directed to the actions of the volitional legal subject.[2]

In this paper, I reconsider the merits of the key text in the development of classical criminology, namely, Beccaria's *Dei delitti e delle pene* (*Of Crimes and Punishments*—henceforth, *Dei delitti*) of 1764. I do so not only because descriptions of classical criminology invariably focus on the life and labors of its anonymous author, the shy and enigmatic member of the Milanese patriciate Cesare Bonesana, Marchese di Beccaria (1738–1794), but also because, as I argue here, the discursive objects of Beccaria's famous treatise have been persistently misrepresented by friend and foe alike.

My thesis about *Dei delitti* unfolds in four stages. First, I claim that in the past 200 years the predominant images of *Dei delitti* have been constructed more in terms of its practico-juridical effects in Europe and colonial America

---

1. By the term "positivist" criminology, I refer loosely to a discourse about crime and criminality that is predicated on the belief that there is a fundamental harmony between the methods of the natural and the social sciences. This discourse views its observational categories as theory independent, and it can assume several forms, each of which, according to its context and object, can be more or less appropriate as a method of inquiry (Beirne, 1987a:1141, n. 3).

2. Some scholars nowadays suggest that because concepts such as "crime," "criminal," and "criminality" were absent from their epistemological universe, classical criminologists such as Beccaria and his followers were not representative of a criminology of *homo criminalis* as such. Rather, the suggestion is that because their concepts were directed to *homo penalis* their labors should be categorized as either "classical penology" or "administrative penology" or even "a theory of social control." For example, Garland argues that it is altogether misleading to designate the work of writers such as Beccaria, Voltaire, Bentham, and Blackstone as "criminology": "their work is essentially the application of legal jurisprudence to the realm of crime and punishment, and it bears no relation to the "human sciences" of the nineteenth century that were to form the basis of the criminological enterprise", (1985:14–15; similarly, see Foucault, 1979:102, 1988; Pasquino, 1980:20–21; Taylor et al., 1973:2–3).

INVENTING CRIMINOLOGY   779

than in terms of its actual discursive features. However, I do not thereby dispute the momentous practical effects exerted by Beccaria's text, the extent of which is indicated in Durkheim's (1901:113) confident assessment "it is incontestably the case that it was . . . *Of Crimes and Punishments* which delivered the mortal blow to the old and hateful routines of the criminal law."[3] Nor do I suggest that *Dei delitti* is to the history of criminology what the Piltdown Man hoax is to the history of physical anthropology. Instead I argue, second, that the persistent misrepresentation of the arguments of *Dei delitti* is actively encouraged by the ambiguity of many of Beccaria's own positions and by the obscure and secretive style of much of his prose—common enough textual practices in the dangerous publishing conditions that existed during much of the Enlightenment. Only with considerable difficulty, therefore, can the nature and intended objects of Beccaria's discourse be discerned. Third, I demonstrate that the chief object of *Dei delitti* is the application to crime and penality of the "science of man," a deterministic discourse implicitly at odds with conventional assumptions about the exclusively humanist and volitional bases of "classical criminology." In making this claim, I fundamentally challenge the existing interpretations of the context and object of Beccaria's book. In so doing, finally, I cast doubt on the very existence of a distinctive "classical criminology." It is a corollary of my argument that those modern-day criminologists who adhere to models of human agency based on "free will" and "rational choice" must look to some discourse other than Beccaria's to discover their intellectual ancestry.

IMAGES OF *DEI DELITTI*

The first copies of *Dei delitti* were printed in Livorno, Italy, and circulated anonymously in the summer of 1764.[4] Beccaria's short treatise of 104 pages was an instant and dazzling success. The first Italian edition was quickly followed by two others and then in 1765, through the intercession of the *philosophes* d'Alembert, Malesherbes, Voltaire, and the Abbé Morellet, a widely read French translation (*Traité des délits et des peines*). By 1800 there had

---

3. See also Maestro (1942:124–151; Paolucci (1963); C. Phillipson (1923:89–106); Venturi (1971:100–116; and Young (1984, 1986).

4. Although he had received a law degree from the University of Pavia in 1758, Beccaria knew very little about criminal law and punishment when he began to write *Dei delitti* in March 1763, and the project itself actually was first suggested to him by Pietro Verri and then developed through discussion with fellow *illuministi* in the *Accademià dei pugni*. Beccaria completed his treatise in January 1764, after working on it for only 10 months. Biographical details of Beccaria's career can be found in Cantù (1862), Landry (1910:7–46), Maestro (1942:51–55, 1973:5–12), Paolucci (1963:ix–xxiii), and C. Phillipson (1923:26).

been no less than 23 Italian editions, 14 French editions, and 11 English editions (3 printed in the United States).[5] Clearly, Beccaria's proposals for the reform of criminal law appealed to a large cross-section of educated society. His disciples included such benevolent and not-so-benevolent despots as Gustavus III of Sweden, Catherine II of Russia, and Empress Maria Theresa of Austria; lawyers and legal philosophers in England like William Blackstone[6] and Jeremy Bentham;[7] republican revolutionaries in colonial America such as

---

5. Which of the several editions of *Dei delitti* represents Beccaria's intended text is not entirely clear. The first Italian edition of 1764 arguably contains the text closest to Beccaria's initial thinking, but it was published only after extensive editing by his friend Pietro Verri. The first French edition of 1765 certainly made the greatest impact on intellectual circles outside Italy, and of the early editions it had by far the largest circulation. However, its translator, the famous Abbé Morellet, made a variety of changes to Beccaria's manuscript without his permission, ostensibly for the sake of clarity of presentation but which perhaps resulted in an undue emphasis on its utilitarian features; for this, Morellet's translation was castigated by the *philosophe* Melchior Grimm (1765a:424–425) and scorned as a perversion of the author's meaning by the anonymous translator of the first English edition of 1767. Yet no compelling evidence (*pace* Venturi, 1971:106–108; Young, 1984:164–165) exists that Beccaria himself was overly concerned either with Morellet's rearrangement of the text or with the effects of the translation. In one of his letters to Morellet, Beccaria (1766:862–863) commented on this very issue in the following terms:

> My work has lost none of its force in your translation, except in those places where the essential character of one or the other language has imparted some difference between your expression and mine . . . I find quite without foundation the objection that your changing the order of my text resulted in a loss of its force. The force consists in the choice of expressions and the *rapprochement* of ideas, neither of which has been harmed.

Nevertheless, the edition of *Dei delitti* used here is the sixth Italian edition of 1766. This is so because all its major arguments are faithful to the original edition, because it appeared not long after the original, and because it was the final edition personally supervised by Beccaria himself. This choice is also favored by the Italian Enlightenment specialist Franco Venturi (1965); fortunately, it has recently been made available in an excellent English translation by Young, and on which I largely depend here.

6. In his *Commentaries on the Law of England*, Blackstone (1769:Vol. 4, ch. 1:3, 4–18) referred to Beccaria as "an ingenious writer," and he praised Beccaria's humanism and his specific recommendations for rules of evidence, for deterrence ("certainty" rather than "severity" of punishment) and a "proportionate scale" of punishments. On the timeliness of Beccaria's ideas for English reformers, and on Blackstone's indebtedness to them, see Beattie (1986:555–557) and Lieberman (1989:209–209). Beccaria's influence on other English reformers, such as William Eden, Henry Dagge, and Manasseh Dawes, is discussed in Green (1985:290–303).

7. Upon reading *Dei delitti*, Bentham exclaimed: "Oh! my master, first evangelist of Reason, you who have raised your Italy so far above England, and I would add above France . . . you who have made so many useful excursions into the path of utility, what is there left for us to do?—Never to turn aside from that path" (cited in Halévy, 1928:21; see also Hart, 1982:40–52). Elsewhere, Bentham wrote of Beccaria that "he was received by the intelligent as an Angel from heaven would be by the faithful. He may be styled the father of *Censorial Jurisprudence*" (1776:14).

INVENTING CRIMINOLOGY   781

Thomas Jefferson and John Adams;[8] and most important, the *philosophes* in France. Among the *philosophes*, Beccaria's ideas were highly esteemed by such luminaries as d'Alembert, Diderot, Helvétius, Buffon, and Voltaire. D'Alembert (1765:313), for example, thought that Beccaria had successfully combined "philosophy, truth, logic, and precision with sentiments of humanity" for which he would gain an "immortal reputation." An astonishing accolade was bestowed on *Dei delitti* when in 1766, and in many subsequent editions, Voltaire's glowing *Commentaire sur le livre des délits et des peines* was appended to Beccaria's text.

Although *Dei delitti* was received with rapture by a large majority of the *philosophes*, some among them greeted it with cautious criticism. While they unanimously endorsed Beccaria's humanitarianism, some disagreed with either the direction or the extent of his specific proposals for reform of the criminal law. Against Beccaria's reticence about the legality of suicide, for example, Voltaire explicitly denied that it was a crime. Against Beccaria's complete opposition to torture, Diderot and others argued that it was justified for the discovery of a guilty party's accomplices. Others protested Beccaria's absolute opposition to capital punishment. Moreover, according to the dour Melchior Grimm (1765:424), Beccaria's proposals were "too geometrical," a vague and overused term that implied a narrow emphasis on probabilism and mathematics. A similar accusation was leveled at Beccaria's work by the Scottish Enlightenment painter Allan Ramsay, who complained that "it is useless to treat penal questions abstractly, as if they were questions of geometry and arithmetic" (n.d.:55).

Worse still, among many jurists in Italy and France, *Dei delitti* immediately became an object of derision and scorn. Beccaria's novel ideas about torture, capital punishment, and equality before the law were condemned as highly dangerous, for example, by Muyart de Vouglans, Daniel Jousse, and the French attorney general Louis Séguier (Maestro, 1942:64–67).[9] Powerful elements in Roman Catholicism also opposed Beccaria's proposals. Thus, in

---

8. Thomas Jefferson, for example, "copied long passages from it in his *Commonplace Book* and used it as his principal modern authority for revising the laws of Virginia" (Wills, 1978:94). In 1770, during his speech in defense of the British soldiers implicated in The Boston Masacre, John Adams pleaded "I am for the prisoners at the bar, and shall apologize for it only in the words of the Marquis Beccaria: 'If I can but be the instrument of preserving one life, his blessing and tears of transport, shall be a sufficient consolation to me, for the contempt of all mankind' " (quoted in Kidder, 1870:232).

9. Maestro (1973:38–39) has outlined the attack made on Beccaria in 1771 by the French jurist Daniel Jousse, in the latter's *Traité de la justice criminelle de France*. Maestro asks, "Why these attacks on Beccaria on the part of the jurists?" and responds "[because] the men who had built their lives, their fortunes, and their reputations on the old customs could not bear to see this young idealist suddenly ruin their edifice." This answer, while correct, fails to specify the precise terms in which the jurists of the *ancien régime* recognized Beccaria's book as such a dangerous threat.

early 1765 the Dominican friar Ferdinando Facchinei—a cantankerous mouthpiece of the Inquisitorial Council of Ten in Venice—published a tract that accused Beccaria of sedition, impiety, and a new heresy, which he termed "socialism"; Facchinei derided Beccaria as "the Rousseau of the Italians" (1765:173; see also Maestro, 1973:35–37). The next year, Beccaria's book was condemned for its extreme rationalism and placed on the papal *Index Prohibitorum*, where it remained for almost two centuries.

Notwithstanding some later retributivist objections to Beccaria's utilitarianism voiced in Germany, the initial furor over *Dei delitti* gradually gave way to a stock of complacent assumptions about the intentions of its author.[10] Chief among them has been the view that the key ideas in *Dei delitti* can be apprehended in terms of their practical effects. An unmediated and necessary association is held typically to exist between Beccaria's intentions, as they were formulated in his text, in other words, and their more or less successful appropriation for the practice of criminal law and criminal justice in the eighteenth century. Since then, most, if not all, sociologists and historians of penology (e.g., Gorecki, 1985:67–68; Jones, 1986:33–57; Mueller, 1990) have read backwards from the effects of the written word to Beccaria's intentions and have thereby made two assumptions about *Dei delitti*. First, they assumed it was primarily a humanist project, inspired by the tradition of the French *philosophes* and motivated by the author's humanitarian opposition to the arbitrariness and barbaric cruelty of European criminal justice in the mid-eighteenth century. Second, they assumed it had as its chief objects the reform of judicial irrationality (including judicial torture and capital punishment) and the institution of a utilitarian approach to punishment based on a calculus of pleasure and pain. In concert, these assumptions have retrospectively led to another, namely, that Beccaria was the founder of classical criminology (e.g., Matza, 1964:3, 13), marked as it is by a penal calculus based on the doctrine of the social contract and couched in the rhetoric of the free legal subject.

This Whiggish consensus has been challenged by recent studies that have attempted to scrutinize the ideological content of *Dei delitti*. In particular, Foucault (1979:73–103, 1988) has argued that neither Beccaria's classical criminology nor its effects were the projects of genuinely enlightened or humanitarian reform. Instead, he has claimed, they were but two among many artifacts peculiar to a new disciplinary power. Following Foucault, a number of other critical assessments of *Dei delitti* have been voiced. The radical pioneering role usually assigned Beccaria within classical criminology has been contradicted, for example, and he has been viewed as allegedly far more conservative than other Enlightenment theorists because he deliberately

---

10. See especially, Kant's (1979:102–107) *Metaphysical Elements of Justice* and Hegel's (1821:70–71) *Philosophy of Right*.

INVENTING CRIMINOLOGY 783

equivocated on such dangerous issues as materialism and spiritualism (Jenkins, 1984; see also Roshier, 1989:16–18). Beccaria is held to have been a champion of aristocratic values that, in his native Lombardy, had been deeply penetrated by the ideology and interests of capitalist agriculture and the new bourgeoisie (Humphries and Greenberg, 1981:224). Beccaria's liberalism, it is claimed, responded to a fundamental difficulty of post-feudal societies: how to prevent the criminality of the masses while masking the fact that the criminal law preserved a class system based on social inequality? Beccaria's solution to this problem is portrayed as a popularization of the legal doctrine "equality before the law," a bourgeois fiction that, simply by doctrinal fiat, lodges criminal responsibility at the level of the individual (Weisser, 1979:133–138). Even Beccaria's intervention in judicial history has been dismissed as a fairy tale, his humanism ridiculed because he did not know that the process of abolishing judicial torture had already been initiated through a decisive transformation of the medieval law of proof (Chadwick, 1981:98; Langbein, 1976:67–68). His attempts to reform the criminal law have therefore been described as fundamental only to the myth of rational sentencing replacing arbitrary injustice (Hirst, 1986:152–155; see also Newman and Marongiu, 1990; Young, 1983).

Many of these assessments of the discourse in *Dei delitti* assume that Beccaria's arguments and ideological presuppositions can be understood more or less exclusively in terms of their manifest effects. Beccaria's intervention in criminal jurisprudence, for example, continues to be regarded as (1) "humanist" because it opposed the barbaric practices of the *ancien régime*, (2) as "revolutionary" because it was in the vanguard of the Italian Enlightenment in exposing religious intolerance, or (3) as "conservative" because it did not travel as far down the road of materialism as others undoubtedly did at that time.

Dei delitti, however, shares with many Enlightenment treatises the fact that the meaning of the author's arguments do not always strike with immediate clarity. To a certain extent, I will suggest, the vivid humanism in the 47 rambling chapters of *Dei delitti* is a mask behind which some of Beccaria's other arguments lie hidden, arguments that can only be discerned with some difficulty and not a little speculation. Accordingly, neither the structure nor the content of Beccaria's discourse should be taken at face value. To understand how and why this is so, something must be known of the conditions of production of *Dei delitti* as a text of the Enlightenment.

READING *DEI DELITTI* AS A TEXT OF ENLIGHTENMENT

A key feature of Italy's Enlightenment was how backward its practitioners believed it to be compared with that of other countries in Europe. "This backwardness was ascribed," Woolf (1979:75) has recorded, "to the stifling effects of the 'official' counter-reformist culture in Italy, to a conformist mentality which led to acquiescence in the teachings of churchmen and lawyers, an acceptance of scholasticism, superstition and curialism" (see also Gross, 1990:258). In matters of religion, science, politics, and economics, the intellectual universe of the *illuministi* was one in which transgressions of the permitted bounds of discourse invited more or less severe censure either from the papacy or from the tiny political cliques that ruled each state.

During the first half of the eighteenth century, in the decade or two prior to the publication of *Dei delitti*, the degree of publicity and openness attending Enlightenment discussion of such matters as religious doctrine, scientific development, and the relationship between them, was largely dictated by the ebb and flow of the political interests of the papacy. Concern about the political divisions of Italy, for example, naturally led to a fierce and threatening debate about the sovereign powers of Church and State, which raised questions about authority over the clergy, the limitation of mortmain, customs duties, and restraint of trade. In the first decade of Benedict XIV's pontificate (1740–1750), Rome opened itself up somewhat to the new culture of science, especially physics and chemistry, in the expectation that science could be applied to the alleviation of chronic economic and social problems in the papal states. Then, during the 1750s, the religious and scientific communities engaged in a heated debate on the nature of faith, the existence of magic, and the remedies for witchcraft. This debate was led by Muratori, the first Italian advocate of scientific history, and it encompassed both the attack on miracles in the *Encyclopédie* by d'Alembert and Diderot and also the discussion between La Mettrie and Maupertuis on the scientific calculation of pleasure and pain. Initially, these and other scientific arguments were couched in the rhetoric of religious doctrine. Rapidly, however, the antagonists in this debate discovered discursive weapons that were even more potent than religion: first Cartesian rationalism, then enlightenment, and finally "reason" (Venturi, 1972:103–129; Woolf, 1979:83–84).

In Beccaria's Milan, the state of Lombardy was subject to the political and economic dominance of the enlightened Austro-Hapsburg ruler Maria Theresa. Under Austrian rule, various aspects of social life in Lombardy were somewhat more liberal than elsewhere in Italy. For example, Maria Theresa had loosened the influence of the Church with the *Giunta economale* and the 1762 Pragmatic Sanction, which required royal consent before papal letters and papal bulls could be entered and published (Roberts, 1960:38). In addition, her representative in Lombardy, Count Firmian—to whom Beccaria would later be indebted for warding off attempts to prosecute him for his book—had enacted a variety of liberal inroads into social and intellectual life, including toleration of debate and discussion by reform-minded *illuministi*.

INVENTING CRIMINOLOGY   785

Beccaria himself was a member of the Milanese *illuministi*. These were typically government officials who sought to create a model bourgeois society that combined spiritual and moral regeneration with and through the materialist advantages of economic growth. However, far from being simple "thermometers of bourgeois opinion," these Milanese reformers envisioned a well-ordered, hierarchical society whose reconstruction would emanate from an enlightened state administration that, although working in alliance with such other powers as the papal administration, could dominate all other power blocs and would include all men of property and education (Klang, 1984:41–46). For the *illuministi*, the problem, both intellectual and organization, was how this collective dream could be implemented.

This problem was the chief focus of the group of Milanese reformers with whom Beccaria mixed in the literary club *Accademià dei pugni* (Academy of Fisticuffs), whose members included the Verri brothers Pietro and Allesandro, the economist Gian Rinaldo Carli, the ecclesiastical law expert Alfonso Longo, and the mathematicians Paolo Frisi and Luigi Lambertenghi. In 1762 the ideas of the *Accademià* began to be published in its critical literary journal *Il Caffè* which, Beccaria (1766:866) later confided, imitated Joseph Addison's *Spectator* in England. Beccaria himself was undoubtedly motivated to join the *Accademià*, and then to compose *Dei delitti*, by his discomfort with the lack of reforms in Lombardy in the domain of criminal law and the administration of justice and also with the continued burden of censorship of the written word. Throughout the Enlightenment, in Italy especially but also elsewhere and with varying degrees of necessity, its practitioners employed ubiquitous trickery to defeat the censor and the police and, in Beccaria's Lombardy, to avoid the prying eyes of the Inquisitorial Council of Ten.[11] Everyday ruses were devised simply to allow heretical, seditious, or egalitarian ideas to be transmitted to the reading public. As with *Dei delitti*, these included anonymous authorship, frontispieces with phoney places of publication, secret printing presses, and an underground network for the distribution and sale of books and pamphlets. Numerous other ploys were designed to cover the truth with a thin veil that would protect a text from hostile eyes. These included the publication of the diaries of imaginary travelers abroad, the translation of imaginary foreign books, and pervasive use of double entendre, which would allow only the *cogniscenti* the pleasure of piercing its message (Darnton, 1979, 1982).

Few works of Italian *illuminism* were able to escape such textual deformities, and the style and the content of the arguments in *Dei delitti* suffered from

---

11. Beccaria himself was painfully aware of the fates of Machiavelli, Galileo, and the historian Giannone (see Beccaria, 1766:863). They published *and* perished! Thus, Pietro Verri wrote in 1765 that for his friend Beccaria the major difficulty in preparing his book was how to publish "such delicate matters without having trouble" (cited in Maestro, 1942:54–55).

them. As a result, a serious difficulty in understanding the arguments of *Dei delitti* is that, like many other Enlightenment texts, it employed an array of devious textual practices, which relied on the cautious dictum that it is better to be a secret witness of Enlightenment than a posthumously acknowledged martyr. Thus, the stated objects of Beccaria's protestations in *Dei delitti* were not the despotic monarchies of contemporary Italy but those of the "state of nature" and classical Rome and Greece (1764:15, 45, 49, 53), and his angry remarks on religious intolerance are utterly devoid of clear temporal and empirical referents. Moreover, in what was more than simply a casual failure to document his sources, Beccaria's text is virtually bereft of intellectual bearings, which, had he openly pointed to them, would have allowed his readers ("the few sages scattered across the face of the earth"—pp. 52–53) the privilege of observing more clearly the precise mast to which he chose to nail his colors. Thus, Beccaria referred to no contemporary sources other than the standard Enlightenment fare of Hobbes (p. 5) and Montesquieu (pp. 4, 5, 28), and even then, no specific reference is made to any particular work.

The lack of formal acknowledgment to other authors creates an immediate hardship for anyone attempting to trace a genealogy of Beccaria's ideas. The voluminous secondary literature on *Dei delitti* has attempted to solve this thorny problem by declaring that it is not in fact a problem at all. Was not Beccaria casually indulging in the free trade of current ideas so prevalent among Enlightenment authors in his day? Can one not read into Beccaria's text the popular views held, if not by all, then by most members of the Enlightenment, and especially by the French *philosophes*?

ENLIGHTENMENT AND ENLIGHTENMENTS

It is not easy to generalize about the eclectic ideas of that period from the middle of the seventeenth century to the last quarter of the eighteenth century that the *philosophes* joyously referred to as "*l'éclairecissement*" and that the taciturn English ironically dubbed "the Age of Enlightenment." It can perhaps be said that all members of the Enlightenment affirmed their belief in the principles of reason, the precision of the scientific method, and the authority of nature; but because there was enormous disagreement about each one of these beliefs, this says little of real substance.[12] Moreover, there was

---

12. In response to religious intolerance, for example, Helvétius, d'Holbach and La Mettrie professed atheism; Condillac, Catholicism; and Diderot alternately embraced both, "according to the state of his nerves" (Knight, 1968:5). Some *philosophes* were ardent materialists; others subscribed to spiritualism. Some were Cartesians, others Newtonians. Some looked to the anthropological state of nature with a romantic nostaligia; others detected in it the sorry aftermath of mankind's fall from grace and the onset of original sin. Some, like Diderot, assented to a limited use of judicial torture. Some opposed capital punishment, but others, like Voltaire and Montesquieu, believed that on certain occasions it was an appropriate device.

INVENTING CRIMINOLOGY 787

not just one Enlightenment but several, and in France, Italy, Holland, Germany, Sweden, Russia, England, Scotland, colonial America, and elsewhere, there existed diverse and sometimes quite incompatible notions of the content and direction of enlightenment.

The objects in Beccaria's text naturally reflected this diversity of opinion, and it is unwise to assume that they had some unitary source. As Beccaria himself suggested, it was in "the choice of expressions and the rapprochement of ideas" (1766:863) that the power of his text resided. His attempted rapprochement occurred with respect to two chief ideas, each of which exerted different effects on his text, and with varying degrees of impact. In concert, both testified to the salient fact that the Italian Enlightenment, which set in relatively late, was unusually under the influence of foreign authors. One was the humanism of the French *philosophes*; the other was the largely unacknowledged influence of the embryonic "science of man" in Scotland.

THE HUMANISM OF THE FRENCH PHILOSOPHES

On more than one occasion, Beccaria openly ackowledged his profound indebtedness to the humanist writings of the French *philosophes*. For example, in a letter to Abbé André Morellet, the translator of the first French edition of his book, Beccaria gushed that "I myself owe everything to French books" (1766:862).[13] Here, he specifically referred to the influence of d'Alembert, Diderot, Helvétius, Buffon, and Hume (p. 864).[14] Among the *philosophes*, it was Montesquieu who exerted the greatest influence on Beccaria's thinking prior to the publication of *Dei delitti*. Thus, Beccaria (1766:865) declared that he had first been converted to the study of philosophy by Montesquieu's *Lettres persanes* of 1721. Moreover, it was on Montesquieu that the only significant textual acknowledgment was bestowed in *Dei delitti*: "invisible truth has compelled me to follow the shining footsteps of this great man" (Beccaria, 1764:4).[15]

---

13. Beccaria at once continued that "they [i.e., French books] developed in my soul feelings of humanity that have been stifled by eight years of a fanatical education" (1766:862). It is significant that Beccaria received from those schoolmasters of Europe, the Jesuits, training in arithmetic, algebra, and geometry, "a fanatical education" as he described it, and one that he shared with anti-Jesuit intellectuals in France, such as Descartes, Montesquieu, Fontenelle, Voltaire, Diderot, Buffon, Condorcet, and possibly, Condillac. See further, Beccaria's comments to d'Alembert on the Jesuits (1765a:860).

14. Beccaria added that he derived many of his ideas from Helvétius's *l'Esprit*, which had alerted him to the misfortunes of humanity (see also note 37); from Buffon, who opened up for him the *"sanctuaire"* of nature; and from d'Alembert: "I know enough about mathematics to appreciate the great discoveries of this celebrated man, and to regard him as the greatest geometer of our century" (1766:865–866). After reading *Dei delitti*, Melchior Grimm thus aptly observed that "M. Beccaria writes in French with Italian words" (1765:330–331). See further, note 20.

15. Significantly, Montesquieu's (1748) *De l'ésprit des lois* is full of misgivings and

Although these few observations are far from conclusive, the influence of the *philosophes* can with reasonable confidence be discerned in the spacious antechamber to Beccaria's edifice, and it is lavishly decorated with their humanist rhetoric. It is demonstrated in two ways. First, Beccaria inherited from Montesquieu—and through Montesquieu, ultimately from the secular law tradition of Grotius and Pufendorf—a desire to disentangle and then sever criminal law and justice from religion. In arguing for the supremacy of the rule of law in human affairs, Beccaria thus rejected any claim that the laws that regulate social relationships derive from Divine Will. For him, it was imperative that sin be demarcated from crime, spiritual powers from temporal powers, and ecclesiastical bodies from secular courts. The Supreme Being who politely haunts the pages of *Dei delitti* is not therefore the omnipotent God the Father of Roman Catholicism but a depersonalized god who has been cast into the nether regions where all other spirits dwell. This god was merely another benevolent despot who could be contemplated "with respect untempered with fear or adoration" (Becker, 1932:50) and whose jurisdiction, for Beccaria, encompassed sins ("offenses between men and God") rather than crimes ("offenses between men and men"). For Beccaria, then, crime— "I do not address myself to sins (1764:73)—is not a theological concept but a social one. Thus, he wrote,

> the true measure of crimes is . . . *the harm done to society*. This is one of the palpable truths which one needs neither quadrants nor telescopes to discover (p. 17).

A second way in which French humanism was manifest in Beccaria's text lay in his rejection of the cruel physical pain inflicted by the judiciary on suspects and on convicted felons. At one point, for example, he drew a stark contrast between "the indolence of the judge and the anguish of someone accused of a crime—between the comforts and pleasures of the unfeeling magistrate . . . and the tears and squalid condition of a prisoner" (p. 36). His strictures in this regard were directed almost exclusively, however, at the practices of judicial torture and capital punishment. Thus, "the torture of the accused while his trial is still in progress is a cruel practice sanctioned by the usage of most nations" (p. 29). More dramatic still, in what was likely a macabre comment on the popular and crowd-pleasing manner of disposing of

---

uncertainties about the thorny problem of free will and determinism. It is instructive, for example, to juxtapose the sort of persistent claim Montesquieu made at the very beginning of his book that "it is absurd to say that "*a blind determinism [fatalité] has produced all the effects that we see in the world*: what could be more absurd than to say that a blind determinism seems to have produced intelligent beings?" (Bk. I:7; emphasis in original) with his materialist analysis of the geographical distribution of various social events in Book XVI. There, Montesquieu actually claimed that such factors as climate and soil influence even sexual inequality and the type and content of laws (1748, Bk. XVI:280–294).

INVENTING CRIMINOLOGY 789

witches and heretics, Beccaria declared that "rational men" object to the distasteful spectacle of "the muffled, confused groans of poor wretches issuing out of vortices of black smoke—the smoke of human limbs—amid the crackling of charred bones and the sizzling of still palpitating entrails" (p. 72).[16] Elsewhere Beccaria confessed (p. 23, and see pp. 4, 29) that he would deem himself fortunate if,

> in the course of upholding the rights of men and invincible truth, I should contribute to saving an unhappy victim of tyranny or of equally pernicious ignorance from suffering and from the anguish of death, then the blessings and tears of that one person overcome with joy would console me for the contempt of all humanity.

Although it was a major impetus to the aims in Beccaria's text, the humanism of the *philosophes* was not at all the sole feature of its discourse. Indeed, at times Beccaria's humanism seems only an incidental feature that was grafted almost in *ad hoc* fashion to other, more significant arguments in *Dei delitti*.[17] Although humanism asserted itself in elegant passages that disavow the physical brutality of criminal law and that adopt a charitable position bent on ameliorating economic inequality, the depth of its textual penetration must not be exaggerated. This is unremarkable, though, if only because the *philosophes* themselves did not often address in their own writings the issues of penality raised in *Dei delitti*. Even in the case of those *philosophes* who did address issues of criminal law and punishment, such as Montesquieu and the Chevalier de Jaucourt (1751), the textual structure of their works resembled unkempt mazes rather than the systematicity to which Beccaria's treatise aspired.

To uncover the principal discursive inspiration behind Beccaria's treatise, one therefore must look elsewhere. It is to be found, I suggest, in the ideas of Enlightenment authors in Britain, especially as they were developed in Scotland.

THE "SCIENCE OF MAN" IN SCOTLAND

I have suggested that, because the publishing conditons in Lombardy were so fraught with danger, Beccaria was forced to conceal some of the intellectual influences on *Dei delitti* and, moreover, some of the arguments within it. Nevertheless, with typical Enlightenment flourish, Beccaria attached to his

---

16. In *Dei delitti*, Beccaria (1764:48–49) argued that capital punishment is justified if (1) an incarcerated citizen is still a threat to society, (2) a citizen's mere existence could produce a revolution dangerous to the state, or (3) a citizen's execution deterred others from committing crimes.

17. Contemporary interest in the humanist aspects of Beccaria's text were probably stimulated by a propaganda campaign mounted by Voltaire (1762a; 1762b; 1763; see also, Maugham, 1928) on behalf of the unfortunate Jean Calas.

text a deliberate clue of extraordinary significance for unlocking the aims of his work. Preceding the text, and prominently displayed on the frontispiece of each of the six editions of *Dei delitti* personally authorized by Beccaria, is an epigram (originally in Latin) from one of the first purveyors of Enlightenment ideas, Francis Bacon (1561–1626): "In all Negociations of Difficulty, a Man may not look to sow and reap at once; But must Prepare Business, and so Ripen it by Degrees" (1632:283).

It is interesting to speculate why Bacon's advice was so highly esteemed by Beccaria that he actually introduced his text with it. An obvious but perhaps superficial explanation is that Beccaria was declaring his intention to practise a virtue that was decidely lacking in other *illuministi*, namely, patience. In other words, although fearing that his proposals in *Dei delitti* might arouse stiff opposition from Church and State, Beccaria nevertheless was secure in the knowledge that they would eventually see the light of day, ripen, and bear fruit, and he was hereby stating as much. Still, an intriguing question remains. If Beccaria chose to introduce his text with a message for the faithful, why did he do so with an epigram from Bacon rather than, say, Montesquieu or Helvétius or Voltaire? Is it only that Beccaria had enormous admiration for Bacon?[18] One of Beccaria's (n.d.1:459–470) unpublished manuscripts, indeed, reveals that with marginal lines and copious notes he devoured several of Bacon's treatises, including *Sermones Fideles, De Dignitate, De Augmentis Scientiarum*, and the *Novum Organum*. Or is it more likely that Beccaria wished to invite his readers to draw a favorable parallel between what Bacon had attempted to do to English law in Elizabethan times and what it was that he intended to do to Italian criminal law in his day? Indeed, to his eighteenth-century Enlightenment disciples, Bacon was admired not only because he was the founder of empiricism and a great philosopher and scientist; to would-be legal reformers, like Beccaria in Italy and William Blackstone in England, Bacon was also revered for his legal theorizing, for his statute consolidation, and for the attempt in his *Digests* to give the law "light" (Lieberman, 1989:181–186). These very purposes were among Beccaria's own, as well, with respect to Italian criminal law. Beccaria

---

18.   Beccaria shared his neglected Baconian heritage with the anti-Cartesian humanist Giambattista Vico (1668–1744), the professor of Latin Eloquence at the University of Naples and one of the most creative social theorists in the entire Enlightenment. In his books *On the Study Methods of Our Time* (1709) and *The New Science* (1725), Vico audaciously applied Bacon's evolutionary and inductivist analysis of nature of natural law, jurisprudence, and history. Vico anticipated the *philosophes* in arguing that, through the judicious use of rewards and punishments, aristocratic laws can turn private vices into public virtues, and thus ensure civil happiness. Moreover, in *The New Science*, his expansive historical analyses suggested that on the "concrete and complex order of human civil institutions, we may superimpose the order of numbers" (1725:339–340; see also, Berlin, 1960). However, few of the *philosophes* themselves bothered to pierce Vico's obscure, convoluted, and tormented style, and in his lifetime he exerted almost no influence.

INVENTING CRIMINOLOGY 791

thus had good reason to pay homage to Chancellor Bacon and to England, "a nation whose literary glory, whose superiority in commerce and wealth (and hence in power), and whose examples of virtue and courage leave no doubt as to the excellence of its laws" (1764:31–32).[19]

The placement of Bacon's epigram must be mentioned not least because of Beccaria's use of it as an introduction to his text. As an introduction, it directs the reader to another dimension of Enlightenment thinking, the powerful presence of which in *Dei delitti* has largely been overlooked (*pace* Wills, 1978:149–151) but which was, I suggest, its central thrust and one that Beccaria had very good reason to hide from Catholic censors. This is the drift toward a science of man that had been inaugurated by enlightenment English philosophers such as Bacon himself, and by Newton and Shaftesbury, and after them by Locke. Later, it was developed even more forcefully in the civic tradition of Scottish authors such as Hutcheson, Hume, John Millar, Adam Ferguson, and Adam Smith.[20] Indeed, in a letter of April 6, 1762, Pietro Verri described his young friend Beccaria as "a profound mathematician . . .

---

19. Beyond the explanations given above, the remote possibility exists that there is even more to Beccaria's prominent placement of Bacon's epigram than meets the eye. Perhaps Beccaria was indulging in another Enlightenment game with his readers, designed not so much to stimulate his readers to seek its textual meaning *between* the lines but *before* them. Perhaps it was not to this particular Baconian passage that Beccaria wished to alert his fellow *philosophes*, but to the one preceding it, which states: "In Dealing with Cunning Persons, we must ever Consider their Ends, to interpret their Speeches; And it is good, to say little to them, and that which they least look for" (quoting Bacon, 1632:282–283). If Beccaria was inviting his readers to "interpret" his own argument, then, given that his opposition to judicial arbitrariness was not hidden in his text, but quite exposed, it is possible that there was some other important, though hidden, feature of his text, to which Beccaria wanted to alert his readers.

20. In Maestro's (1942) *Voltaire and Beccaria as Reformers of Criminal Law*, for example, there is no mention of either Bacon or Francis Hutcheson (1694–1746), and neither John Locke (1632–1704) nor David Hume (1711–1776) merit more than passing mention, although Hutcheson merits a brief comment in his (Maestro, 1973:21) authoritative *Cesare Beccaria and the Origins of Penal Reform*. Similarly, Chadwick (1981:96) writes regarding the Milanese Enlightenment that "Paris loomed much closer. The English and Scottish writers were less important." Venturi (1983) has noticed several fortuitous "parallels" between Beccaria's text and Scottish authors, but he identifies Henry Home, Lord Kames, Ferguson, and Smith rather than Hutcheson.

This is not to suggest that it was only the Scottish philosophers who were concerned to develop a scientific account of society. Far from it. Beccaria's French colleague Jean d'Alembert, for example, typically believed that only his Baconian-inspired "geometry," or "science of man," could unravel intricate religious doctrine, and when he (e.g., d'Alembert, n.d. 1:571–572; n.d. 2:99–114) addressed issues of human rights and duties he did so with the rhetoric of *esprit géométrique* and the methods of the exact sciences. On one occasion, he even argued that "mathematics should be used to subvert the Inquisition. Infiltrate enough geometers into the citizenry of a country oppressed by the Church, and Enlightenment would follow inevitably" (d'Alembert, quoted in Hankins, 1970:14).

with a mind apt to try new roads if laziness and discouragement do not suffocate him" (cited in Maestro, 1942:53). Given the virulent Anglomania that
gripped the Italian devotees of the Enlightenment, it is only to be expected
that Beccaria should have been compared with some English theorist. But it
is most interesting that the comparison was not with a legal reformer, such as
William Blackstone, but with the great scientist Isaac Newton; the most affectionate and admiring nickname given Beccaria by his friends was
"Newtoncino"—little Newton (Gay, 1966:12).

Before I try to demonstrate the influence of certain British authors on Beccaria's arguments in *Dei delitti*, let me offer some anticipatory evidence of this
connection from the period just prior to and contemporaneous with its publication in 1764. To begin with, it must be stressed how unexceptional it is that
Beccaria's discourse drew so heavily on the ideas of Enlightenment authors in
England and Scotland. Among the Italian *illuministi*, they, of all the authors,
exercised enormous influence, the peak of which they enjoyed from the late
1750s to the early 1770s. In much of Italy there was widespread feeling that
the economic and political progress of countries like England, France, and
Holland, was directly linked to the scientific rationalism embedded in the
empiricist discourse of the Enlightenment triumvirate of Bacon, Newton, and
Locke. Although some key works in this tradition had been banned in Italy
by state authorities, the papacy, or both,[21] they were nevertheless widely
available—Bacon and Newton could easily be found in Latin, and French
translations of Locke's *Essay Concerning Human Understanding* and
Voltaire's *Eléments de la philosophie de Newton* appeared in 1700 and 1738,
respectively. Indeed, the work of British authors dominated the conversations and the literary discourse of Beccaria's *Accademià* meetings.
Accademià members regularly read and discussed works by Bacon, Shake-
speare, Swift, Addison, Pope, Dryden, and Locke (Landry, 1910:13–14), and
also by the Scottish philosophers, among whom certainly were Hutcheson
and Hume (Shackleton, 1972:1470–1471).

The subtle complexity of *Dei delitti* cannot be comprehended in all its richness without recognizing the effects on his text of Beccaria's thoroughgoing
admiration for enlightened British writings, especially those in the Scottish
"civic tradition." Beginning with the writings of Andrew Fletcher in the late
seventeenth century, this tradition was concerned above all, and to a degree
that existed in no other country, with the multifaceted relationship between
political institutions and economic progress (Robertson, 1983). This concern,
heightened at the turn of the century by the possibility of enforced union with
England, was directed to a variety of issues, many of which naturally excited

---

21. Locke's *Essay Concerning Human Understanding*, for example, was placed on the
Index in 1734 by Pope Clement XII explicitly because its empiricism threatened religious
belief.

INVENTING CRIMINOLOGY 793

the reformist yearnings of the Italian *illuministi* as well in the middle of the eighteenth century. Chief among these topics were religious toleration, property and industry, the rule of law, constitutional government, justice, and the conditions of social order. Moreover, from about 1750 to 1770 the Scottish civic tradition was pivotal in the rise of a presociological discourse about society, and within that discourse a central place was occupied by the attempt to construct a science of man (Phillipson, 1981; Swingewood, 1970).

It is instructive now to consider Beccaria's other early writings, which, against *Dei delitti*'s bright reception, have generally been ignored. This is unfortunate because, although Beccaria's other writings did not exert much influence, they provide a broader view of his concerns at the time he wrote *Dei delitti*. Prior to the publication of *Dei delitti*, Beccaria published two short tracts, each of which yields some details as to the direction of his thought. In his first work, he (Beccaria, 1762a) addressed the economic problems of the Milanese currency. This essay drew its inspiration from Hume, Sir William Petty (Schumpeter, 1954:298), and especially, he (Beccaria, 1762a:8) admitted, from Locke; here Beccaria (1762a:8) specifically referred to the influence of Locke's *Nuove considerazioni* on his monetary analysis.[22] In another *Il Caffè* essay, Beccaria (1762a) creatively used algebraic formulae to analyze the costs and benefits of the crime of smuggling; here his main question was "given that a certain proportion of smuggled goods will be seized by the authorities, what is the total quantity that smugglers must move to be left with neither gain nor loss?"[23] His answer to this

---

22. "*Nuove considerazioni . . .*" was doubtless Locke's *Further Considerations Concerning Raising the Value of Money* (1695; see also Hutcheson, 1755, Bk.II, Ch. 12). Locke's book had been translated into Italian in 1749 by the Tuscan Abbés Pagnini and Tavanti, although its publication was delayed until 1751, probably because the translators feared that there must have been "some hidden mystery, as for instance that it might not be to the liking of certain important persons" (Venturi, 1963:783; see also Venturi, 1972:230–231). Moreover, it is no small coincidence that in his *Essay Concerning Human Understanding*—available throughout Europe in Latin since the 1690s, Locke had argued, in the context of equating the growth of crime with the rise of money as a universal form of exchange, that those who committed crime did so because they were trying either to assuage an immediate pain or to satisfy an absent pleasure (1689, 1:97–122); see further Schumpeter (1954:297–299) and especially Caffentzis (1989:61–68).

23. Beccaria's algebraic response to this question perhaps inaugurated the idea of indifference theory in modern economics (Schumpeter, 1954:179; see also Beccaria, 1804:551–562). For present purposes, it is fair to say that this idea anticipates Beccaria's attempt in *Dei delitti* to calculate the precise amount of pain needed to deter the pleasure gained from committing a crime. Thus, "the prison sentence of a tobacco smuggler should not be the same as that of a cutthroat or a thief, and the smuggler's labor, if confined to the work and service of the royal revenue administration that he had meant to defraud, will be the most suitable type of punishment" (Beccaria, 1764:64).

In 1765 Beccaria (1765b:858) confessed to Archduke Ferdinand, the Austrian governor of Lombardy, that he had never enjoyed the study of law and that, rather than don the judicial robe, he wanted to serve his country by engaging in sciences more relevant to the

question was probably influenced by his reading of Jonathan Swift's satirical *Gulliver's Travels* (1762b:164).

It has never been properly acknowledged that, like several other continental adherents of Enlightenment (e.g., Helvétius, 1758; Jaucourt, 1751; see also Wood, 1989), Beccaria was inspired by the ideas of the founder of the Scottish Enlightenment, the Glaswegian philosopher Francis Hutcheson, and by Hutcheson's pupil Hume (whose "profound metaphysics" he praised generously: Beccaria, 1766:865). One of Beccaria's (1765c:169) early essays, for example, shows the unmistakable influence of Hutcheson's (1725a:48–51) idea of the beauty of theorems.[24] The influence of Hutcheson on Beccaria's *Dei delitti* far transcends the communality of discursive practices often engaged in by Enlightenment writers. When Beccaria introduced *Dei delitti* with the enigmatic sentence "Mankind owes a debt of gratitude to the philosopher who, from the despised obscurity of his study, had the courage to cast the first and long fruitless seeds of useful truths among the multitude!" (1764:3; see also Scott, 1900:273–274),[25] he was undoubtedly referring to Hutcheson, who had explicitly termed himself "an obscure Philosopher" (Hutcheson, 1725b:vii).

Nearly every page of *Dei delitti* is marked, I suggest, by Hutcheson's towering influence on Beccaria's thinking. It is found in the common metaphors of expression used in *Dei delitti* and in Hutcheson's (1755) *System of Moral Philosophy*;[26] these metaphors are taken from such diverse fields as theology, law, architecture, Newtonian mechanics, and geometry. Hutcheson's influence is also found in the extraordinary correspondence between key recommendations in Beccaria's *Dei delitti* and those in Hutcheson's *System*. Careful comparison reveals that whole sections of *Dei delitti* either restate or develop the proposals for law and criminal justice in Hutcheson's *System*.

---

economic regulation of a state. Thus, from 1769 to 1773 he lectured on political economy at the Palatinate, at the same time beginning a career in government administration in Lombardy, until his death in 1794 (see further Canetta, 1985; Maestro, 1973:81–150).

24.   The same mathematical heresies that led to the condemnation and avoidance for two decades of Hutcheson's work in France at once endeared it to various scholars in Italy. However, in the middle of the century the *philosophes* revived interest in Hutcheson's mathematical approach to utilitarianism: Lévesque de Pouilly, Maupertuis, and Duclos wrote of happiness in Hutchesonian terms, Marc Antoine Eidous published a French translation of Hutcheson's *Inquiry*, and Diderot described his aesthetic ideas in the *Encyclopédie* (Shackleton, 1972:1468–1470). It is almost certain that Beccaria had read Hutcheson's (1725b) *Inquiry into the Original of our Ideas of Beauty and Virtue*, probably in a French translation of 1749 (Scott, 1900:273; see also Robbins, 1968:195).

25.   In the introduction to *Dei delitti*, this exclamation comes on the heels of Beccaria's statement of belief in the utilitarian formula; see further Scott (1900:273–274).

26.   In 1738 Hutcheson had circulated the manuscript of his *System of Moral Philosophy* in Scotland, Ireland, England, and Holland. It had therefore been known on the continent considerably before its actual date of publication in 1755; nowhere was it more popular than in Italy, especially in Lombardy.

INVENTING CRIMINOLOGY   795

Among the most important of these are those that refer to property as the basis of the social contracts (see Hutcheson, 1755:Bk. II, ch. 6:319–322; Beccaria, p. 7); the definition of crime (Hutcheson, Bk. II; ch. 15:86–87, "injury"; Beccaria, p. 17, "harm"; the uniformity of laws (Hutcheson, Bk. II; ch. 15:101–102; Beccaria, pp. 11–12); the simplicity of laws (Hutcheson, Bk. III; ch. 9:322–323; Beccaria, pp. 12–13, 75); the harm inflicted by corrupt public servants and magistrates (Hutcheson, Bk. II; ch. 15:88–89; Beccaria, p. 78); the compensatory use of fines (Hutcheson, Bk. II; ch. 15:88–91; Beccaria, pp. 39–40, but see pp. 34–45); the deterrent nature of punishment (Hutcheson, Bk. II; ch. 15:87, 93–94; Bk. III; ch. 9:333; Beccaria, pp. 23, 33, 47, 50, 74–75); the proportionality of punishment to crime (Hutcheson, Bk. III; ch. 9:331–338; Beccaria, pp. 14–16, 23, 46–47, 55, 64); and opposition to judicial torture (Hutcheson, Bk. II; ch. 15:97; Bk. III; ch. 9:337–338); Beccaria, pp. 29–33, 70–72).

But my chief intention here is not to document in detail the remarkable identity in the respective penal recommendations of Hutcheson's *System* and those of Beccaria's *Dei delitti*. Rather, it is to show that just as much of the specific content of Beccaria's famous treatise is taken from Hutcheson's (1755) *System* so, too, is much of the structure of its argumentation. As discussed below, Beccaria's treatise must thus be placed in a trajectory radically different from the "classical" one conventionally accorded it. In the same way that Hutcheson's *System* contained a progeny of useful truths otherwise known to Beccaria as the new "science of man" so, too, did Beccaria aspire in *Dei delitti* to apply this science to the field of crime and punishment.

THE SCIENCE OF MAN IN *DEI DELITTI*

Some of the arguments of *Dei delitti* embodied a deterministic discourse that, if not for their author then in retrospect, seem decidedly at odds with the classic dependence on free will that is commonly attributed to *Dei delitti*. Among Enlightenment thinkers this discourse was denominated loosely and was signified by such terms as Pascal's *esprit géométrique*[27] and, after mid-century, the Scottish civic tradition's "science of man." Beccaria himself variously referred to it as "geometry," "moral geography," "political arithmetic," "number," and the "science of man." Woven within Beccaria's stylistic eloquence and his passionate humanism is a strong reliance on the discursive use of determinist principles derived from the science of man.

Several key features of the science of man are plainly recognizable in *Dei*

---

27. By the middle of the eighteenth century the term *"esprit géométrique"* had lost much of its original meaning as a mathematical antonym for "the philosophical spirit"; it had become, according to Knight (1968:18–19), "a kind of ritual invocation of a whole cluster of virtues associated with science of all kinds, including the anti-mathematical science of the empirical tradition."

delitti. Chief among them are the doctrines of utilitarianism, probabilism, associationism, and sensationalism. The doctine of utilitarianism operated for Beccaria as a core justificatory argument for establishing "the right to punish," and it is positioned prominently at the very beginning of the text. With it Beccaria attempted to forge linkages, as had Hutcheson before him, among the rule of law, justice, and the economic marketplace. Beccaria employed probabilism, associationism, and sensationalism throughout *Dei delitti*, and he wielded the three doctrines in concert as mechanisms with which to advance various technico-administrative aspects of his chosen penal strategies (or "how to punish").

THE RIGHT TO PUNISH

The point of entry into Beccaria's discourse about penal strategies is provided by his subscription to an economistic form of social contract theory based on utilitarianism and secured through the rule of law.[28] *Dei delitti* begins with a utilitarian argument for "the greatest happiness" cast in the specific context of a plea for the supremacy of the rule of law. Whereas in the past, according to Beccaria, law had most commonly been the instrument of the passions of a few persons, "the impartial observer of human nature [would] grasp the actions of a multitude of men and consider them from this point of view: *the greatest happiness shared among the majority of people*" [*la massima felicità divisa nel maggior numero*] (1764:3).[29] The happiness of "a

---

28. It is reasonable to suppose that Beccaria derived this—the foundation of *Dei delitti*—from the algebraic formulations in Hutcheson's (1725b) *Inquiry into the Original of our Ideas of Beauty and Virtue* (see also Scott, 1900:273–274; Shackleton, 1972:1466–1472). In the first edition of his *Inquiry*, Hutcheson had written "that action is best, which procures the greatest happiness for the greatest numbers; and that worst, which in like manner, occasions misery" (1725b:177–178). In the fourth and final edition, although much else in it had been considerably modified, Hutcheson argued that "the most perfectly virtuous actions" are those "as appear to have the most universal unlimited Tendency to the greatest and most extensive Happiness of all the rational agents, to whom an Influence can reach" (1738:184).

I do not mean to suggest that the utilitarian principle originated in the work of Hutcheson; see, for example, the even earlier formulation by Locke (1689, 1:112)—"the highest Perfection of intellectual Nature lies in a careful and constant Pursuit of true and solid Happiness." Indeed, its roots can be discovered in the works of Cicero (wishing his friend "bonis affici quam maximis" in *De Finibus*) and in that of late Stoics such as Antoninus (see also Scott, 1900:275–277). Alternative contemporary candidates, albeit with far weaker claims than Hutcheson's, were Pietro Verri "[là] felicità pubblica o sia la maggior felicità possibile divisa colla maggiore uguaglianza possibile," 1763:84) and Helvétius ("l'utilité du public, c'est-à-dire, du plus grand nombre d'hommes soumis à la même forme de gouvernement," 1758:Discourse 2, Ch. 17:175). See further the speculations about alternative candidates by Gianni Francioni in *Cesare Beccaria: Opere* (Firpo, 1984, 1:23).

29. Beccaria's wording of this utilitarian slogan differed slightly (*contra* Young's translation of it) both from Hutcheson's original statement and from the version of it later popularized by Bentham, a fact due to its frequent translation from one language to

INVENTING CRIMINOLOGY   797

few illustrious persons" is therefore something Beccaria derided as tyranny (p. 43). To whatever he intended as the content of the otherwise empty utilitarian objective *felicità*,[30] Beccaria attached the condition that if all individual members are bound to society then—as opposed to the original, warlike state of nature—society is likewise bound to all of them by a binding contract of mutual obligation.

> This obligation, which reaches from the throne to the hovel and which is equally binding on the greatest and the most wretched of men, means nothing other than that it is in everybody's interest that the contracts useful to the greatest number should be observed. Their violation, even by one person, opens the door to anarchy (p. 9).

Beccaria harnessed his declared utilitarianism to two mechanisms, which he tended to elevate to the status of ends. The first is the rule of law: "the true foundations of the happiness I mentioned here are security and freedom limited only by law" (p. 62). For Beccaria, law is the condition by which "independent and isolated men, tired of living in a constant state of war and of enjoying a freedom made useless by the uncertainty of keeping it, unite in society" (p. 7). As will be discussed in some detail, Beccaria urged that criminal law especially have various features of formal and substantive rationality, including clarity, logical inclusiveness, and predictability. Beccaria's plea for the rule of law emerged largely *via negativa*, as a result of his disenchantment with the theocentrism of Rome, with its ecclesiastical courts and its inquisitorial practices. Law and justice must develop apart from the activities of religious policing:

> It is the task of theologians to establish the limits of justice and injustice regarding the intrinsic goodness or wickedness of an act; it is the task of the observer of public life to establish the relationships of political justice and injustice, that is, of what is useful or harmful to society (p. 5).[31]

Moreover, Beccaria asserted that those who believe that the intention of the criminal is the true measure of crime are in error because crime can only be measured by "the harm done to the nation" (p. 16) or "to the public good" (p. 15):

---

another—beginning in English (1725, Hutcheson), then to French (1749, Marc Antoine Eidous), to Italian (1764, Beccaria), to French (1765, Morellet), and finally back to English (1768, Priestly). See further Shackleton (1972).

30. In Beccaria's discourse the content of the relationship between the state and its citizenry is never properly spelled out in words like "*felicità*." To him "happiness" seems to have meant both the warm mental sensations associated with individualism—where the public good is the aggregate of individually pursued self-interest—and also such virtues as courage, liberty, justice, and honor.

31. Unfortunately, except for the crime of suicide, Beccaria was otherwise quite circumspect on this issue. About suicide, he argued that "it is a crime which God punishes (since He alone can punish even after death)" (Beccaria, 1764:63).

798   BEIRNE

> Given the necessity of men uniting together, and given the compacts
> which necessarily result from the very clash of private interests, one may
> discern a scale of misdeeds wherein the highest degree consists of acts
> that are directly destructive of society and the lowest of the least possible
> injustice against one of its members. Between these extremes lie all
> actions contrary to the public good, which are called crimes . . . (pp.
> 14–15).

For the achievement of his declared utilitarian objective, Beccaria envisaged a second mechanism, namely, the economic marketplace. In this
respect, he believed that the juridico-political basis of the modern state should
be secured, not through such feudal relics as theocentrism and the divine
right of kings, but through the utilitarian principles of large-scale, bourgeois
commodity exchange. The free economic agent and the subject of law are,
indeed, one and the same individual; the atomized individual who "thinks of
himself as the center of all the world's affairs" (p. 8) is an economic agent
simply reconstituted in juridical terms. Thus, Beccaria argued that although
"commerce and the ownership of goods" are not the goal of the social contract, they can be a means of achieving it (p. 66); *"common utility,"* in other
words, is "the basis of human justice" (p. 16). Beccaria was enthusiastic
about the "quiet war of industry [that] has broken out among great nations,
the most humane sort of war and the kind most worthy of reasonable men"
(p. 3), and he praised "easy, simple, and great laws . . . that require only a nod
from the legislator to spread wealth and vigor" (p. 66). Indeed, the surest
way of securing the compliance of individuals with the law of their nation is
to

> improve the relative well-being of each of them. Just as every effort
> ought to be made to turn the balance of the trade in our favor, so it is in
> the greatest interests of the sovereign and of the nation that the sum total
> of happiness . . . should be greater than elsewhere (p. 62).

Given this relationship, Beccaria's concept of crime as "what is harmful to
society" is likewise intimately linked to the economic marketplace (see also
Wills, 1978:153–154; Zeman, 1981:20). For Beccaria, the social contract
entails that all citizens surrender a portion of their liberty to the state, in
return for which the state protects their right to security and tranquility;
"there is no enlightened man who does not love the open, clear, and useful
contracts of public security when he compares the slight portion of useful
liberty that he has sacrificed to the total sum of all the liberty sacrificed by
other men" (Beccaria, 1764:76). The sum of all these portions of liberty is
thus a "deposit" that no citizen can ever "withdraw" from the "common
store" or from the "public treasury" (pp. 7, 34), and therein lies the basis of
the state's right to punish its subjects:

The mere formation of this deposit, however, [is] not sufficient; it [has] to

INVENTING CRIMINOLOGY 799

be defended against the private usurpations of each particular individual
. . . Tangible motives [are] required sufficient to dissuade the despotic
spirit of each man from plunging the laws of society back into the original chaos (p. 7).

Crime is thus an offense against both law and economic intercourse.
Accordingly, when in *Dei delitti* Beccaria referred to particular crimes, he
only emphasized crimes against property, including theft, counterfeiting,
bankruptcy, smuggling, and indolence. He especially condemned political
indolence (which "contributes to society neither with work nor with wealth"
pp. 41–42) and "timid prudence" (which "sees only the present moment" p.
66). At several points in his discussion of punishment, moreover, he invoked
a symmetry between the aims and conditions of penal servitude and those of
the marketplace. One feature of this symmetry is described as "the faint and
prolonged example of a man who, deprived of his liberty, has become a beast
of burden, repaying the society he has offended with his labors" (p. 49). Elsewhere he urged that "the most fitting punishment [for theft] . . . is the only
sort of slavery that can be deemed just: the temporary subjugation to society
of the labor and the person of criminal" (p. 40).

HOW TO PUNISH

It is not my concern here to outline each of Beccaria's chosen penal strategies but to show how his argumentation regarding them again demonstrates
his adherence to various aspects of the new science of man. Chief among
those aspects were the loosely defined doctrines of probabilism, sensationalism, and associationism.

PROBABILISM

Beccaria's attempt to apply "probability" and "number" to matters of punishment derives from his dependence on the ideas of wise governance held by
British authors such as Locke[32] and Hutcheson[33] rather than by the French

---

32. Locke himself attached great importance to the roles of number, probability, and
mathematics in the analysis of human affairs. "In all sorts of Reasoning," he argued,
"every single Argument should be manag'd as a Mathematical Demonstration" (Locke,
1689, 3:397; see also 1:85, 308–309). It is tempting to suggest that Beccaria also drew
inspiration from the writings of one of Hutcheson's mentors, the English statistician and
physician Sir William Petty (1623–1687). Besides his noted contribution to the development of statistics, Petty was a staunch critic of physical punishments. In Chapter 10 of his
Treatise of Taxes & Contributions, he urged that pecuniary "mulcts" (i.e., fines), made over
to the Commonwealth as "reparations," were far better than physical punishments, which
benefit no one, and actually deprive the state of useful labor. Thus, "Here we are to
remember in consequence of our opinion [that 'Labour is the Father and active principle of
Wealth, as Lands are the Mother'], that the State by killing, mutilating, or imprisoning
their members, do withall punish themselves; wherefore such punishments ought (as much

philosophes.

Near the beginning of *Dei delitti*, Beccaria asserted his intention of "going back to general principles" (pp. 3–4) to uncover the rampant political and judicial errors "accumulated" over several centuries. In a sense, his search for these principles reflected an abhorrence of uncertainty. Thus, he objected to "arbitrary notions of vice and virtue" (p. 4). Sometimes, he complained, "despotic impatience" and "effiminate timidity" transform "serious trials into a kind of game in which chance and subterfuge are the main elements" (p. 24), and he derided "the errors and passions that have successively dominated various legislators" (p. 15). Such errors included the useless tortures "multiplied" with prodigious and useless severity; the punishment of crimes that are "unproven"; and the horrors of a prison, "augumented" by "uncertainty" ("that most cruel tormentor of the wretched" (p. 4). Simultaneously, Beccaria bemoaned the unhappy fact that, unlike "the symmetry and order that is the lot of brute, inanimate matter" (p. 74), "turbulent human activity" and "the infinitely complicated relationships and mutations of social arrangements" are impossible to reduce to a "geometric order devoid of irregularity and confusion" (pp. 74–75; see also p. 5):

> It is impossible to prevent all disorders in the universal strife of human passions. They increase at the compound rate of population growth and the intertwining of public interests, which cannot be directed toward the public welfare with geometric precision. In political arithmetic, one must substitute the calculation of probability for mathematical exactitude (p. 14).

Beccaria's advocacy of probability extended as well to each stage of the criminal justice system, including the clarity of the law itself, judicial torture, witnesses and evidence, jurors, and sentencing practices. In this regard, his remarks were addressed not only to the *illuministi* and *philosophes* but also, especially, to enlightened lawmakers, to "the legislator [who] acts like the good architect, whose role is to oppose the ruinous course of gravity and to bring to bear everything that contributes to the strength of his building" (p. 15). A brief outline of these remarks is now in order.

Beccaria urged that only a fixed and predictable law could provide citizens

---

as possible) to be avoided and commuted for pecuniary mulcts, which will encrease labour and publick wealth" (Petty, 1662:68; cf. Hutcheson, 1755, Bk. II:318–319, 341).

33.   Unlike that of the philosophes, Hutcheson's utilitarianism was explicitly formulated in mathematical and economic terms. Thus, when Hutcheson wrote "that action is best, which procures the greatest happiness *for the greatest numbers*" [emphasis added], he meant it literally and mathematically; when he attempted to calculate the precise incidence of "perfect virtue" and "moral evil," he did so strictly in terms of algebraic equations (1725b:187–193). Indeed, the original title of Hutcheson's *Inquiry* contained the words *"with an attempt to introduce a mathematical calculation in subjects of morality."* This inclination was shared by Beccaria.

with personal security and liberate them from judicial arbitrariness. Thus, "the greater the number of people who understand the sacred law code and who have it in their hands, the less frequent crimes will be, for there is no doubt that ignorance and uncertainty concerning punishments aid the eloquence of the passions" (p. 13). The law itself must be unambiguous because only with "fixed" and "immutable" laws can citizens acquire personal "security": "this is just because it is the goal of society, and it is useful because it enables [citizens] to calculate precisely the ill consequences of a misdeed" (p. 12). Moreover,

> when a fixed legal code that must be observed to the letter leaves the judge no other task than to examine a citizen's actions and to determine whether or not they conform to the written law, when the standard of justice and injustice that must guide the actions of the ignorant as well as the philosophic citizen is not a matter of philosophic controversy but of fact, then subjects are not exposed to the petty tyranies of many men (p. 12).

For minor and less heinous crimes, moreover, there should be a statute of limitations that relieves citizens of "uncertainty" regarding their fate (p. 56); but such time limits "ought not to increase in exact proportion to the atrocity of the crime, for the liklihood of crimes is inversely proportional to their barbarity" (p. 56).

Beccaria's subscription to the doctrine of probabilism throws more light on the question of how *Dei delitti* viewed judicial torture. As discussed above, it was on humanist grounds that Beccaria opposed the practice of interrogating an accused with methods of torture.[34] If in this specific context "humanism" simply connotes a condemnaton of the infliction of physical pain on others, then one is left with some difficulty because Beccaria vigorously supported noncapital corporal punishment (*pene corporali*) "without exception" for crimes against persons and for crimes of theft accompanied by violence (pp.

---

34. Beccaria's arguments on torture were greatly influenced by the counsel of his friend Pietro Verri, whose book *Osservazioni sulla tortura* was only published posthumously in 1804. Whether Beccaria was correct in his assumption that judicial torture was still a widespread practice in mid-eighteenth-century Europe is an interesting question, but one that will not be addressed here. In his provocative book *Torture and the Law of Proof*, Langbein (1976; see also Hirst, 1986:152–154) has fundamentally reinterpreted the history of the transformation of judicial torture in Europe. He claims that the conventional account of the demise of torture through the Enlightenment efforts of Beccaria and others is a fairy tale. His thesis is that there is an unmistakable causal relationship between the abolition of judicial torture and a contemporaneous revolution in the law of proof. He suggests that a fundamental reason why historians have written hardly anything on the importance of changes in the law of proof is that they have uncritically accepted the critical explanations of the eighteenth-century abolitionist writers, who themselves knew very little about these changes or, if they did, did not understand their significance.

37, 40).[35] Yet this apparent paradox can be resolved by stressing that, besides his humanism, Beccaria articulated his opposition to judicial torture in another, even more insistent way. Here he claimed that judicial torture is an inefficient method of establishing the "probability" or the "certainty" of the guilt or innocence of the accused. Accordingly, "the problems of whether torture and death are either just or useful deserve a mathematically precise solution" (p. 23). Elsewhere, Beccaria added that it is "a remarkable contradiction in the laws that they authorize torture, yet what sort of interrogation could be more *suggestive* than pain?" (p. 71):

> The outcome of torture, then, is a matter of temperament and calculation that varies with each man in proportion to his hardiness and his sensitivity, so that, by means of this method, a mathematician could solve the following problem better than a judge could: given the strength of an innocent person's muscles and the sensitivity of his fibers, find the degree of pain that will make him confess himself guilty of a given crime (p. 31).

In place of judicial torture, Beccaria recommended "the real trial, the 'informative' one, that is, the impartial investigation of facts which reason demands" (p. 34).

In respect to witnesses and evidence, Beccaria argued that to determine the guilt or innocence of a defendant more than one witness is necessary because, if one witness affirms the guilt and another denies its, "there is no certainty" (p. 24; see also Locke, 1689, 1:309).[36] A witness is credible if he is "a rational man" and his credibility increases if his reason is undisturbed by a prior relationship with either the defendant or the victim. "The credibility of a witness, therefore, must diminish in proportion to the hatred or friendship or close relationship between himself and the accused" (Beccaria, 1764:24). The credibility of a witness also diminishes significantly as the gravity of the alleged crime increases or as its circumstances become more "improbable" (pp. 24–25). The credibility of a witness is virtually nil in cases that involve making words a crime: "[it is] far easier to slander someone's words than to slander his actions, for, in the latter case, the greater the number of circumstances adduced as evidence, the greater are the means available to the

---

35. Moreover, Beccaria urged that among the serious crimes, those such as infamy, which "are founded on pride, and [which] draw glory and nourishment from pain itself" (1764:41), did not warrant the use of painful corporal punishments.

36. Elsewhere in *Dei delitti*, Beccaria extended to magistrates his idea of the relation between the number of concurring witnesses and the certainty of a verdict. Thus, he wrote about the "corps of those charged with executing the law that "the greater the number of men who constitute such a body, the less the danger of encroachments on the law will be" (1764:78). It should be noted that Beccaria's observations on witnesses, juries, and magistrates were instrumental in the development of a "*science sociale*" by Condorcet (1795b:62–63) and Laplace (1814).

INVENTING CRIMINOLOGY 803

accused to clear himself" (p. 25). Somewhat inconsistently, Beccaria also held that to the degree that "punishments become moderate, that squalor and hunger are banished from prisons, and that compassion and humanity pass through the iron gates . . . the law may be content with weaker and weaker evidence to imprison someone" (p. 54).

For Beccaria, there exists a "general theorem" that is most useful in calculating with certainty the facts of a crime, namely, the "weight of evidence." In unfolding the aspects of this theorem, he argued that (1) when different pieces of factual evidence are substantiated only by each other, the less certain is any one fact; (2) when all the proofs of a fact depend on one piece of evidence, the number of proofs neither augments nor diminishes the probability of the fact; and (3) when proofs are independent of each other, then the probability of the fact increases with each new witness (p. 25). Moreover, Beccaria deemed it ironic that the most atrocious and obscure crimes—that is, "those that are most unlikely"—are the hardest to prove. Such crimes are typically proved by conjecture and by the weakest and most equivocal evidence; it is as though "the danger of condemning an innocent man were not all the greater as the probability of his innocence surpasses the liklihood of his guilt" (p. 58). That is not to say that there are not some crimes that are both frequent in society and difficult to prove—such as "adultery" and "pederasty"—and, in these cases, "the difficulty of establishing guilt takes the place of the probability of innocence" (p. 58). Finally, because the respective probabilities of "atrocious" crimes and of lesser offenses differ greatly, they must be adjudicated differently: for atrocious crimes the period of judicial examination "should decrease in view of the greater liklihood of the innocence of the accused . . . but with minor crimes, given the lesser liklihood of the innocence of the accused, the period of judicial investigation should be extended, and, as the pernicious consequences of impunity decline, the delay in granting immunity from further prosecution should be shortened" (p. 57).

Finally, Beccaria offered some brief comments on jurors and on sentencing practices from the perspective of probabilism. About jurors, he recommended, without explanation, that when a crime has been committed against a third party "half the jurors should be the equals of the accused and half the peers of the victim" (p. 27). About sentencing practices, he warned that "certainty" ought to be required for convictions in criminal cases and that if geometry "were adaptable to the infinite and obscure arrangements of human activity, there ought to be a corresponding scale of punishments, descending from the most rigorous to the slightest" (p. 15).

Many of the strategies in Beccaria's penal calculus, including his key concept of deterrence, are derived not from geometry or probabilism, as such, but from the doctrines of associationism and sensationalism. To these related doctrines in the science of man we now turn.

804   BEIRNE

ASSOCIATIONISM

Beccaria's penal calculus rested on the view that it is better to prevent crimes than to punish them. This can only occur if the law forces potential criminals to make an accurate "association" of ideas between crime and punishment. "It is well established," Beccaria claimed, along with Hume and Helvétius, "that the association of ideas is the cement that shapes the whole structure of the human intellect; without it, pleasure and pain would be isolated feelings with no consequences" (p. 36).[37] Following Hume, Beccaria urged that associated ideas must be in a position of constant conjunction and that they must comprise a relation of cause and effect. Beccaria characterized the nexus of the desired association between crime and punishment in many ways, such as "deterrence" (p. 33), "intimidation" (pp. 23, 29), and "dissuasion" (p. 23).[38] The key properties of the association between crime and punishment are condensed in the following formula, which is the concluding sentence of *Dei delitti*, now appropriately enshrined as the original statement of the principle of deterrence:

> in order that any punishment should not be an act of violence committed by one person or many against a private citizen, it is essential that it should be public, prompt, necessary, the minimum possible under the given circumstances, [and] proportionate to the crimes" (p. 81).

Elsewhere in his text, yet still within an associationist framework, Beccaria expanded on several items in this formula, most notably on the need for prompt, mild, and proportionate punishment. About the promptness of punishment, first, Beccaria believed that the shorter the time period between a crime and chastisement for the crime "the stronger and more permanent is the human mind's association of the two ideas of crime and punishment, so that imperceptibly the one will come to be considered as the cause and the other as the necessary and inevitable result" (p. 36). Delay thus serves only

---

37. The philosophical writings of Hume and Helvétius (both followers of Hutcheson) were among the "French books" to which Beccaria admitted "I myself owe everything" (1766:862; see also 1764:19). About Hume's general influence on *Dei delitti* see, for example, his *Treatise of Human Nature* (1739, especially Bk. 1, Pt. 1 and Pt. 3); specifically, compare Beccaria (1764:19) with Hume (1739, Bk. 1, Pt. 1, s. 4, p. 10). See also Beccaria (1762a, 1766:865), where he praised Hume's "profound metaphysics." Helvétius contributed little that was original to the principle of associationism, although Beccaria's (1766:862) generous comment about Helvétius's influence on *Dei delitti* probably refers to Helvétius's *De l'esprit* (1758:Discourse I, Chs. 1–2; Discourse II, Ch. 15).

38. This is not to suggest that Beccaria's recommendations for penal strategies were based exclusively on an intended purpose of deterrence. At certain points in *Dei delitti*, his equation of crime with social harms also led Beccaria to a posture of retributivism toward criminals. However, given his overwhelming concern with deterrence, Beccaria's retributivism was not and could not have been an important feature of his text (*pace* Young, 1983).

INVENTING CRIMINOLOGY   805

to sever the association between the two ideas. Moreover, the temporal proximity of crime and punishment is of paramount importance if one desires to arouse in "crude and uneducated minds the idea of punishment in association with the seductive image of a certain advantageous crime" (p. 37). About the mildness of punishment, second, Beccaria argued that to achieve its intended effect the intensity of a punishment should exceed the benefit resulting from the crime and that in its application punishment should be "inexorable," "inevitable," and "certain" (pp. 46–47). Cruel punishments, insofar as they destroy the association between law and justice, therefore undermine the aim of deterrence. Finally, about the required proportion between punishment and crime, Beccaria warned that "the obstacles that restrain men from committing crimes should be stronger according to the degree that such misdeeds are contrary to the public good and according to the motives that lead people to crimes" (p. 14; see also p. 15). This is so because, if two unequally harmful crimes are each awarded the same punishment, then would-be miscreants will tend to commit the more serious crime if it holds greater advantage for them. If punishments are disproportionate to crime by being tyrannical (i.e., excessive), then popular dissatisfaction will be directed at the law itself—"punishments will punish the crimes that they themselves have caused" (p. 16).[39] Further, in arguing that "punishment . . . should conform as closely as possible to the nature of the crime" (p. 37), Beccaria implicitly attempted to link the argument about the proportionality of crime and punishment with the desired association among ideas about the type of crime (e.g., theft), form of punishment (penal servitude with forced labor), and virtue of industriousness.[40]

In the context of Beccaria's use of the doctrine of associationism, it is worth returning briefly to his opposition to capital punishment. It is fair to suggest that Beccaria opposed capital punishment not because he thought it cruel, which he did, but because it did not serve the new penal objective of deterrence.[41] He argued instead that a life sentence is a sufficiently intense

---

39.   For this reason, Beccaria therefore suggested that some punishments might even be considered as crimes (1764:17); for example, "it appears absurd to me that the laws . . . commit murder themselves . . . [and] command public assassination" (1764:51).

40.   Interestingly, appearing in a frontispiece engraving in a 1765 edition of *Dei delitti* is the figure of Justice, who is portrayed as combining law and wisdom in the features of Minerva. Justice herself recoils from the executioner's offering of three decapitated heads and instead gazes approvingly at various instruments of labor, of measurement, and of detention. The engraving of Justice was incised for the third edition of *Dei delitti* (1765, Lausanne) and, according to Venturi (1971:105), the sketch for the engraving was completed by Beccaria himself.

41.   Only much later did Beccaria (1792:739–740) argue that the rights of an accused are violated by the death penalty because, once an execution had been carried out, there is no "possibility" of reversal even after proof of innocence.

substitute for the death penalty and that it includes all the necessary ingredients needed to deter the most hardened criminal. "Neither fanaticism nor vanity survives among fetters and chains, under the prod or the yoke, or in an iron cage . . . a lifetime at hard labor" (p. 50). It is thus not the severity of punishment that, for Beccaria, has the greatest impact on a would-be criminal but, albeit in addition to its other characteristics, its duration:

> If someone were to say that life at hard labor is as painful as death and therefore equally cruel, I should reply that, taking all the unhappy moments of perpetual slavery together, it is perhaps even more painful, but these moments are spread out over a lifetime, and capital punishment exercises all its power in an instant. And this is the advantage of life at hard labor; it frightens the spectator more than the victim (p. 50).

SENSATIONALISM

A third hallmark of the science of man engraved in *Dei delitti* is the doctrine of sensationalism. In Beccaria's discussion of the nature of honor, for example, the presence of this doctrine is indicated by a Newtonian metaphor:

> How miserable is the condition of the human mind! It has a better grasp of the most remote and least important ideas about the revolutions of the heavenly bodies than of the most immediate and important moral concepts, which are always fluctuating and confused as they are driven by the winds of passion and guided by the ignorance that receives and transmits them! (p. 19; see also Halévy, 1928:57).

This "ostensible paradox" will disappear, Beccaria (1764:19) continued, only when one considers that

> just as objects too close to one's eyes are blurred, so the excessive proximity of moral ideas makes it easy to confuse the large number of simple ideas that go to form them. Wishing to measure the phenomena of human sensibility, the geometric spirit needs dividing lines. When these are clearly drawn, the impartial observer of human affairs will be less astonished, and he will suspect that there is perhaps no need for so great a moral apparatus or for so many bonds in order to make men happy and secure.

These two passages betray the influence on *Dei delitti* of the doctrine of sensationalism, which, in the course of his unheralded book on aesthetics, Beccaria (1770:81–93; see also Beccaria, 1766:866) explicitly acknowledged having taken from works by Locke and Condillac.[42] Besides the humanism inherent in his widely circulated condemnation of religious persecution and

---

42. Beccaria's (1770) unfinished book *Ricerche intorno alla natura dello stile* was condemned in its French translation by Diderot (1771:60), who politely discounted it as "an obscure work based on a subtle metaphysic."

INVENTING CRIMINOLOGY 807

superstition in *Letters Concerning Toleration*, Locke's sensationalism tended to suggest that all things painful are by definition bad and all things pleasurable, good. Interestingly, his original discussion of the doctrine of hedonism—the pleasure/pain principle as outlined in chapter 20 of his *Essay Concerning Human Understanding*—occurred within the framework of sensationalism; when Locke discussed the status of hedonism in human affairs, he did so in a radically materialistic way, arguing that "pleasure and pain, and that which causes them, Good and Evil, are the hinges on which our *passions* turn" (1689,1:95). Among the *philosophes*, Condillac (1715–1780) was the most ardent champion of the antimetaphysical, empirical tradition of Bacon, Newton, and Locke (Knight, 1968). In his preparatory *Essai sur l'origin des connaissances humaines* (1746), in *Traité des systèmes* (1749), and then in *Traité des sensations* (1754), Condillac developed Locke's doctrine of sensationalism, positing that the human mind is at birth a *tabula rasa*, which operates through sensations. Like Locke, Condillac (1754:338) championed the rigidly materialistic conclusion that "man" is simply what he has acquired through his sensations:

> It is pleasures and pains compared, that is to say, our needs which exercise our faculties. As a result, it is to them that we owe the happiness that is ours to enjoy. We have as many needs as different kinds of enjoyment; as many degrees of need as degrees of enjoyment. And there you have the germ of everything that we are, the source of our unhappiness or of our happiness. To observe the influence of this principle is thus the sole means to study ourselves.

It is difficult to imagine a doctrine more hostile to the doctrine of free will than sensationalism. When Beccaria applied it to criminal justice, sensationalism effectively displaced the volitional subject of Catholic theology and, thereby, denied any active role in human society for the Supreme Being. Beccaria was so fearful of the censor precisely because his text implied that human agents are no more than the products of their sensory reactions to external stimuli. His text, replete as it is with probabilism, associationism, and sensationalism—all directed to the new objective of deterrence—is resolutely opposed to any notion of free will. *Dei delitti* contains a concept of volition, it is true, but it is a determined will rather than a free will: "sentiment is always proportional to the result of the impressions made on the senses" (p. 25). The penal recommendations of *Dei delitti* are not at all predicated, therefore, on the notion of a rational calculating subject who, when faced with inexorable punishment, will weigh the costs and benefits and choose to desist from crime. In this discourse, punishments ("tangible motives") have "a direct impact on the senses and appear continually to the mind to counterbalance the strong impressions of individual passions opposed to the general good" (p. 7).

Sensationalism intersects concretely with Beccaria's chosen penal strategies in three ways. First, it is an extra ground on which judicial torture must be rejected. Beccaria insisted that, in terms of their respective results, the only difference between judicial torture and other ordeals, such as fire and boiling water, is that the former appears to depend on the will of the accused and the latter on a purely physical act. To this he responded that

> speaking the truth amid convulsions and torments is no more a free act than staving off the effects of fire and boiling water except by fraud. Every act of our will is always proportional to the strength of the sense impressions from which it springs. . ." (p. 31).

Sensationalist claims are also inserted into Beccaria's arguments about the nature of deterrence. During his discussion of the appropriateness of prompt punishment, for example, he argued that "that gravity-like force that impels us to seek our own well-being can be restrained only to the degree that obstacles are established in opposition to it" and that "remote consequences make a very weak impression" (pp. 14, 64). Effecting a link with probabilism, he argued that "experience and reason have shown us that the probability and certainty of human traditions decline the farther removed they are from their source" (p. 13). Effecting yet another link, this time with associationist claims, he reflected that

> the magnitude of punishment ought to be relative to the condition of the nation itself. Stronger and more obvious impressions are required for the hardened spirits of a people who have scarcely emerged from a savage state. A thunderbolt is needed to fell a ferocious lion who is merely angered by a gun shot. But to the extent that human spirits are made gentle by the social state, sensibility increases; as it increases, the severity of punishment must diminish if one wishes to maintain a constant relation between object and feeling (p. 81).

Finally, Beccaria attached his belief in sensationalism to a variety of non-penal strategies designed to manipulate and channel sense impressions into law-abiding actions. While penal strategies tend to operate swiftly and dramatically on their subjects, non-penal strategies are designed as positive mental inducements that operate slowly and calmly at the level of custom and habit, or at what is nowadays known as the domain of "socialization." Thus, Beccaria suggested that in order to prevent crimes, "enlightenment should accompany liberty" (p. 76). What precisely he meant by this recommendation is not very clear, but perhaps it was "education," an instrument whose importance he also stressed (pp. 76–79), as did such thinkers as Montesquieu, d'Alembert, Helvétius, Rousseau, and Charles Pinot Duclos. He warned that "the most certain but most difficult way to prevent crimes is to perfect education" (p. 79). By "education," a vague term with no clear institutional or

INVENTING CRIMINOLOGY   809

empirical referent in *Dei delitti*, Beccaria likely intended a process whose outcome, at least, was the gradual inculcation in the citizenry of such attributes as virtue, courage, and liberty—for the encouragement of which he recommended the distribution of prizes (p. 79).

FROM THE SCIENCE OF MAN TO *HOMO CRIMINALIS*

> Morality, politics, and the fine arts, which are respectively the sciences of virtue, of utility, and of beauty, have a greater identity of principles than can be imagined: these sciences all derive from one primary science, the science of man; it is hopeless to think that we will ever make rapid progress in fathoming the depths of these secondary sciences without first immersing ourselves in the science of man (Beccaria, 1770:71).[43]

In addition to the contemporary protestations of certain luminaries, such as Grimm (1765a, 1765b) and Ramsay (n.d.), that Beccaria's treatment of penal questions in *Dei delitti* was "too geometrical," other legal scholars and social reformers of the period more or less clearly understood the proto-scientific intentions of *Dei delitti* and valued it for that very direction.[44] To the French mathematician and *philosophe* Condorcet, for example, Beccaria was one of a select group of scholars—that included the Scottish political economists, Rousseau and Montesquieu—whose works, since the time of Locke, had advanced the moral sciences, or *"mathématique sociale"* and *"science sociale"* as he termed the application of "the calculus of . . . probabilities" to the understanding of human societies (1795b:178; see also Baker, 1975:193).[45] The influential English legal scholar Blackstone observed in his *Commentaries on the Laws of England* that Beccaria "seems to have well studied the springs of human action" (1769:4:17), and he emphatically placed Beccaria's

---

43. In his *Elementi di economia pubblica*, a series of lectures completed at the Palatine School in 1771, Beccaria displayed a keen interest in various aspects of the new statistics of populations that had become a key factor in the development of the science of man. These included statistical tables and comparative evidence on births, marriages, education, and life expectancy (1804:401–433). On the uncanny similarities between Beccaria's *Elementi* and the *Wealth of Nations* by Hutcheson's pupil, the Scottish political economist Adam Smith, see Schumpeter (1954:179–183).

44. Besides Beccaria, Melchior Grimm also attacked Beccaria's mentor Condillac for being "too geometrical" (see Knight, 1968:2–3, 235; and Becker, 1932:83–84).

45. In letters to Beccaria of 1771, Condorcet condemned the injustices of existing criminal jurisprudence and he expressed his desire to follow Beccaria's lead in using mathematics to search for rationality in judicial decision making (cited in Baker, 1975:231–232). Later, he (Condorcet, 1785) recommended to Frederick II of Prussia the application of the "calculus of probabilities" to Beccaria's ideas on capital punishment and on wise legislation. Moreover, although it was perhaps first used in late 1791 by his friend Dominique-Joseph Garat, it was Condorcet who in 1795 popularized the term *"science sociale"* in his *Tableau historique des progrès de l'ésprit humain* (see also Baker, 1975:391). In the *Tableau*, Condorcet (1795b:177–178) referred to *"l'art social"* as one of the sciences.

"humane" reform proposals within the rubric of a new discourse of crime and penality that emerged in Britain in the 1760s and that stressed investigation of the "causes of crime," deterrence, and the correction of offenders.

Indeed, attached to Beccaria's discourse on penal strategies, there is present in *Dei delitti* a very rudimentary attempt to forge some key concepts of an embryonic criminology. Those concepts include "crime," "criminal," and "causes of crime." Quite apart from his innovative approach to the understanding of crime ("the harm done to society"),[46] Beccaria also attempted to identify the criminal as something other than a mere bundle of illegalities. This concept of a criminal operates in concert with and is burdened by Beccaria's humanism and his advocacy of legal rationality, yet it marks, one might say, a movement away from a single-minded focus with how to punish *homo penalis* to a wider "criminological" concern with understanding the situation of *homo criminalis*. An example of this movement occurs when, during an impassioned tirade against unjust laws, Beccaria (1764:51) inserted the following words into the mouth of "a scoundrel":

> What are these laws that I must respect and that leave such a great distance between me and the rich man? . . . Who made these laws? Rich and powerful men who have never deigned to visit the squalid hovels of the poor, who have never broken a moldy crust of bread among the innocent cries of their famished children and the tears of their wives. Let us break these bonds that are so ruinous for the majority and useful to a handful of indolent tyrants; let us attack injustice at its source.

At several other points in his text, as well, Beccaria indicated that criminals and criminal behavior should be understood causally, in material and social terms rather than purely individualistic ones. He suggested, for example, that "theft is only the crime of misery and desperation; it is the crime of that unhappy portion of humanity to whom the right of property . . . has left only a bare existence" (p. 39). It is difficult to know how much to invest in Beccaria's reasoning in passages such as these, other than to say that he seems keen to position illegalities in a quasi-social context. Similarly suggestive reasoning is directed to the crimes of adultery (pp. 58–59), pederasty (p. 60), and infanticide (*infanticidio*) "by a woman" (p. 60).[47]

It must also be said that *Dei delitti* even contains an adumbration of a

---

46. See further *supra*: 22, 33–34, 39–40.

47. *Dei delitti* provides no real clues as to Beccaria's understanding of the gendered position of women before law, although in the chapter on "The Spirit of the Family" Beccaria (1764:43–45) seems to oppose authoritarian (i.e., male-dominated) families ("little monarchies"). Nowhere in his text does Beccaria indulge in the antifeminism of those such as Rousseau and Buffon, although its publication date precludes his participation in the progressive ideas of feminist *philosophes* like Condorcet. On the periodicity of Enlightenment feminism, see generally Clinton (1975).

INVENTING CRIMINOLOGY 811

"dangerous class."[48] This is visible at several points. Thus, Beccaria spoke philosophically of wanting to disabuse those "who, from a poorly understood love of liberty, would desire to establish anarchy" (p. 18) and who are inclined toward "a desperate return to the original state of nature" (p. 47). These unfortunates he described as "the credulous and admiring crowd" (p. 39), "a fanatical crowd" (p. 47), "a blind and fanatical crowd, pushing and jostling one another in a closed labyrinth" (p. 77) that "does not adopt stable principles of conduct" (p. 7). In crowds there resides a "dangerous concentration of popular passions" (p. 22) that is akin to the sentiments in "the state of nature . . . the savage" (p. 74).[49] Its actions include "concealed despotism . . . turbulent mob anarchy" (p. 57) and those events especially

> that disturb the public tranquility and the peace of citizens: matters such as tumults and carousing in public thoroughfares meant for business and for traffic, or such as fanatical sermons that excite the fickle passions of the curious crowd. These passions gather strength from the great number of the audience; they owe more to the effects of a murky and mysterious rapture than to clear and calm reason, which never has any effect on a large mass of men (p. 22).[50]

Ultimately, *Dei delitti* teases its audience with a presociological view of the relation between crime and social organization:

> Most men lack that vigor which is equally necessary for great crimes and great virtues; thus, it seems that the former always coexist with the latter in those nations that sustain themselves by the activity of their governments and by passions working together for the public good, rather than in countries that depend on their size or the invariable excellence of their laws. In the latter sort of nation, weakened passions seem better suited

---

48. The term "dangerous classes" first appeared in France during the Restoration and was popularized by Frégier's (1840) classic study. See further Tombs (1980) and Beirne (1987a:1144–1148).

49. From Beccaria's vague references to social life in the "state of nature," it is very difficult to know whether he appropriated this term from Hobbes's *"bellum omnium contra omnes,"* from *philosophes* such as Montesquieu and Rousseau, or even from the Hutchesonian "mutual offices of good will," all of which are very different notions from Beccaria's.

50. In the following passage Beccaria even indicated a stark contrast between an embryonic dangerous class and the law-abiding citizenry:

> Enslaved men are more sensual, more debauched, and more cruel than free men. The latter think about the sciences; they think about the interests of the nation; they see great examples, and they imitate them. The former, on the other hand, content with the present moment, seek a distraction for the emptiness of their lives in the tumult of debauchery. Accustomed to uncertain results in everything, the doubts they have about the outcome of their crimes strengthens the passions by which crimes are determined (1764:75).

812   BEIRNE

to the maintenance rather than to the improvement of the form of government. From this, one can draw an important conclusion: that great crimes in a nation are not always proof of its decline (p. 58).

CONCLUSION: WHITHER CLASSICAL CRIMINOLOGY?

Less by way of conclusion to this paper than as an invitation for further exploration, several implications must now be drawn about the place of *Dei delitti* in the intellectual history of criminology.

First, I have not disputed the conventional view that Beccaria's advocacy of humanism and legal rationality are important features of his treatise. Rather, I claim that neither the method of *Dei delitti* nor its object can be understood in terms of those tendencies alone. An altogether different tendency, veiled and incompletely developed, actually comprised the kernel of Beccaria's discourse—the application to crime and penality of key principles in the science of man. It is in the framework of that new science that the two major themes of *Dei delitti* (the "right to punish" and "how to punish") are couched as, too, are Beccaria's advocacy of deterrence and his opposition to capital punishment and judicial torture.

Second, contrary to prevailing opinion, the discourse of *Dei delitti* was not erected on the volitional subject of classical jurisprudence, or "free will" as it is often termed. Although Beccaria's view of volitional conduct is not clear in *Dei delitti*, it is possible that, like many of his contemporaries in the eighteenth-century Enlightenment who saw in this no contradiction, he subscribed to a notion of human agency simultaneously involving "free" rational calculation *and* "determined" action. But the concept of an unfettered free will must be relegated along with humanism to the margins of *Dei delitti*. The warriors and wretches who inhabit its pages are not volitional agents but creatures trapped in a web of determinism. The potential criminals in Beccaria's schema "act" like automata; in effect, they are recalcitrant objects who must be angled, steered, and forced into appropriate and law-abiding behavior.[51] But this is only to be expected of a discourse that relies on rigidly deterministic principles concretely manifest in the specific doctrines of probabilism, associationism, and sensationalism. As such, at the very least, the position of *Dei delitti* in intellectual history does not and cannot lie at the center of classical criminology as it is conventionally understood. Nor, however, despite the temptation of focusing on Beccaria's predeliction for the science of man, should it be placed, however precariously, at the beginning of the tradition to which it is commonly opposed, namely, positivist criminology. Beccaria's utterances on crime and penality were never intended—nor

---

51.   See also Beccaria's deterministic account of sexual attraction and adultery, which, like gravity, "diminishes with distance" but, unlike gravity, "gathers strength and vigor with the growth of the very obstacles opposed to it" (1764:59).

INVENTING CRIMINOLOGY 813

could they have been—to inhabit the same positivist terrain as that so eagerly tenanted a century later by his compatriot Cesare Lombroso.[52]

Finally, the very category of a distinct "classical" period in criminology must be reconsidered. "Classical criminology" was not the creation of Beccaria, Bentham, and others, but the retrospective product of scholarly self-aggrandizement. As an identifiable set of assumptions about crime and punishment, classical criminology was not actually denominated as such until the 1870s, and then by another generation of Italian theorists—positivist criminologists such as Lombroso, Garofalo, and Ferri. These thinkers were keen to distance their invention of a scientific criminology from that of Beccaria's "outmoded discourse of free will," either because they failed properly to understand the arguments of *Dei delitti* or, more likely, because it did not suit their own interests to do so. Yet if the discourse of *Dei delitti* is not couched in the rhetoric of classical jurisprudence, if its chief object (the construction of a rational and efficient penal calculus) is not directed to the actions of volitional subjects but to those of automata given by the science of man, and if humanism is a minor rather than a major feature of this discourse, then what is left of the classical edifice? Perhaps very little.

REFERENCES

Alembert, Jean Lerond d'
n.d.1   De l'abus de la critique en matière de religion. Vol. 1:547–572 in *Oeuvres complètes de d'Alembert*. 1821–1822. 5 vols. Paris: A. Belin.
n.d.2   Explication détaillée du Système des Connaissances humaines. Vol. 1:99–114 in *Oeuvres complètes de d'Alembert*. 1821–1822. 5 vols. Paris: A. Belin.
1765   Lettera a Paolo Frisi. 312–314 in Venturi (ed.), *Cesare Beccaria, Dei delitti e delle pene*. 1965. Turin: Giulio Einaudi.

Bacon, Francis
1632   *The Essayes or Counsels Civill and Morall, of Francis Lo[rd] Verulam*. London: John Haviland.

Baker, Keith Michael
1975   *Condorcet: From Natural Philosophy to Social Mathematics*. Chicago: University of Chicago Press.

Beattie, J.M.
1986   *Crime and the Courts in England 1550–1800*. Princeton: Princeton University Press.

---

52. So also must I resist the intriguing temptation of arguing—even in the relative safety of a footnote—that *Dei delitti* should be seen as the first link in a chain that proceeds to Condorcet's obscure *Essai sur l'application de l'analyse à la probabilité des décisions rendues à la pluralité des voix* (1785) and his *Tableau général de la science* (1795a; see also Baker, 1975:227–242; Condorcet, 1785; Hankins, 1985:182–183; Lottin, 1912:362) and concludes with the rise of well-formed, presociological analyses of crime as found in the 1830s in the discourse of moral statistics.

814   BEIRNE

Beccaria, Cesare
    n.d.   Estratti da Bacone: Nota al testo, materiali non pubblicati. Vol. 2:457–473
                in Luigi Firpo (ed.), *Cesare Beccaria: Opere*. 1984. Milan: Medio banca.
    1762a   *Del disordine e de'rimedi delle monete nello stato di Milano nell'anno 1762*.
                Vol. 1:7–34 in Sergio Romagnoli (ed.), *Cesare Beccaria: Opere*. 1958.
                Florence: Sansoni.
    1762b   Tentativo analitico su i contrabbandi. Vol. 1:164–166 in Sergio Romagnoli
                (ed.), *Cesare Beccaria: Opere*. 1958. Florence: Sansoni.
    1764   *On Crimes and Punishments*, trans. David Young. 1986. Indianapolis:
                Hackett.
    1765a   A Jean-Baptiste Le Rond D'Alembert. Vol. 2:859–861 in Sergio Romagnoli
                (ed.), *Cesare Beccaria: Opere*. 1958. Florence: Sansoni.
    1765b   All'arciduca Ferdinando d'Austria, duca di Modena, governatore della
                Lombardia. Vol. 2:858–859 in Sergio Romagnoli (ed.), *Cesare Beccaria:
                Opere*. 1958. Florence: Sansoni.
    1765c   Frammento sullo stile. Vol. 1:167–174 in Sergio Romagnoli (ed.), *Cesare
                Beccaria: Opere*. 1958. Florence: Sansoni.
    1766   Ad André Morellet, le 26 janvier. Vol. 2:862–870 in Sergio Romagnoli (ed.),
                Cesare Beccaria: Opere. 1958. Florence: Sansoni.
    1770   *Ricercne intorno alla natura dello stile*. Vol. 2:63–206 in Luigi Firpo (ed.),
                Cesare Beccaria: Opere. 1984. Milan: Mediobanca.
    1792   Voto per la riforma del sistema criminale nella Lombardia Austriaca
                riguargante la pena di morte. Vol. 2:735–741 in Sergio Romagnoli (ed.),
                Cesare Beccaria: Opere. 1958. Florence: Sansoni.
    1804   *Elemti di economia pubblica*. Vol. 1:379–649 in Sergio Romagnoli (ed.),
                Cesare Beccaria: Opere. 1958. Florence: Sansoni.

Becker, Carl L.
    1932   *The Heavenly City of the Eighteenth-Century Philosophers*. New Haven:
                Yale University Press.

Beirne, Piers
    1987a   Adolphe Quetelet and the origins of positivist criminology. *American
                Journal of Sociology* 92(5):1140–1169.
    1987b   Between classicism and positivism: Crime and penality in the writings of
                Gabriel Tarde. *Criminology* 25(4):785–819.
    1988   Heredity versus environment: A reconsideration of Charles Goring's *The
                English Convict* (1913). *British Journal of Criminology* 28(3):315–339.

Beirne, Piers and Alan Hunt
    1990   Lenin, crime, and penal politics, 1917–1924. Pp. 99–135 in Piers Beirne
                (ed.), *Revolution in Law: Contributions to Soviet Legal Theory, 1917–1938*.
                Armonk, N.Y.: M.E. Sharpe.

Bentham, Jeremy
    1776   *A Fragment on Government*. 1988. New York: Cambridge University Press.

Berlin, Isaiah
    1960   The philosophical ideas of Giambattista Vico. Pp. 156–236 in Harold Acton
                et al., *Art and Ideas in Eighteenth-Century Italy*. Rome: The Italian
                Institute of London.

Blackstone, Sir William
    1769   *Commentaries on the Laws of England* (1783, 9th ed.). 1978. 4 vols.
                London: Garland.

INVENTING CRIMINOLOGY 815

Caffentzis, Constantine George
1989 *Clipped Coins, Abused Words, and Civil Government: John Locke's Philosophy of Money*. New York: Autonomedia.

Canetta, Rosalba
1985 Beccaria economista e gli atti di governo. Pp. 11–27 in *Cesare Beccaria: Atti di governo*. Milan: Mediobanca.

Cantu, Cesare
1862 *Beccaria e il diritto penale*. Florence: Barbera.

Chadwick, Owen
1981 The Italian Enlightenment. Pp. 90–105 in Roy Potter and Mikulás Teich (eds.), *The Enlightenment in National Context*. New York: Cambridge University Press.

Clinton, Katherine B.
1975 *Femme et philosophe*: Enlightenment origins of feminism. *Eighteenth-Century Studies* 8(3):283–299.

Condillac, Etienne Bonnot, Abbé de
17754 *A Treatise on the Sensations*. Pp. 175–339 of *Philosophical Writings of Etienne Bonnot, Abbé de Condillac*, trans. Franklin Philip, with the collaboration of Harlan Lane. 1982. Hillsdale, N.J.: Lawrence Erlbaum.

Condorcet, Marie–Jean–Antoine Nicolas Caritat
1782 Discours prononcé dans l'Académie française le jeudi 21 février 1782. Vol. 1:389–415 in A. Condorcet–O'Connor and M.F. Arago (eds.), *Oeuvres de Condorcet*. 1847. Paris:
1785 Letter to King Frederick II of Prussia, 2 May 1785. Vol. 13:268–273 in *Oeuvres posthumes de Fréderic II, roi de Prusse*. 1788. 15 vols. Berlin: Voss.
1795a Tableau général de la science qui a pour objet l'application au calcul aux sciences politiques et morales. Vol. 1:539–573 in A. Condorcet–O'Connor and M.F. Arago (eds.), *Oeuvres de Condorcet*. Paris: Firmin Didot.
1795b *Tableau historique des progrés de l'ésprit humain*. 1990. Paris: G. Steinheil.

Darnton, Robert
1979 *The Business of Enlightenment: A Publishing History of the Encyclopédie, 1775–1800*. Cambridge, Mass.: Harvard University Press.
1982 *The Literary Underground of the Old Regime*. Cambridge, Mass.: Harvard University Press.

Diderot, Dennis
1771 Des recherches sur le style par Beccaria. Vol. 4:60–63 in *Diderot: Oeuvres complétes*. Paris: Garnier.

Durkheim, Emile
1901 Two laws of penal evolution. Pp. 102–132 in Steven Lukes and Andrew Scull (eds.), *Durkheim and the Law*. 1983. New York: St. Martin's Press.

Facchinei, Ferdinando
1765 Note ed osservazioni sul libro intitolato "Dei delitti e delle pene." Pp. 164–177 in Franco Venturi (ed.), *Cesare Beccaria, Dei delitti e delle pene*. Turin: Giulio Einaudi.

Firpo, Luigi (ed.)
1984 Cesare Beccaria: Opere. 6 vols. Milan: Mediobanca.

816 BEIRNE

Foucault, Michel
1979   *Discipline & Punish: The Birth of the Prison*, trans. Alan Sheridan. New
        York: Vintage.
1988   The dangerous individual. Pp. 125–156 in Lawrence D. Kritzman (ed.),
        *Foucault: Politics, Philosophy, Culture (Interviews and Other Writings
        1977–1984)*, trans. Alain Baudot and Jane Couchman. London: Routledge.

Garland, David
1985   *Punishment and Welfare: A History of Penal Strategies*. Brookfield, Vt.:
        Gower.

Gay, Peter
1966   *The Enlightenment: An Interpretation*. New York: Alfred A. Knopf.

Gorecki, Jan
1985   *A Theory of Criminal Justice*. New York: Columbia University Press.

Green, Thomas Andrew
1985   *Verdict According to Conscience: Perspectives on the English Criminal Trial
        Jury 1200–1800*. Chicago: University of Chicago Press.

Grimm, Melchior
1765a   Examen de la traduction du *Traité des Délits et des Peines de Beccaria par
        Morellet*. Vol. 6:422–429 in *Correspondance littéraire, philosophique et
        critique*. 1878. 6 vols. Paris: Garnier.
1765b   Sur le traité des *Délits et des Peines, par Beccaria*. Vol. 6:329–338 in
        Correspondance littéraire, philosophique et critique. 1878. 6 vols. Paris:
        Garnier.

Gross, Hanns
1990   *Rome in the Age of Enlightenment*. New York: Cambridge University Press.

Halévy, Elie
1928   *The Growth of Philosophical Radicalism*. London: Faber & Gwyer.

Hankins, Thomas L.
1970   *Jean d'Alembert: Science and the Enlightenment*. Oxford: Clarendon Press.
1985   *Science and the Enlightenment*. New York: Cambridge University Press.

Hart, H.L.A.
1982   *Essays on Bentham*. Oxford: Clarendon Press.

Hegel, G.W.
1821   *The Philosophy of Right*, trans. T.M. Knox. 1967. London: Oxford
        University Press.

Helvétius, Claude–Adrien
1758   *De l'ésprit*. Paris: Durand.

Hirst, Paul Q.
1986   *Law, Socialism and Democracy*. London: Allen & Unwin.

Hume, David
1739   *A Treatise of Human Nature*. 1967. Oxford: Clarendon Press.

Humphries, Drew and David F. Greenberg
1981   The dialectics of crime control. Pp. 209–254 in David F. Greenberg (ed.),
        Crime & Capitalism: Readings in Marxist Criminology. Palo Alto, Calif.:
        Mayfield.

INVENTING CRIMINOLOGY 817

Hutcheson, Francis
  1725a   *An Inquiry Concerning, Beauty, Order, Harmony, Design.* 1973. The Hague:
          Martinus Nijhoff.
  1725b   *An Inquiry into the Original of our Ideas of Beauty and Virtue. In Two
          Treatises.* 1738. London: printed for D. Midwinter, A. Bettesworth, and C.
          Hitch.
  1755   *A System of Moral Philosophy.* London: A Millar and T. Longman.

Jaucourt, Chevalier de
  1751   Crime (faute, péché, délit, forfait). Vol. 1:466–470 in Diderot and
          d'Alembert (eds.), *Encyclopédie, ou dictionnaire raisonné des sciences, des arts
          et des métiers.* 1969. 6 vols. New York: Pergamon.

Jenkins, Philip
  1984   Varieties of Enlightenment criminology. *British Journal of Criminology*
          24(2):112–130.

Jones, David A.
  1986   *History of Criminology: A Philosophical Perspective.* New York: Greenwood
          Press.

Kant, Immanuel
  1797   *The Metaphysical Elements of Justice.* Part I of *The Metaphysics of Morals,*
          trans. John Ladd. 1965. Indianapolis: Bobbs–Merrill.

Kidder, Frederic
  1870   *History of the Boston Massacre.* Albany: Joel Munsell.

Klang, Daniel M.
  1984   Reform and enlightenment in eighteenth-century Lombardy. *Canadian
          Journal of History/Annales Canadiennes d'Histoire* 19(April):39–70.

Knight, Isabel F.
  1968   *The Geometric Spirit: The Abbé de Condillac and the French Enlightenment.*
          New Haven: Yale University Press.

Landry, Eugenio
  1910   *Cesare Beccaria: Scritti e lettere inediti.* Milan: Ulrico Hoepli.

Langbein, John H.
  1976   *Torture and the Law of Proof: Europe and England in the Ancien Régime.*
          Chicago: University of Chicago Press.

Laplace, Pierre Simon de
  1814   *A Philosophical Essay on Probabilities,* trans. F.W. Truscott and F.L. Emory.
          1951. New York: Dover.

Lieberman, David
  1989   *The Province of Legislation Determined.* New York: Cambridge University
          Press.

Locke, John
  1689   *Essay Concerning Human Understanding,* and Of the Conduct of the
          Understanding. Vol. 1:1–342 and vol. 3:389–428 in *The Works of John
          Locke.* 1727. London, printed for Arthur Bettesworth.
  1695   *Further Considerations Concerning Raising the Value of Money.* London:
          printed for A. and J. Churchill.

818   BEIRNE

Lottin, Joseph
   1912   *Quetelet: Statisticien et sociologue.* 1967. New York: Franklin.

Maestro, Marcello T.
   1942   *Voltaire and Beccaria as Reformers of Criminal Law.* New York: Columbia
            University Press.
   1973   *Cesare Beccaria and the Origins of Penal Reform.* Philadelphia: Temple
            University Press.

Matza, David
   1964   *Delinquency and Drift.* New York: John Wiley & Sons.

Maugham, Frederic Herbert
   1928   *The Case of Jean Calas.* London: William Heinemann.

Montesquieu, Charles Louis de Secondat
   1721   *Lettres persanes.* 1960. Paris: Garnier.
   1748   *De l'ésprit des lois.* 1973. 2 vols. Paris: Garnier.

Mueller, G.O.W.
   1990   Whose prophet is Cesare Beccaria? An essay on the origins of criminologi-
            cal theory. Vol. 2:1–14 in William S. Laufer and Freda Adler, eds.,
            Advances in Criminological Theory. New Brunswick, N.J.: Transaction
            Publishers.

Newman, Graeme and Pietro Marongiu
   1990   Penological reform and the myth of Beccaria. *Criminology* 28(2):325–346.

Paolucci, Henry
   1963   Translator's introduction. Pp. ix–xxiii in Beccaria, *On Crimes and Punish-
            ments.* Indianapolis: Bobbs–Merrill.

Pasquino, Pasquale
   1980   Criminology: The birth of a special savior. *Ideology and Consciousnness*
            7:17–32.

Petty, William
   1662   A treatise of taxes & contributions. Pp. 1–97 in Charles H. Hull (ed.), *The
            Economic Writings of Sir William Petty.* 1899. New York: Cambridge
            University Press.

Phillipson, Coleman
   1923   *Three Criminal Law Reformers: Beccaria/Bentham/Romilly.* 1975. Mont-
            clair, N.J.: Patterson Smith.

Phillipson, Nicholas
   1981   The Scottish Enlightenment. Pp. 19–40 in Roy Porter and Mikulás Teich
            (eds.), *The Enlightenment in National Context.* New York: Cambridge
            University Press.

Ramsay, Allan
   n.d.   Lettre à A.M. Diderot Vol. 4:56–60 in *Diderot: Oeuvres complètes.* Paris:
            Garnier.

Robbins, Caroline
   1968   *The Eighteenth-Century Commonwealthman.* New York: Atheneum.

Roberts, John M.
   1960   Enlightened despotism in Italy. Pp. 25–44 in Harold Acton et al., *Art and
            Ideas in Eighteenth-Century Italy.* Rome: The Italian Institute of London.

INVENTING CRIMINOLOGY 819

Robertson, John
1983   The Scottish Enlightenment at the limits of the civic tradition. Pp. 137–178 in Istvan Hont and Michael Ignatieff (eds.), *Wealth and Virtue: The Shaping of Political Economy in the Scottish Enlightenment*. New York: Cambridge University Press.

Roshier, Bob
1989   *Controlling Crime: The Classical Perspective in Criminology*. Chicago: Lyceum Books.

Schumpeter, Joseph A.
1954   *History of Economic Analysis*. New York: Oxford University Press.

Scott, William Robert
1900   *Francis Hutcheson*. New York: Cambridge University Press.

Servin, Antoine Nicholas
1782   *De la législation criminelle*. Basel: Schweigenhauser.

Shackleton, Robert
1972   The greatest happiness of the greatest number: The history of Bentham's phrase. Vol. 90:1461–1482 in *Studies on Voltaire and the Eighteenth Century*.

Swingewood, Alan
1970   Origins of sociology: The case of the Scottish Enlightenment. *British Journal of Sociology* 21(2):164–180.

Taylor, Ian, Paul Walton, and Jock Young
1973   *The New Criminology*. London: Routledge & Kegan Paul.

Tombs, Robert
1980   Crime and the security of the state: The "dangerous classes" and insurrection in nineteenth-century Paris. Pp. 214–237 in V.A.C. Gatrell, Bruce Lenman, and Geoffrey Parker (eds.), *Crime and the Law: The Social History of Crime in Western Europe since 1500*. London: Europa.

Venturi, Franco
1963   Elementi e tentativi di riforme nello Stato Pontificio del Settecento. *Rivista Storica Italiana* 25:778–817.
1971   *Utopia and Reform in the Enlightenment*. New York: Cambridge University Press.
1972   *Italy and the Enlightenment*, trans. Susan Corsi. New York: New York University Press.
1983   Scottish echoes in eighteenth-century Italy. Pp. 345–362 in Istvan Hont and Michael Ignatieff (eds.), *Wealth and Virtue: The Shaping of Political Economy in the Scottish Enlightenment*. New York: Cambridge University Press.

Venturi, Franco (ed.)
1965   *Cesare Beccaria, dei delitti e delle pene. Con una raccolta di lettere e documenti relativi alla nascita dell'opera e alla sua fortuna nell'Europa del Settecento*. Turin: Giulio Einaudi.

Verri, Pietro
1763   *Meditazioni sulla felicità*. Milan: Galeazzi.

820   BEIRNE

Vico, Giambattista
    1709   *On the Study Methods of Our Time*, trans Elio Gianturco. 1965.
            Indianapolis: Bobbs–Merrill.
    1725   *The New Science*, trans. T.G. Bergin and M.H. Fisch. 1970. Ithaca, N.Y.:
            Cornell University Press.

Vold, George B. and Thomas J. Bernard
    1986   *Theoretical Criminology*. New York: Oxford University Press.

Voltaire, François–Marie Arouet de
    1762a   Lettre à M. d'Alembert. Vol. 42:78–79 in *Oeuvres complètes de Voltaire*.
            Paris: Garnier.
    1762   Lettre à M. d'Alembert. Vol. 42:167–168 in *Oeuvres complètes de Voltaire*.
            Paris: Garnier.
    1763   Traité sur la tolérance à l'occasion de la mort de Jean Calas. Vol. 25:18–118
            in *Oeuvres complètes de Voltaire*. 1879. Paris: Garnier.

Weisser, Michael R.
    1979   *Crime and Punishment in Early Modern Europe*. Atlantic Highlands, N.J.:
            Humanities Press.

Wills, Garry
    1978   *Inventing America: Jefferson's Declaration of Independence*. Garden City,
            N.Y.: Doubleday.

Wood, P.B.
    1989   The natural history of man in the Scottish Enlightenment. *History of
            Science* 28(1):89–123.

Woolf, Stuart
    1979   *A History of Italy, 1700–1860*. London: Methuen.

Young, David
    1983   Cesare Beccaria: Utilitarian or retributivist? *Journal of Criminal Justice*
            11(4):317–326.
    1984   "Let Us Content Ourselves with Praising the Work While Drawing a Veil
            Over Its Principles": Eighteenth-century reactions to Beccaria's *On Crimes
            and Punishments. Justice Quarterly* 1:155–169.
    1986   Property and punishment in the eighteenth century: Beccaria and his critics.
            American Journal of Jurisprudence 31:121–135.

Zeman, Thomas Edward
    1981   Order, crime and punishment: The American criminological tradition.
            Unpublished Ph.D. dissertation in the History of Consciousness (Political
            and Social Thought), University of California at Santa Cruz.

Piers Beirne is Professor of Sociology and Legal Studies at the University of Southern
Maine. He recently edited *Revolution in Law: Contributions to the Development of Soviet
Legal Theory, 1917–1936*, and is author of the forthcoming *Inventing Criminology: The
Rise of 'Homo Criminalis'*, 1750–1915. With Jim Messerschmidt, he is the author of the
textbook *Criminology* (1991). His current research is on abolitionism.

[4]

BRIT. J. CRIMINOL. Vol. 24 No. 2 APRIL 1984

VARIETIES OF ENLIGHTENMENT CRIMINOLOGY

Beccaria, Godwin, de Sade

Philip Jenkins (*Pennsylvania*)*

This article aims at a fundamental reassessment of the nature and complexity of Classical criminology, and of the radical pioneering role usually assigned to Cesare Beccaria (1738–94). It will here be proposed that Beccaria was a deeply conservative figure who sought to create a criminological system which evaded the dangerously revolutionary and materialist implications of Enlightenment thought. Whatever his original intentions, the result of his work was the creation of a bureaucratic tool. That a thoroughly revolutionary criminology was possible at this time is shown by the extensive writing of the anarchist William Godwin (1756–1836) and the libertine atheist the Marquis de Sade (1740–1814).

The importance of Beccaria's Classical school is beyond question. It was the first naturalistic explanation of crime—one that did not base itself on concepts of sin and demonology. Histories of criminology customarily begin with the publication in 1764 of Beccaria's *Dei Delitti e pene* (*Of Crimes and Punishments*), the immensely influential work which largely inspired the transition from reliance on capital and corporal punishment to dependence on incarceration (see for example Radzinowicz 1966. pp.1–20: Vold, 1979, pp.18–34). Beccaria also emphasised the necessity to control administrative discretion in order to defend individual rights, and argued that fixed and predictable sentences were the best way to ensure an element of certainty for promoting deterrence. After a century of Positivism and the rehabilitative ideal. such ideas have once again come into vogue. so that there was talk in the 1970s of a "Neo-Classical" revival in penology. Classicism is a central issue both for the history of criminology, and for its contemporary development.

Modern accounts of Classical criminology are often descriptions of Beccaria's life and work (Phillipson, 1970). Professor Elio Monachesi wrote in 1955 that "It is not an exaggeration to regard Beccaria's work as being of primary importance in paving the way for penal reform for approximately the last two centuries" (Monachesi. 1972. p.49. Compare Maestro. 1942 and 1973: Heath, 1963: Radzinowicz and King, 1977. pp.1–9: Newman. 1978: Vold. 1979. pp.18–34: Cullen and Gilbert. 1982. pp.28–32, 52–53). Beccaria's influence is undoubted: *Of Crimes and Punishments* achieved instant popularity. and it played a central role in developing concepts of law and crime in both the American and French Revolutions (Wills. 1978, pp.152–153: Hufton. 1980. p.91).

* Assistant Professor. Administration of Justice. The Pennsylvania State University. In writing this article. I have been helped by the comments and suggestions of Gil Geis. Daniel Katkin. James Fox. Gary Potter. and Sean McConville.

VARIETIES OF ENLIGHTENMENT CRIMINOLOGY

But opinions differ as to the profundity of Beccaria's thought, and criticisms have been made by the radical criminological school which has emerged in the last two decades. It was *The New Criminology*—one of the foundation texts of the new school—which pointed out how many issues had been neglected by Beccaria, so it is appropriate to summarise here the argument of this work. First, the radicals point out that the Classical school erred in defining crime only in terms of acts which characterise the poorer classes, so that little attention is paid to the "crimes of the powerful". More important, Classicism assumed a consensus within society about the rationality of property and inequality; it assumed free will on the part of people influenced by their environment: and it failed to understand that the Classical scheme could only be applied justly where there was social and economic equality. *The New Criminology* suggests that Beccaria partially perceived these contradictions, but failed to press them to their logical conclusions. It was then left to nineteenth-century science to understand human behaviour as a function of social environment, and to replace Beccaria's views with a more materialistic and deterministic theory in a "Positivist Revolution" (Taylor *et al.*, 1973, pp.1–10). The modern radical view therefore implies that Beccaria suggested policies extremely advanced and humane for his own day, but lacked the scientific framework to embrace a truly "rational" view of behaviour.

But it is possible to propose a very different etiology for "Classical" theories. It will be argued that the intellectual tendencies of the mid-eighteenth century were apparently moving towards something very like the "Positivist Revolution" in criminology. By about 1760, there were many advanced thinkers who already saw behaviour from a standpoint at once atheist, materialist and determinist. Beccaria's importance was not as a progressive or a revolutionary writer, it was that he succeeded in diverting contemporary thought on crime and punishment in a deliberately conservative direction. His sudden fame can be attributed to the relief of educated society that it was possible to hold rational, "enlightened" views on human behaviour without having to accept radical materialism. Obviously, it is not suggested here that Beccaria was in some sense a conscious "tool of the state", a mouthpiece for a cynical ruling class. His aim was not simply to curry favour with the powerful, still less to make his book a best-seller. He was motivated by an obvious humanitarian concern for current injustices. It just happened that his modest, limited and conservative tract was widely seized upon because it filled an urgent social need.

By the 1750s, Enlightenment thought had advanced to the point at which scholars almost despaired of finding a firm and rational basis on which to justify virtue or obedience to law. Religion had failed—both traditional and liberal—and purely secular solutions also seemed ineffectual. It was at this point that Beccaria published a new synthesis of well-established ideas of contract theory and mutual self-interest, but without the materialist doctrines with which such ideas were often presented. Religion said that crime was inevitable. Enlightened philosophy

PHILIP JENKINS

said it could be cured, but at the cost of accepting thoroughgoing scientific determinism. Now, Beccaria presented ways of removing crime without invoking either extreme. His work achieved great popularity precisely because of its extreme caution on dangerous issues. He had succeeded in providing Enlightenment ideas with an acceptably non-subversive face. This conservative scholarship appealed to absolutist states, to whom it provided an ideological tool of great strength, and modern radical scholarship has also suggested its compatibility to the emerging commercial and industrial order (Humphries and Greenberg, 1981; Rustigan, 1981; Takagi, 1981; Hogg, 1981).

Beccaria's work was only one of the systems that could be erected on Enlightenment foundations, and it will be shown that conservatives of the period were wise to fear the possible consequences of pursuing such ideas to their logical conclusions. Two other criminological systems will be examined, both equally based on the mainstream of Enlightenment thought, yet both far more radical and dangerous to the established order than what we know as mainstream "Classicism". These other systems are the very sophisticated radical theories of Godwin and de Sade.

"Classicism"—the system pioneered by Beccaria and developed by Bentham—was not therefore the only significant Enlightenment view of criminology. Enlightenment criminology was almost as broad a spectrum as that of the twentieth century. To see Classical views alone as representing the side of reform would be like seeing the Californian treatment model of the 1950s as the sole trend in twentieth-century penology. Beccaria's views were only one part of a spectrum that stretched from "mediaeval" savagery and repression on one extreme, to anarchist views like those of current radicalism on the other. The problem is to explain why Beccarian opinions survived as the major representation of eighteenth-century thought on crime: it certainly was not the most faithful heir of the Enlightenment.

Morality and the Enlightenment

Beccaria was working at a time when the mainstream of European philosophy was making it more and more difficult to find rational bases for good conduct. During the eighteenth century, religious dogma and supernatural interpretations had become increasingly unpopular, so that God had become a very distant figure. Before 1740, there had been an optimistic phase when it was believed that there was a benevolent master plan for mankind, guided ultimately by God and manifested through Nature. Religion and self-interest both tended to the same ends, of virtue, pleasure and human happiness. However, this had been a very difficult attitude to sustain, particularly considering the seemingly random bloodshed of the 1750s—the wars in Europe and America, the great Lisbon earthquake of 1755 (Gay, 1966–69). By the mid-century, there was a widespread belief that there was no plan or purpose for humanity, no guiding hand of God or Providence (Wickwar, 1935). Nature might simply be a neutral machine, not caring whether humanity prospered or vanished

VARIETIES OF ENLIGHTENMENT CRIMINOLOGY

into extinction, and certainly exhibiting no concern for any individual. This was the despairing message of d'Holbach's *Système de la Nature* of 1770, but such attitudes had been familiar at least from the mid-1740s (Hampson, 1968: Smith. 1965).

The study of man also tended to suggest a purely materialistic view, in which neither sin nor the supernatural could play a part. At the start of the century, Locke had shown how ideas and values were the result of sense-impressions, with the corollary that improving the social or educational environment could create a better humanity. In the materialistic 1750s, this idea was extended by Condillac to suggest that the mind itself was "merely an agglomeration of ideas which were themselves sense-impressions". Morality and reason were products of environment. a view which strongly tended to lead to moral relativism (Hampson. 1968, pp.26–27. 110–118).

By the 1760s. Enlightenment science and philosophy had reached something like despair. As Professor Hampson summarised their views: "Chance. or the blind determinism of matter in regular but aimless motion. appeared to regulate the operation of the universe and the destiny of man" (Hampson. 1968. p.186). In 1748. Montesquieu's conservative *Spirit of Laws* stressed how behaviour was conditioned by social development. which in turn resulted from economic. geographical and political factors (Montesquieu. 1966). Laws were "the necessary relationships which are determined by the nature of things". In the same year. Hume made a very strong case against the possibility of free will—and therefore (perhaps) against the existence of moral evil. The philosophy of these years was both materialistic and determinist. and it achieved its most adventurous expression in the *De L'Esprit* published by Helvetius in 1758 (Hampson. 1968. pp.119–127: Smith. 1965. pp.13–14).

Beccaria's contemporaries were therefore aware of the range of theories which would influence the development of criminology in the mid-nineteenth century. In particular. they were well used to the idea that behaviour (good or evil) arose from predetermined conditions in the social environment. This tended to destroy any concept of moral responsibility, and it would be this dilemma which in the next century would lead to the theories of Positivism and rehabilitation (Jenkins. 1983a). It would prompt others to suggest that. if crime arose from social conditions. then social revolution might eliminate crime and misery. Might different economic environments also give rise to different moralities for different classes? Clearly. these theories were approaching the Marxist concept of class ideologies: and Marx and Engels drew heavily on the Enlightenment materialist tradition (Taylor *et al.*. 1973. pp.11–23: McDonald. 1976: Engels. 1961).

The Enlightenment philosophers were on very dangerous ground. If there were no higher standards. why should people not seek pleasure. regardless of whether acts are labelled "good" or "evil"? Already in 1750. La Mettrie the materialist had noted that criminals might be just as happy as the virtuous. Again. Nature could not justify virtue: but might

PHILIP JENKINS

it justify evil? Goethe wrote that Nature was "an eternally devouring, eternally regurgitating monster". Might not the criminal or murderer therefore be acting in accordance with its desires (Hampson, 1968, pp.123, 190)?

Moreover, if reason was the only criterion to be applied to society, how could one justify property, authority, government, inequality? New justifications had to be invented for such things, as revealed religion could no longer be invoked with any confidence (Jenkins, 1983b, pp.211–212). The commonest theory found to meet this need was that of the social contract, whereby people had initiated society for self-defence, and to put an end to the "war of all against all". But yet again, there was a serious difficulty. By the 1760s, the most sophisticated version of this theory was that of Helvetius, whose view had the advantage of being rational and secular. It explained obedience to the law in terms of mutual self-interest, and judged actions by the rational standards of utilitarianism. But this theory had grave problems, in that it was intimately bound up with Helvetius's radical views of materialism and determinism. Was there really a simple choice between religious dogma, and a deterministic rationalism which made man the servant of his senses? It was for many an undesirable choice (Hampson, 1968, pp.125–127; Philippson, 1970, pp.44–47).

Crime, Punishment and Beccaria

The views of the Enlightenment had a very wide appeal to educated opinion, even among those who were not prepared to go all the way to atheism and determinism. The newer and more humane views also had social and political appeal. They provided a propaganda weapon for the intelligentsia and the bourgeoisie to attack the Church and aristocracy, classes whose power derived wholly from traditionally "irrational" and religious foundations. This attack was also supported by "Enlightened" monarchs, who stood to gain from the weakening of clerics and lords. Furthermore, by supporting legal or penal reform, absolutist rulers also proved that their power did not rest solely on tradition and heredity: their regimes had social utility, and won the support of influential writers like Voltaire or Montesquieu (we are already in the age when international public relations were an important consideration of policy). Finally, as Professor Rustigan has shown, the humanisation of punishments suited the interests of middle-class groups, and their need for the more efficient protection of property (Rudé, 1972, pp.195–217; Hay et al., 1975, pp.57–58; Foucault, 1977, pp.75–78; Rustigan, 1981).

From the 1740s, Enlightenment theories about punishment began to be put into practice. Elizabeth of Russia abolished capital punishment; Frederick of Prussia banned torture. In France, Voltaire led assaults against a series of acts of judicial barbarity—the Calas affair of 1762, in which a Protestant was falsely accused of murder: the de la Barre case of 1766, when an aristocrat was savagely punished for irreverent and blasphemous acts. As yet, there was little systematic theory about how penal policies should be amended by the new ideas, though Montesquieu's

VARIETIES OF ENLIGHTENMENT CRIMINOLOGY

Spirit of Laws had made some suggestions. It was this gap that Beccaria's book filled in 1764 (Beccaria. 1963: Maestro, 1942. 1973. p.18: Foucault. 1977; Weisser, 1979).

Of Crimes and Punishments did not initiate reforming concern about the justice systems of Europe; and. what is more. it certainly did not put forward the most advanced contemporary thought on the subject of crime and punishment. Quite the contrary: there is something of an effort not to explore the suggestions made by thinkers who had made a profound impact on Beccaria. The reformer emerges as a paradoxical figure, who produced an essentially conservative book in a very radical ambience. For instance. Beccaria's closest friends included Pietro Verri, whose deterministic theories about the origins of human behaviour would be bitterly criticised by orthodox Catholics (Manzoni. 1964: Maestro, 1973, pp.4–12). When Beccaria listed the authors who had influenced him, he mentioned especially Montesquieu, Rousseau. Helvetius. Hume and Diderot, all of whom had faced severe criticisms for the radicalism of their writings, and who often had trouble finding a printer. In the late 1760s, his friends in Paris would include Diderot and d'Holbach. men who had passed from simple scepticism to outright atheism (Beccaria. 1963. p.6; Philippson. 1970. pp.15–18). Such connections help to explain the remarks of modern scholars that Beccaria indulged in "extremely rationalistic presuppositions" or that he wrote with "the iconoclastic fury of youth. all the revolutionary enthusiasm of the enlightened zealot" (Manzoni. 1964. p.xii).

Such claims are implausible. given the place and date at which he was writing. Italy in the 1760s was more liberal than it had been a century earlier. but Beccaria knew well what could happen to radicals who attacked the Church or the established order. The historian Giannone had recently been imprisoned for such a mistake. and Beccaria himself wished "to defend humanity without becoming a martyr". He was even conscious of the more distant shade of Galileo (Maestro, 1973. p.41: Cochrane. 1973. pp.419–483). His sensitivity to charges of radicalism was extreme. and this explains the short preface added to later editions of his work asserting that he was neither an infidel nor a revolutionary. To a modern reader. this is puzzling. Why should he need to assert this obvious fact? (Beccaria. 1963. pp.3–7.)

Beccaria's book was a very innocent piece. but it was handling debates which had led others to much more dangerous conclusions. To understand this. it is first necessary to study the intellectual framework of *Of Crimes and Punishments*. and then see how Beccaria has selected his material. First. his idea of society was based on contract theory: laws were made by compacts of free men, and the guide to be applied in the making of law was utility, "the greatest happiness of the greatest number" *(ibid..* pp.7–13). Society had originated in an ancient state of war, which had led people to band together for mutual defence. In society, they yielded up portions of their freedom to the sovereign. who used punishment to prevent the tyranny of one individual over another. The means for this

PHILIP JENKINS

were "tangible"—that is, implying that conduct was guided by what was felt through the senses (*ibid.*, pp.10–12). It seems at first as though Beccaria were asserting essentially materialist doctrines. A certain social radicalism is also suggested by passages that say laws "have always favoured the few and outraged the many" (*ibid.*, p.42). There would appear to be strong reasons for the vigorous attack on this work by Italian clerics, and by conservative jurists. If it had appeared at any time up to the early eighteenth century, it would have been a revolutionary tract (Venturi, 1971).

But it appeared during the 1760s. At this time, the only line in the book which could have caused surprise was one which stated that the "terrible and perhaps unnecessary right" of property caused poverty, which in turn led to crime. However, there is strong evidence to believe that this was a printer's error, and Beccaria was merely stating that property was a *necessary* and fundamental right (Beccaria, 1963, p.74, n.39). Otherwise, he used a moderately secular framework to explain the foundation of society in an "original contract", but in the most conservative sense of that idea. He must have been aware that in 1762 Rousseau's *Social Contract* had used the same theory to assert that society came before government, and therefore had the right to dissolve governments by the democratic will (Rousseau, 1967). Early in the next century, the American criminologist Edward Livingston would take up Rousseau's suggestion, and use a strongly democratic contract theory to suggest that government could not withdraw inalienable rights. This American "Classicist" was also much more prepared to assert that laws were often abused in the interests of the ruling class, and he denied that absolute sanctity of property had been granted by the "Original Contract" (Mouledoux, 1972, pp.73–74). In Beccaria's work, these ideas remain largely unexplored. By the 1760s, it would be difficult to imagine a less controversial or more cautious version of contract theory.

Again, Beccaria made a statement epitomising utilitarian doctrine, in the phrase that would be made famous by Bentham, "the greatest happiness of the greatest number". But it appears here shorn of the extreme materialist connotations which it would be given by Helvetius or d'Holbach. It was d'Holbach who said that "the only known norm by which reason can judge men and things is their real and lasting utility to our species" (Wickwar, 1935, pp.125–126; Wills, 1979, pp.149–159). In consequence, every attempt must be abandoned to discover God's will about human affairs, nor could a supposed after-life guide human conduct in society. Helvetius too would use social utility as the sole guide of morality, but with an even more controversial implication. His materialism reduced humans to "pleasure-pain calculating machines", who could be mechanically driven by laws or punishments to be good citizens; but, if pleasure was the only goal of the mind, why should this not be achieved through vice or crime? There was no easy answer, and Helvetius's modern biographer comments that this posed the philosophical choice of one or two extremes: by the 1780s, one could choose either de Sade's nihilism or

VARIETIES OF ENLIGHTENMENT CRIMINOLOGY

extreme authoritarianism. It was an unpleasant dilemma. which Beccaria simply ignored—and did so even while claiming that Helvetius was one of the greatest influences on his work (Smith, 1965, pp.14, 223).

All Beccaria's sources raised very difficult questions. which could remove the basic justifications for the working of criminal justice systems. They suggested that people were not responsible for their acts, they they had been led to crime by social injustice. and perhaps that there was no rational reason to prefer virtue to crime. Beccaria provided an acceptable framework which most could accept. It began by using radical language—the social contract, *sensationalism* (in modern terms, "behaviourism"), utility as the guide of conduct. There were enough suggestions of concern about social inequality to appease radicals; but all are presented in an anodyne form. Time after time, we see Beccaria shying away from far-reaching reforms. For instance. he suggested the abolition of capital punishment, which would mean more use of prisons. In the 1740s, La Mettrie's materialism had stressed how the human organism could be altered by the mechanical discipline of such an institution. and Professor Foucault has shown how such theories influenced the invention of the new prison at the end of the century. There was no reason why Beccaria should not have explored these ideas—except that, if he did, he would have had to acknowledge the materialist sources on which he was drawing (Foucault, 1977).

For Beccaria's contemporaries. as for the Positivists of the next century. crime was determined by external circumstances. Helvetius himself had said that moral laws were just as susceptible to rational inquiry as physical laws, and just as predictable (Wickwar, 1935, p.53). For a scholar of the 1760s to create a criminological system based on belief in free will was reactionary, and showed a remarkable willingness to ignore the findings of current social science and psychology. Equally, it is surprising that Beccaria included so little criticism of social inequality as a cause of crime. It would have been by no means unusual for a writer at this time to attack extreme inequality of property. as had Rousseau. Even the conservative Adam Smith remarked that government—and, by implication, criminal law—was intended "for the defence of the rich against the poor" (quoted in Jesilow, 1982, p.319). At the other extreme. the true Enlightenment radicals had already passed to the stage of attacking the right to property *per se*. Once again. Beccaria's Classicism does not appear to be the most radical system that could have been conceived in a benighted and pre-scientific age. It was exactly the kind of moderate and tentative theory that could have been expected from an aristocratic liberal deeply aware of the limitations imposed by one of the most effective systems of censorship of the time. Beccaria knew the radical alternatives to his theory, and may have wished to explore them—but he could not. It was left to the Positivists of the next century to do so.

Beccaria and his Sources

By 1766. Beccaria's associate Pietro Verri had become extremely jealous of the success of *Of Crimes and Punishments*. and he began to make threats

PHILIP JENKINS

to expose Beccaria as a charlatan and plagiarist. Allegedly, Verri himself had inspired the work, while all Beccaria had done was to borrow passages from Montesquieu, Helvetius, Voltaire and Graevius. Verri's claim as it stands is extremely difficult to accept, but a study of the way in which Beccaria used his sources reveals two things: first, he was expressing little that was novel; and second, where he did handle material similar to other writers, he gave it a very conservative slant. It is not suggested that Beccaria was deliberately "sanitising" radical material in order to create a system that would appeal to governments of his day. However, he was forced to be extremely careful in his selection and use of contemporary writers (Philippson, 1970, p.20; Beccaria, 1963, p.xvii).

Naturally, Beccaria found himself covering some well-trodden ground, and some of his observations were so commonplace that it is often difficult to isolate an exact source for them. For instance, when he related the severity of punishments to the repressiveness of a country's legislation and the degree of social injustice, he might have been borrowing the idea either from Montesquieu's *Spirit of Laws* (1748) or Rousseau's *Social Contract* (1762). Repeatedly, we find that ideas associated with Beccaria in Enlightenment debate had originated with Montesquieu, Voltaire, Locke, or else an ancient writer. Montesquieu was an especially influential source for discussions on the separation of powers within a Constitution, on the nature of religious and moral offences, on treason legislation and on torture (such reliance was appropriate given Montesquieu's strong conservative bent). Beccaria had been preceded by Rousseau in his criticism of the frequent use of pardons. Voltaire had attacked existing criminal law systems for their inadequate standards of proof, for secret accusations, the use of torture and excessive recourse to capital punishment—and many other abuses which we find mentioned in Beccaria's work. *Of Crimes and Punishments* was a work of synthesis, not especially one of creativity (Maestro, 1942; Philippson, 1970, pp.51–53).

But Beccaria did not take his ideas intact. For instance, most of the material for his chapter on torture was collected by Pietro Verri, who would later expand this subject into a book. Verri studied historical examples of torture being used to secure confessions to non-existent crimes, and evolved a theory that it was the social and scientific level of a period which determined the extent of the use of torture. He was therefore following the materialists in suggesting that social foundations created legal abuse—and his determinism was severely criticised by nineteenth-century conservatives (Manzoni, 1964). But Beccaria used the material on torture without the theoretical framework. Torture simply illustrated ignorance and inhumanity, not a deterministic theory of society. Again, we can see an effort to avoid serious controversy.

This can be seen most clearly if we compare Beccaria's view of ecclesiastical atrocities with the discussions found in Voltaire or Montesquieu. Beccaria was remarkably restrained here, for he never once mentions the Church overtly. All he can do is attack past persecutions of crimes "wholly imaginary" ... "impossible crimes, fabricated by timid

VARIETIES OF ENLIGHTENMENT CRIMINOLOGY

ignorance" (presumably witchcraft). Again. he criticises the punishment of people for "being true to their own principles" (heresy). Indeed. in a gruesome chapter describing the savage punishment of such offenders for "crimes that have covered Europe with human blood" it is only called "a particular kind of crime". We are left to assume that he meant to discuss heresy and witchcraft. but was restricted by the harsh censorship of Italy (Beccaria, 1963, pp.9. 42–43. 86–87). By contrast. Montesquieu used more powerful language to attack the prosecution of such crimes. and he explicitly names the offences he was dealing with. Moreover, his attack on obscurantism is buttressed with familiar anti-clerical stories from the barbarous Middle Ages (Montesquieu. 1966, pp.187–191: Montesquieu. 1973). Voltaire spent many years fighting the clerical persecutions of protestants or free-thinkers. urged the abolition of offences such as sacrilege, heresy and blasphemy, and campaigned for the suppression of ecclesiastical courts. Once again. Beccaria is seen to have been on the reforming side—but definitely as a conservative force for reform (Philippson, 1970, pp.51–53).

Beccaria's Influence

If Beccaria's work was neither original nor adventurous. why did it have such immediate impact? Every history of penal reform stresses its influence throughout Europe. and how Beccaria and Bentham became the founders of what would remain for a century the main Western school of criminology. It may be suggested that the book was a synthesis of progressive calls for reform. in language likely to have very widespread appeal. It allowed the educated to understand the case for reform. untrammelled by the extreme radicalism which might so easily have become associated with such questions. Again. it helped "Enlightened" monarchs by assuring them that they could readily justify their existence as reformers and humanitarians—but without having to accept beliefs which would threaten all morality and property. Beccaria himself averted charges of radicalism by writing that "the great monarchs. the benefactors of humanity who rule us. are pleased to hear truths expounded. even by an unknown thinker . . .". When the Italian clergy attacked Beccaria. he was defended by the conservative and authoritarian Imperial representative, Count Firmian. Perhaps despite himself. he found himself a close ally of the established order (Beccaria. 1963. pp.xi. 4).

Beccaria's views came to epitomise humane reform from above within the justice system. They were first adopted by Enlightened absolutist monarchs. and were later disseminated alongside the ideals of the French Revolution. The first half of the nineteenth century saw the triumph of Classical ideals in penology. until they came under scientific assault from early Positivism. From the 1820s. evidence from various sources began to accumulate to suggest that human behaviour was determined by social. economic or biological factors: if so. ideologies based on free will and rational hedonism were clearly inappropriate (McDonald. 1976).

PHILIP JENKINS

But was this new synthesis one which had actually been delayed by the conservative nature of Beccaria's writings? Of course, speculation on "what might have been" is perilous, and the Enlightenment lacked the firm statistical basis on which Positivism was based. On the other hand, there is evidence to support the hypothesis proposed here. It can be shown that other writers on crime and punishment actually did pursue the lines of inquiry suggested by the materialists, and by the radical theorists of the social contract. The conclusions they reached during Beccaria's lifetime were based on the same Enlightenment assumptions as Beccaria's, and yet were far more fundamental in their attack on social conventions.

The criticism can be made that it is unfair to compare Godwin and de Sade with Beccaria. They were writing long after *Of Crimes and Punishments*, in a time of dramatic political upheaval. How can it possibly be claimed that such radical theories could have evolved as early as the tranquil 1760s? However, it can easily be shown that these radicals use no ideas as sources that were not familiar to Beccaria and his contemporaries. But for the censorship of the time, the "radical criminology" of the revolutionary years could have emerged as early as the 1760s.

The Criminology of William Godwin

The Classicism evolved by Beccaria has appropriately been described as "administrative and legal criminology" (Vold, 1979, p.26). Beccaria's contribution was to suggest to governments and ruling élites that there could indeed be an administrative or bureaucratic solution to crime, that laws and penal reforms could actually achieve something positive within the existing social framework. But he merely delayed the day when it would be widely accepted that the solution to crime lay only in fundamental social change. This was the dilemma which would be portrayed effectively in the 1790s by William Godwin.

Godwin achieved fame as a radical not only for his writings, but for his family circle: he was the husband of the pioneer feminist Mary Wollstonecraft, the father of the author of *Frankenstein*, and a close friend of Shelley. In his own right, he was most celebrated for his political treatise of 1793: the *Enquiry Concerning Political Justice*, in which can be found most of the doctrines of the anarchism of the next century. This appeared in the turbulent years following the French Revolution, but it was not just a result of that crisis. Godwin had been forming his ideas from 1781, when he had discovered authors like Helvetius, d'Holbach, Rousseau and Hume—essentially the same influences to which Beccaria had been subject. But while Beccaria was careful to use his material in a moderate way, Godwin actually carried these sources to their logical and revolutionary conclusion (Brown, 1926; Woodcock, 1963, Chap. 3; Godwin, 1976).

Godwin was an unashamed materialist, who believed that human behaviour arose from social conditioning. He believed in determinism, the power of "Necessity", although he followed Hume in allowing some role for human choice within the framework of causality. His version of contract theory was both adventurous and novel. He accepted that there

VARIETIES OF ENLIGHTENMENT CRIMINOLOGY

had been some such contract, although he denied that humanity was necessarily subject to any precedents, even of an "Original Contract". Also, he suggested that the people who made the contract might have been gravely disappointed by the atrocities which governments had committed since. For Godwin, humanity progressed towards perfectibility, towards the stage where people could manifest their natural disinterestedness and benevolence, until the day when they could live according to the pure laws of Nature. Rousseau had been quite correct to describe the idyllic state of the "noble savage" in the time before civilisation: but Godwin wished to suggest that this was an ideal which could also be reached *after* the extinction of government and property (Godwin, 1976, pp.69, 75–76, 496–497 note).

By this point, Godwin had moved much further than Rousseau, further than the radical politics of the Enlightenment, and had arrived at true anarchism, which he saw as the natural end of society. It was from this perspective that he launched his attack on punishment and the criminal justice system, in terms which mark a very striking contrast with the work of Beccaria. It is a fascinating demonstration of how two such different writers could follow the same sources and stay within one broad tradition, and yet reach such totally different conclusions.

Godwin devoted the whole of Book VII of *Political Justice* to "Of Crimes and Punishments", the title of which almost certainly refers back to Beccaria's work. Book VII represented almost a tenth of the whole work, a substantial proportion justified because of Godwin's view that punishment and criminal justice were at the core of any political debate. They were the state's last line of defence, and its ultimate *raison d'être*. Godwin rejected all the claims that could be made in favour of the state or its justice system, however extensively they might be reformed. Laws would inevitably favour the rich, as was proved by examples like the taxation or game laws in England or France, or the tendency of laws not to punish socially harmful acts by the rich. Crime was by definition composed of "offences which the wealthier part of the community have no temptation to commit" (Godwin, 1976, pp.631–700).

Godwin believed that crime arose from the property system, as inequality caused poverty. Many people were "continually prompted by disappointment and distress to commit violence upon their more fortunate neighbours" (*ibid.*, p.87). Crime rose in proportion to social inequality. "The fruitful source of crimes consists in this circumstance, one man's possessing in abundance that of which another man is destitute" (*ibid.*, p.731). The amount of crime, and the brutality of punishment, were inversely proportionate to the extent to which a country followed the natural law of mutual aid: "The more the institutions of society contradict the genuine sentiments of the human mind, the more severely is it necessary to avenge their violation." (We may recall the views of radical criminologists in the 1970s that crime rates reflect the degree of repression necessary to preserve the inequalities of a given society) (*ibid.*, p.673).

PHILIP JENKINS

In a society based on gross inequality, it would become necessary to have very severe punishments; and here Godwin draws near to Beccarian ideas, but he retains his characteristic views. He refers to the "humane and benevolent" Beccaria as a pioneer in the attack on barbarous punishments, and includes several passages on Beccarian lines. He opposes capital and corporal punishment, the excessive use of pardons, and the use of law to enforce religious orthodoxy. But it soon becomes apparent that his conclusions are diametrically opposed to Beccaria's, in that he sees no justification whatever for punishment. First, punishment depended on free will and responsibility, and science showed these to be mythical. Assassins were tools of circumstances, no less than the daggers they used. Both were subject to "necessary causes and irresistible motives" (*ibid.*, pp.631–633, 647–653).

Punishment or coercion involved attempts to affect the lowest part of human nature, instead of appealing to higher social instincts. At best, it could only preserve compliance with the simplest minimum standards of behaviour. Punishment "begins with violently alienating the mind from the truth with which we wish it to be impressed." None of the usual justifications for punishment was justified: retribution looked only to what was past and irrecoverable, hence "must be ranked among the most pernicious exhibitions of an untutored barbarism". Incapacitation implied restraint from committing a possible future crime, "the very argument which has been employed to justify the most execrable tyrannies". Deterrence, or general "example", had led to the most extreme brutalities of judicial torture in an attempt to impress the public mind (*ibid.*, pp.635–674).

In all this, Godwin was not in conflict with much of the penological opinion of his age. In the 1790s, American states would begin to follow the example of Pennsylvania and to replace the widespread use of capital and corporal punishment with the institution of imprisonment: and European prisons would begin to be reformed to suit the new "humane" ideals (Ignatieff, 1978; Platt and Takagi, 1981). But Godwin departed massively from the Classical school by his rejection of reformation or rehabilitation as appropriate ideals for a penal system. Coercion could only alienate the mind of the prisoner, regardless of whether this was done with good intentions. It only conveyed a message of "submit to force, and abjure reason. Be not directed by the convictions of your understanding, but by the basest part of your nature, the fear of personal pain, and a compulsory awe of the injustice of others". "To conceive that compulsion and punishment are the proper means of reformation is the sentiment of a barbarian" (*ibid.*, pp.644–669).

Godwin proceeded to attack aspects of contemporary "Classical" reform, notably the "well-intentioned but misguided philanthropy of Mr. [John] Howard" (*ibid.*, pp.676–681). Solitary confinement was "uncommonly tyrannical and severe", because of man's gregarious nature, and it might well be classed as a brutal torture (*ibid.*, p.676). Prison labour was equally barbarous, especially futile work on the treadmill. Godwin summarises

VARIETIES OF ENLIGHTENMENT CRIMINOLOGY

contemporary prison reform within his own country by writing that "the institution of personal slavery has, within a few years, made a considerable progress in the island of Great Britain" (*ibid.*, p.678 note). It is important to emphasise the prophetic value of this criticism. The trends Godwin describes—reform through solitary confinement and hard work—continued to be the guiding principles of western prison systems until the middle of the next century, when they began to be subjected to criticism of precisely the type Godwin had put forward in the 1790s. Before the ideas of Beccaria and Howard had been fully applied, Godwin had already identified their fatal flaws and presented an impressive critique of Classical assumptions. In so doing, he also influenced the widespread radical movement in contemporary England (Evans, 1982, pp.189–192).

Godwin understood the fact that Beccaria could not bring himself to face, that crime arose from factors within society, and could only be removed by changing that society. For Godwin, property itself was the greatest criminogenic institution. "If among the inhabitants of any country there existed no desire in one individual to possess himself of the substance of another, or no desire so vehement and restless as to prompt him to acquire it by means inconsistent with order and justice, undoubtedly in that country guilt could scarcely be known but by report" (*ibid.*, p.89). Such a society could be created by abolishing government and property, by reorganising society on a decentralised parish level, and by recognising that each person had a duty to support the less fortunate. If anyone broke the rules of the new society, then punishment existed as a temporary expedient—but only in so far as the criminal could be restrained. Godwin never accepted the view taken by later radicals that rehabilitation would be appropriate for a democratic society: "Restrain the offender as long as the safety of the community prescribes it, for this is just. Restrain him not an instant from a simple view to his own improvement, for this is contrary to reason and morality" (p.675. Compare Jenkins, 1982).

The Criminology of the Marquis de Sade

To a respectable propertied person in the 1790s, Godwin's ideas must have seemed a great threat, the *ne plus ultra* of radicalism. But in the same years, there appeared in France a series of books which contained even more shocking ideas. These were the works written by the Marquis de Sade between about 1782 and 1797, culminating in *La Nouvelle Justine* and *Juliette* of the latter year. At first sight, it may seem strange to extract any coherent philosophy from the work of one widely regarded as a depraved monster. When Beccaria's book was published in 1764, de Sade was serving the first of many terms of imprisonment, this time for "excesses" committed in a brothel. But the popular image of de Sade omits much of relevance (Lely, 1970; de Sade, 1965).

De Sade's reputation has continued to grow during the present century, both as a literary stylist and as a philosopher who links the Enlightenment with Romanticism. Much in his personal life belies the "sadistic" image. How, for example, are we to explain why such a figure wrote a pamphlet

PHILIP JENKINS

urging the abolition of "the atrocity of capital punishment, because the law which attempts a man's life is impractical, unjust, inadmissible"? It was a system that had never succeeded in repressing crime (de Sade, 1965. p.310). He appealed to "slaughterers, jailers" and others to "prefer the science of understanding man to that of imprisoning and killing him" (de Sade, 1966, p.47). Still more remarkable, he bitterly attacked the institution of imprisonment, which was gaining in contemporary popularity. In particular, solitary confinement makes a man "come out of prison more sly and more dangerous than ever" (de Sade, 1964, p.46). As with Godwin. this was a prophetic insight in the decade in which the Pennsylvania prison system was established—and it left de Sade with a more humane view than either Beccaria or Howard. He urged the new French republican state to adopt far more liberal and permissive laws than the old regime. and not merely for sexual or moral offences (de Sade, 1965, pp.311–315). Few other propagandists of the age (outside the extreme radicals) so fervently urged a reduction of penalties for offences against property. This curious radical advocated a communist state—yet he resigned his judicial office rather than participate in the brutalities of the "Terror" that sought to achieve such a radical solution. Even the extremely pornographic nature of his writings seems less surprising when we understand the strong tradition in late eighteenth-century France of expressing revolutionary sentiments through scatological underground tracts. "Politico-pornography" was a flourishing genre of the time (Darnton, 1976. 1982. 1984).

So de Sade, like Godwin, can be considered as a reformer on the radical wing of Enlightenment criminology, one who pushed to their logical conclusions the speculations of rationalist philosophers. The main influences that we can trace are Helvetius and d'Holbach—the friends of Beccaria and mentors of Godwin—and de Sade's system of belief was predictably atheist and materialist. His great pornographic work *Juliette* includes many pages of some of the most perceptive Biblical criticism written before the present century. and this leads him to conclude that there was no God, no revealed truth. A person was only a material thing. which perished at death. There was no universal cause. and the cosmos was an "assemblage of unlike entities which act and react mutually and successively with and against each other"—an account heavily based on the mechanistic system of d'Holbach and La Mettrie (de Sade. 1966. pp.40–49; de Sade, 1968, pp.43–45, 375–390, 731, 748–750).

This interpretation also applied to human behaviour. which provided the basis for de Sade's "criminology". "All moral effects are to be related to physical causes. unto which they are linked most absolutely: the drumstick strikes the taut-drawn skin and the sound answers the blow" (de Sade, 1968, p.15). In such a behaviourist system, crime arose from our predispositions, what we ate or inhaled, the chemical composition of food—"this is what moves a person to crime or to virtue. and often. to both within the space of a single day". Humans were therefore "the constant slaves of necessity" (*ibid.*, p.15). They sought pleasure. and were unrestrained by any natural law. Indeed, nature might positively encour-

126

VARIETIES OF ENLIGHTENMENT CRIMINOLOGY

age vice and crime, as destruction was clearly part of the natural plan for creation and renewal (de Sade, 1968, pp.170–172, 316–320, 605–606; Aries, 1981, pp.391–392). One might therefore argue that committing destructive acts was merely "natural" behaviour; and if it gave pleasure, there was no reason why such conduct should not be performed. De Sade justified crime—but to do so, he used no idea that was not a philosophical commonplace from the 1750s, and no idea that was not familiar to Beccaria. When we compare the work of the two men, we are surprised not only at the amorality of de Sade but at the restraint and conservatism of Beccaria.

This is also apparent when we examine what the two men had to say about the "social contract". De Sade imagines a primitive age when the world was divided between the weak and the strong. When the strong had seized a certain amount of material goods by theft and violence, society was created to draw a line against further usurpations. Thereafter, anyone who tried to do what the strong had already done was described as a criminal. The weak man agreed to the contract only to safeguard what little he had left, while the strong (or rich) planned to ignore his own side of the agreement. Society and property were simply judicial theft. Punishing theft meant only punishing the weak for trying to retain what had once belonged to him (de Sade, 1968, pp.114–119). During the revolutionary years, de Sade put forward his communist ideas in a pamphlet which would influence the French Left throughout the next century (*ibid.*, p.118; de Sade, 1965, pp.310–316; Kiernan, 1976, p.363).

Crime could be justified in several ways: perhaps Nature drove men to various actions, and it was mere chance which acts were labelled as crime. De Sade quotes extensively from examples of other societies where offences such as adultery or infanticide were considered legal and normal, and suggests that Nature can have laid down no absolute rules. Alternatively, crime might be an act of class revolt, an anarchist gesture. Thirdly, Enlightenment philosophy had been attempting for a hundred years to base virtue on the pleasures of the senses, and the conditioning of the nervous system. But what if one believed that vice and crime contributed an unparalleled nervous stimulus? No rational reasons were left to declare this wrong (de Sade, 1968, pp.33–37, 120–123).

By contrast, punishment had few justifications. Murder might be incited by the determinism of external circumstances, but capital punishment required a cold and impassive act of brutal premeditation. This explains why de Sade urged such moderate penal policies, and why during his period as a Grand Juror he actually refused to convict the majority of those brought before him, even personal enemies who had persecuted him for years (*ibid.*, p.418; de Sade, 1965, pp.27–31). When de Sade portrays enforcers or defenders of the law, they are at least as brutal as his "villains", and indeed the worst characters in his novels are often government officials or ministers (de Sade, 1968, pp.732–740).

De Sade began his career with ideas very far removed from the sober optimism of Godwin, but the two had come to have much in common by

PHILIP JENKINS

the 1790s. Both had come to believe that laws were a worse form of oppression than anarchy, and that property was in itself a fundamental crime against society. Both agreed that "men are pure only in their natural condition" (Foucault, 1965, pp.282–285; de Sade, 1968, p.733). When they reached such conclusions, they were merely carrying on the work of Helvetius, d'Holbach and Rousseau, and applying such ideas to crime and punishment. In their very different ways, they were doing what Beccaria refused to do. The contrast is apparent when we study the moral basis they found for society's right to punish. Beccaria found such a basis in the essential justice and fairness of the social contract and of the states built upon it. Godwin and de Sade anticipated contemporary radicals in denying the existence of this justice, and countered with a conflict model of society. In this view, punishment could only be legitimate once social injustice was abolished. Clearly, it was Beccaria who was most likely to achieve acceptance with the governments of the day, monarchic or democratic.

Not until the 1840s would there once more emerge criminological systems which emphasised determinism and the role of crime as a form of social revolt. Had it not been for Beccaria's success, this might have been achieved decades earlier.

Conclusion

Beccaria had gone as far as he could in urging penal reform, for the next logical steps involved assaults on matters held sacred by the society of his day. One more step towards determinism, and individual responsibility was weakened, as actually occurred with the Positivist movement. One step more towards environmental theories of crime, and appreciation of the role of poverty, and the question arose whether crime was a reasonable response to injustice. Religion forbade accepting the first solution, propertied society rejected the second. But the fact that Beccaria did not pose these questions by no means implied that they were inconceivable without nineteenth-century social science. De Sade shows that they were posed, and Godwin suggests how they could have been incorporated into a serious political programme. By contrast, Beccaria's work stands as a conservative monument, the first great effort to cure crime without curing the society which produced it.

REFERENCES

ARIES, P. (1981). *The Hour of Our Death*. New York: Alfred A. Knopf.

BECCARIA, C. (1963). *Of Crimes and Punishments*. Indianapolis: Bobbs Merrill Co.

BROWN, F. K. (1926). *Life of William Godwin*. London: Dent.

COCHRANE, E. (1973). *Florence in the Forgotten Centuries*. University of Chicago Press.

CULLEN, F. T. and GILBERT, K. E. (1982). *Reaffirming Rehabilitation*. Cincinnati: Anderson.

VARIETIES OF ENLIGHTENMENT CRIMINOLOGY

Darnton, R. (1976). "The High Enlightenment and the Low-Life of Literature in Pre-Revolutionary France", pp.53–87 in Douglas Johnson (ed.), *French Society and the Revolution*. Cambridge University Press.

Darnton, R. (1982). *The Literary Underground of the Old Régime*. Harvard University Press.

Darnton, R. (1984). *The Great Cat Massacre*. New York: Harper and Row.

De Sade, Marquis D.-A.-F. (1964). *Justine*. (Translated by A. H. Walton). London: Corgi.

De Sade, Marquis D.-A.-F. (1965). *The Complete Justine, Philosophy in the Bedroom and Other Writings*. (Compiled by R. Seaver and A. Wainhouse). New York: Grove.

De Sade, Marquis D.-A.-F. (1966). *The 120 Days of Sodom*. (Compiled by A. Wainhouse and R. Seaver). New York: Grove.

De Sade, Marquis D.-A.-F. (1968). *Juliette*. (Translated by A. Wainhouse). New York: Grove.

Engels, F. (1961). "Socialism, Utopian and Scientific", pp.45–82 in A. P. Mendel (ed.), *Essential Works of Marxism*. New York: Bantam.

Evans, R. (1982). *The Fabrication of Virtue: English Prison Architecture 1750–1840*. Cambridge University Press.

Foucault, M. (1965). *Madness and Civilisation*. New York: Random House.

Foucault, M. (1977). *Discipline and Punish: The Birth of the Prison*. London: Allen Lane.

Gay, P. (1966–69). *The Enlightenment* (2 vols). New York: Knopf.

Godwin, W. (1976). *Enquiry Concerning Political Justice*. (Edited by I. Kramnick). London: Pelican.

Hampson, N. (1968). *The Enlightenment*. London: Penguin.

Hay, D. *et al.* (1975). *Albion's Fatal Tree*. London: Penguin.

Heath, J. (1963). *Eighteenth Century Penal Theory*. Oxford University Press.

Hogg, R. (1981). "Imprisonment and Society Under Early British Capitalism", in T. Platt and P. Takagi (eds.), *Punishment and Penal Discipline*. Berkeley, Ca.: Crime and Social Justice.

Hufton, O. (1980). *Europe: Privilege and Protest 1730–89*. London: Fontana.

Humphries, D. and Greenberg, D. F. (1981). "The Dialectics of Crime Control", pp.209–254 in D. F. Greenberg (ed.), *Crime and Capitalism*. Palo Alto, Ca.: Mayfield.

Ignatieff, M. (1978). *A Just Measure of Pain*. New York: Pantheon.

Jacob, M. (1981). *The Radical Enlightenment*. New York: Allen and Unwin.

Jenkins, P. (1982). "The Radicals and the Rehabilitative Ideal". *Criminology*, **20**, 347–372.

Jenkins, P. (1983a). "*Erewhon*: A Manifesto of the Rehabilitative Ideal". *Journal of Criminal Justice*. **11**, 35–46.

Jenkins, P. (1983b). *The Making of a Ruling Class: The Glamorgan Gentry 1640–1790*. Cambridge University Press.

Jesilow, P. (1982). "Adam Smith and White-Collar Crime". *Criminology*, **20**, 319–328.

Kiernan, V. G. (1976). "Private Property in History". pp.361–398 in J. Goody *et al.* (eds.), *Family and Inheritance*. Cambridge University Press.

PHILIP JENKINS

LA METTRIE, J. O. DE (1961). *Man a Machine*. La Salle. IL: Open Court.

LELY. G. (1970). *The Marquis de Sade: A Biography*. New York: Grove.

MAESTRO, M. T. (1942). *Voltaire and Beccaria as Reformers of Criminal Law*. New York: Columbia University Press.

MAESTRO, M. T. (1973). *Cesare Beccaria and the Origins of Penal Reform*. Philadelphia: Temple University Press.

MANZONI, A. (1964). *The Column of Infamy*. (Edited by A. P. d'Entrèves). Oxford University Press.

McDONALD, L. (1976). *The Sociology of Law and Order*. London: Faber.

MONACHESI, E. (1972). "Cesare Beccaria", pp.36–50 in H. Mannheim (ed.). *Pioneers in Criminology*. Montclair, N.J.: Patterson Smith.

MONTESQUIEU, C. L. DE S. DE (1966). *The Spirit of the Laws*. (Translated by Thomas Nugent). New York: Haffner.

MONTESQUIEU, C. L. DE S. DE (1973). *Persian Letters*. (Translated by C. J. Betts). London: Penguin Classics.

MOULEDOUX, J. (1972). "Edward Livingston", pp.69–83 in H. Mannheim. (ed.). *Pioneers in Criminology*. Montclair, N.J.: Patterson Smith.

NEWMAN, G. (1978). *The Punishment Response*. Philadelphia: J. B. Lippincott.

PHILIPPSON, C. (1970). *Three Criminal Law Reformers*. Montclair. N.J.: Patterson Smith.

PLATT. A. and TAKAGI, P. (1981). *Punishment and Penal Discipline*. Berkeley. Ca.: Crime and Social Justice.

RADZINOWICZ, L. (1966). *Ideology and Crime*. New York: Columbia University Press.

RADZINOWICZ, L. and KING, J. (1977). *The Growth of Crime*. London: Hamish Hamilton.

ROUSSEAU, J. J. (1967). *The Social Contract*, and *Discourse on the Origin of Inequality*. (Translated by L. G. Crocker). New York: Simon and Schuster.

RUDÉ, G. (1972). *Europe in the Eighteenth Century*. London: Weidenfeld and Nicolson.

RUSTIGAN, M. (1981). "Reinterpretation of Criminal Law Reform". pp.255–278 in D. F. Greenberg (ed.), *Crime and Capitalism*. Palo Alto. Ca.: Mayfield.

SMITH, D. W. (1965). *Helvetius. A Study in Persecution*. Oxford University Press.

TAKAGI, P. (1981). "The Walnut Street Jail", pp.279–291 in D. F. Greenberg (ed.), *Crime and Capitalism*. Palo Alto. Ca.: Mayfield.

TAYLOR, I. *et al.* (1973). *The New Criminology*. London: Routledge and Kegan Paul.

VENTURI, F. (1971). *Utopia and Reform in the Enlightenment*. Cambridge University Press.

VOLD. G. (1979). *Theoretical Criminology*. (2nd ed.. by T. J. Bernard). Oxford University Press.

WEISSER, M. R. (1979). *Crime and Punishment in Early Modern Europe*. Atlantic Highfields, N.J.

WICKWAR, W. H. (1935). *Baron d'Holbach—A Prelude to the French Revolution*. New York: A. M. Kelley (reprint).

WILLS, G. (1978). *Inventing America*. New York: Random House.

WOODCOCK, G. (1963). *Anarchism*. London: Penguin.

Part II
The Rise of Positivist Criminology

[5]

Adolphe Quetelet and the Origins of Positivist Criminology[1]

Piers Beirne
University of Southern Maine

This article examines the largely unacknowledged contribution of Adolphe Quetelet (1796–1874) to the origins of positivist criminology. Quetelet's labors have previously tended to be misrepresented either as a political project that was an unmediated expression of state and class interests or as a discourse that anticipated the subsequent maturation of Lombrosianism and the Chicago school of ecology. It is suggested here, instead, that Quetelet's social mechanics of crime should properly be understood in terms of its emergence from some of the focal concerns of the domains of penality and the statistical movement which, during the Restoration, coincided in the issue of the regulation of the "dangerous classes." This coincidence informed Quetelet's ideas about the constancy of crime, criminal propensities, the causes of crime, the average man, and social regulation. This article tentatively concludes that Quetelet's multifaceted analysis of crime ultimately fostered a rigid binary opposition between normality and deviation and provided the epistemological core for the dominance of biologism, mental hereditarianism, and economism in positivist criminology.

> Society itself contains the germs of all the crimes committed. It is the social state, in some measure, that prepares these crimes, and the criminal is merely the instrument that executes them. [QUETELET 1835]

During the formative period of social science, Adolphe Quetelet was for half a century one of the most influential figures in Europe, though it is only in astronomy, in statistics, and in meteorology that his reputation as

[1] This paper profited greatly from the generosity of the Institute of Criminology at Cambridge University, which provided me with a visiting scholarship in summer 1985. For their encouragement and for their helpful criticism of an earlier version of this paper, I am indebted to Susan Corrente Beirne, David Garland, Guy Houchon, Alan Hunt, Peter Lehman, Rosy Miller, Sawyer Sylvester, Ian Taylor, and the anonymous reviewers for *AJS*. Unless otherwise indicated, all translations from the French are my own. Requests for reprints should be sent to Piers Beirne, Department of Sociology, University of Southern Maine, Portland, Maine 04103.

a pioneer and seminal thinker is securely beyond doubt. Quetelet's analysis of social organization was frequently pressed into service for a broad spectrum of political and ideological interests: about his *Sur l'homme* (*On Man*) of 1835, Marx wrote in the *New York Daily Tribune* that it was "an excellent and learned work" ([1853] 1956, p. 229), and, of the same book, Durkheim claimed in *Suicide* that its idea of the *homme moyen* (average man) embodied "a theory, moreover, which has remained the only systematic explanation [of] the remarkable regularity with which social phenomena repeat themselves during identical periods of time" ([1897] 1951, p. 300).[2] The historian of science George Sarton has recorded that *Sur l'homme* "was one of the greatest books of the nineteenth century" (1935, p. 4) and that "a great injustice is made when Comte is called the founder of sociology, for Quetelet has better claims to this title than he" (p. 14; see also Landau and Lazarsfeld 1968).

My concern here is not, though, with Quetelet's largely unheralded role in the founding of sociology as such. That unfinished task is larger and more ambitious than mine. In what follows, I restrict myself to outlining Quetelet's contribution to the origins of positivist criminology.[3] This contribution, also, has never properly been acknowledged. The principal biographies of Quetelet (Mailly 1875; Hankins 1908; Lottin [1912] 1969) were written nearly 100 years ago, and none of them has his criminology as its explicit focus. None of Quetelet's writings on crime was translated for the prestigious series of European works published between 1911 and 1918 under the auspices of the American Institute of Criminal Law and Criminology.[4] Neither Quetelet nor any other member of the Franco-Belgian school of criminology of the 1830s was represented in Mann-

[2] Douglas has even suggested that Durkheim's *Suicide* differed only in degree from the principles, methodology, and empirical findings of the moral statisticians and that Quetelet's *Sur l'homme* was "the most influential moral-statistical work of all . . . " (1967, p. 11; see also Giddens 1965, pp. 3–4).

[3] From the outset, let me admit that I do not wish to debate the putative existence of some genuine, correct description of "positivist" relative to the study of crime. This term is nowadays so frequently abused that it tends to be best understood as an epithet—a weapon—directed against those with whom one has political or epistemological disagreement. Positivism has several forms, each of which, according to its context and object, can be more or less appropriate as a method of inquiry. By "positivist criminology," I refer loosely to a discourse about crime that is predicated on the belief that there is a fundamental harmony between the methods of the natural and social sciences, a discourse that views its observational categories as theory independent and that requires a specific form of empirical inquiry in support of its argumentation. Such a description of positivism has its limitations, of course, but it has the singular merit of being the one to which Quetelet himself subscribed.

[4] The Modern Criminal Science Series included works by de Quiros, Gross, Lombroso, Saleilles, Ferri, Tarde, Bonger, Garofalo, and Aschaffenburg.

American Journal of Sociology

heim's (1972) *Pioneers in Criminology*, an important biographical collection that contains essays on lesser figures, such as Maconochie and de Marsangy. Taylor, Walton, and Young's (1973, p. 37) celebrated *The New Criminology* refers briefly to Quetelet but then only in terms of the unsubstantiated assertion that Quetelet and his colleague A. M. Guerry largely effected the transition in penology from free will to determinism (see also Radzinowicz 1966, pp. 29–37). In the most recent histories of criminological theory (e.g., Gibbons 1979; Jacoby 1979; Pelfrey 1980), no mention at all is made of Quetelet.

The sustained neglect of Quetelet's work on crime can in part be explained, somewhat ironically, by the thrust of the cursory recognition accorded him by American criminologists in the 1930s. At that time, two specific claims were made about his work. First, it was claimed (e.g., Lindesmith and Levin 1937, pp. 654–55; Sellin 1937) that Quetelet, rather than Lombroso, had been responsible for rescuing the study of crime from the mire of metaphysics and elevating it to the status of a science and, somewhat paradoxically, that the tradition established by Quetelet gave Lombroso's contemporaries both the standards and the evidence to criticize and reject atavistic ideas of the born criminal.[5] Second, it was claimed (e.g., Elmer 1933; and see Morris 1957, pp. 37–52) that Quetelet and Guerry were the founders, or perhaps the precursors, of the ecological school in crime. Both claims have some merit. It is true, for example, that the strongest critics of Lombrosianism, such as Tarde, Topinard, Manouvrier, and Lacassagne, marshaled their evidence against the idea of the born criminal with generalizations about the effects of the social environment on criminality. It is also true that, in some respects, Quetelet and Guerry anticipated the work of ecological theorists a century later. However, both claims tend to ignore the historical context and thus the originality of Quetelet's own analysis of crime. The effect of the first claim was to characterize Quetelet's intervention in criminology as merely pre-Lombrosian. The effect of the second claim was to make Quetelet's importance hinge on the success of the ecological movement that matured in Chicago in the 1930s, and of which, in fact, Guerry—rather than Quetelet—was usually identified as the precursor (see Shaw and McKay [1942], p. 5). Both claims, therefore, tend to render Quetelet's specific analysis of crime invisible or, at best, derivative.

My intention here, therefore, is chiefly to identify Quetelet's particular contribution to the rise of positivist criminology. This I do by (1) an

---

[5] The intellectual maturation of Lombroso's idea of the born criminal has been charted in great detail by Wolfgang (1972). An excellent account of the "medicalization of deviance" implicit in this idea, and also of the various oppositional currents to it (especially in France), is given by Nye (1984, pp. 97–131).

outline of the historical context of the genesis of Quetelet's *oeuvre*, namely, the conjunction of the apparent failure of French penal strategies and the expansion in the scope of the statistical movement to include empirical social research; (2) a summary of Quetelet's method of inquiry and of the structure and content of his criminology; and (3) an indication of the controversial reception of his writings. Finally, I offer a tentative assessment of Quetelet's place in the development of positivist criminology.

PENALITY AND THE MORAL STATISTICS OF CRIME

Before proceeding to any detailed exhumation of Quetelet's criminology, it is useful to place the genesis of his *oeuvre* in its proper historical context. The emergence of positivist criminology in early 19th-century France should initially be understood as an important effect of the transformation in penal strategies that occurred, rapidly in some spheres and gradually in others, between the middle of the 18th and the beginning of the 19th centuries. Before this transformation, there were the amorphous penal strategies of the ancien régime. These were dictated by a discourse couched in rhetoric about the free legal subject, the transgressions of whom were dealt with by the infliction of brutal physical punishment. The spectrum of the new penal strategies had at its center a network of carceral institutions inscribed with Enlightenment rationalism and the humanism of the philosophes. These institutions were devised as mechanisms of surveillance and were intended to act with the same monotonous precision on their individual subjects as the school, the barracks, and the monastery.[6] Their growing inventory included hospitals, asylums, workhouses (*dépôts de mendicité*), reformatories, houses of correction, and prisons.[7] Their "delinquent" and "pathological" inmates comprised

---

[6] In the Napoleonic era, these strategies operated in concert with a new criminal code (with additional categories of delinquency), a professional *gendarmerie*, a system of passport and identity cards, and an extensive network of paid informers and spies directed by the notorious Minister of Police, Fouché (Foucault 1979, p. 280; Stead 1983, pp. 47–48).

[7] The modern prison system was inaugurated by imperial decree in 1810. Although the socioeconomic characteristics of the prison population were not collected in any systematic way until the 1870s, it is safe to assume that, until at least the 1850s, 80% of prisoners were young, unmarried males from the skilled or unskilled working class (O'Brien 1982, pp. 54–61). Excluding military prisons (*bagnes*) and debtors' prisons, the Restoration established at least five categories of prison, each based on a complex classification of inmates (see O'Brien 1982, pp. 3–51; Petit 1984). Strategically, the prisons isolated delinquents from the law-abiding citizenry; the development of agricultural colonies, transportation, and the galleys carried this strategy to its logical extreme.

American Journal of Sociology

syphilitics, alcoholics, idiots and eccentrics, vagabonds, immigrants, libertines, prostitutes, and petty and professional criminals; their stated objective was moral rehabilitation through the deprivation of liberty. This project has been variously described as "the power of normalization" (Foucault 1979, p. 308), "the fabrication of a reliable person" (Treiber and Steinert 1980), and "the sequestration of unreason" (Doerner 1981, pp. 14–17).

Foucault (1980, pp. 47–49) has proposed, in passages uncharacteristically redolent of instrumentalism, that positivist criminology (of which Quetelet was to be the leading figure) emerged in France in the 1820s as a calculated response to the need for an official and comprehensive discourse that could justify these new strategies of penality. But this view assumes, a priori, an identity (or at least a complementarity) between the intentions of those, like Quetelet, who constructed such a discourse and the conscious objectives of French penal policy. Even if ultimately true, such an assumption does little to illuminate for us either the specific content of this discourse or the theoretical and conceptual maneuvers that were to characterize this period of its adolescence. While it emerged from the state and as a state practice, criminology was not an unmediated expression of state or class interests. Against Foucault, it can be said that positivist criminology emerged from the intersection of two hitherto unrelated domains of state activity. From the domain of penality, criminology secured an institutional position, a measure of financial support, and considerable popular interest in its pronouncements. From the domain of the statistical movement, criminology acquired its intellectual orientation and recognition by the scientific community of its major discursive techniques. The many sites of each of these two domains were almost entirely separate until, during the Restoration (1814–30), they coincided in a common issue. This issue was the apparent failure to normalize the conduct of the "dangerous classes."[8]

That the new penal strategies had significantly failed to do so was apparent in three ways. First, it was implicit in the very existence of a large group of poor, semiproletarian thieves (*les misérables*)—a separate nation within the French nation—whose continued presence among them represented a fearful affront to the sensibilities of the law-abiding citizenry. Frégier (1840; see also Chevalier 1973, p. 448) estimated that the sole means of support for 30,000 Parisians was robbery; Balzac's *Code*

[8] The "dangerous classes" (*classes dangereuses*) was a term that first appeared during the Restoration, although it was not popularized until Frégier's (1840) classic study of urban criminality. Tombs (1980) provides a good account of the stock moral categories on which the term was constructed and of the ways in which it was often invoked to justify military repression.

des gens honnêtes recorded that there were 20,000 professional criminals and as many as 120,000 "rogues" in Restoration Paris. To a certain extent, the social visibility of the dangerous classes was an intractable effect of the new demographic composition of Restoration France. This was most obvious in urban areas such as Paris. Despite a doubling of its population in the half century after 1800, Paris remained structurally intact. It is not difficult to imagine how quickly this immense population increase, in so relatively short a period, led to a far-reaching social deterioration, which was manifest in the incidence of infant mortality and problems of sanitation and sewage, accommodation, food supplies, employment, public order, and crime. According to Chevalier, the sudden change in Paris's population was such that the city's inability to adapt itself to its new composition relegated a large part of the working class "to the furthest confines of the economy, of society and almost of existence itself, in material, moral and, basically, biological circumstances conducive to crime, of which crime itself was a possible consequence" (1973, p. 258).

The new prominence of crime in the description of urban life in France can be attributed to the fear of the criminality of the dangerous classes that endured at all levels of French society throughout the 19th century. Chevalier (1973) depicts Restoration Paris as a city in which the citizenry were engrossed in reports of crime as one of their normal daily worries; during certain cold winters of destitution, the fear of crime turned to panic and terror. Reports of crime were ubiquitously conveyed in newspapers and eagerly devoured by readers; in some cases, such as in the sensational accounts of the police informer (and ex-thief) Vidocq and the poet-bandit Lacenaire, fear was transformed into morbid fascination. Hugo's *Les Misérables* was a brilliant and typical literary example of the fearful attitude toward crime in general; other authors, such as Balzac, depicted the fear of specific forms of crime, such as theft by domestic servants. Popular melodramas about crime were regularly staged in the Boulevard du Temple. This widespread fear of crime was itself exacerbated by working-class insurrections, and, as Tombs (1980, p. 214) has suggested, it quickly became an unquestioned tenet of middle-class thought that crime and revolution were symptoms of the same disease.[9]

In the public concern with crime, the centrality of the dangerous classes was fixed by two further facts. First, in 1815 and for several years thereafter, a sudden increase was recorded in the rate of felony offenses. This increase occurred primarily in theft and disturbances of public order

---

[9] In turn, this assumption led to extreme harshness on the part of juries—whose composition in the 19th century was thoroughly bourgeois in origin—toward those accused of ordinary property crimes (see Donovan 1981).

American Journal of Sociology

(Wright 1983, pp. 48–50; Duesterberg 1979, pp. 29–31); between 1813 and 1820 alone, the number of convictions in the criminal tribunals nearly doubled.[10] A second and even more decisive factor was the increasing rates of recidivism; these implied that the stated rehabilitative object of the carceral institutions had failed. It is difficult to know what degree of accuracy can be attributed to the figures of recidivism before 1835, but the publicity about them was rampant, and they generated much indignation. Indeed, about the recidivism rate in the mid 1820s, the statistical organ of the Ministry of Justice later stressed that "[it was] without contradiction the most important part of the *Compte* because it reveals the inefficacy of repression and the inadequacy of punishment" (*Compte général* 1882, p. 83). According to other contemporary accounts, the rate of recidivism between 1828 and 1834 was 21% or more of those convicted of crimes during this time; before 1831, 38% of those who had left the *maisons centrales* were convicted again, as were 33% of those sentenced to convict ships (Foucault 1979, p. 265; Duesterberg 1979, p. 89). During the July Monarchy (1830–48), the recidivism rates were as high as 45% (Wright 1983, p. 50).

That the carceral institutions had failed to normalize the dangerous classes was therefore confirmed, at least for a fearful and fascinated public, by the rising rates of crime and recidivism during the first years of the Restoration. "In 1820 it was already understood," writes Foucault, "that the prisons, far from transforming criminals into citizens, serve only to manufacture new criminals and drive existing criminals ever deeper into criminality" (1980, p. 40). This failure was the essential condition for the appearance of a vast corpus of studies, instigated both by state bureaus and by private researchers, that sought to uncover the vital statistics of the dangerous classes.[11] It had been understood since the 16th

[10] These increases in recorded criminality can be explained in part by the turbulent transition to peace after Napoleon's final military defeat in 1815. During the 1820s, the *Compte général* recorded a decrease in the crime rate, and this official record is generally supported by Lodhi and Tilly (1973) and Tilly, Tilly, and Tilly (1975). However, Zehr (1976) has more persuasively argued that the declining official rate was deceptive because of the increasing tendency of prosecutors not to follow through on reports of crime and for property crimes to be tried in lower courts as misdemeanors—trends later identified and condemned by Tarde (1886, pp. 61–121). Combining data from correctional and assize courts, Zehr (1976, pp. 34–43, 146 n. 11) reveals a significant increase in all indices of property crime except arson.

[11] Among the vital conditions of the population now subject to regular state scrutiny were mortality, age, occupation, disease, and indigence. At the suggestion of the *administration préfectorale* of the Seine, supported by the Ministry of the Interior and administered by Fourier, the dissemination of these data was institutionalized in 1821 in the *Recherches statistiques de la ville de Paris*. On the "opening up" of the statistical movement during the Restoration, see Fauré (1918, pp. 289–91), Chevalier (1973, pp. 29–69), and Porter (1985).

century that the surveillance and exposure of criminals could be served by enumeration, but it was not until this precise juncture that the application of numerical analysis to penality achieved the status of an accepted science whose object was the structured order of observable facts: "Facts, based upon direct observation and preferably expressed numerically, would decide all questions" (Coleman 1982, p. 123).[12] Statistical inquiry into the dangerous classes began with the circumscribed population of prisoners. Several quasi-governmental, philanthropic, and religious organizations began to investigate prison conditions with the intention of rejuvenating the moral health of the prisoners. In 1819, for example, the *Société royale pour l'amélioration des prisons* reported on such items as the quality of prison construction, diet, clothing, bedding, and infirmaries. The factual information provided by these organizations was supplemented by the inquiries of independent investigators from the public health (*hygiène publique*) movement, the leading figures of which included de Chateauneuf, Parent-Duchâtelet, and Villermé. In 1820, Villermé's *Des prisons*, for example, pointed to the statistical links between gruesome prison conditions, moral degradation, and recidivism; incarceration itself, in other words, was now thought to increase the size of that section of the dangerous classes that was continually shuttled between civil society and prison.

In most of the inquiries into prison conditions, one question was invariably present: "Should (or could) the prisoners be returned to society and, if so, how?" (Petit 1984, p. 137). The resolution of this question could not be obtained, it was soon realized, with information derived exclusively from the facts about prison conditions. From a narrow focus on the prison population, then, the inquiry soon broadened to consider the larger population that passed through successive layers of the administration of justice. Within this broader inquiry the most important development occurred in 1825, the year that the Ministry of Justice initiated the first national statistical tables on crime, the annual *Compte général de l'administration de la justice criminelle en France*. The *Compte* was first published in 1827 under the efficient direction of Guerry de Champneuf (director of criminal affairs) and Arondeau (department head in the

---

[12] Prior to the Restoration, the nascent statistical movement had been discredited because of its use as a naked instrument of political surveillance, especially between the Reign of Terror and the end of the empire. According to Chevalier (1973, p. 49), the census and similar state projects were commonly regarded as thinly veiled attempts by the police to identify suspects; the very announcement of a census unleashed a wave of denunciations. On the professional and institutional setbacks of the statistical movement prior to the Restoration, see Westergaard (1932, pp. 114–16) and Perrot and Woolf (1984); on its insulation from mathematical theory until the Restoration, see Porter (1985).

American Journal of Sociology

Ministry of Justice), immediately after a winter in which the rates of crime and death increased equally and during which public fear and terror throughout Paris were the main themes of police reports and newspaper articles (Chevalier 1973, p. 3). The *Compte* was drawn up from quarterly returns prepared by public prosecutors in every *département*. These were itemized, uniformly printed, and checked for accuracy by the chief administrator of criminal prosecutors in Paris. The tables in the *Compte* were divided into four parts: the first included all prosecutions in the assize courts; the second, the verdicts of correctional tribunals; the third, the verdicts of the tribunals of the police courts; and the fourth, statistical information about the criminal process from other jurisdictions such as the royal courts. For each *département*, the *Compte* measured the annual number of known and prosecuted crimes against persons and property, whether the accused (if prosecuted) were acquitted or convicted as well as the punishment accorded the latter; additionally, it began to record the time of year when these offenses were committed and the age, sex, occupation, and educational status of both accused and convicted. Information about repeat offenders became more and more detailed with each successive year of publication, and new tables were constantly added on the correlations between the nature of offenses and the characteristics of the accused.[13]

Both the Ministry of Justice and a group of social statisticians believed that the data, or "facts," in these tables could one day be used to perfect legislation in civil and moral matters. In his introduction to the first volume of the *Compte*, Minister of Justice Comte de Peyronnet declared that "the exact knowledge of facts is one of the first needs of our form of government; it enlightens deliberations; it simplifies them; it gives them a solid foundation by substituting the positive vision and reliability of experience for the vagueness of theories" (*Compte* 1827, p. x). The dissemination of the *Compte* was quickly followed by the labors of a loosely knit, somewhat amateur movement of moral statisticians, which included the Parisian lawyer and social cartographer A. M. Guerry; the statisticians Villermé, d'Angeville, and d'Ivernois; the Italian geographer Balbi; and the young Belgian astronomer Quetelet. It is to Quetelet's immersion in this movement that I now turn.[14]

[13] The various deposits into and the infrequent withdrawals from the *Compte* between 1827 and the 1880s are chronicled by Perrot (1975, pp. 70–81).

[14] The reader should be made aware that, in the following account of Quetelet's criminology, virtually no reference will be made to any of his writings after 1848, including his widely acclaimed *Physique sociale* (1869). Despite Quetelet's continued propensity to publish, his work after 1848 contains no departures from his earlier analyses of crime; indeed, as Quetelet himself later recorded, "In publishing the first edition of my *Physique sociale*, in 1834 and 1835, I believed it necessary to give a

QUETELET AND THE SOCIAL MECHANICS OF CRIME

At the age of 23, Quetelet received a doctorate in science from the new University of Ghent. His 1819 dissertation, written under the guidance of Jean Garnier, a noted professor of astronomy and higher mathematics, was an important and widely acclaimed contribution to the theory of conic sections. One of Garnier's colleagues went so far as to compare Quetelet's discovery of a new curve with Pascal's discovery of a cycloid (Hankins 1908, p. 455). Later in the same year, Quetelet was appointed to a chair in mathematics at the Brussels Athenaeum. In quick succession, he was, in 1820, elected to and at once revived the moribund Royal Academy of Sciences in Brussels, served as editor, with Garnier, of the influential *Correspondance mathématique et physique*, and helped to create the liberal (and soon-to-be suppressed) *Société Belge pour la propagation de l'instruction et de la morale*. Quetelet's *Traité populaire d'astronomie*, falsely rumored to have been placed on the Catholic *Index Librorum Prohibitorum*, contributed to the spread throughout Europe of popular education in astronomy.

Social Mechanics and the Average Man

These early achievements of the young Quetelet in astronomy and mathematics served as intellectual preparation for his seminal contribution to the new discourse of social mechanics (*mécanique sociale*). The opportunity for this was provided by the Royal Academy, which, in 1823, sent him to Paris to study astronomical apparatuses with a view—vague and often postponed—toward erecting an observatory in Brussels.[15] It was

---

special place to criminal statistics. I have found, to a striking degree, the most conspicuous proof of the confirmation of my ideas about the size and the constancy of social regularities. . . . Today I do not think that I have to change any of my conclusions" (1869, p. 269). Hankins has noted that, after Quetelet suffered a stroke in 1855, his writings "needed the most thorough revision. . . . His books published after 1855, in so far as [they are] new in composition, are full of ambiguous or unintelligible phrases, ill-arranged and very repetitious" (1908, pp. 473–74). Actually, repetitiousness had set in well before the date marked by Hankins; for example, except for the addition of some paragraphs on suicides and dueling, Quetelet's (1842) *Treatise on Man* merely repeats the content of *Research on the Propensity for Crime at Different Ages* ([1831a] 1984). Moreover, the sections on crime in *Physique sociale* (1869) only reiterate work published three decades earlier ([1831a] 1984, 1835); the title was but a reversal of the title and subtitle of *Sur l'homme* (1835), and even the introduction to *Physique sociale*, by the English astronomer Sir John Herschel, had previously appeared in the *Edinburgh Review* in 1850.

[15] This was a difficult period for emigré Belgian intellectuals, marked as it was by the effective submission of Belgium to Franco-Dutch rule and the cultural dominance of the French intelligentsia. Quetelet's interest in social mechanics was probably

American Journal of Sociology

during his months in Paris on this mission that Quetelet was first introduced by the astronomers Bouvard and Humboldt to various currents
in the statistical movement (see Quetelet 1871). From the German administrative *Statistik*, from the French social reformism of Condorcet and
Turgot (among others), and from the English political "state-istics" of
Graunt and Petty, he learned of the general potential for the application
of enumeration to social matter (*matière sociale*). From Malthus's *Essay
on Population*, Villermé's *Des prisons*, Fourier's statistical research on
Paris and its environs in the early 1820s, and, above all, from the work
of his friend and mentor, Laplace, on celestial mechanics (*mécanique
celeste*), on the principles of probabilistic theory, and on the method of
least squares, Quetelet learned how to apply algebra and geometry to
demographic tables.[16] On his return to Belgium from Paris in 1824,
Quetelet engaged in a variety of projects. His first statistical work (1826)
utilized Belgian birth and mortality tables as the basis for the construction of insurance rates. Soon thereafter, he published studies in physics,
astronomy, and mathematics, furnished a commentary on Dutch demographic policies, and submitted plans in Belgium for a national census
and the collection of crime statistics.

In these early works, Quetelet attempted to reveal that the same lawlike, mechanical regularity that had been determined to exist in the heav-
ens and in the world of nature also existed in the world of social facts
(*faits sociaux*). "In following attentively the regular march of nature in
the development of plants and animals," Quetelet reasoned, "we are
compelled to believe in the analogue that the influence of laws should be
extended to the human species" (1826, p. 495). The identification of such
laws in the social world was dependent on statistical calculation: "We can
assess how perfected a science has become by how much or how little it is

---

intensified by the Belgian nationalist movement, but there is no compelling evidence
that he was active in either Belgian or French politics. However, he frequently commented on the professional hardships for himself and for his many protegés brought on
by the 1830 revolution (see Porter 1985, p. 58).

[16] It is very tempting to suggest that the general direction for social-scientific analysis
had been gleaned by Quetelet from writers such as Saint-Simon and the young Comte.
But no references to either appeared in any of his early works. The absence of Comte is
especially puzzling, and, although Lottin (1912, pp. 356–67) correctly points to the
fundamental differences between them, it is difficult to believe that Quetelet had not
been influenced by works such as Comte's *Plan des travaux scientifiques nécessaires
pour réorganiser la société* (1822). Possibly under Fourier's guidance, Quetelet adopted
Comte's term *physique sociale* as the subtitle of his *Sur l'homme* (1835). Later, in his
Cours de philosophie positive, Comte protested the usurpation of the discipline of
social physics by "a Belgian scholar who has adopted it, in recent years, as the title of a
work whose concern is merely simple statistics" (1838, p. 15). Thus did Quetelet force
Comte to invent the neologism "sociology."

based on calculation" (Quetelet 1828, p. 230). This ambitious project Quetelet termed social mechanics (later, in 1835, social physics), and he identified not inexactitude in method but insufficiency of empirical data as the chief obstacle to its realization. Human forces were notoriously susceptible to the influence of "secular perturbations"; only a very large number of empirical observations could reduce the perturbing effect of variation in a particular datum and thereby disclose the aggregate nature of social regularities.

At first, Quetelet sought these regularities in relatively uncomplicated data that were subject to predictable variation and that could be observed directly: mortality rates, the heights of 100,000 French army conscripts, and the chest measurements of 5,738 Scottish soldiers. From his observations, Quetelet (1826, 1829; see also [1831a] 1984, pp. 3–11; 1831b; 1842, pp. 57–72) calculated the average weight and height of his subjects, cross-tabulated these with sex, age, occupation, and geographical region, and then submitted these correlations to the perturbational influence of such factors as "the difficulties, toils and privations experienced in infancy, youth and infirmity." The average value of any given scale was thought by Quetelet to be more accurate, the greater the number of empirical observations. In combination, these average values produced an image of a fictitious, statistically derived creature whom Quetelet termed the average man. "If the *average* man were ascertained for one nation, he would present the type of that nation. If he could be ascertained according to the mass of men, he would present the type of the human species altogether" ([1831a] 1984, p. 3). The average man therefore occupied a place among all men that Quetelet envisaged as analogous to the center of gravity in matter. His calculation of physical averages was undertaken as preparation for the extension of social mechanics to the vital phenomena of moral statistics, namely, to suicide, marriage, and crime.[17]

The Constancy of Crime

Quetelet claimed that the enumeration of the vital phenomena of moral statistics was more complex than the measurement of nonvital, physical

[17] According to Durkheim (1897, p. 300 n. 1), the founder of moral statistics was Pastor Süssmilch. Among the Franco-Belgian statisticians, it was most likely Guerry who first applied the term to the phenomena of crime. Contra Lottin (1912, p. 37), Quetelet first explicitly applied it to his own work in 1842 (1842, pp. 79–80); here, he urged that moral statistics be expanded to include witchcraft practices, torture, and execution for religious reasons, as well as political and religious fanaticism of various sorts. To these items, Quetelet (1869, pp. 232–368) later added intellectual faculties, mental illness (*aliénation*), alcoholism, dueling, and accidental death.

items. Vital phenomena were more complex not only in their individual identities and therefore in their comparability but also, and more important, because they emanated from "certain forces which [man] has at his command from his free will" (Quetelet [1831a] 1984, p. 3). Because human action is volitional behavior, Quetelet suggested that it is reasonable to suppose that the volume of crime would vary from one year to another according to human caprice. This would especially seem to be true of unpremeditated crimes—murders, for example, committed in a quarrel or in fortuitous circumstances. However, Quetelet immediately warns that to argue that the human species is not subject to laws "would be more offensive to the divinity than the very research which we intend to do" ([1831a] 1984, p. 5).

This metaphysical assertion was first elaborated by Quetelet in his *mémoire, Research on the Propensity for Crime at Different Ages* ([1831a] 1984). While being careful to point out that social mechanics can never pretend to discover laws that can be verified for isolated individuals, he states that—when observed indirectly on a great scale through the prism of statistical artifacts such as the *Compte*—the phenomena of crime nevertheless resemble the patterned behavior of physical phenomena.[18] This insight, as we shall see, was to cause Quetelet's contemporaries considerable discomfort. Indeed, Quetelet himself warned that "this way of looking at the social system has something positive about it which must, at first, frighten certain minds. Some will see in it a tendency to materialism. Others, in interpreting my ideas badly, will find there an exaggerated pretention to aggrandize the domain of the exact sciences and to place the geometrician in an element which is not his own. They will reproach me for becoming involved in absurd speculations while being occupied with things which are not susceptible to being measured" ([1831a] 1984, p. 4). Quetelet's understanding of the data in the *Compte* reveals considerable sophistication for his era. Following de Candolle's (1830) short treatise on criminal statistics, Quetelet argues that any

---

[18] Quetelet was the first moral statistician to suggest this resemblance, although his priority was disputed by A. M. Guerry. There was considerable personal animosity between Quetelet and Guerry, an example of which appears at the end of the third book of *A Treatise on Man*, which was directed against Guerry's *Essai sur la statistique morale de la France* (1833). Here, Quetelet writes about his discovery of the constancy of crime: "As this idea has continually presented itself to me in all my researches on man, and, as I have exactly expressed it in the same terms as those of the text, in my conclusions on the *Recherches sur le penchant au crime*, a work that appeared a year before that of A. M. Guerry, I have thought it necessary to mention the point here, to prevent misunderstanding" (1842, p. 96). See also Quetelet's (1842, p. 79) unnecessary comment that Guerry paid insufficient attention to documentary sources.

scientific analysis of crime must assume *"a relationship pretty nearly invariable between offenses known and judged and the unknown sum total of offenses committed"* ([1831a] 1984, p. 17). The size of this relationship, he suggested, would depend on the seriousness of offenses and on "the activity of justice in reaching the guilty, on the care which these latter will take in hiding themselves, and on the repugnance which wronged individuals will feel in complaining, or on the ignorance in which they perhaps will be concerning the wrong which has been done to them" (Quetelet [1831a] 1984, p. 18). Quetelet argued that, if the causes that influence this relationship remain the same, then their representation in official statistics would remain constant; in a later study in Belgium, Quetelet ([1848a] 1984, pp. 19–20; see also Houchon 1976, p. 25) found a constant relationship between crimes known and crimes subject to judicial prosecution between 1833 and 1839. That the ratio of unknown crimes to recorded crimes was, in practice, constant Quetelet inferred from the astonishing regularity in the crime rates between 1826 and 1829 (see table 1).

In addition to the constancy in the annual number of accused and convicted and in the ratios of accused to convicted, of accused to inhabitants, and of crime against persons to crimes against property, Quetelet also points to regularities in the number of accused who failed to appear in the tribunals, in the number of convictions in different types of tribunals, and in the number of convicts sentenced to death, confinement, or forced labor for a term. Even the different methods of murder were shown to be constant from one year to another. He therefore concludes that

> one passes from one year to the other with the sad perspective of seeing the same crimes reproduced in the same order and bringing with them the same penalties in the same proportions. Sad condition of the human species! The share of prisons, chains, and the scaffold appears fixed with as much probability as the revenues of the state. We are able to enumerate in advance how many individuals will stain their hands with the blood of their fellow creatures, how many will be forgers, how many poisoners, pretty nearly as one can enumerate in advance the births and deaths which must take place. [Quetelet (1831a) 1984, p. 69]

Criminal Propensities and the Causes of Crime

The apparent constancy of crime rates recorded in the *Compte* suggested to Quetelet that, whatever the idiosyncrasies of human agency, criminal behavior obeyed laws of the same order as those that regulate the motion of inanimate objects. The disproportionate and relentless presence of certain categories in the *Compte* between 1826 and 1829 also indicated to Quetelet that young males, the poor, the less educated, and those without

TABLE 1

THE CONSTANCY OF CRIME, 1826–1829

| YEAR | ACCUSED (TRIED) | CONVICTED | INHABITANTS FOR ONE ACCUSED | CONVICTED FROM 100 ACCUSED | ACCUSED OF CRIMES | | RELATIONSHIP BETWEEN THE N OF TYPES OF ACCUSED |
					Against Persons	Against Property	
1826	6,988	4,348	4,557	62	1,907	5,081	2.7
1827	6,929	4,236	4,593	61	1,911	5,018	2.6
1828	7,396	4,551	4,307	61	1,844	5,552	3.0
1829	7,373	4,475	4,321	61	1,791	5,582	3.1
Totals	28,686	17,610	4,463	61	7,453	21,233	2.8

SOURCE. – Quetelet ([1831a] 1984, p. 20), abridged.

employment or in lowly occupations had a greater propensity (*penchant*) than others to commit crimes and to be convicted of them.[19] These data seemed to enable Quetelet to take issue with several conventional accounts of the factors that precipitated crime. In particular, he adduced that neither the presence of poverty nor the absence of formal education warranted the monolithic causal importance commonly claimed for them. Against those who asserted the inevitable association of poverty with crime, Quetelet ([1831*a*] 1984, pp. 37–38; 1842, p. 89) pointed out that some of the poorest areas in France (e.g., Creuse) and in the Low Countries (e.g., Luxembourg) had among the lowest crime rates; both areas also had among the highest rates of illiteracy. Far more influential a factor than absolute poverty was the perturbing effect of inequality in wealth. Where great riches are amassed by a few, when an economy suddenly fluctuates, and when thousands of individuals pass rapidly from well-being to misery, "These are the rough alternations from one state to another that give birth to crime, especially if those who suffer from them are surrounded by subjects of temptation and find themselves irritated by the continual view of luxury and of an inequality of fortune which disheartens them" (Quetelet [1831*a*] 1984, p. 38). Moreover, against those who argued that the growth of public education weakened criminal propensities, Quetelet disclosed that those with higher "intellectual states" tended to commit crimes of a relatively more violent nature, such as rape and murder. It was thus an error to suppose that a country would have fewer crimes simply because more children are sent to school there or because more of the population is literate; the departments with the lowest literacy rates, for example, tended to have only average crime rates. However, to those who inferred from this that public education was potentially harmful to society (see Porter 1985, p. 55), Quetelet pointed out that, among the educated, the most educated did not commit relatively more crimes. It was not, therefore, education as such that altered the propensity to crime but the type of education and the presence or absence of "moral instruction" (Quetelet [1831*a*] 1984, p. 37).

For Quetelet, the data in the *Compte* implied that the two factors most prominently associated with criminal propensities were age and sex. In table 2, he tabulated crimes according to the ages of their perpetrators

---

[19] It is important to note that Quetelet's inferences about criminal propensities were drawn exclusively from the data in the *Compte* or, as criminologists from Goring (1913) onward would say, from a single-cell design. While Quetelet (e.g., [1831*a*] 1984, pp. 53, 58) was aware of the need to compare the social characteristics of the population in the *Compte* with those of the general population, it was a comparison he never made. Moreover, Quetelet's representation of the obstacles to such a comparison—and of its significance could it be made—was consistently confined to a methodological rather than a theoretical realm.

American Journal of Sociology

TABLE 2

AGE AND THE PROPENSITY FOR CRIME, 1826–1829

Age	Crimes against		Crimes against Property out of 100 Crimes	Population according to Ages	Degrees of the Propensity for Crime
	Persons	Property			
Under 16	80	440	85	3,304	161
16–21	904	3,723	80	887	5,217
21–25	1,278	3,329	72	673	6,846
25–30	1,575	3,702	70	791	6,671
30–35	1,153	2,883	71	732	5,514
35–40	650	2,076	76	672	4,057
40–45	575	1,724	75	612	3,757
45–50	445	1,275	74	549	3,133
50–55	288	811	74	482	2,280
55–60	168	500	75	410	1,629
60–65	157	385	71	330	1,642
65–70	91	184	70	247	1,113
70–80	64	137	68	255	788
80 and over	5	14	74	55	345

SOURCE.—Quetelet ([1831a] 1984, p. 56).

and divided the number of crimes by the population in the respective age groups. Results show the propensity for committing crime at various ages. This propensity is at its weakest at both extremes of life—in infancy, neither strength nor passion ("those two powerful instruments of crime") is at all developed, and, in old age, their intensity is restricted by the "dictates of reason." The propensity for crime is at its strongest between the ages of 21 and 25—when strength and passions are most intense, and when reason is insufficiently developed to restrain their combined influence. Quetelet perceives a cyclical pattern in his age-specific "steps in the career of crime" between infancy and old age: physical immaturity allows only for crimes such as indecent assault and rape in which the victim offers little resistance; the age of dispassionate reflection seeks more organized crimes such as thefts on the public highways, murder by poisoning, and acts of rebellion; finally, using the little strength that nature has left him, the elderly criminal uses a depraved treachery "to strike his enemy in the shadow" through crimes such as forgery and child molestation.

Quetelet notes (see table 3) that, between 1826 and 1829, there were 23 women for every 100 men who appeared before criminal tribunals. He

TABLE 3

SEX AND THE PROPENSITY FOR CRIME, 1826–1829

	CRIMES AGAINST PERSONS			CRIMES AGAINST PROPERTY		
YEAR	Men	Women	Relationship	Men	Women	Relationship
1826	1,639	268	.16	4,073	1,008	.25
1827	1,637	274	.17	4,020	998	.25
1828	1,576	270	.17	4,396	1,156	.26
1829	1,552	239	.15	4,379	1,203	.27
Average ...	1,601	263	.16	4,217	1,091	.26

SOURCE.—Quetelet ([1831a] 1984, p. 47).

suggests that one could therefore suppose that male criminal propensities were roughly four times greater than those of women. But these propensities do not inform us, Quetelet warns, about the differing seriousness of the crimes committed by each sex. Quetelet therefore notes that the ratio of women to men accused of property crimes was 26:100 but, for crimes against persons, was only 16:100. Assuming the latter to be more serious than crimes against property, Quetelet concludes that French men were at least four times more "criminal" than French women. In trying to explain the difference in criminality between French men and women, he argued that the commission of any crime requires the bringing together of a will (which depends on morality), an opportunity, and the ability to act. Quetelet posited the will of women as more motivated by the sentiments of shame and modesty than that of men. Such an understanding of will would explain not only women's lower propensity to crime in general but also their higher indulgence in infanticide. "As to infanticide, not only does a woman have more opportunities to commit it than a man, but she is in some ways often pushed into it by hardship and almost always by the desire to hide a mistake and escape the shame and contempt of society, which spares the man more in similar circumstances" (Quetelet [1831a] 1984, p. 49). Moreover, women have less opportunity to commit crime because they lead more retiring, less passionate lives and are less often excited by alcohol; their lesser ability to act derives from their lesser strength in comparison with that of men and is reflected, for example, in their differential rate of parricide.[20]

---

[20] Women's lack of visibility in the *Compte* was a reflection of the lenient attitude toward them in the courts throughout the 19th century; women were more often successfully able to plead mitigating circumstances and were rarely sentenced to death. On the difficult explanatory problems that such leniency raises, see Perrot (1975).

American Journal of Sociology

In his first studies of crime, Quetelet was cautious in drawing specific causal inferences from the regularities manifest in the *Compte* because, he lamented, "The causes which influence crime are so enormous and so diverse, that it becomes almost impossible to assign to each its degree of importance" (Quetelet [1831a] 1984, p. 37). Nevertheless, against those who employed eclectic ideas of causality, Quetelet suggested that the many causes of crime can be divided into three principal categories (1846, pp. 157–256). First, there are accidental causes, to which no probability can be assigned and which are manifested fortuitously and are indifferent in their direction. Examples of these include wars, famines, and natural disasters. Quetelet understands their influence within a teleological schema and confines it to "the order of succession of events." Second, there are variable causes, such as free will and personality, that can oscillate between greater or smaller limits. These causes act in a continuous manner, although some variable causes such as climate and the seasons operate only periodically. The intensity and direction of variable causes change as a result of either determined laws or their absence. Finally, there are constant causes, such as age, sex, occupation, and religion. These causes have a fixed probability and act in a continuous manner with the same intensity and in the same direction; evidence for the predominance of this third causal category was adduced by Quetelet from the constancy of crime rates. Quetelet's insertion of criminal behavior into a formal structure of causality was a remarkable advance over the ad hoc, eclectic speculations of his contemporaries. Even more significant, within this formal structure, is the shift of his analysis to a different level, which allows him to claim that, because crime is a constant, inevitable feature of social organization, it was society, France, or the nation itself that caused crime. Thus, "Every social state presupposes, then, a certain number and a certain order of crimes, these being merely the necessary consequences of its organization" (Quetelet 1842, p. 6). Again, "The crimes which are annually committed seem to be a necessary result of our social organization. . . . *Society prepares crime, and the guilty are only the instruments by which it is executed*" (p. 108). Logic aside and with the considerable advantages of hindsight, it can perhaps be argued that Quetelet's intuition that society caused crime marked a profound theoretical departure from the crude realism of public opinion, classical jurisprudence, and the criminal code and flew in the face of the idea that criminals freely chose to engage in wickedness. But, because Quetelet's concept of social organization was based on the idea of society as an aggregate of individuals, his projections about the causal nexus between social organization and crime and of the way in which propensities to crime were translated into criminal actions remained thoroughly conventional. To understand this aspect of his work, we must return to his idea of the average man and the way in which, especially during the 1840s, this concept infiltrated his discourse on criminality.

The Average Man and Social Regulation

In his work of the 1820s and early 1830s, as we have seen, Quetelet determined the average values of the human physique and correlated these with such variables as age and sex, with the result being a description of the bodily characteristics of the average man in a given population. In the early 1840s, especially after he became acquainted with the probabilistic error function in celestial mechanics, Quetelet insisted on the need to present not only the mean of a scale of given characteristics but also the upper and lower limits between which individuals oscillated. Minor or "natural" variation around the mean was then identified by Quetelet as deviation that should attract no unusual attention; extraordinary variation (e.g., the height of giants and dwarfs) he saw as "preternatural . . . monstrous" (1842, p. x). In addition, Quetelet perceived that variation around the mean occurred not randomly but in a determinate order that approximated the principle of the normal distribution in celestial mechanics (1846, p. 114; 1848b, p. ix). This principle, he now surmised, was also applicable to the distribution of all the nonphysical qualities of man.

Quetelet's application of the principle of normal distribution to crime presaged a fundamental redirection of his criminology and led directly to his positing a rigid binary opposition between the statistical mean and "unusual" deviation. Although he inferred from the normal distribution that "every man, therefore, has a certain propensity to break the laws" (Quetelet 1848b, p. 94), it was also evident to him that the criminal propensities of the average man were rarely, if ever, translated into criminal actions. Accordingly, the dispositions of individuals with propensities at the mean were now imbued by Quetelet with the rhetoric of their conformity to law, medical and psychological health, and moral temperance. Quetelet's interpretation of the Aristotelian *differentia* of virtue in the *Nicomachean Ethics* and of Victor Cousin's (1829) *juste milieu* in his *Cours de l'histoire de la philosophie* persuaded him that the average man was one who regularly chose the mean course between the extremes of deficiency and excess. The virtues of the average man thus comprised "rational and temperate habits, more regulated passions, [and] foresight, as manifested by investment in savings banks, assurance societies and the different institutions which encourage foresight" (Quetelet 1842, p. 78). With the noncriminality of the average man. Quetelet frequently juxtaposed the criminality of vagabonds, vagrants, primitives, gypsies, the "inferior classes," certain races with "inferior moral stock," and "persons

American Journal of Sociology

of low moral character." With the virtues of the average man, he juxtaposed the vices of those deviants who engaged in crime. This latter juxtaposition repeatedly informs his work of the 1840s and is found, for example, in his contrast between "an industrious and prudent people [and] a depraved and indolent one" (Quetelet 1842, p. 41). The vices of those who deviated from the average included "the passions for gambling . . . failures . . . the frequenting of coffee houses and low haunts . . . drunkenness" (p. 78). In common with a widespread emphasis on the biological basis of demographic and social facts (Chevalier 1973, pp. 437–41), Quetelet yielded to the notion that unhealthy morality was manifest in biological defects and that those with such defects had high criminal propensities (1842, pp. vi–vii). Crime, he concluded, was "a pestilential germ . . . contagious . . . [sometimes] hereditary" (Quetelet 1848*b*, pp. 214–15).[21]

The practical outcome of Quetelet's criminology was the application of his binary opposition of normality and deviance to the domain of penality. With an insistence that became more urgent with the approach of the 1848 revolution, Quetelet demanded that governments identify the causes of crime in order to reduce the frequency of crime or, if possible, to eliminate crime altogether. "Since the number [of crimes] cannot diminish without the causes which induce them undergoing previous modification, it is the province of legislators to ascertain these causes, and to remove them as far as possible" (Quetelet 1842, p. 108). Because it appeared on the basis of this theory that the same amount of crime was regularly produced by the same causes, Quetelet was optimistic that secular disturbances such as crime could be reduced simply by reducing the intensity of their causes. While legislators could not hope to prevent all crime, there was, nevertheless, "an ensemble of laws, an enlightened administration and a social state such that the number of crimes can be reduced as much as possible" (Quetelet 1846, pp. 357–58).

According to Quetelet, because every government, like every physical body, is confronted by two types of force ("those that are attractive and

[21] This conclusion should be compared with Quetelet's seemingly innocuous statement, voiced much earlier, that "man carries at birth the germs of all the qualities which develop successively and in greater proportions" ([1831*a*] 1984, p. 14). The influence of Gall's and Spurzheim's phrenology on Quetelet here is unmistakable. Gall had been a resident of Paris since 1807, and it is fairly safe to assume that, perhaps through a common network of friends, he and Quetelet either knew each other or moved in the same intellectual circles. It must also be mentioned that Comte himself was one of the earliest members of the *Société phrénologique* and that it was in Gall's phrenology that he hoped to find a mediating principle for his sociology and biology (see also n. 16 above). A biological reading of Quetelet is supported by Durkheim's (1897, pp. 301–2) discussion in *Suicide* of the concept of the average man.

those that are repulsive"), wise statecraft consists in the pursuit of two policies toward crime. First, the state should initiate an appropriate reaction to combat and paralyze the recalcitrant minority with incorrigible criminal tendencies, and, Quetelet suggests, this reaction should involve adherence to the principles of the criminal code, the constant detection and prosecution of criminals, a uniformity in the decisions of juries and judges, and the maintenance of an appropriate relation between the gravity of an offense and the punishment awarded it (1846, pp. 356–57).[22] In addition, ameliorative reforms should be introduced so that "the elements of disorganization . . . those who provoke revolutions" (Quetelet 1848*b*, p. 295) would be prevented from destroying the very basis of the social system. Second, the state should participate in the inevitable progress of civilization by allowing the moral and intellectual qualities of the average man to flourish; to this end, a government should enact and enforce laws to reduce the effect of secular disturbances and to encourage an equilibrium in the social system. "The more do deviations from the average disappear . . . the more, consequently, do we tend to approach that which is beautiful, that which is good" (Quetelet 1842, p. 108).

QUETELET AND HIS CRITICS

According to the discursive standards of his era, Quetelet had demonstrated his mechanistic notions of the constancy of crime, its causes, and its regulation, as well as it was then possible to do. His insistence that crime was an inevitable feature of social organization and, moreover, almost a necessary consequence of it assured his work a widespread notoriety. As Sarton (1935, p. 4) has observed, no one could have carried scientific indiscretion further than by attempting, as did Quetelet, to analyze social transgressions as if they were physical accidents and to consider passions of the soul as if they were abnormalities of the weather. Given public opinion, which identified the criminality of the dangerous classes with working-class failures and rebellion, Quetelet's idea that

---

[22] Throughout his criminology it is unclear whether Quetelet's rather scanty advice on penality was based on the repressive strategies of the ancien régime or on the rehabilitative model of the prison favored in the postrevolutionary era. Despite Quetelet's professed allegiance to free will, a consistent belief in rehabilitation seems to have been precluded by his subscription to the deterministic views (of Villermé and others) that prison life necessarily exacerbated criminal propensities (e.g., Quetelet [1831*a*] 1984, p. 17 n. 6) and that criminality itself was hereditary. More than a decade after Quetelet's death, French criminologists and anthropologists tended to adopt the neo-Lamarckian "degeneracy" model of criminality rather than the Lombrosian "born criminal" type because, as Nye (1984, pp. 101–2, 119–21) has suggested, this position allowed belief in voluntarism and rehabilitation.

criminal propensities were distributed throughout the population was an affront to the moral sensibilities of the law-abiding citizenry. To a judiciary that couched legal responsibility and the application of punishment in the classical discourse about the free legal subject, Quetelet's ideas about the causality of crime amounted to a deterministic heresy, for, if crimes had social rather than individual causes, then perhaps criminals could not be held strictly accountable for their misdeeds.

However, in Quetelet's own lifetime, the recognition of his criminology as such was largely preempted by controversy about the nature of his general contribution to statistical analysis.[23] One facet of the controversy focused on the position that Quetelet was believed to have taken toward free will. In this debate, there was no middle ground between the determinists and the spiritualists, between those who adhered to Quetelet's perceived social determinism and those who preferred to discern a faint promise of social equilibrium through individual moral improvement. To the spiritualists, determinism in any form represented an ungodly opposition to the soul, to Christianity, and to free will. To the determinists, spiritualism was a metaphysical doctrine with roots in the untenable philosophies of German romanticism and naturalism. These competing positions resulted in a rather fruitless debate that continued until the end of the century (Lottin [1912] 1969, pp. 413–58).[24]

Quetelet himself was clearly perplexed by the accusation that his moral

---

[23] In France, Quetelet's criminology contributed to the growth of the empirical tradition represented by such important studies as Fregier's *Dangerous Classes* and Parent-Duchâtelet's *Prostitution in Paris*. The reception of his work outside Belgium and France was generally very favorable, especially in England. John Herschel, e.g., reviewed the broad span of Quetelet's endeavors and argued strongly that, while Quetelet's social mechanics was evidence that statistical progress in the social sciences was less advanced than in the natural sciences, nevertheless, no one had better exerted himself in the scientific collection and analysis of political, social, and moral data; Quetelet's advice on how to repress the violent and rapacious, Herschel continued, "deserves to be written in letters of gold" (1850, p. 37). Indeed, Quetelet's writings on crime continued to exert great influence on work as diverse in content and as separated in time as Henry Buckle's *History of Civilisation in England* (1860) and Charles Goring's celebrated *The English Convict* (1913).

[24] It could not have escaped the attention of the spiritualists that the implicit determinism of *Sur l'homme* had a certain appeal in the 1840s to radical writers such as Marx and Engels (who saw in this book a demonstration of the fundamental links between modern bourgeois society, immiserization, and the amount and sorts of crime). Besides the work of Quetelet and of those such as Marx and Engels, it was only in the workers' newspapers, such as *L'Humanitaire, La Fraternité*, and *Almanach populaire de la France*, that individualist descriptions of criminality were challenged by an alternative analysis that sought the origins of crime in the inegalitarian structure of society itself. Thus, *L'Humanitaire* of August 1841 decreed: "The man who kills you is not free not to kill you. It is society, or to be more precise, bad social organization that is responsible" (quoted in Foucault 1979, p. 287).

statistics assumed human action to be totally devoid of choice and free will. Toward the end of *Research on the Propensity for Crime*, for example, he held out the following promise: "I am far from concluding . . . that man can do nothing for his amelioration. . . . He possesses a moral strength capable of modifying the laws which concern him" (Quetelet [1831a] 1984, p. 69; see also Constant 1961; Dupréel 1942, p. 31). The 1842 English translation of *Sur l'homme* contained a new preface in which Quetelet tried to defend himself against various charges of fatalism, atheism, and materialism. Moreover, at the beginning of this translation, he instructed the publisher to insert a notice to the effect that he was "no theorist or system maker" and that he simply wished "to arrive at truth by the only legitimate way, namely, the examination of *facts*—the incontrovertible facts furnished by statistical data" (Quetelet 1842, p. iv).[25] So sensitive was Quetelet to the charge that determinism necessarily embraced atheism that he frequently affirmed his belief in "the wise influence of divine power." In this way and in others, Quetelet consistently eschewed any explicit interpretation that others, for a wide variety of reasons, wished to foist on his facts.

In addition to the controversy surrounding Quetelet's position on free will, a second controversy stemmed from Quetelet's idea of the average man. To some theorists, this idea—which Quetelet (1848, p. vii) implied was his pivotal concept—was a source of acrimonious debate, scandal, and grief. Against Quetelet's belief that the statistical means of various physical traits could somehow be combined to form an "average," paradigmatic human being, contemporary statisticians made three major objections. The first of these was made in 1843 by the rector of the Académie de Grenoble, the philosopher and mathematical economist Antoine Cournot. Cournot argued that, just as a right triangle cannot generally be formed from the average lengths of the three sides of many right triangles, so too the average man determined from the average physical measurements (of height, of feet, of strength, etc.) of many men would simply be "un homme impossible" (1843, p. 210). Quetelet did not reply to this difficulty.[26] The attack against the average man was continued by

[25] The net cast by antideterminist views included others besides Quetelet. For example, in a paper read to the Statistical Section of the British Association in 1839, Rawson W. Rawson, a follower of Quetelet, complained that "undeserved ridicule has been cast upon some attempts which have been made to show that moral phenomena are subject to established and general laws . . . " (1839, p: 344).

[26] It seems Quetelet never responded to specific criticisms of his work. Only at one point did he (1848a, pp. 13–20) deign to recognize, and then unsuccessfully to dismiss, three charges directed against the broad enterprise of moral statistics: (1) the causes of social facts can never properly be observed because they are too numerous and too variable in their influence; (2) moral facts, unlike other statistical facts, are not compa-

American Journal of Sociology

Jacques Bertillon, professor of demography at the *École d'anthropologie*, who was a pioneer of statistical analysis of the rates of divorce, alcoholism, and suicide and who provided some of Durkheim's theoretical groundwork. Bertillon suggested that an average man, constructed from each of the human attributes, was not a scientific entity but an invention of the imagination. Far from being an ideal of human perfection, Quetelet's average man was the epitome of mediocrity; he could only be a monster, the "type de la vulgarité" (Bertillon 1876, p. 311). A third objection was made by Joseph Bertrand, who argued that Quetelet had defined "man" independently of particular men considered at random. He reasoned that, because the average man must necessarily be average in all his attributes, his features must therefore simultaneously embody the averages of such antitheses as beauty and ugliness. The average man could therefore be neither ugly nor beautiful, neither foolish nor wise, neither virtuous nor criminal, neither strong nor weak, neither brave nor cowardly. Bertrand suggested, perhaps facetiously, that, in the body of the average man, Quetelet would perhaps place an average soul (1889, p. xliii).

To these three objections to Quetelet's idea of the average man, a fourth should be added, namely, the objection made by Émile Durkheim in *Suicide* (1897). Having congratulated Quetelet for pointing to the existence of regularities in social phenomena, Durkheim went on to argue, however, that these cannot be explained by the concept of the average man. The description of social regularities, even if accurate and portrayed in great detail, does not explain them. In the particular case of suicide rates, Durkheim reasoned, this was so for two reasons. First, the fact that 15 out of 100,000 persons kill themselves each year "does not imply that the others are exposed in any degree" (p. 304). Durkheim therefore reminds us that Quetelet's average man was constructed as the arithmetic mean of qualities that occur in varying degrees in all individuals of a given type. But, as with the vast majority of any given population that, in practice, has no propensity to suicide whatsoever, so also, in Quetelet's terms, could it be said that the average man does not kill himself. From this point on, Quetelet's idea of the average man, as a proper object of scientific inquiry, was not to be taken seriously.[27]

---

rable, and one therefore cannot deduce an average from their aggregate; and (3) the study of moral facts must always be incomplete because one can never know everything about the actions—good or bad—of man. Quetelet's response to these difficulties was that, by recognizing their partial truth, he thereby delivered his own work from the criticism implied by these charges.

[27] Attempts have occasionally been made to resurrect Quetelet's concept of the average man, most recently by the French mathematician Maurice Fréchet. Fréchet has suggested that Quetelet's *homme moyen* can be rescued by the more precise concept

CONCLUSIONS

It has been suggested in this paper that Quetelet's criminology included some of the focal concerns in penality and the statistical movement. During the Restoration, these domains coincided in a common issue, namely, the regulation of the dangerous classes. Quetelet's social mechanics of crime emerged almost directly, in other words, from the conjunction of the apparent failure of French penal strategies and the expansion in the scope of the statistical movement to include empirical social research. This conjunction provided the structure and much of the substantive content of Quetelet's criminology. Its structure was formed by the relentless application of the methods of the natural sciences to the moral phenomena reported in the official records of crime. Its content consisted in an empirical examination of the effects of different social environments on the individuals—drawn largely from the dangerous classes—who passed through the successive layers of the administration of justice. In this examination, Quetelet made no theoretical distinction—nor did he even contemplate one—between his own observational categories and those of the state officials who constructed the data in the *Compte général*. The object of Quetelet's criminology was therefore the already constituted problem of the dangerous classes; its outcome was a positivist discourse that fostered a rigid binary opposition between normality and deviation.

Where, then, should Quetelet's criminology be placed in the history of criminological theory? This question has no simple answer. The response to it depends, in part, on the identification of a distinctive set of discursive techniques and objects by which criminology as such can be demarcated from other infant disciplines such as penology, phrenology, and psychiatry. But, since the early history of modern criminology is still largely uncharted terrain, the placement of Quetelet's contribution in its subsequent maturation must, for the present, remain quite tentative. Quetelet's analysis of crime contained, and maybe even fostered, many of the uncertainties and the inconsistencies associated with the transitional phase in French penality between classicism and positivism, between the unbridled legal subject of the former and the overdetermined object of the latter. In the soul of Quetelet's criminal, as in that of Victor Hugo's exconvict Jean Valjean (in *Les Misérables*), there dwelled a primitive spark, a divine element, incorruptible in this world and immortal in the next,

---

homme typique. The latter has two basic qualities: "(1) the typical man of a population will be *the one* individual of this population who excludes all possibility of incompatibility among the different characteristics of this typical man; (2) the typical man ought to be typical in relation to the *ensemble* of his characteristics without being necessarily typical relative to each of them" (Fréchet 1955, p. 327).

American Journal of Sociology

that could be kindled, lit up, and made radiant by good and that evil could never entirely extinguish. Quetelet's criminology cannot be understood exclusively as a part of the positivist reaction to the voluntaristic excesses of classical penology and jurisprudence; at most, Quetelet was a reluctant determinist who neither disowned the classical doctrine of free will nor denied the determinate character of social behavior. Although his presociological discourse was soon to be transcended in fundamental ways by Marx and Weber and, especially, by Durkheim, it is perhaps fair to say that Quetelet provided the positivist core of a deterministic criminology that subsequently dominated the labors of Lombroso, Goring, and Bonger, who emphasized, respectively, biologism, mental hereditarianism, and economism. Moreover, by identifying the existence of lawlike regularities in recorded criminal behavior, by suggesting that crime was subject to causal laws of the order found in the natural sciences, and by implying that criminal behavior was as much a product of society as of volition, Quetelet also opened up the possibility of a sociological analysis of crime. This great achievement was recognized by Durkheim and Fauconnet when they traced to Quetelet the emergence of an autonomous sociology resolutely opposed to methodological individualism: "Social phenomena could no longer be deemed the product of fortuitous combinations, arbitrary acts of the will, or local and chance circumstances. Their generality attests to their essential dependence on general causes which, everywhere that they are present, produce their effects. . . . Where for a long time there has been perceived only isolated actions, lacking any links, there was found to be a system of definite laws. This was already expressed in the title of the book in which Quetelet expounded the basic principles of the statistics of morality" (1903, pp. 201–2).

REFERENCES

Bertillon, Jacques. 1876. "La théorie des moyennes en statistique." *Journal de la société de statistique de Paris* 17:265–71, 286–308.
Bertrand, Joseph. 1889. *Calcul de probabilités*. Paris: Gauthiers-Villers.
Buckle, Henry Thomas. 1860. *History of Civilisation in England*. 2 vols. London: Parker.
Chevalier, Louis. 1973. *Laboring Classes and Dangerous Classes in Paris during the First Half of the Nineteenth Century*. Translated by Frank Jellinek. Princeton, N.J.: Princeton University Press.
Coleman, William. 1982. *Death Is a Social Disease*. Madison: University of Wisconsin Press.
Compte général de l'administration de la justice criminelle en France. 1827. Paris: L'Imprimerie royale.
Comte, Auguste. (1838) 1869. *Cours de philosophie positive*. Vol. 4. Paris: Baillière.
Constant, J. 1961. "À propos de l'école Franco-Belge du milieu social au XIXième siècle." Pp. 303–15 in *La Responsabilité pénale*, edited by J. Léaute. Paris: Dalloz.

Quetelet

Cournot, A. 1843. *Exposition de la théorie des chances et des probabilités*. Paris: Hachette.

Cousin, Victor. 1829. *Cours de l'histoire de la philosophie*. 3 vols. Paris: Didier.

de Candolle, Alphonse. 1830. *Considérations sur la statistique des délits*. Paris: Bibliotheque universelle.

Doerner, Klaus. 1981. *Madmen and the Bourgeoisie: A Social History of Insanity and Psychiatry*. Translated by J. Neugroschel and J. Steinberg. Oxford: Blackwell.

Donovan, James. 1981. "Justice Unblind: The Juries and the Criminal Classes in France, 1825–1914." *Journal of Social History* 15(1): 89–107.

Douglas, Jack D. 1967. *The Social Meanings of Suicide*. Princeton, N.J.: Princeton University Press.

Duesterberg, Thomas J. 1979. "Criminology and the Social Order in Nineteenth-Century France." Ph.D. dissertation, Indiana University.

Dupréel, Eugene. ed. 1942. *Adolphe Quetelet: Pages choisies et commentées*. Brussels: Office de publicité.

Durkheim, Émile. (1897) 1951. *Suicide: A Study in Sociology*. Translated by J. A. Spaulding and George Simpson. New York: Free Press.

Durkheim, Émile, and Paul Fauconnet. (1903) 1982. "Sociology and the Social Sciences." Pp. 175–208 in *The Rules of Sociological Method*, edited and introduced by Steven Lukes. Translated by W. D. Halls. London: Macmillan.

Elmer, M. C. 1933. "Century-Old Ecological Studies in France." *American Journal of Sociology* 39(1): 63–70.

Fauré, Fernand. 1918. "The Development and Progress of Statistics in France." Pp. 217–329 in *The History of Statistics*, edited by John Koren. New York: Franklin.

Foucault, Michel. 1979. *Discipline and Punish: The Birth of the Prison*. Translated by Alan Sheridan. New York: Vintage.

———. 1980. *Power/Knowledge: Selected Interviews and Other Writings, 1972–1977*. Edited by Colin Gordon, translated by Gordon et al. New York: Pantheon.

Fréchet, Maurice. 1955. "Réhabilitation de la notion statistique de l'homme moyen." Pp. 317–41 in *Les mathématiques et le concret*. Paris: Presses universitaires de France.

Frégier, H.-A. 1840. *Des classes dangereuses de la population dans les grandes villes, et des moyens de les rendre meilleurs*. 2 vols. Paris: Baillière.

Gibbons, Don C. 1979. *The Criminological Enterprise*. Englewood Cliffs, N.J.: Prentice-Hall.

Giddens, Anthony. 1965. "The Suicide Problem in French Sociology." *British Journal of Sociology* 16:3–18.

Goring, Charles. 1913. *The English Convict: A Statistical Study*. London: His Majesty's Stationery Office.

Guerry, André-Michel. 1829. *Statistique comparé de l'état de l'instruction et du nombre des crimes*. Paris.

———. 1833. *Essai sur la statistique morale de la France*. Paris: Crochard.

Hankins, Frank H. 1908. "Adolphe Quetelet as Statistician." *Studies in History, Economics and Public Law* 31(4): 443–567.

Herschel, John. 1850. "Review." *Edinburgh Review* 92(185): 1–57.

Houchon, Guy. 1976. "Lacunes, faiblesses et emplois des statistiques criminelles." *Etudes relatives à la recherche criminologique* 14:7–29.

Jacoby, Joseph E. 1979. *Classics in Criminology*. Oak Park, Ill.: Moore.

Landau, David, and Paul Lazarsfeld. 1968. "Adolphe Quetelet." Pp. 247–57 in *International Encyclopaedia of the Social Sciences*. New York: Macmillan and Free Press.

Lindesmith, Alfred, and Yale Levin. 1937. "The Lombrosian Myth in Criminology." *American Journal of Sociology* 42:653–71.

American Journal of Sociology

Lodhi, Abdul Quaiyum, and Charles Tilly. 1973. "Urbanization, Crime, and Collective Violence in 19th-Century France." *American Journal of Sociology* 79(2): 296–318.

Lottin, Joseph. (1912) 1969. *Quetelet: Statisticien et sociologue*. New York: Franklin.

Mailly, Edward. 1875. "Essai sur la vie et les ouvrages de Quetelet." *Annuaire de l'académie royale des sciences, des lettres et des beaux arts Belgique* 41:109–279.

Mannheim, Hermann, ed. 1972. *Pioneers in Criminology*. Montclair, N.J.: Smith.

Marx, Karl. (1853) 1956. "Capital Punishment." *New York Daily Tribune*, February 18, 1853. Reprinted in pp. 228–30 of *Karl Marx: Selected Writings in Sociology and Social Philosophy*, edited by T. B. Bottomore and M. Rubel. New York: McGraw-Hill.

Morris, Terence. 1957. *The Criminal Area*. London: Routledge & Kegan Paul.

Nye. Robert A. 1984. *Crime, Madness, and Politics in Modern France*. Princeton: Princeton University Press.

O'Brien, Patricia. 1982. *The Promise of Punishment: Prisons in Nineteenth-Century France*. Princeton, N.J.: Princeton University Press.

Pelfrey, William V. 1980. *The Evolution of Criminology*. Cincinnati: Anderson.

Perrot, Jean-Claude, and Stuart J. Woolf. 1984. *State and Statistics in France, 1789–1815*. London: Harwood Academic.

Perrot, Michèlle. 1975. "Délinquance et système pénitentiaire en France au XIXe siècle." *Annales: Economies, société, civilisations* 30(1): 67–91.

Petit, Jacques G. 1984. "The Birth and Reform of Prisons in France." Pp. 125–47 in *The Emergence of Carceral Institutions: Prisons, Galleys and Lunatic Asylums, 1550–1900*, edited by Pieter Spierenburg. Rotterdam: Erasmus University.

Porter, Theodore M. 1985. "The Mathematics of Society: Variation and Error in Quetelet's Statistics." *British Journal for the History of Science* 18:51–69.

Quetelet, Adolphe. 1826. "Mémoire sur les lois des naissances et de la mortalité à Bruxelles." *Nouveaux mémoires de l'académie royale des sciences et belles-lettres de Bruxelles* 3:495–512.

———. 1828. *Instructions populaires sur le calcul des probabilités*. Brussels: Tarlier.

———. 1829. "Recherches statistiques sur le royaume des Pays-Bas." *Nouveaux mémoires de l'académie royale* 5:25–38.

———. (1831a) 1984. *Research on the Propensity for Crime at Different Ages*. Translated and introduced by Sawyer F. Sylvester. Cincinnati: Anderson.

———. 1831b. *Recherches sur la loi de la croissance de l'homme*. Brussels: Hayez.

———. 1835. *Sur l'homme et sur le développement de ses facultés, ou Essai de physique sociale*. Paris: Bachelier.

———. 1842. *A Treatise on Man*. Translated by R. Knox and T. Smibert. Edinburgh: Chambers.

———. 1846. *Lettres à S.A.R., le Duc Régnant de Saxe-Coburg et Gotha, sur la théorie des probabilités*. Brussels: Hayez.

———. (1848a) 1984. "Sur la statistique morale et les principes qui doivent en former la base." *Déviance et société* 8(1): 13–41.

———. 1848b. *Du système social et des lois qui le régissent*. Paris: Guillaumin.

———. 1869. *Physique sociale; ou, Essai sur le développement des facultés*. Brussels: Murquardt.

———. 1871. "Des lois concernant le développement de l'homme." *Annuaire de l'observatoire de Bruxelles* 38:205–16.

Radzinowicz, Leon. 1966. *Ideology and Crime*. New York: Columbia University Press.

Rawson, Rawson W. 1839. "An Inquiry into the Statistics of Crime in England and Wales." *Journal of the Statistical Society of London* 2:316–44.

Sarton. George. 1935. "Preface to Volume 22 of Isis (Quetelet)." *Isis* 23:4–24.

Sellin, Thorsten. 1937. " 'The Lombrosian Myth in Criminology'—Letter to the Editor." *American Journal of Sociology* 42:897–99.

Shaw, Clifford R., and Henry D. McKay. 1942. *Juvenile Delinquency and Urban Areas*. Chicago: University of Chicago Press.

Stead, Philip John. 1983. *The Police of France*. London: Macmillan.

Tarde, Gabriel. 1886. *La criminalité comparée*. Paris: Alcan.

Taylor, Ian, Paul Walton, and Jock Young. 1973. *The New Criminology*. London: Routledge & Kegan Paul.

Tilly, Charles, Louise Tilly, and Richard Tilly. 1975. *The Rebellious Century: 1830– 1930*. Cambridge, Mass.: Harvard University Press.

Tombs, Robert. 1980. "Crime and the Security of the State: The 'Dangerous Classes' and Insurrection in Nineteenth-Century Paris." Pp. 214–37 in *Crime and the Law: The Social History of Crime in Western Europe since 1500*, edited by V. A. C. Gatrell, Bruce Lenman, and Geoffrey Parker. London: Europa.

Treiber, Hubert, and Heinz Steinert. 1980. *Die Fabrikation des zuverlässigen Menschen*. Berlin: Ernst.

Villermé, René. 1820. *Des prisons telles qu'elles sont et telles qu'elles devraient être: Ouvrage dans lequel on les considére par rapport a l'hygiène, à la morale et à l'économie politique*. Paris: Mequignon-Marvis.

Westergaard, Harold. 1932. *Contributions to the History of Statistics*. London: King.

Wolfgang, Marvin E. 1972. "Cesare Lombroso." Pp. 232–91 in *Pioneers in Criminology*, edited by H. Mannheim. Montclair, N.J.: Smith.

Wright, Gordon. 1983. *Between the Guillotine and Liberty: Two Centuries of the Crime Problem in France*. New York: Oxford University Press.

Zehr, Howard. 1976. *Crime and the Development of Modern Society*. London: Croom Helm.

[6]

Criminology: the birth of a special savoir

Transformations in penal theory and new sources of right in the late nineteenth century

Pasquale Pasquino

In Chapter 111 of *The Man Without Qualities*, Robert Musil records the 'sensational conversion' to 'the social school of thought' of Ulrich's father, an elderly jurist and member of a 'committee set up by the Ministry of Justice for the purpose of bringing the criminal code up to date', whose theoretical U-turn led to his being denounced by some of his colleagues as a 'materialist' and 'Prussian'.

What had our jurist's ideas been before this point, and what were they now to become? This is the question which I would like to take as my (in some respects arbitrary) starting-point for a discussion of the transformation of penal law towards the end of the nineteenth century.

The epithet 'Prussian', 'maliciously' employed to discredit the old jurist's change of theoretical viewpoint, was at that time a code-word in Kakania (Musil's name for the Austro-Hungarian monarchy) for how not to conduct oneself; but in the vocabulary of his fellow-jurists the word no doubt also had a more precise signification, referring to the *Jungdeutsche Kriminalistenschüle* (Young German School of Criminal Psychologists), whose leading figure, von Liszt, had taken up the Chair in Penal Law at Berlin in 1899.

Our commentary on Musil might well begin with Liszt's inaugural lecture at Berlin (1). But this is itself only a moment of synthesis within a more protracted process, a purely juridical recodification of a wider debate which had shaken the theoretical foundations of law and was beginning to transform the perspectives of jurisprudence throughout the European continent, from Russia to Holland and Italy, namely the debate concerning criminal anthropology. In order to reconstruct this debate, we need instead to begin at the southernmost point of this juridical Europe, at Naples, where fifteen years earlier in 1885 Enrico Ferri had delivered a university lecture on 'The positivist school of criminology' (2). This lecture will provide us with an exegisis of the

17

'sensational' character of the conversion of a jurist who, at the beginning of Musil's Chapter 111, was still of the opinion that 'so far as jurists are concerned, there are no semi-insane people'; it also throws light on the following passage:

> The social view tells us that the criminally 'degenerate' person cannot at all be considered from a moral aspect, but only according to the degree in which he is dangerous to society as a whole. What follows from this is that the more dangerous he is the more he is responsible for his actions. And what follows again from this, with compelling logic, is that the criminals who are apparently least guilty, that is to say, those who are insane or of defective morality, who by virtue of their nature are least susceptible to the corrective influence of punishment, must be threatened with the harshest penalties . . .(3)

Since, as Musil puts it "it is difficult to do justice to justice in brief" (4), I must ask the reader to excuse me if the following account is a little too rapid and perhaps obscure on some points.

We turn, then, to Naples in 1885. At the outset of his lecture Ferri (a personage, or rather a career about whose exemplary significance it will be necessary to say a few words in a moment) states with a reformer's ardour all the major theses of the social school of law. And he formulates them by means of a contrast drawn on a number of crucial points with the then prevailing doctrines of the classical school of legal theory.

A person who commits a crime, says Ferri, is a criminal, (5) that is to say a person who by reason of his psychic and moral constitution is not normal. It is no use looking for the motive of his act: the reason for his crime is, precisely, his criminality. In a sense these few peremptory words mark the registering of a new object of penal science and practice: *homo criminalis*, a new figure engendered outside the sphere of classical penal thought, but which in the course of the nineteenth century gradually advances to its forefront. In order to show that we have to do here with more than a mere fantasy of Ferri's criminological brain, (6) let us cite here just one testimony to the seriousness with which this new object-personage was viewed. At the International Penitentiary Conference of 1925 in London, its President, Ruggles Brise, declared in his opening speech: "In every civilised country, it has been increasingly recognised that the person of the criminal must enter into the concept of law in as much as this concerns the degree of responsibility and the extent and form of punishment, and that consequently it is necessary to undertake the pathological and psychological [and—he might have added—sociological) study of criminals." (7)

The utilitarian tariff
But why should we suppose that this 'criminal' is a novel personage – a

view which may well appear paradoxical given that our penal theory was not invented at the end of the last century? The reason is that in fact the whole classical theory of penal law, whether in Italy with Beccaria, in England with Bentham or in Germany with Anselm Feuerbach in fact posited and assumed the existence of a figure quite different from *homo criminalis*, namely *homo penalis*.

In classical theory, penal justice is constructed around the triangle formed by law, crime and punishment. The relations between these three terms are defined in three canonical formulae: *nulla poena sine lege; nulla poena sine crimine; nullum crimen sine poena legale*: no punishment except on the basis of existing law – an act is punishable only if it violates the law: no punishment without a crime – the existence of a criminal act must be proved; and lastly, a crime consists simply in an infraction defined by law (8).

Let us briefly note the fact that classical penal justice emerged within a double historical movement of a much more general order: on the one hand, the fixing of limits to arbitrary royal power – one should bear in mind here the important phenomenon, often passed over in silence by historians of 'society', of juridical codifications, notably the one carried out, prior to the Napoleonic Codes, by the *Preussisches Allgemeine Landrecht* of 1794, and, parallel to the promulgation of codes, the disappearance of the special decrees and ordinances issued by monarchs, police, parliaments and other administrative instances; and on the other hand, the movement for the defence of law, the affirmation of the duty of one and all to respect the contract which founds civil society. This tendency is exemplified in the writings of Anselm Fuerbach, known as the father of German penal jurisprudence. In his *Lehrbuch des gemeinen in Deutschland gueltigen peinlichen Recht* (Manual of German Penal Law), he writes, at the beginning of Section 8:

> Civil society [*die bürgliche Gesellschaft*] is founded through the union of the wills and powers of individuals which guarantees the liberties of each in respect to others. A civil society organised by submission to a general will and to a Constitution: this is what is meant by a State. Its [the State's] end is the maintenance of a state of legality [*rechtliche Zustand*], that is to say the coexistence of men in accordance with laws. (9)

This, then, in brief, is the double movement within which the classical theory of penal law takes shape.

What interests us here about this triangle of law, crime and punishment is the absence of the figure of the 'criminal'. What occupies its place is the positing of a 'free will' as establishing the subjective basis of the power to punish. Now by its very nature this free will is precisely the faculty which is common to all (i.e. to every juridical subject). As such, it is not the object of a special form of knowledge. Anyone can commit

19

a crime: *homo penalis* is not a separate species, but a function. What serves to explain the actions of *homo penalis* is not criminology but rather a 'general anthropology' (in the now anachronistic sense of a general theory of the human subject) – the same theory, in essence, as that which explains the behaviour of *homo economicus*. This free, and hence responsible will thus completes the circle of classical penal theory without it being necessary to presuppose any special corresponding mode of knowledge apart from the utilitarianism of a "calculus of the goods and evils of this life" (10).

Within the classical regime of penal theory, it will no doubt be said of a man who commits a crime, or rather he himself will say *'video meliora proboque, deteriora sequor'* ['I see and approve the better, I follow the worse' (Ovid)]. *Homo penalis* is nothing more or less than the citizen, the man of the Contract. *Homo penalis* exists as a potentiality in each of us, but is actualised only through such violations of the law as any person may commit simply as the outcome of an erroneous calculation. Now it is precisely this 'rationality' of the old penal order which Ferri, along with many others, will call in question. The discourse of the 'social' or 'positive' school of legal theory is organised around two main poles: the criminal and society. Without being eliminated, the themes of law, crime and punishment recede to a secondary level of importance. Very schematically, we can say that *homo penalis* is joined here by a new subject, *homo criminalis*, which truly constitutes a veritable new species, a separate race of men whose acts are not the results of a false calculation (where imprisonment would be somewhat akin to bankruptcy), but the manifestations of an evil nature. If crime amounts in classical law to a sort of accident of the mind, a confusion of representations, the new legal theory will regard the criminal as an excrement of the social body, at once a residue of archaic stages in the evolution of the species and a waste-product of social organisation. Ferri says, again in his Naples lecture, that the criminal is naturally a savage, and socially an abnormal.

In order to render these dry formulae a little more intelligible, let us consider the social school's analysis and interrogation of one of the two main apparatuses (*dispositifs*) making up the classical penal order, the one which the German jurists termed *Abschreckung*: intimidation, dissuasion, also known as intervention *'ad deterrendum'*. (Concerning the other main apparatus, the prison, I need only refer the reader to Michel Foucault's *Discipline and Punish* (11).)

> Penal laws are the motives which experience shows us to be
> capable of containing or annihilating the impulses which passions
> impart to the wills of men.

> Thus penal laws, by displaying terrifying objects to men whom
> they suppose to be capable of fear, present them with suitable

2 0

motives to influence their will. (12)

These two quotations, drawn not from juridical texts but direct from Holbach's *System of Nature*, illustrate how the juridical utterances of the classical age of law emerge as elements within that discursive practice which I have termed 'general anthropology'. Of course, the apparatus of intimidation presented here by Holbach in its most general form is not new in itself. Hobbes and Puffendorf, among many others, had already written about it; and, after all, the institution of public judicial torture and execution served – and how – a function of intimidation. But what is new and specific to the eighteenth-century reformers is the idea that intimidation, as prescribed by a system in which punishments are graded and modulated in accordance with the diverse forms of crime, coupled not with the exemplary yet discontinuous terror of the supplice, but with the mild yet inexorable and integral efficacy of justice (13), will necessarily tend to exert a pressure on human wills such that the force of the passions can be arrested at the point where contract and law fix the bounds of each person's liberty in relation to that of others. Promote the happiness or interest of each, says Utilitarianism, but within the limits of the law. In other words, intimidation is no longer the threat of a *sovereign power* against whoever may dare to ignore or defy it, but rather has for its basis and instrument *law*, that discreet yet uninterrupted threat which acts through the medium of representations on that particular form of mental representation which comprises the 'calculus of the goods and evils of this life'.

Here is what Bentham has to say on this question in his *Theorié des peines et des récompenses*: "Each individual conducts himself, albeit unknowingly, according to a well- or ill-made calculus of pleasures and pains. Should he foresee that a pain will be the consequence of an act which pleases him, this idea will act with a certain force so as to divert him from that action. If the total value of the pain appears greater to him than the total value of the pleasure, the repulsive force will be the greater; the act will not occur". (14) Two of Bentham's further remarks on this question seem to me to throw light on the punitive rationality of the classical theory. The first occurs in a Chapter entitled 'Fortification of the impression made by punishments on the imagination':

If an abridged edition of the penal code were to be published, illustrated with woodcuts showing the specific penalty laid down for each kind of crime, this would act as an imposing commentary, a sensible image of the law. Each person would then be led to think to himself: this is what I must suffer if I should break this law. (15)

Bentham accordingly rejects as 'ineffective' "those penalties which can produce no effect on the will and consequently cannot serve to prevent similar acts" (16).

21

The second remark I wish to cite concerns the Panopticon, and is of interest here because it shows how the apparatus of the prison itself assumes a signification within the framework of the apparatus of Abschreckung:

> The penal scene is located in the neighbourhood of a metropolis, the place which contains assembled the greatest number of men and of those among them who most need to have displayed before their eyes the punishment of crime. The appearance of the building, the singularity of its form, the walls and moats that surround it, the guard at its gates, all of this serves to reinforce the idea of malefactors confined and punished: the ease of admission could not fail to attract a great number of visitors . . . What a most striking spectacle for the most numerous class of spectators! What a theme for conversations, allusions, domestic lessons, useful stories! . . .And yet the real penalty is less great than the apparent one . . .The punishments being visible, the imagination exaggerates them. (17)

An imaginary theatre of punishments. Anselm Fuerbach is restating the same principle in the more abstract language of Kant's Critique of Pure Reason, when he writes in a paragraph of his manual dealing with 'psychological constraint':

> All breaches of law have their psychological source in sensible nature, in so far as the faculty of desire in man is stirred by pleasure either during the committal of the offence or from the moment of the desire to commit it. This sensible impulsion can be annulled by the fact that each man knows his criminal act will ineluctably lead to an evil greater than that of the loss of pleasure occasioned by the non-satisfaction of the impulse to perform the act. (18)

From deterrence to neutralisation
So much by way of a reconstruction, at any rate with respect to one quite important point, of the theoretical background and juridical *credo* of Ulrich's father, prior to his conversion. We will now try and explain the nature of the conversion itself.

From the 1870s and 1880s, the essential elements of the old penal rationality began to be definitively overturned. Ferri (to confine ourselves to him – but the examples could be multiplied endlessly) argues as follows. Beccaria's theory of punishment as an instrument *ad deterrendum* counterweighting the interest in the committing of crimes is false, both theoretically and practically: practically, because the statistics of crimes and criminals simply continue to increase; theoretically, because the criminal does not think like a normal and honest man such as Beccaria – indeed, we may say that he does not think at all. The criminal cannot be a *homo penalis* because he is not a Man.

What then is to be done, given the impotence of punishments and the rising number of crimes? For Ferri, the answer consists fundamentally not so much in intimidation as in the elimination of the very sources of crime. One must pass from *Abschreckung* to *Unschädlichmachung*, from deterrence to neutralisation. The new penal theory will be concerned far less with dissuading the citizen from law-breaking than with rendering the criminal incapable of harm. The problem which thus comes to be posed is that of the origin or aetiology of crime.

The question of free will had long been the grand showpiece theme of debate among jurists since, as we saw above, it was free will which functioned in classical theory as the subjective foundation of the right to punish. This debate, traversed by arguments of exquisite subtlety and linked from an early date to the alienists' speculations on insanity, went on throughout the nineteenth century. The first authoritative general work on the subject, Vaillant's *De libera voluntate ad delictum necessaria*, was published at Amsterdam in 1837. Enrico Ferri likewise began his university career in 1878 with a theses in 'The theory of the imputability and negation of free will' (19). Here he initially summarises his position by citing a work on determinism by Fouillée where it is stated that "without venturing upon metaphysical considerations, we may justify punishment from a human viewpoint. And this purely social justification has no need to ascend to the absolute truth of things, for it derives from social relations as they exist in fact" (20). Much more than the problematic of free will, the issue here is that of the very basis of the right to punish. In this perspective, it is society, not law or sovereignty, which is seen as being attacked or endangered by crime, or rather by the criminal. The question is whether it is law which is promordial for society – in the sense of being the immediate expression of the will of every subject – or whether law is no more than the secondary and variable codification of the rules of social functioning.

We must pause on this point, since it leads on to the theme of 'social defence' which becomes the slogan of the new penal theory. It is in the writings of the Belgian jurist Prins – who, with Liszt and von Hamel, was to head the International Union of Penal Law at the turn of the century – that one finds the most explicit statement of this theme. But first it should be noted that the problematic, and even the expression 'social defence', are not in themselves new. Soon after 1830, the Italian jurist Carmignani had published an important book entitled *Theory of the Laws of Social Security*. Already here he argues for the replacement of the notions of crime and punishment hitherto assumed as fundamental in penal theory by the new concepts of 'social offence' and 'social defence' (21). Füerbach himself says that the *raison d'être* of punishments is the necessity to avert the dangers which menace social life (22). But since words are not things, or at any rate not practices, we need to examine the question more closely. For Prins, as for Liszt

23

and Ferri, 'social defence' is much more than a verbal formula. It is the keystone of the new penal rationality, one whose central elements seem to me to be the following:

1. Firstly, imputability. The question of the subjective foundation of the right to punish, even it it never disappears from the codes, recedes little by little into the background: "this 'I' [the free will of the subject] is a mystery, and one cannot found the right to punish on a mystery" (23): the axis of responsibility is no longer, as for Kant and the classical legal theorists, reason and its good or bad calculations, but conformity or nonconformity with respect to social life.

2. Secondly, social defence. If the idea of social defence is not new, why are we speaking here of a transformation in the order of penal theory? To answer this question, we need first of all to ask in turn, for each successive stage of penal theory, what the 'society' is which it is sought to defend, and what exactly is meant in each case by the notion of 'defence'.

Let us take the latter point first. Intimidation does not vanish from its place among the elements of the penal apparatus. But it remains no more than an element, and a minor one at that. The social school continues to recognise its value, but only as a means of dealing with what are termed 'occasional delinquents' (in Liszt's word, *Augenblicksverbrecher*). Now this occasional delinquent is only the residue of *homo penalis*: his actions are evil and dangerous, but not his inherent nature. But the true criminal is quite another matter. The defence of society against the criminal will involve what we termed above his 'neutralisation'. We should add that, between the two extremes of residual intimidation for occasional delinquents and neutralisation (tending towards physical liquidation) for hardened criminals (Liszt's *unverbesserliche Verbrecher*), there opens up a vast domain of intervention for what the International Union of Penal Law will term social hygiene, designed to act as a preventive mopping-up of the social breeding grounds of crime.

This new theory of right is thus centred, not on crime considered as a purely anthropological or mental fact, but on the rebellious hordes of the criminal, understood as a social phenomenon. There is a strange paradox here: if it is claimed that criminality is a phenomenon with a social aetiology, how is it possible to say that the criminal has an asocial nature? In reality it is Darwinism which supplies the solution of the paradox. Within the same social organism there can coexist different stages of the evolution of the species; in this sense, society is a mixture of different natures. At the very heart of social evolution and by virtue of that process itself, one can recognise as archaic residues those individuals and groups which, unable to keep up with the proper pace of evolution and left behind by it, endanger by their existence the proper functioning of the whole.

Thus we can begin to see that the society whose defence is in question here is something quite different from Feuerbach's *bürgliche Gesell-schaft*, in which and for which the State of Right acts as the guarantor of law, and where society and law are one and the same, or rather where law – the contract – founds society. By prescribing the limits of sovereign power, law operates a sort of symbolic zeroising of unequal privileges: in real terms, it will function as the act of recognition and formalisation of the great and little machines of *assujettissement* (subjection/subjectification) which come in late eighteenth-century Europe to combine into a relatively unified continuum.

Now the new 'society' conceived of by late nineteenth-century jurists and criminologists is, or so we may suggest, the outcome of the failure of the old liberal programme of laissez-faire and the rule of law. Ever since the Physiocrats, liberalism as an effective governmental rationality had proved impossible to realise, and it was to remain so for the remainder of the nineteenth century at least. The demarcation of the zones of legitimate State interference, the division between its '*agenda*' and its '*non agenda*', had never been satisfactorily established; the policy encapsulated in Quesnay's advice to the King that 'to govern, one should do nothing', turned out to be a difficult and ultimately quite untenable undertaking. Nineteenth-century political strategies were dominated by a 'reforming' current, seeking and finding, not without conflicts and vacillations, the difficult middle path between 'doing nothing' and 'doing too much'. The strength of this current had lain in its capacity to define for governmental activity a space and a legitimation in relation to the different newly emerging social and economic forces. But in the process, the project of a society built out of individual subjects had aborted. The natural society which was supposed to emerge through laissez-faire had failed to materialise. The machines of *assujettissement* had begun to malfunction to the extent of its being said, with Renan, that "nature is unjustice itself" (24). And without a good nature, no government in law is possible.

What then is to serve as the new founding principle? Not subjects or law, but society itself, considered as a complex of conflicts and interests. A society which is not nature but community, *Gemeinschaft*, *Volksgemeinschaft*. Let us now return to the specific problem of penal law. Liszt writes in his treatise that the law exists to defend vital interests. Law-breaking is defined in these terms as "the defective state, demonstrated by the act committed, of the social mentality necessary for life in community . . . my object is to designate the material content of infraction which is not created by law but presents itself to law, and which is thus definable only outside and beyond law. But above the law there exists only society itself, organised in the State. Hence it is here that the principle of infraction is to be sought" (25). Here, then,

25

society emerges as the only meaningful basis for the right to punish, laws being nothing but the changeable mode of codification of society's vital interests. And all the more so because society is regarded no longer as natural but as historical. The theoretical basis on which it will be possible to speak of society will no longer be that of law, but that of a 'historical sociology'. Hence the great role played by the reactivation and development of a whole anthropological knowledge (this time in the modern sense of the term) which will call in question the idea of natural freedom. There will no longer be the possibility of founding society on legal right, since each society that arises in historical space and time produces its own form of legal right, just as it produces its mythology, its culture and, along with everything else, its criminals and its means of defence against them. For the new penal order, society will thus not only be the source of the right to punish but also the immediate source of all right, of all laws, and also of criminality.

Marx, Spencer, Darwin: for Ferri these three names represent, as it were, the epistemological preconditions—to speak in a language other than his—of a criminal sociology. But Gerri often also cites a fourth name, the rather less well-known one of the French psychiatrist B. Morel. There is insufficient space here to discuss this important figure, whose name is closely linked to the theory of degeneracy: one should consult the pages Robert Castel devotes to him in *L'Ordre psychiatrique* (26). I will limit myself to the assertion (which would still need to be demonstrated) that without Morel's theory of instinctive acts, the formation of this special 'savoir' of criminology would have been far less readily accomplished (27).

3. Finally, as the third of the main components of the new penal rationality, we have the figure of the criminal. It too does not just emerge out of nowhere one fine day in the landscape of law. It has diverse ancestors, and a convoluted prehistory. To retrace this would involve the reconstruction of the history of another special knowledge, that of legal medicine. In the eighteenth century Gayot de Pitival had already published a collection in several volumes of remarkable legal cases, accompanied by observations of every kind (28). About a century later, Anselm Feuerbach in Germany does the same thing in his *Darstellung merkwürdiger Criminalrechtsfälle* (29). But the crowd of characters represented in this forensic literature lacks the coherent identity which it will afterwards assume. Neither species nor race, the ancestor of *homo criminalis* we encounter here is a monster alien to nature and society alike. It has yet to become the object of a knowledge: at best, it is classified in such bestiaries as the works of Pitival and Feuerbach as a curiosity or accident, not of spirit but of nature. Later in the nineteenth century, the monster becomes madman and is transposed from the bestiary to the asylum; it comes to figure in all the pamphlets which psychiatrists and jurists started to produce in the wake of the great cases of monstrous or motiveless crime which

erupted in France in the 1820s (30). At the conclusion of a struggle
like that between angel and devil over the soul of the dying, doctors
and judges finally arrived at an understanding. The doctors were to be
accredited as the experts in questions of insanity, while the judges
found themselves rescued by the alienists from the legal dilemmas
which had threatened to cripple the apparatus of justice (31). No doubt
the character of Moosbrugger in *The Man Without Qualities* is the last,
imaginary representative of this lineage of monsters.

But at this point the criminal *per se* is no longer an especially disquiet-
ing figure – except perhaps where he kills a king or prime minister, or
turns anarchist. He becomes an exhibit – as witness the museum of
criminology which Lombroso established in a suite of rooms in Turin
(32), a docile animal which has lost even the privilege of terror. The
figure of the monster had inspired fear because it was itself impervious
to fear. Prins simply says this of criminals: "Is it admissable that society
should be incapable of dealing with its waste-products as industry does
with its? We too can cut down the overheads of social administration,
recycle society's residues and endeavour to keep the loss of strength
to a minimum. Even an inferior organism can prove useful provided one
succeeds in adapting it to an inferior function'." (33).

The essential point is that the genealogical precursors of the criminal
include other figures besides that of the monster, personages the nineteenth century had already learned to live with, from incorrigible children to perverts, from homosexuals to prostitutes (whose physiological
characteristics were tabulated at an early date by Parent–Duchâtelet
(34)) and the common poor, the 'dangerous classes' which social economists never ceased to evoke following Sismondi's discovery of the ills
of industrialism'.

The criminological vocation

It is around this figure of *homo criminalis* that penal theory will
construct its special 'savoir'. It is obliged to do so, because a general
régime of knowledge of man in the manner of Bentham had either
ceased to be, or had yet to become possible (according to the latter
point of view, what remained lacking was works such as those of von
Mises) And this special anthropology will assume, or so I have been
rapidly trying to indicate, a place alongside that of sociology, the
general knowledge of societies. Rusche and Kirchheimer rightly say in
their book *Punishment and Social Structure* that for crimologists of the
late nineteenth century "the science of crime was essentially a science
of society" (35).

Throughout this discussion we have been following the argument of
Ferri's Naples lecture. Who was Ferri? An academic and jurist, a pupil
of Lombroso. Ferri was undoubtedly the most active and best-known

member of the Italian legal school. He had a singular political career. He joined the Socialist Party as a young progressive in the 1880s and played an important role as a leader of its Left or 'maximalist' wing (to which Mussolini also later adhered), becoming editor of the party newspaper *Avanti* from 1900 to 1905. After the coming of Fascism he became a convert to the regime and died in 1929 a Senator of the kingdom. In 1919 he was nominated president of the Royal Commission for the reform of the Penal Code, in 1921 he published a 'project for a Penal Code' (36) which became the basis not only for the Fascist Rocco Code in Italy but also for the codes of other countries including Cuba and the Soviet Union.

From the pre-fascist Italy of Ferri and Prampolini, and the Socialist Party's "confusion of tongues and monstrous accents" (37), let us turn to the University of Berlin and Professor von Liszt's inaugural lecture on the object and method of the penal sciences. In this lecture Liszt enumerates three tasks of the penal sciences, tasks which I will very rapidly summarise.

1. The first task is to establish a pedagogy providing future practical criminologists with the knowledge necessary to accomplish their duties. On this point he remarks that knowledge of the rules of law and justice is not enough. For example, a judge cannot simply confine himself to imposing a prescribed penalty for a specified crime: he will need to adjust the punishment to fit not so much the offence as the criminal subject who has committed it (see his important discussion here of 'variable sentences').

2. The second task is to explain the socio-psychological causes of crime and thereby to demonstrate that punishment is nothing but the specific reaction of society to anti-social acts. Law merely serves to regulate this 'reaction'. This seems to me to be a fundamental formulation of the notion of social defence.

3. The third task goes beyond the field of penal theory and practice as thus defined, it consists in calling on the legislator in the name of the struggle against crime to launch an attack on the very roots of criminality. This is what is termed, in contrast with the generalised strategy of prevention based on *Abschreckung*, specialised prevention, or social hygiene (38).

If, then, classical penal theory derived the juridical apparatus calculated to maintain and reaffirm order, by way of the algebra of a general anthropology which knows no other person but Man, from law as the constitution of liberty and eternal social order, one can perhaps say that the penal theory which establishes itself in the late nineteenth century proceeds from the premise of society as source of life and right to deduce the activity of society as a self-defending subject, via a special anthropology which is at once a symptomatology, a pathology and a

therapeutic for a social body which is prone to all the disorders induced
by subjects who are unreliable (*'infidi'*) because inadequately subjected-
subjectified, and therefore ever dangerous.

If one recalls the remark by Prins cited above, one can see two distinct
lines of development which emerge at this point. One of these leads towards a policy of neutralisation: one can reflect here on Ferri's
proposal to send hardened criminals to reclaim the marshes of Latium
where they would perish of malaria, thereby at once ridding society of
them for good and procuring it an economic gain (39). This suggestion
was indeed put into effect during the Fascist era. The other perspective,
which might be called that of a principle of economy and which is more
explicitly stated by Prins, consists in the minimisation of the cost of
administering social disorders. But clearly this point, where constraints
of space oblige us to break off this history of penal regimes, does not
mark their ultimate stage of development.

To conclude, a word on the nature of this discussion. I would like
briefly to address a problem which has already been posed in regard to
this kind of analysis, and might be formulated thus: what kind of a
history have I been trying to sketch out here? What is it meant to be a
history of? Let us say first of all that we are not dealing with the
history of law or juridical theories properly speaking – to do so it
would have been necessary to analyse, in the case of Germany for
example, not only the work of Liszt but a whole theoretical debate
involving such authors as Binding, Birkmeyer and others. Even less have
I been attempting an overall history of jurisprudence: the point is too
obvious to need labouring.

What I have been trying to do, albeit in a manifestly tentative and pre-
carious fashion, is a history of punitive rationalities and their transformations. Because I am convinced that there is no single, solid plane
of consistency for all historical events, no immovable, nameable funda-
ment of the tree of historical life, and that the real is not immediately
given, I would understand by 'rationalities' that which makes possible
for us an intelligibility of practices, an intelligibility which at once
traverses and is incorporated in these practices. In other words, the kind
of research being attempted in this seminar might be taken as posing
for history, and in the present instance for the history of law, the same
question which Kant posed for 'Reason', a question which might issue
in a mapping of chronologically distinct rationalities and practices that
renders visible at once their modes of functioning, their surfaces of
emergence and their 'limits'. The old Marxist transformation-problem
would thereby come to reoccupy the focal point of this 'critique' – the
latter term being understood in its Kantian sense. But this undertaking
would surely also aim to elicit, in the face of the present and of history,
something other than either a posture of denunciation or the euphoria
of world-historical expectancy. What it would rather be necessary to

29

demonstrate would be the incessant attenuation of historical forms, to reduce (if I may put it thus) history to history. The political benefit which I would hope might be drawn from this enterprise would be to regain contact, via this detour, with present actuality, that is to say, with the possible (40). To be able to do this it will be necessary to silence all that clamorous past which never ceases to din in our ears.

The past and history would then belong to us in the way the landscape belongs to the 'coastwise voyager' in Thomas Mann's *Joseph and his Brothers*, "who finds no end to his journey, for behind each headland of clayey dune he conquers, fresh headlands and new distances lure him on" (41).

Paris, March 1979
Translated by Colin Gordon

Notes

*This paper was written for a seminar on transformations in law during the late nineteenth century, organised at the Collège de France in 1979 by Michel Foucault. I would especially like to thank Professor Paul Veyne of the Collège de France and Professor Antonio Negri of the University of Padua, imprisoned since April 1979 owing to a scandalous prosecution, whose intelligence and learning greatly helped me to find my bearings in an unfamiliar field of research.

1. F. von Liszt, *Die Aufgaben und die Methode der Strafrechtswissenschaft*, inaugural lecture in Penal Law at the University of Berlin, 27.10.1899, in *Strafrechtliche Aufsätze und Vorträge*, Berlin 1905, Vol. II pp.284-298. French edition, Paris 1902.
2. E. Ferri, *La scuola criminale positiva*, lecture at the University of Naples, 1885.
3. Robert Musil, *The Man Without Qualities*, Vol. 2, Chapter 111, p.285. Translated by Eithne Wilkins and Ernst Kaiser, Panther Books, London 1968.
4. Ibid. p.283.
5. This stunning truism recurs almost a century later in R. Merle and A. Vitu, *Traité de droit criminel*, 2nd ed., Paris 1978, p.28: "the delinquent is a human being who commits crimes" (sic).
6. This was the view held for instance by Benedetto Croce, who wrote in his *Logica*, "For every little idea which stirs in a professor's brain, we see a new science born; we have thus been blessed with sociologies, social psychologies . . . criminologies, sciences of comparative literature and so forth, each endowed with its own special methodology" (p.249).
7. Quoted by E. Ferri, 'Le congres penitentiaire international de Londres, *Revue Internationale de Droit Pénal*, 1 Jan, 1926.
8. I believe these formulae first appear in Anselm Feuerbach, *Lehrbuch des gemeinen in Deutschland gültigen Rechts*, 1801. In the 13th edition used here, they occur at Paragraph 20, page 41. Cf. the article on this question by S. Glaser cited by Hayek, 'Nullum crimen sine lege', in *Legislation and International Law*, 3rd Series, Vol. XXIV, London 1942.
9. Feuerbach ibid. p.36.
10. C. Beccaria, *Dei delitti e delle pene*, 1764.
11. See also M. Ignatieff, *A Just Measure of Pain*, London 1978.
12. Holbach, *Système de la Nature*, Vol. 1 Ch. 12, p. 191 and 197, quoted by K. Binding, *Die Normen und ihre Übertretung*, Vol. II, p.25, Leipzig 1877.
13. Cf. M. Foucault, *Discipline and Punish*, London 1979, pp.92f, 101-103.
14. Jeremy Bentham, *Théorie des peines et des récompenses*, edited by Dumont, London 1811. pp.12-13.

15. Jeremy Bentham, *Traités de législation civile et pénale*, 3 vol., Paris 1802, Vol. III, pp.75-76.
16. Ibid. Vol. II, p.381.
17. Jeremy Bentham, *Théorie des peines et des récompenses*, op. cit., p.203.
18. A. Feuerbach, op. cit., Paragraph 13, p.38.
19. E. Ferri, *La teoria dell'imputibilità e la negazione del libero arbitrio*, Firenze 1878.
20. A. Fouillé, *La liberté et le déterminisme*, Paris 1872, Vol. II Para. 3, p.26, cited in Ferri ibid. p.7.
21. G. Carmignani, *Teoria delle leggi sulla sicurezza sociale*, 4 vol., Pisa 1831-32, Vol. I p.21.
22. A. Feuerbach, ibid., Para. 103, p.203.
23. A. Prins, *La défense sociale et la transformation du droit pénal*, 1910, p.10. See also the same author's previous book: *Criminalité et répression*, Brussels, 1886.
24. Renan's words appear as the epigraph to E. de Laveleye and H. Spencer, *L'etat et l'individu ou darwinisme social et christianisme*, Florence 1885.
25. F. von Liszt, *Lehrbuch des deutschen Strafrechts*. Cited here from the French edition, *Traité du droit pénal allemand*, Paris 1911, p.94 and 232-33 note 2; cf. also A. Prins, *Criminalité et répression*, op. cit. p.22.
26. Robert Castel, *L'Ordre psychiatrique*, Vol. 1, *L'age d'or de l'aliénisme*, Paris 1976 pp.276ff.
27. To illustrate this point, two quotations from Morel's *Traité de la médicine légale des aliénes*, Paris 1866, pp.ii-iii and iv. "To suppose that from a juridical or medical point of view a treatise of this kind concerns only the inmates of our asylums, or indeed only those whose palpable insanity is generally recognised by public opinion, would be to misunderstand its aim and scope. Experience teaches us that, over and above madness in the strict sense as described in books and observed in lunatic asylums, madness as it is generally understood in the world, there occur a mass of human actions which by their strangeness, their exceptionally dangerous character, and so to speak their authors' instinctive and reasoned perversity, arouse great perplexity in the minds of judges (. . .) What use to us are the more or less vague definitions of madness, the theories on the degree of criminal responsibility of lunatics and the medico-legal consequences of partial deliria? It is sufficient if we can observe and prove that madness is a disease, a *corporis affectus*, as the masters of antiquity taught; that there is not just one madness, but diverse varieties of this condition; that the lunatic is not an ideal, unique, abstract type (. . .) but that there are diverse categories of lunatics . . ."
28. Gayot de Pitival, *Causes célèbres et intéressantes avec les jugements qui les ont décidés*, Paris 1734-43.
29. A. Feuerbach, *Merkwurdige Kriminalrechtsfälle*, 2 vol., Giessen 1808-11.
30. Cf. *I. Pierre Rivière . . .*, ed. M. Foucault, London 1978.
31. Cf. Robert Castel, 'Doctors and Judges', in ibid.
32. On Lombroso's museum, see F. Colombo's book *La scienza infelice*, remarkable especially for its photographic documentation.
33. A. Prins, *La défense sociale*, op. cit., p.162.
34. Parent-Duchâtelet, *De la prostitution dans la ville de Paris considérée sous le rapport de l'hygiène publique, de la morale et de l'administration*, Paris 1836, 2 vol. See notably Chapter 3.
35. Rusche and Kirchheimer, *Punishment and Social Structure*, New York 1939.
36. E. Ferri, *Relazione sul progetto preliminare di codice penale italiano (Libro I)* Roma 1921, edition in four languages: Italian, French, English and German.
37. Dante, *Inferno*, III 25. Trans. J. Ciardi, New York 1954.
38. Cf. Note 1 above, passim.
39. E. Ferri, op. cit. (Note 2 above), pp.57-58.
40. 'The possible' is meant here in the sense in which Musil writes in *The Man Without Qualities*: "If there is such a thing as a sense of reality, there must

31

also be a sense of possibility" (Vol. 1, Chapter 4, title); I am also thinking especially of the following passage: "The possible, however, covers not only the dreams of nervously sensitive persons, but also the not yet manifested intentions of God. A possible experience or a possible truth does not equate to real experience of real truth minus the value 'real'; but, at least in the opinion of its devotees, a fiery, soaring quality, a constructive will, a conscious utopianism that does not shrink from reality but treats it, on the contrary, as a mission and an invention." Ibid. p.48 (cf. Note 3 above).

41. Thomas Mann, *Joseph and His Brothers*, Part I: The Tales of Jacob, Prelude: Descent into Hell p.3. Penguin Books, 1978. I owe this quotation, among many other things, to my friend E. Galzenati.

[7]

THE BRITISH JOURNAL

OF

CRIMINOLOGY

| Vol. 28 | Spring 1988 | No. 2 |

BRITISH CRIMINOLOGY BEFORE 1935

DAVID GARLAND (*Edinburgh*)*

I

"Criminology", as a professional academic discipline, did not exist in Britain before 1935, and was established only gradually and precariously thereafter. So whatever this essay is about, it cannot be about criminology in quite the sense we think of it today. Instead, it examines some of the lines of emergence of that discipline, and in particular, the theoretical and institutional processes which gave rise to a scientific criminology in Britain. Given the short space available to me here, this can be no more than a very selective account, highlighting a few important currents, while ignoring much that would be essential to a proper genealogy of the subject. My central concern will be to show that the development of British criminology can best be understood by concentrating less upon the spread of ideas from abroad and more upon the ways in which penal and social institutions acted as a practical surface of emergence for this kind of knowledge. What is presented is not an abstracted history of ideas, but instead an attempt to situate criminology within the institutional practices and power relations which have formed its immediate context and foundation. It should be possible, in turn, to situate this history of institutional pragmatics within a wider field of social forces—see Garland (1985)—but no such analysis is attempted here.

By convention, modern scientific criminology[1] is said to have begun with

---

* Lecturer in the Centre for Criminology, University of Edinburgh and currently Visiting Professor at the Center for Law and Society at Berkeley California. I am grateful to Peter Young, Beverley Brown, Phillipe Robert and Roger Hood for their comments on an earlier draft of this article.

[1] The term "scientific" is used in this essay to discuss those forms of talking about crime and criminals which were self-consciously undertaken within a framework derived from natural science. In using the term I intend to distinguish such criminologies from other ones which were phrased in moral, religious or common-sense vocabularies. This uncritical use of the term "science" is intended as an historical attribution, repeating actors' conceptions, not an epistemological evaluation. For a critical discussion of criminology's claims to be a science, see Garland 1985, Ch. 3.

BJC/132   DAVID GARLAND

Lombroso's criminal anthropology in the 1870s, and in one sense this is
true enough, since it was the impact of Lombroso which sparked off the
international congresses and debates of the 1880s and brought the idea of a
criminological science to public prominence for the first time. But criminology
in Britain did not develop out of the Lombrosian tradition. Nor did it derive
from the European movement, despite the way in which Edwardian penal
reforms appeared to follow its lead—even despite the fact that it would later
be a group of European *émigrés* who did most to establish an academic profession of criminologists in this country. In fact the scientific approach to crime
and punishment was not something which Britain reluctantly imported from
abroad. On the contrary, there existed in Britain, from the 1860s onward, a
distinctive, indigenous tradition of applied medico-legal science which was
sponsored by the penal and psychiatric establishments, and it was this
tradition which formed the theoretical and professional space within which
"criminological science" was first developed in this country.[2] If we are to
understand criminology and its social foundations it is important not to confuse
these two traditions, or to collapse one onto the other. In particular, we should
avoid assuming that any criminological work which is "positivist" in style is
somehow derived from the "Scuola Positiva" of Lombroso. Much of the early
British criminology which I will describe falls into the broad epistemological
and methodological categories which we nowadays call "positivist"—but it
had little to do with Lombroso's Positivism, nor indeed with that of Comte.

Lombrosian criminology grew, somewhat accidentally, out of an anthropological concern to study man and his natural varieties. The identification of
human types led Lombroso and others to isolate such types as the genius, the
insane, the epileptoid and the criminal, and to subject them to scientific
scrutiny and categorisation. To some extent this was effectively the rediscrip-
tion in scientific language of distinctions which were already established in
cultural terms, and certainly the excitement which followed Lombroso's
identification of "the born criminal" occurred because his work allowed a
spectacular convergence between human science and the concerns of social
policy. His differentiation of "the criminal type" chimed with deep-rooted
cultural prejudice and also with the real processes of differentiation which
were then being established by the expanding prison system, so that the
apparent policy implications of Lombroso's work immediately became a focus
for widespread attention. But although Lombroso was well aware of the social
policy relevance of his anthropology, and took pains to promote it, he was not,
at first, particularly well informed about the practical realities of crime and
punishment. In consequence, his penology was not just radical and at odds
with current practices: it was also naive and uninformed, demonstrating a

---

[2] There were of course other, indigenous traditions of criminological thought in nineteenth century
Britain, most notably the ecological and social survey work of writers like Joseph Fletcher and Henry
Mayhew. See on this, Lindesmith and Levin (1937), Morris (1957) and Carson and Wiles (1971). This
particular genre was to be retrieved as an important strand in twentieth century British criminology, but it
was not the central, continuous tradition through which the discipline initially developed in this country.
For a comprehensive discussion of early criminology in Britain, see Radzinowicz and Hood (1986), Part I.

lack of familiarity with the normal range of offenders and with the institutions which dealt with them.[3] In fact it is clear that Lombroso had developed his conception of the criminal type more out of theoretical commitment than from practical experience or observation. And although exposure to criticism and his increasing involvement in penal affairs eventually led him to amend his initial framework, and to tone down his more outrageous propositions, it was the clear and unqualified claims of his early work which continued to define the Lombrosian tradition, particularly for those who viewed it from afar.

The psychiatric and medico-legal framework within which Britain developed its early criminological science was different from the Lombrosian tradition in a number of important respects.[4] Unlike anthropology, psychiatry was not concerned to isolate discrete types of human individuals and classify them by means of racial and constitutional differences.[5] Instead, it was a therapeutically oriented discipline based upon a classification system of psychiatric disorders which, like the disease model of nineteenth century medicine, discussed the condition separately from the individual in whom it might be manifested. Within the classification system of morbid psychology there were a variety of conditions which criminals were typically said to exhibit—insanity, moral insanity, degeneracy, feeble-mindedness, etc. But generally speaking, *the* criminal was not conceived as *a* psychological type. Instead the spectrum of psychiatric conditions might be usefully applied to a part of the criminal population: there was no separate criminal psychology or psychiatry, based upon ontological difference.

But more important than this *theoretical* difference was the way in which British psychiatry contrasted with Lombrosian anthropology in its *practical* commitments and its relationship to the institutions of criminal justice. Theorising about the condition of criminals was not done in the abstract, but instead was linked to professional tasks such as the giving of psychiatric evidence before a court of law, or the decisions as to classification, diagnosis and regimen which prison medical officers made on a daily basis. This practical experience was crucial in shaping the psychiatric approach to criminological issues because it ensured that psychiatrists and prison medics were well acquainted with the day to day realities of criminal justice and with the need to bring psychiatric propositions into line with the demands of courts and prison authorities.[6]

[3] For a critical discussion of Lombroso's penology, see the review by Arthur St. John (1912). St. John contrasts Lombroso, who has "never quite thought out the practical part of the subject", with the practical common sense of James Devon and his book *The Criminal and the Community* (1912).

[4] I do not intend to imply here or elsewhere that the criminology of other countries can be accounted for by reference to the Lombrosian tradition. My discussion here relates only to Britain and my intention is to show how the history of British criminology differs from its conventional description—not from that of other countries.

[5] These theoretical differences were not, however, absolute; there was a certain fluidity and overlap between all of the mid-century "sciences of man". Although psychiatry was primarily concerned with mental or psychic phenomena, it was at times intensely "physicalist" in its mode of explanation, and readers of the British psychiatric journals were kept well informed of developments in European anthropology, craniology and biology. The same overlap can be seen in Lombroso's own work, which draws indiscriminately upon all of these different "sciences".

[6] On this process of conflict and adjustment, see R. Smith (1981).

BJC/134   DAVID GARLAND

One can see the developing effects of this professional experience by reading through the psychiatric journals of this period and noting the changing terms in which criminals are discussed. In the 1860s Henry Maudsley and particularly J. Bruce Thomson could write, quite unguardedly, about "the genuine criminal" and "the criminal class", variously calling them "morally insane", "degenerate", "defective in physical organisation—from hereditary causes" and "incurable" in a way which is, for all the world, Lombrosian before Lombroso. Others though, like G. McKenzie Bacon, took care to distinguish between the "wilful" criminal on the one hand, and "the diseased" on the other,[7] and from the 1870s onward, prison doctors such as David Nicolson and later John Baker set about redefining "the morbid psychology of criminals", so as to differentiate a range of conditions rather than a single type. Nicolson emphasised that professional observation made it clear that only a minority of criminals were in any sense mentally abnormal, and he forcibly dispelled any suggestion that the general reformation of offenders was put in question by psychiatric science.[8] At the same time, the wider profession was learning—sometimes to its cost—that the criminal courts would not tolerate any psychiatric evidence which contradicted legal axioms about the general nature of action, or the importance of responsibility for conduct, and it gradually developed a practical *modus vivendi* which aimed to minimise conflict between psychiatry and the legal institutions. By the 1880s, leading figures of the new profession such as Needham, Hack Tuke, Nicolson and the mature Maudsley were able to distance themselves from the kind of embarassing or outrageous claims made by psychiatrists in earlier years—claims which were now being taken up again by the new criminal anthropologists.[9]

The British tradition of scientific thinking about criminals was thus, from an early age, situated within an institutional framework which had the support of the prison establishment and the prestige of medicine behind it. Partly in consequence, it was generally modest in its claims, and very respectful of the requirements of institutional regimes and legal principles. As far

---

[7] See G. McKenzie Bacon (1864); H. Maudsley (1863); J. Bruce Thomson (1867), (1869–70) and (1870–71).

[8] See D. Nicolson ("D.N.") (1872–73) where he stresses the importance of studying "the mental condition of the mass [of prisoners]"—not just the minority of insane or weak-minded inmates. In Nicolson (1873–74) (continued in subsequent volumes) he sets out a typology ranging from the "accidental criminal" to the "habitual and thorough criminal" and talks of the "psychical range" which the population of criminals displays. See also Nicolson (1878–79) where he criticises the claims of J. Bruce Thomson as "rash and misleading and fallacious" (p. 18) as well as Maudsley's tendency to generalise the link between insanity and crime. His concern is with the dangers such exaggerations present to the hope that ". . . there may be found a consentatious principle upon which the law and medical psychology may be able to harmonise in the matter of criminal responsibility" (p. 20). See also John Baker (1888), (1891) and (1896).

[9] See H. Maudsley (1889): ". . . first, there is no general criminal constitution, predisposing to and, as it were, excusing crime; second, . . . there are no theories of criminal anthropology so well-grounded and exact as to justify their introduction into a revised criminal law" (p. 165) and the remarks made in discussion by Dr. Needham and Dr. Hack Tuke (ibid.). See also D. Nicolson (1895) and the discussion by Sir Edmund Du Cane, Dr. Clouston and Dr. Conolly Norman: ". . . any address which exposes the puerilities of criminal anthropology is distinctly an advantage" (pp. 589–590). Finally, see H. Maudsley (1895) where he criticises the "lamentable extravagances" of the latest school of criminology: ". . . although they make the vulgar stare, they make the judicious grieve" (p. 662).

4

as most prison doctors and experienced psychiatrists were concerned, the majority of criminals were more or less normal individuals; only a minority required psychiatric treatment, and this usually involved removing them from the penal system and into institutions for the mentally ill or defective. And although the diagnostic and therapeutic claims of psychiatry changed over time, from an early stage there was a recognition that, for the mainstream of offenders, the normal processes of law and punishment should apply. Compared to the sweeping claims of criminal anthropology, the psychiatric tradition was, by the 1880s, somewhat conservative in appearance.

But conservative or not (and here it depends on point of view) it was within this framework that most scientific-criminological work was done in Britain up until the middle of the twentieth century. It is, for example, almost exclusively within the Reports of the Medical Commissioner of Prisons and of the various Prison Medical Officers that one will find any official discussion of criminological science in the period before 1935. Similarly, most of the major scientific works on crime, written in Britain before 1935, were written by medics with psychiatric training and positions within the prison service, among them J. F. Sutherland (1908), R. F. Quinton (1910), J. Devon (1912), M. Hamblin Smith (1922), W. C. Sullivan (1924) and W. Norwood East (1927).

The first university lectures in "Criminology" delivered in this country—given at Birmingham by Maurice Hamblin Smith from the 1921/1922 session onwards—were directed to postgraduate medical students within a course entitled "Medical Aspects of Crime and Punishment", and long before Mannheim began teaching at the London School of Economics (LSE) in 1935 there were courses on "Crime and Insanity" offered at London University by senior prison medical officers such as Sullivan and East.

As for professional journals, although there was no specialist periodical devoted to criminology before 1950 (if one excludes the crime enthusiast's magazine *The Criminologist*, one issue of which appeared in 1927), a variety of medical and psychiatric journals devoted regular sections to issues of criminological science, above all the *Journal of Mental Science* (JMS), which had a criminological review section and regular articles, and the *Transactions* of the Medico-Legal Association, which from 1933, was renamed *The Medico-Legal and Criminological Review*. In contrast, journals such as *The Sociological Review*, which would later become an important outlet for criminological publications, carried nothing substantial on the subject from its inception in 1908 until the first British publications of Mannheim and Radzinowicz in the late 1930s.

Set against this background, the scepticism which greeted Havelock Ellis' campaign to introduce to Britain the teachings of criminal anthropology can be understood rather differently.[10] It was not, as historians have suggested, that the idea of a scientific approach to crime was culturally alien to the British. In fact Ellis' book was warmly welcomed by eminent representatives of the new scientific spirit such as Francis Galton, and many lay reviewers

---

[10] See H. Ellis : 1890). 1890a, and his "retrospects" section in the *JMS* where he reviewed works on criminal anthropology from 1890 until 1919.

considered it to be of great interest[11]—as, apparently, did the literate public, which continued to buy it through three editions and several print runs. Rather, what the book encountered was a professional scepticism, based not upon anti-scientism but upon a rather different scientific tradition—one which was more modest, more acceptable to the institutional authorities, and was organised by engaged professionals rather than by maverick intellectuals. In his later years, the first Medical Commissioner of Prisons, Sir Horatio Bryan Donkin, gave clear expression to the distinction between the two traditions. Professing some discomfort at having to use the term at all, he contrasted what he understood as "criminology" properly so-called—namely the investigations undertaken by "persons concerned in some way with prison authorities who strive to discover just principles on which to base their work"—with the newer "doctrine and debate on the causation of crime" which he condemned as "theories based on preconceived assumptions regardless of fact".[12] A similar position was still being argued by Norwood East in the 1930s, when he occupied this same leading office.

In fact Havelock Ellis perfectly epitomised Donkin's view of the "theoretical" criminologist, whose knowledge was based entirely on book learning and second-hand doctrine.[13] Of the all criminological experts of this period, he was the only one with no practical involvement or experience, which was why he was able to approach the work of Lombroso, Benedict and Ferri with such unqualified enthusiasm. It was also why he continued to think of men like Maudsley and Nicolson as being forerunners of the Lombrosian tradition, even after they had done their vehement best to distance themselves from it.[14] In the end, Ellis' popularisation of criminal anthropology had little impact upon the thinking of practitioners, though it was important in other ways. His introduction into English of the term "criminology" in 1890 had the effect of firmly associating that name with the "criminal type" doctrines of Lombroso, thereby making it the subject of considerable scepticism, even where the Lombrosian heritage was actually negligible. In the same way, his much-referenced historical account of the subject has tended to link British criminology to criminal anthropology, and to assimilate all indigenous work to this single, European tradition. Less importantly, it was Ellis (followed by Bonger (1936)) who first made the now conventional attribution of the term "criminology" to remarks by Topinard in 1889. In fact the word—or rather its French and Italian equivalents—was certainly in use earlier than this. It was, for instance, the title of Garafalo's major work of 1885.

Interestingly, the only other person to take up the continental writers in the 1890s was the Revd W. Douglas Morrison, a Canadian who became a prison

---

[11] See the anonymous review of *The Criminal* in *The Athenæum*. 6 September 1890. Francis Galton's review appears in *Nature*. 22 May 1890 at pp. 75–76. See also the anonymous review in *The Saturday Review*. 30 August 1890 which doubts the scientific wisdom and practical use of criminal anthropology.

[12] H. B. Donkin (1917) p. 17.

[13] For Ellis' own account of his writing of *The Criminal*, see Ellis (1940).

[14] See Ellis' footnote in "The Study of the Criminal" cited above: "In recent utterances Dr. Maudsley seems to ignore, or to treat with indifference, the results of criminal anthropology. These results are, however, but the legitimate outcome of the ideas of which it is his chief distinction to have been the champion" p. 6.

chaplain at Wandsworth and whose radical criticisms of the system helped provoke the appointment of the Gladstone Committee in 1894. Morrison was responsible for establishing and editing "The Criminology Series", a rather quirky, short-lived venture, which published translations of works by Lombroso (1895), Ferri (1895), and Proal (1898), as well as Morrison's own *Juvenile Offenders* (1896). Significantly though, Morrison's utilisation of these European theorists—as demonstrated in his "Introductions" to their texts and in his own work[15]—placed greatest emphasis upon the penal reform arguments which the new movement provided. Indeed his reduction of the new criminology to a scientific argument for penal reform which could strengthen the evangelical and humanitarian campaign, was perhaps the most characteristic way in which the European tradition was received in this country. When Major Arthur Griffiths, the retired Prison Inspector and one-time delegate to the Congress of Criminal Anthropology in Geneva, 1896, was commissioned to write the first ever entry on "Criminology" for the 11th (1910–11) edition of the *Encyclopaedia Britannica*, he showed the same broad scepticism for the theory of criminal types, together with a cautious interest in the penological ideas which were by now emerging from the movement.

II

The British tradition of institutionally-based, administratively-oriented criminology was, by its nature, a dynamic, evolving tradition. The "criminological" texts which it generated grew out of practical contexts which were forever changing, since institutions continually redefined their operations and took on new concerns, and also because new methods, theories and techniques became available to the professionals responsible for administering them.

Much of nineteenth century criminology, in this sphere, had grown out of the reclassification of selected offenders as being primarily psychiatric cases, rather than criminal ones, either because of moral insanity, or later, because of the less severe but more widespread diagnosis of feeble-mindedness. Underlying this process and the theoretical texts it produced was, of course, the institutional division between the asylum and the prison, or more broadly, between medicine and law. After about 1895 this simple division began to be reformulated to accommodate the much more complex world of penal-welfare institutions, with its more refined classifications and selection procedures, and the allocation of offenders to a greatly extended range of institutions and regimes. One result of this was an important extension of the specialist's role within the system, and a corresponding increase in the production of criminological literature which theorised those new diagnostic and classificatory tasks and the principles upon which they should be based. Such work as *Alcoholism* (1906) by W. C. Sullivan, *Recidivism* (1908) by J. F. Sutherland, *The Psychology of the Criminal* (1922) by M. Hamblin Smith and

[15] See W. D. Morrison (1889) and (1891).

7

BJC/138   DAVID GARLAND

"The Psychology of Crime" (1932) by H. E. Field are significant examples of criminological work derived from this developing context.

In 1919, the new penological emphasis upon individual character and specialised treatment—together with concerns about the large numbers of shell-shocked and mentally disturbed men returning from the War—led the Birmingham Justices to establish a permanent scheme for the clinical examination of adult offenders who came before the courts. Previously such work had been done on an occasional, *ad hoc* basis, and depended upon the skill and interest of the local prison doctor. By appointing M. Hamblin Smith and W. A. Potts, both psychiatrically-trained prison medics, and charging them with these new duties, the Justices (together with the Prison Commission) effectively created a new specialism for applied criminology. Before long, Potts, and particularly Hamblin Smith, were adapting the standard forms of mental tests for use in this specialist area, publishing the results of their clinical studies, and writing extensively about the need for this kind of investigation and its implications for the treatment and prevention of crime. In *The Psychology of the Criminal* (1922) and in a series of articles in the JMS, The Howard Journal and elsewhere, Smith emphasised the importance of criminological study, though for him this meant the kind of clinical examination of individuals which the Birmingham scheme employed.[16] As Britain's first authorised teacher of "criminology", and the first individual to go under the title of "criminologist", it is significant that Smith, too, rejected the search for "general theories" in favour of the "study of the individual".[17] Significantly too, the centres of criminological research and teaching, which he called to be set up in each university town, were envisaged as places where "young medical graduates" would be trained to become expert in the medical examination and assessment of offenders.

Hamblin Smith was also one of the first criminological workers in Britain to profess an interest in psycho-analysis, which he utilised as a means to assess the personality "make-up" of offenders, as well as proposing it as a technique for treating the mental conflicts and abnormalities which, he claimed, lay behind the criminal act. In this respect, Smith met with much official opposition, particularly from W. Norwood East,[18] but there were others, outside the establishment, who were more enthusiastic about the role of psycho-analysis. In the winter of 1922–23 Dr. Grace Pailthorpe voluntarily assisted Smith in the psycho-analytic investigation of female offenders at Birmingham, and went on to complete a 5-year study at Holloway, funded by a grant from the Medical Research Council (MRC). Her Report—completed by 1929, but delayed by the MRC until 1932—and its claim that crime was a symptom of mental conflict which might be psycho-analytically resolved, met with some consternation in official circles (see East 1936, 319) but it excited the interest

---

[16] See M. Hamblin Smith (1921), (1922) and (1925) and the reviews which Smith contributed to the *JMS* in this period. See also W. A. Potts (1921) and (1925).

[17] M. Hamblin Smith 1922 at p. 25.

[18] See, for example, East (1924–25). This kind of opposition seems to have restrained Smith somewhat, as East noted in his obituary: "Hamblin Smith was a convinced determinist and an omnivorous reader of philosophy and speculative psychology, but he retained a clear distinction between assumptions and facts, and his theoretical inclinations never obtruded in his daily duties" East (1936a) at p. 292.

of a number of analysts and medical psychologists who formed a group to promote the Report and its approach. Out of their meetings emerged the Association for the Scientific Treatment of Criminals (1931), which, in 1932, became the Institute for the Scientific Treatment of Delinquency (ISTD).[19]

In fact most of the founder members of this group were in some way or other involved in the new and expanding out-patient sector of psychiatric work, made possible by the opening of private clinics such as the Tavistock (1921), the Maudsley (1923), the new child guidance centres, and eventually, the ISTD's own Psychopathic Clinic (1933) (later moved and renamed the Portman Clinic (1937)). Once again this new field of practice gave rise to its own distinctive brand of criminological theory. The early publications of the ISTD emphasise the clinical exploration of individual personality, and in that sense are continuous with much previous work. But they also manifest a new preventative emphasis, which reflected the fact that the new clinics operated outside the formal penal system, and could deal with individuals before their disturbed conduct actually became criminal. Eventually the group's emphasis upon psycho-analysis, and its open hostility to much official penal policy, ensured that the ISTD remained essentially outsiders, usually operating at arms length from the Home office and the Prison Commission.[20] This outsider status forms an important background to the later decision of the Home Office to establish a criminological institute at Cambridge, rather than under ISTD auspices in London, for although "the formation of such a body was one of the original aims of the ISTD" (Glover 1960, 70) the Home Office appears not to have even considered such an option.

Despite its subsequent neglect, the work of W. Norwood East—particularly *Forensic Psychiatry* (1927) and *The Medical Aspects of Crime* (1936)—better represents the mainstream of British criminology in the 1920s and 1930s. East was a psychiatrically trained prison medical officer who became a leading figure in the 1930s as Medical Director on the Prison Commission, and President of the Medico-Legal Society, and his views dominated official policy-making for a lengthy period. East was himself a proponent of a psychological approach to crime, but he viewed its scope as being sharply delimited, and consistently warned against the dangers and absurdities of exaggerating its claims. In 1934, he established an extended experiment at Wormwood Scrubs, whereby those offenders deemed most likely to respond to psychological therapy— particularly sex offenders and arsonists—were subjected to a period of investigation and treatment by Dr. W. H. de B. Hubert. At the end of five years, East and Hubert's *Report on the Psychological Treatment of Crime* (1939)

[19] According to E. Glover's (1950–51) obituary of Dr. E. T. Jensen, this early group included the following individuals: Dr. E. T. Jensen, Mrs. Charles Tharp, Victor B. Neuberg, Dr. Jennings-White, Dr. A. C. Wilson, Dr. Worster Drought, Dr. David Eder, Dr. J. A. Hadfield, Dr. E. Miller and Dr. E. Glover himself. About the same time that Pailthorpe was completing her research at Holloway, Alice Raven published a number of articles setting out a psychoanalytical approach to crime. See Raven (1928) and (1929). See also Melanie Klein (1927) and (1934). The founding document of this psychoanalytical approach to crime was Freud's "Criminality from a Sense of Guilt" which was first published in 1915.

[20] Emanuel Miller recollects: ".... feeling like a conspiratorial group as the Establishment was hardly sympathetic: early criminological workers such as Norwood East, Hubert and prison administrator Lionel Fox were sympathetic but markedly orthodox" Miller (1970).

BJC/140   DAVID GARLAND

re-affirmed East's view that while 80 per cent of offenders were psychologically normal, and would respond to routine punishment, a minority might usefully be investigated and offered psychological treatment. The Report proposed a special institution to deal with such offenders—a proposal which was immediately accepted but not enacted until the opening of Grendon Underwood in 1962. East and Hubert also recommended that this proposed institution should function as a centre for criminological research, and it is significant that here, when a criminological centre is proposed for the first time in an official Report, it should be envisaged as a psychiatric institution, dealing only with a small minority of offenders.

An important departure from this series of clinically-based, psychiatric studies, was *The English Convict: A Statistical Study*, by Dr. Charles Goring.[21] This work also grew out of institutional routines, insofar as anthropometric measurement was used in prisons for the identification of habitual offenders during the 1890s, but it represented much more than the writing up of daily experience. In fact, in its final, expanded form, the study represents a major development because it signals the use of deliberately undertaken social science research to answer questions posed in institutional practice. The questions taken up here were numerous, and came from a variety of sources. Major Arthur Griffiths had previously suggested that data might be collected to test Lombroso's criminal type hypothesis against the evidence of English prisoners (Radzinowicz and Hood 1986, 20) and this may have been the original motivation of his name-sake, Dr. G. B. Griffiths, who began the work at Parkhurst Prison in 1901. It was probably a belief that other, useful information could be generated—for example, about the numbers of feeble-minded persons in prison, or the effect of prison diet and conditions upon the physical and mental health of inmates—which led Sir Bryan Donkin and Sir Herbert Smalley, the senior medical staff of the prison system, to take up the research and extend it considerably. The work was completed by Dr. Charles Goring, after a lengthy secondment at Karl Pearson's Biometrical laboratory, where he tabulated and analysed a vast quantity of data—motivated, no doubt, by a mixture of scientific curiosity and eugenist commitment.

As its sponsors intended, the study gave a definitive refutation of the old Lombrosian claim that the criminal corresponded to a particular physical type, thus confirming the position which the British authorities had held all along. However Goring's study went much further than this negative finding. In fact, in an important sense Goring's analysis *began* by assuming that there was no criminal type, as such, and although it was not much noticed at the time, his study is chiefly notable for demonstrating a quite new way of conceiving the criminal "difference". In the early part of the book, Goring set out extensive theoretical and methodological arguments which insisted that criminality should be viewed not as a qualitative difference of type, marked by anomaly and morbidity, but instead as a variant of normality, differentiated only by degree. Following the arguments of Manouvrier and Topinard, he pointed out that so-called criminal "anomalies" are only "more or less

---

[21] For a detailed discussion of this work, see Beirne (1987).

extreme degrees of character which in some degree are present in all men".
Moreover, he made it clear that his use of statistical method necessarily pre-
supposed this idea of a criminal characteristics which is a common feature of
all individuals, and he went on to name this hypothesized entity "the criminal
diathesis".

This conception of criminality as normal, rather than morbid or pathological, implied a new basis for criminological science, which Goring vigorously
set forth. From now on, criminology could no longer depend upon the clinical
gaze of a Lombroso and its impressionistic identification of anomalies.
(Goring had, in any case, provided a devastating critique of such methods.)
Instead it must be a matter of large populations, careful measurement and
statistical analysis, demonstrating patterns of differentiation in the mass
which would not be visible in the individual or to the naked eye. His own
study, he concluded, had revealed a significant, but by no means universal,
association between criminality and two heritable characteristics, namely low
intelligence and poor physique.

Although *The English Convict* made a massive impact abroad, and especially
in the U.S.A., in Britain it received a surprisingly muted response which
dismayed both its author, and his mentor, Karl Pearson. On the one hand,
Goring's attack had been centred upon theoretical positions which had little
support in this country; and on the other, it appeared to have policy
implications—eugenic and otherwise—which were not altogether welcome in
official circles. The Prison Commission, while supporting the study's publication as a Blue Book, refused to endorse all of its conclusions. Sir Evelyn
Ruggles-Brise provided a preface to the book which took care to render its
finding compatible with the official brand of penal reform, while Sir Bryan
Donkin distances himself from the study altogether, arguing that "even correct
generalisations . . . . concerning convicted criminals in the mass are not likely
to be of much positive value in the study or treatment of individuals . . . ".[22] In
much the same way W. C. Sullivan, the medical superintendent of Broadmoor,
argued in *Crime and Insanity* (1924) that clinical rather than statistical methods
were the only reliable means to obtaining useful, policy relevant knowledge.
Nevertheless, Goring's major argument—for the importance of statistical
method in criminological research—was, in the long term, taken up by the
British authorities. By the end of the 1930s, the Prison Commission and
the Home Office had each embarked upon large-scale, statistically-based
projects—eventually published as East (1942) and Carr-Saunders *et al.*
(1942)—and this became the characteristics form of government sponsored
research in the years after 1945.

The English Convict was a transitional work. Its conception of criminality as
continuous with normal conduct, together with its statistical sophistication,
opened up new research questions and methods for their solution, and gave
British criminological work a scope and rigour which it had not possessed
before. However its extensive engagement with older questions about

---

[22] Sir H. Bryan Donkin (1919). This article is part of an exchange with Goring, provoked by Donkin's
1917 paper. See Goring's response; Goring (1918).

BJC/142   DAVID GARLAND

"criminal types" and "physical anomalies" meant that for much of the book
its language and concepts were those of a pre-modern idiom—an idiom
which, even in 1913. was not much spoken in this country.[23] A mark of the
book's success is that this idiom quickly became archaic, even in places such as
the U.S.A. where it had once been strong.

                                    III

When later criminologists such as Mannheim and Radzinowicz looked back
upon their predecessors—and being the founders of a profession they were
deeply concerned to establish a proper ancestry—they spent little time discussing the merits of *The English Convict*. Instead, they invariably picked out
Cyril Burt's 1925 study of *The Young Delinquent* as the first work of modern
criminology, and as an exemplar for the profession they were forming.[24] And
indeed even now, more than sixty years after its publication, if one reads the
600 odd pages of *The Young Delinquent* it still seems strikingly modern in a way
which even the best works of this period do not—not least because much of
subsequent criminology was actually formed in its image. It seems appropriate
then, to end this survey by asking what it was about Burt's work which gave it
this major status and its aspect of "modernity".

Burt's book combined the statistical expertise of a Goring with the clinical
experience and practical concerns of workers like Hamblin Smith, Sullivan
and East, but was actually written for a wide popular audience, with a degree
of verve and literary style rarely encountered in a scholarly text. Its analyses
had all the marks of the scientist and disciplined researcher, but it also carried
the transparent common sense of a practitioner who appeared to know his
clients intimately (and compassionately) and who was concerned to specify
viable modes of individual treatment as well as scientific claims about
causation. As such, it could, and did, appeal to the widest range of readers—
not just "criminological workers" but also parents, teachers, social workers,
and social policy-makers—thereby linking scientific criminology into the
other important traditions of writing and thinking about crime. It was a work
which was able to open out criminological science, making it more relevant
and comprehensible to a wider public than ever before.

Like most other British criminological texts, *The Young Delinquent* emerged
from a specific field of practice, but in common with the subsequent work of
the ISTD, and in marked contrast to most previous work in this genre, this
field of practice was outside or on the margins of the penal system, rather than
central to it. In his post as educational psychologist to the London County
Council—the first post of its kind in Britain—Burt was responsible for the
psychological assessment and advising of London's school-child population,

[23] In fact *The English Convict* was widely interpreted as presenting an alternative version of "the criminal
type". See the review symposium in the American *Journal of Criminal Law, Criminology and Police Science*,
Vol. 5 (1914–15) and also W. C. Sullivan (1924) pp. 9–10.
[24] See L. Radzinowicz (1961) pp. 173–176: " . . . it may be said that modern criminological research in
England dates only from Sir Cyril Burt's study of *The Young Delinquent*, first published in 1925. Its excellence
in method and interpretation was at once recognised and it has stood the test of rapidly advancing
knowledge". See also H. Mannheim (1949) at p. 11.

which involved him in examining thousands of individual problem cases—many of them behavioural as well as educational—and making recommendations for their treatment. His books from this period were thus a kind of operational research, reflecting his practice, its problems, and the data he derived therefrom.[25] It was thus an educational rather than a penal surface of emergence which allowed Burt to develop his criminological study around a wider than usual population—notably including pre-delinquents as well as convicted offenders—and which also released his inquiries from the narrowness of penal or prison-based issues. Rather than inquire about specific classifications or distinctions, Burt was interested to specify all the possible sources of individual psychological difference, and thereby to identify the causal patterns which precipitate delinquency and non-delinquency.

The Young Delinquent was based upon the detailed clinical examination of 400 schoolchildren (a delinquent or quasi-delinquent group and a control group), using a technical repertoire which included biometric measurement, mental testing, psycho-analysis and social inquiries, together with the most up-to-date statistical techniques of factor analysis and correlation. Its findings were expansively eclectic, identifying some 170 causitive factors which were in some way associated with delinquency, and showing, by way of narrative case histories, how each factor might typically operate. From his analysis, Burt concluded that certain factors, such as defective discipline, defective family relationships and particular types of temperament were highly correlated with delinquency, while the influence of other factors, such as poverty or low intelligence, while not altogether negligible, had been seriously overstated in the past. His major proposition was that delinquency was not the outcome of special factors operating only upon delinquents, but was rather the result of a combination of factors—typically as many as nine or ten—operating at once upon a single individual. In consequence, the study of criminality must be, above all, multi-causal in scope, while its treatment must be tailored to fit the needs of the individual case.

Although Burt conceived his book as part of a larger study within individual psychology, *The Young Delinquent*, more than any other work, set out the case for an independent, self-constituting discipline of criminology. As glimpsed through Burt's work, criminology was so broad in its eclectic coverage, drawing upon a wide range of sciences and disciplines, and yet so focused in its particular concerns, dealing with the peculiarities of offenders and the institutional complex that surrounded them, that it cried out for specialised expertise. The book suggested a vision of criminological research as an eclectic, multi-disciplinary activity, based upon the clinical study of individuals, and held together by statistical analysis. It also evoked an image of the professional criminologist, conversant with the quirks and characteristics of

[25] *The Young Delinquent* was completed about 20 years before the first occasion on which Burt is known to have falsified data and findings. In his biography *Cyril Burt: Psychologist* (1979), L. S. Hearnshaw describes how Burt's manipulation of data and manufacturing of results occurred at a time when he was out of immediate touch with field research (having lost much of his original data as a result of the war) and was responding defensively against challenges to his deeply held beliefs about the existence and hereditary nature of general intelligence. He was probably also suffering from the psychosomatic condition known as Menseres Disease.

13

BJC/144   DAVID GARLAND

deviant individuals, familiar with the vagaries of institutional practice, and able to translate scientific research into practical advice for the solution of important social problems.[26] Conceived in these terms, criminology could hardly be left as the passing trade of non-specialists from other disciplines, so it is hardly surprising that Burt's book would later hold such great appeal for those who favoured the idea of an independent criminology.

One might pause to reflect here that Burt's rationale for the discipline is based entirely upon the pragmatics of applied science and social necessity. It is a claim that criminological issues are important enough and complex enough to warrant specialised study, not that there is any distinctive object of study which can only be understood criminologically. In this respect it is very different from criminology's original Lombrosian claim that the criminal type is a naturally occurring entity which requires a scientific specialism of its own. And although this conception of criminology as rooted in the needs of social policy is perhaps more realistic and more enduring than one purportedly based upon a division of nature, it does raise questions about the nature of a knowledge which is linked so closely to forms of institutional power and policy. Or at least it should raise such questions: it would be some fifty years after Burt's work before criminologists began to take them seriously.[27]

Burt's work is thus important because it exhibits a framework which academic criminology would later latch onto and form itself around. But it would be historically short-sighted to concentrate too much upon texts which gave criminology its specific configuration at the moment of its professional inception—not least because that configuration has been changing ever since. This essay has concentrated instead upon some of the earlier work which helped prepare a social and institutional space for criminology in Britain. In particular it has discussed the institutionally-linked psychiatric tradition, which can be seen as the crucial route by which the idea of a scientific approach to criminals became implanted—however marginally[28]—in penal practice, in the courts, and in the policy thinking of governmental authorities. To some extent this might be seen as the "official criminology" of the period. It did not represent a general theory of crime, or even a full research programme which might produce one, and it would later be unpopular with academics for precisely that reason. But, as I have stressed, this tradition had no such ambition. Its goal was not general theory but instead particular understanding for specific, practical purposes, and it was bound to conflict with the intellectual ambitions of academic criminology in the 1950s, just as it had done with the continental work of the 1880s.

Criminologists in Britain, before the development of a university-based profession, were characteristically practitioners. Insofar as they had an expertise or a knowledge-base it was a detailed knowledge of the institutional terrain and its requirements, together with a general training in medicine or

[26] In his lecture "Should the Criminologist be Encouraged?" Paterson (1931–32). Alexander Paterson uses Cyril Burt as an exemplar of what "the criminologist" might amount to, given official support.
[27] Matza (1969) drew attention to the way in which criminologists had "separated the study of crime from the workings and theory of the state" (at p. 143). Much of the radical criminology of the 1970's and 1980's can be seen as an attempt to restructure the field so as to overcome this separation.
[28] Pat Carlen (1986) describes the contemporary operation of psychiatry in British prisons.

psychiatry, and later, psychology. It was this practical surface of emergence which largely accounts for the individualised, policy-based and theoretically limited criminology which was characteristic of Britain before 1935.

The history of British criminology has mostly been written by modern academic criminologists who searched in vain for "schools of criminology" and, finding none, have concluded that the subject was painfully slow to develop in this country. In doing so, they echo the complaints of Ellis or Morrison who also did not know, or did not like, the indigenous criminology of this early period. But if we cease to assume that "criminology" can take only an academic form, and instead ask about the ways in which scientific thinking about crime has previously been located in the social fabric, then the foundations of the criminological enterprise will be traced rather differently. By doing so, we can put ourselves in a position to judge the wider implications of these different traditions—their effects as forms of power as well as forms of knowledge.[29] At a time when a renewed vision of criminology as an engaged administrative knowledge has risen up to challenge the 1970s ideal of independent and critical theorising, there may be some value in pursuing this line of inquiry.

David Garland
University of Edinburgh
August 1987

REFERENCES

BACON, G. McKENZIE (1864). "Prison Discipline". *The Social Science Review* (New Series) II.

BAKER, John (1888). "Some Remarks on the Relation of Epilepsy and Crime". *J.M.S.* **XXXIV**, 183–191.

BAKER, John (1891). "Some Points connected with Criminals". *J.M.S* **XXXVIII**, 364–369.

BAKER, John (1896). "Insanity in English Local Prisons 1894–95". *J.M.S.* **XLII**, 294–302.

BEIRNE, Piers (1987). "Carapace, Crab, Cranium Criminal: A Reconsideration of Charles Goring's *The English Convict*." Paper delivered at the British Criminology Conference, Sheffield, July 1987.

BONGER, William Adriaan (1936). *An Introduction to Criminology*. London.

BURT, Cyril (1925). *The Young Delinquent*. London.

CARLEN, Pat (1986). "Psychiatry in Prisons" In P. Miller and N. Rose (eds.), *The Power of Psychiatry*.

CARR-SAUNDERS, A., MANNHEIM, H. and RHODES, E. C. (1942). *Young Offenders*. London.

CARSON, W. G. and WILES, P. (eds.) (1971). *Crime and Delinquency in Britain, Vol. 1*. Oxford.

DEVON, James (1912). *The Criminal and the Community*. London.

DONKIN, H. Bryan (1917). "Notes on Mental Defect in Criminals". *J.M.S.* **LXIII**.

DONKIN, H. Bryan (1919). "The Factors of Criminal Action". *J.M.S.* **XLV**, 87–96.

---

[29] For a discussion of these issues, see Garland (1985a).

BJC/146   DAVID GARLAND

EAST, W. Norwood (1924–25). Report of the Medical Officer of Brixton Prison in *The Report of the Commissioners of Prisons for 1923–24*, pp. 1924–25. Cmnd. 2307 XV, 44.

EAST, W. Norwood (1927). *An Introduction to Forensic Psychiatry in the Criminal Courts* London.

EAST, W. Norwood (1936). *The Medical Aspects of Crime*. London.

EAST, W. Norwood (1936a). Obituary of M. Hamblin Smith *J.M.S.* LXXXII.

EAST, W. Norwood and HUBERT. W. H. de B. (1939). *Report on the Psychological Treatment of Crime*. H.M.S.O. London.

EAST, W. Norwood (1942). *The Adolescent Criminal; A Medico-Sociological Study of 4,000 Male Adolescents*. London.

ELLIS, Havelock (1890). *The Criminal*. London.

ELLIS, Havelock (1890a). "The Study of the Criminal" *J.M.S.* XXXVI.

ELLIS, Havelock (1940). *My Life*. London.

FERRI, Enrico (1895). *Criminal Sociology*. (Vol. 2 in "The Criminology Series"). London.

FIELD, H. E. (1932). "The Psychology of Crime: The Place of Psychology in *the* Treatment of Delinquents". *British Journal of Medical Psychology*. 12, 241–256.

FREUD, Sigmund (1915). "Criminality from a Sense of Guilt" in "Some Character Types Met with in Psycho-analytic Work" in S. Freud: *Collected Papers* Vol 4 (ed. J. Riviere) (1959) New York. (First published in *Imago*. IV (1915–16).

GALTON, Francis (1890). "Criminal Anthropology". *Nature*, 22 May 1890.

GARLAND, David (1985). *Punishment and Welfare*. Aldershot.

GARLAND, David (1985a). "Politics and Policy in Criminological Discourse". *The International Journal of the Sociology of Law*. 13, 1–33.

GLOVER, Edward (1950–51). Obituary of Dr. E. T. Jensen *The British Journal of Delinquency*. 1.

GORING, Charles (1913). *The English Convict: A Statistical Study*. London.

GORING, Charles (1918). "The Aetiology of Crime". *J.M.S.* LXIV, 129–146.

GRIFFITHS, Major Arthur (1910–11). Entry on "Criminology" in *The Encyclopaedia Britannica*. 11th edition.

HEARNSHAW, L. S. (1979). *Cyril Burt, Psychologist*.

KLEIN, Melanie (1927). "Criminal Tendencies in Normal Children". *The British Journal of Medical Psychology*. VII.

KLEIN, Melanie (1934). "On Criminality". *The British Journal of Medical Psychology*, XIV.

LOMBROSO, Cesare (1895). *The Female Offender*. (Vol. 1 in "The Criminology Series"). London.

LINDESMITH, A. and LEVIN, Y. (1937). "The Lombrosian Myth in Criminology". *American Journal of Sociology*. XLII, 653–671.

MANNHEIM, Hermann (1949). Contribution to *Why Delinquency?* published by the National Association for Mental Health.

MATZA, David (1969). *Becoming Deviant*. New Jersey.

MAUDSLEY, Henry (1863). Review of "Female Life in Prison". *J.M.S.* IX.

MAUDSLEY, Henry (1889). "Remarks on Crime and Criminals". *J.M.S.* XXXIV.

MAUDSLEY, Henry (1895). "Criminal Responsibility in Relation to Insanity". *J.M.S.* XLI.

MILLER, Emanuel (1970). "Retrospects and Reflections, 1950–1970". *The British Journal of Criminology.* **10**, No. 4.

MORRIS, Terrence : 1957). *The Criminal Area: A Study in Social Ecology.* London.

MORRISON, W. Douglas (1889). "Reflections on the Theories of Criminality" *J.M.S.* **XXXV.**

MORRISON, W. Douglas (1891). *Crime and Its Causes.* London.

MORRISON, W. Douglas (1896). *Juvenile Offenders.* (Vol. 3 in "The Criminology Series"). London.

NICOLSON, David (1872–73). "Criminal Psychology". *J.M.S.* **XVIII.**

NICOLSON, David (1873–74). "The Morbid Psychology of Criminals". *J.M.S.* **XIX.**

NICOLSON, David (1878–79). "The Measure of Individual and Social Responsibility in Criminal Cases". *J.M.S.* **XXIV.**

NICOLSON, David (1895). "Crime, Criminals and Criminal Lunatics". *J.M.S.* **XLI.**

PAILTHORPE, Grace W. (1932). *Studies in the Psychology of Delinquency.* London.

PAILTHORPE, Grace W. , 1932). *What We Put in Prison, and in Preventive and Rescue Homes.* London.

PATERSON, Alexander ' 1933). "Should the Criminologist Be Encouraged?" *Trans. of the Medico-Legal Society.* **XXVI.**

POTTS, W. A. (1921). "Justice for the Defective Offender". *The Howard Journal.* **1**, No. 1.

POTTS, W. A. (1925). "Delinquency". *J.M.S.* **LXXI.**

PROAL, Louis (1898). *Political Crime.* (Vol. 4 in "The Criminology Series"). London.

QUINTON, Richard Frith (1910). *Crime and Criminals 1876–1910.* London.

RADZINOWICZ, Leon (1961). *In Search of Criminology.* London.

RADZINOWICZ, Leon and HOOD, Roger (1986). *History of the English Criminal Law.* Vol. 5.

RAVEN, Alice 1928). "A Contribution towards a Psychological Conception of Insanity and its Relation to Crime". *The Sociological Review.* **XX.**

RAVEN, Alice (1929). "Murder and Suicide as Marks of an Abnormal Mind." *The Sociological Review.* **XXI.**

ST. JOHN, Arthur (1912). "Criminal Anthropology and Common Sense". *The Sociological Review.* **5**, 65–67.

SMITH, M. Hamblin (1921). "The Birmingham Scheme: A Review". *The Howard Journal.* **1**, No. 1.

SMITH, M. Hamblin (1922). *The Psychology of the Criminal.* London.

SMITH, M. Hamblin (1922). "The Medical Examination of Delinquents". *J.M.S.* **LXVIII.**

SMITH M. Hamblin (1925). "The Psychopathic Personality". *J.M.S.* **LXXI.**

SMITH, Roger 1981). *Trial by Medicine.*

SULLIVAN, W. C. 1906). *Alcoholism.* London.

SULLIVAN, W. C. 1924). *Crime and Insanity.* London.

SUTHERLAND, J. F. , 1908). *Recidivism: Habitual Criminality and Habitual Petty Delinquency.* Edinburgh.

THOMSON, J. Bruce (1869). "The Effects of the Present System of Prison Discipline on the Body and the Mind". *J.M.S.* **XII.**

THOMSON, J. Bruce 1869–70). "The Hereditary Nature of Crime". *J.M.S.* **XV.**

THOMSON, J. Bruce 1870–71). "The Psychology of Criminals". *J.M.S.* **XVI.**

[8]

From Marx to Bonger: Socialist Writings on Women, Gender, and Crime*

James W. Messerschmidt, *University of Southern Maine*

Contemporary socialist criminologists concentrate their analysis of crime on production relations, ignoring the co-determination of reproduction and thus the role gender plays in crime by men and women. The author argues that this omission has occurred by reason of the theoretical work of Marx and Engels, as well as other socialist "criminologists" of the late nineteenth and early twentieth centuries. The importance of the paper lies in its demonstration that the questions raised by these early socialist theoreticians are inadequate for developing a comprehensive theory of crime.

Criminological theory has historically maintained a conceptual blindness, ignoring the best predictor of criminality, *gender*. Gender explains more variance in crime cross-culturally than any other variable, and this "appears so *regardless* of whether officially known or hidden ("true") rates of crime are indexed" (Harris 1977, pp. 3–4). A number of scholars have pointed out this male bias in criminological theory generally (Harris 1977; Klein 1982; Leonard 1982), yet socialist criminology has been practically ignored, with only recent references to its neglect of gender and women (Leonard 1982; Messerschmidt 1986).

While differing specifically in the way they analyze crime, contemporary socialist criminologists have in common a commitment to understanding crime solely in terms of relations of production and class. For example, the leading textbooks from this perspective scarcely consider gender relations (Michalowski 1985; Eitzen and Timmer 1985), and the best known theoretical works of contemporary socialist criminology completely ignore gender and women (Gordon 1971; Quinney 1973; 1980; Chambliss 1975; Spitzer 1975; Greenberg 1981). These criminologists have failed to analyze crime in terms of gender not because of a hidden sexism, but rather, by reason of an uncritical adoption of the theoretical work of Marx and Engels, as well as other socialist "criminologists" of the late nineteenth and early twentieth centuries.

Criminological scholars have analyzed Marx's and Engels' writings on crime (Taylor, Walton and Young 1973; Hirst 1972; Cain and Hunt 1979; Greenberg 1981), and a few have discussed the work of other socialist "criminologists" of the late nineteenth and early twentieth centuries (Greenberg 1981, p. 11; Taylor, Walton, and Young 1973), yet the gender bias of these works has been ignored. This paper fills that void by exhibiting how early socialist writers on crime have historically neglected reproduction (the production of human life through procreation, socialization, and daily maintenance) as being of equal importance with production for understanding crime.

The paper examines Marx's and Engels' views on women, reproduction, and crime. It was these theorists who set the stage for a continued patriarchal dogmatism in early socialist writings on crime by arguing that reproduction is "superstructural" and derived from production. Marx and Engels ignored the fundamental fact that humans must reproduce as well as produce in all societies in order to sustain themselves and society. In short, traditional Marxist social theory is flawed, since, as shown below, production and reproduction, as interdependent structural social relations, constitute the material base of society. This ignoring of the co-determinative nature of the base by Marx and Engels provided a model by which later socialists were to organize their writings on crime. Consequently, this patriarchal bias in early socialist writings on women, gender, and crime has had a significant influence on contemporary socialist criminologists.

To understand the work of early socialists on crime it is important to recognize the cultural and intellectual context of their era. In many ways, contemporary questions on gender (e.g. the relation between economic and gender domination) were the same questions discussed among socialists during Marx's and Engels' day. Many utopian socialist feminists in the early nineteenth century emphasized the mutual dependence of class and gender oppression (Rowbotham 1972, pp. 36–58). Marx and Engels rejected this view, however, arguing that gender oppression was the result of class oppression. Two specific aspects of Marx's and Engels' era informed this rejection: their reliance on, and debate with, classical economics (in which they derived the notion of production as an analytically distinct and socially decisive system), and the dominant Victorian ideology of the nineteenth century (Benenson 1984).

Working within this intellectual and cultural milieu, Marx and Engels abandoned the utopian socialist feminist emphasis on the mutual dependence of gender and class oppression, adopting instead the idea of class as the key to understanding all social phenomena, including women's position in society. Thus, while Marx and Engels were well acquainted with the utopian socialist feminist movement of their time, their approach was different: the oppression of women was not seen as an equally unique phenomenon but a result of class society.

It is within this intellectual and cultural context that the works of Marx and Engels, and as a result, not only Marxist social theory, but early socialist writings on crime, developed. Thus, while I criticize these socialists for the patriarchal nature of their writings, this criticism must be understood within this historical context. There is no assumption here that early socialist theoreticians were supposed to transcend their time and place. However, some early socialist writers—in particular Engels—did attempt an explanation of women's oppression, an explanation which is not only incorrect, but is also still accepted over one-hundred years later by some segments of contemporary socialist criminology. The importance of the following discussion therefore lies in demonstrating that the questions raised by the early socialist "criminologists" are inadequate for developing a modern, comprehensive theory of crime.

Marx and Engels on Women and Reproduction

Marx and Engels said very little about either reproduction or crime. What they did say, however, is important for understanding the direction socialist writings on crime have taken, for it is here where the root of a gender bias in contemporary socialist criminology is grounded.

"Every child knows," Marx (1868) wrote, "that a country that ceased to work would die." Every society must produce food, shelter, and clothing simply to survive. Moreover, according to Marx and Engels, for a society to maintain itself, it must organize its own form of reproduction. It is these two systems that create the conditions for everyday existence. As Engels (1884, pp. 5–6) stated, production and reproduction are central to understanding any society according to "the materialistic conception."

> According to the materialistic conception, the determining factor in history is, in the final instance, the production and reproduction of immediate life. This, again, is of a two-fold character: on the one side, the production of the means of existence, of food, clothing and shelter and the tools necessary for that production; on the other side, the production of human beings themselves, the propagation of the species. The social organization under which the people of a particular historical epoch and a particular country live is determined by both kinds of production; by the stage of development of labour on the one hand and of the family on the other.

Marx and Engels never developed a materialistic perspective accounting for both production and reproduction "as the determining factor in history" (Eisenstein 1979; Flax 1976). Their work concentrates on production and class relations, abstracting away from reproduction and gender relations. Although recognizing the importance of both production and reproduction as codetermining the "social organization under which the people of a particular historical epoch and a particular country live," their analysis subsumes reproduction and the family to the economy and production. In this way, gender relations are made subordinate to class relations and the oppression of women becomes for Marx and Engels simply a reflection of the more important and fundamental class oppression (Eisenstein 1979).

For Marx and Engels, the first division of labor is biologically based in the family. The act of procreation gives rise to a "natural" division of labor in the family that "develops spontaneously or 'naturally' by virtue of natural predisposition (e.g. physical strength), needs, accidents, etc.," (Marx and Engels 1846, p. 51). Discussing the peasant family in *Capital*. Marx (1867, pp. 77–78) noted that this type of family system possesses a "spontaneously developed system of division of labor." The distribution of work and the regulation of labor time of family members "depends upon the differences of age and sex as upon natural conditions varying with the seasons" (p.78). The division of labor in the home, arising from differences in sex and age, is "a division that is consequently on a purely physiological foundation" (p. 351).

Engels (1884) argues further that from the earliest times, this "natural" division of labor results in men producing the means of subsistence while women work in the household. Engels does not view this sexual division of labor as placing women in a subordinate position. Men and women had their own spheres, each vital to the survival of the community. In fact, Engels (1884, p. 113) states that in "primitive" societies women were dominant, and this female supremacy has a material foundation: "The communistic household, in which most or all of the women belong to one and the same gens, while men come from various gentes, is the material foundation of that supremacy of the women which was general in primitive times."

This alleged supremacy is destroyed, according to Engels, by developments in the productive sphere. The invention of agriculture and the domestication of animals greatly expand the forces of production and create a surplus. These developments make engaging in slavery profitable and lead to the emergence of a class society. Engels argues that since these developments occurred in the "male sphere"—production—men came to dominate women. Moreover, because men accumulated wealth, they wanted to pass it on to their children, so men changed a matrilineal communal system to a patrilineal private property system. This overthrowing of "mother right" was for Engels (1884, p. 120), "the world historic defeat of the female sex."

Engels' account suffers from severe anthropological inaccuracies, which is not surprising given the infancy of anthropological research in his time. While it is true in hunting and gathering societies (what Engels calls "primitive" societies) that men hunt, fight wars, and make weaponry, they do not procure all or even most of the raw materials for food, nor the tools that are necessary to carry out this labor. Varda Burstyn (1983), in analyzing a large body of anthropological evidence on the genesis of women's oppression, concludes that female involvement in gathering provides the major and consistent source of food, even in those societies where hunting is accorded greater

382   JAMES W. MESSERSCHMIDT

prestige. Moreover, in horticultural (small scale cultivation) societies, women are primarily involved in cultivation, and therefore provide not only the major and consistent source of food, but also any surplus (Burstyn 1983; Reiter 1975; Blumberg 1978; Fisher 1979). To Engels, however, female labor, for the most part, was unknown, unrecognized, and therefore invisible. In those horticultural societies that produced a surplus, it was women primarily who produced it, but Engels inaccurately portrays this sphere as male. Women's labor was, therefore, both productive and reproductive in hunting and gathering societies.

Engels uses the Iroquois as an example of how the surplus produced by women was appropriated by the community as a whole. However, the Iroquois were atypical and represented only one type of surplus appropriation. In other horticultural societies, the surplus produced by women is appropriated by men and used to increase their social standing. As Rae Lesser Blumberg (1978, p. 36) argues in her analysis of the rise of class and gender stratification, this latter type of appropriation

emerges when men use women's labor in cultivation in order to deliberately produce surplus—and prestige—for their own benefit. Typically, the chief beneficiary is the man for whom the woman labors, in most cases, her husband. . . . In this way, the surplus of one group is appropriated for the benefit of another—the hallmark of class stratification.

In most hunting and gathering societies women maintained control over their productive and reproductive labor power, but with the development of certain kinds of horticultural societies, masculine control of the labor power of women emerged. Female labor began to be manipulated as a scarce good, leading to polygamy becoming prevalent as a family form with a concomitant set of restrictions on female sexual activity. As Burstyn (1983, p. 27) argues, the woman loses control of her sexuality and becomes an "affiliated and controlled wife" in many horticultural societies. Thus, with the development of masculine appropriation of the productive labor power of women in horticultural societies, masculine control over women's reproductive labor and thus sexuality emerges. Economic classes, in the Marxist sense, eventually arise once the greater surplus produced by agriculture and the domestication of animals becomes prevalent. Therefore, the growth of surplus accumulation and the rise of social classes is grounded in women's labor and its appropriation by men, as well as in the control of women's sexuality (Blumberg 1978; Burstyn 1983). Women were the first "producing class" and men the first "appropriating class." With the development of certain types of horticultural societies, incipient patriarchal gender relations emerge, entailing appropriation and domination in both the productive and reproductive spheres.

Engels was evidently unaware that the sexual division of labor was the first "great social division of labor" where an exploiter-exploited relationship existed. Engels ignored the internal dynamics of the reproductive sphere and its codeterminative aspect with production. As a result, Engels' account of "the world historic defeat of the female sex" fails to answer a number of important questions. If his analysis is accurate, why did women not come to dominate since they produced the surplus in horticultural societies? If female supremacy was dominant, as Engels seems to argue, why did women not remain in control? And why do men, who did not bequeath property to their biological children under matrilineality, suddenly desire to do so? The empirical fact is that in most horticultural societies, men appropriate the surplus produced by women.

Engels' failure to analyze accurately the sexual division of labor, and therefore masculine appropriation of female labor, led him to concentrate on, in a limited way, the sphere of production. While he acknowledged the equal importance of production and reproduction in "primitive" societies, his incomplete understanding of production comes to dominate upon the emergence of class society, and reproduction becomes "superstructural" (Engels 1884, p. 72).

In short, Marx and Engels, having failed to analyze the relations between men and women in society, view the relations of reproduction in societies beyond the "primitive" stage as secondary to relations of production and determined ultimately by production. The Marxist materialist conception of history simply excludes the dynamics and effects of gender relations and hierarchy, thereby concealing, rather than illuminating, masculine dominance. While Marx and Engels acknowledge that the sexual division of labor is the first division of labor, they see it as "natural" and unproblematic in and of itself; consequently, they develop the thesis that women's oppression derives from the mode of production, not the codetermination of reproduction and production.

This criticism of Marx and Engels is important not because we would expect them to transcend their time and place, but by reason of the fact that most contemporary socialist criminologists feel that the rudiments of Engels' premise are still valid for explaining the rise of sexual inequality. An example is the work of Julia and Herman Schwendinger (1983, pp. 131–132) who, while pointing out some of the limitations of Engels' argument, still maintain that the major ideas of Engels "appear to be accurate" and these "ideas relate sexual inequality to the evolution of social classes, private property, the family and the state."

Marx and Engels on Crime

Although Marx was primarily interested in political economy, he and

Engels did touch on crime a number of times in their analysis of society. Marx and Engels argued that crime was ultimately the result of capitalist economic conditions. The specific circumstances of industrial capitalism demoralized the proletariat, creating an "immoral" class and thus crime. As Engels (1845, p. 130) states in *The Condition of the Working Class in England*,

> Immorality is fostered in every possible way by the conditions of working class life. The worker is poor; life has nothing to offer him; he is deprived of virtually all pleasures. Consequently he does not fear the penalties of the law. Why should he leave the rich man in undisturbed possession of his property? Why should he not take at least a part of this property for himself? What reason has the worker for *not* stealing?

Marx and Engels argued that a capitalist economic system caused demoralization and immorality, and the working class responds to this by engaging in crime.

Concentrating on the alleged immorality of the working class, Marx and Engels seem to totally ignore crime committed by women. It is perhaps true that Marx and Engels felt working class women were also demoralized and brutalized by the day-to-day experiences under industrial capitalism, yet they ignored their gender specific brutalization and how this may have contributed to female crime. This is particularly evident in Marx's discussion of prostitution. According to Marx, women are not involved in prostitution by reason of their subordinate position in a masculine-dominated society, rather, "prostitution is only a *specific* expression of the *universal* prostitution of the worker" (cited in Jaggar 1983, p. 221). In other words, prostitution results from the exploitation of one class by another, not because of the domination of men over women. Indeed, Marx's characterization of prostitution as a relation of economic domination is puzzling, as Alison Jaggar (1983, pp. 221-222) points out:

> The pimp may exploit the prostitute, but his power over her does not come from his ownership of certain means of production to which she has no access. Other than the physical body of the woman, prostitution requires no elaborate means of production which can be owned by another, and work is not "socialized" through an elaborate division of labor. Alienation is supposed to characterize relationships that are typically capitalist, but prostitution seems closer to slavery.

Clearly, the intent of Marx was not to understand prostitution, female crime, and female oppression, but rather, to use a form of female "deviant" activity to discredit wage labor.

Engels reinforces Marx in his work *The Condition of the Working Class in England* (1845). He begins his chapter "Results of Industrialization" by pointing to the similarity between criminal murder and analogous forms of "capitalist murder." In other words, when hundreds of workers are placed in a position resulting in their "premature and unnatural ends," murder has occurred (Engels, 1845, pp. 108–109). However, while Engels notes the murderous conditions in the capitalist workplace, his concentration is on street crime of the working class, since statistics prove "that the working classes are responsible for nearly all the crime in the country" (p. 147). By reason of the demoralizing effects of capitalism, "everyone sees in his neighbor a rival to be elbowed aside, or at best a victim to be exploited for his own ends" (Engels 1845, p. 149). As Engels (p. 149) concludes, "If the demoralization of the worker passes beyond a certain point then it is just as natural that he will turn into a criminal—as inevitably as water turns into steam at boiling point."

Engels' account of proletarian crime ignores an understanding of the differences between male and female criminality; street crime is simply a class phenomenon, no theoretical account of gender is developed. This occurs because for Engels, women under capitalism do not experience any special form of oppression other than an economic one. According to Engels (1884, p. 137), women's oppression results from her exclusion from social production as the husband maintains his position of supremacy in the household by reason of his economically privileged position. As a result, the "emancipation of women will only be possible when women can take part in production on a large scale and domestic work no longer claims anything but an insignificant amount of her time" (p. 158). Engels (1845, pp. 162–166) argued that as women and children became wage laborers, the authority of the male (husband/father) would be undermined. In fact, Engels (1884, p. 135) states that masculine dominance in the proletarian household no longer has a basis:

> Now that large scale industry has taken the wife out of the home onto the labor market and into the factory, and made her often the breadwinner of the family, no basis for any kind of male supremacy is left in the proletarian household.

By denying women's subordination in working-class families, Marx and Engels simply averted representing women's distinct needs as an equal part of their overall program (Benenson 1984). But in addition, without an understanding of the relations between men and women, there simply cannot exist a theoretical conception of the differences in male and female criminality. Both Marx's and Engels' analyses ignore the objective and subjective experience of dominance and/or subordination as determined by both class and gender. Why is it males who are disproportionately involved in street crimes, and how is this fact related to both the objective nature of power and the subjective experience of masculinity? Marx and Engels not only ignore power in terms of gender relations, and therefore its relation to crime, they also tend to accept masculinity and femininity as given, rather than confronting their origin and how they help to structure particular patterns of crime. This is particularly evident in Engels' discussion of the effects of the factory system on working class women. As Engels (1845, p. 166) states,

> The moral consequences of the employment of women in factories are even worse. In the factories members of both sexes of all ages work together in a single room. It is inevitable that they should come into close contact with each other. The crowding together of a large number of men and women who lack the advantages of moral or intellectual instruction is not exactly calculated to promote the favourable development of the female virtues.

For Engels, women working in factories, and therefore being influenced by persons of "dissolute character," creates the conditions which will permanently injure their morality. In fact, Engels (p. 167) argues that it is the "immorality" in the factory which leads inevitably to prostitution: "most of the prostitutes . . . [have] the factories to thank for their present degradation." Engels (p. 167) made the point that the "moral standards of the factory worker were somewhat lower than the average standard of the working classes," and, therefore, had a discouraging influence on the sexual morality of working class women. In making such an argument, Engels was supporting the Victorian notion that working-class women were nothing more than passive victims of factory conditions. Their "immoral" sexuality was not something they chose, but rather, it was seen as being forced on them by forces outside their control.

   In sum, Marx and Engels clearly attributed crime to economic conditions. By reason of their empirically incorrect understanding of the rise of gender inequality, they ignored the dialectic of production and reproduction, and the subsequent effect the latter, in interaction with the former, may have on human conduct and thus crime. Moreover, although women made up at least half the "demoralized" individuals of the proletariat, Marx and Engels made no attempt to account for their lower crime rate and the types of crimes women commit. They ignored power in terms of gender relations and accepted masculinity and femininity as given. Unfortunately, not only have most contemporary socialist criminologists done exactly the same thing, but many socialists who wrote immediately after Marx and Engels followed closely in their footsteps. In the following section a brief analysis of early socialists who wrote on the topic of crime is presented.

Late Nineteenth and Early Twentieth Century Socialist Writers on Crime

   A number of socialists who wrote on crime immediately after Marx and Engels found themselves in a debate with the conservative, biological positivists of the time. It was essentially the work of Cesare Lombroso (1835-1909) which led to this intellectual altercation. In 1876 Lombroso published *L'Uomo Delinquente* (translated as *Criminal Man*), a work which is grounded in the racial, gender, and class biased notions characteristic of nineteenth century bourgeois thought. Crime was viewed as being biologically based in differences between whites and non-whites, women and men, and the fit (upper classes) and the unfit (lower classes). Crime for Lombroso was the result of the survival of primitive traits and physical stigmata. He used the theories of evolution, such as Social Darwinism, to support the belief that criminals were not only physically different from non-criminals but were also inferior human beings. In other words, his explanation of crime was based on the notion that women, non-whites, and the poorer classes had evolved less than had white upper class men and therefore were more susceptible to primitive urges and crime. As Dorie Klein (1982, p. 39) points out, Lombroso concluded in his work that individuals develop "differently within sexual and racial limitations which differ hierarchically from the most highly developed, the white men, to the most primitive, the non-white women." It was Lombroso's theory which helped to legitimate the rule of capitalist over worker, white over black, and men over women.

A number of socialists who wrote on crime during this time engaged in a "critique" of Lombroso. One was Achille Loria, and Italian socialist who, in a book entitled *Economic Foundations of Society* (1902), discusses the causes of crime in economic terms and then attempts a critique of Lombroso's biological positivism. Property crimes, according to Loria, "are the result of economic conditions and proceed directly from the misery that weights so heavily upon the larger proportion of the population in our richest and most civilised countries" (pp. 107–108). As for "the criminal acts of the rich" Loria goes on, "we must bear in mind that economic conditions exert a corrupting influence upon morals, not only through an excess of misery but also by a superabundance of wealth. The criminality of the rich is therefore, not so independent of the influence of the economic environment as one would think" (p. 109. Thus, for Loria, it is certain conditions resulting from the economic system alone that lead to crime by both the rich and the poor. There is no attempt to understand crime as related to the sexual division of labor.

Loria goes on to criticize Lombroso, but does not attack Lombroso's class bias, racism, and sexism. Rather, he agrees with the assumption that criminals possess inferior physical stigmata. Loria's criticism lies in Lombroso's failure to account for physical stigmata in economic terms. For Loria (1902, pp. 109–110), it was certain economic conditions—"prolonged poverty, hard labor performed by women during pregnancy, malodorous and un-healthful dwellings, insufficient and anti-hygienic alimentation, alcoholism (the fatal corrollary of idleness among the rich as well as the poor), spasmodic work for varying and uncertain wages, the dissolvent influences of indolent and inactive wealth''—that lead to these morbid physical states.

Loria, and other socialist analysts of crime during this time differed from Lombroso and Ferrero in their attention to economic conditions. The writings of Filippo Turati, Bruno Battaglia, Napoleone Colajanni, August Bebel, Paul Lafargue, and Wilhelm Adriaan Bonger analyzed crime purely in economic terms (Greenberg 1981, p. 11).

Probably the most prominent of these early socialist criminologists, however, was Bonger who published *Criminality and Economic Conditions* in 1905. According to Bonger, by reason of a capitalist economic system ''egoism'' arises in all members of society, but certain people in all social classes (the class of criminals) develop a ''criminal thought'' from this egoism, which eventually leads to crime. All forms of criminal activity, such as economic, sexual, political, and pathological crimes are linked to egoism, that is, self interest above the interest of others.

According to Bonger (1905), the mode of production determines whether or not members of a society will be altruistic or egoistic. It is the capitalist mode of production which ''has developed egoism at the expense of altruism'' (Bonger 1905, p. 40). Thus for Bonger, capitalism creates egoism, which leads a number of people in all social classes to adopt criminal thoughts and eventually involve themselves in criminality. Bonger assumes that there are criminals and non-criminals, two different classes of behavior, one of which is motivated by ''criminal thoughts.''

This does not suggest that the writings of early socialists did not contribute to the understanding of crime in capitalist societies. Indeed, socialist analysts were the first to introduce the idea that crime under capitalism is, in part, correlated to economic conditions. In so doing, they went significantly beyond biological explanations by attempting to demonstrate the relationship between the social organization of capitalism and crime.

However, most early socialist writings on crime concentrated on lower class criminality among men. While some did discuss the criminality of women, they attributed this criminality only to economic conditions. If the early socialists who wrote on crime maintained a form of economic determinism, they in addition had no understanding of gender relations and power. Following Marx and Engels, women's position was solely explained in economic terms. Moreover, in their eagerness to identify the economic forces that encouraged crimes such as prostitution, they denied women any role other than that of passive victim. These socialists carried into their theoretical explanations the Victorian image of women as sexual innocents, who fell into illicit sex. They assumed, as did their conservative and liberal counterparts that any sex outside of marriage was so improper and degrading that no woman could choose prostitution. Their emphasis was on how a capitalist economic system turns "good" women into "bad" women, damaging prospects for marriage and proper womanhood. This was clearly not only a condescending view of prostitution, but also of women.

Bonger went somewhat beyond the others, proposing an explanation for why women commit less crime than men. Discussing strength and courage, Bonger (1905, p. 472) concluded that "the average woman of our time has less strength and courage than the average man, and consequently, commits on the average fewer crimes than he." Moreover, women are not involved in "sexual crimes" because "the role of women in sexual life (and thus in the criminal sexual life) is rather passive than active" (p. 473). Bonger fails to provide us with a reason for women's passivity other than implying an inherent female quality. This is likewise apparent in his portrayal of women as lacking in courage.

Bonger acknowledged the oppression of women but makes clear that they are not as oppressed as proletarian males. This consequently leads to less crime. Although the oppression of a woman "forces her to lying and hypocrisy," Bonger argued, the eventual consequences "of her manner of life, in so far as they are harmful to the formation of character, are probably counterbalanced by those which are favorable," that is marriage and the family (Bonger 1905, p. 478). It is this institution which protects women from the outside harmful effects of capitalism. As Bonger (p. 478) continues, "her smaller criminality is like the health of a hothouse plant; it is due not to innate qualities, but to the hothouse which protects it from harmful influences." While it is true that the isolation of females in the home hinders female involvement in criminality (Messerschmidt 1986), Bonger (1905) is unaware of the possibility that the dominance of men over women within the family may also be oppressive to women and therefore contribute to criminality and other types of anti-social behavior by both men and women. Moreover, he fails to explain why specifically it is women, and not men, who are the ones being isolated in the home. This is a prime example of what results from employing a theory which takes gender stratification for granted and looks only to relations of production; that is, relations of production defined in the traditional Marxist way.

For Bonger, women engage in less property crimes because prostitution is more financially rewarding. Bonger finds poverty correlated with involvement in prostitution, while simultaneously attributing this form of crime to an "immoral environment." Bonger (1905, p. 329) is first of all, class biased:

. . . the ranks of prostitutes are in a very large measure recruited from the less well-to-do classes, or where the neglect of children have assumed enormous proportions, and not from the more favored classes where the children are carefully guarded and kept away from unfavorable influences.

Then he blames this immoral environment on proletarian women. Since proletarian women are working outside the home, their children become demoralized:

> The development of capitalism has led to the paid labor of married women, and consequently to one of the most important causes of the demoralization of the children of the working class. When there is no one to watch a child, when he is left to himself, he becomes demoralized (p. 318).

If women were home, where they are supposed to be, children would not become demoralized, and young girls would not become prostitutes. In this regard, it is interesting to note that Marx, Engels, Bonger, and others did not regard male wage labor as the beginning of the dissolution of the family as the agent of child socialization. They objected to the extraction of mothers/wives from the family context but did not apply the same objections to the extraction of fathers/husbands from that context.

By reason of their acceptance of the sexual division of labor as being natural, for Bonger (and others) the demoralization of children in the working class, while connected to capitalism, turns out in the end to be in part the fault of women. By working outside the home, women are calling into question their "natural" place in this division of labor. Therefore, they help to cause delinquency.

Thus, for a number of socialists who wrote on crime during the late nineteenth and early twentieth centuries, economic conditions, not gender stratification, was the cause of crime. Concentrating their discussion on prostitution —a preoccupation common among both conservative and liberal male criminologists—capitalist economic conditions turned "good" women into "immoral" women. And some argued that women's participation in production ruined the family, leading to delinquency amongst their children. For others, women's criminality was ignored altogether. All of these theorists likewise disregarded the role of reproduction and masculine dominance on human behavior and consequently on crime by both males and females. While we must appreciate the unique historical circumstances and therefore gender ideology underlying these writings, we also begin to see where the patriarchal bias in contemporary socialist criminology is rooted.

In summation, Marx and Engels' rejection of utopian socialist feminism involved an important change in nineteenth century socialist thought and analysis. While Marx and Engels identified the problematic and naive nature of the utopian socialist feminist overall program for social change, they simultaneously developed a gender-blind theoretical framework for socialist analysis of not only society, but crime as well. It is important we recognize the unique historical circumstances of gender ideology which underlie the writings of

Marx, Engels, and Bonger, for it is within this context that a suggested patriarchal bias found in contemporary socialist criminology is rooted.

ENDNOTE

*I would like to thank Piers Beirne, Varda Burstyn, and the anonymous referees for helpful comments on earlier drafts of this paper.

REFERENCES

Benenson, Harold. 1984. "Victorian Sexual Ideology and Marx's Theory of the Working Class." *International Labor and Working Class History* 25:1–23.

Blumberg, Rae Lesser. 1978. *Stratification: Socio-Economic and Sexual Inequality*. Dubuque: William C. Brown.

Bonger, Wilhelm. 1905. *Criminality and Economic Conditions*. Boston: Little, Brown and Company.

Burstyn, Varda. 1983. "Economy, Sexuality, and Politics: Engels and the Sexual Division of Labor." *Socialist Studies* 3:19–39.

Cain, Maureen, and Alan Hunt. 1979. *Marx and Engels on Law*. New York: Academic Press.

Chambliss, William J. 1975. "Toward a Political Economy of Crime." *Theory and Society* 2: 167–180.

Eisenstein, Zilla. 1979. "Developing a Theory of Capitalist Patriarchy and Socialist Feminism." Pp. 5–40 in *Capitalist Patriarchy and the Case for Socialist Feminism*, edited by Z. Eisenstein. New York: Monthly Review.

Eitzen, D. Stanley, and Doug Timmer. 1985. *Criminology: Crime and Criminal Justice*. New York: John Wiley.

Engels, Fredrick. 1845. (1968). *The Condition of the Working Class in England*. Stanford, CA: Stanford University Press.

——— . 1884. (1972). *The Origin of the Family, Private Property and the State*. Moscow: Progress Publishers.

Fisher, Ellen. 1979. *Women's Creation*. Garden City, NY: Anchor Press/Doubleday.

Flax, Joan. 1976. "Do Feminists Need Marxism?" *Quest* 3:46–58.

Gordon, David. 1971. "Class and the Economics of Crime." *Review of Radical Political Economics* 3:51–75.

Greenberg, David. 1981. *Crime and Capitalism: Readings in Marxist Criminology*. Palo Alto, CA: Mayfield.

Harris, Anthony R. 1977. "Sex and Theories of Deviance: Toward a Functional Theory of Deviant Type-Scripts." *American Sociological Review* 42:3–16.

Hirst, Paul Q. 1972. "Marx and Engels on crime, law and morality." *Economy and Society* 1:28–56.

Jaggar, Alison. 1983. *Feminist Politics and Human Nature*. Totowa, NJ: Rowman & Allenheid.

Klein, Dorie. 1982. "The Etiology of Female Crime: A Review of the Literature." Pp. 35–60 in *The Criminal Justice System and Women*. edited by Barbara R. Price and Natalie Sokoloff. New York: Clark Boardman.

Leonard, Eileen. 1982. *Women, Crime and Society*. New York: Longman.

Lombroso, Cesare. 1876. *L'Uomo Delinquente*. Milan, Italy: Hoepli.

Loria, Achille. 1902. *Economic Foundations of Society*. London: George Allen and Unwin, Ltd.

Marx, Karl. 1867. (1967). *Capital Vol. I*. New York: International Publishers.

392   JAMES W. MESSERSCHMIDT

———. 1868. "Letter to Dr. Kugelman."

Marx, Karl, and Fredrick Engels. 1846. (1970). *The German Ideology*. New York: International Publishers.

Messerschmidt, James W. 1986. *Capitalism, Patriarchy and Crime: Toward a Socialist Feminist Criminology*. Totowa, NJ: Rowman and Littlefield.

Michalowski, Raymond J. 1985. *Order, Law and Crime*. New York: Random House.

Quinney, Richard. 1973. *Critique of Legal Order*. Boston: Little, Brown and Company.

———. 1980. *Class, State and Crime*. New York: Longman.

Reiter, Rita. 1975. *Toward an Anthropology of Women*, edited by Rita Reiter. New York: Monthly Review Press.

Rowbotham, Sheila. 1972. *Women, Resistance and Revolution*. New York: Random House.

Schwendinger, Julia R., and Herman Schwendinger. 1983. *Rape and Inequality*. Beverly Hills, CA: Sage.

Spitzer, Steven. 1975. "Toward a Marxian Theory of Deviance." *Social Problems* 22:638–651.

Taylor, Ian, Paul Walton, and Jock Young. 1973. *The New Criminology: For a Social Theory of Deviance*. London: Routledge and Kegan Paul.

Chapter 5

Lenin, Crime, and Penal Politics, 1917-1924

Piers Beirne and Alan Hunt

In the fight against crime the reform of social and political institutions is much more important than the imposition of punishment.

—Lenin (1901a:394)

I. Introduction

In this chapter we examine Lenin's pronouncements on crime and penal politics ("penality") during the critical period of early Bolshevik power between October 1917 and his death in early 1924.

Our intent is twofold. First, it is to extend to Lenin's perspective on crime and penal politics our critical analysis of his view of law and the constitution of Soviet society in the previous chapter (Beirne and Hunt, *supra*, chapter 4). In our analysis there we tried to identify Lenin's diverse views about the nature of legal relations in the period of socialist transition between capitalism and communism. The implications of Lenin's various pronouncements about such relations we placed within a broad conception of the constitution of Soviet society. In that conception, we argued, Lenin failed to secure, or even to specify, a coherent space either for an institutional separation of powers or for a juridical (or other) means of sustaining the boundaries between them. This failure, we concluded, greatly contributed to the intensification of authoritarian centralism during the late 1920s which was, afterwards, a defining characteristic of the Stalinist period. However, as will shortly become clear, we largely disagree with the widely held Whig interpretation (see Gouldner, 1977:7–11; Cohen, 1985:38–70) that, within Russian Bolshevism, the link between Leninism and Stalinism was an ineluctable straight line.

What follows here is an exploration of Lenin's view of a specific aspect of

We wish to thank Peter Solomon for his helpful comments on an earlier version of this chapter.

the constitution of Soviet society, namely, the field of crime and penal politics.[1] As we outline, this field was the object of a mass of pronouncements by Lenin in the early years of Bolshevik power. Given his close and apparently domineering relationship with key Bolshevik personnel in the Commissariat of Justice, such as P. I. Stuchka and D. I. Kursky, it is reasonable to suppose that Lenin must have been aware of and have implicitly condoned all of the major shifts in Bolshevik penal strategies (see, for example, Stuchka, 1925; Pashukanis, 1925). With few exceptions, no decree of importance was enacted in this period without Lenin's direct or indirect approval. He himself wrote and revised hundreds of decrees and other legislative instruments, several of which he actually dictated at CPC meetings. Whenever he presided over these meetings, regardless of who subsequently signed the minutes, it was Lenin who personally worded all the decisions (Bratous, 1970).[2] However, as in his discourse on law and the constitution of Soviet society, Lenin rarely analyzed crime and penality as explicit theoretical objects. For this reason, and also for others that lie within the intellectual history of modern criminology (but which cannot concern us here), there has to date been no sustained treatment of Lenin's conception of the field of crime and penal politics either in the literature of criminology and social control or in that of political theory.

Our second, more expository intention here is therefore to describe Lenin's discourse on crime and penal politics. In this discourse we identify three key elements:

(1) a neoclassical view of criminality in socialist and communist societies;

(2) adherence to various progressive features in Bolshevik penal strategies;

(3) a simultaneously coherent and contradictory fusion, within the penal complex, of strategies of law and terror.

Lenin's discourse on crime and penal politics must be situated in the general context of his political theory, important aspects of which include: the relationship between authoritarian and libertarian tendencies, specifically as this was reproduced in his concept of the dictatorship of the proletariat (hereinafter DoP); whether there was a revolution in Bolshevik penal strategies between 1917 and 1923 and, if so, then of what sort and to what extent; and the paradoxical relation between law and terror, especially as it was manifest in specific fields of the penal complex such as ''red terror,'' show trials, and capital punishment. Our underlying thesis is that the origins of authoritarianism in general, and of authoritarian penal practices in particular, were intrinsic neither to the early Bolshevik project nor to Lenin's discourse as its major exponent. Rather, authoritarianism was the unintended consequence of the silences, omissions, and absences in Lenin's political theory and practice, including its libertarian tendencies. Specifically, it derived from the absence of any sustained theory of what we have designated as the constitution of Soviet society. Finally, by way of tentative conclusion, we summarize the lessons provided by Lenin's contribution to the first socialist experiment in the field of crime and penality.

II. Politics, Law, and Penality

Two key tendencies can be identified in Lenin's diverse theoretical views concerning the constitution of Soviet society: an authoritarian tendency and a libertarian one. It is in the terms of the rhetoric supplied by this couplet of authoritarianism and libertarianism that many of the prevailing questions about Lenin's contribution to Marxist political theory have been couched.[3] For example, was Lenin's claim about the emancipatory *aim* of the revolution—"[w]e do not all differ with the anarchists on the question of the abolition of the state" (1917:436)—a clever strategy to gain the much-needed allegiance, prior to their planned annihilation by the Bolsheviks, of ultraleftists such as anarchists and syndicalists? Which aspect of the couplet of authoritarianism and libertarianism was typically dominant, and why? Did Lenin actually subscribe to both tendencies simultaneously? If he did, was this position one of simple contradiction or, rather, a "realist" one that depended on his pragmatic assessment of the configuration of class forces at any given moment?

Such questions can readily be compressed into yet another: What was the relation between authority and liberty in Lenin's extension of theory to the realm of the concrete? An underlying premise of our argument about Lenin's view of crime and penality is that, although for heuristic purposes they can easily be disengaged, for Lenin himself the tendencies of authoritarianism and libertarianism were not concretely separated in practice by some yawning political chasm. On the contrary, they often overlapped and, ultimately, were indissolubly interwoven. Both libertarianism and authoritarianism lay at the heart of Lenin's crucial concept of the DoP, for example, and nowhere did the convoluted interplay of these tendencies penetrate more deeply than in his classic text on the DoP, the much debated *State and Revolution* (Lenin, 1917).

In *State and Revolution*, Lenin urged that an all-encompassing commitment to the DoP was a defining characteristic of Marxism itself (1917:412; and see 1918:231–242). The practical implications of the role that Lenin envisaged for the DoP during the socialist transition therefore comprised a crucial point of reference next to which his pronouncements about crime and penality should be situated. Lenin was adamant that a Marxist commitment to the DoP had to be practiced at three levels. First, he insisted that the DoP must entail a rigorous and rapid conquest of political power by the revolutionary forces so as to prevent the restoration of the old order. At this level, in its conquest of political power, the DoP was to be an exceptional, quasi-military, and temporary phase needed for securing the complete defeat of the old regime, but not in itself constitutive of socialism. Second, Lenin contended that during the DoP the revolutionary forces should not utilize the institutions of the overthrown capitalist state because these were inappropriate for achieving the objectives of the socialist revolution. This contention, in turn, derived from Lenin's broader thesis that there must be a complete rupture between the periods of capitalism and socialism. To effect this rupture the institutions of the old capitalist state needed to be ruthlessly suppressed and then supplanted by proletarian organizations such as soviets.[4] Third, Lenin urged that the DoP should be a constructive period that actively promotes the institutions and social relations for the transition from socialism to communism. Socialism differed from all earlier revolutions not only because it was the first revolution made on behalf of the majority of the population but also because of the principled importance that it attached to a second (i.e., communist) revolutionary transformation. At this level, then, the DoP was to be less negative and coercive than active and educative in its quest for communism.

In Lenin's view, practical commitment to the DoP involved both an uncompromising insistence on the necessity to smash (*razbit'*) the old order and also a determination to unleash the creative energy of the people. It therefore entailed both authoritarian and libertarian practices. Its authoritarianism was largely predicated on Lenin's insistence that the old order must be utterly smashed—because otherwise, like a weed whose roots are left in the soil, it would reassert itself and eventually suffocate the red flower of the revolution. Its libertarianism cultivated both the unleashing of the creative energies of mass popular initiative unfettered by bureaucratic and legalistic restraints, and also the valorization of spontaneous popular participation in democratic processes associated with the concept of "socialist legality."[5]

Only iron-willed discipline, Lenin reasoned, could transform social relations as thoroughly as this. For Lenin, in other words, authoritarianism and libertarianism were integral parts of the same revolutionary struggle. Only the practice of iron-willed authority could ensure the success of the libertarian project.

Let us reiterate our claim that the libertarian and authoritarian tendencies in Lenin's writings and practice were coterminous in such basic concepts as the DoP. In *State and Revolution*, Lenin (1917; and see 1919e:420) viewed the DoP as a transitional period whose political structure was circumscribed in extent and duration. As Medvedev (1981:47–49) has documented, Lenin subscribed to the classical notion of dictatorship rather than to its post-Machiavellian, modern meaning. He conceived the DoP as a transitional period directed to *both* the completion and consolidation of political power *and* the development of alternative participatory democracy within Soviet power. He saw both strategies as being employed simultaneously and coextensively. Whichever tendency became dominant, this interpretation implies, would depend upon the specific and largely unpredictable configuration of historical forces. For example, had no Western military intervention occurred in 1918 and had the Civil War not been so protracted, then the emergent Soviet society would have developed, or at least could have developed, in a far more libertarian direction. Two such directions did in fact have a brief and prefigurative existence. One direction was the radical libertarian trajectory heralded by the 1921 Kronstadt revolt (Avrich, 1970). The other was the coexistence of different modes of production, and the likelihood of a corresponding political pluralism, that emerged between 1921 and 1923 during the early years of the New Economic Policy (NEP). Although we recognize that the absence in Lenin's texts of a politico-constitutional theory could have resulted in very sharp problems for either of these two trajectories, we disagree with the assumption that the path to authoritarianism was inevitable.

Before we examine Lenin's view of crime and penality, our claim about the theoretico-practical fusion of authoritarianism and libertarianism must be contrasted with the otherwise similar thesis of Polan's (1984) book *Lenin and the End of Politics*. We agree with Polan that authoritarianism was deeply imbricated in *both* the authoritarian *and* libertarian traditions. However, our disagreement is not with Polan's conclusion about the dichotomy of authoritarianism and libertarianism within Leninism.[6] It is with his definition of the two tendencies in Lenin's work as existing in *a priori* contradiction with each other rather than, as we argue, as coterminous. Such an *a priori* characterization largely ignores the fact that Lenin rarely employed these tendencies on the same theoretical or temporal plane. Neither Lenin's intentions nor their cultural effects on the project of socialist emancipation, for example, were necessarily contradictory when he asserted both: (a) "[d]ictatorship . . . is rule based directly upon force and unrestricted by any laws" (1918:236), and (b) "legality must be raised (or rigorously observed), since the basis of laws in the RSFSR has been established" (1918a:110). Couplets such as this pervade Lenin's texts.[7] But only if they are extracted from their specific conditions of production can they be adduced as sufficient evidence for a contradictory political project. In short, their theoretical context, their political objects, and their intended effects resided at quite different levels of analysis, and must therefore be understood as such.[8]

Did Lenin's pronouncements encourage in the domain of penality the institutionalization of a systematic authoritarianism during the period of Stalinism? If so, how, and to what extent? It must be recognized, in addressing these questions, that the same fusion of authoritarianism and libertarianism that resided in Lenin's concept of the DoP also inhabited many of his pronouncements on penality. In the domain of penality an important source of this fusion arose in the political linkages that Lenin encouraged between the socialist law of the DoP and the complex of Bolshevik penal strategies. Although similar in form to its bourgeois counterpart, in that each was commonly seen as a set of injunctions with the whole population as its disciplinary object, the socialist law of the DoP was applauded by Lenin (e.g., 1922c:364; see Beirne and Hunt, *supra*, chapter 4) for its explicit subservience to socialist politics (as in class societies, he insisted, it always was) and to the needs of the revolution.

The principled subservience of socialist law to politics during the DoP was manifest in three major ways.[9] First, the dictates of socialist law were envisaged as providing only a temporary basis for the consolidation of Bolshevik policy. As Lenin himself argued, "In a period of transition, laws have only a temporary validity; and when law hinders the development of a revolution, it must be abolished or amended" (1918o:519). A second linkage forged between socialist law and Bolshevik penal strategies was doctrinal and institutional antiformalism. A key point of reference that allowed the Bolsheviks to distinguish between the forms of social regulation which they were creating and the bourgeois law which they replaced was the "principle of the participation of the working and exploited classes . . . in the administration of the state" (Lenin, 1918n:217). The new institutions of socialist justice were therefore to be liberated from the shackles of bourgeois ideology and composed of a popular rather than a professional staff. The temporary and antiformalist nature of Bolshevik law has been widely recognized in the scholarly literature. But in the early years of Bolshevik power the relation of law to penal strategies had a third, largely unrecognized feature—namely, a differential emphasis upon the legal regulation, control, and discipline of the representatives of Soviet power. Indeed, a distinctive feature of Lenin's approach to crime and penality during the DoP was his insistence that a chief object of socialist law should be the soviet official. However, his views on the use of law to regulate the conduct of party and soviet functionaries should be considered in the context of Lenin's overriding political end, namely, the achievement of the future communist society. To his sparse views on this we now turn.

Among many of the Bolsheviks, including Lenin, there was every expectation that because formal law was essentially a bourgeois phenomenon, nonlegal and socialist forms of regulation would emerge with the weakening of capitalist relations of production. Although he occasionally remarked about these new forms of regulation, it must at once be noted that Lenin (e.g., 1917:457), like Marx and Engels before him, opposed detailed descriptions of the future communist society as fanciful utopianism. One reason for this stance was that he was so involved with the immediate problems of socialist construction that he was simply unable to concern himself with the future communist society, the date of whose introduction he was continually forced to postpone. Another reason is the implicit idealism that he believed to inhere in laboratory-like projections of the good society. Thus,

> what distinguishes Marxism from the old, utopian socialism is that the latter wanted to build the new society not from the mass human material produced by bloodstained, sordid, rapacious, shopkeeping capitalism, but from very virtuous men and women reared in special hothouses and cucumber frames. (1918k:388)

Lenin's brief but significant arguments about the nature of communist social relations were the condensed outcome of his prior analyses of politics, bureaucracy, and culture under conditions of the DoP. Lenin (1917:459–474) envisaged the DoP, or the period of socialist construction, as the first phase of communism. During this first phase he saw the period of the DoP as one in which a "new socialist person" was to be created. This was to be accomplished in a variety of ways, but chiefly in the process of work.

We must learn to combine the "public meeting" democracy of the working people—turbulent, surging, overflowing its banks like a spring flood—with *iron* discipline while at work. (1918i:271)

Social classes would gradually disappear during socialist construction and so, correspondingly, would the structural sources of social, economic, and political conflict. People would become increasingly accustomed to collective life. All would learn to participate in public life. In turn, and linked with Engels's attractive claim that under communism "the government of persons is replaced by the administration of things" (1880:147), Lenin argued that when

the more important functions of the state are reduced to such [simplified] accounting and control . . . it will cease to be a "political state" and public functions will lose their political character and become mere administrative functions. (Lenin, 1917:473; see also ibid., 420–421)[10]

We give the name of communism to the system under which people form the habit of performing their social duties without any special apparatus of coercion, and when unpaid work for the public good becomes a general phenomenon. (1919f:284–285)

Under communism one section of society would no longer dominate others because "people will *become accustomed* to observing the elementary conditions of social life *without violence* and *without subordination*" (Lenin, 1917:424).

Lenin's (1917:464) most extended pronouncement about crime in communist society occurred in *State and Revolution*:

only communism makes the state absolutely unnecessary, for there is *nobody* to be suppressed—"nobody" in the sense of a *class*, of a systematic struggle against a definite section of the population. We are not utopians, and do not in the least deny the possibility and inevitability of excesses on the part of *individual persons*, or the need to stop *such* excesses. In the first place, however, no special machine, no special apparatus of suppression, is needed for this; this will be done by the armed people themselves, as simply and as readily as any crowd of civilised people, even in modern society, interferes to put a stop to a scuffle or to prevent a woman from being assaulted. And, secondly, we know that the fundamental social cause of excesses, which consist in the violation of the rules of social intercourse, is the exploitation of the people, their want and their poverty. With the removal of this chief cause, excesses will inevitably begin to "*wither away.*" We do not know how quickly and in what succession, but we do know they will wither away. With their withering away the state will also *wither away*. [emphases in original]

Elsewhere Lenin urged that during socialist construction the DoP should be a dictatorship of the people "without any police" (1920b:352), because the people, the mass of the population, unorganised, "casually" assembled at the given spot, itself appears on the scene, exercises justice and metes out punishment, exercises power and creates a new, revolutionary law. (ibid., 353)

However, it must be stressed that Lenin's concept of communism was far from being an abolitionist one. In two texts which straddle the October revolution, Lenin (1917:395–401; 1918i) recommended that the strategic objective of the withering away of law should not be nihilist or abolitionist in nature. Instead, its objective was to be the construction of a radically new form of social administration in which the state would disappear. The state would increasingly be dissipated as a mechanism of social power when more and, eventually, all citizens participated, without remuneration, in its activities (Lenin, 1918i:272–273). Only under communism, when social classes and the state have disappeared,

will democracy begin to *wither away*, owing to the simple fact that, freed from capitalist slavery, from the untold horrors, savagery, absurdities and infamies of capitalist exploitation, people will *become accustomed* to observing the elementary rules of social intercourse . . . without force, without coercion, without subordination. . . . (Lenin, 1917:462)

III. Penal Strategies in the "Normal" State

The entire range of pre-Stalinist Bolshevik penal strategies has tended to be characterized in the rhetoric of the "straight line" theory referred to earlier in this chapter. In this characterization, prominently employed in the analysis of the carceral archipelago by the otherwise instructive writings of Solzhenitsyn (e.g., 1973:26–39), the origins of the Stalinist labor camps, for example, are firmly identified as the expanded focus of the penal strategies of early Soviet power. But this portrayal mistakenly vilifies much in early Bolshevik history that was genuinely enlightened. Indeed, to look backwards from the depths of the gulags, as Solomon (1980:195) has rightly complained,

is to take a selective or partial view of early Soviet penal history, for the civil war period contained the embryo of another penal policy, a progressive policy, which differed radically from that practiced by the Cheka and OGPU. And it was this progressive policy, not the Cheka's approach, which gained the predominant position during the NEP years.[11]

Although Lenin's own—on balance, unintentional—contribution to the rise of the *gulags* will soon be acknowledged here, it is instructive to indicate, prior to beginning that task, just how enlightened some of the often forgotten "normal" strategies of Bolshevik penality actually were.

In the Neoclassical Vanguard

The Bolshevik theorization of socialist penality embodied, at a very abstract level, various aspects of the terrain of neoclassical criminology emerging elsewhere in Europe (Gsovski and Grzybowski, 1959, 2:926–927; Garland, 1985; Beirne, 1987). The key element in neoclassicism was the compromise established between the overdetermined object of positivist criminology and the volitional legal subject of classical jurisprudence. In Lenin's own implicit theorization, the proper articulation of penal strategies was to be based on a compromise between a positivist concept of crime, on the one hand, and a voluntaristic concept of rehabilitation on the other. While conceptual compromise was the essence of neoclassicism, the many features that clustered around it naturally varied from one country to another.

In the early years of Soviet power, the terms of neoclassicism were erected, first, on the positivist (and largely economistic) assumption that the "causes" of crime lie in exploitative, and especially capitalist, social relations (private property, the capitalist state, ideology, etc.) and second, on the voluntaristic assumption that (except for incorrigible class enemies) the criminal character could be reformed through moral rehabilitation. As we will see, because of his acceptance of the first assumption, Lenin insisted that a chief object of socialist law should be remnants of the old capitalist system and corrupt soviet and party officials. Because of the second assumption, Lenin determined that, with the use of voluntaristic penal strategies associated with socialist construction, it would be possible drastically to reduce the extent of exploitation, violence, and other injustices in the future communist society.

For at least two years after the October 1917 revolution, and despite the publication of numerous decrees in the field of crime and penality, the Bolsheviks were extremely reluctant to articulate in juridical terms the basic concepts underlying their penal strategies. The flexible category of "violation," for example, was often preferred to the legalistic concept of "crime."[12] Juridical concepts such as "guilt" and "responsibility" were condemned as medieval errors, deleted from the vocabulary of criminalization, and replaced by nonlegal concepts such as "social danger" and "social harm." The concept of "punishment," oscillating between repression and education, was retermed "measures of social defense"; "imprisonment" became "deprivation of freedom." The coercive principle of "retribution" was abandoned for the humananistic language of conversion, correction, and reeducation. This doctrinal antiformalism was matched by a desire to deprofessionalize the composition of socialist legal institutions.

Even when compared with other systems of criminal justice elsewhere in Europe, it is fair to say that Russian Bolshevism was in the vanguard of the neoclassical movement. Many of the key strategies of early Bolshevik penality conformed with the neoclassical principles of "rehabilitation" and "individualization." These strategies can be summarized as follows (Dallin and Nicolaevsky, 1947:149–163; Carr, 1960:421–454; Juviler, 1976:35–36; Solomon, 1980:196–199):

- the decriminalization of certain common crimes;
- the use of noncustodial sanctions including fines, suspended sentences, and compulsory work for a great variety of offenses;
- the use of neoclassical principles of sentencing policy that allowed judges to consider a convict's motive, mental capacity, age, social circumstances, and degree of recidivism;
- minimum prison sentences that reflected the aim of rehabilitation rather than retribution, and which led to a reduction in the average length of prison terms actually served;
- a sweeping institutional reform of the prison system, including the introduction of the progressive stage system, semiopen agricultural colonies and educational programs, and socially useful labor (sometimes as a substitute for incarceration) paid at trade union rates;
- a reliance on unsupervised parole; and,
- a great reduction in the use of capital punishment.

Under Lenin's guidance between 1917 and 1923, these innovative policies were inaugurated by the Commissariat of Justice, rapidly and successfully in some spheres but slowly and without visible effect in others.[13] Lenin himself was highly selective in the attention that he gave, or could afford to give, to the various aspects of Bolshevik penality. He rarely concerned himself, for example, with the precise calculus of pain required by neoclassical philosophies of sentencing and incarceration. However, during debates on the 1919 Bolshevik Party Program, Lenin himself urged a reduction in the use of incarceration and he encouraged (1) extensive use of conditional convictions; (2) increased use of public censure; (3) replacement of imprisonment by compulsory labor at home; (4) replacement of prison with educational institutions; and (5) introduction of comrades' courts to handle certain categories of crime (Carr, 1960, 2:421; Bassiouni and Savitski, 1979:189–190).

Lenin recognized that the eradication of the old social order would lead, in the short run, to chaos and to an increase "of crime, hooliganism, corruption, profiteering and outrages of every kind" (1918i:264) during the socialist transition.[14] "To put these down," he continued, "requires time and ... *an iron hand*" (ibid.). This requirement necessitated "[d]ictatorship ... government that is revolutionarily bold, swift and ruthless in suppressing both exploiters and hooligans" (ibid., 265).[15]

From the very beginning of the October revolution, the Bolsheviks distinguished between "ordinary" crimes typically committed by the powerless, and "counterrevolutionary crimes" typically committed by those with military, economic, or political power. Lenin himself was not equally concerned with "every kind" of crime; the traditional crimes of the powerless, for example, commanded very little of his attention. Indeed, during the Civil War years (1918–1920) the Bolsheviks altogether abolished certain of these categories, including abortion, some sexual offenses, and most crimes by juveniles.[16]

In 1923, certainly with Lenin's knowledge and probably with his active consent, a special commission (led by the old Bolshevik Aron Solts and the Moscow prosecutor Shmuel Fainblit) granted general amnesty to large numbers of poor peasants convicted of the crime of home brewing (Solomon, 1981:16; Weissman, 1986). Between mid-1924 and early 1925, just after Lenin's death but presumably with his prior knowledge and tacit approval, there was a massive decriminalization of an even wider set of offenses. These included home brewing for personal use, poaching small amounts of timber for personal use, hooliganism committed for the first time, and petty thefts in factories (Solomon, ibid., 16–17).

In many of Lenin's pronouncements, and in much early Bolshevik practice, the crimes of soviet economic and political cadres were as much an object of criminal law as were the typical crimes of the powerless. An important reason why Lenin condemned "red-collar crimes" (Lós, 1988:147) is that he envisaged a simplified bureaucracy as a crucial feature of postrevolutionary society. Thus, he argued that in addition to the chiefly oppressive apparatus (the standing army, the police, and the bureaucracy), the modern state possesses an accounting and bookkeeping apparatus (banks, syndicates, postal service, consumers' societies, and office employees' unions) which will be "the *skeleton* of socialist society" (Lenin, 1917d:106). Lenin himself was especially concerned with two sorts of crime: (i) economic crimes by war-profiteers and remnants of the old bourgeoisie, and (ii) offenses by state officials, whether bureaucrats or party members, that stemmed from or included the abuse of their political power. For the first sort of crime Lenin reserved his most vehement condemnation. Thus, he suggested that war-profiteers "are the worst that [have] remained of the old capitalist system and are the vehicles of all the old evils; these we must kick out . . ." (19181:468–469). Indeed, one of the very first CEC decrees ("On Workers' Control" of November 1917) ordered that "[t]hose guilty of concealment of materials, products and orders, improper keeping of accounts and other such malpractices are held criminally responsible."[17] In mid-1918, immediately prior to the passage of a new law on embezzlement, Lenin requested that the Commissariat of Justice ensure "speedier and more ruthless court action against the bourgeoisie, embezzlers of state property, etc." (1918m:77). At the same time he demanded the expulsion from the party of judges who had given lenient sentences to four members of the Moscow Commission of Investigation charged with bribery and blackmail (Lenin, 1918h:331, n.317). Again, Lenin insisted that in order to proceed with the nationalization of the banks, "real success must be had" in "catching and *shooting* bribe-takers" (1918i:252; see also 1921g:78). He ordered that "everything must be done" to identify and capture bandits, capitalists, and landowners because they were "saboteurs, who stop at no crime to injure Soviet power" (Lenin, 1919i:556). In June 1921, capital punishment was fixed as the maximum penalty for state officials who aided theft from state warehouses (Hazard, 1951:302).[18] Moreover, it should be stressed that the provisions of the code indicate that the Bolsheviks were more concerned with embezzlement by state officials than by private citizens—the latter could only be punished by incarceration for a period no longer than six months.[19]

Our claim that red-collar criminals (i.e., soviet and party officials) were an important object of Bolshevik criminal law was only implicit in Lenin's writings. Although this claim was never developed theoretically by Lenin himself in the explicit form in which we express it here, it can nevertheless be derived from numerous pronouncements in his writings and speeches. From these it is evident that for Lenin a major object of Soviet law and socialist legality was the disciplining of the agents or representatives of Soviet power. Their somewhat unenviable position derived from Lenin's conception of socialist law as a mechanism for achieving the standards of conduct and responsibility expected of public officials if they were to fulfill their "leading role" as representatives of the most advanced section of the proletariat. Indeed, for all practical purposes, Lenin regarded the encumbents of this role as synonymous with the party membership itself. As occurred so often in Lenin's thought, we find here a mixture of practical exigency and political principle. The practical considerations arising from the immediate requirements of Soviet power entailed reliance upon cadres who were inexperienced, undereducated, and impatient. In this context, it was only to be expected that the agents of Soviet power would commit "errors" and "excesses." Yet these actions provided dangerous ammunition for counterrevolutionary forces, weakened the loyalty of allies, and undermined popular commitment to the socialist project. Accordingly, Lenin reminded the representatives of Soviet power that "the strictest revolutionary order is essential for the victory of socialism" (1917c:241). The violation of legality could have serious political consequences.

> The slightest lawlessness, the slightest infraction of Soviet law and order is a *loophole* the foes of the working people take immediate advantage of, it is a *starting-point* for Kolchak and Denikin victories. (Lenin, 1919i:556)

Similarly, albeit in another context, Lenin stressed the need for the strictest adherence to legality in economic relations with the peasantry so as to preserve and promote the fragile political alliance on which the revolution depended:

> those who contrary to the laws of Soviet power, treat the peasants unjustly must be ruthlessly fought, immediately removed and most severely prosecuted. (Lenin, 1923:502; see also Lenin, 1918j:252; 1919i:556; 1919b; and 1922c)

He argued that the lessons of such mistakes must be recognized and that soviet authorities must investigate, bring to trial, and punish all such "violations" and "excesses." On another occasion (the attempt to develop commodity exchange at the beginning of NEP), Lenin (1921f:387) demanded detailed reports about whether such activities had been investigated and, if so, whether the perpetrators had been punished. In a letter of 1918 to Kursky, he urged that it was essential for a bill to be drawn up prescribing that the penalties for bribery, extortion, and graft should be no less than ten years' imprisonment in addition to ten years of compulsory labor (Lenin, 1918h:331). Significantly, he demanded that differential or exemplary punishments be imposed on party members: "triple penalties should be inflicted on Communists, as compared with non-Party people" (Lenin, 1922:562). Elsewhere, he challenged functionaries in the People's Commissariat of Justice:

> every worker in this Commissariat should be assessed according to his record, on the strength of the following figures: how many Communists have you jailed with triple sentences? . . . How many bureaucrats have you jailed? (Lenin, 1922:562)

Lenin's emphasis on the importance of securing adherence to socialist legality by soviet and party officials was closely associated with his concern about the struggle against bureaucracy. In the period prior to his death he became more strident in his demand for action against the bureaucrats. He ordered that bureaucracy and red tape should be exposed and punished: "We must not be afraid of the courts . . . but must drag bureaucratic delays out into daylight for the people's judgment" (Lenin, 1921:556). He demanded exemplary trials of "the more 'vivid' cases" (Lenin, 1921a:522), and sent numerous missives to the People's Commissariat of Justice for action against red tape and for the reorganization of state control (Lenin, 1918j; 1919c; 1919d:486; 1921b:180; 1921c; and 1922d).

Penality and the Courts

However, the center of Bolshevik penal strategies is not to be found in the differential emphasis on class enemies and red-collar offenders, even though this strategy was arguably Bolshevism's most original feature. Nor, we believe (*pace* Solzhenitsyn), did it lie in the spheres of incarceration and sentencing. Indeed, the precise articulation of these two spheres was conceived by the Bolsheviks as lying at the end point rather than at the center of their policies. At the center of Bolshevik penal strategies were undoubtedly the courts (Hazard, 1960:1–63), the tsarist forms of which Lenin had earlier referred to as "instrument[s] of exploitation" (1918l:464) and "organs of bourgeois rule" (1919j:131; and see Krylenko, 1934:44). Moreover, it was precisely toward the innovative contribution of courts to the revolutionary process that many of Lenin's pronouncements about penality were directed.

One of Lenin's (1901a) earliest commentaries on courts had been sparked by a case of police brutality. Lenin's subsequent attack on the tsarist police was set within the general context of an 1887 law which had removed crimes by and against officials from the jurisdiction of courts sitting with a jury, and which had then transferred them to courts of crown judges and representatives of the estates. In his polemic, he distinguished between the respective merits of "state trials" and "street trials":

Trial by the street is valuable because it breathes a living spirit into the bureau-cratic formalism which pervades our government institutions. The street is interested, not only, and not so much, in the definition of the given offence (insulting behavior, assault, torture), or in the category of punishment to be imposed; it is interested in exposing thoroughly and bringing to public light the significance and all the social and political threads of the crime, in order to draw lessons in public morals and practical politics from the trial. The street does not want to see in the court "an official institution," in which functionaries apply to given cases the corresponding articles of the Penal Code, but a public institution which exposes the ulcers of the present system, which provides material for criticising it and, consequently, for improving it. Impelled by its practical knowledge of public affairs and by the growth of political consciousness, the street is discovering the truth for which our official, professorial jurisprudence, weighed down by its scholastic shackles, is groping with such difficulty and timidity—namely, that in the fight against crime the reform of social and political institutions is much more important than the imposition of punishment. (Ibid., 393–394)

Lenin concluded that street justice was the better form of justice, especially if the citizenry was sufficiently educated to understand and press for its "rights."[20] While Lenin never advocated street justice as a form of proletarian regulation, his polemic here disclosed his abiding preference for a system that was "closer to the people" than formalistic adjudication. Indeed, after the ravages of the Civil War, Lenin stressed that the Russian people had previously experienced courts as external impositions, as exclusively coercive and oppressive. This experience inculcated a negative response, itself part of the general backwardness of Russian civil society that was akin to a "semi-savage habit of mind" and an "ocean of illegality" that was "the greatest obstacle to the establishment of law and culture" (Lenin, 1922c:365).

So important to Lenin was the role of the courts during the DoP that the first legislation on courts (Decree No. 1 on the Court) was enacted only a few weeks after the October revolution, in November 1917. The Decree (as modified several times in the next seven months) dictated the basic elements of the new court system and abolished existing legal institutions such as the Procuracy, the Bar, and all but the most basic of laws.[21] It transpires, in numerous of Lenin's pronouncements, that from the beginning of the revolution the new Bolshevik system of courts was burdened with a heavy political agenda. While the local and people's courts had ordinary crimes as their chief targets, the revolutionary tribunals were created to combat counterrevolutionary forces. By order of Trotsky, in 1917, military disci-pline was to be adjudicated through a system of comrades' courts. Apart from eradicating the old social order, the courts were to be a leading agency for the inculcation and propagation of socialist virtues. As Lenin put it: "the courts . . . have another, still more important task . . . [namely] to ensure the strictest discipline and self-discipline of the working people" (Lenin, 1918n:217; and see 1918c). Thus, Lenin wrote:

> Soviet power . . . immediately threw the old court on the scrap-heap. By that we paved the way for a real people's court, and not so much by the force of repressive measures as by massive example, the authority of the working people, without formalities; we transformed the court from an instrument of exploitation into an instrument of education on the firm foundations of socialist society. There is no doubt that we cannot attain such a society at once. (1918l:464; see also 1921d:351)

Lenin played an important part in forming the structure of the revolutionary tribunals, and he insisted that they be set up to deal with "counter-revolutionaries, bribe-takers, disorganisers and violators of discipline" (1918q:220). He intended that, taken together, these courts would spearhead the elimination of the old social order and also propagate discipline and culture. In the context of addressing the question of how to restore the "discipline and self-discipline" of the masses, Lenin offered some comments about the dual roles of the new courts:

> [S]pecial mention should be made of the important role now devolving on the courts of law. In capitalist society, the court was mainly an instrument of oppression, an instrument of bourgeois exploitation. Hence the bounden duty of the proletarian revolution lay not in reforming the judicial institutions . . . but in completely destroying and razing to its foundations the whole of the old judicial apparatus. . . . The new court has been needed first and foremost for the struggle against the exploiters. . . . But, in addition, the courts—if they are really organised on the principle of Soviet institutions—have another, still more important task. This task is to ensure the strictest discipline and self-discipline of the working people. (1918n:217)

Like socialist legal institutions as a whole, the new courts were intended to be temporary, popular in composition, and selective in their handling of different categories of crime and criminality.[22] The new courts were quite explicitly located at a lower level, and included local (later, people's) courts and revolutionary tribunals. The local courts were devised for civil cases involving suits not exceeding 3,000 roubles and for criminal cases punishable with not more than two years imprisonment. They were to be staffed by a permanent local judge and two alternate assessors who were instructed to abide by the old laws insofar as they had not been abolished by the revolution and contradicted neither revolutionary conscience nor revolutionary legal consciousness.

We can discern several new features about the new courts. First, there was an attempt to politicize their principles of adjudication. For example, in trying cases, the courts were instructed to be guided by extant laws if they had not been annulled by the CEC or CPC and if they did not contradict socialist legal conscience.[23] Again, for both civil and criminal cases the existing courts' rules of procedure were held to be operative only if they did not "run counter to the legal consciousness of the working classes."[24] People's courts were to be free from formal considerations when deciding what evidence to accept as relevant in a given case.[25] In all cases, courts were not to be bound by formal law at the expense of substantive justice.[26] According to Decree No. 3 on the Court (July 1918), which increased the jurisdiction of the local courts, judges were henceforth never to permit formalities to hinder a just decision.[27]

Second, the staff of the new courts was popularized. As Lenin explained about the soviet courts, "we did not have to create a new apparatus, because anybody can act as a judge basing himself on the revolutionary sense of justice of the working class" (1919g:182). Moreover, a note added to Decree No. 2 on the Court declared that the size of the daily fees of assessors was to be determined by the soviets, "bearing in mind the gradual obligatory transition to gratuituous performance by citizens of the state duty of administering justice."

Third, some concern was shown with respect to due process and procedural safeguards. For example, according to Decree No. 2 on the Court, there was to be a limited system of appeals from the new people's courts of 1918 overseen by a Supreme Supervisory Authority in Petrograd.[28] The types of cases that could be appealed were expanded in 1918.[29] In July 1918 the Commissariat of Justice issued an Instruction, signed by Stuchka, about procedure in the people's courts.[30] Procedural rules were largely confined to the pretrial stage and related to jurisdiction, the calling of witnesses, and sufficiency of evidence. These instructions were expanded by the Decree on the People's Court of November 30, 1918, and here we meet the first mention of appeal for procedural errors and violations: decisions could be overturned if court procedure was violated.

However, in certain key respects it is evident that all was not well with the new court structure. Lenin's position about the simplification of state functions produced by popular participation in the courts, for example, probably remained largely exhortatory. According to the Bolshevik Vinokurov (cited in Hazard, 1960:389), by 1924 the courts were largely proletarian in composition: 87 percent of the people's judges and 72 percent of the judges in the provincial courts were of worker or peasant background; 75 percent of the former and 80 percent of the latter were Bolsheviks. But, from the NEP onwards, Lenin's mounting concern with bureaucracy attested to events actually in conflict with the universal participation to which he was committed. Moreover, he never addressed the project of administrative democracy in concrète terms. In 1918 it was provided that old legal officials could still be elected to both judicial and investigation institutions.[31] Thus, exactly how influential Decree No. 1 was in practice is unclear. Stuchka, the second Commissar of Justice, wrote in August 1918 that some jurisdictions had already replaced the old courts before the Decree's enactment, while others had been unable to replace them after it; the central authorities had to content themselves with the issuance of general directives (see further Hazard, 1960:8 and n.16). Lenin himself complained that

> our revolutionary and people's courts are extremely, incredibly weak. One feels that we have not yet done away with the people's attitude toward the courts as something official and alien. . . . It is not yet sufficiently realised that the courts are an organ which enlists precisely the poor, every one of them, in the work of state administration. (1918c:266)

Problems of the composition of the new court structure were exacerbated, moreover, by a certain confusion which Lenin, unintentionally and carelessly, created in the respective jurisdictions of the different courts. For example, he demanded that the People's Commissariat of Justice should push the people's courts to conduct "noisy model trials" (Lenin, 1922:561–562) of those who abused NEP; yet, at the same time, he urged that such trials (specifically, of bureaucratic negligence) should be held in the revolutionary tribunals (Lenin, 1922a). Therefore, there was also an increasing blur between political crimes and ordinary crimes. This was itself intensified by the lack of clear guidelines between the types of crime respectively dealt with by the people's courts and the revolutionary tribunals.

Thus far, we have suggested no more than that in the differential objects of its criminal law lay the seeds of a revolution in the "normal" strategies of Bolshevik penality. In that Bolshevik penality had as its chief objects the illegalities of soviet and party officials, rather than those of the powerless Russian masses, its intentions were arguably quite revolutionary. The neoclassical principles of Bolshevik penality were undoubtedly far more enlightened than either the antiquated policies of the tsarist system or the classical schemes of the Socialist Revolutionaries (SRs), their main rivals for power.

IV. Penal Strategies in the "Exceptional" State

Our concern now is to explore the extent to which Lenin encouraged the use of *exceptional* forms of penal strategies. Was this encouragement linked to, or did it even cause, the low priority accorded to individual civil liberties and lack of legal constraints on party and state power in the subsequent history of Soviet society? E. H. Carr has identified the paradox of the Bolshevik conception of crime as the product of a disordered society and punishment as an act of reclamation and education, on the one hand, and the Bolshevik use of revolutionary terror to combat counterrevolution on the other (1960, 2:421–422).

> The paradox of the tension between ultimate humanitarian ideals and the immediate necessities of a revolutionary situation was . . . particularly acute. The tension could be resolved only on the heroic assumption that the harshest

penalties applied to class enemies were temporary measures necessitated by the
revolutionary struggle for power, and had nothing in common with the permanent
methods and policies of the régime. (Ibid., 421)

By way of responding to this paradox, we should begin by noting that Lenin's
libertarianism was significantly *weaker*, in a specific sense, than his authoritarianism. However, it was not "weaker" because he was less strongly committed to his
libertarianism, but because he failed either to specify or to create the organizational
and institutional forms for its realization. In contrast, Lenin's authoritarianism can
properly be seen as the *dominant* element within Bolshevism precisely because its
manifestations secured early institutional expression. Only in this specific sense,
we suggest, is it correct to identify a strong continuity between Leninism and
Stalinism. Indeed, Lenin's view of the authoritarian dimension of the DoP never
amounted to an endorsement of unbridled violence or to an abstract preference for
centralism. So, Lenin insisted that

> as the fundamental task of the government becomes, not military suppression,
> but administration, the typical manifestation of suppression and compulsion will
> be, not shooting on the spot, but trial by court. (Lenin, 1918i:266)

How, then, can we account for Lenin's encouragement of *specific* facets of the
arsenal of authoritarianism, namely, the various strategies that we have thus far
referred to as those of the "exceptional" state? We will explore this thorny question
by briefly considering his views on three items in the authoritarian inventory: model
(or "show") trials, capital punishment, and "red terror."

Model Trials

Lenin undoubtedly bears some historical responsibility for the Soviet institution of
the model or "show" trial. Consistent with our rejection of the thesis of simple
linearity between Leninist and Stalinist authoritarianism, our view is that Lenin's
use of show trials unwittingly provided the institutional framework later deployed
with such devastating effect in the Stalinist 1930s. However, whereas Lenin
typically conceived of show trials as vehicles of public education, their very
publicity was transformed in the 1930s into a purely repressive mechanism that
served to inhibit and eventually to destroy all possibility of legalized political
opposition.

Model trials do not seem to have been conceived of by Lenin in the same sense
of stagedness as used later in Stalin's show trials. In 1922 Lenin sent instructions
to the People's Commissariat of Justice insisting that "several model trials" be
held in Moscow, Petrograd, and other key centers (1922:561; 1922a). The chief
purpose of these trials was to ensure that counterrevolutionaries knew that their
crimes would be detected, tried, and punished according to law. At the same time,

these trials were to be held in conjunction with educative political meetings and with the widest possible press coverage. Lenin's espousal of these public displays was premised on a belief in their potential educative value in underlining and publicizing the policy and the ethics of socialism. For example, he wrote to the Moscow Revolutionary Tribunal about a case of bureaucratic procrastination that

> it is of exceptional importance—both from the Party and the political stand-point—to have the proceedings in the red tape case arranged with the greatest solemnity, making the trial *educational*, and the trial sufficiently impressive. (Lenin, 1921e:348)

The most important, and the most well known model trial with which Lenin was associated was that of the leadership of the Right Socialist Revolutionaries (SRs) in mid-1922.[32] While allowing that the Bolsheviks acted abominably during the SR trial (see e.g., Burbank, 1986:108–110), it is nevertheless difficult to determine Lenin's conduct in it. According to the very partisan account of Jansen (1982:27), for example, Lenin orchestrated the entire affair, despite his grave illness. Yet others have suggested, implicitly (Carr, 1961, 1:189) or explicitly (Medvedev, 1971:382), that Lenin, who was seriously ill during the whole trial, played no role in it at all, and that it had been instigated by the Chekist leader (Dzerzhinsky), and organized by the General Secretary (Stalin).

The trial of the SRs resulted in considerable opposition from all branches of the international socialist movement, and a delegate from the Comintern—meeting with representatives from the other two Socialist Internationals—agreed that the Soviet government would allow international observers at the trial and that it would not apply the death penalty against any of the defendants. Lenin disagreed with these concessions. But having argued his case, he concluded that, an agreement having been made, the Bolsheviks should adhere to it (Lenin, 1922b:330).[33]

It is perhaps strange that Lenin should have been opposed to the participation of foreign observers since, if nothing else, publicity for the Bolshevik contention about the duplicity of the SRs would have been maximized by the presence of foreign observers. Because such trials were consciously transformed into political events, they necessarily generated demands for observer status from other interested groups. It is perhaps fair to say that Lenin's opposition articulated a persistent Soviet preoccupation with the right to national self-determination—which implied a sharp separation between internal and external affairs. The logic of the show trial, which Stalin understood better than Lenin, was that the greatest impact could be achieved with the maximum internationalization of the proceedings. It seems clear that Lenin had not thought through the logic of the maximum use of show trials as a political strategy, nor did they play anything more than an occasional role in early Soviet political life. Their elaboration and full deployment was, of course, to come later; however, while Lenin's authoritarianism coexisted with his libertarianism in an uneasy and often contradictory tension, no such ambiguity existed in the social order of Stalinism.

Capital Punishment

Any discussion of Lenin's position on capital punishment must acknowledge a cardinal distinction between those who were executed according to the due processes of Bolshevik law, on the one hand, and those who died through extralegal (although often officially approved) means in the course of purges, for example, or during the Red Terror, on the other. In what follows we begin with a discussion of the former.

Although Lenin clearly shared the traditional hostility of Russian progressive thought to state executions, he nevertheless maintained an ambivalent position toward capital punishment.[34] In February 1917 Kerensky's Provisional Government had abolished the death penalty. The abolition was met with unanimous approval, although there was a deafening silence about it in the Bolshevik press (*Pravda* and *Izvestiia*)—a silence that probably indicated a refusal to pay any tribute to the government, rather than any hostility to the measure itself. One month later, with the impending collapse of the Russian army, the Provisional Government restored the death penalty for "traitorous" soldiers at the front. The Bolsheviks, in alliance with the SRs, now campaigned actively for its abolition. However, there is some evidence to suggest that, even at this time, Lenin himself would have supported the retention of the death penalty for class enemies. For example, in a brief discussion of the Petrograd Soviet's resolution to abolish capital punishment, which he supported, Lenin remarked that "the situation would be different if it were a weapon against the landowners and capitalists" (1917f:263).[35]

In one of its first decrees, in November 1917, the Second Congress of Soviets abolished capital punishment. Lenin was not apparently present, although Trotsky reported that at the time Lenin had reservations about the abolition. Moreover, Trotsky attributed to Lenin the observation that "[t]his is madness. . . . How can we accomplish a revolution without shooting?" (1925:133).[36] Trotsky's report of Lenin's attitude is confirmed in one of Lenin's own pamphlets written in mid-1917:

> It is right to argue against the death penalty only when it is applied by the exploiters against the *mass* of the working people. . . . It is hardly likely that any revolutionary government whatever could do without applying the death penalty to the *exploiters*. (Lenin, 1917a:341)

In the early days of the revolution the Bolsheviks tended to be noticeably lenient with their opponents, often being content to disarm them and then to set them free (Carr, 1950, 1:150–162). By Lenin's own account, "[w]hen we arrested anyone we told him we would let him go if he gave us a written promise not to engage in sabotage" (Lenin, 1917b:294). However, the death penalty reemerged as the Civil War intensified, although not through any formal decision. The evidence suggests that the Cheka began to carry out executions in February 1918; the first summary executions were of bandits, speculators, and blackmailers rather than political enemies (van den Berg, 1983:155). In June 1918, the revolutionary tribunals began imposing the death penalty without regard to the absence of any jurisdictional authority to do so. With Wrangel's military activity in the Crimea and with the Poles advancing in the Ukraine, the use of the death penalty became more regular. Now Lenin openly defended capital punishment and advocated its extension to ever wider categories of opponents. During War Communism and the Civil War these new categories included the avoidance of labor service (1918c:33); unlicensed possession of arms (1918d:35); indiscipline in the supply services (1918e:406); prostitution (1918f:349); those assisting the "predatory campaign of the Anglo-French imperialists," if resisting arrest (1918p:114–115); "formal and bureaucratic attitudes to work" in the food-purchasing board (1919:499); and informers giving false information (1918g:115).[37] At the beginning of NEP Lenin also showed a willingness to broaden the categories of those liable for capital punishment; these new categories included "abuse of NEP" (1922:561); assistance to the international bourgeoisie and striving to overthrow the communist system of property by violence, blockade, espionage, financing the press (1922e).

However, in early 1920, after Denikin's defeat, Lenin again placed the abolition of the death penalty on the agenda. The use of terror had only been imposed, he argued, in response to counterrevolutionary terrorism. With victory, he insisted, "we shall renounce all extraordinary measures" (Lenin, 1920:328). In the same month, he referred more cautiously to the same decision to end Cheka's use of the death sentence: "[A] reservation was made at the very beginning that we do not by any means close our eyes to the possibility of restoring capital punishment" (Lenin, 1920a:167). Capital punishment was restored in early May 1920.

Finally, reference should be made to the statutory provisions for capital punishment enacted while Lenin was in power, especially those contained in the RSFSR Criminal Code of 1922. It should be noted that, during the debates prior to enactment of the Code, considerable protest (led by Riazanov) had occurred among the Bolsheviks about the restoration of capital punishment (Adams, 1972:82). While the CEC was preparing the draft, Lenin wrote to Kursky, then Commissar of Justice, urging that the death penalty be used against those assisting the international bourgeoisie (1922e:358; and see van den Berg, 1983:156). The 1922 Code contained a large number (forty-seven) of capital offenses—and to these should be added nine more offenses that violated a decree or an administrative order. Significantly, the language of the Code revealed a serious intent by the Bolsheviks to punish by death an almost unique concatenation of crimes: crimes by and against public officials, counterrevolutionary crimes, military crimes, economic crimes, and crimes against socialist property. Indeed, for only three "ordinary" crimes (robbery, aggravated rape, and aggravated murder) was the death penalty in effect. According to Adams's content analysis of Soviet decrees and statutes relating to capital punishment, these three had a far lower likelihood of being carried out than most other capital offenses (Adams, 1972:89–90).[38]

It is important to draw attention to the consequences of the particular way in which these capital offenses were drafted. Some offenses were defined in such a way as to require no proof either of specific conduct or of determinable intent. Rather, they explictly required ex post facto judgement as to the political ramifications of the conduct complained of. Thus, for example, "sabotage" (*diversiia*) and "wrecking," "participation in a counterrevolutionary organization," "undermining state institutions," and "aiding the international bourgeoisie" were all extremely broad catch-all offenses.[39] Indeed, Lenin's dislike of legal formalism predisposed him to favor broad statutory provisions, of which the avoidance of repressive interpretation could be entrusted to the good sense of the proletarianized courts. There is an obvious naivety in this cavalier rejection of legal formalism, to which we will soon return.

About Lenin's several views on capital punishment, then, it can be said that they entailed a tension unresolved by the explanation that he only accepted its use in the extreme conditions of Civil War. As van den Berg writes, "already under Lenin, the direct relationship between the necessity of terror in a revolution and the death penalty no longer governed actual policy" (1983:156). Once introduced on grounds of expedience, then legitimized, and finally expanded in scope, capital punishment later became so familiar a feature of the political landscape that there was only minimal resistance to its reintroduction as a normal strategy for responding to political disputes.

Red Terror

Both model trials and capital punishment were important parts of the exceptional penal strategies directed to the establishment of Bolshevik hegemony. They were exceptional not only because, unlike the neoclassical strategies of Bolshevism discussed earlier in this chapter, they were understood to embody authoritarian rather than libertarian practices, but also because their use was expected to be of short duration.

The third and most insidious weapon in the arsenal of exceptional penal strategies was undoubtedly terrorism, officially referred to by the Bolsheviks themselves as "red terror." The several organs of red terror were a crucial aspect of Bolshevik penal strategies during and after the Civil War. Institutionally, they included an extensive secret police network (the infamous Cheka), the revolutionary tribunals, and a special system of camps that originally existed in parallel with the prisons of the neoclassical regime. Local units of the Cheka soon comprised a grid covering the entire Soviet Republic—all major cities, county seats, provincial capitals, railroads, ports, and the army (Heller and Nekrich, 1986:65).

As we have seen, Lenin's principled opposition to terrorism before 1917 stands in stark contrast to the emergence, and his own explicit endorsement of, red terror during and after the period of the Civil War.[40] What was involved in Lenin's apparent change of position toward terror?

Prior to 1917, Lenin had emphasized that the struggle for democracy was a necessary stage of development within the prebourgeois political formation of tsarist Russia. In this he differed profoundly from the many Russian political movements which advocated almost unqualified terrorism (Woodcock, 1963:376–400). His clear and unambiguous message was that Russian revolutionaries should campaign without violence for the realization of bourgeois democracy and legality because it offered the most advantageous conditions for the development of the struggle against both tsarism and the bourgeoisie, of whom the latter Lenin (1905:300) insisted were the long-term enemy.[41] Indeed, immediately after the seizure of power, Lenin denied that Bolsheviks had engaged in terrorism. In November 1917, for example, he wrote, "we are accused of resorting to terrorism, but we have not resorted, and I hope will not resort, to the terrorism of the French revolutionaries who guillotined unarmed men" (Lenin, 1917b:294).

Lenin consistently criticized political tendencies that resorted to terroristic forms of struggle. He employed two main arguments against terrorism. Firstly, he argued that it was an essentially petty-bourgeois activity (e.g., Lenin, 1902:471). This was so because it expressed the opportunism of those intellectuals who, lacking systematic contact with either the working class or the peasantry, were inclined to favor spontaneity and sensationalism. As a political strategy, terrorism was opposed to mass political action. Second, he insisted that it was futile to engage in abstract discussions of terrorism "in principle" (e.g., Lenin 1901:19). Against such abstractions, Lenin countered that the issue should be posed in terms of whether or not terrorism was appropriate or harmful "under the present conditions." There is no trace in his extensive discussion of the concept of the DoP of any *general* or principled endorsement of revolutionary terror.

We therefore reject the popular view (e.g. Leggett, 1975) that all along Lenin was a covert authoritarian and that, having secured political power, he at once displayed his "true colors." Rather, we suggest that his endorsement of terror was largely a response to the brutal reality of the "white terror" unleashed by the forces of the counterrevolution.[42] The establishment of repressive organs such as the Cheka and the revolutionary tribunals was an urgent response to the military fact that, barely six weeks after the revolution, southeastern Russia was overrun by Cossack armies and other white forces, western Russia was threatened by the Germans, and the Ukraine was heavily infiltrated by French and British influence. "At the critical moment of a hard-fought struggle," reflects E. H. Carr, "the establishment of these organs can hardly be regarded as unusual" (1950, 1:167–168). Moreover, Chekist energies were at first only directed to (i) the sabotage of Bolshevik administration by the bourgeoisie, (ii) destruction and rioting by drunken mobs and, (iii) banditry "under the flag of anarchism" (see Carr, ibid.).[43] The particular combination of external military intervention and internal civil war added a real desperation to the maintenance of power, and Lenin's urgent telegrams to the "fronts" in 1918 and 1919 reveal the perilous circumstances of Bolshevik power. In these circumstances the resort to terror, for Lenin, was an unavoidable necessity. Characteristically, Lenin made a virtue out of necessity. He thus explicitly argued for the political necessity of resorting to revolutionary terror—red terror, in contrast to the white terror of the counterrevolution.

At the same time, however, Lenin increasingly began to argue for the regularization and even the "legalization" of red terror. He wrote to Zinoviev, for example, only four days before an assassination attempt on his own life, criticizing him for restraining Petrograd workers who wanted to respond with mass terror to the murder of a leading Bolshevik. Instead of restraint, urged Lenin, "[w]e must encourage the energy and mass character of the terror against the counterrevolutionaries" (1918b:336). As an objective, moreover, the regularization of red terror outlasted the most perilous period of the Civil War. Soon thereafter, according to Trotsky's recollection, "at every passing opportunity" Lenin now began to equate the DoP with the absolute necessity of the terror (1925:137–138).[44] About a new article for inclusion in the Criminal Code that would justify and legalize the institutionalization of terror, Lenin wrote to Commissar of Justice Kursky that

> the courts must not ban terror—to promise that would be deception or self-deception—[we] must formulate the motives underlying it, legalise it as a principle, plainly, without any make-believe or embellishment. (1922e:358)

His very next sentence has considerable import:

> It must be formulated in the broadest possible manner, for only revolutionary law and revolutionary conscience can more or less widely determine the limits within which it should be applied. (1922e:358)

From a temporary and exceptional penal strategy, then, red terror had by 1922 been more or less consciously perverted by Lenin and transformed into a normal one. It is not possible here to address either the dimensions or the putative justifications of Lenin's contribution to this double perversion, a tragic transformation the concrete unfolding of which has been presented in great detail elsewhere (e.g., Shub, 1948; Carr, 1960, 2:421–454; Andics, 1969; Bettelheim, 1976). However, we would be remiss if we failed to point out that, when normal and exceptional penal strategies are so conflated, red terror is nothing less than official lawlessness. The very problem of official lawlessness, of which Lenin was so well aware, and which returns us to our original argument about Lenin's inadequate theorization of the constitution of Soviet society, demanded mechanisms of regulation involving a certain degree of separation of powers. The absence of such mechanisms, whilst not in itself authoritarian, created the conditions in which official lawlessness was able to flourish, as it did under Stalinism.

Nowhere were the consequences of the absence of mechanisms for "policing the police" more dire than in the intersection of Chekist practices with the attempted development of neoclassical forms of incarceration. Indeed, the gradual transformation of the enlightened, neoclassical prisons into the infamous system of gulags originated in the indistinct boundaries between the jurisdiction of the courts and the legal (and extralegal) activities of the Cheka—a deadly muddle to which Lenin, with his disdain for legal formalism, decidedly contributed but which, at the same time, he clearly did not intend (Feldbrugge, 1986).[45] During his last attendance at a Party Congress, Lenin (1922g) somewhat obliquely bemoaned the overinvestment of carceral power in the security apparatuses. Far too late, in other words, Lenin himself seems pathetically to have realized that when in the same political project libertarianism and unchecked authoritarianism intersect, libertarianism is inevitably the bloody loser.

V. Conclusion

> Freedom only for the supporters of the government, only for the members of one party—however numerous they may be—is no freedom at all. Freedom is always and exclusively freedom for the one who thinks differently. Not because of any fanatical concept of "justice" but because all that is instructive, wholesome and purifying in political freedom depends on this essential characteristic, and its effectiveness vanishes when "freedom" becomes a special privilege.
>
> —Rosa Luxemburg (1918:69)

In this chapter we have offered what we believe is a necessary palliative to the widely held view that the chief source of the degeneration of Soviet society was the dominance of the authoritarian over the libertarian tendencies within Bolshevism. The authoritarian roots of Leninist penality, we have suggested, lay in *both* the authoritarian and libertarian tendencies within his political thought, and in the specific combination of the two that was manifest in his chosen penal strategies. Within both these traditions there was a failure to advance, either theoretically or concretely, a model of political and constitutional relations that could provide and secure the minimum conditions of democratic life under socialism. These provisions would have needed to include a secure public space for political discussion and political competition. Additionally, they would have needed to specify and to mandate the policing of the boundaries between the different levels of institutional powers and competencies.

An inescapable tension existed between the regularization or legalization of suppression against "counterrevolutionary crimes" and the reliance upon mass initiative and revolutionary conscience to govern the circumstances and the degree of its operation. Ultimately, Lenin's position amounted to an act of political faith in the moral rectitude either of the proletariat as a whole, or of party members and state officials, that legal powers would be applied with circumspection and good judgment. With his disdain for legal formalism, and his tendency to castigate all legally empowered rights as intrinsically bourgeois, Lenin failed to provide any institutional guarantees against the abuse or violation of rules by individual agents of revolutionary power. Such provision, characteristically, is a distinguishing feature of the doctrine of "the rule of law."

But we should not be understood as advancing the naive position that all would have been well if Lenin had insisted on the institutionalization of the rule of law. Commitment to "the rule of law," of course, does not in itself guarantee that official lawlessness is effectively banished. Rather, we hold the view that Lenin can, and indeed must, be criticized for relying on the naive and moralistic view that political commitment can in itself be a guarantee against authoritarian practices by party and state officials. Lenin's position was epitomized in his letter to Kursky in the alternative drafts of the definition of "counterrevolution":

> *Variant 1:* Propaganda or agitation, or membership of, or assistance given to organisations the object of which . . . is to assist that section of the international bourgeoisie which refuses to recognise the rights of the communist system of ownership. . . . (1922ea:358)

> *Variant 2:* Propaganda or agitation that objectively serves . . . the interests of that section of the international bourgeoisie which (as above). . . . (1922ea:359)

Lenin indicated his preference for *Variant 2*. The contrast is clearly posed. The former required both some identifiable conduct and an intention, such as to assist an external political agent. The latter had no requirement either of specified conduct or of intention; it sufficed that there was some conjuncture which could be construed as "serving the interests of the international bourgeoisie." The application of such a rule required great and, we suggest, unreasonable faith in "revolutionary conscience," quite apart from its inherent capacity to spill over into a license for generalized repression.

Lenin clearly attached great significance to a combination of socialist legality, nonlegalistic rules (such as exhortation to revolutionary conscience) and, beginning with the Civil War and War Communism, the several organs of red terror. This combination vividly emerged in a set of draft theses on "strict observance of the laws." Here Lenin urged that "emergency measures of warfare against counterrevolution should not be restricted by the laws." Such measures were subject to what is in essence both a declaratory and reporting condition that

> an exact and formal statement be made by the appropriate Soviet body or official to the effect that the special conditions of civil war and the fight against counterrevolution require that the limits of the law be exceeded. (Lenin, 1918a:110)

This provision was self-evidently dependent upon officials' revolutionary conscience, and Lenin clearly had such a generalized confidence. It may be significant that he was himself prepared to intervene, to demand explanation, or to institute investigation where some irregularity or persecution had been reported to him. However, personal intervention depends on the disposition and prestige of the leader, of the flow of information and access to the leader. Such a system cannot itself be a solution to the supervision and control of exceptional powers.

What emerges from and extends beyond Lenin's practical and exhortatory concern to punish violations by soviet officials is a broad conception of socialist legality as an appeal to an exemplary moral order. How far is it correct to push the analogy between the conception of the party and that of an elect moral agency? Lenin himself would have clearly rejected such an analogy as confusing the role of example and leadership with that of an idealist conception of moral agency. However, it remains true that there was a serious tension in Lenin's thought between a materialism, which rejected concepts like moral agency, and a voluntarism, which emphasized the role of will and determination as final arbiters of the historical process. This dualism is not unique to Marxism but it lies at its core. It is epitomized in Marx's own celebrated dictum that "[m]en make their own history, but they do not make it just as they please" (Marx, 1852, 1:398). Indeed, in *State and Revolution* Lenin was virtually silent about the question of the relation between the party and the masses. His sole mention of this question is pregnant with dangerous possibilities:

> By educating the workers' party, Marxism educates the vanguard of the proletariat, capable of assuming power and *leading the whole people* to socialism, of directing and organising the new system, of being the teacher, the guide, the leader of all the working and exploited people in organising their social life. . . . (Lenin, 1917:404)

The key feature of this formulation is its overinvestment in the voluntarist burden allocated to party personnel. Our contention is not simply a version of a skepticism which denies the very possibility of an organic relation between party and masses. Rather, we have been anxious to focus attention on Lenin's disregard of the need for the institutional protection of legal and political processes from bureaucratic or authoritarian tendencies. These absences are consistent with, but not necessarily justified by, Lenin's sincerely held view that the exceptional measures he advocated were only to be short-lived, a necessary but temporary consequence of the need to secure power and to defeat the counterrevolution in the Civil War.

The libertarian strain in Lenin's thought was undoubtedly conceived as the dynamic element initiating the long road to the communist future. The self-activating participatory democracy of Lenin's conception of communism was accorded no resources apart from its own revolutionary consciousness. Without proper resources it was unable to resist the institutionalization of the dual process of exceptionalism and bureaucratism; it simply had no supports or guarantees outside the voluntaristic inspiration of the revolutionary élan once that institution had itself become an agency of the very exceptionalism and bureaucratism which undercut its revolutionary vocation. Thus, the conjunctural history of the revolution and its institutionalization became the bearer of precisely those processes which first postponed, and then abandoned, the experimental and humanitarian impulse of Bolshevik penal strategies.

Notes

1. According to one secondary source, although we have been unable to confirm this in any original texts, Lenin "gave his approval to the study of crime and penal practices, in the apparent hope that progress would result from such study" (Connor, 1969:28). In our analysis we ignore the many occasions when Lenin used only polemically the vocabulary of crime and penality and with no serious theoretical intent. In *Lenin's Collected Works* we have therefore ignored such meaningless entries as, for example, Lenin's utterance about a conference to found a Third International in August 1917, that "[i]t would be simply criminal to postpone now the calling of a conference of the Left" (1917e:321).

2. These diverse activities still seem to provide theoretical grist for the understanding of crime and penality. Indeed, several recent texts (e.g., Bucholz, Hartman, Lekschas, and Stiller, 1974; Bassiouni and Savitski, 1979:101–129; Avanesov, 1981; Korobeinikov, 1985; and Vigh, 1985) profess to have discovered the relevance of Lenin's pronouncements for a modern-day socialist criminology. According to Bucholz et al., for example, "socialist criminology sees the Marxist-*Leninist* concept of the causes of crime as its principal scientific foundation" (1974:8) [our emphasis]. However, this "Marxist-Leninist" criminology has very little to do with socialism or, indeed, with the respective projects of Marx, Engels, and Lenin. Far from it, it most closely resembles a crude amalgam of biologism and late–1940s structural functionalism, whose combined objects are well-worn and bankrupt concepts like "criminology as science," "causes of crime," "criminal personality," "criminological prediction," and "organization of social prevention."

3. We firmly reject the view that Lenin covertly subscribed to only one aspect of this couplet and that his pronouncements about the other aspect were mere facade. Anticipatory versions of our account of the relation between the authoritarian and libertarian tendencies can be found in the dichotomy of popular initiative/elite direction (Evans, 1987) and the view that Lenin's tracts on the proletarian dictatorship, especially *State and Revolution*, were *genuinely* based "on the audacious project of directly proceeding with and actually encouraging the dissolution of the state" (Harding, 1983, 2:187).

4. However, see Lenin's somewhat different formulation in his lecture "The State" (1919h:488).

5. Lenin's concept of the democratic process referred not only to the democratization of institutions but also, and perhaps more importantly, to the dictatorship of the masses over the exploiters. Every democracy (a term of bourgeois legal ideology), for Lenin, is a class dictatorship; see Balibar, 1977:66–77. Lenin tended to see the concept of socialist legality as a peculiarly socialist form that mediated between democracy and dictatorship and transcended their individual bourgeois components; see Carr (1960, 2:468–471).

6. The conclusions we draw are very much the same as those arrived at by Polan: "The central absence in Lenin's politics is that of a theory of political institutions . . . Lenin's state form is one-dimensional. It allows no distances, no spaces, no appeals, no checks, no balances, no processes, no delays, no interrogations and, above all, no distribution of power" (1984:129).

7. The quotations in the couplet above, for example, which occurred in *The Proletarian Revolution and the Renegade Kautsky* (Lenin, 1918) and the "Rough Thesis of a Decision on the Strict Observance of the Laws" (Lenin, 1918a), respectively, were produced in wholly different circumstances and had altogether different objects. The former was in part directed to factions within German Social Democracy that articulated socialist demands in legalistic terms; the latter was concerned to secure obedience to a socialist legality that avoided the inflexibility of formal law.

8. Polan himself approaches this position with an argument appealing to Weber rather than Lenin: "There are certain situations where the rule of law cannot exist. Clearly, the rule of law cannot be assumed to exist in a society undergoing revolutionary reconstruction. . . . This reconstruction is at very least a time-consuming and complex process. A multitude of contradictory interpretations of the newly dominant ideology will for some time obtain" (1984:113).

9. In almost their first legislative act (Decree No. 1 on the Court), the Bolsheviks (1) abolished the "existing general judicial institutions," including the old hierarchy of tsarist courts, the system of justices of the peace, and the procuracy; (2) invalidated, in a note inserted by Lenin, all existing laws if they contravened CEC decrees or the Bolshevik/SR minimum programs; and (3) established a new court system (see *infra*). The legislative measures of the young Soviet Republic were of various sorts, including largely symbolic decrees such as "To the Population" and "To Workers, Peasants and Soldiers!" About the new decrees Lenin proclaimed, "we shall not regard them as absolute injunctions which must be put into effect instantly and at all costs" (1919g:209). On the difficulties of distinguishing the various forms of Bolshevik law, see Makepeace (1980:75–76).

10. Soon thereafter, Pashukanis (1924) and the commodity exchange school of law elevated this sort of argument to a theoretical foundation for the distinction between "legal" and "technical" rules. By the early 1930s, with the virtual disappearance of public provision for private rights and liberties, the anarchic attractions of this distinction, however brilliant its proponents, turned out to be tragically superficial (Beirne and Sharlet, 1980; Sharlet and Beirne, 1984).

11. The Cheka ("Extraordinary Commission for the Struggle against Counterrevolution, Sabotage and Official Crimes") was formerly established under the leadership of Felix Dzerzhinskii in November/December 1917. See further Levytsky (1972) and Gerson (1976).

12. For example, the foreword to the 1919 *Basic Principles of Criminal Law* (written by the People's Commissariat of Justice) defined criminal law as "rules of law and other measures by which the system of social relations of a particular class society is protected against violations (crimes) through the use of means of repression (punishment)"; see *Sobranie Uzakonenii* (Collection of Laws, hereinafter *S.U.*), RSFSR, 1919, no. 66, art. 590. Not until legislation of 1922 were Bolshevik penal strategies (definition of crime, stated objectives, etc.) given precise definition (*S.U.*, RSFSR, 1922, no. 15, art. 153).

13. In the "temporary instruction" "On Deprivation of Liberty as a Measure of Punishment and on the Method of Undergoing It," enacted on July 23, 1918, the Commissariat of Justice (*Narkomiust*) attempted to systematize many of the early decrees; see *S.U.*, RSFSR, 1917–1918, no. 53, art. 598. This decree focused on the worthiness of corrective labor as a means of reforming criminals. It also introduced a special category of isolated prison for incorrigibles. See further Carr, 1960, 2:421–424.

14. Despite the decriminalization of certain offenses by 1923, the soviet courts were tremendously congested with new criminal cases. Limitations of space preclude proper discussion here of the interesting but probably unresolvable problem of whether the crime rate actually did increase during the early period of Bolshevik power. However, in an important essay that discusses aspects of this question, Solomon (1981; and see Juviler,

1976:30–31) has argued that there was no increase in "actual" criminal behavior after October 1917. Rather, the new criminal cases in the people's courts resulted from the criminalization of certain common misdemeanors previously adjudicated outside the tsarist criminal courts. Van den Berg (1985:9–16) discusses the difficulties involved in estimating both the volume of crime in the 1920s and also the level of judicial repression.

15. Lenin appropriated the term "hooliganism" (*khuliganstvo*) from the tsarist legal and criminological discourse at the beginning of the century; see further Weissman (1978) and Pearson (1983:106–107; 255–256). For both tsarist and Bolshevik purposes the term referred to such diverse activities as public obscenity, the breaking of windows, the stealing of carriage wheels, rape, arson, and murder. In modern Soviet society, "hooliganism" has occupied a dual role in the vocabulary of penality: on the one hand, as a sociomedical description of alcoholism and, on the other, as a rhetorical device to marginalize political dissent.

16. For Bolshevik support of progressive legislation for women, see Goldman (1984:364–366). In January 1918, Lenin supported a decree, despite strong opposition, that raised the age of criminal responsibility from ten to seventeen (Juviler, 1976:25–26; and on his advocacy of the use of "educational" and "medical" institutions for juvenile delinquents, see e.g., Lenin, 1920c:182–183).

17. *S.U.*, RSFSR, no. 3, art. 35, sec. 10, 1917.

18. The crime of embezzlement was specifically introduced by several sections of the first Criminal Code of the RSFSR in 1922. Article 113 of the code referred to "[e]mbezzlement by an official of money or other valuables, which are under his control by virtue of his official position . . ." (quoted in Hazard, 1951:302); this was punishable by deprivation of liberty for between one and ten years. Another paragraph described the exacerbating circumstances (e.g., officials entrusted with special powers, or embezzlement of very valuable state property) that could lead, on conviction, to the maximum sentence of death.

19. Hazard (1951:304), relying on Utevsky (1948:265), argues that "[t]he giving of precise definition to the crime of embezzlement and the campaign conducted against those who committed it seems to have had little effect . . . following the adoption of the 1922 Code."

20. Although Lenin often advocated enforcement of the legal rights available under tsarism, when and where he selectively deemed it politically appropriate, he altogether lacked a coherent view of rights, justice, and civil liberties (see e.g., 1917d:129). After the 1917 October revolution he occasionally referred to "rights," but because he tended to regard them as mere expressions of bourgeois individualism, they played no positive part in his thinking about the means of securing the interests of the Soviet citizenry. See further Lukes (1985:61–70), Hirst (1986), and Beirne and Hunt (1988:579–581).

21. Because he was disturbed by the political arbitrariness of local authorities, Lenin (1922c; see also Timasheff, 1958:9) personally took the initiative in having the procuracy restored in 1922 (*Sobranie Zakonov*, RSFSR, 1922, no. 36, art. 424). The political question of whether or not procurators should be appointed both by the central authority (People's Commissariat) and by local authorities (Gubernia Executive Committee) was not a simple one. Lenin (1922c:363–364) recognized that dual subordination was a mechanism for ensuring the independence of local authorities from bureaucratic centralism. However, he argued (ibid., 365–367) that local procurators should be subordinate only to the central authority on the grounds that a higher principle was at stake, namely, a uniform law for the RSFSR. Lenin seemed genuinely concerned about the "high-handed" conduct of central authorities and, accordingly, he successfully proposed that if procurators challenged the legality of a local authority's decision, then that decision was not (as before) suspended, but subject to judgment in the courts. In reality, however, the result was a

dangerous expansion in the potential abuse of the democratic wishes of local authorities by the central state organs. See further Hazard (1960:230–232).

22. On February 15, 1918, some of the provisions of Decree No. 1 were amended by Decree No. 2 on the Court (*S.U.*, RSFSR, 1917–1918, no. 26, item 420).

23. Decree No. 2 on the Court, *S.U.*, RSFSR, 1917–1918, no. 26, item 420, s. 36. It should be pointed out that, according to Commissar of Justice Stuchka (1925:90), Lenin himself was not particularly attracted to concepts such as "revolutionary legal conscience" and "revolutionary legal consciousness" because they allegedly had no concrete content.

24. Decree No. 2 on the Court, *S.U.*, RSFSR, 1917–1918, no. 26, item 420, s. 8.

25. Decree No. 2 on the Court, *S.U.*, RSFSR, 1917–1918, no. 26, item 420, s. 14.

26. Decree No. 2 on the Court, *S.U.*, RSFSR, 1917–1918, no. 26, item 420, s. 36.

27. *S.U.*, 1918, no. 52, item 589.

28. *S.U.*, RSFSR, 1917–1918, no. 26, item 420.

29. Decree No. 3 on the Court, *S.U.*, 1918, no. 52, item 589.

30. *S.U.*, 1917–1918, no. 53, item 597. See further Hazard (1960:26).

31. Decree No. 2 on the Court, *S.U.*, RSFSR, 1917–1918, no. 26, item 420, s. 39.

32. After the Civil War, the Bolsheviks had declared an amnesty with the Right SRs, legalizing their party in 1919, and allowing publication of their newspaper *Delo naroda*. However, the crimes committed by the SRs against the Soviet government were not trumped up by the Bolsheviks: they included assassination attempts on the lives of Lenin and other Bolshevik leaders in 1918, and in 1920 they organized and led kulak uprisings in many regions (Medvedev, 1973:382; and see Carr, 1966, 1:190). The indictments therefore reflected serious offenses. As Carr writes, "[i]f it was true that the Bolshevik regime was not prepared after the first few months to tolerate an organized opposition, it was equally true that no opposition party was prepared to remain within legal limits. The premise of dictatorship was common to both sides of the argument" (ibid., 190).

33. Lenin may have agreed not to support the death penalty in this particular SR case, but it did not reflect his general view of the appropriate way of dealing with SR counter-revolutionary activities. For example, in a note to Commissar of Justice Kursky, written just before the start of the SR trial and intended as an addendum to the draft preamble of the new RSFSR criminal code, Lenin urged that "I think the application of the death sentence should be extended (commutable to deportation) . . . to all forms of activity by the Mensheviks, SRs *and so on*" (1922f:419). However, in his vague statements to the Eleventh Party Congress it was not at all clear (*pace* Jansen, 1982:34) that Lenin (1922g:282–283; 313) demanded the death penalty for the SRs.

34. E. H. Carr has observed that a "curious essay might be written on the attitude of the Russian revolution to capital punishment" (1950, 1:162). Were such an essay to be written it might begin by showing that Lenin's ambivalence reflected Marx's. On the one hand, Marx (1853:194) complained that "it would be very difficult, if not altogether impossible, to establish any principle upon which the justice or expediency of capital punishment could be founded in a society glorifying in its civilisation"; on the other, he (Marx, 1849:213) described as "heroic" the actions of those who, in the 1848 Hungarian revolution, dared "to oppose white terror with red terror" (Marx, 1849:213).

35. However, it is difficult to know precisely how to interpret Lenin's remark in his polemical speech "Paper Resolutions." Some (e.g., Adams, 1972: n. 30) have argued that Lenin's comment should straightforwardly be understood as support of capital punishment for landowners and capitalists, nothing more and nothing less. But Lenin's argument here, we suggest, was directed not only to the abolition of capital punishment. It was also cognizant of the fact that its restoration would inevitably result in executions not of "landowners and capitalists" but of "the masses" (or "the masses of soldiers" as

suggested in the Petrograd resolution: see *Collected Works of V.I. Lenin*, New York, 1932, vol. 21, no. 1, pp. 292–293).

36. According to Trotsky, Lenin "proposed changing the decree at once. We told him this would make an extraordinarily unfavorable impression. Finally someone said: 'the best thing is to resort to shooting only when there is no other way.' And it was left at that." (1925:134).

37. Van den Berg (1983:157) notes, while refraining from an assessment, that the official number of death sentences was 16,000 during June 1918 to October 1919, and that the military tribunals alone passed 6,543 such sentences between June 1 and October 31, 1920. Estimates of the number of death sentences and of actual executions during War Communism and the Civil War are legion, and it is impossible to assess which of them, if any, are correct.

38. Adams's analysis was not based on actual executions, but on a rating scale derived from the wording of penalty clauses about capital punishment (ibid., 84–85). The rating scale included a spectrum ranging from a mandatory death sentence to a noncapital penalty. Adams's scale clearly shows that military and counterrevolutionary crimes were most likely to result in executions; the three common crimes of aggravated murder, aggravated rape, and robbery were moderately unlikely to result in execution.

39. It should be noted that pressure to abolish the death penalty did not diminish after the 1922 code. Article 33 of the 1922 code was amended five times in the first thirteen months of operation, thereby restricting executions of pregnant women and minors, and introducing a statute of limitations; see Adams (1970:117, n. 45) and Hazard (1960:343).

40. Accounts of the Cheka's punitive measures are nearly always fragmentary and unreliable (Carr, 1950, 1:174); in the spring and summer of 1918 their victims included "insurgents . . . the bourgeoisie . . . officers and gendarmes . . . white-guard[s] . . . kulaks . . . priests" (ibid.).

41. Lenin saw no contradiction between this demand and the recognition that bourgeois democracy provides "the best possible political shell for capitalism" (1917:393). Political forms had to provide a clear but not inevitable series of stages. The achievement of political democracy would secure both a major victory over the autocracy and also an important new stage in the struggle for socialism. "Marxists know that democracy does not abolish class oppression. It only makes the class struggle more direct, wider, more open and pronounced, and that is what we want" (Lenin, 1916:73).

42. By this claim we do not mean to imply that the Bolsheviks were entirely "innocent" in their introduction of red terror. Quite the contrary, as both Lenin and Trotsky often asserted between 1918 and 1921, red terror was a class-based strategy the need for which—in exceptional circumstances—had been amply demonstrated both by the Jacobin terror of the 1790s in France (see, e.g., Carr, 1950, 1:160–165) and the Russian political theory of Peter Tkachev (Weeks, 1968).

43. Inclinations toward shock or revulsion at the measures taken by the Red Army, or by the Cheka, pale in comparison with the repression meted out by the counterrevolution. Within the party, opposition to the Cheka came from both idealists who disapproved of the terror and from functionaries who objected to the Cheka's usurpation of their domains (Carr, 1950, 1:187). The Cheka was abolished in spring 1922, and its functions conveyed to the GPU (State Political Administration). In October 1922 the GPU acquired the right to apply extrajudicial measures of repression, including execution, to "bandits" (Heller and Nekrich, 1986:220). From the Cheka, the GPU inherited its own armed forces, bureaucrats, and camps (including the infamous *Solovki*). However, at the Eleventh Party Congress, the last that he was able to attend, Lenin (1922g; and see Bettelheim, 1976:288) denounced the irregular extension of the scope of GPU.

44. It is a matter of historical judgment, beyond our present concerns, whether the

objective conditions justified the retention of terror.

45. By the summer of 1918 the people's courts, the revolutionary tribunals, and the Cheka all imposed penalties for various sorts of crime; the first was generally concerned with common crimes, the second and third with crimes that threatened state security. Although the people's courts and the revolutionary tribunals were subject to rules of legal procedure, the Cheka was an administrative organ whose scope was quite unrestricted (Carr, 1960, 2:422–423). After a brief period at the end of the Civil War, when there was a movement to unite the jurisdictional bodies for penitentiaries, the NKVD was finally given leading authority in July 1922 (Feldbrugge, 1986:6–7).

In September 1918, the *Decree on the Red Terror* dictated that class enemies should be isolated in detention camps (*S.U.*, 1917–1918, no. 67, art. 710). Lenin first mentioned these camps in a telegram instructing how to suppress an uprising in Penza during August 1918. In it he urged that a reliable force should be organized "to carry out a campaign of ruthless mass terror against the kulaks, priests and white guards; suspects to be shut up in a detention camp outside the city" (1918r:489). The camps originally acted as preventive rather than punitive institutions, and were from the outset controlled by the Cheka, and then administered by Narkomvnudel (RSFSR Commissariat of Internal Affairs, or NKVD). Originally, the Cheka had virtually unlimited powers to detain political offenders, solely, in these camps. But by 1919 their populations began to resemble those of the Narkomiust prison populations subject to forced labor. The original designation of the People's Commissariat of Justice as the body responsible for penitentiaries was changed in May 1919 by two decrees that placed their responsibility under the NKVD or the Cheka. See further Carr, (1960, 2:421–454) and Solomon (1980). The tremendous expansion in the concentration camps under Stalinism occurred, not because of the real difficulties of executing the progressive (Narkomiust) policy "in an unfavorable environment, but because of factors external to penal policy, in particular, the labor demands generated by the decision to pursue forced-draft industrialization" (Solomon, 1980:195).

References

Authors' notes: (i) Unless otherwise indicated, all works by Lenin are from *Lenin: Collected Works* [*LCW*], 1960–1970, Moscow: Progress Publishers. (ii) In the case of entries with two publication dates, the first refers to the original date of publication and the second to the edition that we have used here.

Works by Lenin

(1901) "Where To Begin," *LCW*, 5:13–24.
(1901a) "Beat—But Not to Death (Casual Notes)," *LCW* 4:387–402.
(1902) "What Is To Be Done?" *LCW*, 5:349–529.
(1905) "The Revolutionary-Democratic Dictatorship of the Proletariat and the Peasantry," *LCW*, 8:293–303.
(1916) "A Caricature of Marxism and Imperialist Economism," *LCW*, 23:28–76.
(1917) *The State and Revolution. LCW*, 25:381–492.
(1917a) "The Impending Catastrophe and How To Combat It," *LCW*, 25:319–365.
(1917b) "Speech at a Joint Meeting of the Petrograd Soviet of Workers' and Soldiers' Deputies and Delegates from the Front, November 4 (17), 1917," *LCW*, 26:293–295.
(1917c) "Meeting of the Petrograd Soviet of Workers' and Soldiers' Deputies," *LCW*, 26:239–241.

(1917d) "Can the Bolsheviks Retain State Power?" *LCW*, 26:87–136.

(1917e) "To the Bureau of the Central Committee Abroad," *LCW*, 35:318–324.

(1917f) "Paper Resolutions," *LCW*, 25:261–264.

(1918) *The Proletarian Revolution and the Renegade Kautsky. LCW*, 28:227–325.

(1918a) "Rough Thesis of a Decision on the Strict Observance of the Laws," *LCW*, 42:110–111.

(1918b) "To G. Y. Zinoviev," *LCW*, 35:336.

(1918c) "The Socialist Fatherland Is in Danger!" *LCW*, 27:30–33.

(1918d) "Supplement to the Decree of the Council of People's Commissars: 'The Socialist Fatherland Is in Danger!' " *LCW*, 27:34–35.

(1918e) "Theses on the Current Situation," *LCW*, 27:406–407.

(1918f) "To G. F. Fyodorov," *LCW*, 35:349.

(1918g) "Proposals Concerning the Work of the Vecheka," *LCW*, 42:115.

(1918h) "Letter to D. I. Kursky," *LCW*, 35:331.

(1918i) "The Immediate Tasks of the Soviet Government," *LCW*, 27:235–277.

(1918j) "Telegram to V. V. Kurayev," *LCW*, 35:351.

(1918k) "A Little Picture in Illustration of Big Problems," *LCW*, 28:386–389.

(1918l) "Third All-Russia Congress of Soviets of Workers', Soldiers' and Peasants' Deputies," *LCW*, 26:453–482.

(1918m) "To the Commissariat for Justice," *LCW*, 44:76–77.

(1918n) "Original Version of the Article 'The Immediate Tasks of the Soviet Government,' " *LCW*, 27:203–218.

(1918o) "Fifth All-Russia Congress of Soviets of Workers', Peasants', Soldiers' and Red Army Deputies," *LCW*, 27:505–532.

(1918p) "Telegram to S. P. Natsarenus," *LCW*, 44:114–115.

(1918q) "Concerning the Decree on Revolutionary Tribunals," *LCW*, 27:219–220.

(1918r) "Telegram to Yevgenia Bosch," *LCW*, 36:489.

(1919) "Telegram to the Kursk Extraordinary Commission," *LCW*, 36:499.

(1919a) "Extraordinary Seventh Congress of the R.C.P.(B).," *LCW*, 27:85–158.

(1919b) "To All Members of the Boards and People's Commissars of All the Commissariats," *LCW*, 44:282.

(1919c) "Note to D. I. Kursky," *LCW*, 36:517.

(1919d) "Note to Stalin on Reorganisation of State Control," *LCW*, 28:486.

(1919e) "A Great Beginning," *LCW*, 29:409–434.

(1919f) "Report on Subbotniks Delivered to a Moscow City Conference of the R.C.P.(B.)," *LCW*, 30:283–288.

(1919g) "Eighth Congress of the R.C.P.(B.)," *LCW*, 29:141–225.

(1919h) *The State. LCW*, 29:470–488.

(1919i) "Letter to the Workers and Peasants Apropos of the Victory over Kolchak," *LCW*, 29:552–560.

(1919j) "Draft Programme of the R.C.P.(B.)," *LCW*, 29:97–140.

(1920) "Report on the Work of the All-Russia Central Executive Committee and the Council of People's Commissars," *LCW*, 30:315–316.

(1920a) "Speech at the Fourth Conference of Gubernia Extraordinary Commissions, February 6, 1920," *LCW*, 42:166–174.

(1920b) "A Contribution to the History of the Question of the Dictatorship," *LCW* 31:340–361.

(1920c) "The Prosecution of Minors," *LCW*, 42:182–183.

(1921) "To P. A. Bogdanov," *LCW*, 36:556–558.

(1921a) "Letter to D. I. Kursky and Instruction to a Secretary," *LCW*, 35:521–522.

(1921b) "Ninth All-Russia Congress of Soviets," *LCW*, 33:141–181.

(1921c) "To D. I. Kursky," *LCW*, 45:368–369.
(1921d) "The Tax in Kind," *LCW*, 32:329–365.
(1921e) "To the Moscow Revolutionary Tribunal," *LCW*, 45:348.
(1921f) "Instructions of the Council of Labour and Defence to Local Soviet Bodies," *LCW*, 32:375–398.
(1921g) "The New Economic Policy and the Tasks of the Political Education Departments," *LCW*, 33:60–79.
(1922) "On the Tasks of the People's Commissariat for Justice under the New Economic Policy," *LCW*, 36:560–565.
(1922a) "To D. I. Kursky," *LCW*, 36:576–577.
(1922b) "We Have Paid Too Much," *LCW*, 33:330–334.
(1922c) " 'Dual' Subordination and Legality," *LCW*, 33:363–367.
(1922d) "To D. I. Kursky," *LCW*, 35:533–534.
(1922e) "To D. I. Kursky," *LCW*, 33:358–359.
(1922f) "Addendum to the Draft Preamble to the Criminal Code of the RSFSR and a Letter to D. I. Kursky," *LCW*, 42:419.
(1922g) "Eleventh Congress of the R.C.P.(B.)," *LCW*, 33:259–326.

Other works

Adams, Will (1972). "Capital Punishment in Soviet Criminal Legislation, 1922–1965: A Code Content Analysis and Graphic Representation." Pp. 78–121 in Roger Kanet and Ivan Völgyes (eds.), *On the Road to Communism: Essays on Soviet Domestic and Foreign Politics*. Lawrence: University of Kansas Press.
Andics, Hellmut (1969). *Rule of Terror: Russia under Lenin and Stalin*. New York: Holt, Rinehart, and Winston.
Avanesov, G. (1981). *The Principles of Criminology*. Moscow: Progress Publishers.
Avrich, Paul (1970). *Kronstadt 1921*. Princeton: Princeton University Press.
Balibar, Etienne (1977). *On the Dictatorship of the Proletariat*. Trans. Grahame Lock. London: New Left Books.
Bassiouni, M. Cherif, and V. M. Savitski (eds.) (1979). *The Criminal Justice System of the USSR*. Trans. L. A. Nejinskaya. Springfield, Ill.: Charles C. Thomas.
Beirne, Piers (1987). "Between Classicism and Positivism: Crime and Penality in the Writings of Gabriel Tarde." *Criminology* 25(4):785–819.
Beirne, Piers and Alan Hunt (1988). "Law and the Constitution of Soviet Society: The Case of Comrade Lenin." *Law & Society Review* 22(3):575–614.
Beirne, Piers and Robert Sharlet (1980). "Editors' Introduction." Pp. 1–36 in P. Beirne and R. Sharlet (eds.), Peter B. Maggs (trans.), *Pashukanis: Selected Writings on Marxism and Law*. London: Academic Press.
Berman, Harold J. (1972). *Soviet Criminal Law and Procedure: The RSFSR Codes*. 2nd edition. Trans. Harold J. Berman and James W. Spindler. Cambridge, Mass.: Harvard University Press.
Bettelheim, Charles (1976). *Class Struggles in the USSR. First Period: 1917–1923*. London: Monthly Review Press.
Bratous, S. N. (1970). "Lenin's Ideas on Soviet Law and Socialist Legality." *Review of Contemporary Law* 1:21–46.
Buchholz, Erich, Richard Hartman, John Lekschas, and Gerhard Stiller (1974). *Socialist Criminology: Theoretical and Methodological Foundations*. Trans. Ewald Osers. Lexington, Mass.: D. C. Heath.
Burbank, Jane (1986). *Intelligentsia and Revolution: Russian Views of Bolshevism, 1917–*

134   PIERS BEIRNE AND ALAN HUNT

1922. New York: Oxford University Press.

Carr, E. H. (1950) (1966). *The Bolshevik Revolution 1917–1923*. 3 vols. London: Pelican.

———— (1960). *Socialism in One Country*. 2 vols. New York: Macmillan.

Cohen, Stephen F. (1985). *Rethinking the Soviet Experience: Politics and History Since 1917*. New York: Oxford University Press.

Dallin, David J., and Boris I. Nicolaevsky (1947). *Forced Labor in Soviet Russia*. New Haven: Yale University Press.

Evans, Alfred B. (1987). "Rereading Lenin's *State and Revolution*." *Slavic Review* 46(1):1–19.

Feldbrugge, F. J. M. (1986). "The Soviet Penitentiary System and the Rules of Internal Order of Corrective Labor Institutions in Historical Perspective." *Review of Socialist Law* 12:5–29.

Garland, David (1985). *Punishment and Welfare. A History of Penal Strategies*. Brookfield, Vt.: Gower.

Gerson, Lennard D. (1976). *The Secret Police in Lenin's Russia*. Philadelphia: Temple University Press.

Goldman, Wendy (1984). "Freedom and Its Consequences: The Debate on the Soviet Family Code of 1926." *Russian History/Histoire Russe* 11(4):362–388.

Gouldner, Alvin W. (1977). "Stalinism: A Study of Internal Colonialism." *Telos* 34:5–48.

Gsovski, Vladimir, and Kazimierz Grzybowski (1959). *Government, Law and Courts in the Soviet Union and Eastern Europe*. 2 vols. New York: Atlantic Books.

Hazard, John N. (1951). "Soviet Socialism and Embezzlement," *Washington Law Review* 26:301–320.

———— (1960). *Settling Disputes in Soviet Society*. New York: Columbia University Press.

Heller, Mikhail, and Aleksandr M. Nekrich (1986). *Utopia in Power*. Trans. Phyllis B. Carlos. New York: Summit Books.

Hirst, Paul (1986). *Law, Socialism and Democracy*. London: Allen & Unwin.

Jankovic, Ivan (1984). "Socialism and the Death Penalty." *Research in Law, Deviance and Social Control* 6:109–137.

Jansen, Marc (1982). *A Show Trial Under Lenin*. The Hague: Martinus Nijhoff.

Juviler, Peter (1976). *Revolutionary Law and Order: Politics and Social Change in the USSR*. New York: Free Press.

Korobeinikov, B. V. (1985). "Sociopolitical and Legal Principles of Crime Prevention in the U.S.S.R." *Crime and Social Justice* 23:29–50.

Krylenko, N. V. (1934). *Lenin o sude i ugolovnoi politike, k desiatiletiiu so dnia smerti, 1924–1934*. Moscow.

Leggett, G. H. (1975). "Lenin, Terror, and the Political Police." *Survey* 21(4):157–187.

Levytsky, Boris (1972). *The Uses of Terror: The Soviet Secret Police 1917–1970*. Trans. H. A. Piehler. New York: Coward, McCann & Geoghegan.

Lós, Maria (1988). *Communist Ideology, Law and Crime*. New York: St. Martin's Press.

Lukes, Steven (1985). *Marxism and Morality*. Oxford: Clarendon Press.

Luxemburg, Rosa (1918) (1976). *The Russian Revolution and Leninism or Marxism*. Ann Arbor: University of Michigan Press.

Makepeace, R. W. (1980). *Marxist Ideology and Soviet Criminal Law*. London: Croom Helm.

Marx, Karl (1849) (1973). "The Magyar Struggle." Pp. 213–226 in David Fernbach (ed.), *Karl Marx: The Revolutions of 1848*. New York: Random House.

———— (1853) (1979). "Capital Punishment." Pp. 193–196 in Alan Hunt and Maureen Cain (eds.), *Marx and Engels on Law*. London: Academic Press.

Medvedev, Roy A. (1971). *Let History Judge*. Trans. Colleen Taylor. New York: Vintage Books.

Pashukanis, E. B. (1924). *The General Theory of Law and Marxism*. Pp. 37–131 in P. Beirne and R. Sharlet (eds.), Peter B. Maggs (trans.), *Pashukanis: Selected Writings on Marxism and Law*. London: Academic Press.

———— (1925) (1980). "Lenin and Questions of Law." Pp.133–164 in P. Beirne and R. Sharlet (eds.), Peter B. Maggs (trans.), *Pashukanis: Selected Writings on Marxism and Law*. London: Academic Press.

Pearson, Geoffrey (1983). *Hooligan: A History of Respectable Fears*. London: Macmillan.

Polan, A. J. (1984). *Lenin and the End of Politics*. London: Methuen.

Sharlet, Robert, and Piers Beirne (1984). "In Search of Vyshinsky: the Paradox of Law and Terror." *International Journal of the Sociology of Law* 12(2):153–177.

Shub, David (1948). *Lenin*. New York: Doubleday & Co.

Shvekov, G. V. (1970). *Pervii Sovetskii ugolovnii kodeks*. Moscow: Vysshaia shkola.

Solomon, Peter H. (1978). *Soviet Criminologists and Criminal Policy*. New York: Columbia University Press.

———— (1980). "Soviet Penal Policy, 1917–1934: A Reinterpretation." *Slavic Review* 39:195–217.

———— (1981). "Criminalization and Decriminalization in Soviet Criminal Policy, 1917–1941," *Law & Society Review* 16(1):9–43.

Solzhenitsyn, Aleksandr I. (1973). *The Gulag Archipelago 1918–1956: An Experiment in Literary Investigation*. New York: Harper & Row.

Stuchka, P. I. (1925) (1988). "Lenin and the Revolutionary Decree." Pp. 89–96 in Robert Sharlet, Peter B. Maggs, and Piers Beirne (eds. and trans.), *P. I. Stuchka: Selected Writings on Soviet Law and Marxism*. Armonk, N.Y., and London: M. E. Sharpe.

Timasheff, N. S. (1958). "The Procurators' Office in the USSR." *Law in Eastern Europe* 1:8–15.

Trotsky, Leon (1925) (1962). *Lenin*. "Authorized translation." New York: Capricorn Books.

Utevsky, B. S. (1948). *Obshchee uchenie o dolzhnostuki prestupleniaki*. [A General Study of Crimes Committed by Officials]. Moscow.

van den Berg, Ger P. (1983). "The Soviet Union and the Death Penalty" *Soviet Studies* 35(2):154–174.

———— (1985). *The Soviet System of Justice: Figures and Policy*. Dordrecht, Netherlands: Martinus Nijhoff.

Vigh, Józse (1985). "Thoughts About the Essence of Socialist Criminology." *Crime and Social Justice* 24:154–186.

Weeks, Albert L. (1968). *The First Bolshevik: A Political Biography of Peter Tkachev*. New York: New York University Press.

Weissman, Neil B. (1978). "Rural Crime in Tsarist Russia: The Question of Hooliganism 1905–1914." *Slavic Review* 37(2):228–240.

———— (1986). "Prohibition and Alcohol Control in the USSR: The 1920s Campaign against Illegal Spirits." *Soviet Studies* 38(3):349–368.

Woodcock, George (1963). *Anarchism*. London: Penguin.

Part III
The Growth of Criminology
in the U.S., 1880–1945

[10]

CRIMINAL ANTHROPOLOGY IN THE UNITED STATES*

NICOLE HAHN RAFTER
Northeastern University

Criminologists continue to debate fundamental issues about the nature of their work. Some of the issues were built into the field by the criminal anthropologists who founded it a century ago. By examining the work of major American criminal anthropologists—a nearly forgotten group—one can identify the origins of three enduring problems: criminology's difficulties in (1) establishing its disciplinary boundaries; (2) defining its methods; and (3) deciding whether its primary goal is crime control or the production of knowledge with no immediate use-value. The study of criminology's roots in criminal anthropology cannot settle these debates, but it can put them in historical perspective and clarify their substance.

As criminologists, we have to deal with a number of unsettling issues about the nature of our field. We debate our disciplinary status—some claim a distinct disciplinary identity, others consider themselves specialists within sociology, and yet others view criminology as an area to which biologists, economists, lawyers, policymakers, psychologists, sociologists, and others can all contribute. We contend over methods and whether our field can or should even try to qualify as a science. We also argue about our goals—is our purpose to help control crime or to produce disinterested knowledge?[1]

These issues have been present since criminal anthropologists founded U.S. criminology 100 years ago.[2] Because criminal anthropologists' doctrine of the criminal as a physically anomalous human type has long been discredited, we tend to ignore their work, at the same time overlooking the legacy of professional issues that they, as the first criminologists, bequeathed to us. If

---

* I am grateful to Kathleen Daly and John H. Laub for comments on an earlier draft of this paper and to Jeanne K. Siraco, of Northeastern University's library, for her bibliographical help.

1. We also debate whether any knowledge can in fact be "disinterested." For a review of this issue that relates closely to the production of the type of information discussed here, see MacKenzie (1981:esp. Ch. 2).

2. As a field of inquiry, American criminology is about to reach its centennial; the first U.S. book in the area, a criminal anthropological tract by Arthur MacDonald titled *Criminology*, appeared in 1893. Although copyrighted in 1892 and labeled "second edition," this 1893 publication seems to have been the first book-length version of the work; the 1892 "first" edition was a pamphlet reprint of an article published earlier that year.

Unless otherwise noted, all of this paper's information on publications was derived from the Library of Congress's *National Union Catalog*.

we are to resolve those issues, or even come to grips with and accept them as unavoidable aspects of our field, we must know how we acquired them.

This paper examines an almost unrecognized phenomenon, the U.S. experience with criminal anthropology, in order to expose the roots of key debates within American criminology. I argue that by investigating the interplay between U.S. criminal anthropologists' professionalization of criminology and the kinds of information they produced, criminologists can better grasp the origins of three persistent problems: criminology's difficulties in (1) establishing a clear-cut disciplinary identity; (2) defining its methods; and (3) distinguishing its role as a knowledge enterprise from its contributions to crime control.

This study covers the production and substance of criminal anthropology in the United States over three decades, from 1881, when the first book on the topic (a German translation) appeared, to 1911, by which time leading theorists had rejected the doctrine (e.g., Parmelee, 1911) and begun to favor another biological theory, defective delinquency theory, which equated criminality with mental retardation (for one of the earliest statements, see Fernald, 1909). After defining my terms and describing my basic procedure, I trace the diffusion of criminal anthropology in the United States and suggest why this process sowed confusion about criminology's disciplinary identity. Next, I summarize the substance of U.S. criminal anthropology and show that its promulgators were uncertain about their doctrine's scientific status and unable to separate its positivist methods from its content. In the final section, on solutions to crime, I indicate that criminologists' uncertainty over goals began with criminal anthropologists: some of these earliest U.S. criminologists were less concerned with the knowledge value of their work than with using it to promote eugenic solutions to crime.

TERMS AND METHOD

In what follows I use the term *criminal anthropologists* to refer to writers who held that the worst ("born," "congenital," "incorrigible," or "instinctive") criminals deviate from ethical and biological normality because they are atavisms, reversions to a more primitive evolutionary state. I distinguish between *criminal anthropology in the United States*, defined as all writings endorsing the doctrine published in the United States through 1911, irrespective of the author's nativity or the language in which the work initially appeared, and *U.S. criminal anthropology*, the subset of works authored by U.S. citizens (also called "Americans" for convenience). I do not attempt to improve on criminal anthropologists' loose definitions of *criminals* and *the criminal*, terms they used variously to denote lawbreakers, prisoners, recidivists, and all "degenerates," including the poor and mentally impaired. When I speak of criminology as a discipline or field, I mean only that it is a

CRIMINAL ANTHROPOLOGY   527

branch of knowledge and am concerned not with its organization but its practitioners' claims to be producers of knowledge about crime and criminals.[3] And I use the term *professionalization of criminology* to describe criminal anthropologists' establishment of the field as a new specialty.

It is necessary to say a few words about *positivism*, which criminal anthropologists interpreted somewhat differently than we do. Gottfredson and Hirschi (1987:10) have recently defined positivism as "the scientific approach to the study of crime where science is characterized by methods, techniques, or rules of procedure rather than by substantive theory." Most contemporary positivists would probably agree that their approach is empirical, often but not necessarily quantitative, inductive, and grounded in "belief in an objective external reality" (Gottfredson and Hirschi, 1987:19). Criminal anthropologists, too, emphasized the importance of direct observation and data collection, but as data they accepted folk wisdom, anecdotes derived from creative literature, and analogies between criminals and "lower" forms of life that would no longer be considered "empirical." When they dealt with the "born" criminal, moreover, they equated positivism with materialism (or naturalism), the philosophical position according to which all phenomena can be explained in terms of physical laws, and they espoused an absolute determinism, denying any role whatsoever to free will.

Instead of critiquing criminal anthropologists' methods, I emphasize the methodological assumptions about materialism and determinism that they considered crucial to positivism and that led to their conclusions. When I observe that criminal anthropologists failed to differentiate between their procedures and conclusions, I do so to indicate an aspect of their work that has, as Gottfredson and Hirschi (1987) more generally point out, left the discipline confused about the nature of its science. My interest, in short, lies in criminal anthropology as a discourse rather than the accuracy of its findings. I am concerned with documenting not its methodological sins but the ways in which it laid the basis for some of criminology's ongoing debates.

My central methodological problem was identifying the major U.S. criminal anthropologists. First, I defined them as American authors of book-length works published through 1911 who endorsed the concept of the criminal as a physically distinct, savage human being and who were frequently cited in the primary and secondary U.S. literature on criminal anthropology. I next listed all criminal anthropological books mentioned in the relevant chapters of three important secondary sources: Fink's *Causes of Crime: Biological Theories in the United States, 1800–1915* (1938), Haller's *Eugenics: Hereditarian Attitudes in American Thought* (1963), and Zeman's dissertation

---

3. This conceptualization of *discipline* draws on discussions of the relationship between professions and knowledge production that appear in Abbott, 1988; Bledstein, 1976; Larson, 1977; MacKenzie, 1981.

528   **RAFTER**

on the American criminological tradition (1981). When I excluded books on juvenile crime and general sociology and reduced Arthur MacDonald's many criminal anthropological works to one, his *Criminology*,[4] my list consisted of nine books by eight authors, most of them mentioned in at least two of the secondary sources. I read the nine books to discover whether they frequently cited other works that fit my definition. They did not; rather, they referred (within my definition's confines) mainly to previously published books already on my list. This made me confident that the nine books had indeed been primary vehicles for the doctrine's dissemination and that their authors had been major U.S. proponents of criminal anthropology.

THE DIFFUSION OF CRIMINAL ANTHROPOLOGY IN THE UNITED STATES

To follow the diffusion of criminal anthropology in the United States, one must distinguish among three groups of producers: the Europeans who generated the theory in the first place ("originators"); those who initially gave Americans access to the originators' work ("channelers"); and the Americans who then elaborated on the channelers' materials ("U.S. criminal anthropologists"). Analysis of the diffusion process reveals that few U.S. criminal anthropologists had firsthand contact with the work of Lombroso, the originator on whom they depended most heavily, and that although most were professionals of one sort or another, they had little expertise in social science. As a result, U.S. criminology began without a well-defined research agenda or sense of its disciplinary boundaries.

ORIGINATORS

The first book on criminal anthropology published in the United States, Moriz Benedikt's *Anatomical Studies upon Brains of Criminals*, appeared in 1881, well in advance of any work by Lombroso. A Hungarian who taught in Vienna, Benedikt was inspired to study the cranium and brain of criminals by the work of Franz Joseph Gall, the founder of phrenology; he was also aware of Lombroso's investigations (p. vii). Dissections led Benedikt to conclude that

> THE BRAINS OF CRIMINALS EXHIBIT A DEVIATION FROM THE NORMAL TYPE, AND CRIMINALS ARE TO BE VIEWED AS AN ANTHROPOLOGICAL VARIETY OF THEIR SPECIES, AT LEAST AMONGST THE CULTURED RACES (p. 157, capitalization as in original).

---

4. MacDonald's other substantial works on adult criminals aimed at persuading Congress to establish laboratories for the study of degenerate types and were published by the Government Printing Office, not as trade books.

CRIMINAL ANTHROPOLOGY 529

This finding excited some debate, especially among physicians (Fink, 1938:107–109), on the existence of an anatomically distinct criminal type. But Benedikt's book was too abstruse to have much impact on mainstream U.S. thinking about the causes of crime, and its methodology—brain dissection—was not one that social scientists could easily adopt. In addition, this was Benedikt's only book to be translated into English. Thus, *Anatomical Studies* became little more than a footnote in the work of U.S. criminal anthropologists.

The other originator, Lombroso,[5] exercised far greater influence, but for years Americans knew his work mainly through secondary sources. Lombroso's own writings appeared slowly in English and at first in the form of his introductions to books by U.S. followers and articles. MacDonald's *Criminology* carried one of these introductions; August Drahms's *The Criminal* (1900) another. Subscribers to the journal *The Forum* could read Lombroso's "Criminal Anthropology: Its Origin and Application," an 1895 survey of the field. Portions of one of his major studies also appeared in English in 1895 as *The Female Offender* (Lombroso and Ferrero, 1895), just two years after its initial Italian publication, and this work was reprinted six times before 1911. But Americans who knew only English had to wait another 16 years before they could read a digest of Lombroso's key work, *L'Uomo Delinquente*, the first Italian edition of which had appeared in 1876. This summary, compiled by Lombroso's daughter with his assistance and carrying yet another of his introductions, was published in 1911 as *Criminal Man* (Lombroso–Ferrero, 1911).[6] His *Crime: Its Causes and Remedies* appeared the same year (Lombroso, 1911).

Americans who could not read Lombroso's *oeuvre* in Italian or French translation, then, lacked direct access to it until criminal anthropology's heyday had passed. This meant that those who built on his research usually worked at some distance from their source material. Their own writings were often doubly derivative, dependent on both Lombroso's research and the channelers who gave them access to it.

---

5. I do not deal here with the work of Lombroso's colleagues Enrico Ferri and Raffaele Garofalo, in part because they were so closely associated with him and in part because I could not confidently gauge their impact in the United States. Some U.S. criminal anthropologists cite Ferri (e.g., McKim, 1900), but most were poor footnoters, and I concluded from internal evidence that they had sometimes used secondary sources instead of the Italian originals and French translations that they cite.

Ferri's work became available in the United States relatively early: his *Criminal Sociology* appeared in 1896 and was reprinted frequently thereafter, and *The Positive School of Criminology* was published in 1906 and reprinted in 1910. None of Garofalo's books appeared until 1914, after this study's cut-off point.

6. A French translation, *L'homme Criminel*, became available considerably earlier (1887, 1895). Several U.S. criminal anthropologists cite this translation as their source on Lombroso's work.

530   **RAFTER**

CHANNELERS

Among the channelers who provided access to the originators' works, translators played an important role by determining, through their initiatives, which European works would reach U.S. audiences. Americans might never have heard of Benedikt, for example, had E. P. Fowler, a New York physician, not translated his *Anatomical Studies* from German—a task he undertook, he tells us, to establish "a scientific basis for the prevention of crime" (in Benedikt, 1881:xi). Henry P. Horton, who translated Lombroso's *Crime: Its Causes and Remedies* from French and German sources, helped introduce Americans to Italian criminal anthropology.[7] Horton's significance as a channeler is eclipsed, however, by that of the organization that arranged this translation, the American Institute of Criminal Law and Criminology. Although this professional association was not founded until enthusiasm for criminal anthropology had begun to wane, it immediately evinced a deep and relatively sophisticated interest in biological theories of crime. Criminological historian Leonard Savitz suggests that the organization's publication policies contributed to Lombroso's American "triumph": "the powerful American Institute of Criminal Law and Criminology, very fierce adherents to the Positivist School, translated Lombroso, Garofalo and Ferri, but, of the French environmentalists, only Tarde." Thus, "the monoglot American criminologist" had less access than Europeans to alternative theoretical traditions (Savitz, 1972:xix).

European criminal anthropology further flowed to the United States through a group of writers who, by summarizing the originators' work in English, first alerted Americans to it. Of these, far and away the most influential was Havelock Ellis, author of *The Criminal* (1890). The multilingual Ellis, an English eugenicist, wrote on an enormous range of subjects, from art to sexology. Although *The Criminal* was his only foray into criminal anthropology, it proved to be an extended foray. By 1911 the book was in its fourth edition and had gone through nine printings. For it, Ellis relied on numerous sources but primarily Lombroso's work. *The Criminal* became the well into which many U.S. Lombrosians dipped for data on born criminals.

Very early American reports on Lombroso's research, while much briefer than *The Criminal*, formed yet another channel through which the doctrine passed into the United States. Joseph Jastrow, a psychology professor, produced one of the first articles of this type, "A Theory of Criminality," for the journal *Science* in 1886. Observing that "a change in our view of crime and criminals seems about to take place," Jastrow uncritically outlines Lombroso's theory of criminality as "a morbid phenomenon . . . a defect" (pp. 22, 20), deriving his information from a French review by Lombroso. An 1887

---

7. I have not been able to identify the translators of *The Female Offender* or *Criminal Man*.

CRIMINAL ANTHROPOLOGY 531

paper on "The Criminal Type," published in the *American Journal of Social Science* by William Noyes, a physician at New York's Bloomingdale Asylum, emphasizes the criminal's bad heredity and primitive nature; based on a French edition of *L'Uomo Delinquente* (p. 32), it too is undilutedly Lombrosian.

Criminal anthropology is better digested in two presentations by Hamilton Wey (1888, 1890), the physician at New York's Elmira Reformatory, that introduced members of the National Prison Association to criminal anthropology. Citing Benedikt, the influential English hereditarian Francis Galton, and Ellis as well as Lombroso, Wey supplements his outline of criminal anthropology with data gathered through his own research at Elmira. Wey's relatively critical attitude toward Lombroso's ideas and the fact that he went beyond his European sources make him a transitional figure between the channelers and the first generation of U.S. criminal anthropologists.

U.S. CRIMINAL ANTHROPOLOGISTS

As news of Lombroso's theory spread, many Americans began writing about it. Thus, the third group of producers, U.S. elaborators of criminal anthropology, outnumbered the other two. This group, however, had core members, identified through procedures described earlier; they and their books are listed in Table 1.

The initial book in this series, MacDonald's *Criminology* (1893), was the first U.S. treatise to identify its subject as "criminology" and its author as a specialist in the area.[8] MacDonald asserts expertise by listing his credentials and claiming that his findings have scientific status; he also dedicates his book to Lombroso, "the founder of criminology," who wrote its introduction.[9] For these reasons, *Criminology*'s 1893 appearance may be taken as the U.S. field's starting point. However, as other titles in Table 1 indicate, for some time to come the study of crime and criminals remained intertwined with investigations of other "degenerate" types.

These major American books on criminal anthropology addressed somewhat different audiences, but on the whole were directed toward educated laypeople, especially the growing body of social welfare workers. Henderson designed his *Introduction to the Study of the Dependent, Defective and Delinquent Classes* (1893) as a textbook for college students and welfare workers (p. ix); Parsons' *Responsibility for Crime* (1909), originally a Columbia University dissertation, also seems to have been written for classroom use.[10]

---

8. Although two other titles listed in Table 1 also appeared in 1893, I give MacDonald's book priority due to its 1892 copyright; see note 2, above.

9. This was apparently Lombroso's first U.S. publication.

10. Parsons subsequently published two works clearly designed as textbooks (in 1924 and 1926) and authored no other books.

532   **RAFTER**

Table 1. Major U.S. Books on Criminal Anthropology
                Published 1893–1911

Author	Title	First Date of Publication	Other Dates of U.S. Publication
MacDonald, A.	*Criminology*	1893*	—
Boies, H.	*Prisoners and Paupers*	1893	—
Henderson, C.R.	*An Introduction to the Study of the Dependent, Defective and Delinquent Classes*	1893	1901, 1908, 1909
Talbot, E.	*Degeneracy*	1898	1904
Drahms, A.	*The Criminal: His Personnel and Environment*	1900	—
McKim, W.D.	*Heredity and Human Progress*	1900	1901
Boies, H.	*The Science of Penology*	1901	—
Lydston, G.F.	*The Diseases of Society*	1904	1905, 1906, 1908
Parsons, P.	*Responsibility for Crime*	1909	—

SOURCE: Library of Congress, *National Union Catalog* (Washington, D.C.) for all except Drahms.

*   This book, copyrighted in 1892, is labeled "second edition." However, the first edition seems to have been a 1892 pamphlet that reprinted an article MacDonald published earlier the same year. The *National Union Catalog* lists no third edition. It does refer to a fourth edition, for which it gives a copyright date of 1892 but no publication date. I have been unable to confirm this edition's publication.

Lydston intended *The Diseases of Society* "primarily for professional readers" but hoped it would do "a little missionary work" among "the reading public" as well (1904:9). The other works were written to inform—usually to alarm—the general public. None of the nine books was aimed chiefly at scholars.

The major U.S. criminal anthropologists were all well-educated, male professionals;[11] those commonalities aside, the group was occupationally diverse. Some were social welfare workers (Boies, Drahms, and Henderson), some educators (Henderson, Lydston, MacDonald, and Talbot),[12] some physicians

----

11. That they were all men helps explain why, despite the popularity of Lombroso's *Female Offender*, "the" criminal whom they described was nearly always male.

12. Parsons, too, may have been an educator, to judge from details in the *National Union Catalog*'s listing of his writings, but I was unable to confirm this.

CRIMINAL ANTHROPOLOGY 533

(Lydston, McKim, and Talbot), and some ministers (Drahms and Henderson; MacDonald, too, had studied theology). Professional heterogeneity characterized most of them as individuals as well. McKim held both Ph.D and M.D. degrees; Lydston, a physician, was a university professor and successful writer; Henderson, a minister heavily involved in welfare work, taught sociology at the University of Chicago; MacDonald, a psychologist and specialist in the education of "the abnormal and weakling classes," had studied theology, medicine, psychiatry, and criminology (MacDonald, 1893:title page and unnumbered next page); and Talbot, a professor of dental and oral surgery, held both M.D. and D.D.S. degrees.

This multiplicity of professional backgrounds among the first U.S. criminologists affected the field negatively in the long run. Like Lombroso, who trained as a physician, the Americans came to criminology from the outside, as amateur specialists. This situation was inevitable: Like social science in general, criminology was still in its "formative period" (MacDonald, 1893:271). As yet the field had no "inside," no training program (Kellor, 1901:5) that could give its practitioners a common set of skills or foster consensus on research goals. MacDonald's European studies had included some formal training in criminology, and four of the other authors had had extensive contact with prisoners; but otherwise American advocates of the "new science" (Lombroso–Ferrero, 1911:5) had few qualifications other than an ability to digest their sources and speak knowledgeably. Although they present masses of data, they did no experimental work (also see Garland, 1985:97). Thus, the field they founded initially had no clearly defined kernel of skills or even goals, other than to broadcast versions of criminal anthropology. Nor did they themselves have a uniform professional identity. The result was a discipline that lacked boundaries and continues into the present to overlap with others, such as psychology and sociology.

THE SUBSTANCE OF U.S. CRIMINAL ANTHROPOLOGY

U.S. criminal anthropologists wrote in a context in which the primary experts on criminal matters were legal authorities and penologists. Their own work was not as unprecedented as they claimed, for a tradition of positivist criminological research had been accumulating throughout the nineteenth century, built up by alienists who analyzed the connections between mental disorders and crime (e.g., Ray, 1838), phrenologists who investigated the organic causes of crime (e.g., Farnham, 1846; also see Davies, 1955:Ch. 8; Savitz et al., 1977), and degenerationists, such as Richard Dugdale (1877), who associated criminal behavior with bad heredity. But these forerunners did not present their work as "criminology" nor themselves as "criminologists." Lombroso's followers had to identify a new jurisdiction (Abbott,

1988)—to stake out professional territory, separate from jurisprudence and penology—over which criminologists would have authority. To accomplish this task they used two tactics, first claiming that their approach constituted an entirely new science and then producing information on criminal types that confirmed that claim.

CRIMINAL ANTHROPOLOGY AS A SCIENCE

Echoing Lombroso, the Americans insisted that criminal anthropology had for the first time carried the study of crime across the divide between idle speculation and true science. Noyes's (1887:32) early article heralds the advent of a "new science, which considers the criminal rather than the crime"; Drahms, calling crime a "social disease," claims that "Criminology . . . reaches the dignity of a science by the same right of necessity that gives to the medical profession its place" (1900:xxi–xxii). They did not always label this science "criminology," however. Because the field was just beginning to emerge, through their work, they sometimes preferred to fold the study of criminal man into better accepted sciences—"scientific sociology" (MacDonald, 1893:173), "the science of penology" (Boies, 1901), or the "scientific" investigation of degeneracy (Talbot, 1898:viii). But all considered their work "scientific," by which they meant that unlike earlier commentators on crime, who had included God and free will in the causational picture, they would be materialists, examining only phenomena anchored in the natural world of matter.

Benedikt had made this materialist position explicit by writing that "man thinks, feels, desires, and acts according to the anatomical construction and physiological development of his brain" (1881:vii). A decade later Wey observed, "Of criminologists there are, generally speaking, two schools, the theological or spiritualistic and the material or anthropological" (1890:275; also see Drahms, 1900:22). Lydston (1904:18) contrasted the work of "the sentimental, non-scientific moralist" and that of "the scientific criminologist," whose job was "to reduce the subject to a material, scientific, and, so far as possible, evolutionary basis." With such remarks, criminal anthropologists voiced their determination to uncover the physical determinants of crime.

From their materialism, two methodological conclusions followed. First, criminal anthropologists would use only empirical methods, starting with direct observation instead of theory or metaphysics. They would report on measurements of criminals' bodies made with scientific equipment, such as callipers, the dynamometer, and the aesthesiometer; they would collect information on criminal jargon and tatoos, excerpt passages from confessions, and gather "proverbs expressing distrust of the criminal type" (Lombroso–Ferrero, 1911:50). All such data would be recorded dispassionately. "A large part of the most rigid science," one learns on the first textual page of

CRIMINAL ANTHROPOLOGY   535

MacDonald's (1893:17) *Criminology*, "consists in simple and exact description, which should be given, of course, without regard to any views that one may consciously or unconsciously hold." Materialism implied, second, that criminal anthropologists would use induction to formulate natural laws. Like other scientists, they would build up to whatever theory the facts indicated.

Materialism led criminal anthropologists to their central assumption—that the body must mirror moral capacity. They took for granted a one-to-one correspondence between the criminal's physical being and ethical behavior. Criminals, wrote Boies (1893:265–266), are "the imperfect, knotty, knurly, worm-eaten, half-rotten fruit of the human race," their bodies illustrating "the truth of the reverse Latin adage, *'insana mens insano corpore'*." Nature had made the investigator's task relatively simple: To detect born criminals, one needed only the appropriate apparatus. Degree of criminality could be determined by charting the offender's deformities. The assumption that offenders literally embody their criminality led in turn to criminal anthropology's distinctive collapse of methods and findings. The doctrine's adherents believed that, just as moral worth could be directly read from the body, so too could the body be unmediatedly charted by their documents (see, esp., Green, 1985; Sekula, 1986). Theoretical assumptions did not intervene in either case, for theirs were the methods of science.

THE BORN CRIMINAL

At criminal anthropology's heart lay Lombroso's perception of "the congenital criminal as an anomaly, partly pathological and partly atavistic, a revival of the primitive savage" (Lombroso–Ferrero, 1911:xxii). All nine of the U.S. books in Table 1 reiterate this message. "Criminals," Talbot (1898:18) writes in a typical passage,

> form a variety of the human family quite distinct from law-abiding men. A low type of physique indicating a deteriorated character gives a family likeness due to the fact that they form a community which retrogrades from generation to generation.

Most of the U.S. criminal anthropologists repeat Lombroso's descriptions of the born criminal's physical anomalies—his pointed head, heavy jaw, receding brow, scanty beard, long arms, and so on. They also adhere closely to Lombroso by enumerating the criminal's "psychical" anomalies—his laziness and frivolity, his use of argot and tendency to inscribe both his cell and his body with hieroglyphics, his moral insensibility and emotional instability. Seemingly the most scientific aspect of criminal anthropology, these were also its most sensational findings.

But five of the eight American authors express doubts about the born criminal's existence even while devoting entire chapters to his stigmata. Apparently unable to resist reporting Lombroso's galvanizing findings, these five simultaneously qualify their reports, often without reconciling their enthusiasm for the "new science" with their uneasiness about it. After filling many pages with such statements as "Flesch, out of 50 brains of criminals, did not find one without anomalies," MacDonald (1893:58, 65) confesses that little is known about the relation of "psychical" to organic peculiarities. Henderson (1893:113) lauds Lombroso while warning that his views "are by no means universally accepted as final." Lydston (1904:25–26) masks his ambivalence by mocking the "ultra-materialism" of "so-called criminal anthropologists" and aligning himself with the doctrine's true practitioners. But Drahms (1900) and Parsons (1909) completely fail to harmonize their misgivings about born-criminal theory with their desire to advance it. These first criminologists lacked confidence in the scientific centerpiece of their doctrine. They endorsed a science that even to them seemed shaky.

Insofar as they deviated from Lombrosos's teachings about born criminals, the Americans did so not by rejecting his theory but by supplementing it, particularly by placing greater emphasis on the criminal's weak intelligence. In *Criminal Man*, Lombroso pays little attention to the criminal's mentality aside from stating that "*Intelligence* is feeble in some and exaggerated in others" (Lombroso–Ferrero, 1911:41 [emphasis in original]; also see Lombroso and Ferrero, 1895:170–171). Four of the eight U.S. criminal anthropologists, in contrast, carry Lombroso's implications to their logical conclusion by finding that criminals are intellectually as well as ethically weak, mental as well as moral imbeciles. Talbot (1898:18), for example, draws on evolutionism to explain that "there is truly a brute brain within the man's, and when the latter stops short of its characteristic development, it is natural that it should manifest only its most primitive functions." Lydston (1904:946), noting that "a defective moral sense is most likely to be associated with defective development of the brain in general," concludes that it is "not surprising that the typic or born criminal should lack intelligence" (also see MacDonald, 1893:Ch. 4; Drahms, 1900:72–75). The American concern with the criminal's poor intelligence formed the bridge between criminal anthropology and its successor, defective delinquency theory, which identified criminality with "feeble-mindedness."

The U.S. authors further supplemented Lombroso's work by thoroughly integrating criminal anthropology with degeneration theory. Popular on both sides of the Atlantic, degenerationism attributed the genesis of socially problematic groups—paupers and the insane and feeble-minded, as well as the criminalistic—to an inherited tendency toward organic devolution ("degeneracy," "depraved heredity," "innate viciousness," and other synonyms). (On degenerationism, see, generally, Chamberlin and Gilman, 1985; Pick, 1989.) Lombroso did not immediately realize that degeneration could explain the criminal's bad heredity; at first he relied on the notion of atavism (Parmelee, 1911:xxix; Wolfgang, 1972:247, 249). His American followers, writing after

CRIMINAL ANTHROPOLOGY   537

degeneration theory had had more time to mature, made it the basis for their hereditarianism. Aside from MacDonald (who depends most heavily on European sources), the U.S. authors emphasize that the born criminal comes "of a degenerate line, and that if he have offspring some measure of his innate viciousness will be transmitted" (McKim, 1900:23).

American criminal anthropologists stress the close connections among degenerate types; poverty, mental disease, and crime were but interchangeable symptoms of the underlying organic malaise. "The Degenerate Stock," Henderson (1893:114) explained, "has three main branches, organically united,—Dependents, Defectives and Delinquents. They are one blood." It followed that "vice, crime, and insanity may be regarded as merely different phases of degeneracy which so resemble one another that we are often at a loss when we would distinguish between them" (McKim, 1900:64). The term "criminal anthropology," Haller (1963:16) has pointed out, was "in a sense . . . a misnomer," for the doctrine "was concerned with the nature and causes of all classes of human defects." This was especially true of U.S. criminal anthropology. Wedded to degenerationism, the first American criminologists had no interest in defining the study of crime as a field apart from the study of other social problems.

OTHER CRIMINAL TYPES

Lombroso eventually opened his science to the investigation of a range of criminal types by distinguishing between born criminals and "criminaloids," such as habitual criminals, who do not inherit but acquire the habit of offending; juridical criminals, who violate the law accidentally; and the handsome, sensitive criminal-by-passion, who is motivated by altruism (Lombroso–Ferrero, 1911:Ch. 4). These were, in large part, etiological distinctions: Heredity alone determines the behavior of born criminals, whereas environmental and sociological factors increasingly shape the criminality of higher offender types. Six of the nine U.S. books include substantial material on the etiology of criminal types (there is little or none in MacDonald, 1893; Talbot, 1898; or McKim, 1900). The Americans' typologies, like that of Lombroso, ultimately imply a close correlation between degree of criminality and social class. The positivist approach began by promoting a theory heavy with class content, and the founders of U.S. criminology were unable to separate their methodological assumptions from the substance of their message.

The Americans' commentaries on criminal types fall along a continuum that starts with the very crude typification of one of their first books, Boies's *Prisoners and Paupers* (1893), and ends with the highly developed typology of the series' last work, Parsons' *Responsibility for Crime* (1909). *Prisoners and Paupers* reviews the causes of degeneration at length but does not relate them

to a subsequent discussion of degrees of criminality. Boies had not yet realized that he could explain differences among criminal types in terms of varying causes of crime (cf. Boies, 1901). His typology, moreover, is rudimentary,
identifying merely two sorts of criminals. On the one hand are the "born" or
"incorrigible" offenders, who have "inherited criminality" and constitute
40% of the "criminal class" (Boies, 1893:172–183); the remaining 60% are
"the victims of heteronomy [multiple factors], the subjects of evil associations
and environment" (p. 184). Only the latter can be reformed. Boies vaguely
indicates that incorrigibles can be identified by number of convictions and
offense seriousness (pp. 178, 185), but in this book he mostly avoids the issue
of how to distinguish the hereditary from the heteronomic criminal.

Chronologically and substantively, Drahms's *The Criminal* (1900) marks a
midpoint in the process by which U.S. criminal anthropologists articulated a
hierarchy of criminal types differentiated by the causes of their offenses.
Drahms recognizes three kinds of criminals. The *instinctive criminal*'s "biological, moral, and intellectual equipments are the results of hereditary entail-
ment from prenatal sources" (p. 56). The *habitual criminal* "draws his
inspirational forces from . . . environment rather than parental fountains" (p.
57). And the "essentially social misdemeanant," whom Drahms labels not a
"criminal" but rather a *single offender*, is "possibly as free from the antisocial taint as the average man" (p. 55). "He is a criminal because the law
declares it" (p. 57).

Parsons' *Responsibility for Crime* (1909) culminates this typification process by identifying a plethora of criminal types. Parsons starts with the most
abnormal, the *insane criminal*, after which he describes the *born criminal*
("His normal condition is abnormal . . . he is born to crime. It is his natural
function" [p. 35]); the *habitual criminal* ("he is capable of something else, at
least in one period of his life. The born criminal never is" [p. 36]); and the
professional criminal ("frequently of a high order of intelligence,—often a college graduate. His profession becomes an art in which he sometimes becomes
a master" [p. 37]). Of the next type, the *occasional criminal*, Parsons informs
us that, "Here, for the first time, environment plays an important part in the
nature of the crime committed"; the occasional criminal, moreover, "frequently posseses a keen sense of remorse" and is "frequently a useful citizen"
(p. 41). Parsons' typology ends with the *criminal by passion or accident*, who
is characterized by a high "sense of duty" and "precise motive," unmarred by
anomalies, and in need of neither cure nor punishment (pp. 42–44).

Whereas Boies (1893) had trouble explaining how to differentiate between
criminal types, Parsons (1909) uses explicit criteria, including the frequency
of physical and mental anomalies; degrees of reformability, intelligence, skill,
and remorse; the extent to which environment influences behavior; and the
offender's ability to exercise free will. These criteria, putatively derived from
biology and then used to establish gradations within the criminal class, are in

CRIMINAL ANTHROPOLOGY   539

fact derived from social class and then attributed back to biology. Criminal anthropology has finally unraveled the implications latent in Boies's distinction between hereditary and heteronomic criminals, arriving at a hierarchy of criminal types that corresponds to the social class hierarchy. At the bottom of the scale is the born criminal, rough in appearance and manners, a foreigner or Negro (Boies, 1893:Chs. 6 and 7), uneducated, of poor background, a drinker. At the top stands Parsons' gentlemanly normal offender, anomaly free, a product of not heredity but environment, intelligent and skilled, conscience stricken and reformable.

Criminal anthropologists' "upper" groups, Zeman (1981:390) points out, "made it possible to maintain a sharp separation, not just of degree, but of essence, between the motivation and character of the ordinary respectable citizen and that of the lower-class offender." One can extend Zeman's insight by observing that that "essence" was what criminal anthropologists called "heredity." In the process of distinguishing among types of criminal bodies, they established a biological hierarchy in which worthiness was signified by class attributes.

The criminal anthropologists' biologism had two long-term effects: It gave positivism a bad name, and it slowed the development of sociological approaches to the study of crime. Positivism suffered no immediate harm by making its criminological debut through criminal anthropology, but its initial confirmation of class biases helped make it suspect to mid-twentieth-century criminologists, some of whom rejected any methods that seemed remotely positivistic (see Gottfredson and Hirschi, 1987:esp. 9–10 and 14–17). Moreover, the biologistic and individualistic emphases of the criminal anthropologists, together with their wide-net degenerationism, attracted nonsociological specialists into criminology's domain. Even when they used a multifactorial approach, criminal anthropologists located "the causes of human conduct in the physiological and mental characteristics of the individual" (Parmelee, 1911:xii). This set the stage for the heavy involvement of psychologists, armed with intelligence tests, in the articulation and application of the next criminological theory, that of defective delinquency (e.g., Gould, 1981:Ch. 5), and of physicians and psychiatrists in the subsequent theory of psychopathy. In the long run, criminal anthropology dampened development of sociological approaches to crime and legitimated those associated with biology and psychology. This is one reason why, even today, criminology draws researchers from a variety of disciplines.

CRIMINAL ANTHROPOLOGY AND EUGENICS

Advocating that punishments be tailored to fit the offender types they had identified, criminal anthropologists aimed at making justice as well as criminology a "science" based on the lawbreaker's biology (Parsons, 1909:194).

540   **RAFTER**

Much as some Americans had gone beyond Lombroso in developing aspects of criminal anthropology, so too did some outdo the master in deriving from the doctrine social defense conclusions of the sort that became known as *eugenics*.

According to eugenics theory, a nation can save its stock from degeneration by preventing reproduction of the unfit (negative eugenics) and simultaneously encouraging the fit to produce more offspring (positive eugenics). U.S. criminal anthropologists did not use the term *eugenics*, which had not yet entered the American vocabulary. But some joined the ranks of Americans who had been calling for eugenic measures since the 1870s (e.g., Lowell, 1879; also see Haller, 1963; Rafter, 1992; Tyor and Bell, 1984), employing such synonyms as "the selection of the fittest and the rejection of the unfit" (McKim, 1900:185).

In *Criminal Man* and *Crime: Its Causes and Remedies*, Lombroso argues merely for individualization of consequences: "Punishments should vary according to the type of criminal" (Lombroso–Ferrero, 1911:185). Criminals of passion and political offenders should "never" be imprisoned. For criminaloids, probation and indeterminate sentencing are appropriate (Lombroso–Ferrero, 1911:186–187). Even habitual and born criminals may be improved under the indeterminate sentence; but those who continue to demonstrate incorrigibility should be kept in "perpetual isolation in a penal colony" or, in extreme cases, executed (Lombroso–Ferrero, 1911:198, 208; also see Lombroso, 1911, Pt. III:Chs. 2 and 3). Lombroso makes these last recommendations not to prevent reproduction but "to realise the supreme end—social safety" (Lombroso–Ferrero, 1911:216; cf. Lombroso, 1912:59-60).

Like Lombroso, half of the major U.S. criminal anthropologists show little or no interest in eugenics.[13] The other four, however, champion eugenic solutions. Two support life sentences on the grounds that they will prevent criminals from breeding (Boies, 1893; Parsons, 1909). Several recommend marriage restriction. "The marriages of all criminals should be prohibited, but the utmost vigilance should be exercised to prevent the marriage of the instinctive" (Boies, 1901:239; also see Boies, 1893:280; Lydston, 1904:557–562; and Parsons, 1909:198–199). And some advise sterilization (Boies, 1893, 1901; Lydston, 1904).

The most extreme eugenic solution came from McKim (1900), who objected to perpetual detention due to its costliness and to sterilization partly because it "could not be repeated" (p. 24). For "the *very* weak and the *very*

---

13. Talbot explicitly rejects eugenics (1898:347–348); MacDonald and Drahms recommend life imprisonment to incapacitate born criminals physically but not reproductively. Henderson (1893:229) proposes "a life sentence for recidivists" for mildly eugenical reasons ("to reduce the supply of morally deformed offspring"), but merely in passing.

CRIMINAL ANTHROPOLOGY   541

vicious *who fall into the hands of the State*," McKim proposes "*a gentle, pain-less death*" (p. 188; emphasis in original). Execution by "carbonic acid gas" is the "surest, the simplest, the kindest, and most humane means for prevent-ing reproduction among those whom we deem unworthy of this high privi-lege" (pp. 193, 188). Their disappearance would result in "a tremendous reduction in the amount of crime" (p. 255).[14]

Although there was no necessary connection between criminal anthropol-ogy and eugenics, some of the major U.S. Lombrosians endorsed eugenic applications for their doctrine. In McKim's case in particular, advocacy of eugenic solutions is clearly the author's main purpose (1900:iii–v); Boies's two treatises and that of Lydston are also suffused with eugenic rationales. In these works, science becomes the servant of not just crime control but a highly charged ideology. Their authors treat criminology as a means to an end rather than a science of value in its own right. While most of today's criminologists would be appalled by such overt partisanship (not to mention eugenics theory itself), we remain divided over whether our field can or should even try to produce agenda-free information.

CONCLUSION

Beset by European critics, Lombroso took comfort in his "almost fanati-cal" U.S. following (Lombroso–Ferrero, 1911:xxi). American criminal anthropologists, although they established criminology as a specialized branch of inquiry, were less successful than other early U.S. social scientists (Ross, 1979, 1991) in conceptualizing their field. In part, this difficulty was a function of the way Lombroso's science was transplanted to the United States: Dependent on channelers, such as Havelock Ellis, few American criminal anthropologists had immediate contact with Lombroso's work. Moreover, lacking the skills to conduct social scientific research themselves, they addressed the educated layperson, not scholars, and generated work that soon proved of little value. Even though they cannibalized one another's books, they had almost nothing in common professionally and never agreed on a disciplinary agenda independent of their doctrine. They did share com-mon ground as positivists, but their version of positivism was so tightly tied to materialistic premises that it made even them uncomfortable. When they broke free of biological determinism to use a multifactor approach and develop typologies, they mainly produced guidelines for differential sentenc-ing by social class.

Its origins in criminal anthropology account for some (though certainly not all) of criminology's subsequent problems in defining itself, specifying its

---

14.   Boies and Parsons praised McKim's proposal while reluctantly rejecting it, Boies (1901:53) because he feared that "public sentiment does not yet support the purely scien-tific plan of Dr. McKim," and Parsons (1909:90) because it was too violent.

542   RAFTER

methods, and reaching consensus on goals. True, the field's first members
had to clear new professional terrain, apart from jurisprudence and penology,
but they themselves were unclear about the nature of their authority and the
type of training the next generation should receive. Moreover, as degenerationists, they were disinclined to demarcate the field's contours so as to
exclude noncriminal groups. Their fondness for biologistic and individualistic explanations also kept criminology's perimeters fluid, making it a field into
which specialists from other areas flowed. If one result has been cross-fertili-
zation, ferment, and richness, another has been criminology's lack of disciplinary boundaries.

A closely related problem, lack of agreement on methods and on whether
criminologists can or should try to qualify as scientists, is also rooted in criminal anthropology—in its unexamined methodological assumptions, its collapse of methods with findings, and its advocates' inability to define the
nature (much less practice) of their science. Absence of methodological una-
nimity, too, has contributed to criminology's fertility and flexibility. But it
has also impeded the field's ability to build on past findings and fostered
methodological animosities over the value of positivism. The third problem,
the continuing dispute over whether criminology's main goal should be to
help control crime or to produce knowledge with no direct use-value, can also
be traced to criminal anthropology—to some of its proponents' subordination
of criminology to eugenics. As their overeagerness to turn criminology into
an applied science demonstrates, criminology has from the start been characterized by this tension in goals. The study of criminal anthropology cannot
settle these persistent issues, but it can help us put them in historical perspective and grasp the origins of our disciplinary cleavages.

REFERENCES

Abbott, Andrew
  1988   The System of Professions. Chicago: University of Chicago Press.

Benedikt, Moriz
  1881   Anatomical Studies upon Brains of Criminals. New York: William Wood &
            Company.

Bledstein, Burton J.
  1976   The Culture of Professionalism. New York: W. W. Norton.

Boies, Henry M.
  1893   Prisoners and Paupers. New York: G.P. Putnam's Sons.
  1901   The Science of Penology: The Defence of Society Against Crime. New
            York: G.P. Putnam's Sons.

Chamberlin, J. Edward and Sander L. Gilman (eds.)
  1985   Degeneration: The Dark Side of Progress. New York: Columbia University
            Press.

CRIMINAL ANTHROPOLOGY   543

Davies, John D.
  1955   Phrenology: Fad and Science. New Haven: Yale University Press.

Drahms, August
  1900   The Criminal: His Personnel and Environment—A Scientific Study, with an
            Introduction by Cesare Lombroso. 1971. Montclair, N.J.: Patterson Smith.

Dugdale, Richard L.
  1877   "The Jukes": A Study in Crime, Pauperism, Disease and Heredity; also
            Further Studies of Criminals. New York: G.P. Putnam's Sons.

Ellis, Havelock
  1890   The Criminal. London: Walter Scott.

Farnham, E.W.
  1846   "Introductory preface" to M.B. Sampson, Rationale of Crime. New York:
            D. Appleton & Company.

Fernald, Walter E.
  1909   The imbecile with criminal instincts. American Journal of Insanity
            65:731–749.

Fink, Arthur E.
  1938   Causes of Crime: Biological Theories in the United States, 1800–1915.
            Philadelphia: University of Pennsylvania Press.

Garland, David
  1985   Punishment and Welfare: A History of Penal Strategies. Brookfield, Vt.:
            Gower.

Gottfredson, Michael R. and Travis Hirschi
  1987   The positivist tradition. In Michael R. Gottfredson and Travis Hirschi
            (eds.), Positive Criminology. Newbury Park, Calif.: Sage.

Gould, Stephen J.
  1981   The Mismeasure of Man. New York: W.W. Norton.

Green, David
  1985   Veins of resemblance: Photography and eugenics. Oxford Art Review
            7:3–16.

Haller, Mark
  1963   Eugenics: Hereditarian Attitudes in American Thought. New Brunswick,
            N.J.: Rutgers University Press.

Henderson, Charles R.
  1893   An Introduction to the Study of the Dependent, Defective and Delinquent
            Classes. Boston: D.C. Heath.

Jastrow, Joseph
  1886   A theory of criminality. Science 8:20–22.

Kellor, Frances A.
  1901   Experimental Sociology. Descriptive and Analytical. Delinquents. New
            York: Macmillan.

Larson, Magali S.
  1977   The Rise of Professionalism. Berkeley: University of California Press.

Lombroso, Cesare
  1895   Criminal anthropology: Its origin and application. The Forum 20:33–49.

544   RAFTER

1911   Crime: Its Causes and Remedies. 1918. Boston: Little, Brown.

Lombroso, Cesare
1912   Crime and insanity in the twenty-first century. The Journal of Criminal
            Law and Criminology 3:57-61.

Lombroso, Cesare and William Ferrero
1895   The Female Offender. 1915. New York: D. Appleton.

Lombroso–Ferrero, Gina
1911   Criminal Man According to the Classification of Cesare Lombroso. 1972.
            Montclair, N.J.: Patterson Smith.

Lowell, Josephine Shaw
1879   One means of preventing pauperism. National Conference of Charities, 6th
            Proceedings 1879:189–200.

Lydston, George F.
1904   The Diseases of Society (The Vice and Crime Problem). 1905. Philadelphia:
            J.B. Lippincott.

MacDonald, Arthur
1893   Criminology, with an Introduction by Dr. Cesare Lombroso. New York:
            Funk & Wagnalls.

MacKenzie, Donald A.
1981   Statistics in Britain, 1865–1930. Edinburgh: Edinburgh University Press.

McKim, W. Duncan
1900   Heredity and Human Progress. New York: G.P. Putnam's Sons.

Noyes, William
1887   The criminal type. American Journal of Social Science 24:31–42.

Parmelee, Maurice
1911   Introduction to the English version of Cesare Lombroso, Crime: Its Causes
            and Remedies (1918). Boston: Little, Brown.

Parsons, Philip A.
1909   Responsibility for Crime. New York: Columbia University; Longmans,
            Green, agents.
1924   Introduction to Modern Social Problems. New York: Knopf.
1926   Crime and the Criminal: An Introduction to Criminology. New York:
            Knopf.

Pick, Daniel
1989   Faces of Degeneration: A European Disorder, c.1848—c.1918. New York:
            Cambridge University Press.

Rafter, Nicole Hahn
1992   Claims-making and socio-cultural context in the first U.S. eugenics cam-
            paign. Social Problems 39:17–34.

Ray, Isaac
1838   A Treatise on the Medical Jurisprudence of Insanity. 1983. New York: Da
            Capo Press.

Ross, Dorothy
1979   The development of the social sciences. In A. Oleson and J. Voss (eds.),
            The Organization of Knowledge in Modern America, 1860–1920. Baltimore:
            Johns Hopkins University Press.

CRIMINAL ANTHROPOLOGY 545

1991   The Origins of American Social Science. New York: Cambridge University Press.

Savitz, Leonard D.
1972   Introduction to the reprint edition of Gina Lombroso–Ferrero, Criminal Man (1911). Montclair, N.J.: Patterson Smith.

Savitz, Leonard D., Stanley H. Turner, and Toby Dickman
1977   The origin of scientific criminology: Franz Joseph Gall as the first criminologist. In Robert F. Meier (ed.), Theory in Criminology: Contemporary Views. Beverly Hills, Calif.: Sage.

Sekula, Allen
1986   The body and the archive. October 39:3–64.

Talbot, Eugene S.
1898   Degeneracy: Its Causes, Signs, and Results. New York and London: Walter Scott.

Tyor, Peter L. and Leland V. Bell
1984   Caring for the Retarded in America: A History. Westport, Conn.: Greenwood Press.

Wey, Hamilton D.
1888   A plea for physical training of youthful criminals. National Prison Association, Proceedings 1888: 181-193.
1890   Criminal anthropology. National Prison Association, Proceedings 1890: 274-290.

Wolfgang, Marvin E.
1972   Cesare Lombroso. In Herman Mannheim (ed.), Pioneers in Criminology. 2d ed. enlr. Montclair, N.J.: Patterson Smith.

Zeman, Thomas E.
1981   Order, crime, and punishment: The American criminological tradition. Ph.D. dissertation, University of California, Santa Cruz.

Nicole Hahn Rafter, a professor at Northeastern University's College of Criminal Justice, has published books on prison history, women and criminal justice, and eugenics. She is currently working on a social history of born criminals.

[11]

Contemporary Crises 11: 243–263 (1987)
© Martinus Nijhoff Publishers, Dordrecht – Printed in the Netherlands

Feminism, criminology and the rise of the female sex 'delinquent', 1880–1930

JAMES MESSERSCHMIDT
Department of Sociology, University of Southern Maine, Portland, Maine 04103, USA

Today in the United States (as well as most patriarchal capitalist societies) the state and its juvenile justice system processes primarily young women for specific violations of normative conduct and sanctions them severely. Young women today are far more likely than boys to be arrested and processed for 'status offenses' (behaviors, that, if engaged in by an adult, would not be considered criminal), such as 'indiscriminate sexual intercourse' or what is commonly referred to as 'promiscuity' (Terry 1970; Chesney-Lind 1978; Smart 1976, Shacklady-Smith 1978). Even though the overwhelming majority of females are charged with status offenses (rather than criminal offenses), females are much more likely both to be detained by the state and to be held for longer periods than males (Sarri 1976: 76). As Ann Campbell (1981: 207) wrote in the early 1980s, the reason why young women are penalized 'is associated with society's concern with female sexual behavior'. And more recently, after a careful review of British and North American literature, Mary Eaton (1986: 25) concluded:

> Adolescent girls who come before the court are more likely than their male counterparts to be questioned about their sexual activity, more likely to have their offenses viewed as an aspect of sexual promiscuity, and more likely to lose their liberty for activities which would not be against the law if committed by an adult.

In short, the state today provides a mechanism for reproducing the 'double standard' of sexuality and, therefore, masculine control of female adolescent sexuality.

In this essay, I outline some of the historical precedents for this current state of affairs, namely, the relationship during the Progressive Era (1880–1930) between social feminists, social purists, and criminologists.[1] The late nineteenth- and early twentieth-century feminist movement was involved in a number of moral reforms, in particular an attack on prostitution. Feminists eventually joined in a coalition with the conservative social purity movement to raise the age of sexual consent in an effort to protect young girls from

244

allegedly being forced into prostitution through the so-called 'white slave traffic'. However, the end result was not a decrease in the sexual exploitation of young girls but, rather, the prohibiting of working-class girls' right to engage in heterosexual activity when they pleased, and therefore the creation of a new class of female offenders, teenage sex 'delinquents'.

Feminism, prostitution, and the fight for age of consent legislation

The struggle against regulation

In the 1860s and 1870s feminists organized a campaign against state regulation of prostitution. Susan B. Anthony led the feminist movement by lecturing across the United States on the danger of legalized prostitution (Pivar 1973: 51). Regulationists favored medical control, claiming this would contribute to the preservation of public health. As one of their proponents expounded, 'given man's nature and the laws of health . . . prostitution was a social requisite' (ibid: 56). In the nineteenth century, men in the US were seen as having an excessive sexual 'drive' while women were considered to be asexual. Therefore, according to regulationists, for those men who could not control their alleged sexual 'drive', regulated prostitution would serve as an 'outlet'. This then would protect 'their women', and thus, the family. As Ruth Rosen (1982: 5) points out, 'If men were not to unleash their passions on "young ladies of their acquaintance", or wives too delicate and asexual to cope with their sexual demands, they had to exert heroic self-control; if they failed in these efforts, they could still protect women in their own milieu by going to prostitutes'. Consequently, regulation involving police and medical supervision, was seen by regulationists as being in the best interests of both society and the prostitute (Pivar 1973: 56–57). Regulationists favored compulsory medical examinations for prostitudes rather than the complete suppression of prostitution because the latter was seen as being too costly and would not serve the overall interests of society (Degler 1980: 284–85).

Feminists, on the other hand, argued that regulation forced alleged prostitutes into vaginal examinations and licensing, thus allowing men the freedom to have sex with prostitutes without incurring the risk of venereal disease (Dubois and Gordon 1984: 38). Moreover, they demonstrated as well that regulation did not really protect anyone, since men, who were not inspected, many times were carriers of venereal disease and came into contact with prostitutes who had not yet been infected. For feminists then,regulation in actual practice was masculine-defined in the sense that it served the interests of men (customers) rather than women (prostitutes). As Ellen Dubois and Linda Gordon (1984: 38) further point out, feminist opposition drew not only on their anger at men who bought female flesh, but also reaffirmed their identification with prostitutes victimization. Feminists asserted that all women, even prostitutes, had a right to the integrity of their own bodies.

The regulation of prostitution, feminists argued, simply allowed male clients, doctors, and criminal justice personnel access to and control over women's bodies. The intention of regulation was not to protect society, feminists asserted, but rather, to blame and punish women prostitutes for the spread of venereal disease and allow male 'officials' the arbitrary control of women's bodies. The end result was that the movement against regulation in the US (regulation was already in existence in England and parts of Europe, see Walkowitz 1980a) proved to be so strong and successful that only one city ever tried it – St. Louis – and the experiment here lasted for only four years (Degler 1980: 285).

Cooptation

Yet in the process of defeating regulation, social feminists converged with the emerging conservative social purity movement, eventually being coopted by that movement (Pivar 1973). The social purity movement was an attempt on the part of a variety of individuals from different groups – men and women – to change social attitudes concerning sex. Their aspiration was to achieve a single standard of sexual morality for men and women. In short, the publicly avowed aim was for men to conform to the standards of chastity nineteenth-century US society enjoined on women.

Social purity was the logical outcome in a society dominated by the ideology of conservative Darwinism. Americans, especially in the middle and upper classes, were exposed to the writings of the architect of conservative Darwinism, Herbert Spencer. Spencer, adapting Charles Darwin's evolutionary theory into a social philosophy, argued that the so called 'natural' abilities of the more 'fit' or adaptable members of society would select them out to take control of the society. This 'natural selection' would allow society to progress, as long as the 'detriments' to social progress were efficiently curtailed. Only the *moral* could attain progress, it was the *immoral* who had to be controlled 'to make possible the conditions necessary for general welfare' (Boostrom 1973: 156). In other words, evolutionary progress required a curb on what was termed 'immorality'. It was in this ideological milieu that social purity flourished.

Many social feminists converged with the social purity movement, prostitution eventually being subsumed under the rubric of purification. As David J. Pivar (1973: 63) shows in his work, *Purity Crusade: Sexual Morality and Social Control, 1868–1900,*

246

In the process of active participation, purity reform, at first lacking clear contours, rapidly took shape, with the woman's and purity movements converging ideologically in a common drive for social transformation . . . Prostitution, as an issue, was subsumed by the larger concern for social purification, and the feminist leadership willingly participated in its suppression.

Social feminists, after defeating regulation, joined with the conservative social purity movement to press for the actual abolition of prostitution itself. They began consolidating and expanding their initial victory against regulation into an abolitionist movement containing a program of social purity measures (Vertinsky 1976: 68). As Patricia Vertinsky (ibid: 68–69) argues,

The frequency of ideological exchanges over regulation led many feminist reformers into an expanded interest in social purity. Women came to seek the demise of prostitution as a reformatory measure for the whole of society, and particularly as a means of upgrading, though not radically changing women's traditional role in relation to men . . . The final triumph of such an endeavor would be that of spiritual and brotherly love over animalistic lust.

Between 1885 and 1895 the movement against legalized prostitution changed from a defensive action against regulation to an aggressive campaign for abolitionism. As Pivar (1973: 257) shows, by channeling women into tasks of social purification, the purity leaders defined conservative social objectives for the social feminist movement. Thus, the coalition with the purity movement resulted in *cooptation*, and therefore, 'diminished the importance of the women's movement as a radical movement' (ibid: 258).

The alleged 'white slave traffic' (the idea that prostitutes were physically forced into the business rather than entering it voluntarily), was a major influence on many social feminists. Prostitutes were seen as sexually innocent, passive victims of evil men, which then 'allowed feminists to see themselves as rescuers of slaves' (Dubois and Gordon 1984: 38). The 'white slave' ideology encouraged middle- and upper-class social feminists to challenge the sexual double standard through other women's lives (not their own), therefore focusing their anger on men other than their own husbands (ibid). As Linda Gordon (1976: 118) points out, many feminists

believed that men had developed excessive sexual drives which contributed to the subjection of women and hence limited the development of the whole civilization. From this they drew the inference that excessive sex drive had to be *eliminated*, not merely checked or sublimated, in order to create a pure and sexually equal society.

The abolition of prostitution then would help to create a sexually equal society by ameliorating the problem of male excessive sex drive, raise men to the purity level of women, and therefore contribute to social progress.

The coalition and the age of consent

It was these issues – the 'white slave' ideology, the viewing of prostitutes as sexually innocent, passive victims of evil men, and the understanding that men had an excessive sexual drive – which led the coalition of social feminists and social purists to organize to raise the age of sexual consent; that is, the age at which a young *female* is considered, in law, to be able to consent to sexual intercourse. In this regard, consider Helen H. Gardner's (1895: 196) comments in the *Arena,* writing on the alleged 'sexual innocence' of young women and the 'lechery' of all men.

> There is not, there has never been, there never can be any fact in nature that is not a protest in letters of flame against the infamy of legal enactments which place the innocence and ignorance of childhood at the mercy of licensed lechery... [N]o being who is not too degraded or too utterly mentally and morally diseased to be a safe person to be at large, could wish that a little child, a baby girl fourteen, twelve, aye, ten years of age should be made, as is the case in many of our states, the legal and rightful prey of grown men.

As Gardner (ibid.) went on to argue, the current age of consent laws (which maintained the age as low as 10 in some states) were 'in the interest of the brothel, in the interest of the grade of men who prey upon the ignorance and helplessness of childhood'. And as Vie H. Campbell (1895: 286), President of the Wisconsin Women's Christian Temperance Union (WCTU) added,

> it is time for plain-speaking to reveal to innocent, unsuspecting girlhood the snares that are set to entangle her feet. This long-continued silence is the tributee which unbridled lust has demanded of us; and that we have, without remonstrance, paid it too long, the increasing army of unwarned, unfortunate, helpless victims will bear witness.

By raising the age of sexual consent, social feminists and social purists argued female sexual innocence would be protected and men would be forced to conform to the standards of abstinence nineteenth-century US society demanded of women. In conservative Darwinist ideology, this would thus contribute to social progress.

248

In many states the age of consent for females was set at the age of 10 in 1886. As Frances Willard, a social feminist and social purist who 'made the Womens Christian Temperance Union the largest women's organization in the nation' (Degler 1980: 286) put it, 'we at once declared ourselves determined to "clean house" in a governmental sense, until this record of defilement should be washed away' (Willard 1895: 198). Representatives from each state and territory WCTU went before the legislature with petitions to raise the age of consent (ibid: 199). The WCTU campaign was of course part of a larger feminist effort and Willard (ibid: 204) pointed out how fighting for higher age of consent laws was part of a broader program challenging masculine dominance in society:

> the husband of the modern woman will not have the right to will away her unborn child; to control her property; to make the laws under which she is to live; to fix her penalties; to try her before juries of men; to cast the ballot for her, and, in general, to hold her in the estate of a perpetual minor.

And continuing this line of reasoning, Willard (ibid) went on to state, 'it will not do to let the modern man determine the "age of consent" '.

Through this concerted agitation on the part of social feminists, in coalition with social purists, state after state in the 1890s raised the age of consent (Degler 1980: 288). For example, in Colorado, the age of consent jumped from 10 in 1893 to 18 only two years later. In 1889, Idaho's age of consent was set at 12, by 1895 it was raised to 18. Wyoming's started at 10 in 1886, then went to 14 in 1889, and finally to 18 in 1893 (Pivar 1973: 141–143). By 1900 only two states or territories maintained the age of sexual consent below 14 while twelve had raised it to 18 (Degler 1980: 288). As Dubois and Gordon (1984: 38) point out, like most nineteenth-century feminist causes, 'this one had a radical moment: it communicated an accurate critique of the limitations of 'consent' by women in a male-dominated society'. In other words, social feminists rightly pointed to the power males have over females in US society, and how that power relationship can limit a females ability, in certain situations, to actually 'consent' (eg. adult male/female child; husband/wife; male employer/female employee).

Yet their concentration on young girls alleged passivity and sexual innocence and therefore being the victims of 'white-slavers', blinded many social feminists from understanding the limited choices available to working-class girls in a partriarchal capitalist social order. To be sure, the causes of juvenile prostitution in the nineteenth century are not found solely in an alleged 'white-slave traffic', the sexual innocence of young girls, and the alleged 'excessive' sexual drive of men, but rather in a sexually and economically exploitative social system.

Capitalism, patriarchy, and juvenile prostitution

The 'white-slave traffic' was more myth than reality. While it is true that some women were physically forced into prostitution, 'white-slavery' was most likely 'experienced by less than 10 percent of the prostitute population' (Rosen 1982: 133). The extent of forced prostitution was exaggerated by social feminists and social purists because it served their interests. Simply put, the ideology of 'white slavery' emphasized women's alleged passivity. For them, women would never choose prostitution, theywould only enter it if forced. However, most young women who entered into prostitution, chose to do so because of their position in a patriarchal capitalist society.

In the late 1800s a surplus of youthful labor began to appear in the US. Prior to 1880, children formed an integral part of the labor force in agriculture, manufacturing, and mining. In the nineteenth century, labor scarcity in the US elevated the demand for cheap youthful labor. The earliest cotton mill in the US was operated solely by youthful labor. A journalist visiting this cotton mill early in the nineteenth century stated:

> All processes of turning cotton from its rough into every variety of marketable thread state . . . are here performed by machinery operating by waterwheels, assisted only by children from four to ten years old, and one superintendent [cited in Lebergott 1964: 50].

In 1820, 43 percent of all textile workers in Massachusetts, 47 percent in Connecticut, and 55 percent in Rhode Island were children (ibid.). As the factory system grew, it 'reached out' for youthful labor. However, since the 1840s, the proportion of child labor in manufacturing and mining has continuously and prominently declined, with even a mild decline in agriculture from 1880 to 1910. Furthermore, the overall ratio of child labor in all occupations plunged by two-thirds between 1910 and 1930. The long-run, permanent decline of youthful employment and labor-force participation increased most rapidly in the latter part of the nineteenth century and early years of the twentieth century. Even though the gainfully employed population quadrupled from 1870 to 1930, the number of gainfully employed workers in the ten to fifteen-year-old age bracket declined drastically (Greenberg 1977: 196). Furthermore, there seems to be no association between fertility changes and adolescent worker rates during this timeperiod (Lebergott 1964: 54–56).

This decline in child labor since the 1840s reflected the economic changes in capitalism. A market for such labor fell as those newly formed monopolistic industries underwent rapid technological change. The declining employment of children in factories, mines and agriculture, as a result of monopolization, was a major contribution to a youthful surplus labor problem. And as a result

250

of this, many young women in US society most likely chose to reject unemployment by turning to prostitution. In the nineteenth century, it was expected that young girls would go to work as early as possible in order to contribute to the family income. Therefore, one possible conclusion is that upon losing their jobs, marginalization meant for many, turning to prostitution to help keep the family from an instant slide into poverty. As Linda Gordon (1986: 263) has recently argued, since wage labor was not available,

> Children were encouraged to contribute through casual bits of paid labor, "gleaning", begging, or stealing. In some cases, as soon as the word got out that some man was willing to pay for sexual favors, the number of girls involved would snowball, so eager were they for the coins or treats they might receive. Some parents alleged that they did not know the sources of contributions. Some evidently knew the sources and raised no objections; a few may have participated in the prostitution arrangements.

In addition to unemployment, many young women possibly turned to prostitution because it paid more than the employment that *was* available in the legitimate wage labor force. The average wage for young women in the legitimate wage labor force was between four and six dollars a week. Working as a prostitute however, a young woman could make that amount in one evening. Moreover, many young women expressed disdain for the types of jobs made available to working-class female youth and therefore turned to prostitution (Rosen 1982: Chapter 8). Thus, the social feminist and social purist concentration on prostitution as being the result of force and passivity, obscured the economic and patriarchal conditions working-class women faced. Given those conditions, prostitution was a rational choice.

By ignoring these social structural realities, social feminists failed to demand a radical transformation of the social structure, concentrating instead on state intervention, which as I show below, resulted in the control of working-class female sexuality.

Feminism, criminology, and the rise of the female sex 'delinquent'

The concern with 'flappers'

With the age of sexual consent raised, social purists and social feminists became deeply concerned about the 'illicit' sexuality on the part of adolescent females; that is, females who were now below the age of sexual consent. Social purists and social feminists were highly concerned and 'shocked by the perceptible increase in "flappers", female adolescents in open rebellion against rigid

Victorian sexual standards' (Walkowitz 1980: 133). The self-image of social purists and social feminists was directly challenged by those young women who, while now being under the age of consent, freely engaged in sexual exploration. The sexual habits of this 'small vanguard' was symptomatic of a larger 'sexual revolution' taking place at the beginning of the twentieth century among some segments of society; it was a movement toward free, rather than restrictive, sexuality. As Linda Gordon (1976: 190) argues,

> Unmarried people spent nights together, even lived together; unmarried women took lovers whom they were not even engaged to, often many consecutively, sometimes more than one at a time; a few experimented with drugs such as peyote, and many women drank and smoked with men; sex was discussed in mixed groups; and all these things were done without disguise, even with bravado.

A small group of 'radical' feminists, such as Emma Goldman, Margaret Sanger, and Elizabeth Gurley Flynn, asserted their right to be sexual, to recognize their own sexuality. As Inez Milholland wrote in 1913, 'We are learning to be frank about sex. And through all this frankness runs a definite tendency toward an assault on the dual standard of morality and an assertion of sex rights on the part of women' (cited in Banner 1974: 116).

While most were clearly not feminists, and although for the most part their goal was marriage, 'flappers' were exerting some degree of control over their own sexuality. As Mark Connelly (1980: 39) points out, these young women (flappers) 'had achieved a degree of autonomy outside the context of a male-controlled or domestic setting', consequently leading 'lives markedly different from their mothers'.

For social purists and social feminists, this was a crisis and a sense of emergency pervaded their lives (see Foster 1914). It was men who should change their sexual habits and become more 'pure', not young women altering their behavior in the direction of 'free sex'. Being highly suspicious of sensuality, especially for girls under the age of consent, social purists and social feminists saw it as their duty to now protect the morals of young women. Young women under the age of consent who engaged in any type of sexual exploration were simply now seen as 'immoral'. As Leslie Fishbein (1975: 29) found in her examination of changing feminist views on prostitution in the Progressive Era, 'most feminists were convinced that increasing rather than releasing the taboos on extramarital sex would enhance their position, and they fervently supported social purity campaigns'. Thus, social purists and social feminists made urgent calls for creative new programs to realize and reaffirm traditional morality.

252

The establishment of vice commissions

In response to that call, in the early part of the twentieth century, the major US cities and a number of smaller ones established vice commissions to investigate and publicize within their respective cities, the nature and extent of prostitution and 'sexual immorality' of young women (Connelly 1980: 92). Many of these commissions found sexual 'flapperism" to be a major problem. The Newark Vice Commission reported that there existed in their city a 'large number of girls and young women who sin sexually in return only for the pleasures given or the company of the men with whom they consort' (Newark 1914: 11–12). The Commission went on to point out that these young women 'have no ethical standards and believe that they have as good a right, as it is generally supposed men have, to lead a double life; that they have a right to the pleasure they can gain from their bodies if they can do so without exposure'. The Commission concluded that 'this spirit is growing with alarming rapidity' (ibid. 12). The Syracuse Vice Commission found 'girls, many in number, who go out with men for an evening of pleasure' and then engage in 'intercourse where no money is asked or offered'. According to this Commission, these young women pick up men and boys on the streets, 'and then go to the bed houses, especially to those where they do not have to register. Often this class of girls will go freely with men entirely for pleasure with no economic pressure responsible for driving them to the life' (Syracuse 1913: 67). In Minneapolis, the Vice Commission there found that one of 'the most disturbing phases of the present situation in Minneapolis . . . is the large number of young girls in the streets at night in the downtown sections'. The Commission pointed out that these girls were to be 'found in numbers loitering about the fruit stores, drug stores and other popular locations, haunting hotel lobbies, crowding into the dance halls, the theaters and other amusement resorts; also in the saloon restaurants and the chop suey places and parading the streets and touring out in automobiles with men'. The Commission concluded that the 'situation is unmistakeably sinister', since these young girls were involved in prostitution but many were not, simply being on the road of 'immorality' (Minneapolis 1911: 76–77). A recent historical analysis of Boston came to similar conclusions. Girls in that city would hang out at night – hoping to pick up boys or men – in such notorious places as the Sullivan Square station, Scollay Square in the old West End, the Charlestown Navy Yard, and Revere beach. The girls 'travelled in groups and covered and solicited for each other. They were truant from school, sought out men in bars (and on ships), and generally engaged in provocative behavior' (Gordon 1986: 262).

The Vice Commissions called for novel means of moral control as the solution to this new age of sexual 'flapperism'.

Criminology answers the call

It was the emerging academic discipline of criminology which primarily answered this call, providing the 'scientific' framework for a program perceived as 'moral uplift', but what was in reality the repression of working-class girl sexuality. The 'science' of criminology helped justify state intervention to control the 'immoral flapper', by incarcerating those working-class girls who through their sexual activities, failed to conform to the 'respectable morality'.

A number of criminologists of the time built upon the ideas of conservative Darwinism, rewriting its doctrines to serve their interests. Conservative Darwinism provided criminology with a theory of evolution which justified the 'superior' position of the 'moral ones' (Anglo-Saxon upper-class white males), and the 'necessity' of controlling the 'inferior', 'immoral ones' (working-class European immigrant females). However, a number of US criminological thinkers did not readily accept the leading conservative Darwinist view of Cesare Lombroso on crime and delinquency. While Lombroso argued that crime and delinquency were the result of 'moral degeneracy', he pointed to 'atavism' (or a throwback to an earlier stage of evolution) as *the* cause of this degeneracy. Criminal types, according to Lombroso, could be recognized by their alleged 'atavistic' degenerative body characteristics such as low foreheads, excessive facial hair, large jawbones, high cheekbones, and so on. Prostitutes, for Lombroso, were found to be the most atavistic of all female criminals, and this led to their excessive 'immorality' (Lombroso and Ferrero 1895).

However, for American criminologists of the late 1800s and early 1900s – by reason of the tradition of recognizing social circumstances in the study of crime in the US (Guillot 1943) – the primacy of environmental conditions was seen as 'the chief criminogenic influence on weak degenerative individuals' (Boostrom 1973: 192). These criminologists criticized Lombroso's strict concentration on atavism, while in the process, constructing a *liberal* Darwinist criminology where criminals and delinquents were seen as being *abnormally* conditioned by both biological and environmental factors.

Foremost among these American critics of Lombroso was the University of Chicago criminologist Frances Kellor. Kellor replicated Lombroso's experiments in several prisons and reformatories for women, concluding that the physiology of female criminals and delinquents were not significantly different from non-criminal females. She also criticized Lombroso for ignoring 'the tremendous forces of social and economic environment' (Kellor 1900a: 528). For Frances Kellor (ibid: 533–43, 682) biology, in combination with economic need and the lack of economic opportunity, led to female crime. As she (1900b: 301) pointed out in an article entitled 'Criminal Sociology: The American vs. The Latin School', criminology, as it was being developed in the United States.

254

means not only a study of criminals, within prison walls – of their anatomy, craniums, and physiognomy – but includes an investigation of the criminal's haunts, of his habits, amusements, associates. Neither the phychology nor environmental forces are neglected. In environmental forces are included such as the influence of social and sanitary surroundings, climate, food, light, heat, governmental and economic conditions, occupation; also parental influences, training, education, culture, opportunities, desires, habits, etc.

It was this concentration on both biological and environmental factors which allowed the liberal Darwinist criminologists in the US to advocate special means of controlling the 'degenerate classes'. Since the causes of criminality were beyond the control of the individual, this provided a perfect rationale for the 'expert helper' and 'diagnostician'. As Boostrom (1973: 179) argues,

'Scientific corrections' and 'scientific criminology' were off and running ... and by the time the ideas of Lombroso were finally discredited, the positivistic orientation had already been established as the legitimate approach to the problem of crime. An illusion of a social science which would be indistinguisable from the natural sciences was established. This appealed to those moralistic reformers who aspired to scientific status.

The criminal was now seen as an individual incapable of moral action by both environmental and biological qualities and inadequacies. This moral pathology made the individual ill suited for civilized existence, therefore hindering social progress. What was needed were specialized institutions designed to rehabilitate the 'moral degenerate', making 'them' fit for evolutionary survival. In short, the 'moral invalid' was in need of special treatment (ibid).

As the liberal Darwinist criminology asserted itself, so did arguments justifying the expansion of state control to solve social problems. Progress demanded the correction of the 'degenerate classes'. It became 'the duty' of the state therefore to correct and educate the 'dangerous classes' in order for social progress to occur. As Ron Boostroom (ibid: 198–199) concludes in his study of the emergence of criminology in the United States,

A general welfare state responding in a parternalistic fashion to the diagnosis of social problems provided by elitist reformers was now generally accepted as a worthwhile goal by 'progressive' reformers. Correctional reformers and correctional criminologists began to implement this program of 'benevolent' reform. The juvenile court, probation systems, the indeterminate sentence, and determinate theories of the criminal type; all were products of this movement and were rationalized by the early criminologists.

The state moves in

Part of this movement was special treatment by the state for youth in general, but female adolescent youth in particular. For example, special 'morals' and 'girls' courts were established for the sole purpose of adjudicating prostitutes and sexually recalcitrant girls. Many reformers felt that special courts should be established for girls, with a woman as the judge. A woman judge was needed because, 'to oblige a girl to tell the story of her downfall (most girl delinquents are offenders against sex) to a man, however wise or sympathetic he might be, could only help to destroy such modesty as her experience might have left her' (Rippey 1914: 254). While the idea of a female judge represented a reasonable feminist demand, a special girls court with a female judge would also teach 'such delinquents that there are some matters which are not to be discussed with or before men, or even to be spoken at all, save in hushed whispers of shame' (ibid). The public was 'rigidly excluded' from the courtroom, as the court did not want to futher destroy 'her chances of a useful womanhood' (ibid). These unique and special courts were established in such cities as New York, Philadelphia, and Chicago (Rosen 1982: 19).

It was these special courts, as well as the Juvenile Court, established in both Chicago and Denver in 1899, which became the arena for controlling the sexuality of working-class girls. First, it is clear that the vast majority of children brought before these courts were poor, working class, and usually recent immigrants (Platt 1969, Schlossman and Wallach 1978, Wiley 1915, Sheldon 1981). Additionally, females, as opposed to males, were brought to court for either real or alleged sexuality. In Chicago for instance, between 1899 and 1909, 80.9 percent of the girls, while only 1.6 percent of the boys (the boys were mostly charged with *criminal*, rather than *noncriminal*, offenses), were brought to court for 'immorality' (Breckinridge and Abbott 1912: 28–40). 'Immorality' did not only mean having sexual intercourse, it also included such acts as 'attending tough dances', 'staying out until two or three o'clock in the morning', and masturbation (ibid: 35–36). 'Immorality' therefore meant admitting or being caught in the act of intercourse, or showing through their behavior that they had had intercourse in the past or most likely would in the future.

The courts many times even went to the extent of subjecting girls to a vaginal examination to determine whether or not they had engaged in intercourse. For example, Schlossman and Wallach (1978: 73) cite a case in Milwaukee of a girl named Annagret, who

> like every girl who appeared in court, was subjected to a vaginal examination. The only proof of virginity was an intact hymen. To his own surprise the examining doctor concluded that Annagret was still a virgin, but he

256

informed the court that irritation in her clitoral area indicated that she was a regular masturbator . . . Thus, according to the court, Annagret's masturbatory habits explained her penchant for fantasy and justified labeling her a delinquent.

This same pattern-charging girls, but not boys, with 'immorality'- held true for other parts of the country. For example, between 1907 and 1913 in New Haven, Connecticut, approximately 65 percent of the girls brought to court were charged with 'immorality' (Wiley 1915: 8–9, 15). And in Memphis, Tennessee, between 1910 and 1917 over 30 percent of the females were charged with 'immorality' while only 0.6 percent of the males were (Sheldon 1981: 61–63).

In the 'Girls Court' in Chicago, the case of Angeline (Rippey 1914: 252–256) provides a prime example of who, and what type of behavior, was now being so vigilantly controlled by the state. Angeline, at fourteen, and because of sordid poverty, drunkeness at home, and physical and sexual abuse from her father, left home and obtained a five-dollar a week job in a candy factory. However, because of rent and food, 'She was no better off than she had been at home'. But, 'one dream bade fair to come true – a'fella' rose on Angeline's horizon'. The advances of the 'fella' represented to her 'the opening of a door to hitherto untasted delights', and Angeline eventually engaged in intercourse with the 'strapping young blond teamster'. Her mother, interested in Angeline's income, had her eventually arrested and brought before the female judge in the Chicago 'Girls Court'. The following transpired between Angeline and the Judge (cited in ibid: 253).

'Did no one tell you these things you were doing were wrong, Angeline?' asked the judge.

'No', sobbed Angeline, burying her face in her handkerchief.

'Little girls who run away from home so they can keep the money their mothers need, and live in rooming-houses, and go about with strange men always get into trouble sooner or later', the judge went on.

Angeline threw back her head defiantly. 'I wanted to have some fun', she flashed out. 'I *never* had any fun!'

'Yes, I know', sympathized the judge. 'Every girl needs to have fun, but it must be the right kind. There's fun that's good, you know, Angeline, and fun that's bad'.

'And now, Angeline', the judge concluded, 'would you like to go back home and try again?'

All the wretchedness of Angeline's fourteen dreary, unloved, drudgery-filled years was compressed into her quick, panic stricken cry: 'Oh, I don't *want* to go home! I don't *want* to go home!'

Angeline was sent to a reformatory for girls.

The case of Angeline is important because it exhibits for us the multiplicity of some girls' victimization. Not only were these girls victimized by reformers of another class, they were also – at times – victimized by men of their own class, and even men *and* women of their own families. When these girls roamed the streets, they were extremely vulnerable to sexual victimization – not only rape, but also being tricked, pressured, or bribed into sexual submission to males (Gordon 1986: 261). In other words, for some, their 'immorality' was forced. But in addition to this, many girls were also, like Angeline, victims of sexual abuse by their fathers. Of all the sex delinquent cases for Boston in 1920, 40 percent of the girls alleged incest and another 20 percent alleged nonincestuous rape (ibid: 262). When these girls could not prevent their victimization at home, they attempted to escape – as did Angeline – their families altogether. As Gordon (ibid) points out, 'in their flight from home, incest victims may have been successfully preserving an autonomy vital to their survival'. Yet their resistance was not accepted, as they experienced a new form of victimization: state repression of their own sexuality. The girls were also oppressed by women of their own class and families. For many girls their mothers intensely attempted to control their daughters and used moral purity authority against them. Many girls – as with Angeline – were prosecuted by their mothers. In short, the oppression and victimization of these girls crossed class boundaries.

Reformatories for 'flappers'

Most criminologists argued that both biological and environmental conditions were the cause of juvenile delinquency and female 'immorality' (see Drähms 1900: 282–292, Wiley 1915: 13–15, Breckinridge and Abbott 1912: Chapter 3, Rippey 1914: 255–257). A good example is a study published in *The Journal of Delinquency* by Louise and George Ordahl (1918: 59). They concluded that 'sexual immorality is the most frequent and . . . the most serious offense for which girls are committed'. The conditions which lead to 'immorality' were for the Ordahl's 'considerably complicated', but in general, 'immorality is the result of low intelligence, lack of suitable early training or unfavorable environment, and improper associates' (ibid). The following are a few examples of the 'immorality' studied by the Ordahls (ibid: 61–65).

- This girl states she was immoral with three boys and one old man, just because they asked her.
- While in the factory she became associated with immoral girls, and through their influence became immoral with boys.

258

- While working at the factories, L.D. became associated with immoral girls. She left home, and in company with two other girls, obtained a room and entertained boys.
- While at high school, W.E. became promiscuously immoral and diseased. It appears that somehow a group of high school students became imbued with a pseudo-philosophy of free love and proceeded to live it out to the letter. This girl is, otherwise, apparently a person of good ability and good sense.

While it is clear that many of these 'flappers' experienced very difficult family environments, the criminological account of working-class girl 'immorality' supported the notion that these girls were nothing more than *passive* victims of biological and environmental conditions. Their 'immoral' sexuality was not, to these criminologists, something many freely chose, but rather, it was seen as being *forced* on them by forces outside their control. In short, 'flappers' were not seen by these criminologists as 'sex radicals' rationally attempting to control their own sexuality in a sexually restrictive society, but rather, abnormal and degenerative perverts who needed to be controlled.

As such, these criminologists supported the use of reformatories to 'rehabilitate' these newly, state created, female sexual 'delinquents'. Traditional methods of imprisonment in adult institutions, solely for the purpose of punishment, were seen by Drähms, Wiley, Breckinridge, Abbott, and others, as inadequate for curbing this juvenile delinquency. Punishments, Drähms (1960: 285) argued, 'serve to harden; they rarely cure'. While the police 'should take pride in ridding the streets of the young girlwho is there for immoral purposes' (Wiley 1915: 17), reformatories, specifically designed for youth, providing rational and moral training, was seen as the 'rational and scientific method of dealing with the problem of the rehabilitation of the youthful recalcitrant' (Drähms: 307). Reformatories were seen as the 'moral safequards' of society.

Social feminists joined criminologists and social purity activists to advocate special reformatories for girls and women. Social feminists were concerned with protecting youth from moral weaknesses, and purity activists encouraged criminological reformers to focus on 'loose women'. As Nicole Rafter (1985: 47) points out, the 'social purifiers found an outlet for their program of moral education, and their concern with protecting women, in the women's prison movement'.

Reformatories, for both boys and girls it was argued, should be run by women, as women were seen as especially suited to working with children, particularly those on the 'verge of ruin' (Platt 1969: Chapter 4). Through their architecture and the programs made available, reformatories for youth were to reflect 'the good home life' – nurturing, caring, and above all, moral. Girl reformatories in particular, were to have programs centering around general housework; sewing, cooking, laundry work, dressmaking, training in the care of young children, and beauty culture (Reeves 1929: 299). But in addition to training young women for their predetermined place in society – the home – it was essential that each girl incarcerated receive an extensive program in 'sex education'. As Margaret Reeves (1929: 215) points out in her study of the history of female juvenile reformatories,

> The true purpose of sex education with these delinquent girls is not so much a matter of giving detailed information (though misinformation must be corrected), as of creating the proper attitude toward sex. Most of these girls have had considerable experience in life which they need to forget. With some the sex impulse has been permitted so free an expression that it overshadows all other impulses. Such girls need to be given a different perspective in relation to the whole question.

In short, the 'immoral flapper', through her threatening sexuality, needed to be controlled through 'rehabilitation'. In fact, 'rehabilitation' in the reformatory became the order of the day for the 'immoral' female youth, while males, who engaged in *criminal* acts, were being placed on probation with no institionalization. For example, in the Chicago Juvenile Court, again between 1899 and 1909, 59 percent of the boys were placed on probation, while only 37 percent of the girls were so placed. Yet more striking, 21 percent of the boys were committed to institutions, while 51 percent of the girls were sent to reformatories (Breckinridge and Abbott 1912: 40). In Memphis, females were almost twice as likely to be committed as males, primarily for 'immorality' (Sheldon 1981: 67–69). In Milwaukee, twice as many girls were committed to reformatories as boys (Schlossman and Wallach 1978: 72), and although in New Haven only 31 percent of girls were committed to reformatories between 1907 and 1913, according to Mabel Wiley (1915: 18), this was due to the fact that the courts 'are still far from putting into practice the newer ideas of penology. To a large extent it is still the crime that is punished, rather than the individual reformed'. In short, while girls were charged with 'immorality' and boys appeared in court on *criminal* charges (such as theft and violence), the most severe sanctions were reserved for the girls, incarceration in a reformatory. While social feminists, social purists, and criminologists believed they were helping girls by providing special reformatory care, their 'good intentions do not cancel out the fact that in the course of helping, they gave legal force to a double standard that punished women more severely than men'. (Rafter 1985: 36).

Social feminists and social purity activists supported reformatories for female sexual 'delinquents' because this removed 'flappers' – a source of sexual temptation for boys – from society. Reformatories were also advocated be-

260

cause they allegedly 'protected' young girls from the 'white-slave traffic' and provided a means of rehabilitating the 'fallen' female youth. However, rather than being a program of 'moral uplift', the social feminist/social purity/criminology plan turned out to be a means of controlling working-class girl sexuality.[2] As many young women were attempting to take control over their sexuality, 'reformatories offered a warning that society would still not tolerate girls who showed the same interest in sex as boys and reinforced the traditional belief that "normal" girls were sexually impassive' (Schlossman and Wallach 1978: 91). However, the cases and statements by working-class girls in court and reformatories clearly suggest that they were not the sexually innocent and passive 'little girls' they were alleged to be. What social feminists, criminologists, and social purists obscured was that those whom they sought to protect – working-class girls – did not behave as if they were sexually inert, or for that matter, concerned about the dangers of 'white-slavery'. In fact, we can conclude that most of the girls who were brought to court and sent to reformatories engaged in sexuality out of personal inclination. By first raising the age of consent, and then advocating state sponsored social control for sexually recalcitrant girls, social feminists, in coalition with social purists and now criminologists, denied teenage working-class girls the power to make their own decisions about their sexuality. Social feminists, in short, contributed to the control of women's sexuality and thus the maintenance of patriarchy. 'Flappers' called into question the ideology that women are to be the sexual partner of only one man. Thus, the social control of 'flappers' rested upon and reinforced masculine control of female sexuality.

By the early part of the twentieth century, the state had invested heavily in the custody and 'treatment' of the new female sex 'delinquent'. Between 1860 and 1900, on the average, approximately five new state run female juvenile reformatories were created per decade, for a total of twenty-two. However, between 1900 and 1920, twenty-seven new female state run juvenile reformatories opened in the United States (Reeves 1929: 39). Moreover, nineteenth-century reformatories for female juveniles were expanded in size, staff and clientele between 1910 and 1920, and a number of states began taking over private girls reformatories (Schlossman and Wallach 1978: 70).

Conclusion

During the latter part of the nineteenth century, social feminists were involved in the movement against prostitution. While initially social feminists organized against legalized prostitution to challenge masculine dominance, eventually they aligned themselves with a conservative social force – the social purity movement – in an effort to abolish prostitution itself by, in particular, raising the age of sexual consent. It was the success of this latter effort which set the stage for working class girl sexual repression. By the early part of the twentieth century, when young girls and women began to threaten the sexual status quo – through their attempt to reject traditional sexual norms and control their own sexuality – a discursive alignment between the masculine-dominated state and the social feminist/social purity movement took place. The 'new' liberal Darwinist criminology provided the 'scientific' rationale for that alignment by arguing that in order for society to progress, the 'immoral' had to be controlled and rehabilitated, thus legitimating state intervention 'scientifically'. The program to redistribute power among men and women was lost, and the concentration became rehabilitating the 'immoral flapper'. The end result was that capitalism as an economic system, and patriarchy as a form of gender organization, were buttressed by the creation of a new type of working-class female offender: the teenage sex 'delinquent'. Through the reformatory movement the state contributed to the control of a surplus population of redundant, working-class female youth. But in addition, the state and its newly created juvenile justice system controlled female sexuality by attempting to 'teach' young working-class women early on that their sexuality was not their own. By incarcerating young 'flappers', the state provided a mechanism for reproducing the 'double standard' and therefore masculine control of female sexuality. In short, the desire on the part of social feminists, social purists, and criminologists to protect young working-class girls masked coercive aspirations to control their voluntary sexuality. Thus, reformist feminist energies were eventually channelled – through a coalition with social purists and criminologists – into a conservative and morally repressive movement. As state agencies for social control were expanded, the causes of women's economic and sexual exploitation remained unchanged.

Notes

1. Following historians of the progressive era, I use the terms 'social feminism' and 'social feminist' in this paper to refer primarily to those feminists who attempted to reform society within the existing gender, economic, and overall institutional arrangement, as opposed to 'radical feminists', who were more militant and critical of the social order. However, this does not mean the two groups never advocated the same causes; many times they did. Indeed, it is difficult to categorize some nineteenth-century feminists one way or the other. For example, Charlotte Perkins Gillman, as a 'radical feminist', was very critical of female passivity and 'maleness', yet as a 'social feminist' she spoke out on the alleged dangers of 'excessive sex indulgence'.

2. This does not mean that social feminists and other reformers were always totally repressive. In many instances, young women wanted to be noticed and helped, and occasionally the middle class reformers *were* able to help.

262

References

Anthony, S.B. (1968, 1875). 'Social Purity. In: *Up From the Pedestal*, ed. A.S. Kraditor. Chicago: Quadrangle Books.

Banner, L.W. (1974). *Women in Modern America: A Brief History*. NY: Harcourt Brace Jovanovich.

Boostrom, R. (1973). 'The Personalization of Evil: The Emergence of American Criminology, 1865–1910'. Unpublished Ph.D dissertation, University of California, Berkeley.

Breckinridge, S. and E. Abbott (1912). *The Delinquent Child and the Home*. NY: Russell Sage.

Campbell, A. (1981). *Girl Delinquents*. NY: Basil Blackwell.

Campbell, V.H. (1895). 'Why An Age of Consent?'. *Arena* 12 (July): 285–288.

Chesney-Lind, M. (1978). 'Judicial Enforcement of the Female Sex Role: The Family Court and the Female Delinquent'. *Issues in Criminology* 8, 2: 51–69.

Connelly, M. (1980). *The Response to Prostitution in the Progressive Era*. Chapel Hill: University of North Carolina Press.

Degler, C. (1980). *At Odds: Women and the Family in America From the Revolution to the Present*. NY: Oxford University Press.

Drähms, A. (1900). *The Criminal: His Personnel and Environment*. Montclair, NJ: Patterson Smith.

Dubois, E.C. and L. Gordon. (1984). 'Seeking Ecstasy on the Battlefield: Danger and Pleasure in Nineteenth Century Feminist Sexual Thought'. In: *Pleasure and Danger: Exploring Female Sexuality*, ed. C.S. Vance. Boston: Boutledge and Kegan Paul.

Eaton, M. (1986). *Justice for Women? Family, Court and Social Control*. Philadelphia: Open University Press.

Fishbein, L. (1975). 'Harlot or Heroine? Changing Views of Prostitution, 1870–1920'. *The Historian:* 23–35.

Foster, W.T. (1914). *The Social Emergency*. NY: Houghton Mifflin.

Gardner, H.H. (1895). 'What Shall the Age of Consent Be?'. *Arena* 11 (January): 196–198.

Gordon, L. (1986). 'Incest and Resistance: Patterns of Father-Daughter Incest 1880–1930'. *Social Problems*, Vol. 37, No. 4 (April): 253–267.

Gordan, L. (1976). *Woman's Body, Women's Right: A Social History of Birth Control in America*. NY: Grossman Publishers.

Guillot, E.E. (1943). *Social Factors in Crime: As Explained by American Writers of the Civil War and Post Civil War Periods*. Philadelphia: University of Pennsylvia Press.

Greenberg, D. (1977). 'Delinquency and the Age Structure of Society'. *Contemporary Crises* 1: 189–223.

Kellor, F. (1900a). 'Psychological and Environmental Study of Women Criminals'. *American Journal of Sociology* 5: 527–543, 671–682.

Kellor, F. (1900b). 'Criminal Sociology: The American vs. the Latin School'. *Arena* 23 (March): 301–307.

Lebergott, S. (1964). *Manpower in Economic Growth: The American Record since 1800*. NY: McGraw-Hill.

Lombroso, C. and E. Ferrero. (1895). *The Female Offender*. NY: Appleton.

Minneapolis, M.N. (1911). *Report of the Vice Commission of Minneapolis*.

Newark, N.J. (1914). Citizens Committee on Social Evil. *Report of the Social Evil Conditions of Newark*.

Ordahl, L. and G. Ordahl. (1918). 'A Study of Delinquent and Dependent Girls'. *The Journal of Delinquency* III, 2 (March): 41–73.

Pivar, D.J. (1973). *Purity Crusade: Sexual Morality and Social Control, 1868–1900*. Westport, Conn.: Greenwood.

Platt, A. (1969). *The Child Savers: The Invention of Delinquency*. Chicago: University of Chicago Press.

Rafter, N.H. (1985). *Partial Justice: Women in State Prisons, 1800–1935*. Boston: Northeastern University Press.

Reeves, M. (1929). *Training Schools for Delinquent Girls*. NY: Russell Sage.

Rippey, C.M. (1914). 'The Case of Angeline'. *Outlook* 106: 252–256.

Rosen, R. (1982). *The Lost Sisterhood: Prostitution in America, 1900–1918*. Baltimore: Johns Hopkins University Press.

Sarri, R. (1976). 'Juvenile Law: How It Penalizes Women'. In: *The Female Offender* ed. L. Crites. Lexington, Mass: D.C. Heath.

Schlossman, S. and S. Wallach. (1978). 'The Crime of Precocious Sexuality: Female Juvenile Delinquency in the Progressive Era'. *Harvard Educational Review* 48, 1 (Feb): 65–94.

Shacklady-Smith, L. (1978). 'Sexist Assumptions and Female Delinquency'. In: C. Smart and B. Smart (eds) *Women, Sexuality, and Social Control*. Boston: Routledge and Kegan Paul.

Sheldon, R.G. (1981). 'Sex Discrimination in the Juvenile Justice System: Memphis, Tennessee, 1900–1917'. In: *Comparing Female and Male Offenders* ed. M.Q. Warren. Beverly Hills, CA: Sage.

Smart, C. (1976). *Women, Crime and Criminology: A Feminist Critique*. Boston: Routledge and Kegan Paul.

Syracuse, N.Y., Committee of Eighteen. (1913). *The Social Evil in Syracuse*.

Terry, R.M. (1970). 'Discrimination in the Handling of Juvenile Offenders by Social Control Agencies'. In: P. Garabedian and D.C. Gibbons (eds) *Becoming Delinquent*. Chicago: Aldine Press.

Vertinsky, P.A. (1976). 'Education for Sexual Morality: Moral Reform and the Regulation of American Sexual Behavior in the Nineteenth Century'. Ph.D. Dissertation. University of British Columbia.

Walkowitz, J. (1980). *Prostitution and Victorian Society: Women, Class, and the State*. Cambridge: Cambridge Univerity Press.

Walkowitz, J. (1980). 'The Politics of Prostitution'. *Signs* 6, 1: (Autumn): 123–135.

Wiley, M. (1915). *A Study of the Problem of Girl Delinquency in New Haven*. New Haven, Conn.: Civic Federation of New Haven.

Willard, F.E. (1895). 'Arousing the Public Conscience'. *Arena* 11 (January): 198–202.

12

2

The Etiology of Female Crime:
A Review of the Literature

Dorie Klein

This article on women offenders, a classic in the field, provides an historical overview of the major theories of women and their criminality. This chapter ties in with many points made in the first chapter in Klein's description of how writers have always brought sexist, racist, and classist assumptions to their studies of women criminals. In reading this chapter, pay attention to the rationales and explanations given by different writers over the years to explain why women commit crimes. Consider the arguments which correspond to each of these writers' views.

For the student of women and crime the importance of this chapter is in its discussion on explanations of crime by women and the author's demonstration that these have been neither well-researched nor well-documented. According to Klein, past theories depend on the ultimate idea that criminality is a result of individual characteristics (such as one's biology—read sexuality for women—or psychology). At bottom, this is equally as true for both early as well as many contemporary sociologists. Thus strategies for rehabilitating the offender tend to focus on individual adjustment to the socially acceptable "legal world," not on social change of the broader society itself. Klein, instead, extends her historical analysis to question the impact of the political economy, racism, and sexism on the causes and definitions of female crime.

The criminality of women has long been a neglected subject area of criminology. Many explanations have been advanced for this, such as women's low official rate of crime and delinquency and the preponderance of male theorists in the field. Female criminality has often ended up as a footnote to works on men that purport to be works on criminality in general.

There has been, however, a small group of writings specifically concerned with women and crime. This paper will explore those works con-

36   THE CRIMINAL JUSTICE SYSTEM AND WOMEN

cerned with the etiology of female crime and delinquency, beginning with
the turn-of-the-century writing of Lombroso and extending to the present.
Writers selected to be included have been chosen either for their influence
on the field, such as Lombroso, Thomas, Freud, Davis and Pollak, or
because they are representative of the kinds of work being published, such
as Konopka, Vedder and Somerville, and Cowie, Cowie and Slater. The
emphasis is on the continuity between these works, because it is clear that,
despite recognizable differences in analytical approaches and specific theories, the authors represent a tradition to a great extent. It is important to
understand, therefore, the shared assumptions made by the writers that are
used to laying the groundwork for their theories.

The writers see criminality as the result of *individual* characteristics that
are only peripherally affected by economic, social and political forces.
These characteristics are of a *physiological* or *psychological* nature and are uniformly based on implicit or explicit assumptions about the *inherent nature
of women*. This nature is *universal*, rather than existing within a specific
historical framework.

Since criminality is seen as an individual activity, rather than as a
condition built into existing structures, the focus is on biological, psychological and social factors that would turn a woman toward criminal activity To do this, the writers create two distinct classes of women: good
women who are "normal" noncriminals, and bad women who are criminals, thus taking a moral position that often masquerades as a scientific
distinction. The writers, although they may be biological or social determinists to varying degrees, assume that individuals have *choices* between
criminal and noncriminal activity. They see persons as atomistically moving about in a social and political vacuum; many writers use marketplace
models for human interaction.

Although the theorists may differ on specific remedies for individual
criminality, ranging from sterilization to psychoanalysis (but always stop-
ping far short of social change), the basic thrust is toward *individual adjustment*, whether it be physical or mental, and the frequent model is
rehabilitative therapy. Widespread environmental alterations are usually
included as casual footnotes to specific plans for individual therapy. Most
of the writers are concerned with *social harmony* and the welfare of the
existing social structure rather than with the women involved or with
women's position in general. None of the writers come from anything near
a "feminist" or "radical" perspective.

In *The Female Offender*, originally published in 1903, Lombroso described
female criminality as an inherent tendency produced in individuals that
could be regarded as biological atavisms, similar to cranial and facial features, and one could expect a withering away of crime if the atavistic
people were prohibited from breeding. At this time criminality was widely

regarded as a physical ailment, like epilepsy. Today, Cowie, Cowie and Slater (1968) have identified physical traits in girls who have been classified as delinquent, and have concluded that certain traits, such as bigness, may lead to aggressiveness. This theme of physiological characteristics has been developed by a good number of writers in the last seventy years, such as the Gluecks (1934). One sees at the present time a new surge of "biological" theories of criminality; for example, a study involving "violence-prone" women and menstrual cycles has recently been proposed at UCLA.[1]

Thomas, to a certain degree, and Freud extend the physiological explanation of criminality to propose a psychological theory. However, it is critical to understand that these psychological notions are based on assumptions of universal *physiological* traits of women, such as their reproductive instinct and passivity, that are seen as invariably producing certain psychological reactions. Women may be viewed as turning to crime as a *perversion of* or *rebellion against* their *natural feminine roles*. Whether their problems are biological, psychological or social-environmental, the point is always to return them to their roles. Thomas (1907; 1923), for example, points out that poverty might prevent a woman from marrying, whereby she would turn to prostitution as an alternative to carry on her feminine service role. In fact, Davis (1961) discusses prostitution as a parallel illegal institution to marriage. Pollak (1950) discusses how women extend their service roles into criminal activity due to inherent tendencies such as deceitfulness. Freud (1933; Jones, 1961) sees any kind of rebellion as the result of a failure to develop healthy feminine attitudes, such as narcissism, and Konopka (1966) and Vedder and Somerville (1907) apply Freudian thought to the problem of female delinquency.

The specific characteristics ascribed to women's nature and those critical to theories of female criminality are uniformly *sexual* in their nature. Sexuality is seen as the root of female behavior and the problem of crime. Women are defined as sexual beings, as sexual capital in many cases, physiologically, psychologically and socially. This definition *reflects* and *reinforces* the economic position of women as reproductive and domestic workers. It is mirrored in the laws themselves and in their enforcement, which penalize sexual deviations for women and may be more lenient with economic offenses committed by them, in contrast to the treatment given men. The theorists accept the sexual double standard inherent in the law, often noting that "chivalry" protects women, and many of them build notions of the universality of *sex repression* into their explanations of women's position. Women are thus the sexual backbone of civilization.

In setting hegemonic standards of conduct for all women, the theorists define *femininity*, which they equate with healthy femaleness, in classist, racist and sexist terms, using their assumptions of women's nature, specifically their sexuality, to justify what is often in reality merely a defense of

38   THE CRIMINAL JUSTICE SYSTEM AND WOMEN

the existing order. Lombroso, Thomas and Freud consider the upper-class white woman to be the highest expression of femininity, although she is inferior to the upper-class white man. These standards are adopted by later writers in discussing femininity. To most theorists, women are inherently inferior to men at masculine tasks such as thought and production, and therefore it is logical that their sphere should be reproductive.

Specific characteristics are proposed to bolster this sexual ideology, expressed for example by Freud, such as passivity, emotionalism, narcissism and deceitfulness. In the discussions of criminality, certain theorists, such as Pollak, link female criminality to these traits. Others see criminality as an attempt away from femininity into masculinity, such as Lombroso, although the specifics are often confused. Contradictions can be clearly seen, which are explained by the dual nature of "good" and "bad" women and by the fact that this is a mythology attempting to explain real behavior. Many explanations of what are obviously economically motivated offenses, such as prostitution and shoplifting, are explained in sexual terms, such as prostitution being promiscuity, and shoplifting being "kleptomania" caused by women's inexplicable mental cycles tied to menstruation. Different explanations have to be made for "masculine" crimes, e.g., burglary, and for "feminine" crimes, e.g., shoplifting. Although this distinction crops up consistently, the specifics differ widely.

The problem is complicated by the lack of knowledge of the epidemiology of female crime, which allows such ideas as "hidden crime," first expressed by Pollak (1950), to take root. The problem must be considered on two levels: women, having been confined to certain tasks and socialized in certain ways, are *in fact* more likely to commit crime related to their lives which are sexually oriented; yet even nonsexual offenses are *explained* in sexual terms by the theorists. The writers ignore the problems of poor and Third World women, concentrating on affluent white standards of femininity. The experiences of these overlooked women, who *in fact* constitute a good percentage of women caught up in the criminal justice system, negate the notions of sexually motivated crime. These women have real economic needs which are not being met, and in many cases engage in illegal activities as a viable economic alternative. Furthermore, chivalry has never been extended to them.

The writers largely ignore the problems of sexism, racism and class, thus their work is sexist, racist and classist in its implications. Their concern is adjustment of the woman to society, not social change. Hence, they represent a tradition in criminology and carry along a host of assumptions about women and humanity in general. It is important to explore these assumptions and traditions in depth in order to understand what kinds of myths have been propagated around women and crime. The discussions of each writer or writers will focus on these assumptions and their relevance to criminological theories. These assumptions of universal, biological/psychological characteristics, of individual responsibility for crime, of the necessity for maintaining social harmony, and of the benevolence of the state link different theories along a continuum, transcending political labels and minor divergencies. The road from Lombroso to the present is surprisingly straight.

LOMBROSO: "THERE MUST BE SOME ANOMALY...."

Lombroso's work on female criminality (1920) is important to consider today despite the fact that his methodology and conclusions have long been successfully discredited. Later writings on female crime by Thomas, Davis, Pollak and others use more sophisticated methodologies and may proffer more palatable liberal theories. However, to varying degrees they rely on those sexual ideologies based on *implicit* assumptions about the physiological and psychological nature of women that are *explicit* in Lombroso's work. Reading the work helps to achieve a better understanding of what kinds of myths have been developed for women in general and for female crime and deviance in particular.

One specific notion of women offered by Lombroso is women's physiological immobility and psychological passivity, later elaborated by Thomas, Freud and other writers. Another ascribed characteristic is the Lombrosian notion of women's adaptability to surroundings and their capacity for survival as being superior to that of men. A third idea discussed by Lombroso is women's amorality: they are cold and calculating. This is developed by Thomas (1923), who describes women's manipulation of the male sex urge for ulterior purposes; by Freud (1933), who sees women as avenging their lack of a penis on men; and by Pollak (1950), who depicts women as inherently deceitful.

When one looks at these specific traits, one sees contradictions. The myth of compassionate women clashes with their reputed coldness; their frailness belies their capacity to survive. One possible explanation for these contraditions is the duality of sexual ideology with regard to "good" and "bad" women.[2] Bad women are whores, driven by lust for money or for men, often essentially *"masculine"* in their orientation, and perhaps afflicted with a touch of penis envy. Good women are chaste, "feminine," and usually not prone to criminal activity. But when they are, they commit crime in a most *ladylike* way such as poisoning. In more sophisticated theory, all women are seen as having a bit of both tendencies in them. Therefore, women can be compassionate *and* cold, frail *and* sturdy, pious *and* amoral, depending on which path they choose to follow. They are seen

40   THE CRIMINAL JUSTICE SYSTEM AND WOMEN

as rational (although they are irrational, too!), atomistic individuals making choices in a vacuum, prompted only by personal, physiological/psychological factors. These choices relate only to the *sexual* sphere. Women have no place in any other sphere. Men, on the other hand, are not held sexually accountable, although, as Thomas notes (1907), they are held responsible in *economic* matters. Men's sexual freedom is justified by the myth of masculine, irresistible sex urges. This myth, still worshipped today, is frequently offered as a rationalization for the existence of prostitution and the double standard. As Davis maintains, this necessitates the parallel existence of classes of "good" and "bad" women.

These dual moralities for the sexes are outgrowths of the economic, political and social *realities* for men and women. Women are primarily workers within the family, a critical institution of reproduction and socialization that services such basic needs as food and shelter. Laws and codes of behavior for women thus attempt to maintain the smooth functioning of women in that role, which requires that women act as a conservative force in the continuation of the nuclear family. Women's main tasks are sexual, and the law embodies sexual limitations for women, which do not exist for men, such as the prohibition of promiscuity for girls. This explains why theorists of female criminality are not only concerned with sexual violations by female offenders, but attempt to account for even *nonsexual* offenses, such as prostitution, in sexual terms, e.g., women enter prostitution for sex rather than for money. Such women are not only economic offenders but are sexual deviants, falling neatly into the category of "bad" women.

The works of Lombroso, particularly *The Female Offender* (1920), are a foremost example of the biological explanation of crime. Lombroso deals with crime as an atavism, or survival of "primitive" traits in individuals, particularly those of the female and nonwhite races. He theorizes that individuals develop differentially within sexual and racial limitations which differ hierarchically from the most highly developed, the white men, to the most primitive, the nonwhite women. Beginning with the assumption that criminals must be atavistic, he spends a good deal of time comparing the crania, moles, heights, etc. of convicted criminals and prostitutes with those of normal women. Any trait that he finds to be more common in the "criminal" group is pronounced an atavistic trait, such as moles, dark hair, etc., and women with a number of these telltale traits could be regarded as potentially criminal, since they are of the atavistic type. He specifically rejects the idea that some of these traits, for example obesity in prostitutes, could be the *result* of their activities rather than an indicator of their propensity to them. Many of the traits are depicted as "anomalies," such as darkness and shortness, and characteristic of certain racial groups, such as the Sicilians, who undoubtedly comprise an oppressed group within Italy and form a large part of the imprisoned population.

Lombroso traces an overall pattern of evolution in the human species that accounts for the uneven development of groups: the white and non-white races, males and females, adults and children. Women, children and nonwhites share many traits in common. There are fewer variations in their mental capacities: "even the female criminal is monotonous and uniform compared with her male companion, just as in general woman is inferior to man" (Ibid.:122), due to her being "atavistically nearer to her origin than the male" (Ibid.:107). The notion of women's mediocrity, or limited range of mental possibilities, is a recurrent one in the writings of the twentieth century. Thomas and others note that women comprise "fewer genuises, fewer lunatics and fewer morons" (Thomas 1907:45); lacking the imagination to be at either end of the spectrum, they are conformist and dull . . . not due to social, political or economic constraints on their activities, but because of their innate physiological limitations as a sex. Lombroso attributes the lower female rate of criminality to their having fewer anomalies, which is one aspect of their closeness to the lower forms of less differentiated life.

Related characteristics of women are their passivity and conservatism. Lombroso admits that women's traditional sex roles in the family bind them to a more sedentary life. However, he insists that women's passivity can be directly traced to the "immobility of the ovule compared with the zoosperm" (1920:109), falling back on the sexual act in an interesting anticipation of Freud.

Women, like the lower races, have greater powers of endurance and resistance to mental and physical pain than men. Lombroso states: "denizens of female prisoners . . . have reached the age of 90, having lived within those walls since they were 29 without any grave injury to health" (Ibid.:125). Denying the humanity of women by denying their capability for suffering justifies exploitation of women's energies by arguing for their suitability to hardship. Lombroso remarks that "a duchess can adapt herself to new surroundings and become a washerwoman much more easily than a man can transform himself under analogous conditions" (Ibid.:272). The theme of women's adaptability to physical and social surroundings, which are male initiated, male controlled, and often expressed by saying that women are actually the "stronger" sex, is a persistent thread in writings on women.

Lombroso explains that because women are unable to feel pain, they are insensitive to the pain of others and lack moral refinement. His blunt denial of the age-old myth of women's compassion and sensitivity is modified, however, to take into account women's low crime rate:

42   THE CRIMINAL JUSTICE SYSTEM AND WOMEN

Women have many traits in common with children; that their moral sense is deficient; that they are revengeful, jealous . . . In ordinary cases these defects are neutralized by piety, maternity, want of passion, sexual coldness, weakness and an undeveloped intelligence (Ibid.:151).

Although women lack the higher sensibilities of men, they are thus restrained from criminal activity in most cases by lack of intelligence and passion, qualities which *criminal* women possess as well as all *men*. Within this framework of biological limits of women's nature, the female offender is characterized as *masculine* whereas the normal woman is *feminine*. The anomalies of skull, physiognomy and brain capacity of female criminals, according to Lombroso, more closely approximate that of the man, normal or criminal, than they do those of the normal woman; the female offender often has a "virile cranium" and considerable body hair. Masculinity in women is an anomaly itself, rather than a sign of development, however. A related notion is developed by Thomas, who notes that in "civilized" nations the sexes are more physically different.

What we look for most in the female is femininity, and when we find the opposite in her, we must conclude as a rule that there must be some anomaly . . . Virility was one of the special features of the savage woman . . . In the portraits of Red Indian and Negro beauties, whom it is difficult to recognize for women, so huge are their jaws and cheekbones, so hard and coarse their features, and the same is often the case in their crania and brains (Ibid.:112).

The more highly developed races would therefore have the most feminized women with the requisite passivity, lack of passion, etc. This is a *racist* and *classist* definition of femininity—just as are almost all theories of *femininity* and as, indeed, is the thing itself. The ideal of the lady can only exist in a society built on the exploitation of labor to maintain the woman of leisure who can *be* that ideal lady.

Finally, Lombroso notes women's lack of *property sense*, which contributes to their criminality.

In their eyes theft is . . . an audacity for which compensation is due to the owner . . . as an individual rather than a social crime, just as it was regarded in the primitive periods of human evolution and is still regarded by many uncivilized nations (Ibid.:217).

One may question this statement on several levels. Can it be assumed to have any validity at all, or is it false that women have a different sense of property than men? If it is valid to a degree, is it related to women's lack of property ownership and nonparticipation in the accumulation of capitalist wealth? Indeed, as Thomas (1907) points out, women are considered property themselves. At any rate, it is an interesting point in Lombroso's book that has only been touched on by later writers, and always in a manner supportive of the institution of private property.

THOMAS: "THE STIMULATION SHE CRAVES"

The works of W. I. Thomas are critical in that they mark a transition from purely physiological explanations such as Lombroso's to more sophisticated theories that embrace physiological, psychological and social-structural factors. However, even the most sophisticated explanations of female crime rely on implicit assumptions about the *biological* nature of women. In Thomas' *Sex and Society* (1907) and *The Unadjusted Girl* (1923), there are important contradictions in the two approaches that are representative of the movements during that period between publication dates: a departure from biological Social-Darwinian theories to complex analyses of the interaction between society and the individual, i.e., societal repression and manipulation of the "natural" wishes of persons.

In *Sex and Society* (1907), Thomas poses basic biological differences between the sexes as his starting point. Maleness is "katabolic," the animal force which is destructive of energy and allows men the possibility of creative work through this outward flow. Femaleness is "anabolic," analogous to a plant which stores energy, and is motionless and conservative. Here Thomas is offering his own version of the age-old male/female dichotomy expressed by Lombroso and elaborated on in Freud's paradigm, in the structural-functionalist "instrumental-expressive" duality, and in other analyses of the status quo. According to Thomas, the dichotomy is most highly developed in the most civilized races, due to the greater differentiation of sex roles. This statement ignores the hard physical work done by poor *white* women at home and in the factories and offices in "civilized" countries, and accepts a *ruling-class* definition of femininity.

The cause of women's relative decline in stature in more "civilized" countries is a subject on which Thomas is ambivalent. At one point he attributes it to the lack of "a superior fitness on the motor side" in women (Ibid.:94); at another point, he regards her loss of *sexual freedom* as critical, with the coming of monogamy and her confinement to sexual tasks such as wifehood and motherhood. He perceptively notes:

Women were still further degraded by the development of property and its control by man, together with the habit of treating her as a piece of property, whose value was enhanced if its purity was assured (Ibid.:297).

However, Thomas' underlying assumptions in his explanations of the inferior status of women are *physiological ones*. He attributes to men high amounts of sexual energy, which lead them to pursue women for their sex,

44   THE CRIMINAL JUSTICE SYSTEM AND WOMEN

and he attributes to women maternal feelings devoid of sexuality, which
lead *them* to exchange sex for domesticity. Thus monogamy, with chastity
for women, is the *accommodation* of these basic urges, and women are domes-
ticated while men assume leadership, in a true market exchange.

Why, then, does Thomas see problems in the position of women? It is
because modern women are plagued by "irregularity, pettiness, ill health
and inserviceableness" (Ibid.:245). Change is required to maintain *social
harmony*, apart from considerations of women's needs, and women must be
educated to make them better wives, a theme reiterated throughout this
century by "liberals" on the subject. Correctly anticipating a threat,
Thomas urges that change be made to stabilize the family, and warns that
"no civilization can remain the highest if another civilization adds to the
intelligence of its men the intelligence of its women" (Ibid.:314). Thomas
is motivated by considerations of social integration. Of course, one might
question how women are to be able to contribute much if they are indeed
anabolic. However, due to the transitional nature of Thomas' work, there
are immense contradictions in his writing.

Many of Thomas' specific assertions about the nature of women are
indistinguishable from Lombroso's; they both delineate a biological hierarchy along race and sex lines.

> Man has, in short, become more somatically specialized an animal than women, and
> feels more keenly any disturbance of normal conditions with which he has not the
> same physiological surplus as woman with which to meet the disturbance . . . It is a
> logical fact, however, that the lower human races, the lower classes of society, women
> and children show something of the same quality in their superior tolerance of surgical
> disease (Ibid.:36).

Like Lombroso, Thomas is crediting women with superior capabilities of
survival because they are further down the scale in terms of evolution. It
is significant that Thomas includes the lower classes in his observation; is
he implying that the lower classes are in their position *because* of their
natural unfitness, or perhaps that their *situation* renders them less sensitive
to pain? At different times, Thomas implies both. Furthermore, he agrees
with Lombroso that women are more nearly uniform than men, and says
that they have a smaller percentage of "genius, insanity and idiocy"
(Ibid.:45) than men, as well as fewer creative outbursts of energy.

Dealing with female criminality in *Sex and Society* (1907), Thomas begins
to address the issue of morality, which he closely links to legality from a
standpoint of maintaining social order. He discriminates between male and
female morality:

> Morality as applied to men has a larger element of the contractual, representing the
> adjustment of his activities to those of society at large, or more particularly to the

activities of the male members of society; while the morality which we think of in connection with women shows less of the contractual and more of the personal, representing her adjustment to men, more particularly the adjustment of her person to men (Ibid.:172).

Whereas Lombroso barely observes women's lack of participation in the institution of private property, Thomas' perception is more profound. He points out that women *are* property of men and that their conduct is subject to different codes.

Morality, in the most general sense, represents the code under which activities are best carried on and is worked out in the school of experience. It is preeminently an adult and male system, and men are intelligent enough to realize that neither women nor children have passed through this school. It is on this account that man is merciless to woman from the standpoint of personal behavior, yet he exempts her from anything in the way of contractual morality, or views her defections in this regard with allowance and even with amusement (Ibid.:234).

Disregarding his remarks about intelligence, one confronts the critical point about women with respect to the law: because they occupy a *marginal* position in the productive sphere of exchange commodities outside the home, they in turn occupy a marginal position in regard to "contractual" law which regulates relations of property and production. The argument of differential treatment of men and women by the law is developed in later works by Pollak and others, who attribute it to the "chivalry" of the system which is lenient to women committing offenses. As Thomas notes, however, women are simply not a serious *threat* to property, and are treated more "leniently" because of this. Certain women do become threats by transcending (or by being denied) their traditional role, particularly many Third World women and political rebels, and they are *not* afforded chivalrous treatment! In fact, chivalry is reserved for the women who are least likely to ever come in contact with the criminal justice system: the ladies, or white middle-class women. In matters of *sexual* conduct, however, which embody the double standard, women are rigorously prosecuted by the law. As Thomas understands, this is the sphere in which women's functions *are* critical. Thus it is not a matter of "chivalry" how one is handled, but of different forms and thrusts of social control applied to men and women. Men are engaged in productive tasks and their activities in this area *are* strictly curtailed.

In *The Unadjusted Girl* (1923), Thomas deals with female delinquency as a "normal" response under certain social conditions, using assumptions about the nature of women which he leaves unarticulated in this work. Driven by basic "wishes," an individual is controlled by society in her activities through institutional transmission of codes and mores. Depending on how they are manipulated, wishes can be made to serve social or

46   THE CRIMINAL JUSTICE SYSTEM AND WOMEN

antisocial ends. Thomas stresses the institutions that socialize, such as the family, giving people certain "definitions of the situation." He confidently —and defiantly—asserts:

> There is no individual energy, no unrest, no type of wish, which cannot be sublimated and made socially useful. From this standpoint, the problem is not the right of society to protect itself from the disorderly and antisocial person, but the right of the disorderly and antisocial person to be made orderly and socially valuable . . . The problem of society is to produce the right attitudes in its members (Ibid.:232-233).

This is an important shift in perspective, from the traditional libertarian view of protecting society by punishing transgressors, to the *rehabilitative* and *preventive* perspective of crime control that seeks to control *minds* through socialization rather than to merely control behavior through punishment. The autonomy of the individual to choose is seen as the product of his environment which the state can alter. This is an important refutation of the Lombrosian biological perspective, which maintains that there are crime-prone individuals who must be locked up, sterilized or otherwise incapacitated. Today, one can see an amalgamation of the two perspectives in new theories of "behavior control" that use tactics such as conditioning and brain surgery, combining biological and environmental viewpoints.[3]

Thomas proposes the manipulation of individuals through institutions to prevent antisocial attitudes, and maintains that there is no such person as the "crime prone" individual. A hegemonic system of belief can be imposed by sublimating natural urges and by correcting the poor socialization of slum families. In this perspective, the *definition* of the situation rather than the situation *itself* is what should be changed; a situation is what someone *thinks* it is. The response to a criminal woman who is dissatisfied with her conventional sexual roles is to change not the roles, which would mean widespread social transformations, but to change her attitudes. This concept of civilization as repressive and the need to adjust is later refined by Freud.

Middle class women, according to Thomas, commit little crime because they are socialized to sublimate their natural desires and to behave well, treasuring their chastity as an investment. The poor woman, however, "is not immoral, because this implies a loss of morality, but amoral" (Ibid.:98). Poor women are not objectively driven to crime; they long for it. Delinquent girls are motivated by the desire for excitement or "new experience," and forget the repressive urge of "security." However, these desires are well within Thomas' conception of *femininity*: delinquents are not rebelling against womanhood, as Lombroso suggests, but merely acting it out illegally. Davis and Pollak agree with this notion that delinquent women are not "different" from nondelinquent women.

Thomas maintains that it is not sexual desire that motivates delinquent girls, for they are no more passionate than other women, but they are *manipulating* male desires for sex to achieve their own ulterior ends.

> The beginning of delinquency in girls is usually an impulse to get amusement, adventure, pretty clothes, favorable notice, distinction, freedom in the larger world . . . The girls have usually become 'wild' before the development of sexual desire, and their casual sex relations do not usually awaken sex feeling. Their sex is used as a condition of the realization of other wishes. It is their capital (Ibid.:109).

Here Thomas is expanding on the myth of the manipulative woman, who is cold and scheming and vain. To him, good female sexual behavior is a protective measure—"instinctive, of course" (1907:241), whereas male behavior is uncontrollable as men are caught by helpless desires. This is the common Victorian notion of the woman as seductress which in turn perpetuates the myth of a lack of real sexuality to justify her responsibility for upholding sexual mores. Thomas uses a market analogy to female virtue: good women *keep* their bodies as capital to sell in matrimony for marriage and security, whereas bad women *trade* their bodies for excitement. One notes, of course, the familiar dichotomy. It is difficult, in this framework, to see how Thomas can make *any* moral distinctions, since morality seems to be merely good business sense. In fact, Thomas' yardstick is social harmony, necessitating *control*.

Thomas shows an insensitivity to real human relationships and needs. He also shows ignorance of economic hardships in his denial of economic factors in delinquency.

> An unattached woman has a tendency to become an adventuress not so much on economic as on psychological grounds. Life is rarely so hard that a young woman cannot earn her bread; but she cannot always live and have the stimulation she craves (Ibid.:241).

This is an amazing statement in an era of mass starvation and illness! He rejects economic causes as a possibility at all, denying its importance in criminal activity with as much certainty as Lombroso, Freud, Davis, Pollak and most other writers.

FREUD: "BEAUTY, CHARM AND SWEETNESS"

The Freudian theory of the position of women is grounded in explicit biological assumptions about their nature, expressed by the famous 'Anatomy is Destiny." Built upon this foundation is a construction incorporating psychological and social-structural factors.

Freud himself sees women as anatomically inferior; they are destined to be wives and mothers, and this admittedly an inferior destiny as befits the

48   THE CRIMINAL JUSTICE SYSTEM AND WOMEN

inferior sex. The root of this inferiority is that women's *sex organs* are inferior to those of men, a fact *universally* recognized by children in the Freudian scheme. The girl assumes that she has lost a penis as punishment, is traumatized, and grows up envious and revengeful. The boy also sees the girl as having lost a penis, fears a similar punishment himself, and dreads the girl's envy and vengeance. Feminine traits can be traced to the inferior genitals themselves, or to women's inferiority complex arising from their response to them: women are exhibitionistic, narcissistic, and attempt to compensate for their lack of a penis by being well-dressed and physically beautiful. Women become mothers trying to replace the lost penis with a baby. Women are also masochistic, as Lombroso and Thomas have noted, because their *sexual* role is one of receptor, and their sexual pleasure consists of pain. This woman, Freud notes, is the *healthy* woman. In the familiar dichotomy, the men are aggressive and pain inflicting. Freud comments:

> The male pursues the female for the purposes of sexual union, seizes hold of her, and penetrates into her . . . by this you have precisely reduced the characteristic of masculinity to the factor of aggressiveness (Millett, 1970:189).

Freud, like Lombroso and Thomas, takes the notion of men's activity and women's inactivity and *reduces* it to the sexual level, seeing the sexual union itself through Victorian eyes; ladies don't move.

Women are also inferior in the sense that they are concerned with personal matters and have little social sense. Freud sees civilization as based on repression of the sex drive, where it is the duty of men to repress their strong instincts in order to get on with the worldly business of civilization. Women, on the other hand,

> have little sense of justice, and this is no doubt connected with the preponderance of envy in their mental life; for the demands of justice are a modification of envy; they lay down the conditions under which one is willing to part with it. We also say of women that their social interests are weaker than those of men and that their capacity for the sublimation of their instincts is less (1933:183).

Men are capable of sublimating their individual needs because they rationally perceive the Hobbesian conflict between those urges and social needs. Women are emotional and incapable of such an adjustment because of their innate inability to make such rational judgments. It is only fair then that they should have a marginal relation to production and property.

In this framework, the deviant woman is one who is attempting to be a *man*. She is aggressively rebellious, and her drive to accomplishment is the expression of her longing for a penis; this is a hopeless pursuit, of course, and she will only end up "neurotic." Thus the deviant woman should be treated and helped to *adjust* to her sex role. Here again, as in Thomas' writing, is the notion of individual accommodation that repudiates the possibility of social change.

In a Victorian fashion, Freud rationalizes women's oppression by glorifying their duties as wives and mothers:

It is really a stillborn thought to send women into the struggle for existence exactly the same as men. If, for instance, I imagined my sweet gentle girl as a competitor, it would only end in my telling her, as I did seventeen months ago, that I am fond of her, and I implore her to withdraw from the strife into the calm, uncompetitive activity of my home . . . Nature has determined woman's destiny through beauty, charm and sweetness . . . in youth an adored darling, in mature years a loved wife (Jones 1961:117- 118).

In speaking of femininity, Freud, like his forebearers, is speaking along racist and classist lines. Only upper and middle class women could possibly enjoy lives as sheltered darlings. Freud sets hegemonic standards of femininity for poor and Third World women.

It is important to understand Freudianism because it reduces categories of sexual ideology to explicit sexuality and makes these categories *scientific.* For the last fifty years, Freudianism has been a mainstay of sexist social theory. Kate Millett notes that Freud himself saw his work as stemming the tide of feminist revolution, which he constantly ridiculed:

Coming as it did, at the peak of the sexual revolution, Freud's doctrine of penis envy is in fact a superbly timed accusation, enabling masculine sentiment to take the offensive again as it had not since the disappearance of overt misogyny when the pose of chivalry became fashionable (Millet 1970:189).

Freudian notions of the repression of sexual instincts, the sexual passivity of women, and the sanctity of the nuclear family are conservative not only in their contemporary context, but in the context of their own time. Hitler writes:

For her [woman's] world is her husband, her family, her children and her home . . . The man upholds the nation as the woman upholds the family. The equal rights of women consist in the fact that in the realm of life determined for her by nature, she experience the high esteem that is her due. Woman and man represent quite different types of being. Reason is dominant in man . . . Feeling, in contrast, is much more stable than reason, and woman is the feeling, and therefore the stable, element (Ibid.:170).

One can mark the decline in the position of women after the 1920's through the use of various indices: by noting the progressively earlier age of marriage of women in the United States and the steady rise in the number of children born to them, culminating in the birth explosion of the late forties and fifties; by looking at the relative decline in the number of

50   THE CRIMINAL JUSTICE SYSTEM AND WOMEN

women scholars; and by seeing the failure to liberate women in the Soviet Union and the rise of fascist sexual ideology. Freudianism has had an unparalleled influence in the United States (and came at a key point to help swing the tide against the women's movement) to facilitate the return of women during the depression and postwar years to the home, out of an economy which had no room for them. Freud affected such writers on female deviance as Davis, Pollak and Konopka, who turn to concepts of sexual maladjustment and neurosis to explain women's criminality. Healthy women would now be seen as masochistic, passive and sexually indifferent. Criminal women would be seen as *sexual* misfits. Most importantly, *psychological* factors would be used to explain criminal activity, and social, economic and political factors would be ignored. Explanations would seek to be *universal*, and historical possibilities of change would be refuted.

DAVIS: "THE MOST CONVENIENT SEXUAL OUTLET FOR ARMIES . . . "

Kingsley Davis' work on prostitution (1961) is still considered a classical analysis on the subject with a structural-functionalist perspective. It employs assumptions about "the organic nature of man" and woman, many of which can be traced to ideas proffered by Thomas and Freud.

Davis sees prostitution as a structural necessity whose roots lie in the *sexual* nature of men and women; for example, female humans, unlike primates, are sexually available year-round. He asserts that prostitution is *universal* in time and place, eliminating the possibilities of historical change and ignoring critical differences in the quality and quantity of prostitution in different societies. He maintains that there will always be a class of women who will be prostitutes, the familiar class of "bad" women. The reason for the universality of prostitution is that sexual *repression*, a concept stressed by Thomas and Freud, is essential to the functioning of society. Once again there is the notion of sublimating "natural" sex urges to the overall needs of society, namely social order. Davis notes that in our society sexuality is permitted only within the structure of the nuclear family, which is an institution of stability. He does not, however, analyze in depth the economic and social functions of the family, other than to say it is a bulwark of morality.

> The norms of every society tend to harness and control the sexual appetite, and one of the ways of doing this is to link the sexual act to some stable or potentially stable social relationship . . . Men dominate women in economic, sexual and familial relationships and consider them to some extent as sexual property, to be prohibited to other males. They therefore find promiscuity on the part of women repugnant (Ibid.:264).

Davis is linking the concept of prostitution to promiscuity, defining it as a *sexual* crime, and calling prostitutes sexual transgressors. Its origins, he claims, lie not in economic hardship, but in the marital restraints on sexuality. As long as men seek women, prostitutes will be in demand. One wonders why sex-seeking women have not created a class of male prostitutes.

Davis sees the only possibility of eliminating prostitution in the liberalization of sexual mores, although he is pessimistic about the likelihood of total elimination. In light of the contemporary American "sexual revolution" of commercial sex, which has surely created more prostitutes and semi-prostitutes rather than eliminating the phenomenon, and in considering the revolution in China where, despite a "puritanical" outlook on sexuality, prostitution has largely been eliminated through major economic and social change, the superficiality of Davis' approach becomes evident. Without dealing with root economic, social and political factors, one cannot analyze prostitution.

Davis shows Freudian pessimism about the nature of sexual repression:

> We can imagine a social system in which the motive for prostitution would be completely absent, but we cannot imagine that the system will ever come to pass. It would be a regime of absolute sexual freedom with intercourse practiced solely for pleasure by both parties. There would be no institutional control of sexual expression . . . All sexual desire would have to be mutually complementary . . . Since the basic causes of prostitution—the institutional control of sex, the unequal scale of attractiveness, and the presence of economic and social inequalities between classes and between males and females—are not likely to disappear, prostitution is not likely to disappear either (Ibid.:286).

By talking about "complementary desire," Davis is using a marketplace notion of sex: two attractive or unattractive people are drawn to each other and exchange sexual favors; people are placed on a scale of attractiveness and may be rejected by people above them on the scale; hence they (*men*) become frustrated and demand prostitutes. Women who become prostitutes do so for good pay *and* sexual pleasure. Thus one has a neat little system in which everyone benefits.

> Enabling a small number of women to take care of the needs of a large number of men, it is the most convenient sexual outlet for armies, for the legions of strangers, perverts and physically repulsive in our midst (Ibid.:288).

Prostitution "functions," therefore it must be good. Davis, like Thomas, is motivated by concerns of social order rather than by concerns of what the needs and desires of the women involved might be. He denies that the women involved are economically oppressed; they are on the streets through autonomous, *individual* choice.

52   THE CRIMINAL JUSTICE SYSTEM AND WOMEN

> Some women physically enjoy the intercourse they sell. From a purely economic
> point of view, prostitution comes near the situation of getting something for noth-
> ing . . . Women's wages could scarcely be raised significantly without also raising
> men's. Men would then have more to spend on prostitution (Ibid.:277).

It is important to understand that, given a *sexual* interpretation of what is
an *economic* crime, and given a refusal to consider widespread change (even
equalization of wages, hardly a revolutionary act), Davis' conclusion is the
logical technocratic solution.

In this framework, the deviant women are merely adjusting to their
feminine role in an illegitimate fashion, as Thomas has theorized. They are
not attempting to be rebels or to be "men," as Lombroso's and Freud's
positions suggest. Although Davis sees the main difference between wives
and prostitutes in a macrosocial sense as the difference merely between
legal and illegal roles, in a personal sense he sees the women who *choose*
prostitution as maladjusted and neurotic. However, given the universal
necessity for prostitution, this analysis implies the necessity of having a
perpetually ill and maladjusted class of women. Thus oppression is *built into*
the system, and a healthy *system* makes for a sick *individual*. Here Davis is
integrating Thomas' notions of social integration with Freudian perspectives on neurosis and maladjustment.

POLLAK: "A DIFFERENT ATTITUDE TOWARD VERACITY"

Otto Pollak's *The Criminality of Women* (1950) has had an outstanding influence on the field of women and crime, being the major work on the subject
in the postwar years. Pollak advances the theory of "hidden" female crime
to account for what he considers unreasonably low official rates for wom-
en.

A major reason for the existence of hidden crime, as he sees it, lies in
the *nature* of women themselves. They are instigators rather than perpetrators of criminal activity. While Pollak admits that this role is partly a
socially enforced one, he insists that women are inherently deceitful for
physiological reasons.

> Man must achieve an erection in order to perform the sex act and will not be able to
> hide his failure. His lack of positive emotion in the sexual sphere must become overt
> to the partner, and pretense of sexual response is impossible for him, if it is lacking.
> Woman's body, however, permits such pretense to a certain degree and lack of orgasm
> does not prevent her ability to participate in the sex act (Ibid.:10).

Pollak *reduces* women's nature to the *sex act*, as Freud has done, and finds
women inherently more capable of manipulation, accustomed to being sly,

passive and passionless. As Thomas suggests, women can use sex for ulterior purposes. Furthermore, Pollak suggests that women are innately deceitful on yet another level:

> Our sex mores force women to conceal every four weeks the period of menstruation . . . They thus make concealment and misrepresentation in the eyes of women socially required and must condition them to a different attitude toward veracity than men (Ibid.:11).

Women's abilities at concealment thus allow them to successfully commit crimes in stealth.

Women are also vengeful. Menstruation, in the classic Freudian sense, seals their doomed hopes to become men and arouses women's desire for vengeance, especially during that time of the month. Thus Pollak offers new rationalizations to bolster old myths.

A second factor in hidden crime is the roles played by women which furnish them with opportunities as domestics, nurses, teachers and housewives to commit undetectable crimes. The *kinds* of crimes women commit reflect their nature: false accusation, for example, is an outgrowth of women's treachery, spite or fear and is a sign of neurosis; shoplifting can be traced in many cases to a special mental disease—kleptomania. Economic factors play a minor role; *sexual-psychological* factors account for female criminality. Crime in women is *personalized* and often accounted for by mental illness. Pollak notes:

> Robbery and burglary . . . are considered specifically male offenses since they represent the pursuit of monetary gain by overt action . . . Those cases of female robbery which seem to express a tendency toward masculinization comes from . . . [areas] where social conditions have favored the assumptions of male pursuits by women . . . The female offenders usually retain some trace of femininity, however, and even so glaring an example of masculinization as the 'Michigan Babes,' an all woman gang of robbers in Chicago, shows a typically feminine trait in the modus operandi (Ibid.:29).

Pollak is defining crimes with economic motives that employ overt action as *masculine*, and defining as *feminine* those crimes for *sexual* activity, such as luring men as baits. Thus he is using circular reasoning by saying that feminine crime is feminine. To fit women into the scheme and justify the statistics, he must invent the notion of hidden crime.

It is important to recognize that, to some extent, women *do* adapt to their enforced sexual roles and may be more likely to instigate, to use sexual traps, and to conform to all the other feminine role expectations. However, it is not accidental that theorists label women as conforming even when they are *not;* for example, by inventing sexual motives for what are clearly crimes of economic necessity, or by invoking "mental illness" such as kleptomania for shoplifting. It is difficult to separate the *theory* from the

54   THE CRIMINAL JUSTICE SYSTEM AND WOMEN

reality, since the reality of female crime is largely unknown. But it is not difficult to see that Pollak is using sexist terms and making sexist assumptions to advance theories of hidden female crime.

Pollak, then, sees criminal women as extending their sexual role, like Davis and Thomas, by using sexuality for ulterior purposes. He suggests that the condemnation of extramarital sex has "delivered men who engage in such conduct as practically helpless victims" (Ibid.:152) into the hands of women blackmailers, overlooking completely the possibility of men blackmailing women, which would seem more likely, given the greater taboo on sex for women and their greater risks of being punished.

The final factor that Pollak advances as a root cause of hidden crime is that of "chivalry" in the criminal justice system. Pollak uses Thomas' observation that women are differentially treated by the law, and carries it to a sweeping conclusion based on *cultural* analyses of men's feelings toward women.

> One of the outstanding concomitants of the existing inequality . . . is chivalry, and the general protective attitude of man toward woman . . . Men hate to accuse women and thus indirectly to send them to their punishment, police officers dislike to arrest them, district attorneys to prosecute them, judges and juries to find them guilty, and so on (Ibid.:151).

Pollak rejects the possibility of an actual discrepancy between crime rates for men and women; therefore, he must look for factors to expand the scope of female crime. He assumes that there is chivalry in the criminal justice system that is extended to the women who come in contact with it. Yet the women involved are likely to be poor and Third World women or white middle-class women who have stepped *outside* the definitions of femininity to become hippies or political rebels, and chivalry is *not* likely to be extended to them. Chivalry is a racist and classist concept founded on the notion of women as "ladies" which applies only to wealthy white women and ignores the double sexual standard: These "ladies," however, are the least likely women to ever come in contact with the criminal justice system in the first place.[4]

THE LEGACY OF SEXISM

A major purpose in tracing the development and interaction of ideas pertaining to sexual ideology based on implicit assumptions of the inherent nature of women throughout the works of Lombroso, Thomas, Freud, Davis and Pollak, is to clarify their positions in relation to writers in the field today. One can see the influence their ideas still have by looking at a number of contemporary theorists on female criminality. Illuminating examples can be found in Gisela Konopka's *Adolescent Girl in Conflict* (1966), Vedder and Somerville's *The Delinquent Girl* (1970) and Cowie, Cowie and Slater's *Delinquency in Girls* (1968). The ideas in these minor works have direct roots in those already traced in this paper.

Konopka justifies her decision to study delinquency in girls rather than in boys by noting girls' *influence* on boys in gang fights and on future generations as mothers. This is the notion of women as instigators of men and influencers on children. Konopka's main point is that delinquency in girls can be traced to a specific emotional response: loneliness.

> What I found in the girl in conflict was . . . loneliness accompanied by despair. Adoles-
> cent boys too often feel lonely and search for understanding and friends. Yet in general
> this does not seem to be the central core of their problems, not their most outspoken
> ache. While these girls also strive for independence, their need for dependence is
> unusually great (1966:40).

In this perspective, girls are driven to delinquency by an emotional problem—loneliness and dependency. There are *inherent* emotional differences
between the sexes.

> Almost invariably her [the girl's] problems are deeply personalized. Whatever her
> offense—whether shoplifting, truancy or running away from home—it is usually
> accompanied by some disturbance or unfavorable behavior in the sexual area (Ibid.:4)

Here is the familiar resurrection of female personalism, emotionalism, and
above all, *sexuality*—characteristics already described by Lombroso,
Thomas and Freud. Konopka maintains:

> The delinquent girl suffers, like many boys, from lack of success, lack of opportunity
> But her drive to success is never separated from her need for people, for interpersonal
> involvement (Ibid.:41).

Boys are "instrumental" and become delinquent if they are deprived of the
chance for creative success. However, girls are "expressive" and happiest
dealing with people as wives, mothers, teachers, nurses or psychologists.
This perspective is drawn from the theory of delinquency as a result of
blocked opportunity and from the instrumental/expressive sexual dualism
developed by structural-functionalists. Thus female delinquency must be
dealt with on this *psychological* level, using therapy geared to their needs as
future wives and mothers. They should be *adjusted* and given *opportunities* to
the pretty, sociable women.

The important point is to understand how Konopka analyzes the roots
of girls' feelings. It is very possible that, given women's position, girls may
be in fact more concerned with dependence and sociability. One's under-

56   THE CRIMINAL JUSTICE SYSTEM AND WOMEN

standing of this, however, is based on an understanding of the historical position of women and the nature of their oppression. Konopka says:

> What are the reasons for this essential loneliness in girls? Some will be found in the nature of being an adolescent girl, in her biological makeup and her particular position in her culture and time (Ibid.).

Coming from a Freudian perspective, Konopka's emphasis on female emotions as cause for delinquency, which ignores economic and social factors, is questionable. She employs assumptions about the *physiological* and *psychological* nature of women that very well may have led her to see only those feelings in the first place. For example, she cites menstruation as a significant event in a girl's development. Thus Konopka is rooted firmly in the tradition of Freud and, apart from sympathy, contributes little that is new to the field.[5]

Vedder and Somerville (1970) account for female delinquency in a manner similar to that of Konopka. They also feel the need to justify their attention to girls by remarking that (while female delinquency may not pose as much of a problem as that of boys) because women raise families and are critical agents of socialization, it is worth taking the time to study and control them. Vedder and Somerville also stress the dependence of girls on boys and the instigatory role girls play in boys' activities.

Like Freud and Konopka, the authors view delinquency as blocked access or maladjustment to the normal feminine role. In a blatant statement that ignores the economic and social factors that result from racism and poverty, they attribute the high rates of delinquency among black girls to their lack of "healthy" feminine narcissism, *reducing* racism to a psychological problem in totally sexist and racist terms.

> The black girl is, in fact, the antithesis of the American beauty. However loved she may be by her mother, family and community, she has no real basis of female attractiveness on which to build a sound feminine narcissism . . . Perhaps the 'black is beautiful' movement will help the Negro girl to increase her femininity and personal satisfaction as a black woman (Ibid.:159-160).

Again the focus is on a lack of *sexual* opportunities for women, i.e., the Black woman is not Miss America. *Economic* offenses such as shoplifting are explained as outlets for *sexual* frustration. Since healthy women conform, the individual delinquents should be helped to adjust; the emphasis is on the "definition of the situation" rather than on the situation.

The answer lies in *therapy*, and racism and sexism become merely psychological problems.

> Special attention should be given to girls, taking into consideration their constitutional biological and psychological differences, and their social position in our male dominat-

ed culture. The female offender's goal, as any woman's, is a happy and successful marriage; therefore her self-image is dependent on the establishment of satisfactory relationships with the opposite sex. The double standard for sexual behavior on the part of the male and female must be recognized (Ibid.:153).

Like Konopka, and to some extent drawing on Thomas, the authors see female delinquents as extending femininity in an illegitimate fashion rather than rebelling against it. The assumptions made about women's goals and needs, including *biological* assumptions, lock women into a system from which there is no escape, whereby any behavior will be sexually interpreted and dealt with.

The resurgence of biological or physiological explanations of criminality in general has been noteworthy in the last several years, exemplified by the XYY chromosome controversy and the interest in brain wave in "violent" individuals.[6] In the case of women, biological explanations have *always* been prevalent; every writer has made assumptions about anatomy as destiny. Women are prey, in the literature, to cycles of reproduction, including menstruation, pregnancy, maternity and menopause; they experience emotional responses to these cycles that make them inclined to irrationality and potentially violent activity.

Cowie, Cowie and Slater (1968) propose a *chromosomal* explanation of female delinquency that hearkens back to the works of Lombroso and others such as Healy (1926), Edith Spaulding (1923) and the Gluecks (1934). They write:

> The chromosomal difference between the sexes starts the individual on a divergent path, leading either in a masculine or feminine direction . . . It is possible that the methods of upbringing, differing somewhat for the two sexes, may play some part in increasing the angle of this divergence. (Ibid.:171).

This is the healthy, normal divergence for the sexes. The authors equate *masculinity* and *femininity* with *maleness* and *femaleness*, although contemporary feminists point out that the first categories are *social* and the latter ones *physical*.[7] What relationship exists between the two—how femaleness determines femininity—is dependent on the larger social structure. There is no question that a wide range of possibilities exist historically, and in a non-sexist society it is possible that "masculinity" and "femininity" would disappear, and that the sexes would differ only biologically, specifically by their sex organs. The authors, however, lack this understanding and assume an ahistorical sexist view of women, stressing the *universality* of femininity in the Freudian tradition, and of women's inferior role in the nuclear family.[8]

In this perspective, the female offender is *different* physiologically and psychologically from the "normal" girl.

58   THE CRIMINAL JUSTICE SYSTEM AND WOMEN

The authors conclude, in the tradition of Lombroso, that female delinquents are *masculine*. Examining girls for physical characteristics, they note:

> Markedly masculine traits in girl delinquents have been commented on . . . [as well as] the frequency of homosexual tendencies . . . Energy, aggressiveness, enterprise and the rebelliousness that drives the individual to break through conformist habits are thought of as being masculine . . . We can be sure that they have some physical basis (Ibid.:172).

The authors see crimes as a *rebellion* against sex roles rather than as a maladjusted expression of them. By defining rebellion as *masculine*, they are ascribing characteristics of masculinity to any female rebel. Like Lombroso, they spend time measuring heights, weights, and other *biological* features of female delinquents with other girls.

Crime defined as masculine seems to mean violent, overt crime, whereas "ladylike" crime usually refers to sexual violations and shoplifting. Women are neatly categorized no matter *which* kind of crime they commit: if they are violent, they are "masculine" and suffering from chromosomal deficiencies, penis envy, or atavisms. If they conform, they are manipulative, sexually maladjusted and promiscuous. The *economic* and *social* realities of crime—the fact that poor women commit crimes, and that most crimes for women are property offenses—are overlooked. Women's behavior must be *sexually* defined before it will be considered, for women count only in the sexual sphere. The theme of sexuality is a unifying thread in the various, often contradictory theories.

CONCLUSION

A good deal of the writing on women and crime being done at the present time is squarely in the tradition of the writers that have been discussed. The basic assumptions and technocratic concerns of these writers have produced work that is sexist, racist and classist; assumptions that have served to maintain a repressive ideology with its extensive apparatus of control. To do a new kind of research on women and crime—one that has feminist roots and a radical orientation—it is necessary to understand the assumptions made by the traditional writers and to break away from them. Work that focuses on human needs, rather than those of the state, will require new definitions of criminality, women, the individual and her/his relation to the state. It is beyond the scope of this paper to develop possible areas of study, but is is nonetheless imperative that this work be made a priority by women *and* men in the future.

Notes

1 Quoted from the 1973 proposal for the Center for the Study and Reduction of violence prepared by Dr. Louis J. West, Director, Neuropsychiatric Institute, UCLA: "The question of violence in females will be examined from the point of view that females are more likely to commit acts of violence during the pre-menstrual and menstrual periods" (1973:43).

2 I am indebted to Marion Goldman for introducing me to the notion of the dual morality based on assumptions of different sexuality for men and women.

3 For a discussion of the possibilities of psychosurgery in behavior modification for "violence-prone" individuals, see Frank Ervin and Vernon Mark, *Violence and the Brain* (1970). For an eclectic view of this perspective on crime, see the proposal for the Center for the Study and Reduction of Violence (footnote 1).

4 The concept of hidden crime is reiterated in Reckless and Kay's report to the President's Commission on Law Enforcement and the Administration of Justice. They note:

A large part of the infrequent officially acted upon involvement of women in crime can be traced to the masking effect of women's roles, effective practice on the part of women of deceit and indirection, their instigation of men to commit their crimes (the Lady MacBeth factor), and the unwillingness on the part of the public and law enforcement officials to hold women accountable for their deeds (the chivalry factor) (1967:13).

5 Bertha Payak in "Understanding the Female Offender" (1963) stresses that women offenders have poor self-concepts, feelings of insecurity and dependency, are emotionally selfish and prey to irrationality during menstruation, pregnancy, and menopause (a good deal of their life!).

6 See Theodore R. Sarbin and Jeffrey E. Miller, "Demonism Revisited: The XYY Cromosomal Anomaly," *Issues in Criminology* 5(2) (Summer 1970).

7 Kate Millett (1970) notes that "sex is biological, gender psychological and therefore cultural . . . if the proper terms for sex are male and female, the corresponding terms for gender are masculine and feminine; these latter may be quite independent of biological sex" (*Ibid.:*30).

8 Zelditch (1960), a structural-functionalist, writes that the nuclear family is an inevitability and that within it, women, the "expressive" sex, will inevitably be the domestics.

References

Bishop, Cecil. Women and Crime. London: Chatto and Windus, 1931.

Cowie, John, Valerie Cowie and Eliot Slater. Delinquency in Girls. London: Heinemann, 1968.

Davis, Kingsley. "Prostitution." Comtemporary Social Problems. Edited by Robert K. Merton and Robert A. Nisbet. New York: Harcourt Brace and Jovanovich, 1961. Originally published as "The Sociology of Prostitution." American Sociological Review 2(5) (October 1937).

Ervin, Frank and Vernon Mark. Violence and the Brain. New York: Harper and Row, 1970.

Fernald, Mabel, Mary Hayes and Almena Dawley. A Study of Women Delinquents in New York State. New York: Century Company, 1920.

Freud, Sigmund. New Introductory Lectures on Psychoanalysis. New York: W. W. Norton, 1933.

60 THE CRIMINAL JUSTICE SYSTEM AND WOMEN

Glueck, Eleanor and Sheldon. Four Hundred Delinquent Women. New York: Alfred A. Knopf, 1934.

Healy, William and Augusta Bronner. Delinquents and Criminals: Their Making and Unmaking. New York: Macmillan and Company, 1926.

Hemming, James. Problems of Adolescent Girls. London: Heinemann, 1960.

Jones, Ernest. The Life and Works of Sigmund Freud. New York: Basic Books, 1961.

Konopka, Gisela. The Adolescent Girl in Conflict. Englewood Cliffs, New Jersey: Prentice-Hall, 1966.

Lombroso, Cesare The Female Offender. (Translation). New York: Appleton, 1920. Originally published in 1903.

Millet, Kate. Sexual Politics. New York: Doubleday and Company, 1970.

Monahan, Florence. Women in Crime. New York: I. Washburn, 1941.

[13]

Edwin H. Sutherland's White-Collar Crime in America: An Essay in Historical Criminology

Gil Geis
University of California, Irvine

Colin Goff
University of New Brunswick, Fredericton

Edwin H. Sutherland's monograph *White Collar Crime* has been called "the most significant book ever published in American criminology."[1] Within its pages, Sutherland documents in meticulous detail the criminal actions of the seventy largest American corporations throughout the early decades of the twentieth century. His work on white-collar crime was a hard-hitting exposé of corruption and law-breaking in corporate America, as well as a far-ranging critique of traditional criminological theory. His research flagellated corporate criminal violators and political corruption and was seized with his personal anger and anguish over what he regarded as the parlous state of morality in the upper echelons of American business. This study recreates the various stages of Sutherland's work on white-collar crime and reviews the controversy surrounding the development of his ideas on the subject. In addition, it examines the history of the publishing of his work and its reception in the scholarly and public presses. Based on the relevant published literature, the study also utilizes previously undiscovered archival material and personal correspondence.

Sutherland's monograph, published in 1949, was based on personal research that spanned the three decades of 1920–1950. His earliest research

1

efforts were sporadic, but as his involvement with the subject increased, so did his analytical and conceptual sophistication. Originally, he selected two hundred top corporations and then reduced them to seventy. He began with a study of economic crimes such as misleading advertising, restraint of trade, violations of monopolies, and illegal mergers and then changed his definition of white-collar crime and developed an interest in theoretical background and criticism, including the social, cultural, and psychological makeup of entrepreneurs and corporate officials. In the end, he wanted to show that corporations committed crimes on a normal, everyday basis; and because of their power and acumen and expertise in manipulating the laws that governed them, they were able to avoid being incriminated for their illegal activities. As a result, they were able to keep their illegal activities and those of their employees out of the purview of the criminal courts and the criminal justice system.

The Creation of the Concept of White-Collar Crime

Sutherland's first major presentation on white-collar crime came during his presidential address at the thirty-fourth annual meeting of the American Sociological Society, held in Philadelphia in December 1939. Perhaps the only attendant sociologists who realized the importance of the presentation were a few graduate students from Indiana University who had made the trip to Philadelphia. Sutherland certainly did not disappoint his small entourage. His address continues to have the distinction of being the most widely reproduced American Sociological Society presidential address in its history.

Sutherland's earlier work gave virtually no indication that he would suddenly turn his attention to white-collar crime. The first two editions of his criminology textbook paid no heed to this subject. It was not until the third edition was published in 1934 that Sutherland included a reference to the concept of criminality. In a chapter titled "Indexes of Crime," Sutherland noted that the political and economic realities of American society were changing at a dramatic rate, but that the legal codes were not developing at the same pace. This led to the creation of a new type of criminal, the white-collar criminaloid. "These white-collar criminaloids," Sutherland wrote, "are by far the most dangerous to society of any type of criminals from the point of view of effects on private property and social institutions."[2]

Later, in a speech before the Toynbee Club of DePauw University in Indiana, Sutherland (1956) would say that he had been collecting information on white-collar crimes since 1928, more than a decade before his ground-breaking presidential address. His earliest usage of "white-collar crime" is found in a 1932 article that advocated the use of the concept of "culture" in understanding the crime patterns of immigrants to the United States. Sutherland noted: "It is not suggested as a total explanation of delinquency even in the delinquency area, and it certainly does not explain the financial crimes of the white-collar classes."[3] In the book he coauthored with Harvey J. Locke, *Twenty Thousand Homeless Men* (1936), Sutherland employed the term "white-collar worker" as a classificatory category to distinguish the 7 percent of the people living during the depression in Chicago shelters for unemployed men who had been "professional men, businessmen, clerks, salesmen, accountants, and men who previously held minor political positions."[4] Obviously, the terms *crime* and *white collar* were prominent in Sutherland's professional vocabulary; given his subject matter, their association was almost inevitable.

Where did the term "white-collar crime" originate, and how did Sutherland define it? Sutherland, in the third edition of his textbook, attributed the term "white-collar criminaloid" to E. A. Ross's book, *Sin and Society* (1907). A review of Ross's book, however, shows no use of "white-collar," although the word "criminaloid" was frequently used. Sutherland obviously used "criminaloid" because Ross defined it as an individual who held a position of high status in society and committed a crime. According to Ross: "The immunity enjoyed by the perpetrator of new sins has brought into being a class for which we may coin the term 'criminaloid.'. . . By this we designate those who prosper by flagitious practices which have not yet come under the effective ban of public opinion."[5]

There were assuredly many other writers in the early decades of the twentieth century who testified about the extensive violations of the criminal law by those whose social authority and position protected them to a large degree from publicity, prosecution, or conviction. The majority of these writers were muckrakers, men such as Lincoln Steffens, Gustav Myers, and John T. Flynn, and this fact, too, may have influenced Sutherland to cite E. A. Ross. Sutherland, always the social scientist and intellectual, may have felt strongly about using an academic source in his textbook to put forward such an important criminological idea.

The only other term used by a sociologist that was similar to Ross's "criminaloid" was Albert Morris's notion of "upperworld crime," which appeared in his textbook *Criminology* in 1934. But one point is clear: Sutherland appears to have originated the term "white-collar crime," and criminologists have used his language ever since to denote the crimes of powerful businessmen and other persons who hold positions of social status and engage in criminal activities.

Exactly what Sutherland meant by "white-collar crime" remains vague,

4   CRIMINAL JUSTICE HISTORY

however. Sutherland, who once referred to "white-collar crime" as a "verbal convenience," noted in his 1949 monograph that he meant to employ this term in the sense that Alfred A. Sloan, Jr., did—that is, "principally" to refer to business managers and executives.[6] It is an eccentric reference. Sloan, who had become the president of General Motors Corporation, made a fortune during the halcyon days of the automobile industry. Certainly Sutherland didn't mean to restrict his inquiries to men of Sloan's enormous wealth and power. A biographical sketch of Sloan notes that he characteristically wore collars "of an arresting height and as stiff as a Buick mudguard."[7] Perhaps, if he knew of this, Sutherland was impressed enough with its symbolism to have Sloan represent the class whose crimes form Sutherland's research topic.

The Historical Background of White-Collar Crime, 1930–1934

Sutherland had begun his first organized research into white-collar crimes while he was employed as a researcher in the sociology department at the University of Chicago in 1933. In a letter sent to the Social Science Research Committee of the University of Chicago, Sutherland had requested financial support for a preliminary study of white-collar criminals. His proposal read:

> This study opens a field which is comparatively new. In my opinion be-
> haviouristic studies in the field of crime will be more profitable if the concept of
> crime is divided into smaller and more homogeneous units of some sort. Before
> such smaller units can be defined more information on several types of serious
> crimes, of which the white collar crimes are most important, should be secured.
> The study thus far has been concentrated on embezzlers. Two or more useful
> articles could be written on the basis of the data secured, but it seems preferable
> to pursue the study for a period of several years rather than aim for immediate
> publication.[8]

Thus, at the time of his original application for funds, Sutherland had already accumulated data on one type of white-collar criminal, the embezzler. It is also instructive to emphasize that, at this time, Sutherland seems to have supported the idea of breaking down and isolating various types of criminal acts from each other to gain a better understanding of each one. This, of course, is in marked contrast to his later efforts to develop the grand theory of differential association, which attempted to include and explain all criminal acts.

One month later, on June 25, 1933, Sutherland sent a second letter to the Social Science Research Committee to inform them that he had completed his preliminary studies on white-collar crime:

> Several statistical series showing trends of embezzlement in comparison with
> other crimes against property complete; analysis of all available records in the

office of District Attorney, and of selected cases in the office of the State's Attorney and of fidelity bonding companies; interviews with embezzlers in prison. Valuable material has been secured but the study should be completed.[9]

The fact that Sutherland first used embezzlers as his example of white-collar criminality is probably the result of the trial of Samuel Insull, a Chicago public utility magnate.[10] Insull (1859–1938) was charged by the United States government with twenty-five counts of mail fraud and one additional count of embezzlement in October 1932. The trial, which gained national attention, lasted two months (October–November 1934) and ended with the complete dismissal of all counts and charges. Marshall Clinard, the noted American criminologist, contends that it was Insull's trial that spurred Sutherland into his first study of white-collar criminals, a contention that gains credence by the fact that Insull was the only individual that Sutherland used as an example of an embezzler in both the third and fourth editions of his textbook. Clinard, a student of Sutherland's criminology seminars at the time, also recollects that Sutherland was upset over Insull's statements after the trial, particularly the comment that "every man has a price," and that he had acted only as every banker and business magnate did in the course of business.

Sutherland was astounded when the jury acquitted Insull and found it ironic that an individual of Insull's social standing could be acquitted of all charges even though his crimes involved greater social injury than did the offences of a convicted murderer such as Nathan Leopold—a person who, he thought, would probably never be paroled. What was even more outrageous to Sutherland was the fact that Insull received much more public support for his actions. The mere mention of Leopold's name aroused public outrage, even though Leopold, in Sutherland's opinion, would never again murder. This difference in public sentiment toward Insull and Leopold, he once told a graduate student seminar at Indiana University in the late 1930s, was wrong.[11]

Sutherland was not the only individual astounded by the jury's decision to acquit Insull. John T. Flynn, a member of the same Federal Trade Commission investigating committee that had indicted Insull in the first place, wrote in the magazine *The New Republic* about Insull's full acquittal: "I don't think we manage the vengeance of the financial offender very well."[12] *The Nation* argued in an editorial that the financial decision in the Insull case "illustrates once more the difficulty of sending a rich man to jail, no matter how flagrant his crime."[13]

In 1937–1938, Sutherland employed Fred Strodtbeck, one of his graduate research assistants at Indiana University, to conduct research regarding

6 CRIMINAL JUSTICE HISTORY

the Federal Trade Commission's investigation into public utilities for any information concerning criminal activities. Strodtbeck, now a professor of Sociology at the University of Chicago, having no prior knowledge of big business, found such research a bit tedious. Once a week Strodtbeck would visit Sutherland to go over his notes and discuss their investigations.[14]

One of the chapters in his monograph *White Collar Crime* analyzes the performances and criminal records of fifteen power and light corporations. This is an interesting addition since they—along with transportation, communication, and petroleum corporations—were not included in the list of the seventy largest American corporations that comprised the majority of Sutherland's analysis. Why Sutherland chose to include a chapter on power and light corporations and not the other three industries perhaps can be explained by his animosity to Samuel Insull and his activities in the early 1930s. Sutherland directed some of his severest criticisms toward public utility corporations. He compared them with the Nazis and commented that they were worse offenders than professional thieves because they had the power to influence lawmakers. "Professional thieves," Sutherland wrote, "would not be able to fight effectively against a bill designed to stop professional theft, but the utility corporations have been more powerful than professional thieves and more effective in their efforts."[15] The fact that utility corporations were successful in heading off laws related to fraud did not, in Sutherland's view, make them any less criminal.

Sutherland's study of embezzlers continued throughout his career at Chicago, and, just two months before his departure to Indiana University— where he was to become the chairperson of the Department of Sociology—he sent his final piece of correspondence on this subject to the Social Science Research Committee. The status of this project was discussed in one short line: "materials collected, analysis started; manuscript may be completed at end of one year."[16] It was to take another fourteen years, however, before his material on white-collar crime was to be published, and it would contain only four references to embezzlers.

Indiana University, 1935–1939

The archivist at Indiana University reports no record of Sutherland's research projects between 1935 and 1939. All faculty members were required to complete yearly progress reports on their research projects; given his nature, it is doubtful that he failed to comply. Sutherland's reports may have been lost or mislaid. The development of his thinking on white-collar crime during these four years remains vague, although it is apparent he widened the scope of his analysis of white-collar criminals from embezzlers to that "class which is composed of respectable, or at least respected, business and professional men."[17] A few sociology graduate students who enrolled in Sutherland's criminology seminars during these years recollect that the subject of white-collar crime was a regular topic.[18] Faculty members also discussed the concept quite often in their informal discussions, which they held on a regular basis.

It was during his earlier years at Indiana University that Sutherland incorporated two major changes into his analysis of white-collar crime. The first was at the insistence of a graduate student, Mary Bess (Owen) Cameron, during a criminology seminar in the fall of 1938. Prior to this time, Sutherland had explained white-collar crime as the product of group conflicts over social mores. This was based on his belief that any type of group conflict caused crime; the definition of group conflict included conflicts in relation to such matters as religion, politics, and the standard of living. Cameron argued that this definition was too broad, that it should be narrowed to a more legal basis—namely, group conflict over law. The discussion between Cameron and Sutherland continued on for about a year, ending when Sutherland agreed to incorporate Cameron's point in his explanation of crime. The interchange occurred up until a few months before Sutherland's presidential address, and it was in the speech that the new emphasis was first evident.

The change dramatically altered the focus of Sutherland's work on white-collar crime. He originally had been arguing that white-collar crimes were *morally wrong;* now he stated that such crimes were criminal. But while Sutherland made this important change in his definition of white-collar crime, an element of moralism remained in his approach. The basis of Sutherland's moral stance was his contention that the administration of the criminal law that controlled white-collar offenses was, in fact, biased and unfair since it favored the wealthy and powerful. This, argued Sutherland, was clearly demonstrated by the fact that many white-collar offenses were clearly criminal in terms of their impact, although they were rarely so labeled. Sutherland believed that an act should be criminal (regardless of whether the provisions concerning it were in the criminal law, the civil law, or governmental agency regulations) if it met two requirements: (1) that the law was prescribed by a duly constituted legislative body, and (2) that the legislative body declared the act to be punishable and specified the sanctions that were to be imposed.[19] If these two criteria obtained, then the act should be considered criminal:

> White-collar crime is real crime. It is not ordinarily called crime. . . . It is called crime here in order to bring it within the scope of criminology, which is justified because it is in violation of the criminal law. The crucial question in this analysis is the criterion of violation of the criminal law. Conviction in the criminal court,

which is sometimes suggested as the criterion, is not adequate because a large proportion of those who commit crimes are not convicted in criminal courts. This criterion . . . needs to be supplemented.[20]

Convictions of white-collar offenders in a criminal court were not a good indication of the extent of such offenses because, in Sutherland's view, such offenders were afforded special legal privileges and were not stigmatized as "criminals." White-collar offenders were able to avoid conviction or were apt to be tried in a civil court or before an administrative commission.

Sutherland was preaching during his presidential address rather than basing his argument upon traditional legal principles. But perhaps this accounts for part of the power of his work on white-collar crime, for it transcends the limitations of the legal definition of crime, which would have trivialized his argument. Sutherland's moralistic stance has been described by the criminologist George Vold as a "real plea . . . for a change in the mores basic to attitudes about what is to be considered right or wrong in business practice."[21]

Sutherland also incorporated into his concept of white-collar crime a theoretical addition. This was a methodological technique known as analytical induction, which involved the selection of negative cases to test a theory. Analytical induction maximizes the discovery of negative evidence in order to refine or reject the original hypothesis, theory, or model that was under study. *Negative cases* don't necessarily invalidate the statement under investigation—they can also indicate its limitations. For example, the cause of much delinquent behavior may result from a single delinquent's differential association with other delinquents. But if a juvenile becomes delinquent due to other influences—e.g., the influence of the mass media—these exceptions wouldn't necessarily invalidate the original hypothesis; rather it would limit its inclusiveness to a specific type. The negative case thus becomes the basis for a different explanatory proposition.

Sutherland was introduced to the notion of analytical induction by Alfred Lindesmith, a member of the sociology faculty at Indiana University. Lindesmith had used this technique successfully at the University of Chicago in his Ph.D. dissertation, a study of drug addiction, which at that time was thought to be a result of psychopathological traits found within individuals. Lindesmith's final hypothesis, which he referred to as a "theory," was the result of introducing negative cases to evaluate the dominant explanation of drug addiction. Lindesmith's theory read:

Addiction occurs only when the opiates are used to alleviate withdrawal distress, after this distress has been properly understood or interpreted, that is to say, after it has been represented to the individual in terms of the linguistic symbols and

GIL GEIS AND COLIN GOFF 9

cultural patterns which have grown up around the opiate habit. If the individual fails to conceive of his distress as withdrawal distress brought about by the absence of opiates, he cannot become addicted, but if he does, addiction is quickly and permanently established through the further use of the drug.[22]

Lindesmith encouraged Sutherland to utilize the analytical induction approach in his study of white-collar criminals. Sutherland ultimately applied its principles in his research, and his theory of differential association is based in part upon this methodological technique. Frank Sweetser, another member of the sociology faculty at Indiana University at that time, recollects that Lindesmith "was full of the notion, and introduced it into most methodological discussions in those years."[23]

Sutherland was excited about the concept of white-collar crime because he felt that it supplied the necessary data, or the "negative case," that would ultimately support his theory that crime was learned and not caused by poverty or psychological deficiencies. Since white-collar crime did not fit the other theories—businessmen certainly weren't poverty stricken or pathological, and corporations certainly didn't experience toilet-training problems in their infancy—it created the possibility for a different theory (that is, Sutherland's theory of differential association) to fit the facts about criminality. It was one of Sutherland's favorite statements that "85 percent of anything could not be a cause. It had to be 100 percent or it was not a theory."[24] Indeed, if poverty didn't *always* cause crime, then poverty couldn't qualify as part of a theoretical causal statement.

Sutherland decided to select the occasion of his presidential address to introduce his concept of white-collar crime as a negative case of other theories of crime. He wanted to make his address both a memorable and a scientifically significant one.

The American Corporations and Their Criminal Records; Sutherland's Presidential Address, 1939

The data for Sutherland's presidential address came, not from his earlier research on embezzlers, but from the criminal records of the two hundred largest corporations in the United States. According to the early draft of Sutherland's speech, he checked the list of these corporations (which excluded banking and insurance corporations),

> against the reports of the various commissions which regulate such corporations for the purpose of learning which of these corporations during the last twenty years have had cases before these commissions which might logically have been tried in the criminal courts. To date I have completed only the reports of the Federal Trade Commission and I have found in these that more than one

hundred of the two hundred corporations have been accused of white-collar crimes. I suspect that by the time I have completed all of the available sources very few, if any, of them will show a clean record. Some of them have records which look like those of professional criminals.[25]

By 1939, then, Sutherland had moved from an individual (i.e., the embezzler) frame of reference to an analysis that viewed the corporation as a criminal. How and why he progressed from the individual to the institutional frame of reference is not clear. But by the time his monograph appeared ten years later, embezzlers were relegated to a minor position in the overall context of Sutherland's presentation.

Eight days before he was to read his paper on "The White Collar Criminal" at Philadelphia, Sutherland received the following letter from Croan Greenough, Assistant to the President at Indiana University:

Dear Dr. Sutherland:

I am sending a copy of the paper which you are to read next week at Philadelphia to Mr. Bartley, who will then return it for Mr. Wells to read. I took the liberty of reading the paper myself, and found it one of the most interesting and challenging I have read. I told Mr. Wells about it, and he is genuinely eager to see it when it comes back from the publicity office.[26]

This letter from an Indiana University administrator presages the impact that Sutherland's speech was to have, not only at the American Sociological Society meeting, but in the decades to come.

Sutherland's address, some 5,000 words in length, merits close analysis. The *Philadelphia Inquirer*, in a prominently placed news story on December 28, 1939, the day following the address, took note of Sutherland's talk in terms which suggested that it had pointed to a radical departure from accepted approaches to criminal-behavior theories. The report was headlined "Poverty Belittled as Crime Factor," with the subhead "Sociologist Cites Fraud in Business." Sutherland's audience of economists and sociologists was said to have been "astonished" by the presentation. Certainly the reporter was taken with Professor Sutherland's speech, which he suggested in a figurative sense "threw scores of sociological textbooks into a wastebasket."[27] The *Inquirer* writer's observation would prove more hopeful than prescient.

The *New York Times* also gave Sutherland favorable, albeit more restrained, coverage. Its news report suggested that Sutherland had launched a pointed attack against white-collar criminality. This is the first, though hardly the last, commentary that refused to take seriously Sutherland's patently disingenuous disclaimer at the end of the first paragraph of his paper. Sutherland said that he offered the comparison between crime in the upper class and crime in the lower class "for the purpose of developing theories of criminal behaviour, not for the purpose of muckraking or the reform of anything except criminology."[28] The *Times* story implied that the reporter knew better: he could recognize a muckrake when he saw one.

Perhaps fearing to seem defensive, both the *Inquirer* and the *Times* in their stories gave prominent mention to Sutherland's implied criticism of the press. In many periods, Sutherland asserted, more important crime news can be found on the financial pages than on the front pages of the nation's dailies. The papers also noted Sutherland's scarcely profound observation that white-collar crime of his day was more suave and deceptive than such crime had been in the time of the robber barons. They also found newsworthy the observation that much of white-collar crime was like "stealing candy from a baby"; that is, the matchup between offender and victim was highly uneven.

Following his presidential speech, Sutherland gave one of his students a copy of the address, and wrote on it: "written by Mary Bess Owen, read by Edwin H. Sutherland, and listened to by Lois Marie Greenwood when she wasn't thinking about something else."[29] This copy is now in the possession of Mrs. Cameron; when Lois Greenwood showed it to Mrs. Cameron's husband, the noted literary scholar Kenneth Cameron, he asked if they might have it. This handwritten comment of Sutherland's is indicative of the influence that Mrs. Cameron had upon the development of his thinking on white-collar crime; it was not something he would casually jest about.

Soon after he returned to Bloomington, Sutherland received a personal note from Read Bain, a prominent sociologist who had attended the American Sociological Society meetings in Philadelphia.[30] Bain was ecstatic about Sutherland's presidential address, calling it a "noble" speech and a brilliant piece of work, especially since he had placed white-collar criminals within a general theory of crime. Bain called white-collar criminals the most serious danger to society and the most inept criminals that existed. Bain's comment probably typified the reaction of many sociologists and criminologists; for Sutherland, it no doubt served as a source of inspiration in the coming decade.

Challenging Traditional Views

Much of Sutherland's research on white-collar crime between 1940 and 1945 was supported from the Graduate Research Fund at Indiana University. These funds enabled him to hire graduate students to investigate the frequency and type of corporate violations by analyzing the decisions of criminal and civil courts and governmental agencies and commissions. The graduate students, paid $50 to $60 a month, were instructed to focus upon one particular corporation or groups of corporations in one industry and to record all the relevant decisions for a specified time period. Each decision was copied verbatim by the students onto a separate sheet of paper and then handed to Sutherland, who occasionally wrote his comments concerning the case before placing it into the appropriate file.

The files, which were the basis for Sutherland's empirical work on white-collar crime, are now located in the Lilly Library at Indiana University. Seventy major American corporations were selected for study, and each had its own separate file. Included in the file was an overview of all the decisions that were made against the corporation. Besides court records, Sutherland gained information about the decisions made against the seventy corporations from popular magazines such as the *National Republic* and newspapers, including the *New York Times, Chicago Tribune*, and *Indianapolis Star*.

Sutherland didn't rely entirely on graduate students to compile information about corporations. He also personally reviewed the records of the corporations he had selected for study. Jerome Hall, a faculty member of the law school at Indiana University, recollects seeing Sutherland in the law school library reviewing decisions made against corporations virtually every Saturday morning for a number of years. Sutherland became so personally involved that his wife suggested that he stop working on white-collar crime until after he retired. Sutherland's progress on his final analysis of the white-collar crime data was slowed because of his continuing problem with stomach ulcers, the increasing amount of time his administrative duties as chairman of the Sociology Department were taking, and the fact that the Graduate Research Fund no longer provided him with financial support after 1945.

The majority of the files were complete by the end of 1944, at least to the extent that he could begin to make some initial compilations of his data. Less than a year later, he had finished an analysis of misleading advertising; restraint of trade; labor relations violations; and the infringement of patents, copyrights, and trademarks. He had also started to write the preliminary sections of a manuscript on white-collar crime.

Sutherland's motivation to study white-collar crimes was partly theoretical and partly moralistic. The theoretical purpose of his project was to develop a hypothesis that would include an explanation of all forms of criminal behavior. His scientific motivation arose from his personal dissatisfaction with the historical direction of criminological research and theory. His first sentence in *White Collar Crime* summarized his view of knowledge in criminology up to that time. "Criminal statistics," Sutherland wrote, "show unequivocally that crime, as popularly understood and officially measured, has a high incidence in the lower socio-economic class and a low incidence in the upper socio-economic class."[31]

Challenging the assertion that crime is basically a lower-class phenomenon explained by personal and social pathologies, Sutherland argued that contemporary theories of crime did not "consistently fit the data of criminal behavior . . . because the cases on which these theories are based are a biased sample of all criminal acts."[32] Respectable businessmen who violated the laws in the course of their occupational activities seldom lived in poverty or manifested the social and personal pathologies of lower-class criminals. General Motors Corporation didn't violate the law because of a broken home, or the Aluminum Company of America because of an Oedipus complex. "Such explanations do not apply to these violations of law, whether the violations be considered as behavior of corporations or as behavior of the persons who direct and manage the corporations."[33]

Sutherland believed that any explanation of crime that focused exclusively upon lower-class individuals overlooked the fact that the majority of the members of the lower classes did not commit crimes. Sutherland constantly emphasized that members of the upper class were socially powerful and thus able to avoid prosecution. He noted too that many of the sanctions regulating business were less punitive and rarely treated as harshly as conventional street crime.

As a first step in his effort to explain all types of criminal behavior, Sutherland placed his empirical data on white-collar crime within the framework of the theory of social disorganization. In his article "Crime and Business," he attempted to establish the need for this theoretical orientation by stating that a "hypothesis regarding white-collar crimes is that a crime in any culture area, such as the public utility industry or the medical profession, is a function of the ratio between organization for and organization against criminal behavior in that area."[34] Sutherland was following the ideas advanced by social disorganization theorists who argued that in complex industrial societies there were heterogeneous conflicting norms. In Sutherland's case, his concern was with corporations, and he was interested in the variation in crime rates between different groups of corporations.

Sutherland's paper, "Illegal Behavior of Seventy Corporations," presented at the University of Chicago in 1944, attempted to apply the social disorganization thesis to the crime rates of the leading seventy corporations in the United States. He found that differential social organization tended to promote or limit opportunities for criminal activities based upon a corporation's rank on the list of seventy corporations. More specifically, the number of violations of each particular corporation was, according to Sutherland, related to its position in the "social structure." He concluded that the first fifteen ranked corporations had twice as many adverse decisions made against them as the bottom ranked fifteen. The essential difference for Sutherland, however, was the type of industry with which a particular corporation was associated. He discovered that corporations in similar industries tended to cluster around certain types of violations. In his conclusion, Sutherland argued that corporate violations of the law were similar to high crime-rate areas in cities:

> Big business is similar to the deteriorated area of a city, with its organized crime, its ideology conducive to widespread violation of law, with no loss of status for an offender who is officially pronounced to be a violator of the law. In that sense, position in the social structure determines the opportunity and the need and differential association produces a diffusion among those in the same position of the techniques of violation of law and of the ideologies of criminal behavior.[35]

Once he had established support for the hypothesis of differential social organization, Sutherland proceeded to test a related hypothesis—the transmission of criminal norms among corporate executives. "These two hypotheses must be consistent with each other, if both are valid," Sutherland wrote, "since a crime rate is merely a summation of criminal acts of persons."[36] As a result, Sutherland began to develop his theory of differential association to explain white-collar crime. Both theories appear in the monograph *White Collar Crime*. Sutherland's theory of differential association was presented in the chapter entitled "A Theory of White Collar Crime," while his work on the theory of differential social organization was briefly presented in the chapter "Variations in the Crimes of Corporations."

The other motivating force for Sutherland to research white-collar crime was his moral indignation regarding such offenses. His moral indignation, however, was rarely displayed, probably as a result of the fact that he, at the time of his investigations into white-collar crimes, was caught in a sociological ethos that demanded from him a scientific and value-free analysis.[37] These professional norms no doubt had a strong influence upon Sutherland.

It was on rare occasion that Sutherland displayed any moral indignation over the subject of white-collar crime in published form. In *White Collar Crime*, there is only one passage where Sutherland allowed his emotions to be published. This is when he compared public utility company executives to Nazis.[38] Only one other was located in an extensive search of his files. In an unpublished article on "A & P, Propaganda, and Free Enterprise," Sutherland noted that corporate officials "lusted" for profits, which "per-

GIL GEIS AND COLIN GOFF   15

verted" capitalism.[39] Sutherland's moral indignation reflects a personal distaste for any type of economic system other than free enterprise, although he realized the government might have to regulate the economy to maintain fair competition. Corporations in a free enterprise economic system would probably take advantage of their position in a nonregulated economy to practice "cut-throat" techniques. Sutherland condemned the A & P corporation for its corporate policies, which he believed would lead to a socialist-styled economic system:

> Free enterprise can be maintained in a society only if the economy is controlled by free and fair competition. When free and fair competition breaks down, the society must control by legislation either in the form of regulation or of public ownership. A & P is an illustration of the corporations which have grown big because of profits acquired illegally. If the illegal practices of this corporation continue and expand, they will ruin the independent grocers. . . . A & P . . . has attained its ambition of 25 percent of the grocery trade in many communities . . . they may raise their sights to 40 percent or 60 percent and then expand to other communities. This would be similar to socialism except that the public would have no voice in the industry. . . . A & P . . . is driving the United States . . . away from free enterprise into a socialistic economy.[40]

Some of Sutherland's criticisms directed toward A & P were no doubt valid. The company may have violated the law and did not consider the public interest as a priority in its corporate policy-making. It is, of course, arguable whether the criminal actions of A & P and the other leading American corporations would eventually lead to a socialist-style economic system. Though corporations have continued to violate laws since Sutherland's study, the United States certainly does not have a socialist economy, despite ample government involvement and regulation. Sutherland's fear of socialism in the American economy reveals his moral indignation regarding the white-collar criminals and the possible latent ramifications of their actions. Sutherland was a supporter of capitalism, especially the free enterprise system, and displayed his wrath toward those he thought would destroy it by their illegal activities. Sutherland, indeed, had invested quite a substantial amount of his own personal funds in the stock market. Toward socialists, Sutherland reserved the criticism that "the redistribution of wealth may be highly desirable for other reasons but presumably not as a means of control of crime."[41]

Is White-Color Crime Really Crime? 1945–1949
A major issue for Sutherland to overcome before his manuscript on white-collar crime could be completed was to establish what was exactly meant by

the concept of white-collar crime. Sutherland had initially been criticized for his definition, but it was not until 1945 that he responded to his critics, at least in any published form.[42] His efforts until this time had been theoretical rather than definitional, but the latter issue was of such importance that he included one chapter in his monograph on the subject.

The major source of Sutherland's efforts to deal with the delineation of the term "white-collar crime" was the comments by Paul W. Tappan, a sociologist with legal training, on a paper, "White Collar Offenses," by the sociologist F. E. Hartung, which had been presented at the 1946 American Sociological Society annual convention. Tappan was the discussant of Hartung's paper and launched into a strong critique of the concept, focusing primarily upon the considerable definitional variation among criminologists and the fact that many blurred the distinction between criminal and civil law governing business legislation. Tappan pointed out that the definition of white-collar crime had variously been based upon social class, the inherent wrongfulness of an act, a violation of criminal (as opposed to civil) law, the consequences of an act, and the purposes for which such acts were committed. The definition of white-collar crime, Tappan maintained, was a convenient vehicle for those who wanted to make emotional statements about injustices found in the economic system.[43]

In part, Tappan's criticisms were clearly directed to Sutherland. In an earlier article, "Is 'White-Collar Crime' Crime?" Sutherland had altered his definition of the subject by stating that it was any act that the law described as socially injurious and for which it provided a penalty.[44] Thus, he had made the violation of any law, civil or criminal, a crime when it was "socially injurious" and had a penalty attached to it. Yet, in a letter he sent to Tappan immediately following the 1946 American Sociological Society conference, Sutherland agreed that there was a need for a clear definition of white-collar crime, and, if the definition wasn't grounded upon legal principles, it could be appropriated for propagandistic purposes. Sutherland also told Tappan in the same letter that he hoped to clear up some of the problems associated with the concept, although he never did.

The major difference between Sutherland and Tappan lay in the fact that Tappan insisted that an individual should first be convicted in a criminal court for an offense before the label "criminal" could reasonably be applied. Sutherland outlined his criticism of Tappan's view in a letter to his colleague, Jerome Hall, in the spring of 1947:

> My impression is that Tappan is absurd, and this quite apart from his remarks about "White Collar Crime." For purposes of study of criminal behavior, the important thing is that the behavior be defined as criminal and the procedure

which is used in a particular case is unimportant. His insistence on conviction in the criminal court is important from the point of view of definition of the behavior as criminal. The professional thief with whom I had considerable contact informed me of dozens of occasions on which he picked pockets and for which he was not convicted or even arrested. I do not have the least doubt that he was engaging in criminal behavior on such occasions.

I agree with Tappan that the term "white-collar crime" is used loosely by some [and] . . . should be restricted to those acts which can be justifiably designated as "crimes" from the legal point of view. This problem then goes back to the general principles of the law which define crime.

My position in general is that crime is a legal concept and is defined by general principles rather than by procedures used in a particular case.[45]

Tappan submitted an article, "Who Is the Criminal?" during the summer of 1946 to be considered for publication in the *American Journal of Sociology*. In it, he attacked the vague definitions of white-collar crime that he had previously criticized and appeared to disapprove of Sutherland's empirical work on the subject. However, in his discussion of substantive issues in the field, Tappan concentrated upon the writing of Harry E. Barnes and Negley K. Teeters, who had included a chapter on the concept in their criminology textbook *New Horizons in Criminology* (1943). This chapter, in contrast to Sutherland's rather meticulous and scholarly analysis, employed a popular and nonscientific approach that was criticized by a number of criminologists, including Sutherland. Tappan avoided a head-on confrontation with Sutherland in his article by not dealing with the issue of what is criminal and what is not, the matter that had preoccupied Sutherland.

In a rather surprising move, the editor of the *American Journal of Sociology*, Professor Helen Hughes, sent Sutherland the paper prepared by Tappan for evaluation. Perhaps sensitive to the fact that this was professionally unethical, Sutherland only gently criticized Tappan's paper, although he recommended that it not be published. Tappan's paper, however, did appear in the February 1947 issue of the *American Sociological Review*. Sutherland's review of Tappan's article in its entirety reads as follows:

Tappan's thesis is: Because criminologists often use the terms "crimes" and "criminal" loosely, criminology should be confined to a study of convicted criminals.

The first part of this proposition—that the terms are often used loosely—may be admitted and may be appraised as the author does, as very undesirable. The author does not throw any real light on this part of the proposition and the treatment is in the nature of invective rather than careful scientific analysis. If the first eight pages of the paper had been limited to one paragraph, it would be equally significant. For instance, I should welcome a careful criticism from the legal point of view of the concept of "white-collar crime." The author does not provide this and his statements regarding this concept indicate that he has not read or else not understood my attempt to define the concept in "Is 'White-Collar Crime' Crime?"

Even though the loose usage of these terms were accepted without qualification, this would provide no justification for the last part of the thesis that convicted criminals are the only justifiable object of study in criminology. No one can have a justifiable objection if some criminologist desires to limit his study to convicted criminals. This is very different from the proposition that all other criminologists should do the same thing. Conviction is important from the point of view of the authority of public agencies to administer punishment. It is not important as a definition of criminal behavior.

In general, I do not regard this article as making a significant contribution. Perhaps I should have refused to make an appraisal of this article, since it implies criticism of some of my own work. I have attempted to be as impersonal and objective as possible. I hope you will not depend upon my appraisal alone but will give other appraisals from persons not so intimately involved in the questions.[46]

That same year, in the fourth edition of his criminology textbook, *Principles of Criminology,* Sutherland extended the definition of white-collar crime to include those offenses which "are not even a violation of the spirit of the law, for the parties concerned have been able by bribery and other means to prevent the enactment of laws to prohibit wrongful and injurious practices."[47] Since some groups lacked ethical codes designed to protect the public interest, Sutherland felt that they, too, were committing illegal acts.

This new aspect of Sutherland's definition of white-collar crime frustrated legal scholars. Robert Caldwell, another legally trained sociologist, felt that the concept had now "deteriorated to the point where it can be used to refer to anyone who engages in what an observer considers to be unethical or immoral behavior."[48] The new definition was removed from the fifth edition of *Principles of Criminology* by Donald R. Cressey, who revised the book, and never appeared in the monograph *White Collar Crime.* It may well represent an example of the increasing extent of moral indignation felt by Sutherland toward the unethical businessman, the immoral politician, and the unprofessional doctor or lawyer. But this definition was too subjective to be accepted by most criminologists; it extended well beyond legal boundaries. One of Tappan's statements, made in the article published earlier in the year, is applicable to Sutherland's transient addition to his definition of white-collar crime. The result of such a definition, Tappan maintained, may be a "fine indoctrination or catharsis achieved through blustering broadsides against the 'existing system,' [but] it is not criminology and it is not social science."[49]

The controversy over a proper definition of the concept scarcely detracted from Sutherland's efforts to establish this type of criminal behavior as an important theoretical concern. Sutherland, in his monograph, attempted to stay out of a debate about how white-collar crime should be defined. He merely said that his usage of the term was "not intended to be definitive, but merely to call attention to crimes which are not included within the scope of criminology."[50]

An interesting aspect of Sutherland's development of his ideas on this subject is the fact that he rarely, if ever, interviewed any white-collar criminals. He read whatever case studies became available to him and then tried to fit their ingredients into his definition. Sutherland also scoured novels related to his subject, drew upon his own recollection of his work as a shoe salesman, and carefully read a large number of newspapers and magazines for source material. Sutherland was above all a library researcher on the subject of white-collar crime, no doubt in part because Bloomington, Indiana, was hardly a hub of financial power. Indeed, except for the year that he spent with the Bureau of Social Hygiene in New York City, Sutherland spent virtually all of his life far from the centers of political and economic power (and white-collar crime), where meaningful field work could have been undertaken at the source rather than with second-hand reports. Sutherland could not draw on friendship networks, personal discussions, or similar sources for information and viewpoints about the subject.

By the time of the appearance of Tappan's critique in the February 1947 issue of the *American Sociological Review,* Sutherland had finished his work. He was at that time editor of the sociology series at Dryden Press in New York City. Sutherland sent the manuscript to Stanley Burnshaw, president of the press, who accepted it for publication in 1948. It was taken in its original form, a fact that delighted the author. Sutherland recommended to Dryden that a few statements from prominent criminologists or legal scholars on the dust jacket would be desirable. He suggested that Thorsten Sellin, a criminologist at the University of Pennsylvania, be contacted for his views, as well as Milton Handler, a professor at the Columbia Law School. Handler replied to Dryden that criminal law was outside the range of his specialization, while Sellin enthusiastically stated that all criminologists were awaiting the publication of the book.

Just before he sent his manuscript to Dryden Press, Sutherland made a major alteration. Fearing that his monograph was too "statistical," he decided to render it "scientific" by adding the chapter, "A Theory of White Collar Crime," in which he attempted to explain it by the theory of differential association. By doing this, however, Sutherland trivialized the overall theoretical importance of his monograph. He had originally intended to prove that criminal behavior could be explained by "social facts" instead of by theories based on individual descriptions. By turning to his theory of differential association, he was returning to an individual frame of reference.

A difficulty with applying differential association, then, is that white-collar offenses, however they are defined, are extremely heterogeneous acts and are not susceptible to being understood by means of a rudimentary learning theory, such as differential association. Antitrust violations may resemble Medicare fraud in that the perpetrators have more education than do persons who commit muggings. But the fraud and restraint of trade cannot satisfactorily be explained by differential association. Emphasis upon differential association, in fact, deflects attention from significant ideological matters such as power relationships and other social structural issues.

Sutherland saw no need to make clearcut distinctions among the different types of white-collar crimes. For him, the same theoretical approach would do for any kind of business, professional, or political violation as well as for any other type of criminal law one. He believed that what he saw as sociologically unified groups (e.g., professional thieves) and as logically unified acts (e.g., white-collar crimes) should, for social scientific purposes, be considered analytical units and then all together be understood by means of differential association.[51] Indeed, the theory could no doubt be employed to analyze all human behavior, but it has never been taken at all seriously in other branches of sociology or psychology, despite its continuing vitality in criminology.

A problem developed in the early months of 1949 that almost delayed the publication of the book. The legal counsel for Dryden Press, Nathan Frankel, suggested that corporations might start legal action against the publisher for libel since Sutherland had called many of their actions "criminal," while in fact they had not been tried and found guilty in the criminal courts. Dryden Press brought Sutherland to New York to discuss this issue. Present at the meeting were Sutherland, Stanley Burnshaw, Donald Ambel—a partner in the publishing firm—and Frankel. Frankel pointed out to Sutherland that if the names of the corporations were included in his monograph, any of the corporations could start legal action against Dryden Press. This would leave Dryden moneyless since their accounts receivable would be frozen. Sutherland apparently readily agreed to have the names of the corporations deleted as well as a chapter entitled "Three Case Histories," in which he made a detailed review of the offenses committed by three of the seventy corporations: the American Smelting and Refining Company, the U.S. Rubber Company, and the Pittsburgh Coal Company. In Sutherland's opinion, the impact of the book would not be diminished even if the names were deleted. It would still be apparent to the reader that the normal practices of leading American corporations included extensive criminal activities, which was the main reason for his writing the monograph.

Sutherland rationalized the omissions by saying that they made his book more "objective" and most "scientific." Nonetheless, in a way he had been censored by the same corporations that he had tried to label. But it was really Dryden Press who felt threatened by the power of the corporations. To those who asked Sutherland for the names of the corporations, he sent citations to the court cases where the offenders' identity was easily found. He even looked into the statute of limitations to learn when he could publicly reveal the names of the corporations without fear of a libel suit and discovered that he could do this in the early months of 1953. It was a task he anticipated, but his death soon after the publication of the monograph kept the identities of the corporations protected. Indeed, not until 1983, thirty-four years after the publication of his "revised" monograph, was the unexpurgated version of *White Collar Crime* to be published.

The Critical Reception of *White Collar Crime*

Sutherland's monograph on white-collar crime was the publishing highlight in the field of criminology during the decade of the 1940s. The book was reviewed in a number of sociological and legal journals as well as in at least one popular magazine. Only one reviewer, Hermann Mannheim, was a respected criminologist. His assessment of Sutherland's *White Collar Crime* appeared in *The Annals of the American Academy of Political and Social Science*. Other reviews included those by Selden Bacon in the *American Sociological Review*, Lee M. Brooks in *Social Forces*, William Cole in *Federal Probation*, Robert Sorenson in the *Harvard Law Review*, Thomas Emerson in the *Yale Law Journal*, and an anonymous reviewer in *Harper's Magazine*.

Criminologists and sociologists were the most laudatory and generally reported themselves excited about the research possibilities that this field held. Mannheim was perhaps the most appreciative of Sutherland's work, calling it a "milestone" in the discipline of criminology and stating that it "should become the starting point of a new line of research."[52] Mannheim's accolade for *White Collar Crime* included the statement that Sutherland's "ingenuity, persistence, and courage in studying and exposing its meaning, extent, and danger to society deserve every praise." His one criticism centered upon Sutherland's use of analytical induction. Mannheim felt that Sutherland's "conclusion is hardly justified that if a certain factor is absent in some categories of crime it cannot be regarded as important in any of the others."[53]

Bacon called Sutherland's monograph "daring," for he had "challenged the arbiters of the alleged science of criminology." Bacon pointed out, however, that Sutherland had studied only a select group of offenders in the general category of white-collar crime. For Sutherland, "white-collar" referred only to a select group of corporations and executives, while for Bacon "crime" meant felony, leading him to suggest that a proper subtitle for the monograph would have been "Corporate Felony":

> The general impression of the book for many, however, will be that it is an attack on the male factors of great wealth. It does not appear that this was the author's conscious intention, but restriction of his subject to the very bad (i.e., felonious) actions of only the biggest corporations has its natural consequences. An analogous study might be one labeled *The Broken Family*, which concerned itself exclusively with divorce actions among millionaires. The coloring thus brought on in the present case, however, is explained by the character of criminology; Sutherland is neither sensation-seeker nor socialist. Nevertheless, that our largest corporations are proven the perfect examples of "recidivists" may evoke a lifted eyebrow or two.[54]

Even though *White Collar Crime* was, in Bacon's opinion, "restricted and unbalanced," he praised Sutherland for his attempt to lead criminology "out of a confined and unbalanced field."[55]

Lee Brooks, in his review of *White Collar Crime* for *Social Forces*, wrote that the monograph was "a hard-hitting and informative book, even for those of us long familiar with the point of view."[56] Brooks highlighted the passages in which Sutherland wrote that private collectivism had taken the place of free competition in the United States, and that if government regulation did not succeed any better than it had done with private capitalism, "we may adopt one of the systems in which the public has some representation: socialism, communism, fascism, or large-scale cooperative enterprises."[57]

William Cole called Sutherland's monograph a "valuable addition to the literature in criminology."[58] An anonymous reviewer for *Harper's Magazine* was not so enthusiastic, noting that "institutions, or institutional crimes, can never have the emotional impact of personal crimes, though the former may be just as—or more—reprehensible and injurious to society."[59]

In his review of *White Collar Crime* for the *Harvard Law Review*, Robert Sorenson, a law professor at the University of Nebraska, wrote that Sutherland's work "presents a deadly exposé of a way of life which society complacently accepts."[60] Calling Sutherland's insights "realistic" and "deserving excited promotion rather than mere reviewing," Sorenson was nevertheless critical of the application of the theory of differential association as an explanatory device for white-collar crimes:

> The reviewer's concern, however, is that crime be studied as realistically as possible and that, if we desire to define or study given violations of law, we appreciate their appropriate sources of motive power and effect. Differential association as a theory is adequate only when we fully assess the social forces that make it so.[61]

Emerson also praised Sutherland's work, writing that he felt a "powerful case" had been made by the monograph.[62] In his lengthy, five-page report—the most detailed of any of the reviews—Emerson pointed out that Sutherland had made some surprising errors. These mistakes, he believed, raised some doubts concerning the accuracy of the remainder of Sutherland's monograph and detracted from the overall impact of his argument. Emerson felt that Sutherland's monograph was too quantitative, with the result that he overemphasized "the existence of the violation"[63] while ignoring the importance of ascertaining a violation in the "character and significance in the whole operation of the corporation and in the enforcement of the law."[64] Emerson also believed that Sutherland overstated the need for criminal sanctions against corporations, since "in many cases the criminal sanction is far too cumbersome for practical use and that effective enforcement requires additional and more flexible measures."[65]

In addition, Emerson pointed out that Sutherland had made a few errors of fact, a surprising criticism in light of the author's usual meticulous scholarship. For example, Emerson pointed out that Sutherland had mistakenly asserted that the Norris-LaGuardia Act made collective bargaining obligatory upon the railways; actually, the obligation was imposed by the Railway Labor Act of 1926. Emerson also noted that the War Labor Act did not make collective bargaining mandatory during World War I, as Sutherland had written. There was, in fact, no such statute, and the only obligation arose out of a presidential proclamation. He also pointed out that the National Labor Relations Act was declared unconstitutional in 1937, not 1936 as Sutherland had written. These caveats aside, Emerson wrote appreciatively of Sutherland's monograph, indicating that his work deserved "the most careful and thoughtful consideration."[66]

The two positive law reviews would have pleased Sutherland. He had hoped that his monograph would receive some attention outside the field of criminology so that a wider network of individuals would contribute to the study of white-collar crime. Emerson concluded that Sutherland's "survey poses a crucial problem for American democracy. . . . It is to be hoped that many others will explore the paths he has opened."[67] Sorenson hoped that "as Dr. Sutherland's research is carried forward . . . investigations will be made into the manner in which white-collar criminality sets up chain reactions of still more white-collar crime."[68]

All the scholarly reviews of *White Collar Crime* anticipated more research in the field. Other writers soon followed Sutherland's work on white-collar crime. One of the first published reports was an analysis of the federal government's rationing and price control programs in World War II, published in 1952 and entitled *The Black Market*. In this monograph, Marshall Clinard presented evidence that violations of the federal regulations were so numerous and so extensive that they were, in fact, an alternate source of supply for scarce goods. He also noted that many violators of price regulations included some of the better known and more highly respected commercial corporations in the United States. In his research, Clinard found some support for Sutherland's theory of differential association:

> The majority of World War II black market violations . . . by businessmen appear to have had their origins in behavior learned in association with others. Unethical and illegal practices were circulated in the trade as part of a definition of the situation, and rationalizations to support those violations of law were transmitted by this differential association. Types of violations were picked up in conversations with businessmen and from descriptions of violations in trade journals and the press.[69]

Clinard, however, also argued that differential association could not explain all cases of white-collar crime. Some attention also needed to be given to personality factors: "Such a theory does not adequately explain why some individuals who were familiar with the techniques and the rationalizations of black market violations and were frequently associated with persons similarly familiar, did not engage in such practices."[70]

Frank E. Hartung found, as had Clinard, the same pattern of systematic avoidance and violation in his study of the wholesale meat industry in Detroit. Eighty-two companies, many of them established and respected dealers, were found guilty of 195 violations throughout a four-year period. For some companies, "illegal side-payments" were as much as 15 percent above the established ceiling price for given transactions. These illegal activities produced a profit advantage over and above the possible profits of competitors who observed the regulations and consequently had less meat to sell.[71]

A few other sociological contributions to the study of white-collar crime were published during the first few years after the appearance of Sutherland's monograph. Robert Lane, in his article "Why Businessmen Violate the Law," generally supported Sutherland's theory of differential association by stating that even when the management of a company changes, the participation in illegal white-collar activities usually continues. According to Lane, it "seemed to be the position of the firm, rather than any emotional qualities of its management, which led it to violate."[72] Lane, however, also recognized that individual managers might influence their firms to engage in such crimes, and that a possibility existed that personality characteristics might be important for understanding their causes.

A few years after the publication of *White Collar Crime*, however, interest in the subject waned to the point of almost nonexistence. It was not until the publication of a collection of readings on white-collar crime edited by Gil Geis in 1968 that interest revived. Perhaps the reason for this neglect was Sutherland's use of differential association to explain such crimes. Certainly data to test this hypothesis were difficult to obtain, since corporations refused to allow social scientists to interview their personnel or investigate their records.

Most of the studies of white-collar crime in the 1950s and 1960s portrayed an economy where criminal activity was tolerated and desired by corporations. Social scientists attempted to document the corporate processes that forced employees to violate laws. The literature that emerged was generally atheoretical, relying upon first-person accounts by corporate employees as their data rather than being guided by a grand theory.

A recent review of the criminological literature supports the fact, however, that the field has been virtually ignored since Sutherland's time. A survey of the one hundred most cited scholars in the field found Sutherland's work on white-collar crime to be the fourth most important contribution in criminology. But Sutherland's monograph *White Collar Crime* was ignored in terms of a concomitant count of citations. Becker's *The Outsiders* and Glueck and Glueck's *Unraveling Juvenile Delinquency* were found to have been cited a total of 648 times each. Cloward and Ohlin's *Delinquency and Opportunity* had 535 citations. Sutherland's work on white-collar crime had a mere forty-four.[73] The discrepancy between the scholars' ratings on importance on the one hand, and the actual number of citations in the work on the other, attests to a condition of benign neglect.

In addition, the same study found that out of nearly 3,700 reviewed books and articles, only ninety-two, or approximately 2.5 percent, dealt with white-collar or corporate criminality, even when studies on organized crime were included in the tabulations. If the organized crime studies were removed from the category, no more than 1.2 percent of all writings in criminology dealt with subjects such as corporate crime, fraud, embezzlement, corruption, and bribery.

A study conducted with respect to material included in *Sociological Abstracts* from 1945 to 1972 yielded the same result. In most of the years, there was no more than one article devoted to white-collar crime. The most in any single twelve-month period was nine in 1964, and most of these were on the subject of organized crime. The subject of white-collar crime as a criminological effort appears to have been something of a historical sport.[74]

Undoubtedly, the "importance" rating would have risen had more recent work on white-collar crime been conducted. Recent theoretical advances in the area of organizations has led to a renewed interest in research among criminologists. In this perspective, there is no restricting assumption that corporations "force" their employees to violate the law or that criminal acts are differentially learned. Rather, corporations are seen as presenting extremely tempting structural conditions—i.e., high incentives and opportunities, coupled with low risks—that encourage crime, both by employees and outsiders who seek to enter or use the system for criminal purposes. Examples of studies in the organizational perspective include medicaid fraud, false insurance claims, and securities fraud.

In this type of analysis, the organization is not viewed as benefitting from the crimes it promotes through its structural conditions. The crimes may even be regarded as inimical to organizational goals, though they may go unattended:

> The measures necessary to control internal crime are felt by the system's policy makers to be potentially even more damaging to the system's goals (in most cases, the goal of profit making). Therefore the structural conditions favoring crime are allowed to persist. . . . [This] system involves criminal activity as an unwelcome but unavoidable *cost* of doing business.[75]

Conclusion: The Career of the Concept

Sutherland's monograph revealed that crime was endemic in the American economy. White-collar crimes had permeated the social order to the extent that every corporation Sutherland analyzed had violated at least one law. Due to their power and status, however, corporations were rarely tried in a court of criminal law. They differed from criminals of lesser status in the administrative procedures used in dealing with them, since they were usually tried in administrative courts, far removed from public attention and scrutiny.

This differential application of the criminal law led Sutherland to question the standard criteria used to define criminal behavior. The traditional focus was upon the violation of a criminal law and conviction in a criminal court. Sutherland argued that since white-collar criminals frequently broke the law but were rarely convicted of a criminal offense, a different definition would have to be constructed to incorporate white-collar criminality. He believed that the definition of crime should be changed from those actions that were punished to those that were punishable.

In his analysis of white-collar crime, Sutherland ignored social structural concepts such as capitalism, social class, profit rates, competition, and business cycles. The question of the genesis of the laws governing such crimes in the United States was neglected in favor of a social psychological analysis of individual offenders. This attempt by Sutherland to place his analysis of white-collar criminals into an individual frame of reference is perhaps the most ineffectual aspect of his monograph. He believed that a single theory could explain the entire range of criminal behavior, and he placed that burden on a rather simple collection of statements about human learning that he called differential association. "Favorable" or "unfavorable" learning with respect to the imperatives of the criminal law was viewed by Sutherland as the process that distinguished noncriminal from criminal behavior.

As a result, Sutherland saw no need to make clear-cut distinctions among white-collar crimes. For him, the same theoretical approach would do for any kind of business, professional, or political violation as for any other type of criminal-law offense. Sutherland believed that what he saw as sociologically unified groups (e.g., professional thieves) and as logically unified acts (e.g., white-collar crimes) should, for social and scientific purposes, be considered analytical units and then be regarded together as susceptible to understanding by means of differential association. The theory, however, seems beyond scientific demonstration. Rather than discovering the genesis of criminal behavior, the theory of differential association appears to explain the diffusion of crime.[76] It is significant that the theory could be, with only slight modifications, employed to analyze all human behavior, but that it has never been taken as seriously in other branches of sociological or psychological research as it has in criminology.

The failure to draw distinctions among white-collar criminals led Sutherland to discuss, in some detail, the criminal activities of a shoe salesman, a used-car salesman, a manager of a shoe store, an insurance salesman, and a certified public accountant. With the exception of the accountant, none of the other occupations appears to fit into Sutherland's statement that white-collar criminals were persons "of respectability and high social status."[77] It would have been more congruent with Sutherland's definition if he had delineated the "criminal" careers of such noteworthy American business magnates as Henry Ford, Andrew Mellon, and John D. Rockefeller. Certainly they would have provided better empirical data for Sutherland's study of the malefactors of wealth in American society. Perhaps

28   CRIMINAL JUSTICE HISTORY

his rationale for the selection of "low-status," white-collar occupations is that they served the purpose of making the abstract ideas of his theory of differential association more relevant and concrete to his readers. Such occupations were also more readily discernible in Sutherland's own locale and demographic context. They surely created the impression of the extensive nature of white-collar criminality in the American economy.

Sutherland's interest in white-collar crime over-emphasized the individual criminal rather than the notion of corporations. This was similar to his other work in criminology, where Sutherland also focused upon the actions of individual offenders:

> In Sutherland's work we have a beautiful example of the shift in emphasis from the crime to the criminal. White-collar crimes did not exist before certain legal changes occurred. Why these changes occurred can be determined only by a study of law and society, not by a study of the criminal. The progress and development of criminal law has been due to social and economic historical forces. No evaluation of the personality of the individual criminal is going to substitute for a sociological analysis of crime.[78]

Among the difficulties associated with focusing upon the criminal is that it ignores the degree to which corporations control the legislative apparatus and dictates what is likely to be defined as criminal activity. It bypasses a test of the thesis that the state serves the interests of the corporations when it makes criminal laws regulating their economic activity. By continuing to concentrate upon individual offenders, Sutherland failed to appreciate how the same groups that were to be regulated might influence the regulating agency or turn proposed legislation to their own benefit.

The basis of Sutherland's inability to provide a structural analysis was that he was working within a scientific discipline that had no quarrel with the American economic and social system; and he, as a child of the discipline, had no inclination to offer radical alternatives to existing conditions. Instead, specific reforms, he felt, would enable all citizens to enjoy the benefits of American society and to have ample opportunities for upward mobility. Some businessmen, Sutherland believed, would have to be regulated to control their illegal activities, but the social system was basically good. Little effort, therefore, was made to study the role of the state and its interaction with the economic sector.

It must be recognized, however, that these criticisms are the kinds of backhanded accolades that make significant scholarly work. What must be attended to is Sutherland's determination to singlehandedly create a realm or area of pre-eminent intellectual and policy importance. Perhaps the most significant tribute that he could have ever desired can be found in the statement by the distinguished criminologist, Hermann Mannheim: "There is no Nobel Prize as yet for criminologists, and probably there never will be one, but if it had been available, Sutherland would have been one of the most deserving candidates for his work on [white-collar crime]."[79]

Notes

The authors wish to thank Dianne Bawn for her typing assistance.

1. Donald R. Cressey, *White Collar Crime: The Uncut Version* (New Haven, 1983). Cressey's comment appears on the back cover of the hard bound edition.
2. Edwin H. Sutherland, *Principles of Criminology* (Philadelphia, 1939), 37.
3. Edwin H. Sutherland, "Social Process in Behavior Problems," *Publications of the American Sociological Society* 26 (1932): 59–60.
4. Edwin H. Sutherland and Harvey J. Locke, *Twenty Thousand Homeless Men* (Philadelphia, 1936), 62.
5. E. A. Ross, *Sin and Society* (New York, 1907), 18.
6. Edwin H. Sutherland, *White Collar Crime* (New York, 1949), 9.
7. "Sloan, Alfred Pritchard," *Current Biography* (1940 ed.).
8. *Social Science Research Committee*, Memorandum: Edwin H. Sutherland to the SSRC, Joseph Regenstein Library, University of Chicago, 25 May 1933.
9. *Social Science Research Committee*, Memorandum: Edwin H. Sutherland to the SSRC, Joseph Regenstein Library, University of Chicago, 25 June 1933.
10. Personal inteview with Marshall Clinard, 12 Nov. 1981.
11. Personal interview with Lois Howard, 15 Nov. 1981.
12. John Flynn, "Editorial," *The New Republic*, 12 Dec. 1934, p. 113.
13. *The Nation*, 5 Dec. 1934, p. 631.
14. Personal interview with Fred Strodbeck, 21 Sept. 1981.
15. Sutherland, *White Collar Crime*, 210.
16. *Social Science Research Committee*, Memorandum: Edwin H. Sutherland to the SSRC, Joseph Regenstein Library, University of Chicago, 8 June 1935.
17. Edwin H. Sutherland, "White Collar Criminality," *American Sociological Review* 5 (February, 1940): 1.
18. Personal interviews with Mary Bess (Owen) Cameron, 14 Nov. 1981, and Lois Howard, 15 Nov. 1981.
19. Sutherland, "White Collar Criminality," 9.
20. Ibid., 4–5.
21. George Vold, *Theoretical Criminology* (New York, 1958), 259.
22. Alfred R. Lindesmith, *Opiates and the Law* (Chicago, 1947), 42.
23. Telephone interview with Frank Sweetser, 5 Nov. 1981.
24. Telephone interview with Lois Howard, 28 Mar. 1981.
25. Edwin H. Sutherland, "White Collar Criminality," unpublished manuscript, Indiana University (1939), 4. This is in the possession of Karl Schuessler, Department of Sociology, Indiana University, Bloomington.
26. Croan Greenough, Letter to Edwin H. Sutherland, 20 Dec. 1939; in the possession of Karl Schuessler (n. 25).
27. "Poverty Belittled as Crime Factor," *Philadelphia Inquirer*, 28 Dec. 1939, sec. 1, p. 17, col. 1.

28. "Hits Criminality in White Collars," *New York Times,* 28 Dec. 1939, sec. 1, p. 1, col. 4.
29. Telephone interview with Lois Howard, 28 Mar. 1981.
30. Read Bain, Letter to Edwin H. Sutherland, 30 Dec. 1939; in the possession of Karl Schuessler (n. 25).
31. Sutherland, *White Collar Crime,* 3.
32. Ibid., 6.
33. Edwin H. Sutherland, "The White Collar Criminal," *Encyclopedia of Criminology* (New York, 1949), 514.
34. Edwin H. Sutherland, "Crime and Business," *The Annals of the American Academy of Political and Social Science* 217 (1941): 117.
35. Edwin H. Sutherland, "Illegal Behavior of Seventy Corporations," unpublished manuscript, Indiana University (1944), 20; in the possession of Karl Schuessler (n. 25).
36. Sutherland, "Crime and Business," 117.
37. Leon Bramson, *The Political Context of Sociology* (Cambridge, Mass., 1961), 93–94.
38. Sutherland, *White Collar Crime,* 210.
39. Edwin H. Sutherland, "A and P, Propaganda, and Free Enterprise," unpublished manuscript, Indiana University (1948), 1; in the possession of Karl Schuessler (n. 25).
40. Ibid., 13.
41. Sutherland, "The White Collar Criminal," 514–15.
42. C. C. Van Vechten, "The Toleration Quotient as a Device for Defining Social Concepts," *American Journal of Sociology* 46 (1940): 35–39.
43. Paul R. Tappan, "White Collar Offenses," unpublished manuscript (1946); in the possession of Karl Schuessler (n. 25).
44. Edwin H. Sutherland, "Is White Collar Crime Criminal?" *American Sociological Review* 10 (1945): 132.
45. Edwin H. Sutherland, Letter to Jerome Hall, 5 April 1947; in the possession of Jerome Hall, San Francisco.
46. Edwin H. Sutherland, Letter to Helen Hughes, 17 November 1946; in the possession of Karl Schuessler (n. 25).
47. Edwin H. Sutherland, *Principles of Criminology* (Philadelphia, 4th ed., 1947), 37.
48. Robert G. Caldwell, *Criminology* (New York, 2d ed., 1965), 145.
49. Paul Tappan, "Who is the Criminal?" *American Sociological Review* 12 (1947): 99.
50. Sutherland, "White Collar Crime," 9.
51. Karl Schuessler "Introduction," *On Analyzing Crime* (Chicago, 1974). xxvii.
52. Hermann Mannheim, "White Collar Crime," *The Annals of the American Academy of Political and Social Science* 226 (1949): 244.
53. Ibid.
54. Selden D. Bacon, "White Collar Crime," *American Sociological Review* 15 (1950): 309.
55. Ibid., 310.
56. Lee M. Brooks, "White Collar Crime," *Social Forces* 28 (1949): 216.
57. Ibid.

GIL GEIS AND COLIN GOFF 31

58. William E. Cole, "On Crime in High Places," *Federal Probation* 14 (1950): 57.
59. "White Collar Crime," *Harper's Magazine* 199 (1949): 110.
60. Robert C. Sorenson, "White Collar Crime," *Harvard Law Review* 41 (1950): 80.
61. Ibid., 82.
62. Thomas I. Emerson, "White Collar Crime," *Yale Law Journal* 59 (1950): 584.
63. Ibid., 583.
64. Ibid.
65. Ibid., 584.
66. Ibid., 585.
67. Ibid.
68. Sorenson, "White Collar Crime," 81.
69. Marshall Clinard, *The Black Market* (New York, 1952), 134.
70. Ibid., 25–34.
71. Frank E. Hartung, "White Collar Offenses in the Wholesale Meat Industry in Detroit," *American Journal of Sociology* 56 (1950): 25–34.
72. Robert E. Lane, "Why Businessmen Violate The Law," *Journal of Criminal Law, Criminology, and Police Science* 44 (1953): 63.
73. Marvin E. Wolfgang, Robert M. Figlio, and Terence P. Thornberry, *Evaluating Criminology* (New York, 1978).
74. Stanton Wheeler, "Trends and Problems in the Sociological Study of Crime," *Social Problems* 83 (1976): 528.
75. Martin L. Needleman and Carolyn Needleman, "Organizational Crime: Two Models of Criminogenesis," *Sociological Review* 20 (1979): 521.
76. Schuessler, "Introduction," xxviii.
77. Sutherland, *White Collar Crime*, 9.
78. C. Ray Jeffrey, "The Historical Development of Criminology," in *Pioneers of Criminology*, ed. Hermann Mannheim (Montclair, N.J., 2d ed., 1972), 465.
79. Hermann Mannheim, *Comparative Criminology* (London, 1967), 2: 470.

[14]

The Sutherland-Glueck Debate: On the Sociology of Criminological Knowledge[1]

John H. Laub
Northeastern University

Robert J. Sampson
University of Illinois at Urbana-Champaign

During the 1930s, Edwin Sutherland established the sociological model of crime as the dominant paradigm in criminology and as a result became the most influential criminologist of the 20th century. This article examines Sutherland's debate with Sheldon Glueck and Eleanor Glueck about the causes of crime and the proper focus of social science research. Previously unavailable correspondence and unpublished papers are examined along with published works from the period (1925–45) when Sutherland was developing the theory of differential association and the Gluecks were launching research on criminal careers. The competing paradigms of the Gluecks and Sutherland are also placed in the socio-intellectual and institutional context in which they worked. It is shown that Sutherland's attack on the Gluecks' interdisciplinary research program was driven by: (*a*) a substantive version of sociological positivism that attempted to establish criminology as the proper domain of sociology, (*b*) a commitment to the method of analytic induction, and (*c*) Sutherland's rise to prominence in sociology. In addition, key aspects of the Gluecks' perspective reflecting their own professional interests in law and psychiatry further contributed to sociologists' hostile reaction. Nevertheless, the article presents evidence that the Gluecks' research on such fundamental issues as age and crime, criminal careers, and social control is more correct than commonly believed and, in fact, occupies center stage in contemporary research.

Edwin Sutherland (1883–1950) has been widely acclaimed as the dominant criminologist of the 20th century. Indeed, *Principles of Criminology*

[1] We are grateful to the members of the Manuscript Division of the Harvard Law School Library for their assistance in the production of this paper. We would also like to thank David Bordua, Jan Gorecki, Michael Gottfredson, Robert Alun Jones, Kenna Davis, Janet Lauritsen, and three anonymous *AJS* reviewers for their helpful com-

Sutherland-Glueck Debate

([1924] 1978),[2] *The Professional Thief* (1937a), and *White Collar Crime* (1949, 1983) are classic works still read by students of criminology. It is true as well that most criminologists are familiar with the works of Sutherland's students (e.g., Donald Cressey, Albert Cohen, and Lloyd Ohlin). Moreover, assessments of Sutherland's contributions to criminology are widely available (see, e.g., Cohen, Lindesmith, and Schuessler 1956; Schuessler 1973; and Gaylord and Galliher 1988). The Sutherland legacy in the sociology of crime is thus well established and secure. In fact, as recently as 1979 Gibbons argued that the "evidence is incontrovertible that Edwin Sutherland was the most important contributor to American criminology to have appeared to date." He goes as far as to predict that "it is extremely unlikely that anyone will emerge in future decades to challenge Sutherland's position in the annals of the field" (1979, p. 65). Similarly, Mannheim (1965, p. 470) has suggested that Sutherland receive the equivalent of a Nobel Prize in criminology.

In sharp contrast to the Sutherland legacy stands the work of Sheldon Glueck (1896–1980) and Eleanor Glueck (1898–1972). For over 40 years the Gluecks performed fundamental research in the field of criminology. As shown below, not only did their research provide crucial knowledge on the causes of crime, the Gluecks' research agenda set the stage for battles currently being waged in criminology regarding the proper focus of the discipline and the role of the scientific method. But despite their seminal contributions to the field, the Gluecks' works have been either ignored or criticized—especially by sociologists. As a result, contemporary researchers rarely, if ever, read their original studies. And when perfunctory citations do appear, their purpose is usually to allege fatal flaws in the Gluecks' position. Current debates in criminology have thus emerged as if there were no precedent.

Why have such developments taken place? It is our contention that the accepted fates of Sutherland and the Gluecks are intimately connected and cannot be understood by simple reference to the truth or falsity of their research findings. Instead, the Gluecks' research must be placed in the intellectual and historical context of Sutherland's rise to the position of the dominant sociologist of crime in the 20th century. We argue that

---

ments on an earlier draft. Requests for reprints should be sent to John H. Laub, College of Criminal Justice, 360 Huntington Avenue., Northeastern University, Boston, Massachusetts 02115.

[2] The first edition, published in 1924, was entitled *Criminology*. In 1934 the second, revised edition appeared under the title *Principles of Criminology*. Sutherland alone authored a total of four different editions; the fifth edition (1955) was written with the late Donald Cressey, who remained a coauthor through the tenth edition (1978). All 10 editions of the text have been published by J.B. Lippincott.

American Journal of Sociology

a shift in Sutherland's disciplinary and methodological outlook resulted in a theory that virtually required him to destroy individual-level, or nonsociological, perspectives on crime. The Gluecks advocated a multiple-factor theory of crime, which to Sutherland represented a threat to the intellectual status of sociological criminology. Hence, Sutherland's attack was aimed largely at extinguishing their interdisciplinary model so that sociology could establish proprietary rights to criminology. Although Sutherland's coup was successful at the time and remains so in some circles today, we demonstrate that in important respects it was unfounded and driven by a distorted version of both sociological positivism *and* the Gluecks' research. At the same time we show how the Gluecks' professional interests contributed to their own demise.

To substantiate our claims we examine in detail a previously unanalyzed debate between Edwin Sutherland and the Gluecks about the causes of crime and proper methods of social science research. After a period of initial harmony in the late 1920s and early 1930s, the Sutherland-Glueck exchange became heated and took on the trappings of an intellectual shoot-out that lasted some 15 years. This is the period when Sutherland was developing his famous theory of differential association and the Gluecks were studying the development of criminal careers and the effectiveness of correctional treatment in reducing criminal behavior. The material we analyze includes both published works and previously unavailable correspondence as well as unpublished papers. We uncovered the correspondence and unpublished manuscripts, along with the original raw data for the Gluecks' studies, in the archives of the Harvard Law School Library. The correspondence, unpublished papers, and raw data provide a unique glimpse into the formation and development of some of the major criminological works of our time. As Schuessler has argued, "Sutherland's contribution to criminology consisted as much in his informal papers and letters as in his published writing" (1973, p. xxiii). We believe the same is true of the Gluecks.

We also place the competing research paradigms of the Gluecks and Sutherland in the socio-intellectual and institutional context in which they found themselves. We argue that the formation and substance of their theoretical positions were deeply affected by their respective methodological and disciplinary biases. To understand the latter, we found it necessary to uncover the contextual factors relating to the intellectual climate and social positions to which each party was witness (see esp. Jones 1977, 1986; Camic 1987; Beirne 1987; Laub 1983).

Finally, we reassess the Gluecks' research findings in light of recent criminological advances and the test of time. In so doing we identify four substantive and methodological characteristics of the Glueck perspective that have captured center stage in current research. These include such

salient issues as age and crime, the value of longitudinal research, criminal careers, and social control theory. We show that, although largely
unacknowledged today, the Gluecks' substantive contributions are fundamental to theory and research in the study of crime.

HISTORICAL AND INSTITUTIONAL CONTEXT

The historical context and institutional affiliations of the Gluecks had an
important effect on their methodological stance and later dealings with
Sutherland in three respects. First, unlike Sutherland's, the Gluecks'
educational background was eclectic and interdisciplinary in nature.
Sheldon Glueck in particular was something of an academic maverick.
He first attended Georgetown University (1914–15) and then transferred
to George Washington University where he received his A.B. degree in
the humanities in 1920. He went on to receive an LL.B. and LL.M. from
National University Law School in 1920. After being denied admission
to Harvard Law School, Glueck subsequently entered the Department
of Social Ethics at Harvard University, which was an interdisciplinary
precursor to the sociology department (see Potts [1965] for a fascinating
description of that department). There he received an A.M. in 1922 and
Ph.D. in 1924.[3] Eleanor Glueck's academic terrain was similarly
eclectic—after attending Barnard College (A.B. in English, 1920) and
working in a settlement house in Dorchester, Massachusetts, she enrolled
in the School of Education at Harvard and took an Ed.M. degree in 1923
and a doctorate (Ed.D.) in 1925.[4] (Both Sheldon and Eleanor Glueck
were also given honorary doctorates by Harvard University in 1958.) As
a team the Gluecks were thus not beholden to any one discipline in an
"a priori" sense, and, as a result, they published extensively in the
leading journals of criminology, social work, psychology, sociology, education, law, and psychiatry.[5] As will become more apparent below, the
price they paid for such an interdisciplinary outlook was steep. Indeed,
as Geis recognized over 20 years ago, "the Gluecks belong to no single
academic discipline, and they are suffering the déclasse fate of aliens and
intruders" (1966, p. 188).

    Second, the Gluecks' social positions within the academic community

[3] Sheldon Glueck's (1925) Ph.D. thesis crosscut the interests of sociology, law, and
psychiatry, focusing on criminal responsibility, mental disorder, and criminal law.
[4] Eleanor Glueck's early research focused on the sociology of education (community
and schools) and the evaluation of research methods in social work (1927, 1936; see
also Gilboy 1936 and Vaillant 1980).
[5] A bibliography of the Gluecks' works from 1923 to 1963 is published in Glueck and
Glueck (1964).

American Journal of Sociology

were unique at the time and would be even today. After teaching a few years in the Department of Social Ethics at Harvard, Sheldon Glueck was appointed to the Harvard Law School as assistant professor of criminology in 1929. He became a full professor in 1931 and was appointed the first Roscoe Pound Professor of Law in 1950 (*Current Biography Yearbook* 1957). Sheldon Glueck's position as a professor of criminology in a law school was an unusual institutional arrangement that led him to a somewhat isolated and "outcast" perspective. Specifically, although law professors and students do not often conduct (or reward) social science research, that was his specialty and main interest. Moreover, research on the causes of crime was a particular anomaly in the law school setting, though it should be noted that during the 1930s the Harvard Law School had a tradition of research on the administration of justice (e.g., the Cleveland Crime Survey and the Harvard Crime Survey). Sheldon Glueck's institutional arrangement was a structural constraint in yet another crucial respect—there was no opportunity to train Ph.D. students who might carry on the Gluecks' research agenda.[6]

Perhaps more salient was the institutional treatment accorded Eleanor Glueck. Although armed with a doctorate in education and a prolific publishing record,[7] Eleanor Glueck was unable to secure a tenured faculty position or any teaching position at Harvard. In fact, she was employed from 1930 to 1953 as a research assistant in criminology at the Harvard Law School.[8] Some 20 years after her appointment as a research assistant she was "promoted" to research associate in criminology in 1953, a position she retained until 1964. At the same time, from 1929 to 1964, she was codirector of the project on the causes and prevention of juvenile delinquency.[9] In short, Eleanor Glueck's entire career at Harvard University consisted of a social position akin to what many Ph.D. candidates face today *before* graduation. As such, she was an outcast from mainstream academia at Harvard.

The third fact central to understanding the Gluecks' approach was

[6] The contrast to the structural arrangement of Edwin Sutherland with regard to graduate students is important and is addressed further below.

[7] Eleanor Glueck received her doctorate in educational sociology at the Harvard Graduate School of Education, the only school at Harvard at that time that admitted women.

[8] Harvard Law School did not admit women as students until 1950; it was the last Ivy League school to do so. Even then, it has been noted that during the 1950s and 1960s women at Harvard Law School were "treated like members of an alien species" (Abramson and Franklin 1986, p. 10).

[9] Although the Gluecks' research was carried out under the auspices of the Harvard Law School, their research was funded by numerous private foundations. Eleanor Glueck spent an enormous amount of time on this fund-raising activity.

that their intellectual mentors were a diverse group drawn from a variety of disciplines and all unusual thinkers in their own right. The group included such figures as Roscoe Pound, Felix Frankfurter, Richard Cabot, Bernard Glueck, William Healy, Augusta Bronner, and Edwin B. Wilson. This diversity of intellectual influence is evident throughout the Gluecks' research careers. Early on, the Gluecks were influenced personally as well as professionally by Sheldon Glueck's older brother, Bernard Glueck. The latter was a forensic psychiatrist at Sing Sing Prison and had a long-standing interest in crime (see B. Glueck 1916, 1918). Perhaps equally important, it was Bernard Glueck who arranged the first meeting between one of his graduate students, Eleanor Touroff, and Sheldon Glueck.

At Harvard the Gluecks were influenced by Richard C. Cabot, a professor in the Department of Social Ethics. It was in a seminar with Professor Cabot that the idea for a study of 500 offenders from the Massachusetts Reformatory first originated. Cabot's own research utilized the follow-up method in assessing the accuracy of diagnoses of cardiac illnesses (see Cabot 1926). Sheldon Glueck noted that in the field of penology no studies had been done assessing the posttreatment histories of former prisoners. Excited by the prospects of such research, Cabot arranged financing for the Gluecks' research, which culminated in *500 Criminal Careers* (1930).

Felix Frankfurter served as director of the Harvard Crime Survey in 1926 and was also quite influential in the Gluecks' early studies. In fact, the Harvard Crime Survey, of which *One Thousand Juvenile Delinquents* (1934a) is volume 1 in a series of reports, can be seen as an early model of scientific inquiry in the social sciences. According to Frankfurter, the survey was "not an agency for reform" but a contribution of scientific knowledge to society in the areas of criminal behavior and social policy that "heretofore had been left largely to improvisation, crude empiricism, and propaganda" (1934, p. xii). Moreover, Frankfurter (1934) believed that the formulation of the problem and use of the scientific process to address the problem would eventually lead to prudent social policies. This general perspective can be found in all the Gluecks' research.

William Healy and Augusta Bronner probably wielded the most influence in the Gluecks' intellectual history. The Gluecks had met Healy and Bronner, who were the directors of the Judge Baker Foundation, when they first arrived in Boston, a meeting facilitated in part by Bernard Glueck. The Gluecks had read Healy's *The Individual Delinquent* (1915) and were favorably disposed to his research. At the same time, Healy was interested in issues relating to Sheldon Glueck's doctoral thesis and was one of the reviewers who encouraged its publication by Little, Brown

American Journal of Sociology

(S. Glueck 1964, p. 319). Most important to the Gluecks was the "scientific attitude" of Healy and Bronner and, in a memorial address for Healy, Sheldon Glueck stated that he was "a major catalyst of our work" (1964, p. 319). Like the Gluecks, Healy focused on the individual as the most important unit of analysis, embraced a multiple-factor approach in the study of crime causation, and utilized knowledge across a variety of disciplines (see Healy 1915; and Healy and Bronner 1926). In fact, Snodgrass (1972, p. 326) has referred to *Unraveling Juvenile Delinquency* (Glueck and Glueck 1950*a*) as "essentially a modernized *Individual Delinquent.*"

In short, three factors worked together to develop a fiercely independent, interdisciplinary, and even iconoclastic outlook on the part of the Gluecks. In particular, interdisciplinary educational training, coupled with Sheldon Glueck's unusual position in the law school and apparent gender discrimination against Eleanor Glueck, served to create almost a bunker mentality on the part of the Gluecks, especially regarding Harvard sociology.[10] The Gluecks were also constrained by their lack of involvement in the training of graduate students. Added to this was the intellectual diversity of a set of colleagues who fostered empirical research beyond the confines of any one discipline. It is only within this context that we can now understand the Gluecks' theoretical and methodological perspective.

The Glueck Perspective

During their 40-year career at the Harvard Law School, the Gluecks produced four major data bases relating to crime and delinquency. The first was the study of 510 male offenders from the Massachusetts Reformatory during the period 1911–22. These offenders were studied over a 15-year span, which resulted in three books (Glueck and Glueck 1930, 1937*a*, 1943). A second although similar study of women incarcerated at the Women's Reformatory resulted in the publication of *Five Hundred Delinquent Women* (1934*b*). A third major research effort focused on a sample of juveniles who had been referred by the Boston juvenile court

[10] Harvard sociology in the 1930s has been described as "intellectually ill-defined" (Camic 1987, p. 425). The powers that did exist (e.g., Sorokin, Parsons, and Homans) certainly did not consider the study of crime to be central to the mission of sociology (see Faculty Committee Report 1954, and Cohen's interview in Laub [1983]). In fact, the parallel between Parsons's pursuit of general sociological theory at Harvard (see Camic 1987) and Sutherland's at Indiana is striking. It should also be noted that both Sheldon and Eleanor Glueck were Jewish. One can speculate that discrimination against Jews at Harvard University (see Laub 1983, p. 185) may have also contributed to isolating the Gluecks from the mainstream academic community.

to the Judge Baker Foundation (the existing court clinic at the time). These results were published in *One Thousand Juvenile Delinquents* (1943a), and a follow-up analysis 10 years later produced *Juvenile Delinquents Grown Up* (1940). The results of these studies are summarized in a volume entitled *After-Conduct of Discharged Offenders* (1945). Finally, the work the Gluecks are best known for is *Unraveling Juvenile Delinquency* (1950a). This major study of the formation and development of criminal careers was initiated in the 1940s and involved a sample of 500 delinquents and 500 nondelinquents matched case-by-case on age, race/ ethnicity, general intelligence, and low-income residence—all classic criminological variables thought to influence both delinquency and official reaction. Over a 17-year period the Gluecks conducted an extensive follow-up of the original *Unraveling* sample, which resulted in the publication of *Delinquents and Nondelinquents in Perspective* (1968; see also Glueck and Glueck 1970).

The Gluecks' methodological approach to the study of crime can be characterized by three distinct features. The first is an emphasis on longitudinal and follow-up prediction studies, including, when possible, control groups for comparative purposes. Second, the Gluecks' work emphasized a criminal career focus, especially the study of serious persistent offenders (1950a, p. 13). Related to this was the Gluecks' thought that the study of the formation, development, and termination of criminal careers was an important research priority, and that the causes of the initiation of crime were distinct from the causes of continuing crime and processes of desistance (Glueck and Glueck 1930, p. 257; 1934b, p. 282; 1945, p. 75, n. 1). Third, the Gluecks stressed the importance of collecting multiple sources of information (e.g., parent, teacher, self-report) in addition to official records of delinquency.

As for substantive findings, the Gluecks, like Goring ([1913] 1972), uncovered the important relationship between age and criminality. They argued that age of onset was a key factor in terms of etiology and policy and that career criminals started very young in life. The Gluecks also stressed that crime declined substantially with age. Specifically, in all of their research the Gluecks found that, as the population of offenders aged, their crime rate declined. Furthermore, even among those who continued offending, the seriousness of the offenses declined (Glueck and Glueck 1940, 1943, 1945, 1968). The Gluecks sought to understand the age-crime curve in terms of maturational reform. As we will see, not only was the relationship between age and crime one of the major sources of their battle with Sutherland, it foreshadowed a contemporary debate along similar lines.

Research by the Gluecks also revealed the stability of delinquent patterns over the life cycle. They argued that the data showed "beyond a reasonable doubt that, in all of life's activities considered in this inquiry, the men who as boys comprised our sample of juvenile delinquents have continued on a path markedly *divergent* from those who as juveniles had been included in the control group of nondelinquents" (Glueck and Glueck 1968, pp. 169–70). The Gluecks' hypothesis regarding the stability of deviance would also turn out to be a major sticking point with those advocating a sociological perspective.

According to the Gluecks, the most important factor that distinguished delinquents from nondelinquents in early life was the *family*. In particular, the Gluecks (1950*a*) developed a prediction scale of delinquency that centered on family variables—disciplinary practices, supervision by parents, and child-parent attachment. Those families with lax discipline combined with erratic and threatening punishment, poor supervision, and weak emotional ties between parent and child were found to generate the highest probability of delinquency. Although a focus on the family was to become extremely unpopular in sociology during the 1950s and 1960s, it was one of the Gluecks' major interests.

Perhaps most important, the Gluecks promoted a multidisciplinary perspective and had little patience for those criminologists who were wedded to any one particular discipline. As a result the Gluecks rejected unilateral causation whether sociological, biological, or psychological in focus and embraced instead a multiple causal approach that emphasized differentiation between offenders and nonoffenders. This approach is seen most clearly in *Unraveling*, in which they focused not only on the family, but on school, opportunities (peers and use of leisure time), formal sanctions (e.g., arrest, probation, prison), personality development, temperament, and constitutional factors such as body structure (e.g., mesomorphy). As they stated, "The separate findings, independently gathered, integrate into a dynamic pattern which is neither exclusively biologic nor exclusively socio-cultural, but which derives from an interplay of somatic, temperamental, intellectual, and socio-cultural forces" (1950*a*, p. 281). The Gluecks, along with Healy (1915; see also Healy and Bronner 1926), thus established the multiple-factor approach to the study of crime.

Overall, the Gluecks were stubbornly driven by what their data revealed and refused to pigeonhole their interpretations into any one disciplinary box, tempted though they were. This emphasis on fact gathering prevented them from ever developing a systematic theoretical framework. As they argued, "Neither 'hunches' nor theoretical speculations, can conjure away the facts, even though those facts may not fit neatly into various preconceptions about human nature and crime causation" (1951, p. 762). Their mode of analysis was thus to cross-tabulate all possible factors with delinquency (cf. Lazarsfeld 1955). As a result, *Un-*

raveling is very difficult to read and seems to present nothing but table after table. As Geis has noted, "The paradox of studies by the Gluecks: they do such good work so badly" (1970, p. 118; see also Laub and Sampson [1988] for a review of the methodological criticisms of *Unraveling*).

We will return later to the validity of the Gluecks' major research findings regarding such issues as age and crime, family processes, and the stability of crime and deviance across the life course. For now, we hope to have established the basic Glueck perspective and placed it in the historical and institutional context specified above. In similar fashion we turn our attention next to the Gluecks' major contemporary and critic.

The Initial Sutherland Perspective

In 1924 Edwin Sutherland published the first edition of the now-classic *Principles of Criminology*.[11] At the time Sutherland was an untenured assistant professor of sociology at the University of Illinois in Urbana. His education was also in sociology—receiving a Ph.D. from the University of Chicago in 1913. It may thus come as a surprise to learn of Sutherland's original position on the causes of crime. This is easy to miss, for criminologists today cite the later editions of *Principles* (see n. 2 above), in which the theory of differential association is laid out. But this strategy fails to reveal the magnitude of Sutherland's shift in thinking. The shift, ironically enough, was to come from a multiple-factor approach clearly stated in the first 1924 edition.

Although commonly viewed as a macrosociologist of cultural conflict (see, e.g., Kornhauser 1978), in 1924 Sutherland began by specifying what he considered to be the proper unit of analysis in criminology—the individual. As he noted, "knowledge can be secured best by the individual case study." He also argued for the comparison of "criminal and noncriminal populations" (1924, p. 86). Moreover, in an intriguing section of *Principles* entitled "Plan for Study of Causes of Crime," Sutherland outlines the "ideal" data-collection strategy in criminology. This would include "detailed records of the development of personalities," which "need to be very detailed and pursued from early infancy to old age" (1924, pp. 86–87). This strategy would also extend to "mental and

[11] It should be pointed out that, according to Gaylord and Galliher (1988), writing this text marked the beginning of Sutherland's career in criminology. His Ph.D. thesis focused on "Unemployment and Public Employment Agencies" and his overall substantive interests at the time seemed to be in areas of political economy and political science (Lindesmith 1988, p. xi).

American Journal of Sociology

educational tests," as well as interviews with parents, teachers, and a full recording of all "conduct disorders." It is interesting that this is exactly the sort of methodological strategy followed by the Gluecks.

Sutherland was later to become vehemently antipsychiatry, but there was little evidence of this stance in his early writings on the substantive predictors of crime. For example, he noted the association between psychopathic personality and criminality and, in fact, argued that "there is good reason to believe that the psychopathic personalities, and especially those of the egocentric type, will get into difficulty with other people more frequently than the average individual" (1924, p. 123). Sutherland, like the Gluecks, also maintained that the family was a crucial variable in understanding delinquency: "Those homes with extremely rigid discipline, extremely lax discipline, or inconsistent discipline are developing many children with personalities that are socially undesirable and incline toward delinquency" (1924, p. 147). And, perhaps most ironic, Sutherland acknowledged openly the potential effects of biology on delinquency, noting possible mediating effects of social factors (1924, p. 180). Much like the Gluecks would later argue, Sutherland wrote that "it is not the physical defect itself that produces delinquency, but the social and other conditions surrounding the defective person" (1924, p. 180). In the 1920s Sutherland was thus a multiple-factor theorist. He in fact admitted as much, stating later in an address to the Ohio Valley Sociological Association, "I had a congeries of discrete and co-ordinate factors, unrelated to each other, which may be called multiple-factor theory" (in Schuessler 1973, p. 14).

Sutherland's favorable inclination toward the multiple-factor perspective also extended to his early communication with the Gluecks. The early correspondence between the Gluecks and Sutherland covered the period from February 26, 1929, to May 15, 1936. There are more than 40 pieces of correspondence over this time period.[12] Our inspection of the full body of materials reveals a cordial relationship between professional colleagues. The topics of discussion included parole prediction and the role of mental defects and crime, among others. They also shared ideas and factual information. What is most noteworthy though is Sutherland's strong praise for the Gluecks' work. For instance, in response to the forthcoming publication of *500 Criminal Careers,* Sutherland wrote, in a letter dated September 27, 1929, that the book was "a very great contribution to the literature and methods of criminology" (Sutherland 1929). In the same letter Sutherland did raise some points of "minor

[12] This correspondence can be found in the Eleanor T. and Sheldon Glueck Joint Papers and the Sheldon Glueck Papers, Harvard Law School Library, Cambridge, Mass.

importance" with regard to statistical computations and the Gluecks' interpretation of research on parole prediction with respect to weighting factors. Overall, however, the tone of the letters was upbeat, and, as late as a May 4, 1936, letter, Sutherland praised the Gluecks and expressed "astonishment" at their publication record (Sutherland 1936).

The Gluecks in turn praised Sutherland's work. For instance, in *500 Criminal Careers* (1930), the Gluecks discussed problems in major textbooks in the field with regard to assessment of recidivism rates. However, the Gluecks (1930, p. 7) noted that "E. H. Sutherland, in *Criminology*, does not fall into this fallacy of careless generalization in the direction of optimism." Similarly, with regard to Sutherland's second edition of *Principles of Criminology*, Sheldon Glueck's correspondence with Sutherland's publisher (J. B. Lippincott) stated that the text was "unquestionably the most satisfactory" on the subject and that Sutherland wrote with "objectivity," "temperateness," and "rational eclecticism" (S. Glueck 1934).

SHIFTING TIDES: THE SUTHERLAND-GLUECK DEBATE

Beginning in 1937, Sutherland began to shift his thinking and, as a consequence, his attitude toward the Gluecks' research. The buildup was slow at first and began with a review by Sutherland (1937*b*) of the Gluecks' *Later Criminal Careers*. The *Later Criminal Careers* (Glueck and Glueck 1937*a*) study was the second in a series focusing on 510 offenders released from the Massachusetts Reformatory. This particular book described the second five-year follow-up period after parole (1928–32). Sutherland's attention was centered largely on the two major conclusions of the study. First, improvement in behavior over time was attributed by the Gluecks "primarily to aging or maturation." And second, the major obstacle to reform through maturation was argued to be psychological dysfunction. Sutherland also critiqued almost every methodological aspect of the study, claiming, in a two-page review, that the information gathered was "scanty," that few of the offenders were "observed" firsthand, and that "the purpose of these studies has not been defined" (1937*b*, p. 185). His comments are interesting because an earlier study by the Gluecks (1930), identical in nature, had been praised by Sutherland (1934*b*, pp. 511, 546–47).

As to the substance of the findings, Sutherland strongly attacked the conclusion that "the reduction of delinquency was due to aging or maturation" (1937*b*, p. 185). He unambiguously stated that "there is no justification for this conclusion, either in statistics or logic. Aging, as the mere passing of time, has no significance as a cause" (1937*b*, p. 185). But Sutherland was even more perturbed by the Gluecks' psychologically oriented conclusion that mental and/or emotional difficulties impeded the process of reformation among former prisoners. Although as shown above he once agreed with this position, Sutherland argued that "this is the least satisfactory part of the book." He goes on to maintain in a few short sentences, and without documentation, that the psychiatrist at the institution (who made the evaluations *before* the follow-up when postrelease behavior was measured) had "a heavy case load and little time for careful examinations, and also had a general bias toward interpretation of delinquency as due to mental pathology" (1937*b*, p. 186). Ignoring the crucial fact that the classifications had predictive validity (Glueck and Glueck 1937*a*, pp. 127, 198–212), Sutherland dismissed the results ("no confidence can be placed in this") and the overall conclusions of the book, which he claimed "are doubtful" (1937*b*, p. 186).[13]

Despite its largely negative tone, Sutherland's review in the influential *Harvard Law Review* was only the tip of the iceberg. Sutherland's review was in fact culled from a longer, unpublished manuscript entitled "The Gluecks' *Later Criminal Careers:* An Appraisal by Edwin H. Sutherland" (1937*c*). This original paper was 18 pages in length and was circulated among criminologists, including the Gluecks. The paper was read at the annual meeting of the Sociological Research Association on December 30, 1937, in Atlantic City.[14] An edited version was later published after Sutherland's death in *The Sutherland Papers* (Cohen et al. 1956, pp. 291–307). In the original piece, located in the Gluecks' archive at Harvard University, Sutherland critiqued in a forceful tone the Gluecks' conclusions regarding aging and maturational reform. He also began to express new views that foreshadowed his conversion to analytic induction (described in more detail below) as a methodological tool. With regard to the association between age and crime he wrote, "There is no statistical procedure by which a statistically significant association can be translated into a cause. . . . Moreover, the passing of time no more explains reformation than it explains the genesis of a depression or the election of an old man to the Senate" (1937*c*, p. 12).

[13] For a published point-by-point response to the Sutherland review by a colleague of the Gluecks' from the Harvard Law School, see Hall (1937, pp. 389–93).

[14] According to correspondence from Sutherland to Eleanor Glueck on January 11, 1938, the session was chaired by Ernest Burgess and was devoted to a discussion of *Later Criminal Careers* based on papers by Sutherland and C. E. Gehlke. Sutherland wrote, "I read the principal parts of your paper to the group, reading at least two-thirds of it" (1938). This statement was in response to a request in a letter to Sutherland from the Gluecks dated December 14, 1937: "If you plan to present your paper in its original form, we are sure you will do us the courtesy of having our reply read at the same meeting" (Glueck and Glueck 1937*c*). Whether the Gluecks actually expected Sutherland himself to read their reply to his critique of their book at a meeting organized to discuss their book is, to say the least, unclear.

More generally, Sutherland expressed his distaste for the factual search for the correlates of delinquency in a longitudinal perspective. He argued that it was of utmost importance that researchers first present a thesis and then attempt to test it. Noting his disregard of the search for key facts, Sutherland followed up his unpublished critique with a letter, dated December 4, 1937. Sutherland wrote to Sheldon Glueck about *Later Criminal Careers*, "You would have been much safer if you had presented your factual data without the thread of theory, but in my opinion research work of that factual nature are safe but useless. Every research study should, I believe, be organized around general propositions or general theory, and unless it can be so organized it is relatively futile" (1937*d*).

It is interesting that this passage reveals that Sutherland recognized the Gluecks were not sheer empiricists. Indeed, in his longer review he refers to the Gluecks' "theory of criminal behavior" and that they "fail to prove their hypotheses" (1937*c*, p. 17). In any case, Sutherland castigated the collection of empirical data without theory, yet at the same time rejected the Gluecks' substantive framework on age and crime and maturational reform. Paradoxically, in fact, he accused the Gluecks of trying to prove a preconceived theory of persistent criminality (1937*c*, pp. 3–4).

The Gluecks were sufficiently concerned with Sutherland's critique that they responded (Glueck and Glueck 1937*b*) with a 25-page document that, to our knowledge, was never published. This response was titled "Analysis of Prof. Sutherland's Appraisal of *Later Criminal Careers*" and is dated December 13, 1937. It is surprising that the correspondence shows that some portion of the Gluecks' rejoinder was read by Sutherland himself at the 1937 meeting of the Sociological Research Association (see n. 14 above). In the response the Gluecks countered that they were not trying to prove any preconceived theories regarding age and crime: "We have no criminologic axes to grind. We search for facts as accurately as possible and on the basis of the findings we arrive inductively, and not *a priori*, at certain conclusions. The statement from *Later Criminal Careers* that you quote on pages 3 and 4 [of the unpublished critique] is not a preconception with which we started our work; it is a theory suggested by the evidence emerging from the facts" (1937*b*, p. 3). In the full response they also answered, point by point, Sutherland's "minor" criticisms regarding the number of cases followed up as well as other issues.[15]

---

[15] It is rather ironic to note that in the same year Sutherland was criticizing the Gluecks for their small sample size ($N = 454$), he published *The Professional Thief* (1937*a*), a case study of one. More generally, Sutherland conducted little, if any,

American Journal of Sociology

They expressed more puzzlement, however, at Sutherland's views on methodology. In the Lazarsfeld tradition, the Gluecks tried to establish an age-crime relationship by ruling out (controlling for) other factors associated with age. Although admittedly crude by today's standards, the Gluecks' analysis was straightforward—after they had analyzed several competing variables, age and also psychological adjustment seemed to best predict desistance from crime. Their response to Sutherland reflects the Gluecks' general empirical stance:

> Your statement (page 12) that "there is no statistical procedure by which a statistically significant association can be translated into a cause" is a well known truism in a sense; but the illustration you give [age cannot explain the election of an old man to senate] is obviously absurd and is assuredly not analogous to the association of aging with behavior. While it is true that the mere association of two factors does not necessarily mean that one is causal of the other, it is also true that in every field of science an association between factors that ought, in reason and experience, to be related does give the basis of a valid inference as to causation. . . . If one could not ever make such an inference from statistical associations, it is hard to see how any science would be possible. [1937*b*, pp. 12–13]

They went on in great detail to argue that the age and psychological relationships with crime were robust and met the conventional methodological standards of the time.

One is thus led to wonder, as the Gluecks probably did, what exactly was responsible for Sutherland's newfound rejection of their work. We believe the answer lies in the confluence of three important factors relating to the changing socio-intellectual context of the late 1930s—(*a*) analytical induction, (*b*) sociological positivism, and (*c*) the rising social position of Sutherland in the sociological profession.

Analytic Induction

According to Alfred Lindesmith, a colleague and close friend of Sutherland, subsequent editions of Sutherland's criminology text (in 1934, 1939, and 1947) sought to "improve and correct the multiple factor theory represented by the 1924 edition" (Lindesmith 1988, p. xi). Specifically, the 1939 and 1947 editions were "designed to substitute . . . differential association theory for that of multiple factors. . . . During this same period Sutherland's reputation soared, and his criminological textbook

---

original empirical research on juvenile delinquency. Although presumably not intentional, this insulated his work from the sort of methodological criticisms aimed at the Gluecks.

Sutherland-Glueck Debate

has dominated the field for more than half a century" (Lindesmith 1988, p. xi).

A number of factors have been alluded to as being important in this transformation (see Schuessler 1973, pp. 13–29; Gaylord and Galliher 1988, chaps. 5 and 6). These include the publication of the Michael-Adler report (1933), which highly criticized existing criminological research; a meeting chaired by Dean Beardsley Ruml of the University of Chicago on the state of criminological knowledge, at which Sutherland could not state any positive generalizations about the causes of crime; Sutherland's work on *The Professional Thief* (1937a); the influence on Sutherland's thinking of the work of Charles H. Cooley relating to social processes; the development of analytic induction by Alfred Lindesmith; Sutherland's collaboration with Thorsten Sellin for the Social Science Research Council and the subsequent publication by Sellin of *Culture Conflict and Crime* (1938); and finally, his colleagues at the University of Chicago and Indiana University.

Of these factors the most crucial from our perspective was the development of analytic induction by Alfred Lindesmith, a former student of Sutherland's at the University of Chicago. Lindesmith joined the Sociology Department at Indiana University in 1936 and became known for his research on drug addiction (Lindesmith 1947) and his new method of scientific inquiry. Sutherland succinctly noted the influence of Lindesmith and his methodological outlook.

> When Lindesmith came to Indiana University . . . I became acquainted with his conception of methodology as developed in his study of drug addiction. According to this conception, an hypothesis should fit every case in the defined universe, and the procedure to use is: State the hypothesis and try it out on one case; if it does not fit the facts, modify the hypothesis or else redefine the universe to which it applies, and try it on another case, and so on for case after case. The methodology consists in searching for negative cases, one negative case disproving the hypothesis. Although this involves several cases, it is not concerned with averages, standard deviations, or coefficients of correlation. The methodology assisted me greatly in formulating problems and in testing hypotheses. [In Schuessler 1973, pp. 17, 18]

According to Gaylord and Galliher (1988), Sutherland had reached a theoretical impasse in the early 1930s—he was unable to make sense of multiple causes or factors and multiple-factor theory. Analytic induction provided Sutherland with a methodology that he believed allowed the development of a universal generalization that would explain *all* criminal behavior (Sutherland and Cressey 1955, pp. 68–69; see also Turner 1953). Specifically, this method led Sutherland to extract common elements and organize the heretofore diverse set of facts that criminological research

American Journal of Sociology

had generated into the single theoretical abstraction of "differential association" (Gaylord and Galliher 1988, p. 116; Matsueda 1988, pp. 277–80).[16]

Moreover, by embracing analytic induction as *the* scientific method, Sutherland's development of a general theory of crime causation included a rejection of multiple-factor theory as, among other things, unscientific. As a result the Gluecks' methodology as well as their substantive interest in multiple factors of crime causation were dismissed by the new Sutherland perspective. This conversion is clearly seen in the 1947 edition of *Principles of Criminology*, in which Sutherland argued (p. 3) that "any scientific explanation consists of a description of the conditions which are always present when a phenomenon occurs and which are never present when the phenomenon does not occur."[17]

One can argue that Sutherland had adopted what Hirschi and Selvin (1970) have termed "the false criteria of causality." In large measure, Sutherland's critique of multiple-factor approaches generally, and the Gluecks' research specifically, rests on "false criterion 1." "Insofar as a relation between two variables is not perfect, the variable is not causal" (1970, p. 129). The implication of this point is striking. "Perfect association implies single causation, and less-than-perfect association implies multiple causation. Rejecting as causes of delinquency those variables whose association with delinquency is less than perfect thus implies rejecting the principle of multiple causation" (Hirschi and Selvin 1970, p. 130). As they argued, this criterion of noncausality is inappropriate.[18] In a somewhat different vein, Turner (1953) argues that studies using analytic induction fail to provide empirical prediction.

[16] According to Sutherland, criminal behavior, like noncriminal behavior, is learned in interaction with other people: "A person becomes delinquent because of an excess of definitions favorable to violation of law over definitions unfavorable to violation of law" (Sutherland and Cressey 1955, p. 78). Sutherland also strongly emphasized culture in his analysis of crime, arguing that society consisted of a number of diverse groups with varied cultures. Underlying the phenomenon of criminal behavior is the principle of culture conflict, which leads to differential association, which in turn leads to criminal behavior (see also Matsueda 1988). Sutherland eventually developed nine propositions of differential association (see Sutherland and Cressey 1955, pp. 77–79).

[17] During the 1950s Albert Cohen, a student of Sutherland, also wrote a sharp critique of multiple-factor theory (Cohen 1970). See Hirschi and Selvin (1970) and Hirschi (1973) for a response to Cohen's critique.

[18] Hirschi and Selvin (1970, p. 130) note that precedent for demanding the "perfect criterion of causality" can be found in Michael and Adler's (1933) critique of criminological research. This report was influential in shaping Sutherland's thinking about criminological theory and research (Gaylord and Galliher 1988).

Sutherland-Glueck Debate

With respect to the notion of cause, the Gluecks "recognized that certain influences may be regarded as causal in a statistical sense of high probability" (Glueck and Glueck 1974, p. 44; 1952, pp. 164–69) and thus followed a widely accepted probabilistic model of social science methodology—that is, association, causal order, and lack of spuriousness (see Hirschi and Selvin 1967). (For an illustration of their use of cause see *Unraveling* [1950*a*, pp. 281–82].) In sharp contrast, Geis and Goff have noted that "it was one of Sutherland's favorite statements that '85 percent of anything could not be a cause. It had to be 100 percent or it was not a theory.' Indeed, if poverty didn't *always* cause crime, then poverty couldn't qualify as part of a theoretical causal statement" (1986, p. 9).

It is difficult to overestimate the significance of Sutherland's scientific view for the field of criminology. As Hirschi has highlighted, "Perhaps the outstanding event in the intellectual history of theories of cultural deviance was not a decision about the nature of man, but a rather ordinary appearing decision [by Sutherland] about the nature of scientific explanation: 'I reached the general conclusion that a concrete condition cannot be a cause of crime, and that the only way to get a causal explanation of criminal behavior is by abstracting from the varying concrete conditions things which are universally associated with crime.' Sutherland decided that every case of crime should be explained by the theory he proposed to construct" (1969, pp. 13–14). As Hirschi points out, Sutherland's view that "only concepts can be causes leads to misinterpretation of empirical results and ultimately to the view that the quest for causes is futile" (1969, p. 13, n. 38; see also Hirschi and Selvin 1967, pp. 130–33, 177–83). Although some readers will certainly disagree with the Hirschi-Selvin position on criteria of causal research, it is nonetheless the case that virtually no empirical research today in criminology is guided by analytic induction.

Sociological Positivism

A second, and equally important, factor in explaining Sutherland's changing conception of theory was his use of a particular form of sociological positivism. Traditionally, when social scientists think about positivism there is a tendency to focus on issues of cause and effect, empirical data, replication, and public statement of research methods. In this sense positivism does not fix the concepts to be used in explanations of phenomena, and it guarantees success to none of its constituent disciplines (Gottfredson and Hirschi 1990, p. 49). However, Gottfredson and Hirschi go on to argue that positivism as practiced in the 20th century has actually

American Journal of Sociology

been used as a *substantive* perspective as well as a method of knowing. Specifically, the major error of modern positivism has been the "tendency to confuse the interests of one's discipline with the interests of scientific explanation" (1990, p. 73). In the study of crime, for example, they are able to document the proprietary interests of biology in heritability, psychology in personality, and sociology in social class (Gottfredson and Hirschi 1990, chaps. 3–4). They argue that, by fusing positivism with such "a priori" concepts, the rival disciplines virtually require that research outcomes be consistent with their estimate of their own importance in the behavior at issue.

Nowhere is this more true than in understanding why Sutherland deemed it necessary to attack the Gluecks' work. The Gluecks were gaining widespread readership and, with the exception of Sutherland, praise.[19] More important, Sutherland saw the multiple-factor approach, with its inclusion of such individual-level factors as age and mental capacity, as a threat to a substantive version of sociological positivism. As Gottfredson and Hirschi argue, "Criminology, which came to be dominated by sociology, eventually saw the destruction of individual-level correlates as a prerequisite to 'truly social' theorizing" (1990, p. 70, n. 3). Thus, sociological positivism as practiced by Sutherland did not attempt to establish the sociological causes of crime *independent* of individual-level factors in the Durkheimian tradition. Rather, crime was viewed by Sutherland as a social phenomenon that could *only* be explained by social (i.e., nonindividual) factors. As a result, Sutherland "explicitly denied the claims of all other disciplines potentially interested in crime" (Gottfredson and Hirschi 1990, p. 70).[20]

When combined with Sutherland's adoption of analytic induction, it was then possible for him to interpret all phenomena in a manner consistent with a pure sociological theory of differential association (see also Matsueda 1988). As Hirschi and Gottfredson have argued elsewhere, "Sutherland invented or adapted standards of scientific adequacy that

[19] For example, Walter Reckless, a noted sociologist at Ohio State University, argued in a review of *Juvenile Delinquents Grown Up* that the Gluecks were "pre-eminent in this field of research" (1941, p. 736). Although critical of key aspects of the Gluecks' research, Reckless concluded that, "in spite of shortcomings which inevitably greet pioneer attempts at forecasting, the Gluecks' persistence in their endeavor to explain and to predict criminal outcome by the method of factoring is courageous and praiseworthy" (p. 738). Similarly, Donald Taft, a sociologist at the University of Illinois, wrote in a review of *Later Criminal Careers* that "this valuable book . . . illustrate(s) the importance of long-time criminological research" (1937, p. 940). Further, Taft emphasized the "painstaking type of research which the Gluecks—more than any other investigators—are furnishing" (p. 941).

[20] Sutherland even went so far as to express regret that nonsociologists received funds for research in criminology (see Cohen et al. 1956, p. 270).

Sutherland-Glueck Debate

permitted an ad hoc interpretation of research findings in ways consistent with the theory of differential association" and thus that "the genius of Sutherland . . . was that as he produced a theory of criminality, he simultaneously produced a science to protect it from research results and from competitive theories" (1980, p. 10). This model effectively insulated Sutherland's theory from the results of empirical research based on a multiple-factor approach by defining the necessary and sufficient causes of crime. Hence, with the 1939 edition of *Principles* as a backdrop, criminology became a field closed to the possibility that disciplines other than sociology might have something to contribute (Gottfredson and Hirschi 1990, p. 70).

It is important to recognize here that the error of positivism when interpreted as a substantive theory of crime was not sociology's alone—it was embraced by biology, psychology, and economics as well. The difference, however, is that sociology was successful in its attempt to take over the study of crime (for details, see Gottfredson and Hirschi [1990]; and Gaylord and Galliher [1988]).[21] Sutherland's leadership role in this action was widely recognized—so much so that Robert Merton even compared Sutherland's *Principles of Criminology* to such disciplinary classics as Samuelson's *Economics* and Gray's *Anatomy* as books that "leave an enduring impress on generations of students" (1971, p. vii).

Defending the Sociological Perspective

That Sutherland became the warrior for sociology's coup of criminology was also linked to his social position and rising influence in the sociological discipline. In 1935 he moved from the University of Chicago to Indiana University as head of the Department of Sociology. Exercising a leadership position there, he went on to become president of the American Sociological Association in 1939. In 1940 he was elected president of the Sociological Research Association. He was also elected president of the Ohio Valley Sociological Society in 1942.

As argued in a recent paper by Galliher and Tyree (1985, p. 111), Sutherland was driven by a strong "anti-psychiatry ideology," and he saw this issue as a "professional turf" concern in making the case for a sociological criminology with himself as its leader (see also Gaylord and

[21] In this regard it is interesting to note Sheldon Glueck's bitter and hostile reaction: "The most confident and severest critics have been a group whose writings have the tone of fire-breathing chevaliers eager to do battle for that purest queen of the exact sciences, Sociology, to which the authors of *Unraveling Juvenile Delinquency* allegedly did not pay adequate tribute" (1960, p. 284). The Gluecks clearly did not take criticism well.

American Journal of Sociology

Galliher 1988; and Goff 1986). Sutherland's intentions were not lost on his contemporaries either. As his former colleague Karl Schuessler writes: Sutherland had a "bias against psychiatry" (1973, p. xvii) and "did not broaden his theoretical model to accommodate biological and psychological factors. In fact, he was severely critical of those criminologists who stretched their framework to include every possible factor, however disparate those factors might be" (1973, p. x). Clearly, it came to serve both Sutherland's interests and those of the discipline to establish proprietary rights in the study of crime.

There is also little doubt that Sutherland accurately perceived his own role in spearheading the sociological undermining of the Gluecks. Indeed, in a manner destined to embitter the Gluecks, Sutherland alone reviewed almost all of their books in professional journals (mainly law reviews) in the 1930s and 1940s. In a letter to Sheldon Glueck dated February 11, 1944, Sutherland even wrote, "I refused three invitations from journals to review your *Criminal Careers in Retrospect* because I did not desire to acquire an institutional status as a critic of your work." However, he goes on to say that he did in fact write the review when he "felt that it would be possible to write a review which would be relatively formal" (1944*b*).

His 1944 letter also continued the dismissal of individual-level correlates of crime that was consistent with the new outlook of the 1939 edition of *Principles*. While writing to Sheldon Glueck to "assure you that I have a most kindly personal attitude toward you," he went on to criticize the relevance of age to crime, arguing that the relationship was only "slightly more than chance." Sutherland also attacked the Gluecks' long-standing hypothesis concerning the stability of antisocial behavior over the life course. In particular, he contradicted his 1924 book and argued that "I believe that you do not demonstrate that these childhood characteristics have more than a slight relationship to behavior in middle age" (1944*b*, p. 2). In fact, Sutherland repeated his earlier charge that this "was a preconception and not a finding" (1944*b*, p. 2; see also Sutherland's formal review [1944*a*]).

In addition, Sutherland placed the Gluecks' research in the same camp as William Sheldon and E. A. Hooton, two researchers at Harvard interested in the biological causes of human behavior (see Cohen et al. 1956, pp. 270–326). The result was that the Gluecks were perceived as being interested in *only* the biological basis for criminal behavior. It is no surprise, then, that the most controversial aspect of the Gluecks' research vis-à-vis sociology was their inclusion of constitutional factors—especially body structure—in the study of crime. Indeed, sociologists have always had a long-standing aversion to biological explanations of human behavior. As Rowe and Osgood note, "In most sociological treat-

Sutherland-Glueck Debate

ments of crime and delinquency, genetic explanations are either ignored or ridiculed" (1984, p. 526).

Ironically, however, the Gluecks never posited a deterministic biological model. They argued instead that biological features set the context for social forces. That is, the Gluecks were interested in how social factors mediated the undeniable differences among individuals in such crime-relevant characteristics as strength. As Sheldon Glueck argued, "Those criminologists who call attention to variations in the strength of different hereditary drives and controlling mechanisms do not claim that criminalism *per se* is inherited, but merely point to the too-often sociologically-underemphasized if not ignored biological fact that, in the eyes of nature, all men are not created equal and that some, because of certain traits useful to the kind of activities involved in criminal behavior, probably have a higher delinquency *potential* than others" (1956, p. 94).

Sutherland also failed to recognize that the Gluecks were as critical of the work of Sheldon as was Sutherland himself. For example, in a review of Sheldon's *Varieties of Delinquent Youth* (1949), the Gluecks stated, "Space limitations do not permit us to illustrate [the] deficiencies . . . in the work under review" with respect to standard canons of science (1950*b*, p. 215). The Gluecks went on to totally dismiss the conclusions made by Sheldon, in large part because of an inadequate sampling design (1950*b*, p. 215). In a similar manner, Sutherland (1951) argued that Sheldon's research methods were suspect and his research failed to establish the physical differences between offenders and nonoffenders. In particular, Sutherland, like the Gluecks, pointed out that the "manner of selecting cases . . . effectively prevents [Sheldon] from reaching valid conclusions regarding delinquency." (1951, p. 10). Thus, not only was Sutherland's equation of the Gluecks with biological determinists such as Sheldon and Hooton (see, e.g., Sutherland and Cressey 1978, pp. 123–24) an error of sociological positivism, Sutherland's wholesale rejection of biological influences on human behavior appears to be at odds with current knowledge (see esp. Rowe and Osgood 1984; Udry 1988; Cohen and Machalek 1988).

Sutherland's final and probably most severe attack on the Gluecks concerned forms of data collection and analysis. Quite simply, Sutherland went so far as to imply that the Gluecks fudged their data. His claim was expressed in several ways. In a published review he implied that the Gluecks used ex post facto psychiatric evaluations and thus that the mental diagnosis was "necessarily" associated with the behavior (Sutherland 1937*b*, p. 186). More damning were "informal" comments made in the 1937 review circulated among colleagues across the country. He stated, "When the data and methods are examined, they are found to be completely untrustworthy" (1937*c*, p. 14), and he specifically charged

American Journal of Sociology

that the Gluecks "must have made their classification after the delinquency or nondelinquency of offenders during the second period was
already known to them, as well as after the failure to meet economic or
family responsibilities and the other aspects of behavior during the second
period were already known to them. The classification is therefore nothing except an expression of the authors' a priori conception of the relationship between overt behavior and mental condition. Nothing except
clerical errors could have prevented a high correlation between mental
abnormality and persistence in criminal behavior" (1937*c*, pp. 15–16).
With this alleged fatal flaw, not only could the Gluecks' data be dismissed, but their entire substantive framework, as judged by Sutherland,
"breaks down completely" (1937*c*, p. 17).

The Gluecks appeared quite aware of the underlying message of Sutherland's criticisms. As they wrote in their 25-page rejoinder, "You distinctly imply that we have somehow manipulated our materials to get
the result for which we were looking from the beginning. This is a very
serious charge to make and we are wondering how you could possibly
have arrived at it. It is very startling, to say the least, that . . . you could
infer that we manipulate our materials" (1937*b*, p. 20). The Gluecks
argued that the charge ought to be "ignored as undeserving of notice",
but since Sutherland had, in their words, the "temerity" to make it
(1937*b*, p. 20), they countered with the obvious fact that Sutherland
ignored: "It seems quite self-evident that the psychiatrists who made the
examinations at the different hospitals throughout the country at different
times and without the knowledge that the Gluecks would come along
many years later, and make follow-up studies did not conspire with us
beforehand to see that the unreformed would have a higher incidence of
mental deviation than the reformed. They could not possibly have
known, when they made the examinations, which of the men would
many years later turn out to be recidivists and which would reform,
(1937*b*, p. 20). The rest of their response rebutted in detail the thrust of
Sutherland's criticisms.

Sutherland's tenaciousness in striving for a pure sociological reading
of the evidence extended to his own work as well. For example, in a
detailed examination of the origins and development of Sutherland's *The
Professional Thief* (1937*a*), Snodgrass argues that "Sutherland over-
estimated the class-origin of the professional thief" and "virtually ignored . . . Jones' addiction to narcotics" (1973, pp. 11, 13). Snodgrass's
evaluation of this can be interpreted as Sutherland's use of a misguided
sociological positivism:

> A possible, but perhaps uncharitable, explanation for this omission might
> be the common theoretical association of drug dependence with psychologi-
> cal maladjustment. Sutherland's sociological interpretation would have

been considerably weakened, or at least challenged, had he revealed to the
reading audience that professional thieves were often "dope fiends," as
they were known then, who shot-up with the drugs obtained from the
money earned in their work. Sutherland was with this book also opposing
the psychological school by attempting to picture thieves as mentally stable.
Evading the drug issue was perhaps a way of supporting his sociological
explanation and avoiding a psychological controversy. [1973, p. 15]

Similarly, Galliher and Tyree (1985) examined Sutherland's research
on the origins of sexual psychopath laws and found that he ignored evidence contrary to his hypothesis. Moreover, Galliher and Tyree discovered "curious lapses and inconsistencies in the evidence he [Sutherland]
marshaled in support of his conclusions" (1985, p. 100). More specifically, they argue (1) that Sutherland did not systematically review the
newspapers from the states he discussed, (2) that his conclusions about
the press were based on a very selective sample of sensationalistic pieces,
especially lurid magazine articles, and (3) that he ignored critics such as
Tappan, Inbau, and Gault who questioned his claims. The selective
attention to facts was attributed to Sutherland's strong "antipsychiatric
ideology" (1985, p. 110).

We emphasize that, in our view, Sutherland was not driven by individual maliciousness or intentional dishonesty in his own work or in his
attack on the Gluecks. Rather, Sutherland's behavior may be seen as
socially conceived by the factors analyzed above—a substantive version
of sociological positivism fused with a false criterion of causality supplied
by analytic induction. In conjunction with his rising social position as
the leading sociologist of crime, it seems less surprising that Sutherland
selectively interpreted evidence in the process of dismantling the competition. In fact, it seems fair to suggest that Sutherland actually believed
the Gluecks' data *had* to be wrong and the sociological perspective portrayed in the idea of differential association right.[22]

THE TRANSMISSION OF ACCEPTED WISDOM

Despite the unproven nature of Sutherland's charges against the Gluecks,
the damage was done and took on a life of its own that remains to this
day in sociology. The momentum was facilitated in large part by the
social and institutional context within which both parties operated. Hav-

---

[22] It is beyond the scope of this paper to evaluate the research bearing on the validity
of differential association theory. Besides, this has been done elsewhere—for excellent
arguments that take opposing views see Kornhauser (1978) and Matsueda (1988). It
will come as no surprise to learn that the Gluecks did not think much of differential
association. At one point Sheldon Glueck referred to the idea of differential association
as "puerile" and as a "roof without a house" (1956, pp. 92, 99).

American Journal of Sociology

ing access to the benefits offered by a graduate sociology department, Sutherland became something of a magnet for Ph.D. students who would go on to carry the torch of differential association theory and a disregard for the Gluecks' research. In particular, Donald Cressey was a student of Sutherland's at Indiana University who later coauthored six editions of *Principles*. But there were also other prominent graduate students such as Albert Cohen and Lloyd Ohlin who were deeply influenced by Sutherland. As Cohen remarked in an interview with Laub (1983) about Indiana University in the late 1930s, at the height of the Sutherland-Glueck debate, "I would say all of the better graduate students were in criminology. They were all studying with Sutherland. There was a sense that the department of sociology at that particular time was really the breeding ground of theory. You were there at the source. The most exciting things in criminological theory were happening right there and they all somehow had to do with differential association. Differential association was theoretically the end of the world" (Laub 1983, p. 186). Cohen's remarks seem entirely apt in describing Sutherland's dedication to differential association and inculcating a generation of students that would do likewise. Indeed, Cohen noted that Sutherland "functioned as a kind of a guru" (Laub 1983, p. 186).

The Sutherland mystique even extends to the imputation of laudatory motives on the part of Sutherland in his judgments of the Gluecks. For example, Snodgrass has written that "Sutherland's obsession with honesty is no small reason for why he got into such a fracas with the Gluecks" (1972, p. 227). Schuessler writes that "he [Sutherland] was uncanny in his ability to spot errors in statistical logic and patient in locating the trouble—witness his unraveling of the Gluecks" (1973, p. xxxv). Similarly, Geis and Goff note that Sutherland's "writings are unsparing in their exposure of false syllogism, sloppy logic, the unsupported inference, and the generalization rooted in infancy rather than fact" (1983, p. xxi). Finally, Snodgrass (1972) argues that in his review (1934*b*) of *One Thousand Juvenile Delinquents* Sutherland "was one of the first to point to the Gluecks' exaggerations and omissions of data," and he goes on to state, without any documentation, that this is "a charge which has subsequently been repeated and enlarged, and a *fact* which might insure that [the Gluecks'] research will come to be discredited, if not disregarded, by future students and historians of the discipline" (1972, p. 244; emphasis added).

At the same time, key aspects of the Gluecks' perspective as well as their own particular institutional/historical context also contributed to their demise. We have identified six specific reasons why sociology, especially after Sutherland's death in 1950, was so hostile to the Gluecks' work. First, the Gluecks had a tendency to infuse their works with moral statements that reflected middle-class biases. For instance, in regard to the management of income, the Gluecks wrote that families of delinquents were "living from day to day, borrowing without thought of their ability to make reimbursement and showing little comprehension of the value of limiting their expenditures to conform to a meager income" (1950*a*, p. 108). On all accounts, the Gluecks simply viewed delinquents and their families as inferior. Moreover, although the Gluecks' data were derived from multiple reports describing actual behaviors, the Gluecks often injected moral judgments in their summary coding scheme using categories such as good, fair, and poor to describe these behaviors (see Glueck and Glueck [1950*a*] for numerous examples).

Second, as mentioned above, the Gluecks were atheoretical in their approach to the study of crime. But more than that, the Gluecks were *antitheory*. Although they emphasized an empirical tradition and sought to identify any and all characteristics that may be related to crime and delinquency, they regarded abstract theory as idle speculation and not useful from a scientific view. Thus, the Gluecks did not present a theory of crime or even any systematic theoretical ideas in their numerous works. In fact, their idea of a theoretical statement was to present a "tentative causal formula or law" that merely summarized their findings distinguishing offenders from nonoffenders (see Glueck and Glueck 1950*a*, pp. 281–82).

Third, despite embracing a multiple-factor approach, the Gluecks downplayed or ignored traditional sociological variables like stratification, peer group, culture, and community characteristics. As Snodgrass has noted (1972, p. 9), the Gluecks' focus was "bio-constitutional and psycho-social." Specifically, the Gluecks downplayed social factors (e.g., delinquent associates) in favor of morphology, temperament, and early family influences (see Glueck and Glueck 1943, p. 69; 1950*a;* 1956; 1962; 1968, p. 170). Overall, the Gluecks' research reflected a restricted range of interest in key sociological variables presumed to be related to crime.

Fourth, recall that Sheldon Glueck was a law professor and Eleanor Glueck a soft-money research assistant. By function of their social position within the academic institution, the Gluecks were precluded the opportunity to train graduate students and develop the sort of following that Sutherland had. Quite simply, no one had a stake in defending the Gluecks. We believe this context is crucial in understanding the transmission of Sutherland's legacy.

Fifth, our review of the Glueck papers, especially their personal correspondence (i.e., notes and letters), leads to the conclusion that the Gluecks suffered from social awkwardness and a severe difficulty in public relations. Whereas Sutherland was well liked and perceived to be "humble" and "gentle" (see Laub's [1983] interviews with Cressey, Co-

American Journal of Sociology

hen, and Ohlin), the Gluecks were stubborn and pompous and had great difficulty accepting any criticism of their work, justified or not, as something other than a personal attack on their integrity (see also S. Glueck 1960). This no doubt impeded their attempts to establish a cadre of supporters.

Sixth, and perhaps most important, the Gluecks' research was driven by pragmatic concerns. More precisely, they sought to influence social policy through the use of their prediction tables in two distinct ways. One was to improve the process of decision making by judges, probation officers, parole boards, and military officials.[23] The second was to identify potential delinquents at school age or perhaps even as early as age two and three (see E. Glueck 1966; and Glueck and Glueck 1959) in order to provide therapeutic intervention. For example, the Gluecks argued that the selection of potential delinquents at an early age "would make possible the application of treatment measures that would be truly crime preventive" (1950*a*, p. 257). Moreover, the Gluecks promoted this interest in the popular literature as well as in scholarly books and journals (see, e.g., Glueck and Glueck 1952; Morgan 1960; Callwood 1954; and Dressler 1955).

The Gluecks' research on prediction has been severely criticized on methodological grounds (see, e.g., Reiss 1951; Hirschi and Selvin 1967; and Laub and Sampson 1988). However, this interest reflected their professional interests and intellectual history. Although at the time sociology was not explicitly linked to social policy, such practical applications were the norm for the discipline reflected in the background of the Gluecks—law, psychiatry, education, and social work. In addition, this pragmatic orientation was consistent with the interests of the Gluecks' mentors such as Bernard Glueck and William Healy. Thus, through their interest in prediction techniques, the Gluecks promoted an emphasis on individual-level analysis and advocated the penetration of psychiatric expertise into the formal systems of social control. In fact, Sheldon Glueck maintained that "dynamic psychiatry offers the greatest promise of any single discipline for the discovery of the complex causes and motivations of emotional, intellectual, and behavioral maladjustment and for developing effective prophylactic and therapeutic techniques. For the psychiatric approach necessarily deals with the blended *interplay* of the forces of nature and nurture, instead of grossly overemphasizing innate predisposition, on the one hand, or external environment and general cultural influences, on the other" (1962, p. 158).

[23] For an overview of prediction research in the criminal justice area, see Glueck and Glueck (1959); for an application of the prediction tables in the military, see Schneider et al. (1944).

The Gluecks even envisioned a criminal justice system based on "the rational exercise of discretion enlightened by the reports of psychiatric, psychological, and social workers who ought . . . to be indispensable adjuncts to criminal courts and to classifying agencies and correctional establishments" (S. Glueck 1962, p. 139). Furthermore, the Gluecks encouraged the use and expansion of court clinics and child guidance centers. The result of this concern with social policy and the explicit promotion of the professional interests of the field of psychiatry was to further alienate the Gluecks from mainstream sociology as reflected by the works of Sutherland.[24]

Having placed the Sutherland-Glueck debate in social and historical context, we now turn to a brief assessment of the Gluecks' legacy. If Sutherland and common wisdom are correct (see also Snodgrass 1972, p. 244), then the Gluecks' research should have long ago faded into irrelevance. As it turns out, it is not even necessary to rely on the Gluecks' own defense to show the exaggerated nature of Sutherland's critique. Indeed, it is ironic that, despite numerous personal flaws and narrowly conceived professional interests, the Gluecks' substantive research in criminology remains strong.

A REVISIONIST ASSESSMENT OF THE GLUECKS' RESEARCH

The Gluecks could not have known the implications of their work for modern criminology. To speak of their "contributions" to present research is thus, as shown by Jones (1977, pp. 282–89), to commit the error of "presentism." We avoid this tendency by assessing the *validity* of their research methodology and substantive conclusions—that is, do they stand up to external verification? Moreover, to the extent that the current research agenda in criminology is simply an unacknowledged version of the Gluecks', the validity and importance of their work is further increased. Our assessment is based on a brief overview of four fundamental claims made by the Gluecks that, as detailed above, were dismissed by Sutherland.

Age and crime.—In a recent and highly cited article in this *Journal*, Hirschi and Gottfredson (1983) have argued that the age-crime relationship is one of the strongest in criminology and is generally invariant across time and space. Specifically, Hirschi and Gottfredson have con-

---

[24] It should be pointed out that the Gluecks' research was well received and respected in European countries (Snodgrass 1972, p. 330). This may reflect the fact that, historically, European criminology was dominated by the legal and medical professions in contrast to the United States where criminology was dominated by sociology (see Mannheim 1972, p. 2).

American Journal of Sociology

tended (see also Gottfredson and Hirschi 1986) that crime declines with age and that this pattern holds true even for the most active offenders (career criminals). Their evidence is based on a comprehensive review of extant data on the age-crime relationship covering many different cultures and time periods.

Whether or not the age-crime curve is "invariant" across time and space, the research literature clearly shows that the Gluecks were correct about the fundamental *importance* of age, and that their evidence collected over 40 years ago remains some of the best available on the subject. As Gottfredson and Hirschi concluded, "The Gluecks' data are corroborated by other sources" (1988, p. 50, see also pp. 39, 49). Even the most vocal critics of Hirschi and Gottfredson agree, unlike Sutherland, that age is an important predictor of crime and have also turned explicitly to the Gluecks' data for insight (see, e.g., Blumstein, Cohen, and Farrington 1988, pp. 12–13).

Criminal careers and longitudinal research.—The field of criminology is currently embroiled in a bitter dispute over the value of longitudinal research and the criminal-career paradigm. The spark for this dispute was the publication of a recent report by the National Academy of Sciences (NAS; Blumstein et al. 1986) wherein it was concluded that longitudinal research was necessary to study the causes of criminal careers. Moreover, the NAS report called for major new research initiatives to estimate four parameters of the criminal-career paradigm: *participation* (the distinction between those who engage in crime and those who do not), *frequency* (the rate of criminal activity of those who are active), *seriousness* of offenses committed, and *career length* (the length of time an offender is active). It is argued that valid estimates of these parameters are needed to determine effective crime-control policies in terms of selective incapacitation and individual deterrent effects (Blumstein et al. 1986, pp. 202–4). However, Gottfredson and Hirschi (1986, 1987, 1988) have forcefully attacked the NAS report, basically by claiming that longitudinal research is unnecessary and that selective incapacitation is impossible to achieve.

It is much beyond the scope of this paper to resolve the debate over longitudinal research and criminal careers. However, it is not necessary to do so to acknowledge that the Gluecks were the first to systematically put forth the criminal-career paradigm. As noted earlier, the Gluecks originally made the distinction between frequency and participation, arguing that the causes of recidivism were different from the causes of onset (Glueck and Glueck 1930, 1934a, 1945). They were also the first criminologists to collect longitudinal data on a large scale, follow offenders over long periods of time, study career length, and, unbeknownst to most, suggest the policy of selective incapacitation (Glueck and Glueck 1945, pp. 106–8; 1968, p. 166).

In short, regardless of whether one agrees with the current emphasis in criminology on criminal-career research and longitudinal designs (for opposing viewpoints, see Blumstein et al. [1988] and Gottfredson and Hirschi [1988]), there can be little doubt that such an emphasis basically revives the Gluecks' original arguments. In point of fact, the most adamant critics of the criminal-career paradigm attribute its origin to the Gluecks (see Gottfredson and Hirschi 1988, p. 39).

Stability of crime and deviance.—One of the Gluecks' early and major contributions to criminology was their hypothesis of stability of crime and deviance across the life course. Unlike Sutherland, who saw criminality as an ever-changing construct dependent on changing social influences, the Gluecks documented the relative stability of between-individual differences in crime. The Gluecks' hypothesis can be seen as one of "longitudinal consistency," which concerns "the extent to which individuals in a group retain their relative position on a certain dimension or characteristic . . . at different points in time" (Olweus 1979, p. 852). As they argued in a section of *Delinquents and Nondelinquents in Perspective* aptly titled "The Past Is Prologue," "while the majority of boys originally included in the nondelinquent control group continued, down the years, to remain essentially law-abiding, the greatest majority of those originally included in the delinquent group continued to commit all sorts of crimes in the 17–25 age-span" (Glueck and Glueck 1968, p. 170). In a related argument, the Gluecks' also hypothesized that early life experiences had strong effects on crime in the adult years.

What do the data say? The evidence on longitudinal consistency is unequivocally clear—antisocial behavior is a remarkably stable phenomenon (Loeber 1982; McCord 1979; Robins 1966; Olweus 1979; Huesmann et al. 1984; Gottfredson and Hirschi 1990). For example, Olweus reviewed over 16 studies on aggressive behavior and found "substantial" stability. More precisely, the correlation between early aggressive behavior and later criminality averaged .68 for the studies reviewed (Olweus 1979, pp. 854–55). Loeber completed a similar review of extant literature in many disciplines, concluding that a "consensus" has been reached in favor of the stability hypothesis: "Children who initially display high rates of antisocial behavior are more likely to persist in this behavior than children who initially show lower rates of antisocial behavior" (1982, p. 1433). In probably the most influential study of its kind, Huesmann et al. (1984) studied the aggressiveness of 600 subjects, their parents, and their children over a 22-year period. They concluded that "early aggressiveness was predictive [correlation of .50 for males] of later serious

American Journal of Sociology

antisocial behavior, including criminal behavior, spouse abuse, traffic violations, and self-reported physical aggression. Whatever its causes, aggression can be viewed as a persistent trait that may be influenced by situational variables but possesses substantial cross-situational constancy" (1984, pp. 1120, 1128).

Finally, McCord (1979) and Robins (1966) demonstrated the powerful effects of early-life experiences on later adult behavior. In fact, McCord showed that predictions of *adult* criminality based on childhood family experiences were more accurate than predictions based on the individuals' juvenile criminal records (1978, p. 1485). Sutherland's protestations notwithstanding, the Gluecks' early hypothesis of stability, later confirmed in *Delinquents and Nondelinquents in Perspective* (Glueck and Glueck 1968), has itself been confirmed by an impressive body of interdisciplinary research.

Social control, the family, and delinquency.—Hirschi's (1969) influential *Causes of Delinquency* stated the now widely cited reformulation of assumptions about human nature implicit in differential association theory. As he argued, the question is not why do they do it, but rather "Why *do* men obey the rules of society: Deviance is taken for granted; comformity must be explained" (1969, p. 10). Consider now Sheldon Glueck's earlier conceptualization of the problem, which also directly contradicts differential association theory: "What is there to be learned about simple lying, taking things that belong to another, fighting, and sex play? . . . One must conclude that it is not delinquent behavior that is learned; that comes naturally. It is rather *non*-delinquent behavior that is learned. . . . Law-abiding character formation is a hard-won process" (1956, pp. 94–95). The Gluecks were thus early proponents of a social-control perspective, arguing that the child must be socialized to overcome natural asocial or antisocial impulses. Although unsystematic, the Gluecks' notion of social control led them to study the role of families, schools, opportunities (e.g., peers and use of leisure time), and formal sanctions in explaining crime and delinquency.

Of all the factors they studied, however, the Gluecks clearly focused most attention on the *family*. They identified the key predictors of delinquency as inconsistent and/or lax disciplinary practices by parents, low supervision and monitoring of the youth's behavior, and attenuated attachment between parent and child (1950a, p. 261). These same family process factors have subsequently been shown to be sturdy and strong predictors of juvenile delinquency in a variety of settings—including different time periods, geographic location, age groups, and methodology (see esp. Farrington and West 1981; Robins 1966; Hirschi 1969; Patterson 1982). And in the most exhaustive review available on families and crime, Loeber and Stouthamer-Loeber (1986, pp. 37, 120) conclude that "aspects of family functioning involving direct parent-child contacts" are the most powerful predictors of delinquency and other juvenile conduct problems.

We have also reanalyzed the raw data from the Gluecks' *Unraveling Juvenile Delinquency* from the vantage point of (*a*) recent theoretical advances on the family (e.g., Hirschi 1969, 1983; Patterson 1982) and (*b*) recent advances in multivariate techniques. The results (see Laub and Sampson 1988) demonstrate that the strongest predictors of delinquency are the same family variables identified by the Gluecks as the most important correlates of delinquency over 30 years ago—discipline, supervision, and attachment. Not only do these results correspond with current research *and* theory, they confirm the Gluecks' own analyses.

Overall, then, major areas of the Gluecks' research—age and crime, longitudinal research/criminal careers, stability of crime and antisocial behavior, and social-control theory with a focus on family processes— have been shown to be either (*a*) essentially correct or (*b*) currently dominating the research agenda in criminology. Moreover, despite their methodological shortcomings, which were real and cannot be overlooked (see Laub and Sampson 1988, pp. 357–61), researchers have replicated the Gluecks' basic findings using new methods and procedures on their original data. Therefore, while the Gluecks' research has been *disregarded* by sociologists, as Snodgrass (1972, p. 245) predicted, it has not been *discredited* by subsequent research. Indeed, if the Gluecks' data and analysis were so poor and/or fudged as Sutherland claimed, it is virtually impossible that their findings would have been replicated time and time again by external investigators using other data and by our analyses of their original data.[25]

CONCLUSIONS

There is no doubt that Edwin Sutherland made substantial contributions to the field of criminology, especially in the areas of white-collar and professional crime and the development of the theory of differential association. Unlike other contemporaries (e.g., Clifford Shaw, Henry

---

[25] We also conducted a detailed validation of the Gluecks' data from the *Unraveling* study. Using the original handwritten interview schedules currently preserved at the Henry A. Murray Research Center of Radcliffe College in Cambridge, Mass., we successfully reconstructed the full longitudinal data set and found the data to be consistent with published reports as well as our own logical consistency checks. Moreover, we were able to trace and interview several members of the Gluecks' original research team for the *Unraveling* study, including Richard LaBrie, Mildred P. Cunningham, Sheila Murphrey, and Mary H. Moran. Taking all this information into account, we uncovered no evidence of anything other than meticulous data collection.

American Journal of Sociology

McKay, Thorsten Sellin) Sutherland was also one of the first to offer a systematic theory that attempted to explain individual-level as well as macro-level differences in crime. He is thus appropriately revered as one of the most important criminologists to date, and his work continues to influence modern research (see Matsueda 1988).

Nevertheless, this state of affairs should not blind us to the brute force of Sutherland's critique of the Gluecks' work. Reflecting broader concerns about the shape and image of criminology in society, Sutherland's criticisms stemmed from his rejection of the multiple-factor approach, his adherence to a substantive version of sociological positivism, and his position as the dominant criminologist of the 20th century. When supplied with a false criterion of causality offered by his conversion to analytic induction, Sutherland felt free to dismiss the Gluecks' empirical contributions to criminological knowledge.

The power of Sutherland's critique is hard to overestimate. To this day sociological positivism is dominant and the Gluecks are often seen as relics of a distant past. Having been reified by the academic community, the Gluecks' fate has become so much a social fact that the best-selling criminology text in America (Siegel 1989), with over 1,000 references and 550 pages, cites the Gluecks but once. In true Sutherland tradition, the citation is to mesomorphy—by linking the Gluecks' work to "Lombrosians and other biological determinists" it is summarily rejected as "methodologically unsound" and "invalid" (Siegel 1989, p. 126). By contrast, our analysis has provided a revisionist assessment of the Gluecks' contributions to fundamental issues in criminological research that reaches the opposite conclusion.

Perhaps more important, however, our paper demonstrates the need to understand the processes by which knowledge is socially constructed. In particular, through a contemporary look at the Sutherland-Glueck debate we have provided new insights into the historical and intellectual context of criminological thought. Our findings support recent developments in intellectual historiography, which asserts that classic works in the history of ideas cannot be dealt with according to ordinary processes of causal explanation, but that their understanding presupposes a grasp of the authors' intentions and that this in turn requires the reconstruction of the conventions governing discussion of the issues of concern (see esp. Jones 1977; 1986, p. 618; Beirne 1987).

Moreover, we extended this approach to include an investigation of not only the historical context of the Sutherland-Glueck debate but the social positions and institutional settings they occupied within that context (see Camic 1987). We showed that the formation and substance of both Sutherland's *and* the Gluecks' positions were deeply affected by their respective methodological, disciplinary, and even institutional biases. To Sutherland, the Gluecks' multiple-factor approach to crime represented a symbolic threat to the intellectual status of sociological criminology of which he was the leader, and hence his attack on the Gluecks' interdisciplinary thought served the larger interest of sociology in establishing proprietary rights to criminology. To the Gluecks, Sutherland represented abstract theorizing about crime from a unilateral (i.e., sociological) perspective. Moreover, this general theory was divorced from any social policy designed to prevent and control delinquency. Given the Gluecks' interest in using predictive techniques for pragmatic ends as well as their own lofty views of the importance of their research, they had no choice but to rebut Sutherland's critiques and launch a counterattack on all criminologists who disagreed with their position. The accepted fates of Sutherland and the Gluecks are thus interwoven and cannot be understood simply by reference to the truth *or* falsity of their research findings but instead must be placed within the social and institutional context of their debate.

In sum, our efforts support Jones's sobering yet penetrating conclusion: "For surely it is curious that, at the same time that modern sociologists struggle to expand their imaginations and thus to develop new ideas to account for the complexities of human behavior, there is nothing of which we are more ignorant than the nature of the process by which such ideas emerge, are received, grow, change, and are eventually surpassed" (1977, p. 311). This is perhaps nowhere more true than in criminology, where "new" developments are constantly offered in what seems to be a collective amnesia about the past. We hope to have counteracted this tendency by specifying the social foundations of one of the major developments in criminological knowledge this century.[26]

REFERENCES

Abramson, Jill, and Barbara Franklin. 1986. *Where They Are Now: The Story of the Women of Harvard Law 1974*. New York: Doubleday.
Beirne, Piers. 1987. "Adolphe Quetelet and the Origins of Positivist Criminology." *American Journal of Sociology* 92:1140–60.
Blumstein, Alfred, Jacqueline Cohen, and David P. Farrington. 1988. "Criminal Career Research: Its Value for Criminology." *Criminology* 26:1–35.
Blumstein, Alfred, Jacqueline Cohen, Jeffrey Roth, and Christy Visher, eds. 1986. *Criminal Careers and "Career Criminals."* Washington, D.C.: National Academy
Cabot, Richard C. 1926. *Facts on the Heart*. Philadelphia: Saunders.
Callwood, June. 1954. "Will Your Youngster Turn to Crime?" *Maclean's Magazine*, September 15.

[26] See Beirne (1987) for a sociological account of the 19th-century origins of positivist criminology.

American Journal of Sociology

Camic, Charles. 1987. "Historical Reinterpretation of the Early Parsons." *American Sociological Review* 52:421–39.

Cohen, Albert K. 1970. "Multiple Factor Approaches." Pp. 123–26 in *The Sociology of Crime and Delinquency*, 2d ed. Edited by Marvin Wolfgang, Leonard Savitz and Norman Johnston. New York: Wiley.

Cohen, Albert K., Alfred Lindesmith, and Karl Schuessler, eds. 1956. *The Sutherland Papers*. Bloomington: Indiana University Press.

Cohen, Lawrence E., and Richard Machalek. 1988. "A General Theory of Expropriative Crime: An Evolutionary Ecological Approach." *American Journal of Sociology* 94:465–501.

Current Biography Yearbook. 1957. "Glueck, Sheldon and Eleanor Touroff" 18:10–12. New York: H. W. Wilson.

Dressler, David. 1955. "You: The Newly Married—the Young Parent Can Prevent Delinquency." *Everywoman's Magazine*, September.

Faculty Committee Report. 1954. *The Behavioral Sciences at Harvard*. Eleanor T. and Sheldon Glueck Joint Papers. Harvard Law School Library, Cambridge, Mass.

Farrington, David P., and Donald West. 1981. "The Cambridge Study in Delinquency Development." Pp. 137–45 in *Prospective Longitudinal Research*, edited by S. Mednick and A. E. Baert. Oxford: Oxford University Press.

Frankfurter, Felix. 1934. Introduction to *One Thousand Juvenile Delinquents*. Sheldon and Eleanor Glueck. Cambridge, Mass.: Harvard University Press.

Galliher, John F., and Cheryl Tyree. 1985. "Edwin Sutherland's Research on the Origins of Sexual Psychopath Laws: An Early Case Study of the Medicalization of Deviance." *Social Problems* 33:100–113.

Gaylord, Mark S., and John F. Galliher. 1988. *The Criminology of Edwin Sutherland*, New Brunswick, N.J.: Transaction.

Geis, Gilbert. 1966. "Review of *Ventures in Criminology*." *Journal of Criminal Law, Criminology, and Police Science* 57:187–88.

———. 1970. "Review of *Delinquents and Nondelinquents in Perspective*." *Crime and Delinquency* 16:118–19.

Geis, Gilbert, and Colin Goff. 1983. Introduction to *White Collar Crime: The Uncut Version*, by Edwin H. Sutherland. New Haven, Conn.: Yale University Press.

———. 1986. "Edwin H. Sutherland's White-Collar Crime in America: An Essay in Historical Criminology." *Criminal Justice History* 7:1–31.

Gibbons, Don. 1979. *The Criminological Enterprise: Theories and Perspectives*. Englewood Cliffs, N.J.: Prentice-Hall.

Gilboy, Elizabeth Waterman. 1936. "Interview with Eleanor Touroff Glueck." *Barnard College Alumnae Monthly* 26:11–12.

Glueck, Bernard. 1916. *Studies in Forsenic Psychiatry*. Boston: Little, Brown.

———. 1918. "A Study of Six Hundred and Eight Admissions to Sing Sing Prison." *Mental Hygiene* 2:85–151.

Glueck, Eleanor. 1927. *Community Use of Schools*. Baltimore: Williams & Wilkins.

———. 1936. *Evaluative Research in Social Work*. New York: Columbia University Press.

———. 1966. "Identification of Potential Delinquents at 2–3 Years of Age." *International Journal of Psychiatry* 12:5–16.

Glueck, Sheldon. 1925. *Mental Disorder and the Criminal Law*. Boston: Little, Brown.

———. 1934. Letter to H. H. Bingham, October 5. Sheldon Glueck Papers. Harvard Law School Library, Cambridge, Mass.

———. 1956. "Theory and Fact in Criminology." *British Journal of Delinquency* 7:92–109.

———. 1960. "Ten Years of *Unraveling Juvenile Delinquency:* An Examination of Criticisms." *Journal of Criminal Law, Criminology, and Police Science* 51:283–308.

———. 1962. *Law and Psychiatry: Cold War or Entente Cordiale?* Baltimore: Johns Hopkins University Press.

———. 1964. "Remarks in Honor of William Healy, M.D." *Mental Hygiene* 48:318–22.

Glueck, Sheldon, and Eleanor Glueck. 1930. *500 Criminal Careers*. New York: Knopf.

———. 1934a. *One Thousand Juvenile Delinquents*. Cambridge, Mass.: Harvard University Press.

———. 1934b. *Five Hundred Delinquent Women*. New York: Knopf.

———. 1937a. *Later Criminal Careers*. New York: The Commonwealth Fund.

———. 1937b. "Analysis of Prof. Sutherland's Appraisal of *Later Criminal Careers*." Sheldon Glueck Papers. Harvard Law School Library, Cambridge, Mass.

———. 1937c. Letter to Edwin Sutherland, December 14. Eleanor T. and Sheldon Glueck Joint Papers. Harvard Law School Library, Cambridge, Mass.

———. 1940. *Juvenile Delinquents Grown Up*. New York: The Commonwealth Fund.

———. 1943. *Criminal Careers in Retrospect*. New York: The Commonwealth Fund.

———. 1945. *After-Conduct of Discharged Offenders*. London: Macmillan.

———. 1950a. *Unraveling Juvenile Delinquency*. New York: The Commonwealth Fund.

———. 1950b. "Review of Sheldon's *Varieties of Delinquent Youth*." *Survey* 86:215.

———. 1951. "Note of Plans for Further 'Unraveling' Juvenile Delinquency." *Journal of Criminal Law, Criminology, and Police Science* 41:759–62.

———. 1952. *Delinquents in the Making*. New York: Harper.

———. 1956. *Physique and Delinquency*. New York: Harper.

———. 1959. *Predicting Delinquency and Crime*. Cambridge, Mass.: Harvard University Press.

———. 1962. *Family Environment and Delinquency*. London: Routledge & Kegan Paul.

———. 1964. *Ventures in Criminology*. Cambridge, Mass.: Harvard University Press.

———. 1968. *Delinquents and Nondelinquents in Perspective*. Cambridge, Mass.: Harvard University Press.

———. 1970. *Toward a Typology of Juvenile Delinquency*. New York: Grune & Stratton.

———. 1974. *Of Delinquency and Crime*. Springfield, Ill.: Thomas.

Goff, Colin. 1986. "Criminological Appraisals of Psychiatric Explanations of Crime: 1936–1950." *International Journal of Law and Psychiatry* 9:245–60.

Goring, Charles. (1913) 1972. *The English Convict*. Montclair, N.J.: Patterson Smith.

Gottfredson, Michael, and Travis Hirschi. 1986. "The True Value of Lambda Would Appear to Be Zero: An Essay on Career Criminals, Criminal Careers, Selective Incapacitation, Cohort Studies, and Related Topics." *Criminology* 24:213–34.

———. 1987. "The Methodological Adequacy of Longitudinal Research." *Criminology* 25:581–614.

———. 1988. "Science, Public Policy, and the Career Paradigm." *Criminology* 26:37–55.

———. 1990. *A General Theory of Crime*. Stanford, Calif.: Stanford University Press.

Hall, Livingston. 1937. "A Reply to Professor Sutherland's Review of *Later Criminal Careers*." *Harvard Law Review* 51:389–93.

Healy, William. 1915. *The Individual Delinquent*. Boston: Little, Brown.

Healy, William, and Augusta F. Bronner. 1926. *Delinquents and Criminals: Their Making and Unmaking*. New York: Macmillan.

American Journal of Sociology

Hirschi, Travis. 1969. *Causes of Delinquency*. Berkeley: University of California Press.

———. 1973. "Procedural Rules and the Study of Deviant Behavior." *Social Problems* 21:159–73.

———. 1983. "Crime and the Family." Pp. 53–68 in *Crime and Public Policy*, edited by James Q. Wilson. San Francisco: Institute for Contemporary Studies.

Hirschi, Travis, and Michael Gottfredson. 1980. "Introduction: The Sutherland Tradition in Criminology." Pp. 7–19 in *Understanding Crime*, edited by Travis Hirschi and Michael Gottfredson. Beverly Hills, Calif.: Sage.

———. 1983. "Age and the Explanation of Crime." *American Journal of Sociology* 89:552–84.

Hirschi, Travis, and Hanan C. Selvin. 1967. *Delinquency Research: An Appraisal of Analytic Methods*. New York: Free Press.

———. 1970. "False Criteria of Causality." Pp. 127–40 in *The Sociology of Crime and Delinquency*, 2d ed. Edited by Marvin Wolfgang, Leonard Savitz, and Norman Johnston. New York: Wiley.

Huesmann, L. Rowell, Leonard Eron, Monroe Lefkowitz, and Leopold Walder. 1984. "Stability of Aggression over Time and Generations." *Developmental Psychology* 20:1120–34.

Jones, Robert Alun. 1977. "On Understanding a Sociological Classic." *American Journal of Sociology* 83:279–319.

———. 1986. "Durkheim, Frazer, and Smith: The Role of Analogies and Exemplars in the Development of Durkheim's Sociology of Religion." *American Journal of Sociology* 92:596–627.

Kornhauser, Ruth Rosner. 1978. *Social Sources of Delinquency*. Chicago: University of Chicago Press.

Laub, John H. 1983. *Criminology in the Making: An Oral History*. Boston: Northeastern University Press.

Laub, John H., and Robert J. Sampson. 1988. "Unraveling Families and Delinquency: A Reanalysis of the Gluecks' Data." *Criminology* 26:355–80.

Lazarsfeld, Paul F. 1955. "Interpretation of Statistical Relations as a Research Operation." Pp. 115–25 in *The Language of Social Research*, edited by Paul F. Lazarsfeld and Morris Rosenberg. New York: Free Press.

Lindesmith, Alfred. 1947. *Opiate Addiction*. Bloomington: Indiana University Press.

———. 1988. Foreword to *The Criminology of Edwin Sutherland*, by Mark S. Gaylord and John F. Galliher. New Brunswick, N.J.: Transaction.

Loeber, Rolf. 1982. "The Stability of Antisocial Child Behavior: A Review." *Child Development* 53:1431–46.

Loeber, Rolf, and Magda Stouthamer-Loeber. 1986. "Family Factors as Correlates and Predictors of Juvenile Conduct Problems and Delinquency." Pp. 29–150 in *Crime and Justice: An Annual Review of Research*, vol. 7. Edited by Michael Tonry and Norval Morris. Chicago: University of Chicago Press.

Mannheim, Hermann. 1965. *Comparative Criminology*. Boston: Houghton Mifflin.

———. 1972. *Pioneers in Criminology*, enlarged 2d ed. Montclair, N.J.: Patterson Smith.

Matsueda, Ross L. 1988. "The Current State of Differential Association Theory." *Crime and Delinquency* 34:277–306.

McCord, Joan. 1979. "Some Child-rearing Antecedents of Criminal Behavior in Adult Men." *Journal of Personality and Social Psychology* 37:1477–86.

Merton, Robert. 1971. Foreword to *Masters of Sociological Thought: Ideas in Historical and Social Context*, by Lewis Coser. New York: Harcourt Brace Jovanovich.

Michael, Jerome, and Mortimer J. Adler. 1933. *Crime, Law, and Social Science*. New York: Harcourt Brace.

Sutherland-Glueck Debate

Morgan, Thomas B. 1960. "Now We Can Spot Delinquents Early." _Think Magazine,_ March, pp. 2–6.

Olweus, Daniel. 1979. "Stability of Aggressive Reaction Patterns in Males: A Review." _Psychological Bulletin_ 86:852–75.

Patterson, Gerald. 1982. _Coercive Family Process._ Eugene, Oreg.: Castalia.

Potts, David P. 1965. "Social Ethics at Harvard, 1881–1931: A Study in Academic Activism." Pp. 91–128 in _Social Sciences at Harvard, 1860–1920._ Cambridge, Mass.: Harvard University Press.

Reckless, Walter. 1941. "Review of the Gluecks' _Juvenile Delinquents Grown Up._" _American Journal of Sociology_ 46:736–38.

Reiss, Albert J., Jr. 1951. "Unraveling Juvenile Delinquency. II. An Appraisal of the Research Methods." _American Journal of Sociology_ 57:115–20.

Robins, Lee. 1966. _Deviant Children Grown Up._ Baltimore: Williams & Wilkins.

Rowe, David, and D. Wayne Osgood. 1984. "Heredity and Sociological Theories of Delinquency: A Reconsideration." _American Sociological Review_ 49:526–40.

Schneider, Alexander J. N., Cyrus W. LaGrone, Jr., Eleanor T. Glueck, and Sheldon Glueck. 1944. "Prediction of Behavior of Civilian Delinquents in the Armed Forces." _Mental Hygiene_ 28:456–75.

Schuessler, Karl, ed. 1973. _Edwin H. Sutherland on Analyzing Crime._ Chicago: University of Chicago Press.

Sellin, Thorsten. 1938. _Culture Conflict and Crime._ New York: Social Science Research Council.

Sheldon, William H. 1949. _Varieties of Delinquent Youth: An Introduction to Constitutional Psychiatry._ New York: Harper.

Siegel, Larry. 1989. _Criminology,_ 3d ed. Minneapolis: West.

Snodgrass, Jon. 1972. _The American Criminological Tradition: Portraits of the Men and Ideology in a Discipline._ Ann Arbor, Mich.: University Microfilms International.

———. 1973. "The Criminologist and His Criminal: Edwin H. Sutherland and Broadway Jones." _Issues in Criminology_ 8:1–17.

Sutherland, Edwin H. 1924. _Criminology._ Philadelphia: Lippincott.

———. 1929. Letter to Sheldon Glueck, September 27. Sheldon Glueck Papers. Harvard Law School Library, Cambridge, Mass.

———. 1934a. _Principles of Criminology,_ 2d rev. ed. Philadephia: Lippincott.

———. 1934b. "Review of the Gluecks' _One Thousand Juvenile Delinquents._" _Journal of Criminal Law, Criminology, and Police Science_ 25:144–46.

———. 1936. Letter to Sheldon Glueck, May 4. Sheldon Glueck Papers. Harvard Law School Library, Cambridge, Mass.

———. 1937a. _The Professional Thief._ Chicago: University of Chicago Press.

———. 1937b. "Review of Gluecks' _Later Criminal Careers._" _Harvard Law Review_ 51:184–86.

———. 1937c. "The Gluecks' _Later Criminal Careers:_ An Appraisal by Edwin Sutherland." Eleanor T. and Sheldon Glueck Joint Papers. Harvard Law School Library, Cambridge, Mass.

———. 1937d. Letter to Sheldon Glueck, December 4. Sheldon Glueck Papers. Harvard Law School Library, Cambridge, Mass.

———. 1938. Letter to Eleanor Glueck, January 11. Sheldon Glueck Papers. Harvard Law School Library, Cambridge, Mass.

———. 1944a. "Review of Gluecks' _Criminal Careers in Retrospect._" _American Bar Association Journal_ 30:142.

———. 1944b. Letter to Sheldon Glueck, February 11. Eleanor T. and Sheldon Glueck Joint Papers. Harvard Law School Library, Cambridge, Mass.

———. 1947. _Principles of Criminology,_ 4th ed. Philadelphia: Lippincott.

American Journal of Sociology

————. 1949. *White Collar Crime*. New York: Dryden.
————. 1951. "Critique of Sheldon's *Varieties of Delinquent Youth*." *American Sociological Review* 16:10–13.
————. 1983. *White Collar Crime: The Uncut Version*. New Haven, Conn.: Yale University Press.
Sutherland, Edwin H., and Donald R. Cressey. 1955. *Principles of Criminology*, 5th ed. Chicago: Lippincott.
————. 1978. *Principles of Criminology*, 10th ed. Philadelphia: Lippincott.
Taft, Donald. 1937. "Review of Gluecks' *Later Criminal Careers*." *American Sociological Review* 2:940–41.
Turner, Ralph. 1953. "The Quest for Universals in Sociological Research." *American Sociological Review* 24:605–11.
Udry, J. Richard. 1988. "Biological Predispositions and Social Control in Adolescent Sexual Behavior." *American Sociological Review* 53:709–22.
Vaillant, George E. 1980. "Glueck, Eleanor Touroff." Pp. 278–80 in *Notable American Women: The Modern Period*, edited by Barbara Sickerman and Carol Hurd Greer. Cambridge, Mass.: Harvard University Press.

[15]

THE BRITISH JOURNAL
OF
CRIMINOLOGY

Vol. 16   January 1976   No. 1

CLIFFORD R. SHAW AND HENRY D. McKAY: CHICAGO CRIMINOLOGISTS

JON SNODGRASS (*Los Angeles*) *

THE sociological studies of juvenile delinquency conducted by Clifford R. Shaw and Henry D. McKay in the 1930s and early 1940s were considered extremely important contributions to criminological thought in their day and continue to be highly regarded in the social sciences today. The persisting interest in their work is reflected in the fact that *Juvenile Delinquency and Urban Areas*, their most comprehensive book, has been updated recently with new chapters by McKay and re-issued as a paperback, along with an introduction by James F. Short, Jr. (Short, 1972). Also, it is common to find Shaw and McKay's articles reprinted in modern anthologies (Radzinowitz and Wolfgang, 1971; Voss and Peterson, 1971).

The contributions of Shaw and McKay can be divided into three main areas: (a) collection of autobiographies of juvenile delinquents, (b) research on the geographical distribution of delinquents and (c) creation of a delinquency prevention programme known as the Chicago Area Project (CAP). These efforts were actually integrated theoretically: the geographical material located delinquency in " high delinquency areas", contiguous to commerce and industry and usually near the centre of the city. The autobiographies illustrated an individual case in one of the areas, and the CAP was a community organisation movement which attempted to reform the areas in the interest of delinquency prevention.

* Asst. Professor, Dept. of Sociology, California State University.

1 I am very grateful to a great number of people who gave me information and materials to compose this article. In particular, Henry D. McKay received me very warmly and provided ample time for discussion and access to the files of the old Institute for Juvenile Research. Mrs. Hetta Shaw, William P. Shaw, Rita Shaw, Anthony Sorrentino and James R. Bennett were also very generous with time and materials. I would also like to thank Gilbert Geis, Terry Kendal and Dawn Baker for assistance, affection and support in completing this manuscript.

JON SNODGRASS

Little critical attention has been paid to Shaw and McKay, today or in the past, with the exception of reviews of technical-methodological issues. This paper attempts to provide an overview and criticism of their work. A biographical sketch preceding the analysis affords information about the background of two " social pathologists " and the social conditions under which their ideas developed. A critique follows which attempts to pinpoint theoretical limitations in their ecological studies which have been overlooked to date. The final part presents analysis of the CAP. The relationship between biographical origins and criminological ideas and practices is most developed in this section. Because of space limitations, no analysis of the life history material is presented in this paper. It is hoped that this article will serve as a small contribution to the history of criminological thought and provide some information about two important figures in, and the kind of work which developed out of, the Chicago School of sociology.

The work of Shaw and McKay within criminology was a part of a larger movement in the social sciences usually known as " the social ecology school ". The school was centred in the Sociology Department at the University of Chicago, and was principally under the direction of Robert E. Park and Ernest W. Burgess. As University of Chicago students in the early 1920s Shaw and McKay's attention was drawn to the study of the city itself, and especially to those portions which constituted " social problems ". " Social ecology " provided a general theoretical orientation to explain the causes of social problems in terms of ecological laws. The Sociology Department encouraged fieldwork, empirical research, participant observation and first-hand contact with residents and areas of the city. The efforts of Shaw and McKay in criminology were only one of a number of sociological studies which used ecological theory and case study methods to investigate " urban behaviour ". The same basic orientation was used by Dai in the study of opium addicts, Cavan of suicides, Faris and Dunham of mental disorders, among numerous others (Faris, 1967, 64–67).

The Backgrounds of Shaw and McKay

Clifford R. Shaw and Henry D. McKay, two farm boys who came to Chicago in the 1920s to undertake graduate work in sociology at the famous university, were both born and brought up in rural, mid-western areas of the United States, both received Christian upbringings, and both attended small, denominational country colleges. Shaw was from an Indiana crossroads that barely constituted a town, and McKay was from the vast prairie regions of South Dakota. Following graduate school, Shaw and McKay worked together for 30 years as a research team at the Institute for Juvenile Research near the Chicago Loop.

Although their social origins were quite similar, the personalities of the two men were strikingly different. McKay was the quiet statistician, a man who stayed removed at the Institute and plotted the maps, calculated the rates, ran the correlations and described the findings which located empirically and depicted cartographically the distribution of crime and delinquency in Chicago. Shaw, on the other hand, was an activist, who " related " to

CLIFFORD R. SHAW AND HENRY D. McKAY: CHICAGO CRIMINOLOGISTS

delinquents and got their life stories, and an organiser who attempted to create a community reform movement. McKay was the professional scholar and gentleman—polite, kind, thoughtful—an academic out to prove his position with empirical evidence. Shaw was the more emotional practitioner, a professional administrator and organiser—talkative, friendly, personable, persuasive, energetic and quixotic—out to make his case through action and participation.

Clifford R. Shaw

Shaw, the fifth of 10 children, was born in August 1895 in Luray, an Indiana farm community 30 miles south-east of Muncie. " A dozen little old-fashioned houses snugly hidden among the hills " is the way Shaw once described it. " The houses were neatly and compactly gathered in four right angles made by the intersection of two roads." [2] Shaw's father owned and cultivated an eighty-acre tract of land, owned the small general store, and often worked as a harness-maker and shoemaker. Although Shaw represented his family as poor dirt-farmers, it appears that they were more substantial small-town people; Republican, Scottish-Irish, Protestant, established in Indiana for several generations.[3]

Shaw began school when he was seven and went irregularly until he was fourteen. " At that age I was forced to leave school and work on the farm with my father " Shaw wrote. The reasons why he was " forced " to leave school are not completely known; perhaps his labour was needed at home, apparently he had not done especially well, and there is some indication that his departure was not totally involuntary. Shaw's disenchantment with farming grew over the next several years. He studied vocabulary while working behind the plough, read books at night, longed for brighter lights, and aspired to the ministry.

During public addresses Shaw often, and somewhat fondly, mentioned his own childhood delinquencies in Luray. In one of these, he was caught stealing stove bolts from the blacksmith's shop in order to repair a toy wagon. The blacksmith shook him upside down by the heels, Shaw said, and the bolts fell to the ground. This experience was used to illustrate the typical small-town reaction to delinquency—the blacksmith then helped him repair the wagon.

When Shaw was 15, a Methodist minister from Adrian College in Michigan spoke at the Luray church and encouraged him to pursue his studies. " He told me that there was opportunity for a young man to work his way through college without much financial aid." That fall, Shaw went off to Adrian to study for the ministry.

---

[2] This, and several following quotations, are from a handwritten autobiography by Shaw, probably done in the summer of 1919 in connection with his application to gain admission to the University of Chicago. They should be read with Shaw's goal in mind.

[3] Shaw wrote further: " My father was a man of medium size, of kind yet firm disposition, and was not very free toward his children. He had always worked hard to provide a living for the members of his family. He has always lived on a farm, depending upon renting land from neighbors and giving half of the proceeds for rental. His education was very scant and as a result, hard manual labor has been the only source of financial income he has had. This fact of my parents' financial status has had a very marked influence upon the course and thought of my life."

3

JON SNODGRASS

The religious education, however, prompted a deconversion. Shaw was exposed to more liberal ideas than he had known in his home community. While he remained a non-institutional Christian in principle all his life, Shaw gave up the ministry and left the church. His experiences at Adrian created a deep conflict: " By the end of my junior year I had abandoned the thought of becoming a minister. This radical change in my life-purpose was due to the fact that my religious views were quite liberal and could not find favor in the church to which I belonged, and secondly, I found that I had idealized the ministry as a profession and on finding that my previous conception of the minister was wrong, I suddenly became very intolerant with the profession. My attitude toward ministers and ministerial students became very inimical, especially if their religious views were conservative. My attitude toward religion in general was very hostile. I even came to the place where I considered religion a barrier to the progress of humanity."

In the spring of 1917, after his junior year, and while his mind was still very unsettled, Shaw went from God to arms and joined the U.S. Navy. He was trained at Johns Hopkins University as a pharmacist's mate for the submarine corps, but the war ended before he went to sea. In the fall of 1918, he returned to Adrian to complete the A.B. The next year, having fallen backwards out of the church, Shaw fell forward, as it were, into graduate school in sociology, at the University of Chicago. This shift in career line further substantiates C. W. Mill's (1962) frequently-cited observation that many of the " social pathologists " were " fathered " by the rural, protestant ministry. In Chicago, Shaw lived in a settlement, " The House of Happiness ", in an Eastern European neighbourhood, near the inner city. This introduction to the slum sections served to awaken a consciousness to the starker realities of American social life. Similarly, we know that Edwin H. Sutherland, who came to Chicago out of a background resembling Shaw's, once wrote: " When I became an officer of the Juvenile Protective Association I saw for the first time in my life the conditions of life in the immigrant sections of a large city. These impressed me very much, as had some of the earlier literature I had read (Jacob Riis, etc.) and I developed a somewhat radical attitude." (Sutherland, 1973). The qualification " somewhat radical " was entirely appropriate both for Sutherland and for Shaw. The experience " liberalized " the conservative orientation " naturally " acquired in their rather strict home communities.

From 1921 to 1923, Shaw worked part-time as a parole officer for the Illinois State Training School for Boys at St. Charles. From 1924 to 1926, he was employed as a probation officer at the Cook County Juvenile Court. He continued course work at the University through 1924. Shaw did not complete the Ph.D., mainly because of the language requirement, though he was awarded an honorary Doctor of Laws degree from Adrian in 1939. Toward the end of his graduate studies, Shaw was offered a professorship at McGill University, and nearly took it to be nearer his prospective wife, a Smith graduate who had practised social work in Chicago and then returned to Boston. She agreed to marriage and to return to Chicago, however. They had two children. Shaw subsequently taught criminology, in addition to his

4

CLIFFORD R. SHAW AND HENRY D. McKAY: CHICAGO CRIMINOLOGISTS

research at the Institute, at the George Williams College and the Central Y.M.C.A. College and, after 1941, at the down-town centre of the University of Chicago. He belonged to and participated in professional organisations only briefly in the early part of his career.

In 1926, The Behavior Research Fund made provisions for a research section at the Institute for Juvenile Research. The Institute was formerly the Chicago Juvenile Psychopathic Institute, directed by the well-known criminologist William Healy.[4] The Psychopathic Institute was taken over officially by Cook County in 1914 and by the State of Illinois in 1917. In the 1920s it was renamed the Institute for Juvenile Research and the Sociology Department became the site for Shaw and McKay's researches. Shaw was appointed Director in October 1926 and Henry D. McKay, who had known Shaw as a fellow graduate student, was employed in January 1927 as a clerical research assistant.

Henry D. McKay

McKay was born near Orient, in Hand County, South Dakota, on a 300-acre farm, in December 1899. His grandfather immigrated from Scotland in 1873 and his father had migrated from Minnesota in 1883. It is not surprising then that ideas of race and nationality, migration and immigration, played a large role in his criminology. McKay was the fifth in a family of seven children. In addition to farming, his father was active in county politics. The family was religious, but not as strongly as was Shaw's. McKay worked on the farm and attended public schools, prior to receiving an A.B. from Dakota Wesleyan University.

McKay arrived in Chicago to do graduate work four years after Shaw (1923). He stayed only one year before leaving to teach and study at the University of Illinois. At Illinois, he became acquainted with, though he did not study under, Sutherland, who had begun teaching there in 1919. A very close friendship developed over the years. McKay married in 1926 and had one daughter. He returned to Chicago in 1926 and took courses intermittently through 1929, but did not complete his degree for the same reason as Shaw.

The major question which haunted McKay over the years was whether race and nationality had an effect on delinquent behaviour. He now has long outlived the excitement over this issue in criminology, and publishers considered his overdue manuscript, devoted entirely to the subject, likely to prove unprofitable. The McKay and Shaw researches originally answered this question firmly in the negative by repeatedly showing that the delinquency rates for each nationality were high only while the group resided in a deteriorated area. As assimilation took place and the nationalities were dispersed to outlying areas of Chicago, their delinquency rates approximated to those of " native Americans ". Thus, crime and delinquency were caused by the social conditions, not by racial and ethnic origins. The generalisation broke down, however, when assimilation was not the natural course for black

[4] A biographical sketch and analysis of Healy's work is available in Jon Snodgrass (1972, pp. 58–123).

5

JON SNODGRASS

Americans. Stuck in the ghetto, blacks had crime rates that remained high over generations. This not only threatened the generalisation, it also implicated American society. Stubbornly, trying to support his thesis in regard to blacks as well, McKay persisted with the calculation of rates with each decennial issue of the national census. Finally, the 1960 delinquency rates began to show that for a few ghetto areas on the south and west sides of Chicago, delinquency had declined. (McKay, 1967). This finding tended to vindicate the generalisation and exonerate American society. It took a few decades longer, McKay thought, but delinquency dropped as the black American was " accepted " and as the black community was " stabilised ". When last interviewed in 1972, McKay was patiently waiting for the rates based on the 1970 census further to confirm this trend.

Shaw and McKay

The character of Shaw and McKay's intellectual and research relationship changed over the years. Until the initiation of the CAP in 1932, the writing and research seem to have been shared. Afterward, Shaw's contribution fell off sharply, perhaps partly as a result of his involvement in the sociology department and the action projects, but also because of his health. Although he was rugged in appearance, Shaw's health progressively declined; this lessened his activism and dampened his reputation during the last decade of his life. Shaw was a spent man in the process of being forgotten toward the end. Paradoxically, his death resurrected his contributions and standing in the field. Shaw reached the peak of his creativity and productivity before he was 40; McKay's intellectual maturity seemed to develop more slowly, and was sustained over a longer range of time. The characterisation of Shaw as the hot crusader and McKay as the cool researcher is drawn mostly from the 1932–45 period.[5] At the Institute, McKay took over more and more responsibility for correspondence, memoranda, progress reports and other written material (including the books), many of which were for Shaw's signature or presentation. McKay has described Shaw's activities during this period: " Shaw was a great organiser. He kept a research department alive throughout a long depression, and a great war, which is no mean achievement. First as a participant in the Behavior Research Fund and later as director of the Chicago Area Project he developed private sources of support which were coupled with the State facilities with which both of us were connected. Clifford coupled charisma with organisation talent with very interesting results " (McKay, 1971).

Shaw was an impressive and extraordinary figure. He had a charming and

---

[5] The division of labour between Shaw and McKay was once described by McKay in the following terms: " . . . About the division of labor between Mr. Shaw and myself, . . . I fear that I cannot answer your inquiry in a satisfactory manner. For I suspect that any collaborative report is more than the sum of its parts and any effort to divide the whole into parts is genuinely impossible. A major publication as you know, requires the development of a situation where the work can be carried on, the conceptualisation of a study or studies, the gathering and analysis of the data, the preparation of the report, and finally the details of the publication. It would be foolish to argue that we shared all these tasks equally. The work was divided, but the division was made in the interest of expediency and efficiency and did not indicate necessarily our basic interests and enthusiasms. For this reason I am unwilling to formulate any statement about how the work was divided since the impression made by such a statement is essentially false " (B. Mannheim, 1953, p. 15).

6

CLIFFORD R. SHAW AND HENRY D. McKAY: CHICAGO CRIMINOLOGISTS

affectionate personality, organisational and leadership ability and a talent for obtaining funds. Friends often jested that it was a pity he became a sociologist, for the world thereby lost one of its ablest con-men. Shaw perhaps exemplifies Gouldner's (1973, p. xiii) remark that the Chicago reformer ". . . was soon recognised as a kind of hustler, on the make in his own way. . . ."

Great affection and respect were accorded Shaw by almost everyone he came to know, and this reverence seems to have grown over the years. In 1967, for instance, there was a memorial service in Chicago to commemorate the tenth anniversary of his death. Outside the movement he founded there was criticism, however. Professional social work resented the utilisation of untrained, indigenous workers, a fundamental element in his philosophy of prevention. Shaw and Joseph Lohman parted company (for unknown reasons). And Saul D. Alinsky, an early community organiser for the CAP near the Chicago stockyards, later fired by Shaw, differed sharply on the goals and type of direct action required for social change.[6]

Alinsky once characterised the activities of the area projects in the following terms: " Finally, I quit Joliet and took a job with the Institute for Juvenile Research, one of those outfits that were always studying the causes of juvenile delinquency, making surveys of all the kids in coldwater tenements —with rats nibbling their toes and nothing to eat—and then discovering the solution: camping trips and some shit they called character building " (Alinsky, 1972, p. 68).

Shaw's organisation was never in direct conflict with the political and economic leaders of Chicago. He co-operated with and used these men and their institutions to obtain funds and support for community organisation. He worked between the top industrial and civic leaders, and local " natural " leaders. His activities in this position verged on manipulation, albeit " altruistic " manipulation, for and against both sides. This is the level, too, at which Shaw was a " field worker "; he had much less contact with the " common people " in the community. One confidential investigation of the CAP expresses Shaw's method very well: " . . . he really wants to help those who are poor and who live in the ' blighted ' areas of our city. His method is any method that will work. Consequently, he discovers the ' influential ' people and uses them, no matter their personal or moral standards. Ward politicians, tavern keepers and gamblers serve his purpose, along with priests, industrialists and capitalists " (anonymous).

It may be claimed that community organisation was a courageous undertaking, and perhaps the only realistic alternative, in his day. Had Shaw's health held out, he might have become a national figure. The CAP survived him and had an impact on public policy when they became the prototype for delinquency prevention and welfare programmes of the Kennedy-Johnson era. It is conjecture, however, to suggest that by the 1960s Shaw would have no longer been a Shawist, either in theory or action, and would have moved to a more radical posture.

---

[6] For an understanding of some of the differences which divided Shaw and Alinsky, see Sanders (1970, p. 25) and a long letter from Shaw in August 1942 to Sheldon Glueck, quoted in Snodgrass (1972, pp. 137–138).

7

JON SNODGRASS

Shaw was a kind of within-system politico-missionary. He used " pragmatic " political management in an attempt to form legendary communities
of the past. He saw no incompatibility in pragmatism serving idealism. He
was a charismatic in a rational age. Rather than founding a spiritual movement, as he might have done in an earlier period, he abandoned Christianity,
borrowed many of its principles and values, and attempted methodically to
create a community reform movement ostensibly based on science. An early
worker has remarked that in the enthusiasm of the formative days many felt
as acolytes, zealously hoping to kindle a popular return to hamlets and ethical
humanism within the confines of the city. Shaw was an apostle of community
organisation as a way of saving an American city from its own inherently
great capacity for generating physical deterioration and social disorganisation.

Shaw was known for his identification with, and for the kindness and
generosity with which he treated, the subjects of his life's work. He was a
" delinquent sympathiser " able to relate to and create trust in all manner of
" deviant " individuals. Several delinquents eventually became his close
friends. One, who had written an autobiography published by Shaw,
remembered in 1971 the closeness of their friendship with the comment:
" We were such good friends, I'm sure that if hell is a bad place, Shaw will
send me the message."

Shaw's ability to stimulate authorship was remarkable. As McKay has
written: " I believe that he was at his very best when interviewing juvenile
delinquents from whom he got ' the whole story ' very quickly without any
duress. With delinquents I have never been sure whether he joined them or
they joined him. At any rate, many young offenders produced life stories for
him, some of which were published " (McKay, 1971). There are currently
more than 85 unpublished life-histories of varying quality and in varying
stages of completion still in the files of the Institute for Juvenile Research.[7]

Shaw's appearance and mien contributed to the impact and success
which he had, both organisationally and interpersonally. An insightful
vignette of Shaw comes from "the Jack Roller", Shaw's most famous delinquent and one of his best friends. Shaw encouraged the Jack Roller to write
an autobiography which subsequently became a " classic " in criminology.
(Shaw, 1930.) This description of Shaw was written by the Jack Roller one
week following Shaw's death (on August 1, 1957), in a letter of consolation
to Mrs. Hetta Shaw: " As a boy of twelve, I just met Cliff, back in 1921. He
worked then at the Juvenile Court as well as at the settlement House on 31st
Street. I remember quite vividly his splendid bearing, being rugged of build,
and tall of stature with a thick mane of dark hair, and quite handsome too.
However, he particularly impressed me with his sincere manner and a
geniality that at once captured my confidence, and that I must say was a big
thing, since at that time I had spent over half my twelve years in institutions
and was very much on the defensive. Instinctively I knew him as a friend..."

There are some amusing and some puzzling contradictions in Shaw's

[7] James R. Bennett, at the Institute for Juvenile Research, is presently making use of these autobiographies and also collecting more recent autobiographies for comparative purposes.

CLIFFORD R. SHAW AND HENRY D. McKAY: CHICAGO CRIMINOLOGISTS

biography. Never very organised in his personal life, he persistently attempted to create organised communities. He was an agnostic trying to create Christian order, a pragmatist seeking an ideal, a former delinquent turned delinquent reformer, and a reluctant writer who tried to get almost everyone to write. He was an individual ardently against delinquency and crime with more than a hint of being a " legitimate " confidence man himself. No doubt in some respects Shaw was an enigma to himself.

The Ecological Studies

In Shaw and McKay's ecological studies, the residences of official delinquents (and other kinds of offenders, and other behavioural forms of " social pathology ") were plotted on maps of Chicago. "Spot maps", with one spot per delinquency case, showed the actual residential distribution. " Rate maps " showed the number of offenders per hundred individuals of the same age and sex in square mile areas. " Radial maps " showed the rate of delinquency at regular intervals along major axes drawn from the city centre. " Zone maps " showed the rates of delinquency in concentric zones drawn at one-mile intervals from the city centre.

A major finding indicated that the highest concentration of delinquent residences was in the " transitional zone ", the area surrounding the central business district, an " interstitial area " in transition from residence to business and industry. It is often overlooked, however, that delinquent residences were also found outside the transitional zone, in other areas which were similarly characterised by build-ups of business and industry; for instance, along both sides of the north and south branches of the Chicago River, around the Union Stock Yards, and around the south Chicago steel mills. There was not only an inner-zone concentration, but also a correspondence between the distribution of delinquency and the distribution of business and industry; wherever there were centres of commercial development, areas of social pathology seemed to surround them.

Another major finding was a " gradient tendency " in which delinquency rates declined regularly with increasing distance from the city centre toward the suburban periphery. When the analysis was extended to 20 other large American cities, the two major findings of concentration and gradient proved to be applicable in these urban areas as well as Chicago.

To interpret their findings, Shaw and McKay relied most heavily upon the general concept of " social disorganisation ", the breakdown of social controls in the " communities " located in the transitional zone. The invasion by business and industries from the centre of the city into the former residential areas created a wake of social disorganisation in its advance which disturbed social cohesion and disrupted traditional conduct norms, Shaw and McKay explicitly and repeatedly mentioned industrial invasion as a primary source of communal disorganisation, although other sources, *e.g.* the influx of successive waves of highly mobile immigrant groups, were additional contributing factors, though not unrelated to business expansion. Shaw and McKay took " social disorganisation " for granted, however, and located the causes of delinquency predominantly in the internal conditions within the

9

JON SNODGRASS

disorganised areas, *i.e.* culture conflict, delinquent traditions, gangs, and interpersonal conflict within families.

A most striking aspect of Shaw and McKay's interpretation, then, is the absence of attempts to link business and industrial invasion with the causes of delinquency. The interpretation stayed at the communal level and turned inward to find the causes of delinquency in internal conditions and process within the socially disorganised area.

Thus, their interpretation stopped abruptly at the point at which the relationship between industrial expansion and high delinquency areas could have gone beyond the depiction of the two as coincidentally adjacent to one another geographically. The interpretation was paralysed at the communal level, a level which implied that either the residents were responsible for the deteriorated areas, or that communities collapsed on their own account. Instead of turning inward to find the causes of delinquency exclusively in local traditions, families, play groups and gangs, their interpretation might have turned outward to show political, economic and historical forces at work, which would have accounted for both social disorganisation and the internal conditions, including the delinquency. Needless to say, the interpretation as it stood left business and industry essentially immune from analysis, imputation, and responsibility in the causes of delinquency.

The ecological studies usually made no comment about the joint distribution of delinquency and industry, beyond the fact that the two impinged upon one another. The following quotation, however, actually disputes a causal relationship between the two; the location of industry is regarded merely as an index to the location of a high delinquency area: " Proximity to industry and commerce is an index of the areas of Chicago in which high rates of delinquents are found. However, it is not assumed that this proximity exists because industry and commerce are in themselves causes of delinquency. It may be assumed, however, that the areas adjacent to industry and commerce have certain characteristics which result from this proximity and which serve to differentiate them from the areas with low rates of delinquents " (Shaw, 1932.) Industry's relationship to delinquency was no more than a landmark by which the whereabouts of high delinquency areas might be pinpointed.

The transitional zone, Shaw and McKay noted, came about through the expansion of the central business district. Owners of land and property in the interstitial area retained ownership knowing that land values would go up and that eventually wealthy enterprises would pay handsome prices for the territory as more and more of it was required for expansion. They refrained from making new investments in construction and refused to make " wasteful " repairs on the property since the buildings would be demolished sooner or later to make way for the expansion. Land values remained high, but property rentals stayed comparatively low. Over time the areas deteriorated. Into these slums were drawn impoverished migrants and immigrants who struggled for an existence by performing the menial work in the central city, whose meagre wages enriched the absentee landlords and whose children in large numbers became the " notorious " delinquents.

CLIFFORD R. SHAW AND HENRY D. McKAY: CHICAGO CRIMINOLOGISTS

A number of observations could have been made about this " process " (even the term " transitional " implied that it was a process that took place without conflict). The most obvious was the " discrepancy " in the distribution of land, property, power, wealth, health and longevity between the residents of the high delinquency area and the business elites of the commercial centre. The fact that life resources were held by one class, the fact that landowners allowed their property to deteriorate, the fact that capitalist enterprises and other vaunted institutions invaded and destroyed communities, that this " process " was carried out " legitimately " and without concern for human dislocation and welfare, and that the residents were politically impotent and resourceless (and could offer no resistance) are all " points " unmentioned and apparently unnoticed.

By way of contrast, it may be noted that the " Gold Coast " was the only area in the transitional zone preserved from invasion and destruction. It was safeguarded by the power, wealth, and social prominence of its inhabitants. Zorbaugh has described this section: " Such is the Gold Coast. For in Chicago, all that is aloof and exclusive, all that bears the mark of *l'haute société*, is crowded along the strip of " drive " between the Drake Hotel and Lincoln Park, or along the quiet, aristocratic streets immediately behind it. Here is the greatest concentration of wealth in Chicago. Here live a large number of those who have achieved distinction in industry, science, and the arts. Here are Chicago's most fashionable hotels and clubs. Here live two thousand of the six thousand persons whose names are in the social register of Chicago and its suburbs, and these two thousand include in their number those who are recognized as the leaders of "society". (Zorbaugh, 1929.) The Gold Coast was the sanctuary for the elite who were in many instances directly responsible for the conditions in the high delinquency area. When Shaw and McKay took notice of the Gold Coast, again, they merely observed descriptively that it stood in " vivid contrast " to the surrounding areas (Shaw and McKay, 1972, p. 26).

In the last analysis, Shaw and McKay's interpretation of the geographical material took a curious shift and located the ultimate cause of deteriorated areas in ecological laws. In doing so, the interpretation skipped over dominant institutions and invested industrial invasion with a " naturalistic " philosophical justification. The process which created the transitional zone was an inherent one, a part of the general ecological metabolism and organic development of the city. After all, these were called "natural areas". It was not the decisions, actions and policies of business executives, landowners and political officials which created these miserable sections of Chicago; it was the laws of nature: " (The community) has resulted from the natural processes involved in the growth and expansion of the city " (Shaw and McKay, 1938; p. 97). Or: " In a like manner, the physical, economic, political and cultural conditions which obtained in the community were functions of larger processes of competition, segregation and differentiation within the life of the city as a whole " (Shaw and McKay, 1938; pp. 358–359). The " plant-like " metaphor had the benevolent hand of nature regulating the process. The laws of nature created a cheap labour market, human

JON SNODGRASS

degradation and exploitation, and pre-ordained that one would have slums and delinquency. How consoling for those in power, resting comfortably in the Gold Coast to know that nature had predestined the expansion and legitimated the exploitation! The " spiritual " shift in the theory averted any human action that might be responsible for the process, and any human action that might seek to combat it; one would hardly attempt to organise politically to overcome or overthrow the laws of nature.

The Chicago Area Project 40 Years Later

The Chicago Area Project began in 1932 in three high delinquency areas. A field worker from the Institute for Juvenile Research would enter the community to form councils of local residents which tried to organise the neighbourhood for civic betterment and delinquency prevention. The CAP began on a small scale as a private organisation and expanded over the years. Some CAP councils continue in operation to the present day. From its inception, the CAP raised its own funds but was staffed and administered by state personnel. Eventually, the State of Illinois took over the CAP as part of its general delinquency prevention programme.

The CAP stressed the importance of maintaining the autonomy of the community. An effort was made to avoid the imposition of Anglo-Saxon, middle-class standards on residents. The aim was to " stimulate " community organisation without engineering and controlling it and to " spark " the latent potential for community control. Thus, the field worker was to act as a " catalyst ", the leadership was to be " indigenous ", the council was to be composed of local residents, and management and planning were to be carried out by the residents. There was hope for a wide basis of local, democratic participation.

Shaw believed that communities had existed in the transitional zone prior to the expansion of industry, though the accuracy of this belief is open to question. It seems likely that community and neighbourhood were often used as just another expression for geographical area. Whether or not communities ever had prevailed, the purpose of the organisation fostered by the CAP was to build or rebuild communities. Shaw wanted to restore village life and tradition to city folk. The major tenet underlying the projects was the belief that organisation reinstated all the natural social control inherent in traditional communal life.

Community organisation as the method of correction, the analogy between the CAP and the folk community, and the connection between this method and Shaw's personal life-history, are evident in the following lengthy quotation:

> Many of my ideas about delinquency seem to spring from the situation in which I found myself as I grew up. I grew up in the county in what was, in the real sense of the word, a community. In this situation, people were brought together by certain ties of long acquaintance and friendship, by certain common beliefs and interests. There was something under the surface which made it possible for them to rise to meet a crisis or disaster when the occasion

CLIFFORD R. SHAW AND HENRY D. McKAY: CHICAGO CRIMINOLOGISTS

arose. If there was an illness or death or if someone's home burned, there was a reaction among all the people of the community.

One night in January, when I was about eight years old, the house next to our home burned to the ground, and it seemed sure that our house would also go. Within a few minutes, 400 or 500 people from all over the area had collected, and they organised a bucket brigade, passing water to the men who had climbed to the top of our house. Bucket after bucket of water was poured, until they succeeded in saving the house.

It was a tragic experience which I had that night, seeing the flames come up over our house. I will never forget the fear, the anxiety, and the anger; neither will I ever, ever forget that our house was saved by something called a community or a neighbourhood. A group of people united by a deep bond of friendship, of affection, and of common interest, saved our house.

That is what we are talking about. That is the idea behind the community committees here and in the different sections of the state, wherever we find groups of people living in these little areas who realise their common dependence upon each other, and who appreciate the fact that they can create moral values, spiritual values, and community values by their common efforts.

The community in which I grew up taught me to know and respect its ideas, its ideals, and its values. Not that I was not a delinquent! I was a thief; the sheriff never caught me, but I stole. One of the boys that I knew habitually stole. But these were little things, unimportant exceptions, and they did not seriously interfere with the process through which the community impressed its values upon me. None of my elders ever told me so in words, but I was not very old when I knew that it was all right to steal a chicken to roast, but that to steal one to sell was a serious crime.

I think that we may perhaps be able to build this kind of community in these little neighbourhood areas, and in this way provide the kind of social situation in which all children may grow up as normal and reasonably happy human beings (Shaw, 1951; pp. 69–70).

Shaw was then a folk-idealist waging an imaginary war with urban-industrial reality. The model underlying his projects was turn of the century Indiana farm town. Throughout his life persisted a country boy's fascination and distaste, an attraction and a repulsion, regarding the enticing vice and sins of delight in the city. Rural, small-town life preserved middle-class, Christian, democratic values and habits. Shaw had come to the city to reveal, with missionary zeal, that all that vice, crime and corruption were bred, not just in the city, but right outside its centre. The fact that delinquency rates "thinned" as one travelled the gradient towards rural Illinois was not empirical alone; it had a solid basis in Shaw's personal history and ideology. The gradient implied that the further away one went, the fewer pathologies one found. Back home in rural Indiana, one did not find delinquency, but wild-oats and corn-bred mischievousness (" little things, unimportant exceptions "). Upstate and downtown, serious delinquency was bred massively in the streets. Beating city blocks into county squares and turning passive city people into active townsmen, creating " little neighbourhoods "

13

JON SNODGRASS

just outside the Chicago Loop was the ideal Shaw sought, and was the agrarian conservatism that lay at the base of his criminology.

Shaw's goal was to create community cohesion by having " little groups of neighbours " participate in various activities and projects. The actual goals of the CAP, however, were remarkably vague. No doubt this vagueness derived in part from the desire to leave the precise formulation of aims to the discretion of the people. But discretion veered almost exclusively towards matters that were internal. Points of contact and organisation around economic, political and social matters in the larger city were not evident.[8] " The specific activities conducted by the Area Project are in most respects the same as those conducted by organisations such as boys' clubs, the Young Men's Christian Association, settlements, and parks. Included are camping, baseball, football, basketball, boxing, movies, ping-pong, pool and billiards, small table games, music, dramatics, handicrafts, printing, newspaper work, and club discussions " (Shaw and Jacobs, 1939; p. 45).

Shaw ardently believed that organisation itself rendered the purpose of organisation quite secondary; any internal aim which united the residents and reinstated the bonds of social control would do. Organisation itself was the dominant goal and the dominant good. Concentration on the inside, however, detracted from and disregarded the economic and political sources of delinquency arising from the outside, and left them to run their course.

Shaw was aware of the external sources and was uncertain whether local organisation around social activities might achieve change. " In conclusion, it should be emphasised that the socio-economic conditions which are probably responsible for delinquency in the areas in which the Area Project is operating, are the product of influences which are city-wide in their scope. It is not known, therefore, just how far the reorganisation of life in local areas can be achieved without reorienting the social and economic life of the city itself " (Shaw and Jacobs, 1939, p. 5). It is surprising, given the awareness of external sources, that the projects did not attempt to deal with them directly. The CAP was not an overt political organisation fighting for fundamental rights and an effective voice in Chicago politics, nor was it oriented towards dealing with the industrial invasion, or the economic and physical conditions that the invasion created. The CAP was designed for social activities instead of social action.

A major thrust of Shaw's work was not in changing conditions in the high delinquency areas, but in lifting nationalities out of them. This was done despite the fact that Shaw, of all people, knew that the upward mobility of

---

[8] Shaw and McKay recognised that fundamental changes in political and economic conditions were necessary to prevent delinquency. Shaw wrote: " Any great reduction in the volume of delinquency in large cities probably will not occur except as general changes take place which effect improvements in the economic and social conditions surrounding children in those areas in which the delinquency rates are relatively high " (Shaw and McKay, 1972; p. 441.) Shaw was aware that crime and delinquency were an integral part of the life of the larger city. In a mimeographed report on the Area Project, he suggested that the vice and prostitution in the transitional areas were " in no sense a purely local responsibility. . . . In a sense, they are located in specific areas for the convenience of the entire city. The local population plays a negligible role in subsidising gambling and prostitution." He also stated: " Crime is not a matter of personal or neighborhood blame. It appears rather as an infectious growth within the whole social structure. . . ." (Shaw, 1943; pp. 36 and 40).

CLIFFORD R. SHAW AND HENRY D. McKAY: CHICAGO CRIMINOLOGISTS

one national group out of the areas, into the suburbs and into the middle class, left the same area open for a succeeding immigrant group; one nationality rose up and out while another took its place. Time and again Shaw and McKay noted that the areas and delinquency were relatively unchanged despite alterations in population composition; this was, indeed, perhaps the central finding of their work. In this respect, they attempted to console various nationalities, suggesting that with time and initiative, the economic discrimination and their days in court would eventually vanish. One ethnic group followed another, as though one generation's confinement in the transitional zone, labouring in factories and locked in jails, was the sentence one paid for full acceptance into American society. Any consolation this theory might have offered expired, however, when black southern immigrants came to rest, after World War I, for successive generations at the bottom of the Chicago social structure.

The CAP was consistently concerned with goals for uplifting the community by self-help from within. The organisation was not addressed to broader types of social action and in particular did not seek to deal directly with the forces destroying and disorganising the community.[9] The continual expansion of industry and institution, outward in space and ever more profound in depth of effect, received not the slightest attention. Active opposition to the industrial invasion was very remote for, after all, industry was not considered to be causally related to delinquency. Shaw attempted to prop up and repair the community from the inside, while its walls were " progressively " wrecked and bulldozed from the outside—a curious posture for a man standing in the rubble and who believed that treatment programmes had to deal directly with the actual forces producing delinquency.

The neglect of invasion is perhaps best illustrated by the transition in land use in the Near West Side, one of the three areas in which the CAP first began. Today, the eastern portion is dominated by the University of Illinois at Chicago Circle, " Mayor Daley's School ". Sherman's study of the Near West Side Community Committee in 1946 notes: " In the course of a half-century, there have been great changes on the West Side. . . . The whole area east of Halsted Street seemed to be awaiting the commercial and industrial invasion. This did take place over the years, so that now the whole area east of Halsted Street, which was once a seething mass of humanity, is now almost devoid of residential dwellings. This section has been given over almost completely to business establishments and small factories " (Sherman, 1946; pp. 38–9).[10]

[9] Betty Mannheim's study of the CAP recognised this: " The committees are adept at solving local problems, yet, despite their willingness, they are unable to deal with the wider aspects of the social process. They cannot call a halt to urbanisation and to the industrialising processes which contribute to the break-down of social controls, which create areas of housing shortage, slum conditions, unemployment, and similar conditions. They do, however, facilitate the understanding of these processes on the part of local residents, and thus enable them to cope with the more visible effects of the disintegrative forces. The committees may have some delaying influence and hence can be of use in promoting adjustment even if they are unable to remove the basic disruptive cause. In a sense, they are more of a stop-gap than a radical remedy, and therefore it seems that Shaw's theory does not strike at the roots of the problems of modern society " (B. Mannheim, 1953; pp. 138–139).

[10] A study of the " Addams " area took place in a portion of the Near West Side. The researcher explained that " after a few months in the area, I mentioned to some people that I wanted to write a history of the neighborhood before the city ' tore it down ' " (Suttles, 1970; p. 31).

15

JON SNODGRASS

The CAP was too intimately tied to industry to combat it: its Board of Directors was composed of leading " civic-minded " businessmen, the CAP's financial support came in part from business contributions (and indirectly from business through the United Fund). It was also supported at times by foundations (Rockefeller, Wieboldt, and others).

The CAP was cosmetic rather than surgical; the approach was almost trivial in the face of the realities of Chicago politics and economics. The philosophy of the Board of Directors and the futility of the CAP approach is captured in the following transcription of a conversation between McKay and Sutherland in 1935. McKay is speaking: " . . . the businessmen who are on the boards want to be told that they are doing something important by their contributions and hours of conferences and that their philanthropy is curing the evil. Consequently, they state during one year that they have done a certain amount of work; next year they must report a little more, and the next year still more; and it thus becomes cumulative until their reports of accomplishment have no relationship whatever to their actual accomplishments. But this is what the board wants to hear anyhow, and it makes no difference to them that the conditions which they are trying in this trivial manner to correct are largely due to their own every-day behavior " (Shaw and McKay, " Chicago Area Projects ").

Another conversation recorded at the same time between Shaw and Sutherland reveals the deep reservation which Shaw had about the effectiveness of the projects. Two of the grounds for his pessimism are quoted below:

> " I hear that you are contemplating an area project in Indiana. Why don't you leave the poor people alone? We are pretty well convinced now that we are not going to accomplish anything in our area projects. There are several reasons for this:
>
> . . .
>
> Third, why should anyone object if they are delinquent? It might be an excellent thing if the delinquents did make organised raids on the Gold Coast. There may be only one way to settle things, that is, by organised power. That seems to be the way it works now. Fourth, the Gold Coast businessmen who are leaders of our projects are not evidently better than the people in the neighbourhood. They knowingly misrepresent things because this makes a good story on the coast and helps to raise money. I can see the reasons why the welfare organisations are so dishonest in their reports; they have to be dishonest to satisfy the boards and to raise money. If we were dependent on local finances, I can very well conceive that within a few years we would be just as petty and dishonest as the rest of the organisations we see " (Shaw and McKay, " Chicago Area Projects ").

This passage discloses a radical understanding with regard to the Gold Coast that was never displayed in the projects themselves or in Shaw's formal writings. It also shows, of course, how hampered the projects were by their funding and business ties.

The CAP was actually a measure designed to curb delinquency, not industry, in the interim between initial invasion and complete succession. It

CLIFFORD R. SHAW AND HENRY D. McKAY: CHICAGO CRIMINOLOGISTS

was a palliative attempting to bring temporary stability to the areas to control delinquency until the area was no longer in transition. There was no quarrel with the invasion, only with the ensuing disorganisation, and thus Shaw had community members occupied in innocuous organisations while industrial leaders proceeded with business as usual. Beneath it all lay the assumption that the expansion and prosperity of industry took ultimate precedence over the preservation of community. Industry proceeded without hindrance. In an ironic way, the projects protected the property and equipment of the very concerns which were the root causes of the disorganisation and delinquency. Such mild alleviation even within the logic of the theory probably only aggravated the origins of delinquency. The concern with playgrounds, summer camps and carnivals mistook the incidental for the essential. Shaw and McKay thus unwittingly contributed to the decline of community and the rise of delinquency the very outcomes they fundamentally sought to oppose. While searching for what might create community, they ignored what they knew full well destroyed it.

The judgment may seem harsh, but the concentration on internal organisation and neglect of the political and economic realities of slum residents stems from the fact that there was less concern with rights and welfare than with behaviour control, less concern with community prosperity than with community constraint. The highest priority was given to establishing local social control. The logic of community organisation underscored the normative more than the reformative, the internal constraints of organisation rather than the external benefits that organisation might achieve. The rationale for the sports programme emphasised discipline more than recreation or education. The study of the family and delinquency centred on the breakdown of primary group controls. There is a final irony that cuts straight across many of the values Shaw and McKay espoused: some of the procedures of the CAP are uncomfortably reminiscent of the coercive techniques commonly associated with authoritarian political régimes; for instance, taking down the names and addresses of all the boys in an area and organising block councils in order " to have little groups of neighbours living in the same block who can meet with us when a boy gets into difficulty and thus bring to bear upon that case some public disapproval of his act " (Shaw, 1933, p. 31).[11] The Chicago Area Project was first and foremost a disciplinary force, designed to inculcate values, socialise behaviour, and to achieve an accommodation of slum residents to the conventional order. The projects sought fundamentally to force individuals to adapt to American society.

---

[11] Another example: " Last week we had the case of three boys charged with burglary. We had a juvenile police officer there. We sat down with each boy and his parents and that little committee in the block in which he lived, and talked over that whole question. Those boys know now that there are certain persons in that neighborhood who disapprove of their behavior and who are interested in them. We are attempting to bring that sort of public opinion to bear on these cases of beginning delinquency " (Shaw, 1933, p. 31).

JON SNODGRASS

REFERENCES

ALINSKY, SAUL (1972). " Interview." *Playboy* 19 (March).

ANONYMOUS (n.d.). " Report on the Investigation of the Area Project." Type-written.

FARIS, ROBERT E. L. (1967). *Chicago Sociology*: 1920–1932. Chicago: University of Chicago Press.

GOULDNER, ALVIN W. (1973). Foreword to *The New Criminology*, by Ian Taylor, Paul Walton and Jock Young. London: Routledge and Kegan Paul.

MANNHEIM, BETTY (1953). *The Chicago Area Project: In Theory and Practice.* Unpublished Master's Thesis, University of Illinois.

McKAY, HENRY D. (1967). " A Note on Trends in Rates of Delinquency in Certain Areas of Chicago." *Juvenile. Delinquency and Youth Crime.* President's Commission on Law Enforcement and Administration of Justice. Washington: U.S. Government Printing Office.

McKAY, HENRY D. (1971). Letter to Snodgrass. March 3.

MILLS, C. WRIGHT (1962). " The Professional Ideology of Social Pathologists." *Power, Politics and People.* Edited by Irving Louis Horowitz. New York: Ballantine Books, Inc.

RADZINOWICZ, LEON AND WOLFGANG, MARVIN E. (eds.) (1971). *The Criminal in Society.* New York: Basic Books.

SANDERS, MARION K. (ed.) (1970). *The Professional Radical: Conversations with Saul Alinsky.* New York: Harper and Row.

SHAW, CLIFFORD R. (1930). *The Jack-Roller: A Delinquent Boy's Own Story.* Chicago: University of Chicago Press.

SHAW, CLIFFORD R. (1932). " Housing and Delinquency." *Housing and the Community—Home Repair and Remodeling.* Edited by John M. Grimes and James Ford. Washington: The President's Conference on Home Building and Home Ownership.

SHAW, CLIFFORD R. (1933). " Neighborhood Program for the Treatment of Delinquency." *Quarterly of the Minnesota Education, Philanthropic, Correctional and Penal Institutions* 33 (Sept.).

SHAW, CLIFFORD R. (1943). " The Area Project." Mimeograph. (November 9).

SHAW, CLIFFORD R. (1951). " From the Inside Out: Self-Help in Social Welfare," General Session, Illinois Federation of Community Committees. *Twentieth Annual Conference on Youth and Community Service.* State of Illinois: Dept. of Public Welfare.

SHAW, CLIFFORD R. AND JACOBS, JESSE A. (1939). " The Chicago Area Projects." *Proceedings of the 69th Annual Conference of the American Prison Association.* New York: American Prison Association.

SHAW, CLIFFORD R. AND McKAY, HENRY D. (n.d.). " The Chicago Area Projects." Unpublished.

SHAW, CLIFFORD R. AND McKAY, HENRY D. (1938). *Brothers in Crime.* Chicago: University of Chicago Press.

SHAW, CLIFFORD R AND McKAY, HENRY D. (1972). *Juvenile Delinquency and Urban Areas.* Revised edition. Chicago: University of Chicago Press.

SHERMAN, ROCHELLE D. (1946). *The West Side Community Committee: A People's Organization in Action.* Unpublished Master's thesis, University of Chicago.

CLIFFORD R. SHAW AND HENRY D. McKAY: CHICAGO CRIMINOLOGISTS

SNODGRASS, JON (1972). *The American Criminological Tradition: Portraits of the Men and Ideology in a Discipline*. Unpublished Ph.D. dissertation, University of Pennsylvania.

SUTHERLAND, EDWIN H. (1973). " Fields of Interest." *On Analyzing Crime*. Edited by Karl Schuessler. Chicago: University of Chicago Press.

SUTTLES, GERALD D. (1970). *The Social Order of the Slum*. Chicago: University of Chicago Press.

VOSS, HARWIN L. AND PETERSON, DAVID M. (eds.) (1971). *Ecology, Crime and Delinquency*. New York: Appleton Century Crofts.

ZORBAUGH, HARVEY (1929). *The Gold Coast and the Slum*. Chicago: University of Chicago Press.

19

Name Index